VICTIMS OF MEMORY

MARK PENDERGRAST spent over three years researching and writing *Victims of Memory*. His previous book, *For God, Country and Coca-Cola* (1993) was named a Notable Book of the Year by the *New York Times*. A Harvard graduate, Pendergrast lives in New England.

International praise for *Victims of Memory*:

'According to Pendergrast, the witchhunt of alleged sexual abusers, by means of memories supposedly repressed in childhood and recovered years later in therapy, has claimed several million victims in the USA, and well over 100,000 in Britain. Mark Pendergrast's *Victims of Memory* describes the phenomenon in depth, drawing on extensive interviews with accusers and accused and the therapists who wittingly or unwittingly helped cause the accusations. It also draws on wide research into the myths which have made possible a delusion that has destroyed families and lives. Freud has a great deal to answer for, Pendergrast convincingly argues. But so has the infinite suggestibility of the human mind. This book is both closely reasoned and passionate and should help reverse a terrible, and terrifying, trend.'

FRANCES HILL, author of *Delusion of Satan*

'*Victims of Memory* constitutes the most ambitious and comprehensive, as well as the most emotionally committed, of all the studies before us. Pendergrast devotes the most effort to analyzing the contemporary Zeitgeist in which the recovery movement thrives.'

FREDERICK CREWS, *New York Review of Books*

'Perhaps the most comprehensive study of the recovered memory movement . . . [Pendergrast's] book, richly documented and informed throughout by a sense of history, is both wise and profound.'

RICHARD WEBSTER, *Why Freud Was Wrong*

'*Victims of Memory* is . . . a comprehensive study of a disturbing phenomenon which began to sweep the U.S. in the mid-eighties, reaching Britain in the early nineties.'

SARAH STRICKLAND, *Observer*

'An impressive display of scholarship . . . Pendergrast demonstrates a laudable ability to lay out all sides of the argument.'

DANIEL SCHACTER, *Scientific American*

'Pendergrast even-handedly presents the different sides [and] *all* the different positions with empathy.'

Psychological Reports

'Anyone touched by the subject of repressed memories would do well to read this book.'

BRUCE EINSPRUCH, *Journal of the American Medical Association*

'The most thorough account of the debate yet produced.'

Psychological Science

'By far the most thorough journalism [of three current books on the recovered memory debate] appears in *Victims of Memory*'

KATY BUTLER, *Los Angeles Times*

'Explosive material – massively researched and lucidly argued.'

ANN DIAMOND, *Montreal Gazette*

'Powerful and impassioned, *Victims of Memory* should be essential reading for all counselors, clients, parents and children. Whatever side of the controversy you stand on, this book will shake you up and force you to re-examine your assumptions.'

BRUCE WILSON, *Vancouver Sun*

'In his impassioned, richly literate and thoroughly researched book, Pendergrast tells an appalling, heart-breaking horror story of the forces of mental health gone berserk. This is a courageous, terrifying, and necessary book.'

FRANK PITTMAN Psychiatrist, *Psychology Today* columnist

VICTIMS
OF MEMORY

*Incest Accusations and
Shattered Lives*

MARK PENDERGRAST

HarperCollins*Publishers*

HarperCollins*Publishers*
77–85 Fulham Palace Road
Hammersmith, London, W6 8JB

First published in the USA by Upper Access Books, 1995, 1996

The revised British edition published by HarperCollins*Publishers* 1996
1 3 5 7 9 8 6 4 2

ISBN 0 00 255684 7

Set in Linotype Janson by
Rowland Phototypesetting Ltd,
Bury St Edmunds, Suffolk

Printed and bound in Great Britain by
Caledonian International Book Manufacturing Ltd, Glasgow

For my wonderful daughters, with infinite love.
May this book be the first step
toward renewed dialogue and reconciliation.

Contents

Acknowledgments

MANY THANKS TO the following people for reading various portions of the manuscript and providing valuable commentary that helped to shape the final product: Irene Angelico, Alexander Bodkin, Brent Cohen, Paul Foxman, David Galland, Melody Gavigan, Marylen Grigas, Jonathan Harris, Margaret Jervis, Suzanne Johnson, Michael Kenny, Stephen Lindsay, Elizabeth Loftus, Andrew Meacham, Bill Mitchell, Sherrill Mulhern, Debbie Nathan, Ulric Neisser, August Piper, Larry Ribbecke, Dan Schacter, Paul Schumacher, Margaret Singer, and Saul Wasserman. Of course, they do not necessarily agree with all statements in *Victims of Memory*.

Others who provided articles, information, or expertise include: Ralph Allison, Gerald Amirault, Patty Amirault, George Bergen, Sanford Block, Peggy Buckey, Joseph deRivera, Chris Dodge, Elizabeth Feigon, Elaine Foster, Pamela Freyd, Frank Fuster, George Ganaway, Felicity Goodyear-Smith, Gina Green, Evan Harrington, Kimberly Hart, Roma Hart, Steven Hassan, Anna Hunter, Lawrence Langer, Susan Leighton, Stephen Lindsay, Anita Lipton, Matt Love, Maria Luise, Harry MacLean, James McGaugh, Paul McHugh, J. Gordon Melton, John Morton, Paul Okami, Karen Olio, Britt Pendergrast, Nan Pendergrast, Judith Peterson, Harrison Pope, Dennis Powers, Don Read, Morton Schatzman, Nancy Schoerke, Roger Scotford, Howard Shane, Patty Sheridan, Ray Souza, Shirley Souza, Herbert Spiegel, Larry Squire, Kathy Swan, Ralph Underwager, Elie Wiesel, Linda Meyer Williams, and the late Nicholas Spanos.

I am particularly indebted to British journalist Margaret Jervis for her invaluable research and for her insights into how the sex abuse hysteria developed in the U.K., and to British scholar Richard Webster, author of *Why Freud Was Wrong*, for his encouragement, generosity, and example.

I wish I could name all of the therapists and other anonymous correspondents who shared their painful life stories with me. Regardless of their attitudes toward the recovered-memory controversy, I value their willingness to talk with me openly about a difficult subject. Thanks to Survivors of Incest Anonymous, the False Memory Syndrome Foundation, and the British False Memory Society for helping me to locate many of those I interviewed.

I took advantage of the wonderfully efficient interlibrary loan system here in Vermont and received cheerful, prompt service, particularly from Linda Willis and Norma Lemieux at the Midstate Regional Library in Berlin and Cynthia at the Waters Memorial Library in Underhill. I also thank the staff at the Trinity College Library in Burlington, Vermont, for their excellent collections on Freud, feminism, sexual abuse, and other subjects.

I owe much to those who helped me through this difficult time of my life: my grief group, my local Quaker Clearness Committee, gatherings of other parents who have lost their children, several compassionate professional counselors, my good friends and family, and, especially, my partner Betty, for her unstinting love and support.

To my first primary editor, Jim Peck, much gratitude for once again bringing his wit, insight, and grammatical pedantry to the task of making this the best possible book. I owe a huge debt to Steve and Lisa Carlson at Upper Access Books in Hinesburg, Vermont, who initially took on this project and provided further editing, typesetting, publicity, advice, and hand-holding.

Philip Gwyn Jones and Toby Mundy, my editors at HarperCollins in London, have been unstintingly patient and helpful with contacts in the U.K. Working with them has been a professional and personal pleasure.

MARK PENDERGRAST

A Note on Name Changes

THROUGHOUT THIS BOOK, the names of private individuals (such as incest survivors, their therapists, retractors, accused parents, and so on) have been changed to protect their privacy. Other details, such as their locations of residence, have also been altered. The exceptions to this rule (such as those whose names have previously been identified, well-known researchers, and those who have requested that their correct names be used), should be apparent in the text. When pseudonyms are used, any similarity to the name of a real person is coincidental and unintended.

Your face beams
In my dreams
'spite of all I do.
Everything
Seems to bring
Memories of you.

Popular song lyric from 1930

NOTICE ON PRODIGY,
A COMPUTER BULLETIN BOARD (1992)

I had a strange experience a week ago and wondered if this has ever happened to anyone else. 2 weeks ago in therapy, I tried to get in touch w/my inner child, but was unable to do so. I felt silly trying to find a 'safe place' and didn't want to deal with such a spoiled brat anyway. I felt bad that I couldn't do it, like I let my therapist down. Last Monday night, I tried to do it at home on my own. I sat cross-legged on the bed, with the lights off, and burned a stick of incense to help me relax. I visualized myself as a child and found my safe place, but it didn't progress much beyond that. Having used self-hypnosis tapes for weight loss, I tried some of those techniques—deep breathing, relaxing the entire body, etc. I let my mind wander, and I noticed my lips feeling kind of swollen and bruised; numb. I felt a fullness in my mouth and had to breathe only through my nose. Then my head seemed to be moving by itself. I began to panic, but I knew I had to continue, to see where it would lead. I had my hands clasped in front of me, and it was like some force beyond my control was loosening and separating my fingers. My hands unclasped, and my arms started to raise up and out to my sides, as if someone were spreading my arms out and pinning me down. I felt myself leaning back into a reclining position, and then I had the vague sensation of something penetrating me. I don't know what happened then—it just stopped. I never got any clear visuals, or smells, or anything else; I'm one of those 'dramatic' people, and the adult in me has written this off as hysteria. It never became really frightening for me, more like an intellectual exercise, but my therapist says I tend to intellectualize my abuse. I tried to re-create the experience the next day (and last night) to prove that I was just making it up, but I couldn't do it. Have any of you ever had a similar experience? I'd be grateful for any input/feedback you can give me.

Thank you,
Rebecca

Foreword

ANYONE COULD HAVE a false memory. In fact, inaccurate memories occur to *everyone*, in some form, because every act of memory is simply our best effort at imaginative reconstruction.

My first therapist, who was so successful at implanting the memory that my father molested me, never used sodium Amytal, hypnosis, guided imagery, or any memory aid other than pressure and suggestion. My first false memory was a vague image that anyone might have – a dark outline of my father looming above me. That picture was all I had to go on for a long time, until I sought hypnosis, and then the vague picture became a series of sharp, horrible images. I thought that the original picture was obscure because I was just not *trusting* enough yet, and I didn't feel *safe* enough to get it all out in the open. I didn't think I'd get better, or that my symptoms would go away, until I could successfully 'abreact' the episode, reliving it with full emotion. For three years, I completely believed that my father had committed incest on me.

Misinformation from therapists or books can provide a powerful formula for changing any person's entire belief system. That is what *Victims of Memory* is about: how perfectly normal people like me could come to believe in such horrible delusions, and how responsible therapists and critics can bring an end to this madness. Mark Pendergrast, himself an accused parent, has written a much-needed book. As an investigative journalist and scholar, Mark has delved into the complicated social, cultural, and individual factors that lie behind the accusations. If I had been able to read a book like this *before* seeking therapy, I believe I could have been spared years of anguish.

Everyone involved in this mess is suffering – not only the accused, but the patient who recovers the memories, as well as other family members and friends. We are all left with the residue of what I call emotional vigilantism.

The accused are marked forever, even if they were lucky enough to have been vindicated.

The self-identified 'incest survivors' who believe that they were abused for years, but had completely forgotten about it, struggle with the loss of their families and of their very identity. They have been forced to rewrite their pasts.

Others who continue to suffer are the 'stragglers' – those who never progress beyond vague feelings, but who waste years in recovery groups straining for a memory of abuse so that they can hang their problems on it.

The retractors must rebuild their lives and change from helpless, frightened victims to realistic adults taking responsibility for themselves and their problems. Fortunately, for me and many other retractors, a new personal power comes from within. I know now that I am the master of my life, not the victim of some external events that supposedly happened to me 30 years ago.

The therapists, too, are going to need our compassion as they struggle with the terrible things that they have done to their patients. I wouldn't want to bear their guilt.

The phenomenon of recovered memory is much more widespread a problem than most people realize at this point. Even though the media are just now giving it the attention it deserves, we have a long way to go in understanding how memory works and separating facts from popular beliefs. Our culture appears to be searching for simple solutions to very complex problems, and it is all too easy to latch on to early sexual abuse trauma theory as a one-size-fits-all answer.

There are no simple answers. *Victims of Memory* provides no fool-proof solutions, but it is a giant first step towards understanding a seemingly inexplicable phenomenon, one that will engage psychologists, sociologists, anthropologists and other scholars for many years to come. They will all want to understand how, in a technologically sophisticated culture near the end of the 20th century, millions of perfectly sane people came to believe in monstrous events that never took place. We who have lived through it can bear witness. I was one of those who accused my innocent father. Mark Pendergrast, who can personally tell us what it feels like to bear the brunt of such an accusation, has written a wise, compassionate book for all of us. Read it with care. This book could change your life.

MELODY GAVIGAN,
Editor, *The Retractor Newsletter*

Introduction to the British Edition

Childhood is less clear to me than to many people ... for no reason that I know about, certainly without the usual reason of unhappy memories. For many years that worried me, but then I discovered that the tales of former children are seldom to be trusted. Some people supply too many past victories or pleasures with which to comfort themselves, and other people cling to pains, real and imagined, to excuse what they have become.

LILLIAN HELLMAN, *Pentimento* (1973)[1]

There is no question that sexual abuse in 'civilized' countries is far more prevalent than anyone was willing to admit just a decade ago. Despite the immense amount of publicity given to the subject in recent years, it is still likely that real incidents of sex abuse are woefully under-reported, because victims are often too fearful or ashamed to reveal it.

At the same time, however, there is growing evidence that illusory memories of sexual abuse are being unintentionally promulgated and 'validated' by misguided therapists, resulting in devastating grief and irrevocably damaged family relations.

When you are accused of sexual abuse in our society, at least during the late 20th century, you are automatically presumed guilty unless proven innocent beyond a shadow of a doubt – a virtual impossibility.

Watching the American television program *Sixty Minutes* in 1986, I remember closely observing Ray Buckey, his sister, his mother, and his grandmother, all accused of sexually abusing their young charges at the McMartin Preschool in California, and thinking, 'So this is what perverted child molesters look like.' They denied everything, yet dozens of innocent children accused them of horrendous acts. To me, Ray Buckey's attempts to remain calm indicated sociopathic callousness. His wheelchair-bound grandmother, who expressed outrage at the charges, protested too much, I thought. They were obviously guilty. Why would so many pre-schoolers make up grotesque stories of rape, slaughtered animals, and satanic rituals? I dismissed the notion of their innocence out of hand.

Yet it has become quite clear now that Ray Buckey and his family were innocent, and that the children were led to make their accusations by extensive, coercive questioning by adults, as I document in Chapter 9. Buckey, after five years of unjust incarceration, has been released and is trying to rebuild his life. Now in his late 30s, he plans to go to law school.

I imagine that some readers opening this book will begin with that same supposition of guilt regarding me that I once harbored for the Buckeys. Both of my adult daughters – first one, then the other – have cut off all contact with me, based on vague, unspecified allegations of childhood sexual abuse. (Though I would like to find out what they think I did and discuss it with them, they will not allow any communication.) Why would they take such drastic measures if there were no basis for the allegations? Even if they did stumble into some misguided therapy, the reader might infer, there surely must be a kernel of truth to my daughters' allegations. I must have done *something*.

At first, I tortured myself with these same thoughts, as did most other accused parents I interviewed. My only real defense is the truth. I didn't sexually abuse my children. In hindsight, I know that I wasn't a perfect parent. But then again, neither are most parents. Raising children is the most important and most difficult job on earth, and it is even more challenging in the aftermath of a divorce. There are many things I would indeed apologize for, if only I could, but they were normal human foibles.

I did not want to write this book. It's much too painful. The truth is, I *had* to write it. I finally realized that what has been termed 'false memory syndrome' (FMS)* was destroying not only my children's very identities and my relationship with them, but millions of other families as well, throughout the English-speaking world.

I tried to drop this book, but it wouldn't go away, and it wouldn't let me write anything else, despite my first editor pleading for another business book to follow my history of Coca-Cola, and despite repeated rejections from the major New York publishing houses. As an investigative journalist, it seemed clear to me that this was an issue that needed investigation, and I needed to pursue it to the best of my ability before

---

* The term 'false memory syndrome' has been widely criticized because it has not yet been officially recognized as a psychiatric term and because the word 'false' is pejorative. I use it for lack of any better term, but I have avoided using the term 'false memories' where possible.

re-focusing on other issues. A small publisher in Vermont – Upper Access Books – took on the project and published the first edition of *Victims of Memory* in the United States in February, 1995.

I knew from the outset, however, that the book would be fraught with problems. Given my personal situation, would I be able to represent both sides of the story without appearing grossly prejudiced? Could I approach the subject with an open mind? Could I really understand what those in recovered memory therapy were going through?

Now that I have spoken with so many of those whose lives have been irrevocably altered by recovered 'memories,' I believe that I do understand what these women (and many men) have suffered through. I have come to feel the utmost compassion for all who are involved in this phenomenon.

In interviewing therapists with whom I disagreed, I strove to listen wholeheartedly, to understand what they saw and felt, and I have let them speak for themselves in these pages. Most of them mean well. In all interviews, I represented myself as a journalist interested in exploring the issue of sex abuse, particularly as it related to memories recovered as adults. I did not reveal that I myself had been accused, since that would have tainted the interviews or made them impossible to conduct. My listening and interpretive skills must have been fairly good. 'Gee,' one therapist told me two hours into our interview, 'you'd make a pretty good therapist yourself. You understand this material better than most of my colleagues.'

Similarly, I tried to be extremely sensitive to feelings and stories of 'incest survivors' as I listened to them, even when they described what seemed to me to be well-rehearsed fantasies rather than real memories. Their pain and confusion, their anger and loneliness, their need for love and understanding were all touchingly real. They speak for themselves in these pages.

Here, too, are the disturbing voices of retractors – those who have come to believe that their former accusations were false – with their inevitable rage at former therapists and their guilt and shame over the treatment of their parents.

And, of course, I have listened to agonized parents who have lost their children because of accusations of incest. I have been inspired by their struggles (often at an advanced age) to come to grips with this seemingly inexplicable situation, by their fortitude and courage, and by their continued care and love for their children despite everything.

It is unfortunate that any mention of the phrase 'sex abuse' instantly polarizes those on both sides of this argument. I hope that this book will serve as a kind of dialogue within its pages. Readers will hear in detail from those on all sides of this volatile issue and, although I express my informed opinion, they are free to make their own judgments. In my concluding chapter, I have made tentative suggestions for how reconciliation of all parties might take place.

One of the ironic tragedies of this movement is its supposed affiliation with 'feminism.' Because most of those recovering memories of abuse are women, those who question the memories are labeled sexists. Yet what is really happening here? These therapists specialize in making women feel helpless, dependent, wounded, incomplete, and fundamentally flawed. Does that sound familiar? Women's lives are being harmed by a movement that feminists should abhor.

One Canadian retractor has written poignantly about her own recovered memory experience, in which she became convinced that she had multiple personality disorder. 'It robs women of all power and control over themselves. If I really hated women and wanted to keep them in a completely powerless and childlike state, the best way to do that would be to remove their faith and trust in their own minds and make them dependent.' That is precisely what happens in this form of 'therapy,' which frequently manages, quite literally, to turn women into helpless infants. 'At most MPD gatherings, accommodations are made for those who feel themselves losing control,' this retractor writes. 'These arrangements are exactly like the nurseries set up in churches in case the infants begin to fuss, with coloring books and crayons. And these are for grown women!'[2]

That brings us to the subject of pronouns, a volatile issue nowadays. Since women constitute the vast majority of those who have recovered 'repressed memories,' I refer to any such generic 'survivor' as female throughout the text (e.g., 'When a woman first enters therapy, she . . .'). Ellen Bass and Laura Davis directed *The Courage to Heal*, their controversial book about repressed memories, specifically to women, though they acknowledged that men are also sexually abused. Since *Victims of Memory* is, among other things, a corrective to that book, I consider it important and intellectually honest to address women directly as well, though many men have certainly suffered through the same experiences.

One more point on this touchy subject. Along with social psychologist Carol Tavris (and most scientifically controlled studies), I believe that men and women have much more in common, as members of the same species, than they display genetic differences.*³ The current repressed-memory hunt has breathed life into one of the most damaging and sexist traditions in our culture – the subtle message to women that they can gain power and attention *only* through the *victim* role. That does *not* mean that they are inherently passive, dependent, or hysterical, but it *does* mean that the current hunt follows in that tradition.

Just as I do not want to be branded a sexist, I also do not intend this book to be taken as a broadside assault on all therapists. Many counselors provide needed help and understanding for people in emotional turmoil. I praise those therapists who help clients deal with current life issues, who look to the past (without rewriting it) only in order to understand the present, and who gently nudge their clients toward responsible, mature independence.

I should note, however, my lost admiration for Sigmund Freud and his theories. As an English major at Harvard in the late '60s, I embraced the *ego* and the *id* as wonderful metaphors that helped illuminate literature. My senior honors thesis was drenched in Freudian symbolism. Curiously, my work on the Coca-Cola history rang the first alarm bells for me. Freud appears in *For God, Country and Coca-Cola* as an ambitious young physician who identified cocaine as a wonder drug, introducing it to his friend Fleischl, with fatal consequences.

Now I have come to realize, as you will read in some detail near the end of Chapter 10, that Freud created a magnificent intellectual edifice, a self-contained, self-validating psychological theory, but that it rested on untested hypotheses. Worse, he pressured and manipulated his patients into 'proving' his presumptions.

Perhaps I am too harsh on a fallen hero. After all, we owe Freud for numerous psychological insights, including the realization that human beings are not always rational animals. We sometimes deflect our troubled emotions onto innocent bystanders or ourselves. Through introspection and thoughtful analysis of our past, we can better understand our motivations in the present.

Yet I can't shake my outrage with Freud for any number of inappropriate diagnoses and self-justifications, after he actually made his clients worse rather than better. As readers will see in Chapter 10, Freud sanctioned a preposterous operation on a patient's nose, then blamed her for 'hysteria' when she nearly bled to death as a result. It is, of course, odd that the 'feminist' incest survivor movement should embrace Freud's

* See Carol Tavris, *The Mismeasure of Woman* and Cynthia Epstein, *Deceptive Distinctions*.

concept of repression, while other feminists have justifiably criticized the Viennese patriarch for his ludicrous theories about penis envy.

I hope for a wide audience for this book, including scholars already familiar with research on memory and hypnosis. *Victims of Memory* is, however, aimed primarily at the intelligent general reader. I imagine that this reader might think, just as I once did, that the human brain houses every memory somewhere, just ready to pop out, that hypnosis is a sure way to aid recall of the past, or that multiple personality disorder is a common response to trauma. I have attempted to correct such misconceptions and to 'cover the waterfront,' so to speak. In doing so, I am sure to have missed some of the subtleties or important historical antecedents. Each of the theoretical chapters of this book could easily be expanded into a book of its own. As an overview and synthesis of this disturbing social phenomenon, however, I believe this book fills a unique need.

In preparing this British edition of *Vicims of Memory*, I have been fascinated by the way in which American psychiatric fads and social concerns have spread with astonishing rapidity throughout the English-speaking world. There is a paradoxical historic symmetry involved here. Near the end of the two-century-long European witch craze, the Puritans imported witch-hunting to North America. As a result, in 1692, twenty innocent people were put to death in Salem, Massachusetts. Three hundred years later, we Americans returned the favor by exporting the paranoid search for mythical satanic ritual abuse cults, repressed incest memories, and child sex rings.

As this book documents, the American virus was, to some degree, carried by 'experts' who ventured across the Atlantic to share their views with British colleagues. More than that, however, the ground was prepared by the printed word. Not since *The Malleus Maleficarum* was published a few years after Gutenberg's invention have we seen such evidence of the power of books to affect lives. In particular, *The Courage to Heal* has spread the gospel of recovered memory, but it spawned many imitators.

I can imagine the smug reaction of some readers in Britain and the Commonwealth. 'Ah, those crazy Americans! They trot off to therapy whenever they suffer the slightest mishap. No wonder they believe all this rubbish so readily. We may have a small problem over here, but it's nothing to worry about.' Well, maybe. Certainly, the recovered memory problem in the United States is far worse than anywhere else in the world, in part because of the American search for the 'quick fix,' and the relentless pursuit of that ever-elusive state called 'happiness.'

But sex abuse hysteria, in the form of children's cases and recovered memories, is far more prevalent than most people realize in the United Kingdom, New Zealand, and Australia. In part, the Commonwealth countries are fortunate that the initial drama was played out in the United States. Because of the extensive American media coverage, some British reporters expressed skepticism of recovered memories earlier in their process. British journalist Margaret Jervis, who has been critical of the sex abuse hysteria from its onset, isn't so sure of her colleagues. 'This whole field is blighted by a number of "blueprint" cases which are regarded as proven through convictions but which are extremely suspect,' she wrote to me in 1996. 'If the level of hysteria about sexual abuse in the U.K. has not reached the heights of the U.S., neither has the level of skepticism.' Indeed, the 1990s have witnessed an explosive growth in the therapeutic industry in Great Britain. As I document in Chapter 13, over 100,000 British families have probably been blown apart by false allegations of sexual abuse.

Why has the notion of 'massive repression' been so readily accepted in the literate world? Why did 97 per cent of British psychologists express belief that recovered memories of abuse are 'essentially accurate' in a survey published in 1995 by the British Psychological Society? Clearly, Americans cannot be blamed for such a widely held belief system. It goes back to Freud, who wrote, after all, in German. For over a hundred years, pseudoscientific Freudian myths have permeated Western beliefs.

Indeed, the sex abuse hysteria virus has spread from multiple directions, not just the United States. For instance, New Zealand therapist James Bennett ventured to England in 1986 to indoctrinate disciples in his extremely disturbing version of recovered memory therapy. (*See the interview with Hamish Pitceathly, Chapter 5*.) Rosemary Crossley's 'facilitated communication,' a kind of human ouija board using severely handicapped children, was exported from Australia to the United States in 1989, resulting in many false accusations of sexual abuse. (*See Chapter 3*.) Swiss psychologist Alice Miller was a formative influence in the recovered memory movement. And Czech Stanislav Grof took his 'holotropic breathwork' – a form of hyperventilation often leading to 'memories,' along with violent shaking, gagging, vomiting, and speaking in tongues – to the USA in 1967, but it has now found its way, along with other alarming techniques, to the Findhorn Foundation in Scotland.[4]

In other words, no one should get too smug about 'those crazy Americans.' Instead, we should examine how human beings – wherever they may live – can come to believe in destructive untruths. How can well-intentioned people cause such grievous harm? How can the past be rewritten with such ease? These are questions that transcend national borders.

During the summer of 1995, I ventured to England to conduct interviews with British recovered memory therapists, 'survivors,' accused parents, and retractors. The stories I heard were, unfortunately, all too familiar to me. The interviews are filled with the jargon of the international 'recovery' movement – *violated boundaries, healing, denial, dysfunctional families, inner child, emotional incest* – and with the same swift severance of family relations. Shock, grief, fear, terror, and rage are universal human reactions to this horrifying and unnecessary drama. May it all end soon. When I took taxis in London, I learned that the cabbies had to pass a stringent series of tests before they were certified as possessing "The Knowledge". It struck me as ironic – and lamentable – that British taxi drivers are better trained than British psychotherapists. If you want to get from Victoria to the Strand, you are in capable hands. But *caveat emptor* to anyone who opens his or her vulnerable mind to a psychotherapist untutored in the science of human memory.

Fortunately, since the initial U.S. publication of this book, the entire shaky edifice of recovered memory therapy has begun to crumble. The tenor of the debate over recovered-memory therapy has changed in fundamental ways. American courts have begun to put the scientific validity of recovered memory on trial, and found it wanting. People who have been victimized by this form of therapy are increasingly coming out and seeking compensation for their suffering. In the U.S., over two hundred lawsuits have been filed by retractors against their former therapists, and that number is certain to swell dramatically in the next few years, as more and more people realize that they were 'had' by this misguided form of therapy.[5] I hope that some day, we will look back at this tragedy as a fascinating aberration in late-20th-century history, and that this book will help to provide answers to the inevitable question: 'How could this have happened?'

Unfortunately, that day is probably still far in the future. Those who believe in recovered memory therapy have not given up their dogma, rhetoric, or belief system. Rather than facing the overwhelming evidence that a sizeable number of their profession have violated the Hippocratic oath – 'First, do no harm' – the professional associations have reacted to the controversy by looking the other way, while trying decorously to cover their behinds. The beleaguered American Psychological Association, for instance, has stockpiled a war chest of $1.5 million to polish psychologists' tarnished images, rather than cleaning house. The British Psychological Society has dismissed induced memories as a minor problem and is lobbying to pass a bill giving the Society sole ownership of the title 'psychologist.' One is tempted to ask the professional societies, as one brave soul finally confronted Joseph McCarthy in the U.S. Senate in the 1950s: 'Have you no decency? At long last, have you no sense of decency?'

One regret that I have is that American media attention to my book has centered inordinately on my personal situation. Even favorable reviews often perceived the book as an effort to exonerate myself, to defend myself against unfair allegations. One reviewer, for instance, concluded that *Victims of Memory* was 'a genuine labor of love and social justice, an impressive blend of outrage, empathy, and scholarly distance.' Yet she also began her review by calling it 'an author's effort to assert his innocence.' Wrong. I had no need to defend myself. No one knew anything about my family's sad situation, nor would have, if I had not chosen to write this book.

I *did* hope to reach my children, and I pray daily that they will call or write. But the main reason I wrote the book was to put a stop to the destruction of minds, lives, and families and to explore the fascinating workings of the human mind.

I was a professional journalist long before my children cut off contact, and using a book to try to exonerate myself would be quite unprofessional. Beyond that, it would be an impossible task. I don't even know the specifics of what I am accused of, and even if I did, there would be no way to prove my innocence in a book.

In the first U.S. edition, I included a chapter detailing how my youngest daughter first entered therapy in college and retrieved a 'memory' of being molested by a man living in our household when she was nine. Two years later, she apparently identified me, too, as her abuser and told her older sister, who promptly entered therapy herself and cut off contact with me as well. When I called my ex-wife to find out what was going on, she screamed at me, told me that both children were retrieving more and more memories, and hung up.

At the end of the first edition, I included a letter to my children, hoping they might read it and that it would facilitate reconciliation. To protect their privacy, I changed my daughters' first names, calling them Stacey and Christina. They had changed their last names, so nothing in the book would identify them.

My primary motive in telling my own family's story was intellectual honesty. The book is a work of investigative journalism, which needs to be judged on its own merits. I interviewed people in all situations, with a wide range of informed opinions, and tried to represent them all fairly and honestly. I did not begin my research as a dispassionate observer, however, but began looking into this issue in order to understand what had happened to my own family. Readers had a right to know that.

But the fact that I told my personal story in some detail, despite the protection of my daughters' privacy, has inflamed passions among some, and has distracted from the larger societal issues. It has also led to rumor and innuendo that quickly crossed the Atlantic to England. I was astonished when a British psychotherapist informed me that one of his colleagues had heard that Mark Pendergrast was a 'confirmed pedophile.' When I finally tracked the rumor down, I found it had come from an American psychologist who did not know me or my book. She had been referring to someone else. Similarly, in her British newsletter, *Accuracy About Abuse*, Marjorie Orr, the well-known astrologer, erroneously printed a letter, stating it was written by one of my daughters, when it was not. She subsequently printed an apology.[6]

When *The Sun*, a North Carolina literary magazine, ran an excerpt of my personal account, the magazine received numerous letters to the editor concerned with my guilt or innocence, rather than the validity of recovered memory. Despite the love and affection I expressed in the article, one letter-writer accused me of conducting a 'terrorist attack' on my children. The only totally negative critique of *Victims of Memory* that I have seen appeared in the *Village Voice*, concentrating solely on my own situation. I was accused of failing to understand that my children see a 'different reality.'

Believe me, I do understand that my children and I see different realities. I would like nothing better than to sit down with them and talk again. I'd like to re-establish the things that we can agree on. I accept that there may always be significant issues on which we will never see eye to eye. But if we can just start talking again, even if we agree to disagree about massive repression of sexual abuse memories, I'll be grateful.

As a result, I have eliminated the personal chapter and the letter from this edition of the book. That shouldn't detract from the value of the book. My contribution to the debate on recovered memory is my investigative journalism and scholarship, not my personal story, which, though tragic, is unfortunately not terribly unusual or unique.

I would also like to comment on my affiliation with the American False Memory Syndrome Foundation, which was founded early in 1992 to provide information for distraught accused parents, mental health professionals, and all those caught up in the repressed memory phenomenon. I am tremendously grateful to the FMS Foundation, and I am a member of the organization. When I discovered its existence late in 1992, it provided a lifeline for me. As another parent told me, 'It has turned an incomprehensible personal tragedy into a somewhat understandable social phenomenon.'

However, neither the FMS Foundation nor its counterpart, the British False Memory Society, sponsored this book, nor did they have any control over its contents. I cannot vouch for the innocence of all families that have joined either group (though I seriously doubt the accuracy of any cases based on 'massive repression' of abuse memories). Nonetheless, it is quite clear that these organizations and their excellent newsletters have provided an invaluable service. It is unfortunate that the Foundation has been extensively demonized and villified by those who believe firmly in repressed memories. In the face of such anger and prejudice, it is little wonder that my personal situation has been used against me.

In every other respect, the response to this book to date has been gratifying. It is probably the most important thing I will ever write. I have heard from people all over the world thanking me, telling me that I had written as if I knew their personal stories. These letters have come from accused parents, retracting children, ex-spouses, siblings, and incest victims who have always remembered their abuse.

In the past few months, I have traveled across America, giving speeches, submitting to media interviews, and talking with psychology students, lawyers, and therapists. Wherever I go, I usually stay in the homes of accused parents who inevitably unburden themselves of their stories. I have watched videos of their children from happier times, and we have cried together about the incredible, awful transformations that took place when their children started therapy.

On two separate occasions, accused parents who also happened to be Holocaust survivors told me that losing their children was even worse than what they had endured in the concentration camps. I questioned whether they could really mean that, and both vehemently asserted that they did.

The horror stories appear to have no end. Each is familiar yet unique; almost routine now, yet still unbelievable. I have come to realize how heavily involved the so-called Christian therapy community has become in recovered-memory efforts, in the English-speaking world. The problem extends to virtually every denomination – evangelical, Catholic, Anglican, mainstream Protestant, Jewish, and others. 'What is scary,' one concerned therapist wrote to me recently, 'is that Christian visualization facilitators are almost unreachable, because they are sure God is behind all the revelations of abuse they produce.' Scary indeed.

Another common thread is how this type of therapy destroys marriages. In great pain, many former spouses (mostly men) have come to me after speeches to explain how they completely believed and supported their wives throughout the initial stages of memory therapy. In case after case, the process destroyed first their sex lives, then their marriages.

I have also heard from a great many retractors, whose first-hand reports provide the most compelling and disturbing evidence of the havoc that recovered-memory therapy plays in the lives of those who come to believe that they were raped throughout their childhoods and had repressed all such memories. 'I really believe,' one retractor wrote to me, 'that if *Victims of Memory* had been out there when I was still seeing my therapist, that it would have made a difference in my life. It just addresses so many concerns that I had, I wouldn't have been able to live with the on-going questions the therapist refused to address.'

The single most poignant moment came for me when a young woman approached me after a speech and said, 'I found your book by accident in a bookstore. I was just browsing and it called out to me. I read it, and called my parents for the first time in five years. I just wanted to thank you.'

As bad as the recovered-memory mess is, I have come to a greater understanding that its close relative – the false allegations dragged out of small children – is just as harmful. More than ever, I am glad I included the chapter, 'And A Little Child Shall Lead Them (and Be Led).' These two phenomena – recovered memory therapy and the coercive questioning of young children – are the result of the same therapeutic 'mindset' that assumes guilt and then presses toward a fore-gone conclusion. All of the children's denials are disregarded until they 'disclose' under enormous pressure. Just as adults' memories are rewrit-ten, so are young children's recollections molded by therapists and social workers.

In all too many cases, the two phenomena are directly linked, as in the Massachusetts case of Ray and Shirley Souza, documented in Chapter 9. While in recovered memory therapy, the Souzas' daughter had a dream about them abusing her, which she considered proof. She then warned her sister and sister-in-law that Mom and Dad were evil sex offenders. Thus started the intensive questioning of the grandchildren.

The number of innocent people who have been jailed is overwhelming and disheartening. In their recent book, *Satan's Silence* (Basic Books, 1995), Debbie Nathan and Michael Snedeker listed 57 such American cases, and they are only the better known. I hear frequently from new people who are languishing in prison, desperate for help, and I feel powerless to do much for them. I listen carefully, never assuming immediately that they are innocent, but many of their cases sound all too familiar. Most involve the coercive interviewing of young children, or the 'refreshed memory' of adults who went for therapy.

I'd like to think that I got everything right in this edition of *Victims of Memory*, but of course, with issues this complex and events constantly changing the equations, the ultimate book on the subject cannot be written until the recovered-memory controversy becomes a curious blip in human history. Tragically, that is something that will not occur in the near future.

Meanwhile, life continues to be an arduous odyssey for all of us human beings, adrift on this lovely planet, sometimes clinging together to a life raft, sometimes falling off to swim or drown alone. Let us learn, over and over again, to be kind to one another in our inevitable imperfections and insecurities. As William Blake, my favorite poet and philosopher, put it in 1793:

> Mutual Forgiveness of each Vice,
> Such are the Gates of Paradise.

MARK PENDERGRAST 1996

VICTIMS
OF MEMORY

CHAPTER ONE

How to Become a Survivor

Two postings on Prodigy, a computer bulletin board:

Jan. 1, 1993. Hi everybody, my name is Gretchen. I am from Germany and in the States for about 16 months now. I am 30 years old, married and after 4 miscarriages in 18 months we went to marriage counseling. I also have a sexual problem, no desire at all. The counselor and a therapist are both convinced that I was sexually abused as a kid, but I don't remember anything. They said it is probably so bad, that I had to block it out or it would have killed me. Now I am running around and try to remember . . . I know I was hit every day, I was the only child. But sexual abuse never occurred to me at all . . . God, I have so many questions and hope somebody will answer me and share their experience with me.*

Jan. 1, 1993. Dear Gretchen, You're not alone in this! I had no memories of being sexually abused until about one and a half years ago. About 3 years ago, I started reading books on the subject and every 'effects' list described me to a T! I didn't have any memories, but I just had a really strong feeling that something happened . . . When I stopped thinking of memories in visual terms, I started to realize that I was remembering things all the time. Reactions, feelings, panic attacks, fears & phobias are all memories . . . Reading books on sexual abuse is a really good way to retrieve memories. Pay attention to what you react to. For example, I was reading *The Obsidian Mirror* and she was talking about how her abuser had stuck monopoly pieces inside of her. I had a panic attack when I read that and then had flashbacks of a similar incident happening to me. Books that I would recommend are #1 *The Courage to Heal* (this is the BEST book – very validating if you have no memories).

---

* The grammatical errors in this quotation were in the original. Readers may assume that all misspellings or other errors within direct quotations, throughout this book, are from the original source. I make this note here, rather than interrupting the text with the standard 'sic.' Also, throughout this book, when words are italicized within direct quotations, they were italicized in the original source, unless otherwise noted.

The widespread search for repressed memories of sexual abuse began to mushroom in the United States and Canada in 1988, and in Great Britain in 1990, with the publication in 1988 of *The Courage to Heal*, by Ellen Bass and Laura Davis, which informs readers: '*Forgetting* is one of the most effective ways children deal with sexual abuse. The human mind has tremendous powers of repression. Many children are able to forget about the abuse, *even as it is happening to them.*'[1]* They continue: 'You may think you don't have memories, but often as you begin to talk about what you do remember, there emerges a constellation of feelings, reactions, and recollections that add up . . . . To say, "I was abused," you don't need the kind of recall that would stand up in a court of law.'**[2]

In this chapter, we will examine how *The Courage to Heal* and other popular books encourage illusory memories of sexual abuse – mostly in women, though an increasing number of men are now recovering 'memories.' At first blush, false accusations of incest seem hard to imagine. How, outside of a brainwashing prisoner-of-war torture compound, could people be convinced of such a horrendous delusion, particularly if their relationships with their parents were once warm and loving? How could perfectly normal women come to have vivid memories of fondling and oral sex at the age of three, or frequent sexual intercourse with their fathers as teenagers, or prolonged immersion in satanic sex cults, if these events never took place?

---

* Citations to *The Courage to Heal* refer to the 1992 second edition. A third edition came out in 1994. The essential message remains the same.

** Unfortunately, such 'constellations' of feelings, reactions and recollections, once they have grown to 'memories,' do often stand up in courts of law, mostly in America. They have served as the sole evidence in lawsuits against parents and others. In many cases, elderly parents have chosen to settle out of court rather than go through the financial and emotional stress of a trial. Others have been found guilty on the basis of emotional but uncorroborated testimony of adult children and their therapists. Over half of the states in the U.S. have changed their laws in response to belief in 'repressed' memories of sex abuse, allowing people to sue parents for events alleged to have occurred decades before. In many cases, the statute of limitations has been changed so that a suit can be filed after the 'memories' emerge. In England, more limited statutes of limitation remain in force, though it appears likely that the European Human Rights Court will follow the American lead and allow 'delayed discovery' cases to go forward.

4

THE HORROR OF REAL INCEST

Before reviewing *The Courage to Heal* in detail, it is necessary to understand how and why Ellen Bass, with her collaborator Laura Davis, came to write it.* In the 1970s, during the early days of the women's movement, the horrifying extent of sexual abuse and incest first began to surface, although children had been subjected to such abuse for all of recorded history. Up until then, official statistics claimed a tiny incidence in the general population. In one 'definitive' 1955 study, researchers estimated that there were only 1.1 cases of incest per million persons.[3] Even where incest did occur, it was often minimized or even sanctioned by male psychologists. Some victims were told that they were only fantasizing, based on Freud's presumptions about Electra and Oedipus complexes. Freud thought that all children between ages three and six go through a stage of sexual desire for the opposite-gender parent (*see Chapter 10*).

During Freud's Victorian era, child prostitution was widespread, with virgins bringing top dollar because of the fear of syphilis. In England, a 14-year-old was worth £100, but parents could sell a beautiful preadolescent for £400. In his 1885 newspaper exposé, journalist W. T. Stead reported being sickened by the sight of children, three to five years old, being chloroformed before serving as sex partners for adult men. Around that time, the anonymous author of *My Secret Life* complained of the difficulties of penetrating prepubescent girls, though he had no moral compunctions about it. 'It is the fate of such girls to be fucked young,' he asserted, 'neither laws social or legal can prevent it.'[4]

Sex historian Vern Bullough points out that the Industrial Revolution brought a sharp increase in the sexual abuse of prepubescent children.

---

* Bass appears to be the primary author of *The Courage to Heal*. Laura Davis, her collaborator, was a student in her class and contributes her own story of how she retrieved repressed 'memories' of abuse at the hands of her grandfather, now deceased. Together, the two authors are a publisher's dream – a Survivor literature industry unto themselves. Davis has written two contributions on her own: *The Courage to Heal Workbook* leads people step-by-step through the process of becoming a Survivor, while *Allies in Healing* tells friends and mates how to support and believe the newly identified Survivor. Bass has also written a children's book called *I Like You to Make Jokes With Me, But I Don't Want You to Touch Me*. Finally, there is a slim mini-version of the main volume called *Beginning to Heal*.

Until then, such activity seems to have been relatively rare, although sexual relations between adults and adolescents have always been common and, frequently, culturally sanctioned.* In modern times, however, there are more documented cases of adult males assaulting younger children. As a newspaper reporter in 1949, Bullough observed a two-and-a-half-year-old girl who was 'taken to surgery with a mangled vagina and a damaged urethra.' She had been raped by her father. His editor refused to publish the story, saying he ran a 'family newspaper' unfit for such items.[5]

Four years later, the famed Kinsey report, *Sexual Behavior in the Human Female* (1953), revealed that 24 per cent of respondents 'had been approached while they were pre-adolescent [13 or younger] by adult males who appeared to be making sexual advances, or who had made sexual contacts with the child.' Despite this alarming statistic, the authors implied that the victims were responsible: 'Repetition [of preadolescent contacts with adults] had most frequently occurred ... with relatives who lived in the same household. In many instances, the experiences were repeated because the children had become interested in the sexual activity and had more or less actively sought repetitions.'**[6] They concluded that there was really nothing to worry about: 'We have only one clear-cut case of serious injury done to the child, and a very few instances of vaginal bleeding which, however, did not appear to do any appreciable damage.' Wardell Pomeroy, one of the Kinsey report authors, went even further in 1976, telling a *Penthouse* interviewer: 'Incest between adults and younger children can also prove to be a satisfying and enriching experience, although difficulties can certainly arise.'[7]

With some male psychologists expressing such opinions, it is little wonder that women and many men were finally becoming vocally outraged by the 1970s. In 1975, Susan Brownmiller published *Against Our Will: Men, Women and Rape*. Although her book was primarily a

---

* For further histories of child sexual abuse, see Rush, *The Best-Kept Secret*; Wasserman and Rosenfeld, 'An Overview of the History of Child Sexual Abuse'; and Breiner, *Slaughter of the Innocents: Child Abuse Through the Ages and Today*.

** To some degree, Kinsey's observations may have been valid, though his minimization of incestuous activity was not. In *Long-Range Effects of Child and Adolescent Sexual Experiences* (1992), Allie Kilpatrick concluded from a study of 501 women that 55 per cent had experienced some form of sexual contact with adults when they were children, mostly involving hugging and kissing. 'The partner that most women had as children ... is an unrelated male,' Kilpatrick concluded. 'Most women are active in initiating the experience both as children and as adolescents.'

6

blistering attack on male attitudes toward rape, Brownmiller also made the connection with incest: 'The unholy silence that shrouds the inter-family sexual abuse of children and prevents a realistic appraisal of its true incidence and meaning is rooted in the same patriarchal philosophy of sexual private property that shaped and determined historic male attitudes toward rape.'[8]

Incest victims began to speak out in women's groups and in books. In 1974, Ellen Bass, a young feminist creative writing instructor, received a crumpled half-sheet of paper from a shy student. 'Her writing was so vague, so tentative,' Bass recalls, 'that I wasn't sure what she was trying to say, but I sensed that it was important.' Slowly, with encouragement, the student wrote about the pain of her father's sexual assaults. Shortly afterward, probably because their teacher shared similar stories, one woman after the other wrote horror stories for Bass. 'I was stunned by the number of women who had been sexually abused,' she says. 'I was deeply moved by the anguish they had endured.'[9*10]

In 1978, Bass and five women from her Boston writing workshops began collecting stories for an anthology. Their timing was perfect. That same year, Louise Armstrong published *Kiss Daddy Goodnight*, which included many incest accounts, and therapist Sandra Butler's *Conspiracy of Silence: The Trauma of Incest* came out. Other books and articles quickly followed, authored by David Finkelhor, Christine Courtois, Florence Rush, Judith Herman, Elizabeth Ward, Angie Ash, and others. Swiss psychologist Alice Miller exerted a tremendous influence when her work about traumatized children was translated into English. By the time Bass published her 1983 anthology, incest was a subject of great interest among the general public.

Very little of this early material about incest mentioned repressed memories, though Freud had made the concept of repression a theoretical given. Most of the women who were finally speaking out had never had any trouble remembering that they had been abused. It was all too real for them. Their problem was being *unable to forget it*. Even the title of the 1983 Bass anthology, *I Never Told Anyone*, implied that although

---

* In 1983, when she published the incest anthology, Bass identified so strongly with the stories that sex with her husband became impossible. 'There were times when I could not bear to be touched. Too many stories of too many fingers, tongues, penises of adult men slipping into little girls' vaginas made it impossible for me to open my body to a man. I lost interest in sex.' She subsequently got divorced, declared herself a lesbian, and currently lives with an incest survivor – though whether her lover recovered 'repressed memories' or not is unclear.

7

the victims of incest had remained silent all these years, they had never forgotten. Often, they revealed confused, mixed feelings about their experience. Jean Monroe, whose father fondled her breasts from the time she was nine until her teens, spoke of the 'terrible betrayal' of her trust, but she also said, 'As an adult I've always been very happy sexually. Somehow I got an affirmative sense of my own personal sexual power from my father.'[11]

The notion of repressed incest memories had been quietly growing during the 1970s, however. In 1975, for instance, the director of a Philadelphia sex offender program told an audience of psychotherapists: 'If the sexual attack is dealt with improperly or repressed it may cause serious psychological problems.' Louise Armstrong's *Kiss Daddy Goodnight*, published in 1978, contained the story of Jenny, who told her: 'Until about a year ago I had no awareness that any of it had happened. I had completely removed it from any form of consciousness.' Indeed, Armstrong herself 'recovered' a memory of oral sex that purportedly occurred when she was 14.[12] And Sandra Butler's *Conspiracy of Silence* contained the story of Evelyn, who was 'flooded with [incest] memories which had been repressed ... Even now, the memory has an unreal feeling to it.'[13]

Consequently, it is not surprising that a few of the women in the 1983 Bass anthology also talked about having repressed all memory of their abuse. 'My healing began with my simultaneous decision to accept myself as a lesbian and to enter therapy,' wrote Yarrow Morgan. In therapy, she recovered forgotten memories of abuse by her mother and father while she was still in her crib. Similarly, 'R.C.' dreamed and recovered memories of how her father forced oral sex upon her from the time she was four until she was 11. 'I have met and loved my rage,' she said. She too had recently 'come out' as a lesbian and was completing a master's degree in counseling.[14]

Morgan's and R.C.'s stories – and their attitudes – signalled a fundamentally different kind of incest memory, wrapped in mystery, horror, rage, and gender politics. They contrasted sharply with the stories of always-remembered incest, which described the molestation within the context of daily life. For example, in describing her always-remembered abuse, Jean Monroe remembered: 'Suddenly the bedroom door bangs open and the children come running down the hallway. Daddy hastily closes my top and slides back in his chair.' Relieved, she escaped his fondling to join a game of hide-and-seek.[15]

By comparison, repressed-memory stories such as Yarrow Morgan's often described the abuse scenarios in some detail – Yarrow recalled 'a pink and purple worm-like thing'[16] – but they did not mesh with everyday life circumstances. Rather, they involved unremittingly negative and violent violations. Often, such 'recovered memories' asserted that the abuse began in early infancy, while the always-remembered accounts usually began around age nine or later.*[17]

THE SEARCH FOR LOST MEMORIES

Something odd had happened between the late 1970s and the early 1980s. The appalling extent of real abuse, and the reluctance of many women to disclose it, had led some therapists to conclude that many women had *repressed* all memory of their abuse. After all, as Florence Rush had pointed out, Freud had initially helped to uncover incest memories through hypnosis in the mid–1890s, only to reverse himself and declare his findings invalid. What if Freud had been right in the first place? The hunt for buried memories was on, particularly in Massachusetts.

Judith Herman, a Harvard-affiliated psychiatrist and feminist, actively encouraged women to recall abuse. In 1981, she published *Father-Daughter Incest*, which, like the 1983 Bass anthology, primarily told stories of women who had always recalled their abuse. Its index did not contain references to memory, repression, or dissociation. Herman had already come to believe in the existence of massive repression, though, citing the case of a 25-year-old who came to an emergency room with anxiety attacks and a vivid fantasy of being pursued by a man with a knife. 'It later emerged in psychotherapy,' Herman wrote, that a sexually harassing boss had 'reawakened previously repressed memories of sexual assaults by her father.' From ages 6 to 14, she now recalled, she had been forced to masturbate him, but she had managed to forget all about it until that moment.[18]

In her 1981 book, Herman referred to 'an informal network of

* As sex-abuse researcher David Finkelhor has pointed out, 'Almost all studies report statistics showing that children are more vulnerable to sexual abuse starting in the preadolescent period between ages 8 and 12.' In addition, most molesters are male. In contrast to these well-documented facts, 'recovered memories' often deal with violent and repeated abuse of much younger children, and *mothers* are frequently accused of the offenses.

therapists in private practice in the Boston area,' all of them staunch feminists who now began to hunt for repressed memories.[19*20] Throughout the early 1980s, in Herman's individual and group therapy, women used hypnotic age regression, dream analysis, and induced 'flashbacks' to retrieve their repressed memories. Ellen Bass, who had served as a mental health counselor in Boston, was undoubtedly part of the informal network trading stories of lost memories, and she took them with her to California.

Clinical psychologist Denise Gelinas, who co-founded and directed the Incest Treatment Program at a hospital in Springfield, Massachusetts, was also part of the network. In 1983, Gelinas published 'The Persisting Negative Effects of Incest,' a very influential article, in the journal *Psychiatry*.[21] In it, she described the 'subtle and varied' repercussions of incest, including depression, low self-esteem, alcohol or drug abuse, anxiety, and marital difficulties. The effects of incest, Gelinas stated, 'are so persistent they can emerge many years after cessation of abuse, and so pervasive they can blight the victim's past, present and future.' Once therapists identified potential victims, 'previously repressed memories begin to emerge and become available for work,' the psychologist wrote. 'Recognition of the patient as an incest victim allows the therapist to see the affect and memories as the potentially curative, cathartic emergence of a long-buried traumatic neurosis.'

The following year, Judith Herman and Emily Schatzow published an article entitled 'Time-Limited Group Therapy for Women with a History of Incest.' It was a curious paper. At first, it appeared that Herman and Schatzow had chosen 30 *bona fide* incest victims for group therapy. It soon became apparent, however, that many participants did not actually recall abuse, but had been referred by other therapists as likely candidates for memory retrieval. 'We may have been overzealous in encouraging ambivalent women to join a group,' the authors opined. In fact, the first goal proposed by group members was 'recovery of memories,' while other women described their goal differently: 'I just want to be in the group and feel I belong.' During the third or fourth session, 'the leaders introduced the idea of telling the incest story in more detail,' which resulted in 'discharge of a great deal

---

* Herman almost certainly included Ann Burgess, a Boston psychiatric nurse, in her 'informal network.' Burgess, who in the late 1970s had studied men convicted of having sex with groups of adolescent boys, coined the term 'sex rings,' which led to the myth of widespread ritual abuse cults ferrying children about for their nefarious pleasure. Burgess also helped promote the use of children's drawings to diagnose sexual abuse.

of feeling.' Finally, after rehearsal of their memories set off a 'chain reaction,' another session was devoted to 'shared fantasies of revenge.'[22]

Also in 1984, Jeffrey Masson published *The Assault on Truth: Freud's Suppression of the Seduction Theory*, in which he popularized the idea that Freud had been right when he hypnotized his patients (or applied his 'pressure method') and encouraged them to recall repressed memories of incest. Freud coined the term 'abreaction' to describe what he considered an emotional reliving of forgotten trauma, and for a while he believed he had found the key to his patients' problems in life.[23] Masson vilified Freud for a failure in moral courage in abandoning the theory. Masson's work provided an important scholarly cornerstone for the nascent Incest Survivor Movement and its renewed search for repressed memories. Soon modern therapists would once again encourage 'abreactions.' (*For a critique of Freud's seduction theory, see Chapter 10.*)

Meanwhile, Judith Herman's 'informal network' had extended well beyond the Boston area. It snaked its way across the United States, up into Canada, jumped the ocean to Great Britain, and reached halfway around the world. In 1978, New Zealand therapist Elizabeth Ward visited the United States, where she formed close ties with colleagues in an incest clinic. Back in Australia, she began working in the Canberra Women's Refuge, forming an incest group in 1979. 'The American experience,' she wrote, 'had "taken the scales from my eyes." ' In 1984, the London-based Women's Press published Ward's book, *Father-Daughter Rape* in which she called for 'an end to the patriarchal nuclear family,' suggesting it be replaced by 'matriarchal skills and values.' Though most of Ward's informants had always recalled their abuse, there were hints that recovered memory cases were just around the corner. 'Just recently I've remembered this part,' said Sonia. 'I find it hard to remember a lot of detail – I'm sure that's because I've blocked it out,' asserted Virginia. In her book, Ward referred to an 'international network of feminist caring' and to 'women's movement "speak-outs" in many countries.'[24]

That same year, a Welsh press published feminist Angie Ash's *Father-Daughter Sexual Abuse: The Abuse of Paternal Authority*, a slim radical feminist broadside based on her masters dissertation, which relied heavily on U.S. sources. It identified incest as the inevitable result of the 'patriarchy.'

Also in 1984, 60 million viewers tuned in to an ABC made-for-

American-TV movie called *Something About Amelia*, in which the 'something' bothering the teenage girl turned out to be incest.[25] Her wealthy, well-respected, good-looking father was forcing his daughter into sexual relations. The national attention was riveted on this obscene, hidden problem.

Particularly in England, the emotionally-charged word 'incest' came to be used for virtually any sexual contact with children. In 1981, Incest Survivor Campaign literature redefined incest as 'the sexual molestation of a child by any older person perceived as a figure of trust or authority,' explaining that 'blood relationship and taboo are red herrings.' Incest was simply 'the abuse of power.' By 1983, the organization was claiming that 20 per cent of the British female population were incest survivors.[26]

In the meantime, the idea that someone could completely forget horrendous abuse, then suddenly recall it years later, had been popularized in *Michelle Remembers*, a 1980 account of how Michelle Smith, a depressed young Canadian woman of 27, sought therapy with psychiatrist Lawrence Pazder in the wake of three miscarriages. A psychology major in college, she had a long history of nervous complaints, stemming in part from a childhood spent with an alcoholic father. Her mother had died when Michelle was 14, and her father gave her to her grandparents to raise.

Under the charismatic care of Dr. Pazder, Michelle began to 'remember' lurid scenes from her childhood under a kind of auto-hypnosis. Although he did not consciously invite her fantasies, it is clear from the book (written by therapist and patient, who have subsequently divorced their respective spouses and married one another) that Pazder encouraged a dependent relationship based on his believing everything he heard. 'The only way people were really helped,' Pazder thought, 'was to allow them to go into their feelings.' Not only that, 'he had the strongest sense that he and Michelle were about to embark on something significant.'[27]

Indeed they were. Michelle eventually convinced herself and Pazder that she had repressed memories of grotesque abuse at the hands of a satanic cult, led by the devil himself, when she was five years old. Her mother had actively participated in the cult. Throughout her months of 'remembering,' Michelle disclosed that she had been held naked in a cage full of snakes, that the sadists had burned and butchered stillborn babies and fetuses in her presence, killed kittens, and forced her to perform lurid sexual acts. At one point, they surgically attached horns to her head and a tail to her spine. Finally, Michelle supposedly was allowed to go home with her mother and promptly repressed the memory of her trauma until she felt safe enough to recall it with the sympathetic Dr. Pazder.[28]*

By the mid-'80s, the disturbing evidence of actual incest was increasingly publicized. Back in 1978, Diana Russell had conducted a survey of 930 randomly selected women in the San Francisco area. Her researchers conducted lengthy interviews. None of them fished for repressed memories. Russell published the results in 1986 as *The Secret Trauma: Incest in the Lives of Girls and Women*. Her findings were shocking. Using a fairly moderate definition of incest (unwanted actual or attempted sexual contact between relatives), she found that 12 per cent of the women had been incest victims before the age of 14. The mean age at which incest occurred was just over 11 years old. The prevalence rate for *all* sexual abuse, including extra-familial, was 28 per cent for those under 14. Using somewhat broader definitions (including experiences with exhibitionists as well as other unwanted non-contact sexual experiences), the figure rose to 48 per cent before 14.[29] A similar study of 248 random women, conducted by Gail Wyatt in Los Angeles, confirmed Russell's findings.[30]**[31]

Since that time, many figures about sex abuse have been thrown around – some much lower, others higher. Much depends on the definition of incest. Step-fathers are apparently more likely to molest their step-daughters, for instance. The U.S. incidence of incest in which biological fathers have intercourse with their children appears to be 1 per cent or less, according to several independent studies.[32] Regardless of the particular figure one chooses to believe, it is clear that the incidence of incest and other sexual abuse is alarmingly high. As Russell

---

* *Michelle Remembers* fails to mention Michelle's two sisters, neither of whom recalls any abuse. A family friend describes the mother as a woman 'whose whole life was for her children and nothing else. You couldn't have a nicer, more charming person.' Other claims fall apart when examined closely. For instance, a neighbor and former teacher recalls Michelle Smith attending first grade regularly in 1955 just when she was supposedly locked in a basement for months at a time.

** Russell's and Wyatt's studies have been criticized, however, on several grounds, among them: (1) Russell instructed interviewers to ask, 'How upset were you by this experience – extremely upset, somewhat upset, or not very upset?' There was no allowance for the possibility that the episodes were experienced as positive in any way, such as between brother and sister with mutual consent. (2) Incest was defined too broadly, as including *any attempted* sexual contact between relatives, *no matter how distant the relationship*. (3) The figures most frequently cited were inflated by including unwanted sexual approaches during adolescence (before the age of 18).

asserted, it appears to have profound consequences for many victims, affecting, to one degree or another, their ability to trust, to form relationships, to hold jobs.

It is almost impossible for a man to conceive of how threatened a woman feels in our society. Walking down the street, women are constantly aware, at some level, that they are vulnerable to attack. One of my daughters, for instance, barely escaped a rape when she was in college. Two teenage boys trapped her in an elevator in a campus building. Fortunately, she fought them off and got away when the doors opened, but it was a frightening and traumatic event for her.

While Diana Russell's book helped to alert the public to the extent of sex abuse, it also, unfortunately, helped promote the idea that many memories of abuse might have been relegated to the subconscious. 'Repression is a common protective mechanism employed by victims of all ages,' Russell asserted, 'but particularly victims of childhood traumas . . . Deliberate silence on the part of the victim and all who know about this trauma is more common. This silence makes repression all the more likely to occur.' She referred to a 1985 speech Judith Herman made to the American Psychiatric Association, claiming that those who were abused in very early childhood or who had endured violent abuse were most likely to resort to 'massive repression.'[33]

The following year, Cathy Ann Matthews, an Australian clergyman's wife in her fifties, published her first-person account of recovered memories, providing a role model for many other such books in years to come. Clearly influenced by Elizabeth Ward's work at the Canberra Women's Refuge, Matthews' book began unequivocally: 'Repression has burst its bonds.' Though she had previously remembered 'a fairly normal childhood, externally happy [in] an ordinary everyday suburban home,' she now believed that she had endured years of incest. 'Now, as though doors have been flung open, those first fifteen years of my life are bursting forth with an agony almost beyond endurance.'[34]*

By the mid-'80s, the idea that incest victims routinely repressed their memories had also filtered inland in the United States from Massachusetts and California and found purchase in the American heartland. In 1985, for instance, Mary Ann Donaldson, a therapist in Fargo, North Dakota, published her report on women in group therapy, many of

---

* Matthews expanded her original 1986 book and published it in 1990 as *Breaking Through*. The same year, an Australian docudrama of the same name riveted television viewers.

whom had recovered 'memories' in the process of therapy. 'The therapist should provide a safe environment,' Donaldson wrote. 'To break through the powerful denial, a process of memory recollections is a starting point.' She quoted one client, who reported her experience as 'very, very intense – the day that it first surfaced in the office I felt that it was happening to me right then.' Donaldson cautioned that after the initial revelation of abuse, 'the memories, perceptions about memories, and feeling reactions must be experienced in doses.' She recommended group therapy for its 'quickly developing intensity.'[35]

In 1987, Judith Herman published 'Recovery and Verification of Memories of Childhood Sexual Trauma' in *Psychoanalytic Psychology*, a widely cited professional paper that emphasized the extent and validity of repressed incest memories. (*For a critique of Herman's paper, see Chapter 2.*)

By that time, the idea of recovered memories had spread to England as well, where social workers were warned that sessions with children using anatomically correct dolls might trigger 'reliving of suppressed sexual abuse in the interviewer's own childhood.'[36] The following year, in 1988, a British television documentary, *The Nightingale Roars*, told the story of middle-aged Constance Nightingale, who had, for most of her life, according to one credulous critic, 'blocked from her memory a childhood of terrible abuse.'[37]*

The time was ripe for a major popular book on repressed memories. Indeed, many other threads came together to prompt Ellen Bass and Laura Davis to write *The Courage to Heal* in 1988 (published in the U.K. in 1990). There was, for instance, the mass hysteria over sex abuse in day-care centers. In 1983, frightened, suspicious parents of children attending the McMartin Preschool in California had taken their offspring to therapists. The preschoolers, after repeated questioning and prodding, came to believe that their teachers were monsters who had violated them in fantastic ways, and soon many other day-care centers were closed down and their employees jailed. (*See Chapter 9, 'And a Little Child Shall Lead Them'*) Other factors included the victimology movement, the fragmentation of the modern family, and other social pressures. (*See Chapter 11, 'Why Now?'*)

The time was ripe, and Ellen Bass, creative writer and feminist, was

---

* Constance Nightingale subsequently died, but now Nightingale Books, a Shrewsbury publisher named in her honor, distributes American recovered memory and ritual abuse books in the U.K.

the perfect person to synthesize and popularize the Incest Survivor Movement, along with her student Laura Davis. Their critics complain that Bass and Davis have no training in psychology, but that hardly mattered. Plenty of *bona fide* psychologists and social workers believed precisely the same things, though they might have used fancier terminology and published in academic journals. What Bass and Davis wrote was not so much a psychological primer, however, as it was a religious creed.

THE COURAGE TO ACCUSE

It is impossible to exaggerate the influence that *The Courage to Heal* has exerted. Most of the women I interviewed told me that they had read the book not just once, but obsessively, over and over again. 'I keep it on my bedside table. Like the Bible.' That comes from a 'Survivor'* quoted in the frontispiece of the 1992 edition. Another wrote, 'In the moments when I am most alone, I pick up your book and know that there is understanding.' For those who always recalled sexual abuse but who were afraid to talk about it, *The Courage to Heal* may well provide much-needed support and encouragement to seek help. Unfortunately, it has also served as reinforcement for questionable recovered memory theories and techniques. It is worthwhile, therefore, to understand exactly what Bass and Davis have to say in this book, which has sold over 750,000 copies in several editions.

Much of *The Courage to Heal* may be useful for those who really were abused, although even for them, the degree of rage that it encourages is probably unhealthy. The real trouble with the book, though, is that women who *think* they might have been abused, but who don't remember it, are the primary intended audience. In the introduction, Bass and Davis write, 'Often the knowledge that you were abused starts with a tiny feeling, an intuition. It's important to trust that inner voice and work from there. Assume your feelings are valid.' They assert that this is the beginning of an inevitable progression. 'So far, no one we've talked to thought she might have been abused, and then later discovered that she hadn't been. The progression always goes the other way, from

* Throughout this book, I have capitalized the term 'Survivor' to identify those who have recovered 'repressed memories' of sexual abuse and labeled themselves incest survivors.

suspicion to confirmation. If you think you were abused and your life shows the symptoms, then you were.'[38]*

The authors promise that reading their book will be a 'cathartic healing experience,' but they warn that in the process, many women 'have also reported feeling terrified, furious and anguished.' Others experience nightmares and flashbacks. But that's only to be expected. No pain, no gain. In fact, 'if you breeze through these chapters, you probably aren't feeling safe enough to confront these issues.' Eventually, however, women who suffer through all of this will be whole and healed – and that is the *only* way they can become whole and healed.[39]

In the first chapter Bass and Davis write, 'The long-term effects of child sexual abuse can be so pervasive that it's sometimes hard to pinpoint exactly how the abuse affected you. It permeates everything: your sense of self, your intimate relationships, your sexuality, your parenting, your work life, even your sanity. Everywhere you look, you see its effects.' By addressing female readers as 'you,' the authors automatically draw them in, presuming that they have indeed been abused. Then Bass and Davis ask a number of questions which, if answered in the affirmative, presumably indicate that someone was a victim of sexual abuse.

> Do you feel powerless, like a victim? . . . Do you feel different from other people? . . . Do you have trouble feeling motivated? . . . Are you afraid to succeed? . . . Do you feel you have to be perfect? . . . Do you use work or achievements to compensate for inadequate feelings in other parts of your life? . . . Do you have trouble expressing your feelings? . . . Do you feel confused much of the time? . . . Are you prone to depression? . . . Do you ever use alcohol, drugs, or food in a way that concerns you? . . . Do you feel alienated or lonely? . . . Do you find that your relationships just don't work out? . . . Do you find yourself clinging to the people you care about? . . . Do you expect the people in your family to change?[40]

The list of questions goes on at some length. But other than the most well-adjusted and boring person on earth, who *wouldn't* answer some

---

* I know from watching her on talk shows and from talking to her that Bass has now heard from several such women, retractors who no longer believe that they were abused, other than by therapists and by reading suggestive books. The third edition of *The Courage to Heal* features a very slight modification, saying that the progression *usually* goes from suspicion to confirmation and that if you think you were abused and your life shows the symptoms, there's a *strong likelihood* that you were. (Italics added.)

of these questions affirmatively? Sure, I sometimes feel powerless. I seem to be different from other people, and I often feel awkward and confused. Yes, I work hard. Sometimes I'm lonely and depressed. *Of course* I cling to the people I care about. It is an easy leap from there – if you are vulnerable, which is a good bet if you've picked up *The Courage to Heal* – to think 'Oh, my gosh! I must be an incest victim!' Bass and Davis reinforce this belief. 'If you feel overwhelmed reading this chapter, remember that you have already lived through the hardest part – the abuse itself. You have survived against formidable odds.' It's hard not to admire the way the authors have subtly transformed the reader. Not only are you a secret incest victim, but a Survivor, a hero.

Their next chapter, 'Coping,' reinforces this first lesson in victimhood and Survivorship. 'Coping is what you did to survive the trauma of being sexually abused,' Bass and Davis assure the reader. Such management skills can include just about anything. 'You may have become a superachiever, excelling in school and taking care of your brothers and sisters at home. You may have forgotten what happened to you.' Other coping skills include minimizing and rationalizing the abuse, or denying that it happened. Although the authors don't use the word 'dissociation,' they describe how abused children sometimes 'actually leave their bodies and watch the abuse as if from a great distance.' Other coping devices include mental illness, suicide attempts, or addictions.[41]*[42]

Bass and Davis identify another more widely hailed coping mechanism: eating disorders. If you are overweight, it's because you were sexually abused and you're protecting yourself, rendering yourself unattractive. The same logic applies to anorexia: 'If [incest survivors] don't grow breasts, develop full hips, become curvy, they won't be attractive.' On the other hand, bulimia is interpreted quite literally as a way of throwing up the past. 'As children, many survivors had fingers, penises, and objects shoved into their body openings. You may have had a penis shoved into your mouth. You may have gagged or vomited.'[43]

In short, there is hardly a human characteristic or problem that will not suffice to prove that you were abused or that you are coping. Even denying abuse is proof that it happened.

Having thus prepared the reader, convincing her that she was prob-

---

* Nowadays, people can claim an addiction to virtually anything, including not only alcohol and drugs, but sex, food, sleep, overwork, gambling, television viewing, shopping, and other human activities. 'We're coming up with new addictions every day,' one therapist cheerfully explains. All of these 'addictions' can, of course, be traced back to repressed memories of abuse.

18

ably abused, Bass and Davis describe 'The Decision to Heal' and 'The Emergency Stage.' It is evident from an introductory quotation that 'healing' is pretty scary stuff. 'If you enter into healing, be prepared to lose everything,' this Survivor says. 'Healing is a ravaging force . . . It rips to shreds the structures and foundations I built in weakness and ignorance.' If this is healing, then some people might prefer to remain ill.

Yet the warning is necessary, because the authors quite clearly want their readers to embark on a very painful journey. Only when all their fundamental assumptions are destroyed, when their family relationships lie in ruins, will they develop their new identity as Survivors.

The quotes from women going through this process are revealing, horrifying, and sad:

- It was hard to make that leap . . . I was giving up a person [myself] who was really a very viable, powerful, self-reliant human being . . . Into what void would I be thrown if I let go of this stuff? I felt like a raw muscle walking around for a long time.
- For a long time, I felt like a victim of the process . . . The whole thing felt out of my control, like being swept up in a hurricane.
- Breaking through my own denial, and trying to fit the new reality into the shattered framework of the old, was enough to catapult me into total crisis. I felt my whole foundation had been stolen from me. If this could have happened and I could have forgotten it, then every assumption I had about life and my place in it was thrown up for question.
- I just lost it completely. I wasn't eating. I wasn't sleeping . . . I had terrible nightmares about my father. I was having all kinds of fantasies . . . Physically, I was a mess. I had crabs. I hadn't bathed in a month. I was afraid of the shower.[44]

Bass and Davis admit that the process they recommend as necessary *often* destroys marriages and intimate relationships. 'It can even be hard to sleep, to eat, or simply to stop crying.' They quote another Survivor with approval: 'You can't go back. You can't unremember,' she says, then adds wistfully, 'I spent so many years not hurting at all.' In other words, 'healing' is likely to turn a basically happy life into a painful one. The authors justify this by asserting that 'deciding to actively heal is terrifying because it means opening up to hope.'[45]

During this 'emergency state,' which Bass and Davis say can last for years, Survivors often experience 'a profound sense of disorientation.'

They cut off relations with everyone except other Survivors, who understand what they are going through, and their therapists. 'I dropped everything else in my life,' writes one woman. 'It was like there were large six-foot-high letters in my living room every day when I woke up: INCEST!' Another explains why she dropped all of her old friends: 'I had no energy to deal with other people or their problems ... The people I used to call up and say, "Hi. Let's go roller skating," I didn't bother to call any more.'[46] Instead, the all-wise therapist becomes the center of their lives, a replacement for the lost father and mother: 'The only thing that saved me when I felt totally cut off from everything was that I had my therapist's phone number written many places, all over my house,' writes one Survivor.[47]

Bass and Davis get to the heart of the matter in 'Remembering,' a chapter in which they describe what repressed memories feel and look like. 'Often the memories are vague and dreamlike,' they explain. They will appear disjointed, in fragments. 'You may not know exactly when the abuse began, how old you were, or when and why it stopped.' They describe flashbacks as very brief moments of reliving the abuse, like a slide show in which you get only the briefest glimpse and must guess the progression of what comes before and after.

Bass and Davis recommend 'regression,' carefully avoiding the term *hypnosis*, which might scare some people. They quote a Survivor who began to talk in 'a five-year-old's voice, using words and concepts that a five-year-old might use.' Various stimuli can 'trigger' a memory, according to the authors – a touch, smell or sound. Your nightmares can provide clues to the abuse. Or, they say, 'The body remembers what the mind chooses to forget,' adding that 'memories are stored in our bodies, and it is possible to physically reexperience the terror of the abuse.' Consequently, if you have pelvic pains, feel that you are suffocating and can't breathe, or manifest other bodily complaints, they may be memories.

Reading books such as *The Courage to Heal*, or watching television talk shows in which Survivors recount their stories, help to produce memories, according to Bass and Davis. 'As the media focus on sexual abuse has increased, more and more women have had their memories triggered.' A strong reaction to someone else's story is a give-away. 'Often women become very uncomfortable (nauseated, dizzy, unable to concentrate, emotional) when they hear another survivor's story and realize that what's being described happened to them too.'[48]

Life situations can affect the timing of recovered memories. The birth of a child, a divorce, a father's death, or other transitions can help bring the material to consciousness. Sometimes when your child reaches the same age that you were at the time of the abuse, the memories are triggered.

Regardless of how the memories surface, though, Bass and Davis say that it is important to 'feel the feelings.' Unless you really get into your pain, unless you scream and yell and hurt and cry, it isn't good enough. You aren't really experiencing it all, and it won't get out of your system. 'You must feel, even if it sends you reeling.' One Survivor put it this way: 'These memories are literally stored in my body, and they've got to get out. Otherwise, I'm going to carry them forever.'[49]

Even though you must experience all this feeling, however, Bass and Davis explain that the process of reassembling the disparate memory fragments can be intellectually stimulating, 'a lot like putting together a jigsaw puzzle or being a detective.' They quote a Survivor: 'Part of me felt like I was on the trail of a murder mystery, and I was going to solve it. I really enjoyed following all the clues.'[50]

These clues can often, over time, lead to multiple perpetrators. 'The more I worked on the abuse,' one Survivor explains earnestly, 'the more I remembered. First I remembered my brother, and then my grandfather. About six months after that I remembered my father. And then about a year later, I remembered my mother.' Eventually, she managed to implicate her entire family. 'Even though it was traumatic for me to realize that everyone in my family abused me, there was something reassuring about it.' But what could possibly be reassuring about this? 'My life suddenly made sense,' she says.[51] Now she can find a simple explanation for every unhappy feeling she has ever had.

Despite every effort to find these elusive memories – obsessing over every bodily pain, every dream, every emotional twinge – some women, Bass and Davis lament, still can't quite dredge up memories of abuse. 'If you don't remember your abuse,' they console readers, 'you are not alone. Many women don't have memories, and some never get memories. This doesn't mean they weren't abused.' At this point in the book, Bass and Davis may have convinced readers that if they have any problems at all, then they were, in all likelihood, sexually abused. Just because they don't remember it – that should be no obstacle. 'If you don't have any memory of it,' the authors continue, 'it can be hard to believe the abuse really happened. You may feel insecure about trusting your intuition and want "proof" of your abuse.' If that happens, just give it some time. 'The unconscious has its own way of unfolding that does not always meet your demands or your timetable.'[52]

Bass and Davis quote a woman – 'her story is a good model' – who has never retrieved her abuse memories but has managed to rationalize that failure. 'I obsessed for about a year on trying to remember,' this Survivor relates. Tired of trying, she thought to herself, 'All right, let's act *as if.*' So she simply decided to act *as if* she had memories and not worry about it. After all, 'I had the symptoms. Every incest group I went to I completely empathized. It rang bells all the time.' When she occasionally worried that perhaps she was accusing her father unjustly, she prompted herself, 'Why would I be feeling all this anxiety if some-thing didn't happen?' So, she concludes confidently, 'I'm going with the circumstantial evidence, and I'm working on healing myself.' She goes to incest groups where, when she admits shamefacedly that she has retrieved no specific scenes, people are still sympathetic.[53]

Having perhaps convinced their readers that they really were sexually abused, Bass and Davis attempt to prevent any backsliding in the chapter, 'Believing It Happened.' It is inevitable, they write, that you will ques-tion your memories at first. 'Often in the beginning stages, belief in your memories comes and goes.' Don't worry, though. 'One practical way to validate your abuse is to look at your life. If you see the effects of abuse . . . you can trust that your belief is sound.' In order to maintain this belief system, the authors recommend attending support groups with other Survivors who will 'validate' the memories and reinforce them.[54]

They then relate the story of Emily. 'When confronted with the abuse, her parents denied everything and her father offered to see a counselor, take a lie detector test, anything, to prove his innocence.' What's wrong with that? Plenty. Whenever Emily talked with her parents, she became ill. 'The conflict between what she knew inside and what they presented was too great.' The solution? Try to sort all of this out with her parents with a good counselor? Try to understand the pain and confusion her father is experiencing, and appreciate his efforts to reconcile? No. 'It was only when Emily broke off all communication with her family and established a consistent relationship with a skilled therapist who believed her that she stopped doubting herself and got on with her recovery.' Bass and Davis conclude with words worthy of theologians: 'Believing doesn't usually happen all at once – it's a gradual awakening.'[55]

The next few chapters simply reinforce these familiar lessons. Join a

Survivors' group. Rehearse your memories, repeating them, writing them down, making them more real. Cherish those people who support your new belief system, but jettison those who express even the slightest doubt. 'There is a weeding out that goes on in relationships,' Bass and Davis write. 'Some people may be threatened. Some will go blank or be shocked. These people may be reminded of their own abuse . . . . Some people will be horrified. Some may not even believe you initially. Some may be incredibly rude.'[56] For many relatives who did not react in the precisely prescribed manner, reading this passage explains why they were cut off even though they were not accused themselves, and even though they reacted with horror and empathy. They were simply 'weeded out.'

Following pop guru John Bradshaw,* Bass and Davis spend another chapter encouraging women to contact their wounded, innocent 'child within,' to reconnect with 'her softness, her sense of trust and wonder.' Essentially, this entails a literal regression to childhood in which adult women decorate whole rooms as though for a five-year-old. 'I'm going to build a tent out of bed sheets and we'll [referring to herself and her inner child] sit inside and read stories by flashlight,' one Survivor writes. 'There will be glow-in-the-dark stars on the tent ceiling too. Oh, I love being little!'[57] In its most extreme form, the search for 'inner children' sometimes leads to a belief in multiple personalities, as we will see later.

After a brief chapter on mourning the loss of 'the fantasy that your childhood was happy,' Bass and Davis cut to the heart of the therapy. In the chapter 'Anger – The Backbone of Healing,' they whip women into a towering rage against their supposed perpetrators. 'Anger doesn't have to be suppressed or destructive,' they write. 'It can be both a healthy response to violation and a transformative, powerful energy.' If women can't 'get in touch' with their anger, Bass and Davis suggest working themselves into it. 'A little like priming the pump, you can do things that will get your anger started. Then, once you get the hang of it, it'll begin to flow on its own.' To get going, women should imagine an innocent child being raped, or read Survivor anthologies. Listen to other people's stories. 'You can hear their fury and be incited.' Sometimes, just 'physically taking an angry stance, making menacing gestures and facial expressions' will prompt the proper mood. 'Therapy and support groups can be ideal places for stirring up anger.' Similarly, you

* For an extended critique of John Bradshaw's thought, see Chapter 12.

can break old dishes, pound on your bed with a tennis racket, or just scream a lot.[58]

Bass and Davis consider it therapeutic to fantasize castrating or murdering the perpetrator, but they warn that carrying out such acts could land you in jail. Better to sue the bastard. 'Another woman,' they add helpfully, 'abused by her grandfather, went to his deathbed and, in front of all the other relatives, angrily confronted him right there in the hospital.'[59]

Mothers are not exempted from this flood of rage. Only if they were lucky enough to have been divorced early on, or if they completely believe the accusing daughter and separate now, are they likely to escape blame. 'You do have a right to be angry at your mother,' Bass and Davis write. 'Mothers of abused children are often fearful, self-protective and denying.' Consequently, 'if your mother didn't protect you, looked the other way, set you up, or blamed you, you are inevitably carrying some feelings of anger.' Unless your mother *also* abused you, the authors urge some moderation. 'You must not direct *all* your anger toward her. The abuser deserves his share.' Parceling out rage shouldn't be the problem, though. 'As you allow yourself to know the genuine depth and range of your anger, you will find there's enough to go around.'[60]*[61]

Once their Survivors are properly enraged, Bass and Davis encourage them to confront their abusers, though they add a disclaimer that no one should feel unduly pressured into a confrontation. There are numerous reasons for confronting – to make the perpetrator suffer, to extract revenge, to break the silence, or to demand money. 'When you confront the abuser or disclose your abuse, you are deciding to give up the illusions . . . You must be willing to relinquish the idea that your family has your best interests at heart.'[62]

They encourage thorough preparation before such a confrontation, starting with friends and siblings who are 'most likely to be allies.' Then, 'you set the boundaries, you pick the timing, you pick the turf . . . You can role-play possible scenarios in therapy or with supportive friends. Practice saying the things you want to say and responding to different

---

* As Carol Tavris convincingly documents in her book, *Anger: The Misunderstood Emotion* (1982), 'getting in touch with your anger' and releasing it is not necessarily a constructive or therapeutic activity. Despite the conventional psychological wisdom that regards anger as some sort of internal object in need of venting, Tavris points out that the emotion 'is as much a political matter as a biological one.' Often, ventilating our rage does not provide a catharsis. It simply makes us more angry. Tavris suggests an alternative remedy: developing a sense of humor.

reactions. You can write out the things you want to get across and memorize the essential points.' The confrontation can take place in person, at a therapy session, or through a letter or phone call. One Survivor stood in the receiving line at her older brother's wedding and passed out sealed envelopes containing her accusations against him. Whatever method you choose, Bass and Davis say, make it a surgical strike. 'Go in, say what you need to say, and get out. Make it quick.'[63]

It isn't necessary to wait until you have really clear memories. 'If your memories of the abuse are still fuzzy,' however, 'it is important to realize that you may be grilled for details.' One Survivor's aunt, for instance, had the audacity to suggest in a letter: 'These are very serious charges and you had better present some factual evidence to back it up.' Do not be dismayed by such unreasonable demands. 'You are not responsible for proving that you were abused.'[64]

If you decide not to confront ('Your parents may be paying your tuition at school, and you can't yet afford to be economically self-sufficient'), you can still satisfy your hatred in other ways. Write a nasty letter but don't mail it unless you decide to. 'Do not be reasonable . . . Be as angry and hurt and blunt as you want.' Draw a picture of your abuse and publish it in a Survivor newsletter. Burn a photo of your father. Get a friend to act out the perpetrator role in a psychodrama, while you confront him.[65]

Finally, Bass and Davis deal with the delicate topic of forgiveness, of which they clearly disapprove. 'You may never reach an attitude of forgiveness, and that's perfectly all right . . . Why should you? First they steal everything else from you and then they want forgiveness too? Let them get their own. You've given them enough.' Some Christian Survivors may have been brainwashed by church sermons, but they shouldn't worry. 'If there is such a thing as divine forgiveness, it's God's job, not yours.'[66]

Bass and Davis also counsel counselors. 'Believe the survivor,' they admonish. 'You must believe that your client was sexually abused, even if she sometimes doubts it herself. Doubting is part of the process of coming to terms with abuse. Your client needs you to stay steady in the belief that she was abused.' This is part of the necessary validation. 'If a client is unsure that she was abused but thinks she might have been, work as though she was.' Remember, 'no one fantasizes abuse.' The therapist must act as a 'witness.' 'Validate anger as a sane, healthy response.' If the Survivor wishes to confront her abuser, 'help her to prepare thoroughly. And if possible, be available to facilitate confrontations.' Above all, Bass and Davis stress one important commandment: 'Be willing to believe the unbelievable.'[67]

The Courage to Heal continues for over 500 pages, finally winding down with case studies of 'Courageous Women' and, in the 1992 edition, a lengthy 'Resource Guide' with over 600 books, support groups, organizations, newsletters and audiovisuals on incest, ritual abuse cults, meditation, outdoor programs for survivors, multiple personalities, male survivors, abuse by siblings – you name it, it's there. There's even a board game, 'Survivor's Journey.' Only in America could an entire Incest Survivor industry have sprung up so quickly to relieve frightened, angry women – and their insurance companies – of their money.

There's even a section telling women how to order vibrators and other sex toys. Throughout *The Courage to Heal*, there are selections that border on pornography – all of it lesbian or masturbatory. 'Slowly I spread my legs, opening myself up, positioning myself under the stream of water which falls down, caressing my vulva. I feel the heat, the fire of life, creep into my solar plexus, spreading warmly into my thighs and buttocks.' Or, 'My palms engulf your breasts, your fingernails cruise across my belly. We rock until you lie on top of me. You press your knee against my cunt, whisper I want you Baby.'[68*69]

The Courage to Heal encourages women to become lesbians as part of the politically correct expression of Survivorship. With few exceptions, the examples of relationships given in the text involve only women. References to healthy sex with men are few and far between. 'If you were abused by a man, you may find male genitals scary or repulsive,' write Bass and Davis, both lesbians themselves. Later, the authors use the same kind of suggestive approach to lesbianism as they do with repressed memories. 'If you think you might be a lesbian but the idea scares or disturbs you, what you're feeling is natural. It's common to have doubts and questions in the coming-out process. Try reading about lesbians who are comfortable with themselves. Read coming-out stories.' Besides, the authors explain, there's a lot more to being a lesbian than mere sex. It's a way of life. 'There's music, art, politics. There's a culture, a supportive community. There's an emotional, philosophical, and spiritual connection to women.'[70]

Of course, there's nothing wrong with masturbation or sex between

---

* In another surprising passage, Bass and Davis reveal that 'many [Survivors] masturbate while reading incest literature.'

women. Nonetheless, the message conveyed by *The Courage to Heal* is, at best, confusing. Over a decade ago, lesbian poet Adrienne Rich wrote an essay complaining about 'compulsory heterosexuality.'[71] That was certainly a valid grievance. Today, however, many women must feel that it is virtually compulsory to become a lesbian in order to become a true Survivor. Not only that, but there is an implication that a history of sexual abuse *produces* this sexual orientation, thereby stigmatizing it as somehow not a free choice or genetic predisposition, but one more coping mechanism, a reaction to trauma. It is precisely this sort of thinking that gay men and women have fought for years. Lesbianism as a sexual choice is fine – but as a creed that encourages a generalized hatred of men and a search for repressed memories of abuse, it is disturbing.*[72]

OTHER SURVIVOR LITERATURE

The Courage to Heal has spawned a seemingly endless stream of books, articles, newsletters, organizations, and TV movies about repressed memories of sexual abuse – how to extract them, how to cope with them, how to get back at the perpetrators. They repeat the same injunctions to contact inner children, vent rage, squelch doubts, and terminate family relationships. The titles themselves tell quite a story. Go into your local bookstore, and in the 'Recovery/Addiction' section you'll find books such as *Toxic Parents* by Susan Forward (1989) and *Divorcing a Parent* by Beverly Engel (1990). I will only skim some of the more important and widely quoted Survivor books here.

Secret Survivors, by E. Sue Blume (1990), is famed primarily for its 'Incest Survivors' Aftereffects Checklist,' which includes 34 items, many of which are quite common, such as a 'pattern of ambivalent or intensely conflictive relationships,' depression, phobias, anger issues, 'feeling crazy, feeling different,' low self-esteem, eating disorders, fear of the

---

* In an interesting essay called 'What We're Rollin Around in Bed With,' lesbians Amber Hollibaugh and Cherrie Moraga complain that the feminist movement has idealized lesbian relationships too much, with a vision of 'egalitarian sexuality, where we could magically leap over our heterosexist conditioning into mutually orgasmic, struggle-free, trouble-free sex. We feel this vision has become both misleading and damaging to many feminists, and in particular to lesbians ... Who can really live up to such an ideal?'

dark, swallowing or gagging sensitivity, or even wearing too many baggy clothes. Some 'aftereffects,' such as 'desire to change one's name' or 'humorlessness or extreme solemnity,' seem to be *products* of therapy or reading too many Incest Survivor books rather than symptoms. Others appear to include the entire population, such as number 17: 'High risk taking ("daring the fates"); inability to take risks.' That pretty much covers every contingency. And, of course, there's number 26, the one sure symptom of repressed memories: 'Denial, no awareness at all.'[73]

It is hardly surprising, then, that Blume writes, 'At any given time, *more than three quarters of my clients* are women who were molested in childhood by someone they knew.' Of course, most of them didn't realize they were Survivors until Blume convinced them. 'Many, if not most, incest survivors *do not know* that the abuse has even occurred!' She adds that 'most survivors need many years, and often many therapists, before they can face the truths of their past.' Blume then begins to rope in her reader. 'The incest survivor may appear to be . . . successful, talented, appealing, even happy. Yet underneath, she may feel as if she were rotting . . . If you are reading this and looking at your own life, you may be experiencing uneasiness, even sudden fear. You may suddenly begin to cry. The intensity of your reaction may confuse you, especially if it is accompanied by a strong denial – "No! This couldn't have happened to *me!*"[74] Naturally, Blume asserts that such a reaction proves that the reader was, indeed, abused.

According to Blume, almost any woman could qualify as an incest victim, even without dragging up memories of fondling, forced oral sex, or intercourse. 'Must incest involve intercourse?' she asks. 'Must incest be overtly genital? Must it involve touch at all? The answer is no.' She elaborates: 'There are many other ways that the child's space or senses can be sexually violated. Incest can occur through words, sounds, or even exposure of the child to sights or acts that are sexual but do not involve her.'[75]

In 1989, the year before *The Courage to Heal* became widely available in the U.K., Scottish rape crisis counselors Liz Hall and Siobhan Lloyd published the British equivalent, *Surviving Child Sexual Abuse: A Handbook for Helping Women Challenge Their Past.* Their influential book repeated all of the stereotypical beliefs about repressed memories and how to unearth them. Their list of symptoms included 'headaches, stomach problems, chronic backache, psychosomatic pains and illness, cystitis, asthma and eczema,' as well as epilepsy, insomnia, nightmares, eating disorders, and 'over-positive descriptions of childhood.' Many children who were sexually abused learned to deal with the abuse 'by denying its reality,' they asserted, 'by dissociating themselves from it or by repressing it partially or completely.' Nor is this uncommon. 'Such total amnesia frequently occurs though there are often clues that something unpleasant has happened in a woman's childhood.'

Hall and Lloyd warned that emerging abuse memories might be 'vague and without much detail' at first, but that counselors must encourage them and must themselves *believe the memories*. They should ask potential Survivors questions such as, 'You have been describing a number of difficulties that are often found in women who report that they were sexually abused as children. I wonder if this has ever happened to you?' Then, memories should be elicited using journals, artwork, or oral disclosure. It helps to tell the woman that 'everyone has a child within her. A woman should be reassured that "her" child was abused and needs to tell a safe and trusted adult.' When the client expresses doubts about the reality of such memories, she should be reassured that 'the main issue is that this memory/thought is bothering her' and that 'only by breaking the silence about her memories will they lose some of their pain.' The authors recommend incest survivor groups as good places to discover and process new memories.[76]

Other important Commonwealth Survivor books include:

Rescuing the 'Inner Child': Therapy for Adults Sexually Abused as Children, by Penny Parks (U.K., 1990). Parks is an American incest survivor who played a key role in importing recovered memories and inner child work into the United Kingdom.

Breaking Through: No Longer a Victim of Child Abuse, by Cathy Ann Matthews (Australia, 1990). This is an expanded version of the 1986 book, *No Longer a Victim*, an Australian account of recovered memory.

Dance With the Devil, by Audrey Harper, with Harry Pugh (U.K., 1990). A born-again evangelical Christian, Harper related her recovered memories of serving as a 'brood mare' in a satanic cult. The first British book on satanic Survivorship, this had enormous influence.

Seven for a Secret: Healing the Wounds of Sexual Abuse in Childhood, by Tracy Hansen (U.K., 1991). This is a 'Christian' book about how to retrieve sex abuse memories.

Children for the Devil: Ritual Abuse and Satanic Crime, by Tim Tate (UK, 1991). This controversial book was withdrawn by the publisher following legal action but continues to influence social workers looking for supposed ritual abuse cases. Tim Tate was largely responsible for an influential 1989 television program on satanic abuse.

The Filthy Lie: Discovering and Recovering from Childhood Abuse, by Hellmut Karle (UK, 1992). A British case history by a respected psychologist, this book gave a boost to recovered memories and multiple personality disorder (MPD).

Surviving Secrets, by Moira Walker (UK, 1992). Walker is a Leicester psychologist and a leading trainer among health professionals. This book espouses belief in recovered memories and ritual abuse.

EMOTIONAL INCEST

Sue Blume's broad definition of incest has become part of the Survivor dogma. If your father ever walked around naked, if he ever discussed his own sex life with you, if he walked into your bedroom without knocking, if he looked at you in what you considered a lustful manner,[77] if he commented on your growing breasts, if he hugged you a little too long, if you overheard him making love – that was incest. In fact, even if he did none of those things, he may simply have loved you too much, for the wrong reasons. 'To the casual observer,' writes Patricia Love in *The Emotional Incest Syndrome* (1990), 'the parents may appear loving and devoted. They may spend a great deal of time with their children and lavish them with praise and material gifts. But in the final analysis, their love is not a nurturing, giving love – it's an unconscious ploy to satisfy their own unmet needs.'*[78]

When Love writes about 'emotional incest,' she is not simply employing a metaphor. She believes that she is identifying another form of real incest, which Kenneth Adams calls 'covert incest' in his similar book, *Silently Seduced* (1991). 'These are strong words, I know,' writes Love, 'but I use them advisedly. Just as children are powerless against

---

* In a way, the idea that people could sexually abuse their offspring simply by *looking* at them in the wrong way has a long history in many societies – the so-called 'evil eye' phenomenon.

a parent's sexual advances, they are powerless against an emotionally invasive parent.' She describes Gwen, a well-educated client who at first saw no problem with her father. 'All she saw was what she had gained from the relationship – praise and affection, extra privileges, patient tutoring, and shared confidences.' Systematically, therapist Love destroyed that love, twisting it into confusion and then hatred. 'The difficult task I faced in the coming weeks was to help Gwen see the negative consequences of this excessive devotion. It would be unsettling for her to see how she had been harmed by her relationship with her father, but confronting this fact would give her insight into her puzzling emotional problems.'[79]

Like so many of these books, Love's begins with a checklist to see whether you were a 'Chosen Child,' a victim of emotional incest. If you answer 'yes' to three or more, that means you qualify:

1. I was the source of emotional support for one of my parents.
2. I felt closer to one parent than the other.
3. I got the impression a parent did not want me to marry or move far away from home.
4. Any potential boyfriend or girlfriend was never 'good enough' for one of my parents.
5. I felt I had to hold back my own needs to protect a parent.
6. I felt responsible for my parents' happiness.
7. I sometimes felt invaded by a parent.
8. One of my parents had unrealistic expectations of me.
9. One of my parents was preoccupied with drugs/alcohol, work, outside interests, or another sibling.
10. One of my parents was like my best friend.

Almost anyone would identify with three or more of those statements. Being human, most parents are sometimes unhappy and let their children know it, seeking emotional support from them. It is almost inevitable that a child will, at times, feel closer to one parent than another. Most parents aren't ecstatic at the thought of their offspring moving far away, just as they may be critical of the potential mate a child brings home. In the crucible of the nuclear family, every child sometimes feel invaded. I don't know of any parent in the world who doesn't have 'unrealistic expectations.' The list of preoccupations – drugs, alcohol, work, outside interests, another sibling – would qualify almost anybody. And is it *bad* for a parent to be a best friend as well?

31

There is, of course, much that is true in these books. In many marriages or divorces, a father or mother may rely much too heavily on children for emotional support. In such situations, children can feel acute responsibility beyond their years. While this phenomenon is unfortunate, however, it is fairly normal and widespread, and it is *not* incest, emotional or otherwise.*

In some ways, I find these books as insidious as *The Courage to Heal* and its ilk.**[80] To be a victim of 'emotional incest,' you don't have to drag up any new memories. As recovered-memory therapist Renee Fredrickson notes, one moment a client thought of her extended family as 'a hardworking, family-oriented group of people that she grew up admiring, loving, and laughing with.' But then 'the kaleidoscope shifted, and she suddenly saw an incest family, complete with abusers, alcoholics, and emotionally damaged people.'[81]

In other words, you simply have to shift your perception of always-remembered childhood events such as back rubs, games of chase, or ghost stories, turning them into evidence of long-lasting abuse. Even the positive aspects of parenting – love, devotion, praise, pride, honesty, emotional support, treating children as real individuals instead of minor dependants – are taken as evidence of abuse by Patricia Love. At least Love doesn't encourage readers to cut off all relationship with their parents. 'You don't have to like your parents; you don't have to agree with them on important issues; you don't have to have similar tastes or values. All you need to do is see them and accept them for who they are.'[82] That's the sort of common sense that children have to re-learn every generation. Parents are not perfect.

Unfortunately, Kenneth Adams, in *Silently Seduced*, is more blaming.***[83] He encourages the same sort of rage, augmented by support

---

* Many parents face particular difficulties along these lines in the wake of a divorce, as Judith Wallerstein points out in her landmark 1989 book, *Second Chances: Men, Women, and Children a Decade After Divorce*. 'When a marriage breaks down,' she writes, 'most men and women experience a diminished capacity to parent. They give less time, provide less discipline, and are less sensitive to their children, being caught up in the personal maelstrom of divorce and its aftermath. Many parents are temporarily unable to separate their children's needs from their own.' Wallerstein also noted that 'many children assume responsibilities well beyond their years as they undertake to psychologically advise and physically nurture a troubled parent.'

** *The Courage to Heal* does mention 'emotional incest' in passing, though only for the woman who decided to act 'as if,' because she couldn't find any more satisfactory memories.

*** Adams' book offers a grab-bag of Recovery Movement clichés. 'Covert incest' leads to addictions. 'The list is endless. One can become addicted to anything.' It involves 'the murder of their souls.' One of his clients made the triumphant progression from covert incest to recovering repressed memories that were 'validated through her dreams.'

groups, as do Ellen Bass and Laura Davis. 'Let go of your idealized image of the seductive parent,' he urges. 'Acknowledge that the attention you received was violating and abandoning.' He wants clients to 'set boundaries and separate' from parents. 'If you feel guilty, which is likely, remind yourself it is not your job to be your parent's spouse. Expecting it to be your job is a violation and abusive. You also may need to have no contact at all with this parent for a while.' At least Adams sees reconciliation as a possibility. 'In time as you work through these feelings and set appropriate boundaries, your feelings of love and compassion for your parent may return.' Forgiveness may be in order, he says, but 'it is important that you not forgive too soon.'[84]

As a child of the '60s, I suspect that the attitudes of my contemporaries have made my generation particularly susceptible to charges of emotional or sexual abuse of our now-grown children. Ellen Bass herself, who is roughly my age, in 1983 wrote the following about the parenting of her daughter Sara:

> When she was a toddler and her father or I were undressed, drying off from a shower or putting our clothes on in the morning, she would sometimes comment on our genitals, saying 'vagina' and patting my vagina, or 'penis' and touching her father's penis. We would say, 'Yes, that's my vagina,' or 'Yes, that's my penis,' let her pat for a moment, and continue drying or dressing. I consider this healthy. She is curious about the world, and genitals are part of it.[85]

Frankly, I find that somewhat disturbing. In interactions between adults and children, I have always felt that touching, let alone 'patting,' of genitals is inappropriate, particularly in our culture.*[86] But I did share the larger view that Bass expressed at that time: that the human body is natural and wonderful, that children should be comfortable with their bodies, and that occasional nudity was not a big deal. Today, such

* I discussed this matter with a friend of mine, an anthropologist. He pointed out that in some cultures, it is considered perfectly normal for children to touch their parents' genitals or vice versa. In various cultures in the past (Peru, Egypt, Persia), outright incest was even sanctioned. According to a 1992 article by anthropologist Claudia Konker, 'In a variety of contemporary cultures it appears that adults may affectionately sniff, kiss, blow upon, fondle, and praise the genitals of young male and female children.' Of course, we do not know what effect such ministrations have upon the children's development or attitude toward sex.

attitudes are interpreted in retrospect by Bass's followers as incest, emotional or otherwise.

MEN CAN BE SURVIVORS, TOO

'Emotional incest' is more of an equal-opportunity accusation than the physical variety. Men can complain about how their mothers smothered them with invasive affection just as often as women can identify breached boundaries.

One of the constructive results of the Survivor Movement has been the recognition that boys, too, have been subjected to widespread sexual abuse for centuries. Because of cultural influences in our society, boys and men are less likely to come forward with their stories. While the true incidence of abuse of boys is unquestionably higher than anyone conceived until recently, however, the search for repressed memories is just as hazardous for men as for women.

Although *The Courage to Heal* is directed exclusively toward women, men, too, have been finding their own repressed memories of actual abuse, with a proliferation of books directed specifically to their cases.

In *Victims No Longer* (1988), Mike Lew provides the male equivalent to *The Courage to Heal*, with Ellen Bass writing the foreword. 'When clients tell me they have no recollection of whole pieces of their childhood,' therapist Lew comments, 'I assume the likelihood of some sort of abuse.' Many of his clients arrive at his doorstep already intent on recovering memories. 'If only I knew for certain,' they tell him, 'then I could deal with it. It's the uncertainty that's so hard.' Although Lew cautions them that simply retrieving the memories may not make them completely well, he gladly helps clients along, suggesting 'hypnosis, psychodrama, guided imagery, psychoanalysis, meditation, massage, or any other combination of mind and body work.'[87]

Like their female counterparts, male Survivors must give up the myth of a happy childhood. 'The adult survivor may remember his childhood as having been perfect,' Lew writes. 'He may paint over the grim details with softer colors. When a client presents "too perfect" a picture of childhood, I find that it is usually a good idea to look further.' Lew gives examples of how various men's memories were first triggered. 'I was having a massage,' one Survivor writes, 'and when he had me turn over onto my stomach I began to shake uncontrollably.' Such catalysts

34

may result in clear memories or simply 'the feeling that something happened.'[88]

The rest is all quite familiar to anyone who has read *The Courage to Heal*. Lew encourages confrontation after much rehearsal. 'If you choose to provide advance notice, you will need to consider how much information you are going to supply about the subject of the meeting. Remember, this confrontation is *for your benefit alone*.' Therefore, you need to manipulate the situation in your favor. 'This isn't a debate or a jury trial. There is no need to argue.'[89]

Lew even provides a model accusatory letter from Ivan, complete with memories 'from my birth to age four-and-a-half,' in which the sadistic mother cut the child with a knife. This was so scary that Ivan forgot it completely for decades. 'You may have done the same,' he confidently informs his mother. 'Whatever you've chosen to do with your memories, I can't stand mine anymore. This really happened. To me. So, if you draw a blank, reach back and try to see it.'[90] Ivan sent copies of the letter to his uncle, brother, father, therapist, minister, and selected friends.

Like Ellen Bass and Laura Davis, Mike Lew has spawned imitators. In 1990, for instance, Mic Hunter published *Abused Boys: The Neglected Victims of Sexual Abuse*, in which he describes the familiar process of repression, dissociation, and recovery. The most compelling portions of the book, however, are the personal testimonials at the end. 'My name is Greg, and I am a recovering incest victim,' one begins, in imitation of an Alcoholics Anonymous meeting. 'I am writing my story to say that what happened to me was real, my feelings are valid.' He sought counseling, depressed because of a job demotion. 'My memories of the incest only started to surface after I had been in therapy for a while,' he tells us. 'Even now my memories are few and sketchy.'[91]

Sonny Hall had been in therapy for 14 years, but 'it is only in the last year that I have known that I am recovering from incest.' Allen, another survivor, lay on his bed one night trying to find his memories. 'I laid there trying to listen to my body, my spirit.' He worked himself up into a panicky state until he began gagging. 'It was then I knew the awful truth: I was getting in touch with recalling the abuse I had suffered at my father's hands.' His father, he thought, had stuck his finger in his rectum while choking him. 'So many questions answered: why I hated turtleneck sweaters, neckties; anything on my throat brought me back at some level to my father choking me.'[92]

Some of the stories in *Abused Boys* reveal more about the therapeutic climate than about abuse. 'All my girlfriends eventually told me about how they had been sexually abused as children,' Jim reveals. When he himself went to therapy, his counselor pounced on an apparently normal family story, saying, 'That sounds like sexual abuse to me.' In subsequent sessions, the therapist would identify yet another example of sexual abuse that had somehow eluded Jim. Another self-described Survivor, Kent, first found a male therapist who seduced him sexually, then one who convinced him that his father had anally raped him.

One story, however, does not mention repressed memories and is probably a true account. Unlike the others, it does not involve mystical, fragmentary memories from early childhood. When he was 16, Daniel's new stepmother seduced him. 'I was ecstatic, guilty, frightened, and ashamed. I fell in love with her.'[93]

A TEXTBOOK FOR MEMORY INVENTION

While *The Courage to Heal* may be the bible of the Incest Survivor movement, *Repressed Memories: A Journey to Recovery from Sexual Abuse* (1992), by clinical psychologist Renee Fredrickson, is its potent textbook. If you are determined to create abuse memories *ex nihilo*, this is the book for you.

'Denial is overcome only by patient growth in the opposite direction,' Fredrickson states. 'In reading this book, whenever you find yourself worrying – "What if I'm wrong?" – try to always ask yourself the opposite question – "What if I'm right?"'[94]

Fredrickson relates the story of Carolyn, who gradually came to believe that her father had molested her. 'Her anger and grief were enormous. For months she suffered emotionally, physically, and spiritually. She had crying jags, eating binges, suicidal feelings, and bouts of depression.' Fredrickson unquestioningly assumes that all of these were symptoms of abuse rather than results of therapy. 'I never felt like my problems were connected to my past,' Carolyn told her. 'To be honest, they still don't seem related.'[95]

Another patient exclaimed during a session: 'But I feel like I'm just making this up!' Fredrickson ignored her concern. 'I urged her to continue, explaining that truth or fantasy is not of concern at the beginning of memory retrieval work.'[96]

On cue, Fredrickson provides the now familiar 'symptoms' of abuse

– 'failed relationships, depression, anxiety, addictions, career struggles, and eating disorders,' adding that 'the list is as varied as the human spirit' – or imagination. 'Let yourself know what the most hopeless or shameful problem in your life is,' she advises. 'Try saying to yourself three or four times a day for one week, "I believe this problem is about my repressed memories of abuse." After a week, write down or talk over with a friend how you see the problem now. Speculate on how it may relate to how you were abused.' You don't have to be mentally ill or overtly disturbed to have been sexually abused. 'Most people who have repressed memories are not odd or weird. As a matter of fact, most are models of normalcy. This form of amnesia lurks in the background of millions of ordinary, high-functioning Americans.'[97]

Members of the family system all fit neatly into three categories, according to Fredrickson: offender, denier, or victim. 'Sexual abuse is always intergenerational,' she flatly states, 'and everyone in a sexually abusive system takes one of these roles.' Noting that 'even the most apparently healthy family can have depths of sickness that astound outsiders,' she urges the reader to make a list of nuclear and extended family members. 'List any problem or dysfunction you know of or suspect . . . Err on the side of overstating problems, rather than on the side of denial . . . Signify their role and yours using O for offender, D for denier, and V for victim.'[98]

Fredrickson encourages women to believe that they were abused as infants by several perpetrators. 'How old do you think you were when you were first abused? Write down the very first number that pops into your head, no matter how improbable it seems to you . . . Does it seem too young to be true? I assure you it is not.' She asserts that 'dissociation always occurs during abuse,' and that, further, 'abusers are usually dissociated during the abuse, too.' In other words, not only would the victim forget the abuse, so would the perpetrator – or perpetrators, as the case may be. 'Multiple abusers increase the likelihood of memory repression. The sheer number of abusers becomes overwhelming.'[99]

Fredrickson primes potential Survivors to become suspicious of any stray feelings they may have. 'Bedrooms, bathrooms, basements, and closets are common places where sexual abuse occurs, so be alert to reactions to those places or to objects in them. Ordinary household items that can be vaginally or anally inserted are often used during abuse, like bottles, sticks, or penis-shaped foods or objects.' Once such paranoid visions are implanted, almost anything can become evidence or a 'trigger' for memories of abuse. Buying a cucumber at the grocery store can engender panic. 'Extraordinary fear of dental visits is quite often a signal of oral sexual abuse.'[100]

The heart of *Repressed Memories* describes specific methods for retrieving abuse memories, including guided imagery, dream work, journal writing, body work, hypnosis, art therapy, and rage work. The author's description of 'imagistic memory work' – actually a form of hypnosis – is detailed and revealing. First, under the guidance of a therapist or friend, you seat yourself, close your eyes, and relax, breathing deeply. Try to picture some kind of abuse. 'If nothing surfaces, wait a bit, and then give your best guess in answer to the questions [of your guide]. If you feel resistance or skepticism, try to go past it.' Afterward, your guide should follow up with questions to 'fill in any blanks.' You should consider any scene you envisioned as a 'freeze-frame photograph' out of sequence. 'You want to develop a sequenced slide show, showing the action from beginning to end.' At first, 'you may be hesitant because you are in a new situation and do not understand what is being asked of you.' But don't worry, it will come. It's important to understand that this is an exercise in imagination. 'You are not trying to stimulate your recall memories. Instead, you need to let yourself imagine or picture what might have happened to you.'[101]

Some dull subjects have a hard time with this process. 'Occasionally, you may need a small verbal push to get started. Your guide may suggest some action that seems to arise naturally from the image you are picturing.' The guide should always remember to use the present tense, to increase the feeling that this visualization is actually happening right now. As a helpful example, Fredrickson quotes one suggestible subject: 'Vera was remembering being tied spread-eagled on a table with her grandfather looming over her, holding a knife in one hand and a live rat in another.' Vera picks up the story: 'He cuts the rope from around my neck and starts to shove the rat in my mouth. I am squirming, trying to get away, and he says, "Do you want the rat or me?" Then he puts his penis in my mouth.'[102]

After getting the hang of it, visualizing abuse should be a breeze, according to Fredrickson. 'Once through the initial pitfalls, sequencing proceeds smoothly for a time. You will be able to freely share your images and awarenesses. Action builds, and you become deeply engaged in the process, curious to find out what your mind will picture.' In other words, at this point, the supposed Survivor realizes that she has become the heroine of her own internal movie. She is fulfilling her therapist's expectations, and she will be praised for reporting abuse – the more gruesome, the better. 'The most traumatic act of the abuse,' Fredrickson explains, 'is usually the act that culminates in the orgasm of the offender. At this point, you are completely dissociated . . . and you may say such things as, "I must be making this up," or "I'm just saying what you want me to say." Repressed memories rarely seem real when they first emerge.'[103]

I will not inflict much more of this kind of thing on the reader. Fredrickson interprets dreams, body memories, hypnosis, and art therapy in the same inimitable fashion. Everything confirms abuse. If her patients want to seek some sort of confirmation, such as pediatric records, they are discouraged: 'You can . . . become too caught up in seeking external proof rather than internal relief. External proof of repressed memories is elusive, buried under the massive weight of the family's denial system.' Like Bass and Davis, Fredrickson says that 'you cannot wait until you are doubt-free to disclose to your family . . . Once you make the decision to go ahead, the actual disclosure is an empowering experience . . . Avoid being tentative about your repressed memories. Do not just tell them; express them as truth. If months or years down the road, you find you are mistaken about details, you can always apologize and set the record straight.'[104]

Finally, if your parents steadfastly deny everything, perhaps it's just that they don't remember it either. 'Do not retreat. You may want to suggest that the abuser has repressed all memory of the abuse . . . A suggested response might be to look him or her in the eye and say, "You and I both know that what I am saying is true." '[105]

Not all self-help authors take such an extreme position. For instance, Wendy Maltz, author of *The Sexual Healing Journey: A Guide for Survivors of Sexual Abuse* (1991), doesn't think that *forcing* repressed memories is a good idea. 'Don't try to force recall,' she advises. 'Memories will emerge when you are ready to handle them.' Unfortunately, such a 'moderate' position is in some ways more persuasive than the forceps method advocated by Fredrickson.*[106] Simply telling a client that she *may* have memories, and that they will come up on their own, is enough to set the obsessive mind-search in gear. Maltz helps it along. 'If you

---

* I stole the forceps metaphor from social worker Mitch Bobrow, who wrote a 1993 article entitled 'Helping Sexually Abused Clients to Remember: the Use of Forceps in Psychotherapy.' He recommended 'using a directive and forceful psychotherapeutic tool [to] help shorten a client's recovery process.' Bobrow's method consists of relaxing the client and then asking, over and over again, 'What happened to you? What happened to you?'

feel ready to investigate your memories of sexual abuse, the following exercises may help you.'

After telling women to think about their earliest sexual experiences and to pay close attention to sexual dreams and fantasies, Maltz comes to the clincher: 'Spend time imagining that you were sexually abused, without worrying about accuracy, proving anything, or having your ideas make sense. As you give rein to your imagination, let your intuition guide your thoughts.' As they visualize the hypothetical abuse, women should ask themselves what time of day it is, who is there, what sort of touch is happening, what emotions are raised, and the like. 'Who would have been likely perpetrators?' she adds.[107]

THE ACADEMICS

Thus far, I have primarily cited popular authors. What about the more serious studies by Ph.D. types, with footnotes and four-dollar words? Surely, they do not accept this same oversimplified dogma, do they? Unfortunately, many do, conveying the same concepts as Bass and Fredrickson (herself a Ph.D., actually). Well-known 'experts' such as Lenore Terr, Roland Summit, John Briere, Karen Olio, Christine Courtois and many others have published almost identical material, though their writing styles are less sensational. The most influential of the academics is Judith Lewis Herman, who helped to promote the concept of repressed memories in the first place. Her magnum opus, *Trauma and Recovery* (1992), garnered glowing reviews. Laura Davis, co-author of *The Courage to Heal*, calls Herman's book 'a triumph.'

Much of *Trauma and Recovery* is an accurate description of post-traumatic stress disorder (PTSD) and a review of literature about trauma in general, from war to the Holocaust to rape. Unfortunately, Herman's book is polemical and slanted by ideological zeal from the outset. In her introduction, Herman equates repressed individual memories with societal problems: 'Denial, repression, and dissociation operate on a social as well as an individual level.' Her logic allows her to equate 'vast concentration camps created by tyrants who rule nations' to 'small, hidden concentration camps created by tyrants who rule their homes.'[108] In some cases, this equivalency may hold true, but there is a fundamental distinction. No one completely forgot the Holocaust, though some neo-Nazi revisionists have attempted to write it out of history. Yet Herman assumes that millions of women have managed to erase all conscious memory of abuse from their minds.

There is a stock answer to this observation. The context, Herman says, is all important. Because prisoners lived in Dachau or Auschwitz continuously, the experience was impossible to forget. But a child, terrorized by Daddy every night, has to get up every morning to a make-believe world of a smiling father presiding over the middle-class breakfast table. She cannot handle this enormous disparity, so she represses the memories of abuse.

In her ninth chapter, 'Remembrance and Mourning,' Herman repeats some by-now familiar concepts. Traumatic memories will return in fragments, like 'a series of still snapshots or a silent movie.' The task in therapy is to 'provide the music and words,' with the therapist playing the role of 'witness and ally, in whose presence the survivor can speak of the unspeakable.' Unlike our usual concept of a neutral counselor, Herman emphasizes that 'the moral stance of the therapist is ... of enormous importance. It is not enough for the therapist to be "neutral" or "nonjudgmental."' Instead, the professional must 'affirm a position of moral solidarity with the survivor.'[109]

Even though the initial memories may seem unreal, the therapist must help to 'reconstruct the traumatic event as a recitation of fact. Out of the fragmented components of frozen imagery and sensation, patient and therapist slowly reassemble an organized, detailed, verbal account, oriented in time and historical context.' Herman approvingly quotes a fellow counselor: 'We have them reel it off in great detail, as though they were watching a movie, and with all the senses included. We ask them what they are seeing, what they are hearing, what they are smelling.' At the same time, Herman encourages her clients to *feel* their violation and rage. 'The recitation of facts without the accompanying emotions is a sterile exercise.' She recommends 'flooding' sessions in which 'the patient narrates a script aloud to the therapist, in the present tense, while the therapist encourages him to express his feelings as fully as possible.'[110]

The therapist also 'facilitates naming and the use of language.' In other words, if you *call* something abuse, if you learn the proper jargon – repression, dissociation – you're halfway there on the journey to a new worldview. Herman quotes a Survivor's advice: 'Keep encouraging people to talk even if it's very painful to watch them. It takes a long time to believe. The more I talk about it, the more I have confidence that it happened, the more I can integrate it.'[111]

Even with such rehearsal, 'both patient and therapist must develop tolerance for some degree of uncertainty, even regarding the basic facts of the story. In the course of reconstruction, the story may change as missing pieces are recovered.' Everyone must learn to 'live with ambiguity.' Herman gives the example of Paul, a 23-year-old who described his abuse in a pedophilic sex ring to an excited female therapist. 'Paul suddenly announced that he had fabricated the entire story.' He threatened to quit therapy unless she believed him, but the wily therapist managed to bring Paul around. 'I can't pretend to know what happened,' she told him. 'I do know that it is important to understand your story fully, and we don't understand it yet. I think we should keep an open mind until we do.' Eventually, Paul came to believe that 'his recantation was a last-ditch attempt to maintain his loyalty to his abusers.'[112]

Several people, including accused parents, have told me that Judith Herman is really quite reasonable, since she warns in one brief paragraph that 'therapists have been known to tell patients, merely on the basis of a suggestive history or "symptom profile," that they definitely have had a traumatic experience . . . In some cases patients with only vague, nonspecific symptoms have been informed after a single consultation that they have undoubtedly been the victims of a satanic cult.'[113] While such cautionary words are welcome and laudable, the rest of Herman's advice clearly urges therapists to search for repressed memories – just wait until the third or fourth session before you validate the abuse.

Even in this one cautionary paragraph, Herman goes on to say, 'The therapist has to remember that she is not a fact-finder and that the reconstruction of the trauma story is not a criminal investigation. Her role is to be an open-minded, compassionate witness, not a detective.' Yet lawsuits are in fact built on such cases. Families, lives, careers are destroyed because of what happens in one of these 'open-minded' therapy sessions.

Later, Herman recommends the judicious use of hypnotic age regression, sodium Amytal, psychodrama, group therapy, and dream analysis. Like Bass and Davis, she discourages forgiveness and encourages rage, quoting a dialogue from a group therapy session:

MELISSA: I'd like to break his knees with a bat.
LAURA: He deserves it. I've had fantasies like that.
MARGOT: Go on. Don't stop now!
MELISSA: I'd like to start methodically on one knee and then move

on to the next. I chose that because it would make him feel really helpless. Then he'd know how I felt.[114]

In short, one shouldn't worry about whether one's memories are truthful or not, but it's good to react violently to them.

RITUAL ABUSE AND MULTIPLE PERSONALITIES

The most extreme claims of repressed memories involve supposed ritual abuse, and they frequently lead to a diagnosis of multiple personality disorder, otherwise known as MPD. First 'diagnosed' around the turn of the century (*see Chapter 10*), multiple personalities were considered rare until the publication of *The Three Faces of Eve* by Thigpen and Cleckley in 1957. Their book told the story of 'Eve,' in reality Christine Costner Sizemore, who ultimately graduated from 3 to 22 different internal personalities. But it was *Sybil*, published in 1973 and made into a popular movie in 1977, that really spawned the modern crop of multiples and provided the cornerstone for an assumed background of sexual abuse. Sybil came to Dr. Cornelia Wilbur as a severe anorexic and soon revealed a second side of herself named Peggy. Over time, 16 different entities emerged, all having 'split' from the original because of horrendous sexual and physical abuse.

With the publication in 1980 of *Michelle Remembers*, already mentioned, the element of satanic ritual abuse was added, along with the possibility of demonic possession. Also in 1980, psychiatrist Ralph Allison published *Minds in Many Pieces*, in which he described an exorcism of one of his multiple personality patients. The same year, the third edition of the *Diagnostic and Statistical Manual of Mental Disorders (DSM-III)* , published by the American Psychiatric Association, first recognized multiple personality disorder as a bona fide psychiatric disorder. Because American insurance companies will pay only for mental illnesses sanctioned by the *DSM*, multiple personalities suddenly became lucrative and acceptable in the United States and Canada. The 1980s witnessed a veritable explosion of MPD cases in North America, though many of them were diagnosed by a small cadre of 'specialists' including Richard Kluft, Robert Mayer, Bennett Braun, Philip Coons, Eugene Bliss, Colin Ross, Cornelia Wilbur, and Frank Putnam. Curiously, while the majority of therapists are women, most of the MPD specialists are

43

men. Before 1980, there were only 200 or so references to multiple personalities in the professional literature. Since then, over 25,000 people have been diagnosed with the disorder.[115]

While theorists such as Bass and Herman speak primarily about repression, the MPD specialists prefer to identify 'dissociation' as the primary method of forgetting abuse. In their model, the memories never reach normal consciousness and, therefore, are never forcibly pushed down into the subconscious. Instead, the abuse is so awful that the victim's mind cannot survive if it remains aware. Therefore, the mind splits off, or dissociates, forming alternate personalities to 'take' the abuse. Usually, these 'alters,' as the internal identities have come to be called, are not aware of the 'core personality' or of one another, and the core is equally amnesic toward its alters.

Surprisingly, many MPD clients appear to be 'high-functioning,' seemingly normal individuals who are themselves completely unaware that they harbor multiple alters. Only under hypnosis or through sugges-tive interviewing do they reveal themselves to the savvy therapist, who can then question each personality, calling them forward in turn. The therapists are usually alerted to the possibility of MPD when their patients report an inability to remember whole chunks of their child-hood. These cases often progress in stages. First, the patient reveals simple repressed memories of abuse, often by a father or grandfather. Then, hints of far-worse horrors surface. Eventually, these patients remember ritual group abuse, often involving worship of Satan. In a group setting, they were subjected to hideous sexual and physical abuse. As part of the ritual, babies were hacked to death and eaten, blood and urine drunk, feces consumed, and every other conceivable horror experienced. As a flier from Survivors of Incest Anonymous puts it, 'the physical component usually includes torture, at times maiming and disfigurement, and even death. The sexual component of Ritual Abuse is often violent, purposefully painful, intended to degrade and dehumanize, and to orient the victim toward sadism.'[116]

These ritual abusers routinely turn out to be some of the parents' best friends – bowling buddies, fellow Elks, or the local bridge club. In other words, some of the worst abusers are pillars of the community. Often, the doctors in the group helped to dispose of the telltale remains, erasing all hospital records of the birth. These satanic cults would go to any length to confuse their victims. Often they dressed up in bizarre fashion, so that if the children reported what had occurred, no one would believe them. 'Mind control' methods such as strobe lights, electrical shocks and hypnotic spells were used to make the victims forget or dissociate. Finally, they were told repeatedly, 'This never happened. You will never remember this.'

The Survivors of SRA (satanic ritual abuse) consequently regard themselves as a sort of elite inside the Incest Survivor community. They've seen it all. They've suffered monstrously, beyond belief. Their interior beings include not only the standard wounded inner children, but an entire host of strange alters, often including animals, the opposite sex, and spiritually uplifting 'inner self helpers' who serve as gatekeepers and guides. An MPD Survivor has the opportunity to speak in different voices, to discover layers and layers of personalities, and to garner hushed respect and sympathy.

Many such Survivors have no desire to 'integrate' their personalities. They prefer to speak not of a 'disorder,' but of a multiple-personality 'dignity.' They revel in their own internal community, a kind of self-contained 12-step group. They write poetry, sing songs, and paint exotic portraits of their abuse. Like William Adams, one American MPD song-writer and singer, they may use a singular name on the album cover or poetry collection, but they refer to themselves in the plural. 'A concert of my music,' Adams says, 'is a concert of many hearts and minds, for I am actually we. Our songs are a testimony to both the incredible agony that we all lived through in our childhood, to the amazingly creative way we coped with abuse.'[117]

For the sensation-hungry media, stories of ritual abuse have been a godsend, beginning with a 1985 20/20 American TV program, 'The Devil Worshippers.' A 1988 Geraldo Rivera TV special on ritual abuse really got the ball rolling, as did the publication of *Satan's Underground* in the same year, a first-person account by Lauren Stratford, a Survivor who had retrieved previously forgotten memories. By 1993, the horrifying, titillating tales of unspeakable ritual abuse hit the front covers of *Ms. Magazine* and *Vanity Fair*. The *Ms.* cover depicted an innocent infant in a devil serpent's coils, admonishing the reader to 'BELIEVE IT! Cult Ritual Abuse Exists.' The story, 'Surviving the Unbelievable,' was written by the pseudonymous Elizabeth Rose. The reader has to search very carefully to deduce that the author did not remember all of this horror until quite recently. She believes that she was abused by her mother and aunt in an intergenerational cult when she was four and five years old.

'My mother became pregnant a few months after I was inducted into the cult,' Rose writes. Seven months later, her labor was induced by a cult doctor. 'Two days later, I was forced to watch as they killed my baby sister by decapitation in a ritual sacrifice . . . followed by a communion ritual, during which human flesh and blood were consumed.' She goes on to assert that her mother and best friend were both gang-raped repeatedly. 'Other sexual abuse includes the raping of young girls or infants. Both girls and boys may be sodomized or penetrated with symbolic objects, such as a crucifix, or with weapons.'[118]

Although the *Vanity Fair* piece purports to present a more 'balanced' viewpoint, author Leslie Bennetts clearly believes the stories. In 'Nightmares on Main Street,' she uncritically accepts 34-year-old Aubrey's 'memories of secret satanic rituals practiced by Aubrey's family on the dark nights when her parents, grandparents, and neighbors wore robes and carried torches.' Aubrey's memories include repeated impregnations and early induced labors, after which her babies were sacrificed and consumed. Bennetts also writes of Tiffany, another Survivor whose 'body alone provides some form of corroboration,' since it exhibits 'a baffling array of unexplained scars and other injuries.' Tiffany calmly asserts: 'The first rape was when I was two; my father had molested me before that, but this was the first actual penetration, and he cut my vagina with a knife in order to achieve that. I have the scars.'[119]

While MPD did not flourish outside North America, the satanic ritual abuse scare did, largely through training seminars offered in 1988 in England by U.S. 'experts' such as therapist Pamala Klein and Chicago police detective Jerry Simandl. In July of 1989, a British television program, 'Cook Report: The Devil's Work,' appeared to substantiate alarming claims that satanic cults were abusing children all over England.[120] Soon, British therapists such as Valerie Sinason and Phil Mollon were hearing tales of grotesque ritual sexual abuse and murder from female clients. Sinason edited a professional book, *Treating Survivors of Satanist Abuse*, which was published in 1994. Similar horror stories and therapeutic interest spread to New Zealand and Australia.

ENTERING THE MAINSTREAM: 'THE TERRIBLE TRUTH'

By the early 1990s, belief in an epidemic of repressed memories had become what academic sociologists term an 'urban legend,'*[121] a piece

---

* The classic book in this field is *The Vanishing Hitchhiker: American Urban Legends and Their Meanings*, by Jan Harold Brunvand (1981).

of folklore that is commonly accepted as true. Because that phraseology implies that such rumors persist only in cities, I prefer the term 'contemporary legend.'

Many such legends were debunked during this period, once they were proven, indisputably, to be untrue. The actor who had played 'Mikey' in the Life Cereal commercials went on TV to assure people that he had not been killed by 'Pop Rocks' candy exploding in his stomach. New York City sewer workers explained that baby alligators flushed down toilets had not turned the sewer system into the Everglades. Pepsi drinkers could rest assured that they would not find hypodermic needles in their soft drinks. But acceptance of repressed memories and satanic cults remained, with few coming forward to challenge the evidence, or lack thereof.

Nursing journals featured articles about how to spot possible repressed memories. Police departments and psychological associations offered seminars on ritual abuse. Joan Baez sang a song about satanic cults. Gloria Steinem embraced her inner child and the concept of repression.[122] Actress Roseanne Barr Arnold discovered in therapy that she had been abused in her cradle, trumpeting her new status as a Survivor on talk shows, then wrote a book declaring that she housed multiple personalities named, among others, Piggy, Fucker, and Bambi.[123] Heidi Vanderbilt published a lengthy diatribe on incest and repressed memories in *Lear's*.[124] Weekend retreats* promised to help women retrieve their memories.[125] Made-for-TV movies such as *Ultimate Betrayal* sympathetically portrayed 'real life' cases of recovered incest memories.[126]

Perhaps most frightening, the dogma had flowed from popular self-help books to well-honed fiction that presented engaging, believable

---

* In *The Healing Woman*, a monthly newsletter for Survivors, Caroline Spear described a 1994 weekend workshop, where 26 women gathered to recover memories and rage. 'Emotions are a physical expression and will remain in the body if they are not felt,' the workshop leader explained. 'And if these unfelt emotions are negative, they will stay inside like pockets of toxins and will eventually make us very sick – with cancer or disease.' Nervous about whether she would live up to expectations, Spear announced that 'I had no childhood' because of her abuse. Then she whacked a big punching bag with a baseball bat. 'Is there something there? I am almost remembering,' she thought. 'Was there something about a baseball bat? I am enraged that my own mind has to protect me and keep my own memories from being remembered.' She didn't come up with anything, so she just hit the bag anyway, yelling 'YOU BASTARD! I HATE YOU! YOU HAD NO RIGHT!' When she sat down, another participant smiled at her, touched her arm, and said, 'You were magnificent.'

characters suddenly remembering abuse. *A Thousand Acres* (1991), Jane Smiley's story of a constricted Midwestern farm family, won the Pulitzer Prize and the National Book Critics' Circle Award. Ginny, the protagonist, has repressed all memory of her father's abuse, while her sister Rose has always remembered it. Finally, on page 228, Ginny experiences a 'flashback' to her teenage years, while lying on her childhood bed: 'Lying there, I knew that he had been in there to me, that my father had lain with me on that bed, that I had looked at the top of his head, at his balding spot in the brown grizzled hair, while feeling him suck my breasts.' She jumps up, but she knows that there are more memories to come. 'Behind that one image bulked others, mysterious bulging items in a dark sack, unseen as yet, but felt.' Smiley enshrines all the familiar stereotypes. 'I remembered that he carried a lot of smells – whiskey, cigarette smoke, the sweeter and sourer smells of the farm work.' Ginny always assumed a 'desperate limp inertia' during these sex scenes, which she miraculously banished from her consciousness until years later.[127]

Good fiction can be more convincing than truth. One critic praised Smiley for her 'persuasive and powerful voice,' and he was right. The *Boston Globe* called her characters 'hauntingly real.' *Publishers Weekly* stated that the plot remained 'always within the limits of credibility.' One close friend of mine, who knew about my situation, told me I ought to read the book because it had repressed memories in it. 'But these are real,' she assured me, 'because her sister always remembered it.' I had to remind her that this was a work of fiction.

Finally, popular magazines ran articles such as 'The Terrible Truth,' which appeared in an October 1992 issue of *Self*, written by A. G. Britton, a beauty editor for the magazine. I will end this chapter with a summary of this article, since it provides a telling case study to which I will refer in future chapters.

In 1989, the 33-year-old Britton lost her job, had a miscarriage, and sank into a 'heavyhearted depression I couldn't shake.' She sought therapy, as she had at several other times in her life since her late teens. 'During one session,' she wrote, 'it popped out of my mouth that I may have been sexually molested when I was young.' She had a disturbing dream, but no real memories. 'It was all very vague, but my therapist said that whenever a person suspects abuse, it most likely did occur.'[128]

Britton may not have read *The Courage to Heal* at this point, but she almost certainly had absorbed the dogma – whether consciously or not

– including the idea that dreams can reveal abuse. Her therapist further encouraged the idea that she had probably been abused. Consequently, the progression of the story from here on is all too predictable. Once the suspicion was planted, it grew.

Britton began to experience mysterious ailments – her left leg and arm grew numb. 'I saw doctors and physiotherapists and chiropractors, but no one could find anything physically wrong with me.' She experienced anxiety attacks, more depression, and a 'free-floating rage.' She sought out yet another counselor. 'During the very first visit to my new therapist, she told me it sounded as if I were suffering from Post-Traumatic Stress Disorder.' After seeing this therapist for six months, 'the episodes of distress had come to dominate my life. If I didn't remember the trauma that was feeding them, I was afraid I would be consumed by them.'

Like the woman on the computer bulletin board quoted at the beginning of this chapter, Britton decided that she had been having 'memories' all along 'in symbols, body problems, emotions that seemed to come from nowhere . . . , in the automatic closing of my throat when eating a pleasant food.' Then one day, exhausted, she lay down for an afternoon nap. 'Suddenly, my body went numb, and I felt a tremendous pressure on my chest. I couldn't breathe. I tried to relax, but the feeling got worse. Then I had a vision of what looked like a huge, hairy burned potato close to my face.' When she reported this experience to her therapist, 'she confirmed what I already knew: I had experienced my first [real] memory. "It sounds like fellatio," she said. I felt something crumble within me.'

After this, a 'siege' commenced. 'It was as if an earthquake were ravaging my very being, leaving my subconscious open to the world . . . I had only the foggiest sense of what was real and what were my memories.' Her symptoms and anxiety attacks grew worse. She began to lose weight. 'Terror would shoot through my body, making me feel as if I were being lifted off the ground.' Britton decided to change therapists yet again, since she wasn't getting any better. She sought out Dr. Straker, a psychiatrist she had seen years before. 'He explained how repressed memory emerges: first in the body, then in the emotions and finally as actual memory.' Straker medicated Britton, but she continued to experience what she interpreted as flashbacks.

'I would lose the ability to speak. My tongue would get all gummed up as if I were an infant. I wouldn't be able to read or spell. My body would become listless, and my motor control felt askew . . . I would have an incredible urge to bite through things.' She and Straker concluded that she was reliving her infancy between the ages of six months and two years, including the pain of teething. She experienced 'strange and uncontrollable fears.' She dreamed of ripping apart a bulbous fish with her teeth. In another dream, she tasted something salty.

Finally, after all this preparation, Britton had her first 'fully realized, intellectual memory' in which she saw herself, barely over a year old, at the beach. 'My father was pinning my arms up over my head so that they were pushed against my ears in a painful way. He was relentlessly shoving his penis in my mouth. In a rage, I was trying to bite it off.' She could now explain everything. 'There it was: the answer to 30 years of pain and anguish and confusion.' Her father had molested her from the time she was six to eighteen months old, she decided. Following this breakthrough, the memories began to come back more easily. 'I remembered sitting in my crib, watching my father come at me with instruments in his hand, his fingers smelling of antiseptic.'

Britton's parents had separated when she was not yet two, and her father died when she was 16. Her mother appeared to corroborate her memories. 'She said my father had been a very troubled man and seemed to have an addict's sex drive.' And, in fact, he *had* taken care of his infant daughter much of the time. 'He had convinced her he was a better father than she was a mother.'

Now, Britton bravely proclaims herself a Survivor. 'I'm still reclaiming parts of my life that had been lost in the fog,' she explains. 'My tragedy will always be there. I was raped of my childhood.'

CHAPTER TWO

The Memory Maze

> Great is this power of memory, exceedingly great. O my God, a spreading limitless room within me. Who can reach its uttermost depth? Yet it is a faculty of soul and belongs to my nature. In fact I cannot totally grasp all that I am.
>
> ST. AUGUSTINE, 399 A.D.[1]

We've all experienced sudden, seemingly involuntary recall of incidents, faces, and emotions from the past. Triggered by a particular perfume, a snatch of melody, a photograph, or a voice on the telephone, our pasts can sometimes rush back with surprising intensity and vividness. 'Why, I hadn't thought of Mrs. Carnes in years,' you might say. 'I remember that teacher so clearly now, it's just as if she were in the room with me.' Recalling that second-grade class, you might also flash on Steve Barber, the creep who always chased you and called you names, and the hot flush of fear and anger can be sudden and fresh.

It is, therefore, certainly not beyond the realm of possibility that someone might either forget or actively 'repress' an unpleasant memory, a traumatic event that would pop back into consciousness years later with the proper stimulus. Memory researchers have long recognized that people tend to rewrite their pasts to some degree, making themselves into heroes or transforming their family trips from bickering sojourns into golden moments. Because we often view our personal pasts through rose-colored glasses, isn't it intuitively reasonable to think that the incest survivor accusations may all be true? How many of us are living with versions of our pasts that are essentially myths of happy childhoods, or fabrications to defend our fragile egos?

In the following pages, I'll summarize what researchers have found regarding repression and dissociation. Unfortunately, from the standpoint of pure science, these concepts have been neither absolutely proven nor absolutely disproven. It is usually impossible to corroborate either Survivors' memories of incest or their parents' anguished denials.

The alleged events purportedly took place decades ago, and, except for the group abuse envisioned in ritual-abuse scenarios, there would usually have been no witnesses other than parent and child. Few pedophiles seduce their victims in public. By its very nature, sex abuse is a private, hidden act. Therefore, determining guilt or innocence is usually a matter of emotion, character, and conviction.

Similarly, belief in the concept of repression comes down to – well, just that: *belief*. Because there is no way to verify it, and because the stakes are so high, both sides of the debate over repressed memories tend to become polarized, angry, vociferous, and dogmatic. I'll try to avoid such a polemical stance, although as an accused parent myself, I certainly do not believe in the validity of my own children's accusations. Having come to know quite a few parents in similar situations, I doubt their guilt as well. Finally, having reviewed literature such as *The Courage to Heal* and the other disturbing material presented in the previous chapter, I can see how induced memories of abuse could come to seem quite real. Still, I must look at all sides, particularly because I know how prevalent *real* incest and other forms of abuse are. I would hate to think that anything I write could, in any way, provide cover for perpetrators or contribute to the silencing of real victims.

RECONSTRUCTING THE PAST

One thing should be made clear at the outset. Those who make accusations based on 'recovered memories' are not consciously lying, even if their version of the past may be incorrect. For them, the memories are real, sometimes even more compelling than memories of actual events from childhood. Given that, how can anybody argue that *all*, or at least *most*, of these 'memories' are inaccurate? Any explanation of how delusional memories can occur must include an examination of how our minds recall the past.

Without our memories, how would we define ourselves? Memories *are* who we are. Arguably, it is our capacity to remember and reflect on the past that separates us from other animals. Because we can recall the past and project it into the future, we understand cause-and-effect, we can create hypotheses. Memory allows us to be scientists, poets, storytellers, and creators.

But there is also a darker side to this capacity to remember and interpret past events, smells, and sounds. We nurture the inevitable pain and suffering we encounter, seeking explanations, and incorporating them into our self-concepts. We know that something similar might happen again. Because we see ourselves as active agents in the world, creating our own environments and destinies, we think that we must prevent some future disaster. In short, we worry. We have known pain, disappointment and abuse, and we nurse and rehearse their effects. We are historians.

Dream and nightmare, creative joy and paranoia, nostalgia and terror – all seem central to the human experience, and all rely on thoughts and interpretations of the past. This would probably be true even if our memories served as absolutely accurate recording devices and we all agreed on shared events. In fact, however, our minds, mini-lightning storms of tiny electrical currents snapping over billions of synapses awash in a sea of hormones, still defy our understanding.[2] Little wonder, given this compelling description by science writer Philip J. Hilts:

> The neurons, then, are like minute sea creatures, packed side to side like tiny bristles, several hundred billion of them in the whole cranial vault, and each in a frenetic state of decision or indecision. Each bristle has thousands of fine filaments to connect to others, and with the billions of cells, times the thousands of filaments, times the different signals which may pass between each reaching tentacle and another, there are, all told, tens to hundreds of trillions of tender signaling junctions formed among neurons.[3]

We do not, in other words, record the past in neat computer-like bits and bytes. It is almost impossible to discuss the mechanisms of memory without employing misleading metaphors. Plato compared the mind to a wax writing tablet, the advanced technology of his era. For Freud, the brain functioned something like a giant plumbing system or steam engine, with uncomfortable material stashed away in the cesspool of the subconscious and leaking out when the pressure reached a critical point. Modern researchers have used other metaphors: the mind as a giant filing cabinet, videotape, or computer.[4]

The trouble with all such comparisons is the implication that we remember everything that has ever happened to us – every smell, sound, sensation, joy or trauma has been encoded somewhere in the brain, and, if only the proper command or button is pushed, it will all come flooding back. Pop psychologists have repeatedly promulgated this notion, as in this passage from *Unlocking the Secrets of Your Childhood Memories* (1989): 'Every experience we've had since birth has been recorded and tucked away safely in our brains. Like the most sophisticated computer in the world, the brain retrieves [memories] we need when we need them.'[5][*][6]

But the brain does not function that way, as every modern memory researcher knows. 'One of the most widely held, but wrong, beliefs that people have about memory is that "memories" exist, somewhere in the brain, like books exist in a library, or packages of soap on the supermarket shelves,' writes psychologist Endel Tulving, 'and that remembering is equivalent to somehow retrieving them. The whole concept of repression is built on this misconception.'[7]

British experimental psychologist Frederic Bartlett first made this point in his classic 1932 text, *Remembering: A Study in Experimental and Social Psychology*. 'Some widely held views have to be completely discarded,' he asserted, 'and none more completely than that which treats recall as the re-excitement in some way of fixed and changeless "traces."' To the contrary, he held that remembering is 'an imaginative reconstruction, or construction, built out of the relation of our attitude toward a whole active mass of organized past reactions or experience.' Based on his experiments, Bartlett concluded that our memories generally serve us well, not by offering photographic recall, but by selectively sampling experience and molding it so that our lives have purpose and meaning. 'In a world of constantly changing environment, literal recall is extraordinarily unimportant.'[8] In other words, the human species has evolved a brain that is adaptable, nimble, versatile and imaginative, but not always accurate. We literally 're-member,' patching together the puzzle bits of our past.

Because of this tendency toward 'best guesses,' many of us display 'source amnesia' or source misattribution for a particular memory, even of quite recent events.[9] For instance, I am often quite sure I've told a friend something, when in fact I told someone else. Source amnesia is far more common with distant events, however. Thus, it is fairly common to construct a memory that encompasses details from several sources, including, perhaps, family photos, real memories of a bedroom, stories

---

* The concept of permanent memory traces isn't particularly new. In 1777, German philosopher Johann Nicolas Tetens wrote: 'Each idea does not only leave a trace ... somewhere in the body, but each of them can be stimulated – even if it is not possible to demonstrate this in a given situation.'

we have heard, or movies we have seen. Then the memories can seem quite accurate. A reconstructed incest abuse memory may, for instance, contain the always-remembered feel of a father's stubble against a child's tender face during a goodnight kiss, or the smell of his after-shave. That may be combined with a grotesque, stereotyped scene from a book or movie to form a coherent but misleading narrative.

In addition, we forget a good deal more than we remember. That's why one common method employed by recovered-memory therapists works so well. They ask clients to recall their childhoods in detail, looking particularly for 'missing chunks of time.' If a client cannot recall anything about third and fourth grade, for instance, that supposedly indicates that massive abuse took place during that time, so terrible that the memory had to be repressed, or an alternate personality had to be created. This explanation is quite convincing until one examines how memory works. Normally, we recall the highs and lows of our lives, with very little in between. It isn't surprising, then, that people don't remember much from their childhoods. Most of us don't, unless cued with a particular name, smell, or event. At that point, someone who didn't recall third grade at all might suddenly realize that he or she remembers quite a bit from that time, such as a pet dying, a particular vacation, or a change in bedrooms.

Not only do we simply forget a good deal, our versions of the personal past are highly colored by our own emotions and family myths. Most of us recognize that our siblings tend to recall the same events from quite different perspectives. I may remember those touch football games with great fondness, for instance, whereas for my brother they were pure torture.

After recounting a salient memory of her childhood, the narrator in Sue Miller's 1990 novel, *Family Pictures*, admits that her memory is faulty:

My sister Liddie says it's *her* memory, her story, one she told me much later . . . And yet it seems as clear to me as a picture I might have taken. I could swear this was exactly what happened. But that's the way it is in a family, isn't it? The stories get passed around, polished, embellished . . . And, of course, there's also the factor of time. Of how your perspective, your way of telling the story – of seeing it – changes as time passes. As you change.[10]

The classic Japanese film *Rashomon* makes the same point, allowing four characters who witnessed a violent episode to recall different versions, filtered through their own biases and perspectives.[11]

We are also quite capable of projecting emotions and reinterpretations backward through time, and of creating absolutely clear memories of events that never occurred. This comes as shocking news to everyone, because it threatens our cherished sense of self. Who should know better than *we* what *we* have experienced?

Yet our memories are infinitely more suggestible and malleable than we would like to believe.[12] A 1952 study dramatically illustrates the point. Twelve subjects in group therapy were asked to recall childhood memories involving parents, siblings, and sexual experiences. The Freudian therapist conducting the study was particularly interested in stories about rejecting fathers and flirtatious little girls. The memories were transcribed onto a pack of cards, shuffled, and presented to the subjects from three months to four years later. *None of the patients could identify all of their previously reported memories.* On average, they correctly recalled *half* of them.[13]

Given the proper stimulus and the awful surmise that our parents did something really reprehensible to us – buried in the mists of our murky childhood memories – *we could all come to believe in the reality of grotesque events that never took place.* That, in fact, is what may have happened to millions of frightened, confused, angry adults in the English-speaking world in the final years of the 20th century.

As long ago as 1923, German psychiatrist Karl Jaspers noted that 'nearly all memories are slightly falsified and become a mixture of truth and fantasy.' Jaspers specifically addressed the creation of illusory memories. 'With the phenomena of false memories, the patient gets a sudden image of a previous experience that has all the vivid feeling of a memory, but in actual fact nothing, not even a slender basis for it, is really remembered. Everything is *freshly created*.' His work was published in an English translation in 1963, but it appears that few American psychologists learned much from it.[14]

Because of what Frederic Bartlett called an 'effort after meaning,' we tend to rewrite our pasts to make them match our current attitudes and opinions. Our memories, Bartlett noted, 'live with our interests and with them they change.' Thus it isn't surprising that memories 'display invention, condensation, elaboration, simplification and all the other alterations which my experiments constantly illustrated.'[15] Bartlett did not, of course, assert that memories bore no relationship to real events of the past. He posited that we can indeed recall specific details, particularly through words and visual images, but we weave those bits into a reconstructed narrative.

Our unique language capacity allows us to communicate, not only with one another, but with ourselves. In one sense, *we use words to tell ourselves the constantly reinvented story of our lives.* We are, pre-eminently, a species of internal novelists. That explains our insatiable desire to write and read imagined stories, which distill and interpret experience and render it meaningful. It is, as Bartlett put it, 'the struggle to get somewhere, the varying play of doubt, hesitation, satisfaction and the like, and the eventual building up of the complete story accompanied by the more and more confident advance in a certain direction.'[16]

When we struggle to remember events from our lives, we begin with a general attitude or framework, then fill in the gaps with probable dialogue and detail. Or, as psychologist Stephen Crites puts it: 'To the extent that a coherent identity is achievable at all, the thing must be made, a story-like production with many pitfalls, and it is constantly being revised, sometimes from beginning to end.'[17]

Similarly, we can summon up fragmentary visual images and edit them into an internal movie of our lives. 'The immediate return of certain details is common enough,' Bartlett wrote, 'and it certainly looks very much like the direct re-excitation of certain traces.' Once these images pop up, 'the need to remember becomes active, an attitude is set up.'[18] From these beginnings, a visual scenario develops, the psychic camera rolls, and the imagination – whose root word, after all, is 'image' – takes over. Indeed, recent brain-scan research indicates that our brains treat visualized fantasies quite similarly to sights we actually witnessed.[19] In a way, then, we become expert actors in the internal drama of our own lives. At first, these memories may seem tentative, but with repeated visualization, or the verbal repetition of the stories, they become more real. *Memory, then, is largely a product of rehearsal.*

Given this background, much of the advice in *The Courage to Heal* and other Survivor literature becomes more understandable and frightening. Again and again, Survivors are urged to visualize the abuse scenarios as slide shows, videos, or movies in their heads, running them mentally until they become real. Similarly, they are encouraged to repeat their abuse stories, giving them concrete language, making them real. Writing a story down gives it more of an objective reality. Ellen Bass and Laura Davis specifically recommend following the lead of Irena Kelpfisz, who, as they note, 'developed an exercise that enables you to piece together things you can't possibly know about your history or the history of your family. This form of "remembering," which [Kelpfisz] calls "imaginative reconstruction," can be a valuable tool ... Although you write about things you couldn't realistically know, the result often seems chillingly real.'[20]

In a classic example of circular thinking, Bessel van der Kolk, a Harvard psychiatrist who defends the reality of repressed memories, explains that he believes a story if it *sounds* good. 'If you read a great book and the characters are true to life, that's how people really feel and interact with each other.' Van der Kolk compares true recovered memories to a good novel; he relies on 'the internal coherence of the story, how it all hangs together,' to determine its believability.[21] In 1895, Sigmund Freud made the same kind of observation. 'It still strikes me as strange that the case histories I write should read like short stories.' He even admitted that they 'lack the serious stamp of science,' though Freud usually claimed that his stories and hypotheses were based on the purest science.[22]

In *Dancing With Daddy* (1991), Betsy Petersen recounts how she utilized the Kelpfisz process to 'remember' her abuse. Like Van der Kolk, she came to believe the memories because they made a good story. During therapy, she became obsessed with the idea, '*I'm afraid my father did something to me.*' She had a 'sense of urgency,' wanting to *know* for sure. Consequently, she decided to make it up. 'I had no memory of what my father had done to me, so I tried to reconstruct it. I put all my skill – as reporter, novelist, scholar – to work making that reconstruction as accurate and vivid as possible. I used the memories I had to get to the memories I didn't have.'[23] Using what she already knew about her father – a calm, didactic physician who wore steel-rimmed glasses – she wrote a short story called 'Surgeon's Hands,' set in 1945, in which she imagined him abusing her in her crib when she was three years old:

> I lie there with his fingers crawling over me. I keep jerking, I can't help it, jerking under his fingers. I think it hurts, but I'm not sure. My flesh is so soft down there, so different from the firm skin all over the rest of me. He rubs against the bars of the crib and his eyes cross and roll up behind his glasses. Suddenly he groans and slumps over the bars. His finger stops moving. Is he dead?[24]

Re-reading what she had written, Petersen 'began to scream and curse and cry. I cried so hard I wet my pants.' She took this self-generated horror to be evidence that her imagined scenario was true. 'The feelings that came up for me were so intense I felt they must be grounded in some reality.' Her therapist encouraged her. 'I wanted to believe it: I wanted not to be crazy,' Petersen explains. Subsequently, 'wanted or not, memories came' in the form of daydreams as she lay in the sun on a couch. 'I sink into the welter of images, and there is a moment when one of them sharpens, and I can see it clearly. Then it drifts out of focus again and disappears.'[25]

Bartlett would have understood Petersen's description, because he observed that visual images tend to appear as isolated fragments. 'The course of description, when images abound, is apt to be more exciting, more varied, more rich, more jerky,' he noted. 'There is an image, and meaning has to be tacked on to that, or, perhaps more accurately, has to flow out of it, or emerge from it, before words can carry the process further.' This method of reconstruction has the evolutionary advantage of surmounting mere chronological logic. It permits intuition, inspiration, and poetry. 'A man can take out of its setting something that happened a year ago, reinstate it with much if not all of its individuality unimpaired, combine it with something that happened yesterday, and use them both to help him to solve a problem with which he is confronted today.' Unfortunately, when that 'problem' involves a suspicion of incest, its 'solution' can be devastating. As Bartlett explained, 'The device of images has several defects that are the price of its peculiar excellences.'[26]

PSYCHOLOGICAL TURF WARS

Ever since Freud, the psychology profession has split itself into two camps – the experimental and the clinical – each viewing the other with suspicion, condescension, and, quite often, contempt.

The experimental psychologists conduct research in controlled conditions, attempting to prove or disprove particular hypotheses regarding mental phenomena. By changing one variable at a time, they try to isolate particular cause-and-effect sequences. In trying to explore the human psyche, however, they are largely hampered by ethical constraints. No one, for instance, would look with favor upon a scientist who raised a human child without any touch or affection, just to see how it fared. Therefore, when Harry Harlow conducted his famed experiments to determine the importance of early nurturing touch, he maltreated monkeys instead.[27] Similarly, experimental psychologists often use rats, frogs, guinea pigs, or other animals, manipulating them in the name of science, then slicing up their brains and peering at them through microscopes. By doing so, they hope to arrive at conclusions that might be legitimately applied to humans.

Memory and mind researchers have, however, been able to use human subjects, as long as they did not abuse them. Until the last decade – with the exception of Frederic Bartlett's work – most experiments involving memory concentrated on rote learning of meaningless material. The human subjects risked only the abuse of boredom. Few of the experiments applied to the real world of conflicted emotions and difficult decisions. As Ulric Neisser commented in a 1978 speech, 'If X is an interesting or socially significant aspect of memory, then psychologists have hardly ever studied X.'[28] Endel Tulving agrees. 'There is exceedingly little in the hundred years' worth of mainstream memory research that is relevant to the repressed memories controversy.'[29] Now, however, memory researchers such as Neisser, Elizabeth Loftus, and Nicholas Spanos have conducted intriguing experiments with human subjects, trying to cast light on how we recall and interpret events from our lives.

The experimentalists tend to distrust the clinicians, who generalize from their anecdotal experience with clients and make assertions without controlled scientific proof. This split within the field became pronounced in the early part of this century when Sigmund Freud, the ultimate clinician and systematizer, posited the existence of various mental drives and defense mechanisms, all based on his experience with a limited patient pool. As psychologist J. Victor Haberman wrote in 1914, 'These mechanisms have in no way as yet been shown to exist,' adding that 'the method employed by Freud to prove their existence is scientifically false.'[30]

Haberman complained that American clinicians had uncritically accepted Freudian theories, publishing scores of questionable articles. 'In most, absolutely no attempt is made at more than the mere statement of cases,' he asserted. 'Were a man to make a bold statement as to a new method of cure in carcinoma, sharp criticism would be applied to his work and his announcement; but the American Freudist may publish the very quintessence of inanity and it is accepted without challenge or comment.'[31] Not much has changed since 1914. Freud's fundamental tenets, the experimental psychologists note, have never withstood scientific scrutiny. They are simply convincing myths until proven otherwise. As one critic asserted in 1975, 'Psychoanalytic theory is the most stupendous intellectual confidence trick of the 20th century.'[32]

The clinicians, on the other hand, complain about their experimental colleagues, hiding in their Ivory Tower labs, trying to draw conclusions from timid, limited experiments on college students. What do they know about real life? The clinicians pride themselves on their active involvement with individual clients whose life stories pour out during therapy sessions. Sure, the therapists sometimes read about experimental evidence, but it seems worlds away from their practice, from the real needs of their patients. The experimental psychologists may dismiss a case study as mere 'anecdotal' evidence, but that one person's history is unique, indubitable. And when clinicians see hundreds of such patients, many of whose cases seem to verify Freud's theories about transference, denial, and repression, who is to tell them that they cannot draw valid conclusions, just because they don't wear white coats and carry on double-blind experiments?

Until recently, this turf war between psychologists didn't mean much to the average layperson. Since the publication of *The Courage to Heal*, however, the battle over esoteric theories and evidence for and against repression has become a life-or-death issue for millions of people – the patients and therapists who believe in recovered memories, and the devastated parents accused of incest that they claim never occurred. In court, 'expert' psychological witnesses such as Lenore Terr or Elizabeth Loftus have swayed juries toward crucial decisions. Because of such testimony, innocent people may have been jailed or fined, or the guilty may have gone free. Consequently, these convoluted arguments over obscure psychological mechanisms have dramatic real-life consequences.

REPRESSION: FOR AND AGAINST

In a 1989 speech to his peers, experimental psychologist David Holmes reviewed numerous laboratory attempts to prove the existence of repression. 'Despite over 60 years of research involving numerous approaches by thoughtful and clever investigators,' he concluded, 'at the present time there is no controlled laboratory evidence supporting the concept of repression.' He could not say with certainty that people did not repress memories, because it is impossible to prove a negative;

similarly, no one can disprove the existence of ghosts. But he suggested that it might be appropriate to abandon the theory, filing it under 'interesting but unsupported.' Holmes suggested, somewhat facetiously, that a cautionary truth-in-packaging label should be inscribed in therapists' waiting rooms: 'Warning. The concept of repression has not been validated with experimental research and its use may be hazardous to the accurate interpretation of clinical behavior.'[33]

Holmes knew that his conclusions would be dismissed by the clinicians, who, he noted, would argue that the laboratory research was 'contrived, artificial, sterile, and irrelevant to the "dynamic processes" that occur in the "real world."' He also noted, however, that when the experimental results initially appeared to validate repression, the clinicians were eager to embrace them. Only when further experiments cast doubt on the concept did they disregard the laboratory. Holmes then went on the offensive. 'The clinicians retreat to their consulting rooms for evidence for repression, but what evidence have they produced there?' Only 'impressionistic case studies . . . unconfirmed clinical speculations.'*[34] Finally, he referred to a videotape shown during the conference that was supposed to demonstrate repression in a client. 'But there was no agreement between the conferees concerning when, or even if, repression had occurred [in the video].'

The experiments described by Holmes involved college students remembering various words. In one such experiment, subjects were first tested for recall of a group of nouns. Then one-third of them were told that most of their responses were signs of 'serious pathology.' Another third were told that their answers indicated high creativity and leadership potential. The final third received neutral feedback. The first two groups displayed poorer recall than the final control group. Once the deception was explained, all three groups showed comparable levels of recall. 'From these results,' Holmes said, 'it was concluded that decreased recall following stress was due to interference rather than to repression.'

From the clinicians' viewpoint, however, this experiment proves nothing of the sort. Any number of other factors could be at play, including repression, which has also been defined as 'motivated forgetting.' And regardless of what the experiment shows, it is difficult to see

* Holmes would undoubtedly agree with one 1910 cynic who, commenting on various psychological theories, noted 'a curious similarity in their appeal to their own clinical experience . . . The exponents of the sexual theory, the suggestion theory, the sleep theory . . . alike appeal to experience for confirmation of their opinion, *and find it*.'

how it applies to incest memories. Some of Holmes's adult subjects were mildly 'traumatized,' but certainly the test situation is not comparable to the violent sexual abuse of a child. On the other hand, how could one ethically replicate such trauma in an experimental setting?

'PROOF' FOR REPRESSION

On the other side of the debate, three studies have been widely cited to 'prove' the prevalence of repressed memories of sexual abuse. The first two rely on self-identified Survivors and consequently do not contribute much to the debate, but they deserve mention because they have been quoted prominently elsewhere.

In 1987, Herman and Schatzow published a study of 53 women attending their therapy groups.[35] Of those, 64 per cent reported that they had forgotten at least some of their abuse before recalling it years later in therapy; 28 per cent had 'severe memory deficits.' Most of their 'memories' were recovered in the highly emotional hothouse atmosphere of the group process. 'Participation in group proved to be a powerful stimulus for recovery of memory,' Herman wrote, adding that it was sometimes necessary for her to intervene to 'slow the process' when it got out of hand.

Herman and Schatzow claimed that the majority of these stories were confirmed in some manner. 'Twenty-one women (40 per cent) obtained corroborating evidence either from the perpetrator himself, from other family members or firm physical evidence such as family members, or from physical evidence such as diaries or photographs. Another 18 women (34 per cent) discovered that another child, usually a sibling, had been abused by the same perpetrator. An additional five women (9 per cent) reported statements from other family members indicating a strong likelihood that they had also been abused.' That sounds impressive until closely examined. Unfortunately, we are dealing with apples and oranges here. Yes, in one case, Andrea's stepfather admitted to 'fooling around' with her, but she had *always* remembered the abuse. More typical is the case of Doris, who 'regressed' during group sessions and was 'flooded with memories which included being raped by her father and being forced to service a group of her father's friends while he watched.' Doris reported that her younger sister had once asked her, 'Did Daddy ever try anything funny with you?' She took this as corroboration, though the discussion went no further.

The trouble with confirmations such as these is that they are unverified and second-hand. We have only the word of the accusers, eagerly and uncritically accepted by their therapists. In group, Claudia had recalled 'being handcuffed, burned with cigarettes, forced to perform fellatio, and having objects introduced into her rectum and vagina' between the ages of four and seven. Claudia supposedly searched her brother's room and found handcuffs and a diary 'in which he planned and recorded his sexual "experiments" with his sister in minute detail.' It is impossible to know whether this is an accurate account or not, because the case reports are 'composites,' according to the authors. Certainly, if Claudia had produced this diary, it would serve as horrifying evidence of the alleged crimes. But we have only Claudia's word for this, and she was under pressure to please Herman and Schatzow by coming up with some confirmation.[36]

Given what we know about Judith Herman and her belief system (*see Chapter 1*), it is not difficult to imagine that she would accept virtually anything as validating the memories. A woman could tell her mother that she recalled incest by her uncle, and the mother might say, 'I always knew there was something funny about him.' A sibling, upset and alarmed by her sister's allegations, might enter therapy intent on 'remembering' similar incidents. When she, too, found buried memories, this would be taken as corroboration rather than an extension of the suggestion process.*

Similarly, Briere and Conte's 1993 study of 450 male and female Survivors relied on a 'clinical sample' recruited by therapists.[37] Of these, 59.3 per cent reported amnesia regarding the abuse at some time before the age of 18. Compared to those who had always remembered their abuse, the patients who had recovered repressed memories generally reported molestation at an earlier age and over a longer time span. They were victimized by multiple perpetrators who used more violent techniques. These findings fit neatly with Survivor dogma. The more

---

* I wrote to Judith Herman, asking her to set up anonymous interviews with any clients who might provide confirmed stories involving repressed memories. She declined. Outright fabrications in such cases may be more frequent than one would think, by the way. During the witch craze, for instance, many subjects surreptitiously loaded their mouths with pins so that they could vomit them up on cue. Similarly, in one recent case, an accusing daughter forged a threatening letter from her father.

horrible, the more gut-wrenching the abuse, the more likely that it would be forgotten.

However, to an outside observer, an alternative explanation seems just as plausible, if not more so. Briere and Conte's findings may indicate that nearly 60 per cent of their sample were never abused at all. Under the influence of their therapists and books such as *The Courage to Heal*, they may have come to believe in imagined memories which, not surprisingly, were more violent and included more perpetrators than the memories that real incest victims had never forgotten. As we have seen, patients are actively urged to imagine brutal scenes, multiple offenders, and years of repressed abuse. With therapists such as Renee Fredrickson encouraging women to visualize abuse at extremely early ages, it is natural that this sample would 'remember' back to the crib.

The third study, conducted by sociologist Linda Meyer Williams at the Family Research Laboratory of the University of New Hampshire, is far more interesting.[38] From 1973 to 1975, the U.S. National Institute of Mental Health funded a study of sexual assault victims who had been brought to a city hospital emergency room in a major northeastern city. Nearly two decades later, Williams and her researchers located and interviewed 129 women from the study – without telling them exactly why. Instead, the subjects were simply told that this was a follow-up study on women who, as children, had received medical care at the city hospital.

During the extensive interviews, which averaged three hours, the women were questioned about their childhoods and adult lives. After 'sufficient rapport' was established, the interviewers asked the women to report any instances of sexual abuse that they could recall. The questions were posed several times in different ways, following the methodology first used by Diana Russell in the study already described in Chapter 1. Of the 129 women in the study, *38 per cent failed to report* the specific incidents documented by their hospital visits. Williams, who calls her findings 'quite astonishing,' clearly thinks that she has found evidence of repression. She believes that 'women who were abused in early childhood – and who are now more likely to have forgotten the abuse – will recall the abuse in the next several years.'

There are, however, other ways to interpret her data. Sixty-eight per cent of those who did not report the specific target incident *did* report other instances of sexual molestation. It seems safe to assume that anyone who was *routinely* subjected to incest might not remember every single time it occurred. In other words, we may not be dealing with 'repression' so much as a particular incident lost in a flood of repeated abuse. Eliminating those cases brings the sample down to 12 per cent who did not report the incident and failed to report any other abuse either. It would be interesting to examine the ages of that smaller sample, which Williams does not analyze separately. Eleven victims out of the total sample were three years old or younger at the time of the abuse, while another 31 were between four and six. Because few people remember specific events that occurred prior to the age of four, it seems plausible that many of those who did not recall the abuse were simply not old enough.

There are other possible reasons for non-reporting. For some, the abuse may not have been traumatic enough to report in the context of this particular interview. Sexually abused children, fondled by an otherwise nurturing family member, do not always experience the incident as abusive.*

Alternatively, some may have recalled the abuse and chosen not to report it. Others may simply have forgotten it. We do not remember everything – even every bad thing – that has ever happened to us. It is not necessary to assume that such forgetting involves psychological defense mechanisms. In one U.S. government study, for instance, 14 per cent of those involved in a car accident did not recall it a year later. Similarly, over 25 per cent of those in another study did not remember a hospitalization after a year. Are these surprising statistics the result of mental avoidance, conscious non-reporting, repression, or simply bad memory?

Late in 1995, Linda Williams published an ancillary paper based on the same survey of 129 women.**[39] This one involved 75 women who *did* recall the 'index' event. Of these, 12 reported that there was a time when they did not recall the sexual abuse. None of these cases are examples of 'massive repression.' Five of them involved women who were only two or three years old at the time of the abuse, making their 'memory' of the event extremely doubtful, since the abuse came during the period of infantile amnesia (*see the end of this chapter*). It is likely, in

* The fact that some children are not traumatized by an adult's sexual attentions is acknowledged even by feminist researchers such as Diana Russell and Allie Kilpatrick. This fact does *not* mean that sexual abuse of children is ever 'all right.'
** In the same journal, Bessel van der Kolk and Rita Fisler published a study of 36 childhood trauma victims solicited through newspaper advertisements. Of these, 15 (42 per cent) claimed 'significant or total amnesia for their trauma at some time in their lives.' Like most retrospective studies, this one tells us very little, particularly since the authors provide no further details.

66

these cases, that they were told about the abuse later and then incorporated these stories as their own 'memories.' Two of the cases involve four-year-olds who were supposedly raped – yet doctors failed at the time to find medical evidence of abuse. Since penile penetration of a four-year-old not only leaves scars, but is often life-threatening, we have to question the veracity of these events. Other cases may not involve actual amnesia so much as not thinking about the memories. One woman, for instance, reported that 'when she is happy, she forgets.'[40]

One of the problems with self-reported periods of amnesia involves a kind of chase-your-tail logic. Williams' research assistants asked these women, 'What was your age at the time you forgot and the time you remembered?' But how do you remember when you forgot something? By definition, you can't. How can you recall how long you didn't remember? All you can logically say is, 'I suddenly remembered this incident. I had not thought about it for years.' In the case of limited events that were not perceived as particularly traumatic at the time, it isn't surprising that they would be forgotten and then recalled later. Such may have been the case with Kim, a seven-year-old whose teenage step-brother snuck into her bed and masturbated against her. She recalled the incident at 22 when she was reminded by her cousin that she had been abused.

Of the studies that purport to indicate the reality of repression, then, the Williams studies are definitely the most credible, but they fall far short of proof.[41] It is instructive to compare her first published study to a 1990 report entitled 'Child Abuse: Adolescent Records vs. Adult Recall,' by Donna Della Femina et al., which bears a striking similarity. Femina and her co-authors interviewed 69 subjects who had reported abuse nine years earlier while jailed. Of these, 26 failed to mention their traumas. In other words, 37.7 per cent did not report abuse that was known to have occurred – almost exactly the same percentage as in the Williams study. But Femina and her cohorts went one step further and re-interviewed those who failed to report, trying to find out why. The answers had nothing to do with repressed memories. The commonest explanations were 'a sense of embarrassment, a wish to protect parents, and a desire to forget.'[42]

One final study, published in 1994, deserves mention, because one of the three investigators was Elizabeth Loftus, one of the most prominent repressed-memory skeptics.[43] She and two colleagues questioned 105 New York City female graduates of a drug abuse program. Fifty-seven, or 54 per cent, reported some form of childhood sexual abuse. Of those who were abused, 52 completed a further questionnaire about their memories. Ten of this group claimed to have forgotten the abuse for a time prior to recalling it. In other words, 19 per cent of the women could be interpreted as having repressed their memories. Again we are left with inconclusive evidence, however. We are not told whether the abuse was violent or mild, one-time or ongoing, or at what age it occurred. As Loftus noted, 'It would be fruitful to probe further to find out how and when that [memory] recovery came about.' According to the study report, all of these women had been involved in 12-step programs as well as individual and group counseling. It would be surprising if some of them had not retrieved 'memories' – whether true or confabulated – during that suggestive process.*[44]

LENORE TERR: STORY-TIME

In her 1994 book, *Unchained Memories: True Stories of Traumatic Memories, Lost and Found* (1994), psychiatrist Lenore Terr purports to prove the existence of repressed memories. She does not. Instead, she offers a few anecdotal cases, served up with a tantalizing mix of irrelevant biological studies, presented as if they provide valid experimental underpinnings for her assertions. In her prologue, Terr explains that she decided to write the book 'in short-story style because that format is enjoyable and relatively uncomplicated.' Her stories do make compelling, simple reading, but the unwary reader is likely to swallow Terr's pet theories as though they were proven facts.

Terr made her name by studying the Chowchilla, California, children who were kidnapped and buried alive for two days in 1976. 'I found that every one of the kidnapped children retained detailed, precise memories of what had happened, even in [a] later study,' Terr writes. That should surprise no one. But Terr has now concluded, based on a 1988 report on 20 children who were repeatedly abused before the age of five, that *repetition* will *diminish* recall. She terms a single traumatic event

---

* I asked Elizabeth Loftus whether she felt this study indicated the reality of repressed memories, and she responded that she wrote the questions for the study back in 1991. 'In retrospect, I don't think asking people whether they forgot for awhile tells you much. Roseanne Barr Arnold claims to remember her mother molesting her when she was six months old. If she were in our sample, she would probably answer "Yes" to the question. How would we interpret that?'

'Type I,' and numerous such assaults 'Type II.' She asserts that a child 'well rehearsed in terror' by Type II trauma would probably repress all of the memories.[45]

Her evidence for this theory is questionable. While the Chowchilla children ranged from 5 to 14 years of age, all of Terr's 'Type II' subjects were under 5 years old at the time of their abuse. Over half of them were below the age of three. Because almost no one remembers *anything* from that time of life, it is not necessary to theorize about repression to explain the lack of recall.

Terr says that she can spot 'behavioral memories' of very early trauma, even without verbal reports, but her interpretations of children's play are subjective – and biased by what she already expects to find. In one case where she failed to spot telltale signs, she did not already know that the child had supposedly been abused. She explains: 'I probably did not see any behavioral memories in her case because I was not yet looking.'*[46]

Most behavioral psychologists would disagree with the Type I/Type II theory, citing the concept of classical conditioning. The more often the same terrible thing happens to people, the more likely that they will remember it and react with dread and fear. Rather than continuing to believe that Daddy is a wonderful man, in other words, abused children would exhibit automatic fear because of the association between Daddy and unpleasant events. The children might not remember each precise event, but they would certainly know that they had been repeatedly traumatized. Memory researcher Larry Squire, who is quoted in Terr's book as though he agreed with her conclusions, told me that 'she twisted my data for her own ends' and that her Type II theory 'doesn't make any sense to me at all. She says you would remember one event but forget multiple incidents. I would think it would be the other way around.'[47]

Indeed, if we are to believe Terr's theory, then many of the same Chowchilla children who vividly recalled being buried alive for two days would forget all about it if they were entombed on a monthly basis. Every time, they would march down into the sunken vehicle blithely unaware, protected by the marvelous defense mechanism of Type II massive repression.

* Terr's 1988 study becomes even more suspect when she reveals that one subject was abused as a seven-month-old 'satanic worship victim' – almost certainly a false allegation, since there has never been any evidence to validate such widely rumored 'satanic' cults (*see Chapter 6*).

A representative example of the case studies in Terr's book is that of one Gary Baker (a pseudonym), who came to believe that his mother had thrown him into an irrigation ditch, nearly let a train run over him, locked him in a refrigerator, held his head in a toilet, masturbated with a white dildo in front of him, and stuck a red baseball bat up his rectum. Terr accepts all of these recovered memories as accurate, without question. One hot, humid day at the end of a five-hour drive, soon after his girl-friend dumped him, Gary saw three sudden images, including the red baseball bat. Then he blacked out. He soon entered therapy and retrieved the rest, running the images like color videos in his head. His brother Barry eventually located his own repressed memories of being locked in a freezer chest, which constituted sufficient confirmation, although no one else in his family believed Gary.

Also, 'as a kid, Gary could hold a note on his saxophone longer than anybody else at school,' so that proved that he was thrown into an irrigation ditch, where he learned to hold his breath.

In the same chapter, Terr cites a shock-aversion study conducted on fruit fly larvae. Five days following their aversive shocks, after their metamorphosis into flies, they still remembered their training. What, one may inquire, does this have to do with repressed memories? 'Eight electroshock cycles to a fruit fly larva suffice to alter the behavior of the adult fly,' Terr writes. 'One drowning attempt can change a child's life.'[48]

That strikes me as quite a leap. I don't think that most of us need a fruit fly experiment to prove to us that attempting to drown an infant is a truly horrible thing to do. Because the adult flies weren't hypnotized to determine whether they could recall their abuse as larvae, the study says nothing about repressed memories of human beings.

MISS AMERICA AND OTHER FAMOUS VICTIMS

Three well-publicized cases are often cited as anecdotal evidence of massive repression, so they deserve at least brief examination.

The 1958 Miss America, Marilyn Van Derbur Atler, reported in 1991, when she was 53, that her father had routinely sexually violated her from the age of five until she left for college. She said that she had repressed all knowledge of the abuse for a few years, remembering it at age 24.[49]

Thirty-nine-year-old Brown University public policy professor Ross Cheit says he woke from a 1992 dream feeling a 'powerful presence' in the room, which he identified as William Farmer, an administrator of the San Francisco Boys' Chorus summer camp, which Cheit had attended in the late 1960s. Later that day, he recalled repeated molestation by Farmer. After some investigation, Cheit confronted Farmer by telephone, taping the conversation, and the former camp administrator admitted molesting him. Both criminal and civil suits are moving forward against Farmer.[50]

In a similar case, Frank Fitzpatrick, a Rhode Island insurance adjuster, recalled sexual abuse by James Porter, a former Catholic priest, who had been his confessor in 1962 when Fitzpatrick was 12 years old. When Fitzpatrick contacted other altar boys, they, too, recalled abuse. To date, over 100 Father Porter victims have come forward. He has been tried and convicted of sexual abuse.[51]

As convincing as these cases may sound, they do not prove the existence of massively repressed memories. Marilyn Van Derbur Atler's case is of great interest, because her oldest sister, Gwen Mitchell, says that she was sexually abused by her father and never forgot it. I interviewed Gwen, and her story sounds convincing, though there is no physical proof. When she was seven, Gwen says she woke to find her father masturbating her. Until she left home at 18, he continued periodically to fondle her while he masturbated to climax. Gwen learned to turn her body off. She did not respond sexually during the abuse. She never told anyone about it, but she always recalled it vividly. 'I used to plot his murder in egregious ways in the dark.'[52]

Until Marilyn told her that she, too, had recalled being abused, Gwen told me, 'I thought I was the only one. Mother used to say that he liked me the best. He called me the Countess, so I believed I was special and the only one.' Now, Gwen believes that Marilyn did indeed repress her memories. She thinks that perhaps she, too, repressed memories of actual intercourse, which she does not recall.

Nonetheless, Gwen's experience does not prove that Marilyn was raped for years and forgot it. Marilyn claims that her father was raping her from age 5 until age 18 and that she had absolutely no conscious memory of the abuse. She would kiss her boyfriend (now her husband) Larry chastely good night, from the time she was 15 until 18, then go into her bedroom to be raped by her father, and forget it all by the next morning.

While Marilyn Atler says that she initially recalled her abuse at age

24, after years of gentle prodding by DeDe Harvey, a family friend and counselor, her saga is a bit more complicated. According to her own testimony, she *really* began recovering memories when she turned 40 in 1984 and experienced a debilitating form of psychosomatic paralysis. 'My memories and feelings surfaced and overwhelmed me with anguish from 1984 through 1988.' For several years, she did what she terms her 'work,' which included over 100 deep massages and rolfing sessions, at least 60 acupuncture sessions, 50 sessions of hypnosis, neurolinguistic programming, dance therapy, bioenergetics, self-defense therapy, small group meetings of incest survivors, inner-child work, and frequent sessions with her therapist. She also read 'hundreds of articles and 72 books' on incest. Her night terrors finally stopped in 1988 when she was put on anti-depressant medication.[53]

One could certainly surmise that as a young adult, Atler may have pushed painful childhood memories to the background in order to concentrate on her busy role as college student and beauty queen. But that's very different from the massive memory repression required by Atler's current beliefs about her past. There are several possibilities. (1) Marilyn Atler may not have been sexually abused by her father, but after somehow learning about, or sensing, her sister's experience, she developed a belief in her own memories. (2) Atler may have been fondled in the same manner as Gwen and attempted to 'forget' about it while she pursued fame as Miss America. Though she did not forget, she denied it to herself until she was 24. Then, when she was 40, she actively pursued more violent 'repressed memories' of events that never occurred. (3) Atler's recovered memories may all be accurate.

From my discussions with Ross Cheit, I am convinced that he did indeed recall incidents of sexual abuse after the passage of many years, but it is unclear to me how frequently he was molested. Cheit believes the incidents occurred nightly during the month of August in 1968, when Bill Farmer was the camp administrator. He also thinks that another incident occurred the previous year, when Farmer visited the camp briefly.

Cheit's memories were not particularly traumatic when they came back to him. Mostly, he was embarrassed and experienced a 'visceral uneasiness.'* He had genuinely liked Farmer, and their sexual encoun-

---

* Cheit clearly believes that the long-forgotten molestation was at least partly responsible for his life problems. He had entered therapy a few months before recalling the abuse, although he insists that his therapist never suggested the possibility of sexual abuse. 'I was very unsettled, more than ever before in my life. I felt somehow adrift, as if some anchor in my life had been raised. I had doubts about my marriage, my job, everything.'

ters were not altogether unpleasant for him. It was only months later, when his therapist suggested that he purchase a book about male survivors, that Cheit reframed his experience. 'It was such a stark title, *Abused Boys*, and here I was holding it in this public place. I felt like a kid with *Playboy*, ashamed to be holding it, and everyone would know why I was going to buy it.' For the first time, he said to himself, 'This book is about me. I was an abused boy. I couldn't say words like "molest" without cringing.'[54]

Curiously, Cheit had always recalled another sexual incident at the camp in which a black counselor kissed him on the lips. He was repulsed and got away quickly. Cheit does not know why he forgot about his experience with Farmer and always remembered this kiss. 'I find it puzzling, that's for sure,' he told me.

I would guess that Cheit always remembered the kiss because he found it revolting and therefore memorable. His sexual initiation with Farmer, on the other hand, was not particularly upsetting. 'I didn't dread it,' he told me. 'I wasn't thinking, "Oh, my God, he's going to come in again." There was some feeling of apprehension about it, but it was more tied up with guilt and confusion about sex.'

Despite recalling his sexual abuse years after it occurred, Ross Cheit does not know whether to call his memory 'repressed' or not, nor does he necessarily believe the kind of massive repression reported by other Survivors in which years of abuse were supposedly siphoned off from consciousness.

As with Cheit, it appears beyond dispute that Frank Fitzpatrick was indeed molested by a trusted adult figure, Father James Porter. But, as with Cheit, it is questionable whether this memory was truly 'repressed.' In a 1993 speech, Fitzpatrick said that he 'didn't really forget' his rape, but pushed it out of his consciousness for many years. In other words, although he has played an important role in making public serious abuse, his case may add little to the repressed-memory dispute.*[55]

* Since the 'Father Porter case' has been so widely hailed as proof of recovered memory, I have made a concerted effort to interview Porter victims. According to Massachusetts psychiatrist Stuart Grassian, who has conducted a survey of 43 Porter victims, 18 per cent reported 'no thoughts' of the abuse until triggered by media reports or calls in 1992. That apparently means that eight of the subjects had completely forgotten the abuse, though the questionnaire's wording is not altogether clear on this point. According to Grassian, most of those were molested in only a single instance, and he could not say whether they involved traumatic penetration. Despite my repeated requests, however, neither Fitzpatrick nor Grassian would put me in contact with Porter victims, and Fitzpatrick, who plans to write a book on the subject, would not talk to me about his experience.

It may also be worth noting that two of these accusers seem to enjoy the spotlight of publicity. Marilyn Van Derbur Atler spent years as a 'motivational speaker' before coming forward as a polished Incest Survivor. She clearly relishes the role, comparing herself to Jonas Salk, discoverer of the polio vaccine, or Julie Andrews running through fields in *The Sound of Music*, or a 747 jet with all engines screaming. 'Thirty-three years ago, I won a title that became an extension of my name,' she said just after announcing her allegations. 'Until May 8, 1991, I was Miss America. As of May 8 and forever more, my name is Marilyn Van Derbur Atler, Incest Survivor.'[56] Frank Fitzpatrick has made an avocation out of his Survivor status. He founded Survivor Connections, Inc., where he receives calls about satanic cult allegations and preaches against the 'sin of forgiveness.'[57]*[58]

There is certainly nothing wrong with seeking publicity to combat the very real horrors of incest and other forms of sexual abuse. But as well-known as their stories are, none of these famous victims has provided real evidence for the repressed-memory theory.

CASES OF REAL DENIAL

Whenever falsely accused parents protest their innocence, they are inevitably labeled 'in denial,' implying that they really did commit incest and are simply incapable of admitting it. This unfair characterization has made many critics of repressed memory automatically reject the entire concept of denial. Yet there *does* appear to be a human tendency to deny unpleasant reality, and at times the power of denial can be truly astonishing.

In 1938, famed psychologist Milton Erickson wrote of two cases in which women whose traumatic experience was well-documented subsequently denied that reality. Although we have here second-hand testi-

---

* Psychiatrist Elizabeth Feigon suggests three possible reasons that people might claim to have recovered memories of abuse, when in fact they had always remembered their experience: (1) They must claim repressed memories to collect money in a lawsuit; otherwise, the statute of limitations would have run out. (2) Now that repressed memories are so popular, people are ashamed to admit having known all along and not told. (3) Those who have always remembered may yearn for the attention, drama, and sympathy available to those with recovered memories.

mony over half a century old, it is nonetheless worth examining, since Erickson's observations are compelling.[59]

In Case 1, Erickson described two girls, ages 9 and 11, who were arrested in a raid on a whorehouse, along with 12 male patrons and the girls' parents, who prostituted their own children. Full confessions were obtained from the parents, patrons, and children. 'In addition,' Erickson wrote, 'medical examination of the girls disclosed numerous bruises and injuries [and] that they had been subjected to vaginal and rectal coitus and infected with syphilis and gonorrhea, both rectal and vaginal.'

Erickson interviewed the girls four times, with two months between each interview. During the first interview, conducted during the first week of their institutionalization, 'both told their story readily, easily and completely, manifesting much unhappiness over and repugnance to their experiences.' They expressed 'great satisfaction' over the punishments given to the adults, including their parents. At the same time, they recalled 'pleasurable, though guilty, feelings' about their sexual experiences.

By the third interview, four months later, the girls did not want to talk about the sexual abuse, but 'seemed to be interested only in immediate matters. Questioning about their past experience elicited an utterly inadequate account, in which even major details were denied or greatly minimized. Rectal coitus was emphatically and resentfully denied by both.' Now there was no pleasurable recollection, only repugnance. 'Ma wouldn't let anybody do those things,' one of the girls said.

By the time of the final interview, six months later, 'strong resentment was expressed over my interest in the story,' Erickson observed. No information was given spontaneously other than the declaration that it was 'all a lot of nasty lies.' The girls defended their parents. They stated that 'some bad men came to the house, but nothing bad happened.' Erickson concluded that 'they seemed to have no real recollection of the whole experience as an actual happening in their own lives. At no time could their sincerity or their full belief in their statements be doubted.'

Case 2 also involved denial, though not of sexual abuse. A young man on parole was driving his girl friend to a motel when, because of his reckless driving, the car overturned and burst into flames, pinning the young woman underneath. 'The man freed himself but made no effort to rescue his companion,' Erickson wrote. Passing motorists rescued the girl, but she was severely burned. At the trial, the girl testified against her boy friend with 'much bitterness and hatred.'

Eight months later, however, she changed her mind and tried to secure a retrial, saying that she had given misleading testimony. 'She's nuts!' the man told Erickson. 'She told the truth the first time.' He didn't want a retrial, since he feared a longer sentence. When Erickson interviewed the girl, he found her 'obviously sincere.' She now believed that 'the man had exerted every effort possible to rescue her' and gave a detailed account which Erickson considered 'a process of retrospective falsification and misconstruction.' She explained that her long period of hospitalization had given her time to realize how mistaken she had been. 'No human being would do such a thing nor could anybody endure being so treated,' she said. She emphasized that to be deserted under such circumstances would be 'intolerable.'

What are we to make of these cases? In Case 2, it appears that we do indeed have testimony to the malleability and suggestibility of memory. In this case, the woman has reconstructed her past, reinventing her boy friend's behavior after the accident, rehearsing it in her mind until it became real to her. She could not bear to think that he would abandon her.

In Case 1, it is not quite as clear that the two girls had literally rewritten their past. It appears likely that they were sick of talking about it and resented Erickson's repeated visits and insistence that they again recount the unpleasant events. Nonetheless, it is clear that they were 'in denial' about their parents' behavior and the extent of their abuse. Quite probably, the two girls contributed to one another's new version of reality by discussing it and reshaping their past collectively.

Do these cases provide proof for the concept of repression? No, but they do speak to the human capacity to rewrite the past and to deny reality.

ELIZABETH LOFTUS: 'THAT WOMAN'

Frederic Bartlett's work on memory spawned other research, though much of it was ignored in the United States until Elizabeth Loftus and Ulric Neisser reclaimed it.*[60] (Of particular note is the work of Donald

---

* Neisser, a psychology professor at Emory University in Atlanta, is famous, among other things, for debunking 'flashbulb' memories, which purport to preserve important moments in nearly photographic form. While most people think they remember exactly where they were and what they were doing when Kennedy was assassinated or when the *Challenger* exploded, Neisser has shown that they are in fact wrong most of the time.

Broadbent, Alan Baddeley, R. Conrad, Graham Hitch, Endel Tulving, Larry Weiskrantz, and others who sustained and enlarged on the Bartlett tradition.)[61] Loftus, a University of Washington psychology professor, became fascinated with the malleability of memory early in her academic career. Her conclusions sound remarkably similar to Bartlett's: 'Every time we recall an event, we must reconstruct the memory, and with each recollection the memory may be changed – colored by succeeding events, other people's recollections or suggestions, increased under-standing, or a new context.' Memory, she asserts, is 'an amoeba-like creature with powers to make us laugh, and cry, and clench our fists. Enormous powers – powers even to make us believe in something that never happened.'[62]

In 1974, Loftus published an article entitled 'Reconstructing Memory: The Incredible Eyewitness' in *Psychology Today*, mentioning how testi-mony on her research had helped acquit a defendant. Within days, defense lawyers were clamoring for her services. Consequently, for the last two decades, Loftus has become a fixture in courtrooms as well as psychology labs. On the stand, she routinely annoys prosecutors, explaining how easy it is to bias a line-up by showing the witness a photograph of the suspect beforehand; how 'unconscious transference' – confusing a person seen in one situation with someone in an entirely different context – can lead to false identifications; how our memory fills in gaps according to our expectations.[63]

In the classic Loftus experiment, subjects (usually college students) were shown a series of slides depicting a car that turned right at an intersection with a yield sign, then hit a pedestrian on the crosswalk. Half of the subjects were given misleading information embedded in questions asked immediately after the viewing. 'Did another car pass the red Datsun while it was stopped at the stop sign?' As a result, over 80 per cent of the test subjects later asserted that they had seen a stop sign rather than a yield sign.[64] Over the years, Loftus has conducted hundreds of increasingly sophisticated experiments on memory distor-tion on more than 20,000 subjects.[65] During the course of her work, she has created quite a few mental artifacts, as she wrote in a 1992 article: 'People have recalled seeing nonexistent items, such as broken glass, tape recorders, and even something as large and conspicuous as a barn [in a bucolic scene that contained no buildings at all], and have recalled incorrect traits for items they did see, such that a clean-shaven man developed a mustache, straight hair became curly, a stop sign became a yield sign, and a hammer became a screwdriver.'[66]

Loftus has concluded that 'misleading information can turn a lie into memory's truth ... It can make people confident about these false memories and also, apparently, impair earlier recollections. Once adopted, the newly created memories can be believed as strongly as genuine memories.' Loftus asserts that such mental distortion does not rely on particularly unusual traits or circumstances. In fact, she and a co-author once boasted that they could create a 'brave new world' of manufactured images: 'Give us a dozen healthy memories [and] we'll guarantee to take any one at random and train it to become any type of memory that we might select ... regardless of its origin or the brain that holds it.'[67]

Never one to flee from controversy, in 1990 Loftus wound up testifying in a landmark court battle based on Eileen Franklin Lipsker's 'recovered memories' of how her father, George Franklin, had raped and murdered her friend Susan Nason in 1969 when both girls were eight years old. The case has been meticulously reported by Harry MacLean in his book, *Once Upon a Time*. On the stand, Loftus explained that memory is not like a videotape recorder; that stressful events can cause fewer details to be recalled; that witnesses often incorporate new facts into old memories. She pointed out that the more frequently erroneous memories are repeated, the more confident the reporters become.[68] During cross-examination, however, Loftus had to admit that none of her experiments dealt with repressed memories of traumatic events. Sure, someone might mistake a peripheral detail such as a yield sign rather than a stop sign, but none of her subjects failed to remember the main events. No one forgot that a car had hit a pedestrian.

At the same trial, psychiatrist Lenore Terr's folksy style won over the jury. Terr recounted her theory of Type I and Type II memories and asserted that a mind holding repressed memories of trauma was like an abscess waiting to burst. Once it pops out, it will be as clear as the event itself. Terr stated with great confidence that she could tell whether someone's memory was true or false, based on the level of detail, emotional involvement, and presenting symptoms.[69][*][70] The jury found George Franklin guilty, and the case has been widely hailed as 'proof' of repressed memories.

Loftus remained unconvinced. George Franklin had unquestionably

---

[*] Terr presents her own highly colored version of the Eileen Franklin case in *Unchained Memories*, including the misinformation that Susan Nason's autopsy revealed semen in her vagina.

been a terrible father who had physically, emotionally, and perhaps sexually abused his wife and children. But whether Eileen's memories were accurate or not remained a question. For one thing, as Harry MacLean documents in his book, Eileen's story kept shifting, changing. First she said that the memory had appeared in a dream, then that she visualized the scene during therapy sessions while hypnotized. When she found that such testimony would be inadmissible, she asserted that she had never been hypnotized and had instead remembered the murder spontaneously when her five-year-old daughter looked up at her.* That had supposedly triggered the hidden memory of Susan Nason's immobilized gaze just before George Franklin crushed her head with a rock.[71]

Many other details of Eileen's memory metamorphosed as time went by, including a clearly visualized black molester with an afro whom Eileen then magically transformed into a white friend of her father's. MacLean also described how Eileen bathed in the sympathy and attention which the trial brought her. (On this point, at least, MacLean and Terr agree. In her book, Terr describes Eileen 'glowing like the moon' in the company of sympathizers.)[72]

What MacLean did not understand at the time he covered the trial, however, was how therapists in the late 1980s were actively encouraging their clients – especially those with relationship troubles – to believe that repressed memories of sexual abuse were the true cause of their problems. Seeking help for her troubled marriage and depression over a miscarriage, Eileen saw two counselors who helped her retrieve such incest memories: clinical psychologist Katherine Rieder and marriage and child counselor Kirk Barrett. Over the course of a year, beginning in the summer of 1988, Rieder, who specialized in 'codependency issues,' helped Eileen recover her first sexual abuse memories relating to her father (she visualized him inserting his finger into her vagina when she was six or seven). Later, when Eileen switched to Barrett, who held a masters in psychology, she remembered the murder scene as well as actual incestuous intercourse.[73]

Barrett's testimony takes up less than a page of *Once Upon a Time*. MacLean describes him as 'soft-looking, a mellow Teddy bear, with a tanned, pillowy face.' The therapist explained in a low, soothing voice how, during five sessions in June and July of 1989, Eileen had recovered

* MacLean suggests that Eileen may have gotten the idea for this final version from Lenore Terr, who had appeared with her on a *Today Show* segment. Terr had stated that repressed memories could be triggered when 'one's own child is the age one was at the time of the event in the first place.'

her memories of the murder. During his testimony, a juror, reporter, and research assistant fell asleep.[74] While his monotone made for a boring witness, it undoubtedly served him well as a hypnotist.

MacLean himself now realizes that he missed this crucial point. 'Quite frankly,' he wrote in a letter to me, 'I didn't know enough to suspect that memories of childhood sexual abuse could be therapeutically induced. That information didn't hit the public arena until the False Memory Syndrome Foundation came into existence, and I certainly never encountered it in my research or interviews. The Franklin case would be fascinating were it to be re-tried today.'*[75] MacLean was not alone. Leaving the courtroom, Elizabeth Loftus didn't know anything about *The Courage to Heal*, but she was determined to pursue the suspect area of recovered memories.

But how could she show experimentally that memories of sexual abuse or other traumas could be implanted? If she succeeded, the experiment itself would constitute a form of mental abuse, convincing the innocent subject that something horrible had happened to him or her. Aside from her own ethical concerns, the Human Subjects Committee at the University of Washington would never allow such an experiment. The problem appeared insurmountable, but Loftus devised a clever analogue. She suggested that her research assistants, such as Jim, tell a younger sibling, such as 14-year-old Chris, that he had been lost in a shopping mall (a mythical event) when he was 5 years old, but that a nice man wearing a flannel shirt had found him and brought him back to their parents.

Two days later, Chris remembered how he had felt that day. 'I was so scared that I would never see my family again. I knew that I was in trouble.' Two weeks later, Chris had rehearsed the memory in some detail, filling in the gaps. He recalled, with some emotion, how he had been frightened and cried. He had created an image of his rescuer, who was bald and wore glasses. Even after he was 'debriefed' and told that the story wasn't true, Chris clung to it. 'Really? I thought I remembered being lost . . . and looking around for you guys. I do remember that, and then crying, and Mom coming up and saying, "Where were you? Don't you ever do that again." '[76] Six subjects – 25 per cent of the pilot

---

* Since MacLean wrote those words, the decision against George Franklin has been overturned, based primarily on the jury not being told that Eileen Franklin had access to newspaper accounts containing all the details of the crime she 'remembered.' Franklin remained in prison, on $1 million bail, until prosecutors announced that they were dropping all charges, following DNA tests that cleared Franklin of one murder charge.

sample, ranging in age from 18 to 53, developed memories of being lost in a mall at the age of five.

Therapists such as Judith Herman and Karen Olio scoff at Loftus' experiments. 'The notion that therapists can implant scenarios of horror in the minds of their patients is easily accepted because it appeals to common prejudices,' Herman says.[77] Olio dismisses the false mall memories as irrelevant. Anyone could believe in such a common, mild trauma. That's very different from repressed memories of sadistic sexual abuse. The two events aren't comparable. Although 'suggestions can affect us – perhaps influence our choices at the supermarket, maybe even our vote for president – to claim that such suggestions have fundamentally and falsely altered an entire client population's understanding of themselves and their histories seems grossly exaggerated,' Olio concludes.[78]

As a result of her experiments and her outspoken criticism of therapists who lead their patients to believe in incest that may never have occurred, Loftus has become the lightning rod for the controversy over the 'backlash' against the Recovery Movement. One prosecutor called her a 'whore,' and an accuser's mother told her she was joining hands with the murderers and rapists of the world. Returning from a recent conference, Loftus found herself seated next to a therapist who, when she discovered her seat-mate's identity, swatted Loftus while shrieking, 'You're that *woman!* You're that *woman!*'[79]

Yet Loftus is, herself, a victim of childhood sexual abuse. When she was six years old, her babysitter used to rub her arm gently, which was comforting and pleasant. One night, though, 'he took his pants off, pulled my dress off over my head, and removed my underpants. He lay down on the bed and pulled me on top of him, positioning me so that our pelvises touched. His arms circled around me. I felt him pushing against me, and I knew something was wrong. Embarrassed and confused, I squirmed off him and ran out of the room. After that, there is only blackness ... My memory took him and destroyed him.'[80] Clearly, Loftus recognizes the horror of sexual abuse and how it can indeed distort the memory. On the other hand, she never forgot this incident.

Loftus understands how insidious personal memories can be, particularly when a trusted authority figure such as a family member or therapist validates them. At a family reunion, one of Loftus' uncles told her that when she was 14, she had been the one to find her mother's drowned body. Although she was initially sure that the story was untrue, 'I actually started to think maybe I did,' she recounts. Over the next few days, she began to visualize the scene: her mother floating face down in the pool, young Beth's approach and horror. Perhaps this explained why she was so upset whenever she thought about her mother. Maybe it even accounted for her compulsive workaholic nature, trying to avoid this primal scene. Soon afterwards, however, her brother called to tell her that her uncle had been mistaken.[81]

Although she has been vilified by the Survivor Movement, Loftus has tried to take a moderate stand. She does not deny the possibility that repressed memories may exist. In fact, she expresses a belief in them, employing her own definition. 'If repression is the avoidance in your conscious awareness of unpleasant experiences that come back to you, yes, I believe in repression.' That is not the same mechanism hypothesized in most of these cases, however, as she points out. 'If it [repression] is a blocking out of an endless stream of traumas that occur over and over that leave a person with absolutely no awareness that these things happen, that make them behave in destructive ways and re-emerge decades later in some reliable form – I don't see any evidence for it. It flies in the face of everything we know about memory.'[82]*

WILDER PENFIELD, KARL LASHLEY, AND
THE SEARCH FOR THE ENGRAM

One of the fallacies that Elizabeth Loftus fights against is the notion that memories reside in specific places in the brain, ready to pop out under the proper stimuli. In the 1930s – and continuing through the 1950s – Wilder Penfield, a Montreal neurosurgeon, stumbled onto 'proof' of such localization while operating on epileptics. To help locate the damaged area of the brain, Penfield would stimulate various points of the temporal lobe with a weak electric current. He found that when he electrified a particular point in the brain, some of his patients spontaneously recalled what he took to be specific memories. In 1969, he wrote that 'neuronal connections . . . can be followed again by an electric current many years later with no loss of detail, as though a tape recorder had been receiving it all.'[83]

Penfield's assertions were gobbled up by the popular press, and they continue to influence many psychologists and laymen, who believe that

---

* Outspoken California social psychologist Richard Ofshe agrees with Loftus, going even further in denying the existence of what he terms 'robust repression.'

his findings prove his contentions. Yet the 'memories' Penfield evoked are problematic for a number of reasons. First, they were reported by epileptic patients whose brains were not working normally. Second, during Penfield's long career, only 40 patients out of 520 – 7.7 per cent – whose temporal lobes were stimulated reported having such memories. Third, the 'flashbacks' reported by the patients were not necessarily replications of real events that had occurred in their pasts. One patient, for example, visualized her own birth. Another said she 'seemed to be at the lumberyard,' even though she had never been near one in real life. As Ulric Neisser pointed out, these were probably 'synthetic constructions and not literal recalls.' Fourth, stimulation of precisely the same spot produced the same memory *only* if the probes were conducted in rapid succession. Otherwise, different responses arose.

Loftus suggests that 'these so-called memories, then, appear to consist merely of the thoughts and ideas that happened to exist just prior to and during the stimulation.'[84]

Another problem with Penfield's reports was his own attitude about them. They excited him, and he let his patients know this. This could easily have led to distortions in reporting, because the patients knew the expectations he had that they would 'remember' something. 'I think I saw the river,' one patient offered hopefully. 'I had a little memory – a scene in a play,' another said. The eager surgeon took all such reports as proof that he was probing the mysteries of the mind. 'I was more astonished, each time my electrode brought forth such a response.' While acknowledging that another neurologist interpreted such episodes as 'dreamy states' or 'psychical seizures,' Penfield asserted, 'It was evident at once that these were not dreams. They were electrical activations of the sequential record of consciousness, a record that had been laid down during the patient's earlier experience. The patient "relived" all that he had been aware of in that earlier period of time as in a moving-picture "flashback." '[85] Nearing the end of his career, Penfield expressed a somewhat mystical attitude about the human brain, asserting that 'the mind may be a distinct and *different essence*.'[86]

Penfield believed that he had discovered the elusive 'engram,' a word coined by Harvard psychologist Karl Lashley in the 1920s. During the same decades when Penfield was zapping his patients' gray matter, Lashley was training rats to run in a maze, then cutting out different portions of their brains and turning them loose in the maze again. As expected, the rats didn't perform as well the second time. But what vexed Lashley was his inability to find any particular portion of the brain that contained the full memory or ability to remember the maze. He kept hoping that when he snipped the crucial area, the rat would just stumble randomly around the maze, completely at a loss. But it didn't happen. Regardless of which cortical section he removed, the results were the same. In 1929, he wrote that 'the maze habit, when formed, is not localized in any single area of the cerebrum.' Another 20 years of maze running and rat mutilation failed to alter his findings. In 1950, Lashley concluded that 'somehow, equivalent traces are established throughout the functional area,' adding that 'all of the cells of the brain must be in almost constant activity, either firing or actively inhibited.'[87]

Lashley died in 1959, but he would be pleased to know that subsequent testing indicates that synapses fire like fireflies all over the brain when it is learning or trying to recall something. Or, as biological memory expert Larry Squire puts it, '*all* cortical regions are involved in both processing and memory storage, though always within functionally specified domains.' Not only that, but each mini-ensemble of neurons can encode more than one piece of information, each with its own electrical or chemical activity pattern. There appears to be great potential for biological interference with memory. 'Memory for whole events is stored widely,' Squire writes, 'not in a single location; literal or biologic forgetting can occur, so that recollection of past events is a reconstruction from fragments, not a veridical playback of past events.'[88] Although other tests indicate that some skills and emotions are somewhat localized, it appears that a specific 'memory' simply does not exist at one particular point in the brain.*[89]

Bartlett was right when he talked about a 'schema' to which the mind refers. Whenever we remember something, we literally reconstruct it, grabbing tiny bits of imagery and information from millions of neurons that interconnect in a vast and complex web. Until that moment, the memory cannot be said to 'exist' at all. As one science writer has put it, 'it is only potential, latent, a wraith implicit . . . It is a ghost in the machine.'[90]

---

* Studies of 'split-brain' subjects – epileptics whose corpus callosum was surgically severed – indicate that the right and left sides of the brain can act independently. The right side specializes in nonverbal, spatial, intuitive thought, while the left side offers language expertise. But that does not mean that all language, for instance, resides in one brain hemisphere. Instead, several anatomical regions contribute to every thought in dynamic interplay. As science writer Jeremy Campbell notes, 'a simple concept like "grandmother" may be spread out across a region of the [neural] network.'

IMPLICIT AND STATE-DEPENDENT MEMORY

Thus far, I have been speaking of memory in its commonly understood form, what the specialists call *episodic* or *declarative* memory – our ability to recall the personal past and tell someone what happened. Recovered memory therapists have, however, latched onto another type of memory which, because it cannot be articulated in words, is termed *non-declarative* or *implicit* memory. Like much research on the unseen, scientists have deduced the existence of implicit memory and how it works primarily by observing the behavior of organically damaged patients such as H. M., a Connecticut man who, at the age of 27 in 1953, underwent radical brain surgery to cure his severe epileptic seizures. Most of his hippocampus and amygdala and part of his temporal lobe were removed. The tragic story of H. M. is movingly and thoroughly recounted by Philip J. Hilts in his remarkable book, *Memory's Ghost*.[91]

As a result of the surgery, H. M. displayed severe but specific memory deficits. He can remember his birthday, the names of his teenage girl friends and other events of his youth, but he fails to recognize his current doctor, whom he sees every day. It turns out that the hippocampus is a kind of way-station where short-term declarative memory is processed, then farmed out to other parts of the brain. Without it, H. M. cannot construct long-term memories, though his pre-operational experience remains safely in neuronal connections elsewhere in the cerebral lobes.

There *is* one kind of subtle long-term memory that H. M. can master, however. When presented with the same puzzle day after day, he cannot consciously recall having seen it before – yet his performance steadily improves. Here is evidence that a form of implicit memory is at work, and that it relies on a separate brain area. Researchers have named this *procedural* memory, the ability to perform a particular act without consciously remembering it. Another form of implicit memory involves the emotions. In 1889, for instance, Sergei Korsakoff, who first identified organic amnesia, noticed that while one of his patients had no explicit memory of an electrical shock, he subsequently sought to avoid the black box that administered it.[92]

More recently, Harvard psychologist Daniel Schacter has studied implicit memory.[93] Schacter concludes that 'mood effects on implicit memory may be greater than those on explicit memory' and that 'information on which [people] operate could affect performance and behavior implicitly, without any corresponding phenomenal awareness.'[94] Moreover, in normal subjects without organic brain damage, implicit and explicit memory probably work in tandem. In the case of 'state-dependent' or 'mood-dependent' memories, the implicit, unconscious awareness may be triggered when a person gets into the same emotional or physical state. Reinstating the context in which an event took place has indeed been shown to improve memory in many cases.[95] Some research psychologists and biologists believe that such research *might* apply to the retrieval of repressed or dissociated trauma memories, though Schacter has emphasized that the findings are 'no more than suggestive.'[96] The hypothesis holds that while the conscious mind may not recall the trauma, the hidden, implicit memory of the abuse remains.

Therapists and researchers eager for scientific underpinnings for their belief in massive repression have embraced implicit memory. Thus Lenore Terr writes in *Unchained Memories*: 'One wonders if many of the mute night child's memories were laid down as nondeclarative, or implicit, memories. Such memories could not have been retrieved in words.'[97] Yet such an explanation requires a huge leap of intellectual faith, jumping from brain-damaged patients and studies of word-association to forgotten incest memories. The evidence – derived from hypnosis, multiple-personality cases, and psychogenic amnesia – is highly suspect, as I document in Chapters 3 and 4, and probably stems more from suggestibility and expectation than from any form of real memory, implicit or otherwise. Yes, implicit and state-dependent memories exist, but that does not mean that a woman who hates bananas is necessarily reacting subconsciously to a memory of her father's erect penis, as many trauma therapists believe.

Schacter, who has conducted studies on two 'multiple personality disorder' (MPD) subjects, is now much more skeptical of the phenomenon. 'It has only become apparent in the past few years, largely through the repressed memories controversy, just how powerful the iatrogenic [doctor-induced] influences on memory can be,' he wrote to me recently. 'I would be much less likely now to consider studying an MPD patient than I was six or seven years ago. It is abundantly clear now that some of the recovery therapists have created enormous problems for patients and society. Indeed, implicit memory, rather than reflecting the existence of repressed memory, may sometimes be the basis for constructing false memory.'[98] Schacter was quoted in *The New York Times* in May of

1994, warning how 'the confabulator picks out a bit or piece of an actual memory, but confuses its true context, and draws on other bits of experience to construct a story.'[99]

Psychologist John Kihlstrom, who has co-authored articles on amnesia and memory with Schacter, agrees. 'The evidence is just not there [for the validity of recovered memories]. There is, to my knowledge, not a single published study that [has] attempted to verify the memories recovered by hypnosis and drugs.' He adds that 'in the final analysis, memory isn't like reading a book; it's like *writing* a book from fragmentary notes.' In the cultural atmosphere that has produced *The Courage to Heal*, therapists have grasped at implicit memory as the 'scientific' justification for what Kihlstrom calls a 'peculiarly perverse logic.'[100] Context can indeed affect memory, not only by cuing a forgotten item, but by creating an expectation. As one researcher on state-dependent memory recently wrote, 'The role of context on false recognition has been largely neglected.'[101]

NEUROSCIENCE AND REPRESSED MEMORIES

In the last decade, scientists concerned with the mysterious inner workings of the brain have produced many interesting studies. None either prove nor disprove the existence of repressed memories, though work on the chemistry of highly emotional memories tends to verify the 1891 observation of philosopher and psychologist William James: 'What interests us most vividly at the time is . . . what we remember best. An experience may be so exciting emotionally as almost to leave a scar on the cerebral tissues.'[102] In other words, strong emotions (whether positive or negative) produce strong memories, less subject to distortion and decay than normal memory.

The research of James McGaugh, Larry Cahill, Joseph Ledoux and others all confirm this finding.[103] Epinephrine, more commonly known as adrenaline, is released by the brain when we are stressed. This hormone apparently causes a chain reaction in which other hormones called 'endogenous opiates' (natural opium-like substances produced by the brain) go to work in the thalamus and amygdala, parts of the limbic system situated near the hippocampus. The amygdala, seat of emotion, reinforces the work of the hippocampus, which transfers short-term into long-term memory. It appears that emotional memories are recorded on two simultaneous and somewhat independent tracks – implicit and declarative – that mutually reinforce one another.

From an evolutionary standpoint, this finding makes perfect sense. Humans need to be able to respond appropriately to future situations. By reinforcing a biological mechanism for recalling highly emotional events better than others, evolution guarantees that we will be able to seek out pleasurable situations in the future and avoid unpleasant, dangerous ones. It also helps explain the survival mechanisms that produce post-traumatic stress disorder (PTSD) in which those who have undergone profound trauma sometimes suffer from involuntary, intrusive memories. Indeed, as several researchers have noted, 'the hallmark symptom of PTSD is the reliving or recollection of the traumatic event in the form of intrusive thoughts.' That is certainly what Holocaust historian Lawrence Langer concluded in his book, *Holocaust Testimonies: The Ruins of Memory.*[104]

The research also shows, however, that massive doses of epinephrine actually *impair* memories. Because these experiments have used artificially high amounts of the hormone in non-human subjects, however, it is not known whether we can naturally release such lethal doses from the adrenal medulla. The most suggestive results on humans stem from the apparent effect of glucocorticoids (a class of steroid hormones secreted by the adrenal glands) on the hippocampus. Glucocorticoids are released when the body is under stress, and, in large amounts, they appear to damage neurons in the hippocampus. It is therefore hypothetically possible that stress from sexual abuse would indirectly lead to incomplete memories. Such conclusions are, as Daniel Schacter puts it, 'intriguing speculations.'[105] Even if true, such damage to memory would be universal rather than particular, according to psychologist Larry Weiskrantz. 'There is no evidence that any such secretion would block or weaken a *specific* memory. In other words, having a slightly shrunken hippocampus is bad across the board.'[106]

In addition, damage to the hippocampus would not explain how missing memories could be retrieved later. As neuroscientist James McGaugh puts it, 'Even if we can release these high doses that impair memory, that would provide no explanation for recovered memories – they are, like Clementine, lost and gone forever.'[107]

In a recent issue of *Discover* Magazine, well-respected neurobiologist (and psychiatrist) Eric Kandel wrote an article in which he strongly suggested a biological, scientific foundation for a belief in massive repression. His co-author was his daughter, Minouche Kandel, a feminist lawyer active in the California clemency effort for battered women who kill their partners.*[108] The Kandels reviewed the theory of implicit memory, then discussed rat studies indicating that large doses of endogenous opiates weaken memory storage. 'Such studies give us a biological context for considering how traumatic memories might be suppressed in humans,' the Kandels wrote.[109]

The Kandels finished the article – daughter Minouche perhaps writing the conclusion – by complaining about 'media and academic critics ... using the wedge of doubt to publicly discredit the very existence of delayed memories,' criticizing them as part of a 'backlash,' and ending with a rousing quote from Judith Herman.

Eric Kandel has spent his career studying the behavior of the sea slug *Aplysia*. He chose the slug because of its extremely simple nervous system and has systematically sought to discover what he calls the 'cellular alphabet' of learning. I won't go into his experiments in detail but will merely point out that some other memory researchers, such as Steven Rose in *The Making of Memory* (1992), have criticized Kandel for his reductionist approach. Kandel once gave a talk, for instance, on the theme, 'Psychotherapy and the Single Synapse.'[110]

Although Eric Kandel is a giant in the field of memory research, in this case he wrote outside his expertise within that field. Indeed, it is ironic that he appears to rely in part on the rat studies of James McGaugh, who is himself extremely critical of the notion of repressed memory. Kandel may have been unduly influenced by his daughter's politics.

Harvard psychiatrist Bessel van der Kolk has gone even further than Eric Kandel in asserting the scientific validity of recovered memories. Van der Kolk even professes a belief in the widely discredited notion of 'body memories,' which he christens with the more scientific-sounding label 'somatic memory' in his 1994 article, 'The Body Keeps the Score.'[111]**[112] Van der Kolk reviews an impressive array of studies

---

* The Kandels began their article with the case of Jennifer H. (Hoult) as an example of true recovered memories. Jennifer's 'memories,' however, arose in therapy with an unlicensed psychotherapist whom she saw for relationship problems. During guided imagery sessions, she pictured her father molesting her. 'It was like ... on TV if there is all static,' she explained. 'I slowly opened my eyes in the session and I said, "I never knew that happened to me."'

** The extent to which such pseudoscientific notions have permeated therapeutic thought is alarming, as one recent survey of 38 counselors' beliefs in 'body memories' revealed. One therapist, for instance, asserted that 'within each cell there's a mitochondria that has the capacity for recording events.'

on the biological and neurological effects of trauma, most of which support the fact that traumatic memories are difficult to forget. Indeed, van der Kolk writes that PTSD patients often 'get mired in a continuous reliving of the past.' He quotes Pierre Janet, who noted that 'certain happenings . . . leave indelible and distressing memories – memories to which the sufferer continually returns, and by which he is tormented by day and by night.'

Yet van der Kolk grasps at studies of implicit memory to conjecture that many traumatic memories are completely forgotten at the conscious level, only to be recalled indelibly at the 'somatosensory level' as 'visual images or physical sensations.' Unlike the fragile conscious memory, he posits, these implicit memories are 'impervious to change.' Throughout his hypothetical constructions, van der Kolk slips in tell-tale conditional words – 'catecholamines *could* stimulate active coping mechanisms'; 'state-dependent memory retrieval *may* also be involved in dissociative phenomena in which traumatized persons *may be* wholly or partially amnestic'; 'intense affect *may* inhibit proper evaluation and categorization of experience.' [*Italics added.*]

The ultimate problem with van der Kolk's attempts to provide a scientific basis for massive repression/dissociation is that they are self-contradictory. Even if we ignore the overwhelming evidence that extreme trauma is remembered consciously all too well, it is difficult to understand how conscious memories would ever be retrieved in his scenario. According to van der Kolk, such explicit memories would be destroyed by an overabundance of glucocorticoids and other stress hormones. Then how are they to be 'triggered,' if they are not there? In other words, van der Kolk cannot both destroy his cake and eat it too.

Candace Pert is another brain biochemist whose work is often cited as 'proving' the existence of 'body memories.' In 1986, she wrote an article examining how 'neuropeptides,' opiate-like hormones used in the brain, were also found elsewhere. 'We discovered,' she wrote, 'that the receptors [for neuropeptides] were scattered throughout not only the brain but also the body.' Her conclusion? 'In the beginning of my work, I matter-of-factly presumed that emotions were in the head or the brain. Now I would say they are really in the body as well,' though she admitted that 'some scientists might describe this idea as outrageous.' At the end of her article, Pert joined the ranks of scientists-turned-mystics, espousing her belief in immortality because 'mind and consciousness would appear to be independent of brain and body.'[113]

While it is true that there are receptors for various hormones scattered throughout the body, that does not mean they hold emotions *per se*, and certainly not memories. As James McGaugh points out, 'No one can seriously doubt that fear, love, joy, horror, etc., are expressions of brain activity.' While hormones such as adrenaline 'have important actions in the periphery,' he adds, 'they do not create memories there. The concept of "body memories" is nonsense, if by that you mean that memories are stored outside of the central nervous system. The notion that because there are receptors for neuropeptides located outside of the brain, there is also memory at those receptors, is at best a very strange hypothesis for which there is no evidence.'[114]

In short, although some scientists believe in the concepts of massive repression, dissociation, and body memories, there is no good evidence for these concepts. Although I am not a neuroscientist, I am aware that *no one really knows* how the mind works. We have the merest hints and guesses, based primarily on studies with monkeys, rats, chickens, and other simpler life forms such as sea slugs.

Unfortunately, scientists are human beings, too, and they sometimes jump to seductive conclusions, especially if the conclusions fit their hypotheses and place them on the cutting edge. 'The history of many scientific subjects is virtually freed from . . . constraints of fact,' Stephen Jay Gould wrote in *The Mismeasure of Man*. 'Some topics are invested with enormous social importance but blessed with very little reliable information. When the ratio of data to social impact is so low, a history of scientific attitudes may be little more than an oblique record of social change.'[115]

In Peter Huber's 1991 book, *Galileo's Revenge*, he describes the hallmarks of what he terms 'junk' or 'pathological' science:

Pathological science often depends on experiments at the threshold of detectability, or at the lowest margins of statistical significance. The claims frequently emerge from a body of data that is selectively incomplete; wishful researchers unconsciously discard enough 'bad' data to make the remaining 'good' points look important. That the measurements are at the very threshold of sensitivity is an advantage, not an obstacle: data that don't fit the theory are explained away; those they fit are lovingly retained. Professional statisticians call this 'data dredging.' Dredging is easiest in loose and formless mud. Thus, pathological science does best when recording swings in mood, disruption of brain-wave patterns, and things of that sort.[116]

History has repeatedly taught us that scientists are not immune to cultural and social influences. The phrenologists of the early 19th century were convinced that they could determine human character by studying the shape of the head, for instance. Much more recently, in the 1940s and 1950s, reputable scientists and physicians sanctioned prefrontal lobotomies to attack the problem at its source, thereby turning thousands of patients – mostly women – into placid mental zombies.[117]

In the 1960s, memory researchers thought they had discovered the 'molecules of memory' and could simply inject RNA from rats or worms into their peers and 'teach' them previously learned skills. As memory researcher Steven Rose notes, these experiments could 'all be explained by inadequate statistics, faulty experimental design, [and] overenthusiastic interpretation of ambiguous results.'[118]

Contrary to popular belief, scientists may be *more* prone to stubborn, dogmatic beliefs than other humans, because they often spend their entire professional lives devoted to a single hypothesis.*[119] In addition, scientists are clearly influenced by their social milieu. Some establish credibility through real discoveries and then veer into quackery. As Freud critic Richard Webster has written, 'many "great" scientists have gone on to create significant pseudo-sciences,' adding that 'sometimes the prestige and authority which they have earnt through their genuine contributions to science has both encouraged them along the path of folly at the same time that it has silenced or eclipsed their critics.'[120] We must therefore be wary of accepting the latest 'scientific' hypothesis 'proving' the reality of repressed memory.

William James got it right over a hundred years ago when he quoted Charles Richet, another psychologist: 'Who of us, alas! has not experienced a bitter and profound grief, [an] immense laceration?' he wrote. 'In these great griefs, the present endures neither for a minute, for an hour, nor for a day, but for weeks and months. The memory of the cruel moment will not efface itself from consciousness.'[121]

---

* While unfair to most scientific endeavors, Mark Twain's devastating humor does apply to some, including repressed memory theorists: 'there is something fascinating about science. One gets such wholesale return on conjecture out of such trifling investment in fact.' One is also reminded of an instructive dialogue from *Through the Looking Glass.* 'I see nobody on the road,' said Alice. 'I only wish I had such eyes,' the king replies. 'To be able to see Nobody! And at that distance, too! Why, it's as much as I can do to see real people in this light!'

THE CONNECTIONIST COMPUTER MODEL

During the '60s and '70s, computer scientists believed that they could replicate the brain's functioning, producing 'artificial intelligence' equal to the ability of human beings. After all, a computer's switching element responds much more quickly than does the relatively slow brain synapse. But the programmers failed miserably, largely because they assumed that computers, with their central processing units and specific memory sites, worked like the brain. In the 1980s, however, programmers began to imitate the 'connectionist' brain model, hooking up their computers in 'massively parallel' fashion. Rather than attempting to program one computer memory with the 'right' answer, they challenged their computers to think. By hooking up 300 'artificial neurons,' each a minicomputer, one programmer produced 'NETtalk,' which gradually taught itself to read aloud.[122]

In his thought-provoking book, *The Improbable Machine* (1989), Jeremy Campbell discusses how the connectionist model has revolutionized not only computer programming, but our notion of how and why the mind works. 'We are systematically illogical and biased,' he writes. 'The world in which the brain evolved is a great deal more untidy and less circumscribed [than a serial computer], full of ambiguity, deceit, problems that sprawl in ungainly fashion . . . information that is incomplete or contradictory.' As a result, one's mind readily accepts 'imperfect information, generalizing, filling in the missing parts from its large reserves of worldly knowledge.'

As Campbell repeats in a variety of ways, we don't think logically, and we rely largely on stereotyped generalizations, fitting experience into preordained categories. Human memory is 'much less reliable than a computer, but it is vast, and associative by its very nature. Human memory cannot help but connect one thing it knows with another thing it knows. It puts the world together in such a way that, given just a small fragment of information, it can amplify that fragment instantly.' Consequently, 'the mind is a bundle of paradoxes. It has insight, but at the cost of more-or-less frequent errors. It harnesses the "vice" of prejudice in order to make new discoveries about the world.'[123]

We have, in other words, come full circle, back to Frederic Bartlett. Campbell concludes that 'the mind thrives and flourishes on gaps; it tolerates great gaping holes in what it hears and reads, because it is so adept at filling in the holes with what it knows.' As an example, Campbell asks us to consider the following two sentences: 'A man wearing a ski mask walked into the bank. One of the tellers screamed.' While a computer would not understand why the teller screamed, most of us would immediately apply a 'bank-robber schema,' and we would probably be correct. Of course, as Campbell points out, 'the bank in question could have been in Aspen, Colorado, and the teller might have screamed because she saw a mouse run across the floor.'[124]

In most conditions, the brain works pretty well, even though it relies not so much on logic as on interpretations of generalized experience. And it turns out that the language we use is fundamental to the thinking and remembering process. Words serve as mini-schemata, calling up different connotations and memories. Thus, in one of Elizabeth Loftus' experiments, subjects who were asked to describe two cars 'smashing' together reported fictitious broken glass, while cars that just 'hit' didn't evoke this error.[125] 'Language is the mirror of the mind,' Campbell asserts, and it explains much of our 'associative' thinking. 'The mind seems to be metaphorical to its foundations.'[126]

But how does all of this apply to the millions of 'Survivors' who have retrieved what they believe to be memories of incest? For better or worse, our society has now produced an 'incest schema' that leaps to assumptions based on incomplete information. Consider these two sentences: 'The father sat on his daughter's bed. He said, "I love you so much, Princess," and kissed her goodnight.' In the 1950s, that would have called up a Father-Knows-Best schema. Nowadays, it calls up potential incest. Metaphors such as 'emotional incest' have become literally accepted truth. Once the mind's normal schemata of 'loving family' or 'happy childhood' are systematically destroyed through reading and therapy, an alternative connection is made. 'My therapist thinks I came from a dysfunctional family. I am very unhappy. I have all of these symptoms they talk about. All these books can't be wrong. I think maybe I was abused. Therefore, I probably was abused. It's only a matter of finding the memories.'

As Campbell concludes, 'Memory becomes interpretation. It is not a filing cabinet, nor a set of index cards, but a hermeneutical system. A cue that triggers a memory is a sort of puzzle that has to be solved, a riddle with multiple possible answers that must be disentangled so that the right answer pops out.' Unfortunately, when the 'puzzle' is predefined – 'I think maybe I was sexually abused but repressed the memory' – the right answer *doesn't* pop out. 'In remembering,' writes Campbell, 'people not only distort and interpret information from the past so as to make it fit what they know or believe in the present; they seem to add new information. The more distant the event, the more material the mind adds.'[127]

MEMORY PALACES AND HAUNTED HOUSES

Before the invention of the printing press, humans honed the art of mass memorization to pass on oral traditions – an art which has lasted to this day in one form or another, and which yields intriguing parallels with the guided imagery technique of recovering traumatic memories. The ancient methodology relies on the associative nature of the brain, as Frances Yates has documented in *The Art of Memory*. Around 500 B.C., Simonides left a feast just before the roof caved in, crushing his fellow revelers. He discovered that he could identify the roomful of mangled corpses on the basis of where each banqueter had been sitting at table before the roof caved in.[128] Similarly, 16th-century Jesuit Matteo Ricci could build a 'memory palace' in his mind and store different bits of information in different rooms. By 'hiding' a different fact or memory image behind a sofa here or a gargoyle there, Ricci could then walk through the room and 'retrieve' them in the desired order.[129]

Perhaps significant to our understanding of the repressed memory phenomenon, bizarre sexual imagery seemed to provide helpful associations for Christian philosophers such as Albertus Magnus, who suggested that 'we should imagine some ram, with huge horns and testicles, coming towards us in the dark.'[130] During the Renaissance, the memorists turned mystical, focusing their systems on the memory of a pre-existent Divine Source. The new art of memory made common cause with magic, alchemy, numerology, astrology, radical symbolism, and piety. Memory became associated with vivid imagination. The guided-imagery search for repressed memories, in which people search through mental rooms until they find frightening molestation, follows in this tradition.

INFANTILE AMNESIA AND PREVERBAL ABUSE

Jean Piaget, the famous child psychologist, had a vivid memory of a traumatic event that took place when he was two years old. 'I was sitting in my pram, which my nurse was pushing in the Champs Elysees, when a man tried to kidnap me. I was held in by the strap fastened around me while my nurse bravely tried to stand between me and the thief. She received various scratches.' Piaget recalled how her face looked, how a crowd gathered, how a policeman with a white baton appeared, how the would-be kidnapper fled. But the entire episode turned out to be a fabrication. When Piaget was 15, his former nurse, newly converted to the Salvation Army, wrote to the family confessing that she had faked the scratches. There had been no kidnapper. Piaget concluded that he must have heard detailed accounts of the story as a child and created his own 'visual memory' of an entirely fictitious event.[131]

This anecdote illustrates how we can create vivid memories of events that never occurred. Most experimental psychologists would not have believed in Piaget's 'memory' in the first place, however, because of the well-known if little-understood phenomenon of infantile amnesia. Very few people remember much before the age of five. And hardly anyone – except people who, like Piaget, visualize a possible scenario – remembers anything at all before the age of three.*[132] Freud offered a dubious psychological explanation. He believed that intense infantile sexual conflicts must be repressed, though he offered only his own rather idiosyncratic self-analysis as evidence for his opinion.

However, Freud also referred to an interesting survey conducted by V. and C. Henri and published in 1897. The Henris obtained the self-reported earliest memories of 123 respondents. The majority (88) recalled an event between the ages of two and four. As Freud noted, 'the most frequent content of the first memories of childhood [in the Henri study] are on the one hand occasions of fear, shame, physical pain, etc., and on the other hand important events such as illnesses, deaths, fires, births of brothers and sisters.' In rare instances, simple

* Recently, Ulric Neisser and Elizabeth Loftus, the two prominent memory researchers, have crossed swords over the issue of infantile amnesia. Neisser and a cohort published a study in which they claimed that childhood memories might begin as early as two. Loftus questions the Neisser study, asserting that 'these apparent memories are the result of educated guesses . . . or external information acquired after the age of two.'

images apparently devoid of emotional content were reported, such as a bowl of ice set on a table. Despite the infrequency of these blander images, Freud chose to deal only with them, asserting that they were 'screen memories' for disturbing events too difficult for the child to face.[133]

Because my family moved to a new home when I was five, I can roughly date my earliest memories to when I was three or four. My experience appears to validate the Henris rather than Freud. One day I walked up the hill to our home and bent over to pick up a particularly smooth black stick. It surprised me by wriggling away; it was a long black snake sunning itself, not a stick. When I told my mother, she explained that in Georgia, black snakes weren't poisonous, and I shouldn't worry about it. I also remember the neighbor's boxer, who barked at me through a chain-link fence. And I recall being at a friend's house and running around his dining-room table as he chased me with a hatchet. Although Freud would no doubt have had a wonderful time interpreting the phallic snake, it was really only a snake, albeit a startling one.

Others have interpreted infantile amnesia without Freud's recourse to far-fetched theories. Some scientists hypothesize that the infant's nervous system has not developed sufficiently to encode memories. As we have seen, memories are lodged throughout the brain, but the hippocampus and prefrontal cortex appear to play crucial roles. Because those structures mature several years after birth, it is reasonable to assume that early memories simply fail to find a physical purchase. Others believe that the narrative or cognitive self, with its time sense and focus on life's milestones, doesn't develop until three or so, which matches Piaget's concept of a 'preoperational period.'[134]

According to linguist Noam Chomsky and neuropsychologist Eric Lenneberg, children are born with the structures necessary for language acquisition, but the brain must develop the skill within a critical early period, or it never will. Cases such as Genie, a girl kept a prisoner in a speechless household until she was 12, appear to confirm this theory. Although Genie subsequently mastered isolated words and phrases, she never learned syntax and could not express herself meaningfully. This finding suggests that fairly sophisticated language may be necessary for the formation of permanent memories. 'Language is a logic system so organically tuned to the mechanism of the human brain that it actually triggers the brain's growth,' Russ Rymer, author of the book *Genie*, concludes. 'What are human beings? Beings whose brain development is uniquely responsive to and dependent on the receipt at the proper time of even a small sample of language.' Similarly, visual memory seems to develop slowly.[135]

Regardless of the reasons, the reality of infantile amnesia would appear to be beyond dispute. Many therapists and their patients, however, firmly believe that they can remember back to the crib – and what ghastly memories they are! Because the baby possessed no language to describe what was being done to it, therapists inform their patients that they must interpret 'body memories' and vague images. Thus, in 'The Terrible Truth' (see Chapter 1), A. G. Britton came to believe that her constricted throat, feeling of weight on her chest, and visions of hairy potatoes were 'memories' of her father forcing sex on her between the ages of 6 and 18 months. Similarly, actress Roseanne Barr Arnold believes that she was abused, beginning at six months.

It is difficult to give much credence to such stories, although there is no way to disprove them. The image of an innocent baby being molested is powerful and disgusting, and it is certainly true that the infant could not tell anyone.

In the compelling 1995 Frontline documentary 'Divided Memories,' a mother described how she discovered that her husband was forcing oral sex on her five-year-old daughter.[136] When confronted, he admitted it and vowed to stop. The mother never mentioned it again to the daughter, who forgot it. Years later, when the young adult daughter was having difficulties, the mother decided to tell her about the sexual abuse. Now the daughter is convinced that she has remembered it and that it explains many of her troubles.

It is not altogether surprising that a five-year-old would forget sexual abuse of limited duration, since it occurred on the cusp of infantile amnesia. It is questionable, however, whether the young adult actually recalled the abuse years later. Given the information that it occurred, it is natural that she would struggle to picture it and convince herself that she had indeed remembered it.

Infantile amnesia is a troubling subject. It is natural to *want* to believe that if somebody does something horrible to a baby, there will be a way to find out about it later and hold the perpetrator accountable. If such memories could be reliably recovered, justice could be served. Sadly, the opposite seems to be true: the only 'memories' of infancy are later constructions that can lead to unjust accusations against innocent people.

As much as I have come to distrust Freud, one of his conclusions appears justified: 'It may indeed be questioned whether we have any memories at all *from* our childhood: memories *relating to* our childhood may be all that we possess.'[137]

COMMON-SENSE CONCLUSIONS

Having examined cogent experimental and anecdotal evidence, let me state my opinion. This is, I admit, simply my personal conclusion.

In my view, the notion that human beings could be *repeatedly* abused and then completely forget about it defies common sense. I do not believe that a woman could reach the age of 25, 35, or even 55 thinking that she had a relatively normal childhood, only to 'discover' through recovered memories that her father had fondled her at 2, forced her into oral sex at 7, intercourse at 11, and taken her for an abortion at 14. Even if such massive repression *were* possible, the victims would surely be psychotic – not the relatively normal women who are unearthing these 'memories.'*

Dr. Paul McHugh, head of the Department of Psychiatry at Johns Hopkins, agrees. 'Repression on this scale calls for an astonishing power of mind,' he observes. 'It is implausible on its face, lacks confirmation by research, and ... is usually proposed to patients during therapy without any effort to check any facts.'[138]

I believe that some form of repression *may* occur for one-time traumatic events. Certainly there are many documented cases of temporary amnesia following a severe shock to the psychic system.**[139] Usually, however, the memory loss is temporary, lasting only a few days, and it is clear that something is wrong with the sufferer.[140] Even in these instances, it is unclear how many cases are genuine. 'It is well known,' psychologist Daniel Schacter writes, 'that a non-trivial proportion of cases that present with functional retrograde amnesia turn out to be

---

* Even Freud, the father of repressed-memory theory, believed that large-scale repression used up so much of a person's limited store of energy that it preempted normal functioning as a human being.

** I am considering only 'psychogenic amnesia' here, not 'organic amnesia,' a loss of memory due to brain damage. Some cases of organic amnesia – particularly those resulting in wartime – have been mistakenly attributed to pure psychological causes, however.

deliberately simulated.'[141] British psychiatrist Charles Symonds went so far as to state, 'I suspect that all so-called hysterical fugues [i.e., amnesia] are examples of malingering.'*[142] It is more likely, however, that many cases of amnesia are not conscious deceptions. Rather, they are unconscious role playing, acting out a socially accepted method of avoiding an unpleasant reality.

It is possible that single sexual abuse encounters – or those of limited duration – may be intentionally forgotten or 'repressed,' only to be recalled later in life. If the event in question was truly traumatic, however, experimental evidence indicates that it would probably be remembered. Thus, children who witnessed a parent being murdered all recall it vividly, as one would expect. Rather than forgetting it, the children suffer intrusive memories, just as Vietnam veterans often suffer from unwanted memories.[143] In other words, if memory repression truly does occur, it is likely to happen only for a limited number of incidents, which were not perceived at the time as being particularly traumatic.

While such normal forgetting or psychological defense mechanism may work once, however, I do not think it would apply to repeated abuse. The original horror, unacceptable to the consciousness, would become commonplace. Far from blocking out all memories, the abused daughter would think, 'Oh, no, here comes Daddy again.' She would not forget all such incidents.

Yet every argument for the theory of massive repression assumes some variation of Lenore Terr's Type I/Type II analysis – that repeated and extremely horrible abuse is likely to be forgotten, while more minor, isolated incidents are likely to be remembered.**[144] In other words, day after day, a teenager will happily welcome her abuser, not remembering the terrible things he did the day before, or the day before that, but years or decades later, on a therapist's couch, the horrible truth will come pouring out in minute detail.

* Symonds delivered a stock speech to his amnesic patients: 'I know from experience that your pretended loss of memory is the result of some intolerable emotional situation. If you will tell me the whole story, I promise absolutely to respect your confidence, will give you all the help I can, and will say to your doctor and relatives that I have cured you by hypnotism.' This approach, he asserted, never failed.
** Most recovered memory theorists appear to believe that sexual abuse is a special form of trauma, more susceptible to massive repression than other stressors. One amusing cartoon points up the absurdity of this logic. A masked burglar holds a gun on his male victim, who looks shocked. The legend beneath reads, 'And now, to make sure you don't remember this robbery, I'm going to have to sexually abuse you.'

Science may never be able to prove, absolutely, that this theory is false in every instance. But it is contrary to both common sense and to whatever objective evidence we have about how human memory works.

CHAPTER THREE

How to Believe the Unbelievable

'I can't believe that!' said Alice.
'Can't you?' the Queen said in a pitying tone. 'Try again: draw
a long breath, and shut your eyes.'
Alice laughed. 'There's no use trying,' she said. 'One can't
believe impossible things.'
'I daresay you haven't had much practice,' said the Queen.
'When I was your age, I always did it for half-an-hour a day. Why,
sometimes I've believed as many as six impossible things before
breakfast.'

LEWIS CARROLL, *Through the Looking-Glass*[1]

Given that our memories can fool us sometimes, it is still hard to
understand why or how people would *want* to believe that their parents
committed such awful acts upon them.

But it clearly isn't a matter of *wanting* to believe. I have come to
regard the initial incest suspicion as being a kind of mental kudzu seed
– perhaps a perverse analogue to Jesus' parable of the sower and the
seed. A few decades back, some bright agronomist imported this nifty
Japanese vine to my native Georgia, hoping to halt erosion and provide
cheap cow fodder. The insidious kudzu, with its broad, shiny green
leaves, now covers entire forests, swallowing trees whole. While cows
may indeed eat the stuff, I suspect a few of them have been enveloped,
too, along the way.

Repressed memories seem to grow in the same way. It doesn't take
much – just a small seed, planted in your fertile brain by a television
program, a book, a friend, or a therapist. Maybe, just maybe, all of your
problems stem from childhood incest. Maybe you've forgotten it. Maybe
that's why you are uncomfortable at family reunions. Maybe. No, no,
that's insane! Forget it, not Dad, not Mom! You try to dismiss the idea.
But it won't go away. It takes root, sends out creepers, and grows. Soon
the mental kudzu is twining out of your ears, sending roots down to
your gut, taking over your life. It's true! Your worst fears were justified!

Numerous types of 'evidence' are used to provoke and 'prove' the reality of repressed memories. These include hypnotic regression, sodium Amytal, dreams, visualizations, bodily pangs or marks, panic attacks, or just general unhappiness. I will review each of them in turn, but it is important to understand that debunking one method or symptom really isn't the point, because another can easily take its place. Once the seed is planted, once the idea takes hold, it doesn't matter what method is employed. The results are almost foreordained.

HYPNOSIS: MEMORY PROD OR PRODUCTION?

After both of my children cut off contact with me, I thought that maybe I really *had* done something horrible to them and had repressed the memory myself. So I went to a hypnotist. Like most people, I thought that when you sank into a deep hypnotic trance, you could magically tap into your dormant subconscious, unlocking long-forgotten memories. Fortunately, I went to an ethical hypnotist who did not lead me into believing I had committed incest on my children. She failed, however, to tell me how questionable memories are when 'uncovered' in hypnosis. I discovered that fact during my research.

From its inception – covered in Chapter 10 – hypnosis has caused considerable controversy and spawned innumerable myths. One thing that experts agree on, however, is that memories retrieved under hypnosis are often contaminated mixtures of fantasy and truth. In many cases, outright 'confabulations' – the psychologists' term for illusory memories – result. Here is an unequivocal passage from the 1989 fifth edition of the *Comprehensive Textbook of Psychiatry*:

> An overwhelming body of research indicates that hypnosis does not increase accurate memory, but does increase the person's willingness to report previously uncertain memories with strong conviction. Furthermore, the hypnotized individual has a pronounced tendency to confabulate in those areas where there is little or no recollection; to distort memory to become more congruent with beliefs ... and fantasies; and to incorporate cues from leading questions as factual memories. Finally there is a high likelihood that the beliefs of the hypnotist will somehow be communicated to the patient in hypnosis and incorporated into

what the patient believes to be memories, often with strong conviction.[2]

Psychologist Robert Baker observes that 'confabulation shows up without fail in nearly every context in which hypnosis is employed.' No experimental study has ever provided evidence that hypnosis helps unlock real memories, although, as one researcher put it, 'It is difficult to disregard totally the wealth of anecdotal reports extolling the virtues of hypnotic memory enhancement.'[3] Perhaps, then, hypnosis can enhance both real memories and fantasies. Baker does not agree. 'I carried out a number of laboratory studies over a period of three and a half years,' he writes. 'My results in all cases showed no improvement in either memory or incidental memory as a result of hypnosis.' On the contrary, Baker concludes that 'the hypnotist may unwittingly suggest memories and create pseudomemories, i.e., vivid recollections of events that never happened.'[4]

The reason that memories retrieved under hypnosis are suspect goes to the very definition of the process, which invariably includes the concept of suggestion. Clark Hull and A. M. Weitzenhoffer defined hypnosis simply as 'a state of enhanced suggestibility.'[5] When a subject agrees to be hypnotized, he or she tacitly agrees to abide by the suggestions of the hypnotist. This state of heightened suggestibility can work quite well if the goal is to stop smoking, lose weight, enhance self-esteem, reduce perceived pain, or improve one's sex life. But it is *not* an appropriate method for retrieving supposedly repressed memories, as psychiatrist Martin Orne and psychologist Elizabeth Loftus have repeatedly stressed in courtroom settings.

Orne asserts that hypnosis is a technique that 'greatly facilitates the reconstruction of history, that allows an individual to be influenced unwittingly, and that may catalyze beliefs into "memories."' He emphasizes that 'we cannot distinguish between veridical [true] recall and pseudomemories elicited during hypnosis without prior knowledge or truly independent proof.' Loftus has said virtually the same thing. 'There's no way even the most sophisticated hypnotist can tell the difference between a memory that is real and one that's created. If you've got a person who is hypnotized and highly suggestible and false information is implanted in his mind, it may get imbedded even more strongly. One psychologist tried to use a polygraph to distinguish between real and phony memory but it didn't work. Once someone has constructed a memory, he comes to believe it himself.'[6]

Consequently, numerous psychologists have recognized that reality is routinely distorted under hypnosis. Theodore R. Sarbin and William C. Coe have referred to hypnotism as 'believed-in imaginings,' while Ernest R. Hilgard calls the process 'imaginative involvement.' J. P. Sutcliffe characterized the hypnotic subject as 'deluded' in a purely descriptive sense. Jean-Roch Laurence and Campbell Perry assert: 'Hypnosis is a situation in which an individual is asked to set aside critical judgment, without abandoning it completely, and is asked also to indulge in make-believe and fantasy.'[7]

The hypnotized subject is not the only one who is deluded. The hypnotist who believes that he or she is delving for hidden memories takes an active part in the shared belief system. Both hypnotist and subject are engaged in a tacitly accepted mini-drama in which they act out prescribed roles. Psychiatrist Harold Merskey has defined hypnosis as 'a maneuver in which the subject and hypnotist have an implicit agreement that certain events (e.g. paralyses, hallucinations, amnesias) will occur, either during the special procedure or later, in accordance with the hypnotist's instructions. Both try hard to put this agreement into effect.' He notes that 'there is no trance state, no detectable cerebral physiological change, and only such peripheral physiological responses as may be produced equally by non-hypnotic suggestion or other emotional changes.'[8] Laurence and Perry concur, explaining that 'the EEG [brain wave] of a hypnotized person is formally indistinguishable from that of a person who is relaxed, alert, with eyes closed.'[9]

Eric Greenleaf observes that 'the pretense of hypnotist-operator is a sort of shared delusion which both patient and therapist participate in.' He states that the methods of hypnotic induction are 'more like following the rules of social procedure than ... chemical analysis.' Robert Baker puts it more bluntly: '*There is no such thing as hypnosis.*'[10] Numerous experiments have demonstrated that all of the mysterious hypnotic phenomena, such as pain reduction, posthypnotic amnesia, blindness, paralysis, and the like, are simply part of a subject's belief system and, with the sanction of the authority – the hypnotist – they can all magically reverse themselves.*[11]

I am not trying to imply that 'hypnosis,' whether a real state or not,

---

* Modern psychologists disagree about whether hypnotism involves a 'trance state' or not. Ernest Hilgard and Herbert Spiegel are the leading proponents of the 'state' theory, while Nicholas Spanes argued that hypnosis was simply a form of role playing. All agree, however, that whether hypnotic subjects enter trance or not, they are liable to create pseudomemories.

does not have a profound effect, however. The human imagination is capable of incredible feats, so that subjects under hypnosis can even will away their warts.[12] And it does not have to be called 'hypnosis' to have the same effect. Guided imagery, visualization, sodium Amytal interviews, relaxation exercises, breathing exercises, and prayers to God to reveal abuse are all actually forms of hypnosis. When someone is relaxed, willing to suspend critical judgment, engage in fantasy, and place ultimate faith in an authority figure using ritualistic methods, deceptive scenes from the past can easily be induced.

Hypnotism entails a powerful social mythology. Just as those 'possessed' by demons believed in the process of exorcism, most modern citizens of 'civilized' countries believe that in a hypnotic state, they are granted magical access to the subconscious, where repressed memories lie ready to spring forward at the proper command. Hollywood movies have reinforced this mythology, beginning with a spate of amnesia-retrieval dramas, such as Hitchcock's *Spellbound*, in the 1940s. A good hypnotic subject therefore responds to what psychologists call 'social demand characteristics.' As Baker puts it, there is a 'strong desire of the subject to supply the information demanded of him by the hypnotist.'[13] Psychiatrist Herbert Spiegel says it more directly: 'A good hypnotic subject will vomit up just what the therapist wants to hear.'[14]

The hypnotist is often completely unaware that he is influencing the inductee, but what psychologists term 'inadvertent cuing' can easily occur, often through tone of voice. 'It is incredible,' wrote French psychologist Hippolyte Bernheim in 1888, 'with what acumen certain hypnotized subjects detect, as it were, the idea which they ought to carry into execution. One word, one gesture, one intonation puts them on the track.'[15] Simply urging 'Go on' at a crucial point, or asking 'How does that feel to you?' can cue the desired response. A person who *agrees* to play the role of the hypnotized subject is obviously motivated to believe in that role and act it properly. As hypnotist G. H. Estabrooks wrote in 1946, 'the subject is very quick to co-operate with the operator and at time almost uncanny in his ability to figure out what the operator wishes.'[16] This goes double for clients in psychotherapy who are desperately seeking to locate the source of their unhappiness. If the therapist has let them know, either subtly or directly, that they can expect to find scenes of sexual abuse while under hypnosis or through guided imagery, they are likely to do so.

In the introduction to *Theories of Hypnosis: Current Models and Perspectives* (1991), editors Steven Jay Lynn and Judith W. Rhue summarize the views expressed by the majority of the contributors: 'Hypnotic behavior is interpersonal in nature . . . Subjects' sensitivity to the hypnotist, subtle cues, and the tacit implications of hypnotic communications have a bearing on how they respond.' Further, they note that 'subjects may engage in self-deception, may be unaware of the intrapsychic and contextual determinants of their actions, and may engage in behaviors that fulfill suggested demands with little awareness that they are doing so.'[17]

Experimental psychologists have long understood that false memories can be implanted during hypnosis. In 1891, Bernheim suggested to a hypnotized subject that his sleep had been disturbed the night before by a neighbor who 'coughed, sang, and then opened the window.' After the session, the patient elaborated on this illusory event, even adding how someone else had told his neighbor to close the window. Bernheim then told him that the scene had never happened, that he had dreamed it. 'I didn't dream it,' the patient protested indignantly. 'I was wide awake!'[18]

Laurence and Perry performed a similar experiment in 1983. Under hypnosis, subjects were asked to relive a night from the week before. During this experience, they were asked whether they had been awakened by loud noises. The majority took the hint and described the sleep interruption in some detail. After the hypnotic session, most of them continued to express a belief in the sounds. Even after they were told that the hypnotist had suggested the incident to them, they insisted on their reality. 'I'm pretty certain I heard them,' one subject stated. 'As a matter of fact, I'm pretty damned certain. I'm positive I heard these noises.'[19] The sequence of these comments is revealing. In three sentences, we hear the subject rehearsing his convictions, progressing from 'pretty certain' to 'positive.' Similarly, those intent on recovering memories of incest are usually unsure of their newly envisioned scenes at first. It is only with rehearsal and reinforcement that the memories gradually come to seem real and convincing.

Canadian psychologist Nicholas Spanos performed an interesting extension of the above experiment, trying to show that the implanted memories weren't 'real,' but were instead the result of role playing. As the authoritative hypnotist, he first got his subjects to agree to the memories, then reverse themselves, then agree again, then reverse themselves. By doing so, Spanos asserted that the pseudomemories were never truly believed, but were simply reported in compliance with role expectations. Yet by the end of the confusing process, four of his eleven subjects still insisted that they had really heard the phantom noises.[20] Here, Spanos appears to have missed the vital importance of rehearsal and reinforcement in the production of false memories. If 36 per cent of his subjects still believed in the 'memories' without a therapist insisting on their truth, what kind of results would you get when any doubts are dismissed as attempts to deny the awful truth?

One of the characteristics of well-rehearsed hypnotic confabulations, in fact, is the utter confidence with which they are eventually reported.[21] Such memories tend to become extraordinarily detailed and believable with repetition. 'The more frequently the subject reports the event,' Martin Orne has written, 'the more firmly established the pseudo-memory will tend to become.' As a final caution, he warns that 'psychologists and psychiatrists are not particularly adept at recognizing deception,' adding that, as a rule, the average hotel credit manager is a far better detective.[22]

Unfortunately, clinical psychologists and other therapists appear to have little interest in playing detective, even when they realize that hypnosis often produces false memories.* It is easy to see how the current disastrous situation evolved, given the attitude of psychologists such as Roy Udolf, who wrote the *Handbook of Hypnosis for Professionals* in 1981. 'There is little support in the experimental literature,' he wrote, 'for many of the clinical claims made for the power of hypnosis to provide a subject with total eidetic [accurate] imagery-like recall of past events.' Nonetheless, he went on to assert that 'the kind of memory that hypnosis could logically be expected to enhance would be . . . affect-laden material that the subject has repressed . . . [i.e.,] traumatic early experiences.' Moreover, Udolf concluded that it doesn't matter whether such elicited memories are accurate or not. 'A memory retrieved under hypnotic age regression in therapy may be quite useful to the therapeutic process even if it is distorted, inaccurate, or a total fantasy as opposed to a real memory.'[23]

---

* Most therapists, whether trauma specialists or not, object strenuously to the notion that they should 'play detective' or encourage their patients to do so, seeking external corroboration for the 'narrative truth' revealed in therapy sessions. The trouble is, some therapists already *are* playing detective by unearthing these supposed trauma memories. They encourage a belief system that has dramatic effects in the real world and *then* invoke their intuitive, subjective therapy stance.

AGE REGRESSION: LET'S PRETEND

One of the most convincing forms of hypnosis, to the observer and the subject, is age regression, in which a client is taken back in time to a sixth birthday or a traumatic incest incident at age four. During such regressions, to all appearances, the adult disappears, replaced by an innocent waif. The subject often speaks in a childish, high-pitched lisp. Handwriting becomes large and primitive. Pictures appear stick-like and lack perspective. During the reliving of a childhood trauma, a client might scream just as a toddler would and, if frightened enough, might wet her pants.

Yet there is overwhelming evidence that 'age regression' is simply role playing in which an adult performs as she thinks a child would. As Robert Baker puts it, 'instead of behaving like real children, [they] behave the way they *believe* children behave.'[24] Psychologist Michael Nash has reviewed the empirical literature on age regression and has concluded that 'there is no evidence for the idea that hypnosis enables subjects to accurately reexperience the events of childhood or to return to developmentally previous modes of functioning. If there is anything regressed about hypnosis, it does not seem to involve the literal return of a past psychological or physiological state.' Even when hypnotically regressed subjects perform credibly, normal control subjects do just as well. As final evidence that hypnotic regression involves simple role enactment, Nash points out that 'equally dramatic and subjectively compelling portrayals are given by hypnotized subjects who are told to progress to an age of 70 or 80 years.'[25] Most people would agree that such age progression involves more fantasy than accurate pre-living.*[26]

---

* In 1954, psychiatrists Robert Rubenstein and Richard Newman came to the same conclusion when they successfully 'progressed' five subjects into the future under hypnosis. 'We believe that each of our subjects,' they wrote, 'to please the hypnotist, fantasied a future as actually here and now. We suggest that many descriptions of hypnotic regression also consist of confabulations and simulated behavior.' Incredibly, however, *they exempted repressed memories* from this logic: 'We suspect, however, that our doubts do not apply to the reenactment of traumatic past experiences.'

PAST LIVES AND UNIDENTIFIED FLYING FANTASIES

Hypnotism has similarly proven indispensable in the search for past lives and in 'remembering' UFO abductions. Although nothing is impossible – maybe we really can remember former incarnations,* and perhaps aliens actually do snatch us out of our beds – most readers will probably be more skeptical of such claims than of recovered incest memories. Yet the similarities are startling, including the reliving of sexual abuse while under hypnosis. Past-life therapists (such as Katherine Hylander, whose interview appears in Chapter 5) take people back before their births to previous centuries in which they were raped, tortured, or maimed.[27] Only by recalling and reexperiencing these terrible traumas can they be mentally healed in this life.

'It is extremely common,' Jungian therapist Roger Woolger wrote in *Other Lives, Other Selves* (1987), 'for childhood sexual traumas also to have past-life underlays. I have frequently found that the therapeutic exploration of a scene of childhood sexual abuse in this life will suddenly open up to some wretched past-life scenario such as child prostitution, ritual deflowering, brother–sister or father–daughter incest, or else child rape in any number of settings ranging from the home to the battlefield.' As an example, Woolger quoted one his clients who recalled a scene in a Russian barn during a previous life in which she was an 11-year-old peasant girl: 'They're raping me. They're raping me. Help! Help! HELP! There are six or seven of them. They're soldiers.'[28]

Hypnotic regression to past lives has a venerable history, reaching back to 1906. Under hypnosis, Miss C., a British 26-year-old, relived the life of Blanche Poynings, a friend of Maud, Countess of Salisbury in the late 14th century. She gave verifiable names and details. When closely analyzed, a previous source for the information was finally revealed. Miss C. had read *Countess Maud*, by Emily Holt, when she

---

* The ultimate age regression in *this* life is, of course, to the womb. In 1981, psychiatrist Thomas Verny wrote *The Secret Life of the Unborn Child*, offering examples of just such a feat. Under hypnotic regression, one of his patients reported the following placental message: 'I am a sphere, a ball, a balloon, I am hollow, I have no arms, no legs, no teeth ... I float, I fly, I spin.' Similarly, one Survivor claimed in a 1993 lawsuit that her therapist had helped her remember prenatal memories. Another therapist helped a patient access a memory of being stuck in the Fallopian tube, which explained her 'stuckness' in adult life.

was 12. She had unwittingly taken virtually all of the information for her 'past life' from the novel.[29]

For quite a while, the search for previous existences died down, but it received a boost in 1956 with the publication of *The Search for Bridey Murphy*. As with every well-documented case, it turned out that Virginia Tighe, the American woman who convincingly relived the life of the Irish Bridey – even reproducing her brogue – had indeed delved into her subconscious. However, what she pulled up was not a previous lifetime, but conversations with a Bridie Murphy Corkell, who had once lived across the street.

Theodore Flournoy, who debunked the earliest past-life regressions, coined the term *cryptomnesia* for this inadvertent mixing of prior knowledge with past lives.*[30] Elizabeth Loftus calls the same process 'unconscious transference,' while other psychologists use the term 'source amnesia.'[31]

Regardless of what we call the phenomenon, it offers intriguing evidence that the mind is indeed capable of storing unconscious memories that can be dredged up during hypnosis, though Virginia Tighe's memories of her neighbor presumably weren't 'repressed,' because they weren't traumatic. Those who are recounting tales of their previous lives invariably have read a book, seen a movie, or heard a story about that era or personality. Given the expectation that they will relive another life, their fertile imaginations combine this knowledge with other mental tidbits to create a feasible story. Those who are told to expect some trauma in a previous life add an appropriate rape, suffocation, or burning at the stake to the stew. This is probably not, in most cases, a conscious process of confabulation, because the subjects insist that they have no knowledge of the particular historical period. Similarly, people who are retrieving repressed memories of abuse routinely combine reality with fantasy. They mix their own childhood photographs, stories they have heard, real memories, and stereotyped scenes from *Sybil* or *The Courage to Heal* into a satisfactory scene.

As a further indication of human credulity, among the earliest

---

* When he was president, Ronald Reagan proved to be a master of cryptomnesia. The movies in which he had acted appeared to be irretrievably mixed in his mind with reality, so that he frequently repeated fictional stories as if they had actually occurred. At one point, he even asserted he had personally taken documentary concentration camp footage at Dachau following World War II, even though Reagan did not venture outside the United States at that time. As biographer Garry Wills noted, however, 'Reagan's war stories are real to him.'

practitioners of past-life regression was Colonel Albert de Rochas, who hypnotized clients near the turn of the century. Rochas thought he could literally *progress* his clients into the future.[32] Perhaps if we can *pre-live* the traumas that will be forthcoming in our lives, we might heal ourselves properly now – and confront the evil perpetrator before he has a chance to act!

Similarly, although I consider UFO abduction memories to be far-fetched products of hypnosis, many well-educated, otherwise rational professionals, including Temple University history professor David Jacobs and Harvard psychiatrist John Mack, believe in such events. They have proof. They have heard their clients recall the abductions while hypnotized. In his 1992 book, *Secret Life: Firsthand Documented Accounts of UFO Abductions*, Jacobs describes his clients in terms that should sound familiar by now:

> They were all people who had experienced great pain. They seemed to be suffering from . . . a combination of Post-Traumatic Stress Disorder and the terror that comes from being raped. Nearly all of them felt as if they had been victimized. As I listened to them, I found myself sharing in their emotionally wrenching experiences. I heard people sob with fear and anguish, and seethe with hatred of their tormentors. They had endured enormous psychological (and sometimes physical) pain and suffering. I was profoundly touched by the depth of emotion that they showed during the regressions.[33]

Similarly, in *Abduction: Human Encounters with Aliens* (1994), John Mack is impressed by 'the intensity of the energies and emotions involved as abductees relive their experiences,' in which they report being grabbed against their will and 'subjected to elaborate intrusive procedures which appeared to have a reproductive purpose.' Mack acknowledges the similarity to repressed memories of sexual abuse. In one case, he says, a woman went to a therapist 'for presumed sexual abuse and incest-related problems. Several hypnosis sessions failed to reveal evidence of such events.' Instead, however, she recalled being abducted by aliens when she was six. Mack stresses that the UFO therapist must have 'warmth and empathy, a belief in the ability of the individual to integrate these confusing experiences and make meaning of them . . ., and a willingness to enter into the co-investigative process.'[34]

For abductee therapists, that willingness leads to a memory retrieval process that sounds awfully familiar to those who have listened to recovered memory Survivors. Here is one alien abductee's description of the experience:

> It was . . . common for us to seek [memories] out where they were
> – buried in a form of amnesia. Often we did this through hypnosis
> . . . And what mixed feelings we had as we faced those memories!
> Almost without exception we felt terrified as we relived these trau-
> matic events, a sense of being overwhelmed by their impact. But
> there was also disbelief. *This can't be real. I must be dreaming. This
> isn't happening.* Thus began the vacillation and self-doubt, the alter-
> nating periods of skepticism and belief as we tried to incorporate
> our memories into our sense of who we are and what we know.[34a]

I am sure that David Jacobs and John Mack feel real empathy for these people, who truly believe that they have been taken to UFOs and forcibly subjected to bizarre sexual experimentation.*[35] But their findings seem only to confirm what is already known about hypnotism – that subjects tend to 'remember' whatever the hypnotist is looking for. The pain is real – regardless of whether the memories are of past lives, UFO abduc-tions, or incest by parents – but it was usually prompted and encouraged through the dubious means of hypnotic 'regression.' Investigators such as Jacobs and Mack dupe themselves and others because they genuinely want to *help* people, especially if, in the process, they can feel that they are also exploring uncharted territory.

FACILITATED COMMUNICATION AND
THE HUMAN OUIJA BOARD

That same combination – yearning to save the helpless victim while venturing near the cutting edge of an exciting new discipline – has

---

* John Mack's *Abduction* follows the same basic pattern as that described by Jacobs. His hypnotized subjects reveal that the aliens took sperm and egg samples and inserted probes into their vaginas, anuses, and noses. Mack's aliens, however, are ultimately benign, trying to save humans from ecological disaster. The expectancy effect appears to be at work here: Mack has long been an activist for environmental causes. It appears that his expectations are sometimes quite overt. One reporter invented an abduction story that Mack eagerly accepted. Prior to her hypnotic sessions, he 'made it obvious what he wanted to hear,' according to her.

resulted in the questionable practice of 'facilitated communication,' known familiarly as 'FC,' which purports to allow those afflicted with autism and cerebral palsy to write their thoughts.

In 1989, Syracuse University education professor Douglas Biklen brought the technique back from Australia, where it had been invented by Rosemary Crossley. Not surprisingly, millions of parents latched onto the hope provided by FC. In a few short years, it has become a near-religion.

In this technique, a 'facilitator,' usually a special education teacher, helps support the hand or arm of the autistic child. By sensing where the hand wants to go, the facilitator can help guide the finger to the appropriate letter on a keyboard. According to its advocates, this method has, miraculously, allowed those formerly locked in a silent world to communicate. Students who appeared to have IQs hovering around retarded levels could suddenly write essays on Shakespeare and learn calculus.

Unfortunately, carefully conducted, controlled experiments have shown conclusively that FC is a fraud, even though it was presumably advanced with honorable intentions.[36] It works only when the facilitator knows the answer and can see the keyboard. When an autistic child and a facilitator are shown different objects, the facilitator invariably types what she has seen. If only the child is shown an object, the correct answer is never forthcoming.* These results have shocked and saddened many facilitators, who genuinely believed in the process. Others, including Biklen, refuse to give up on it, convinced that FC works only in non-stressful, non-experimental conditions, with the proper established rapport, so that it can never be tested.

The flap over FC might simply be an alarming example of a human Ouija board if false allegations of sexual abuse had not sprung from the process.[37] In over 70 cases across North America, Europe, and Australia, autistic children have typed out messages that are an exact verbal analogue of the role enactments we've just seen in hypnotic age regression. 'Dad suk my prik,' a typical example reads. 'He give luv to my butt.' Douglas Biklen is largely responsible for such allegations, because he warns his trainees to be on the lookout for abuse. In his 1993 book, *Communication Unbound*, he writes that 10 out of his initial 75 students – i.e., 13 per cent – alleged sexual abuse through FC.[38]

---

* In the rare cases in which FC produces a correct word or phrase, all subjects could already read and write independent of facilitation.

Biklen is mild, however, compared to some FC proponents, who have written that 'there is a better than 100 per cent likelihood that a disabled child will be molested before he or she is eighteen. Facilitated Communication is confirming those statistics.'[39] Primed with such expectations, the facilitators suspect that the helpless, non-communicative autistic child – a perfect victim for abuse – is being molested at home.[40] And so the facilitated accusations pour out. In some cases, autistic girls with intact hymens have supposedly been subjected to hundreds of parental rapes.

The allegations generated by facilitated communication serve as a metaphor for the repressed memory search. Although the facilitator may not be consciously creating the accusations, the words are in fact coming directly from the facilitator's mind, not the child's. In similar fashion, therapists may have no idea that they are implanting memories of abuse.

In every introductory psychology textbook, college freshmen can read the story of Clever Hans, the ingenious horse. Using flash cards and counting frames, his owner, one Herr von Osten, had taught Hans to read, add, and subtract. By 1904, after four years of intensive tutorials, the horse could answer questions put to him about geography, history, science, literature, math, or current events. Hans tapped his hoof a certain number of times for each letter, and he tossed his head up and down for 'yes' and from side to side for 'no.'

Herr von Osten was thoroughly convinced that his horse was a genius. So were many eminent psychologists and zoologists, who walked away from demonstrations as believers. After all, Hans answered questions correctly even when his owner was nowhere near. The equable equine even got the right answers when questions were asked in languages other than his (presumably) native German. Only psychologist Oskar Pfungst remained skeptical. Like researchers on facilitated communication, he found that Hans could only answer correctly if the questioner knew the answer. He eventually discovered that Hans could not answer any questions when he wore a blindfold. It turned out that the horse was picking up subtle, inadvertent cues from his audience – a raised eyebrow or glance upward when the proper number of hoof-taps had been reached, a slight nod or shake of the head to indicate 'yes' or 'no.' Hans was indeed a gifted horse, but not in the way Herr von Osten thought. So, too, are hypnotic subjects gifted – with vivid imaginations and the capacity to pick up on subtle, inadvertent cues.[41]

DREAM WORK

Ever since Joseph saved Egypt by properly interpreting the Pharaoh's dreams – and probably long before that – humans have sought deep meaning from the strange stories they picture in their sleep. In our dreams, anything is possible. We can fly, jump through time, read other people's thoughts. Animals can talk, objects appear and disappear quickly, one thing metamorphoses quickly into something else. Sometimes our dreams are exciting, sexy, or soothing. Often, they are bizarre and frightening. What are we to make of them?

No one really knows, not even the most renowned dream researchers who shake people awake to ask what they're experiencing when their REM (rapid eye movements) indicate that they are in an active dreaming state. J. Allan Hobson, a Harvard psychiatrist and dream expert, believes that dreams represent 'creative confabulations.' In his books, *The Dreaming Brain* and *The Chemistry of Conscious States*, Hobson explores how molecules such as amines control our waking consciousness, while acetylcholine appears to dominate our dream state. We do not remember our dreams (other than those we rehearse immediately upon awakening) because the necessary amines aren't available. Our dreams do not represent real-life events. Rather, the chemicals in our brains apparently throw us into a dreaming state automatically every 90 minutes or so. 'Every mental product (including dreams) is in some way meaningful,' Hobson wrote to me in 1995, 'but meanings cannot be confidently determined by either face-value reading or by complex decoding.'[42]

Such cautions have not prevented various dream interpreters, including Freud, from asserting with great authority that dream ingredients symbolize certain objects, emotions or events. For example, a skyscraper represents a penis. In the second century, Artemidorus used the same kind of logic. For him, a foot meant a slave, while a head indicated a father. The kinky ancient Egyptians apparently dreamed frequently of sexual congress with various animals. One papyrus explained, 'If an ass couples with her, she will be punished for a great fault. If a he-goat couples with her, she will die promptly.'[43]

Modern trauma therapists also use sexual dreams as a form of interpretation. They tell their clients to be particularly aware of any night visions that could be interpreted as sexual abuse. This is called 'dream work.' Not too surprisingly, such dreams are often forthcoming.

'Oh, my God!' the woman reports in therapy. 'It's all true! In my dream last night, my Dad and uncle were taking turns having sex with me. And I was just a little kid!' Such dreams are taken as recovered memories and are presumed to represent literal truth, even though some events seem unlikely – in one well-publicized case, for instance, a daughter recalled being raped by her mother, who was equipped with a penis.[44]

But if these dreams don't necessarily stem from repressed memories of actual events, where do they come from? From the same place that spawns hypnotically guided fantasies – the fertile and overwhelmed imagination. Here is someone feverishly working on her memory recovery, reading books describing horrible abuse, her life consumed with the possibility that her father did something to her. As Calvin Hall noted in *The Meaning of Dreams*, 'It has been fairly well established that some aspects of the dream are usually connected with events of the previous day or immediate past.' It is not surprising that someone with an obsession about incest would dream about it. Hall also warned that 'dreams should never be read for the purpose of constructing a picture of objective reality,' but therapists and patients eager for repressed memories ignore such advice.[45]

The role of *expectation* in all aspects of memory recovery is crucial.* What we expect to see, we see, as Joseph Jastrow observed in his 1935 classic, *Wish and Wisdom*: 'Everywhere, once committed by whatever route, the *prepossessed* mind finds what it looks for.'[46] Elizabeth Loftus tells the true story of two bear hunters at dusk, walking along a trail in the woods. Tired and frustrated, they had seen no bear. As they rounded a bend in the trail, they spotted a large object about 25 yards away, shaking and grunting. Simultaneously, they raised their rifles and fired. But the 'bear' turned out to be a yellow tent with a man and woman making love inside. The woman was killed.[47] As psychologist Irving Kirsch notes, 'response expectancy theory' explains how 'when we expect to feel anxious, relaxed, joyful, or depressed, our expectations tend to produce those feelings.'[48] At its extreme, such a mindset can even lead to self-induced death, as has been well-documented among tribes in which those under a powerful curse fulfill it by wasting away and dying, unless some way to reverse the curse can be found.[49]

---

* Expectancy theory also explains so-called 'automatic writing' about sex abuse. Women are told to keep journals and just write whatever comes to mind. Repressed memories are then supposed to pour out from the subconscious. Indeed, when dreadful scenes scribble themselves onto the page, they seem to come out of nowhere, but they are, in fact, products of suggestion.

Similarly, when we expect to have a particular type of dream, we tend to perform accordingly. As Jerome Frank notes in *Persuasion and Healing*, patients routinely give their therapists the dreams they want. 'The dream the therapist hears is, of course, not necessarily the one the patient dreamed,' Frank explains, 'since considerable time has usually elapsed between the dream and its report. One study compared dreams reported immediately upon awakening with the versions unfolded before a psychiatrist in a subsequent interview. Any material the patient anticipated would not be approved was not recalled.'[50] In his classic 1957 text, *Battle for the Mind*, psychiatrist William Sargant described an acquaintance who had entered first Freudian, then Jungian therapy. 'His contemporary notes show that dreams he had under Freudian treatment varied greatly from those he had under Jungian treatment; and he denies having experienced the same dreams before or since.' Sargant concluded: 'The increased suggestibility of the patient may help the therapist not only to change his conscious thinking, but even to direct his dream life.'[51]

Therapist Renee Fredrickson certainly believes in such directives. 'You can also prime your dream pump, so to speak,' she writes in *Repressed Memories*. 'Before you go to sleep at night, visualize yourself as a little child . . . Then suggest that your inner child show you in a dream what you need to know about the abuse.' Nor does the dream abuse have to be obvious. Fredrickson describes how Diane reported a dream in which 'she was on her hands and knees in a kitchen, washing the floor. Floating in the air were green U-shaped neon objects. Her father was standing next to a large mirror over the sink, watching her.' Eventually, Diane interpreted her dream as follows: 'My father raped me in the evenings when I was cleaning the kitchen . . . He would make me crawl around naked while he watched in the mirror. I also believe the green neon things are about a time he put a cucumber in me.'[52]

SLEEP PARALYSIS

Another fascinating form of semi-dream, which typically occurs in the twilight state between waking and sleeping, accounts for many 'repressed memories.' The psychological term is either a 'hypnogogic' or 'hypnopompic' state, respectively referring to the time just before sleep or prior to waking, but more commonly it is just called 'sleep paralysis.'

During this curious in-between semi-conscious state, people often report chilling visions.*

Robert Baker describes the phenomenon: 'First, the hallucinations always occur [just] before or after falling asleep. Second, the hallucinator is paralyzed or has difficulty moving ... Third, the hallucination is usually bizarre ... Finally, the hallucinator is unalterably convinced of the reality of the entire event.' The vision's content is often related to the dreamer's current concerns. In one study, as many as 67 per cent of a normal sample population reported at least one experience of sleep paralysis, with its attendant hallucinations.[53] Many people experience sleep paralysis during the day, particularly if they take afternoon naps. Those with narcolepsy – a relatively common disorder characterized by brief involuntary periods of sleep during the day, with difficulties resting at night – are particularly prone to these frightening hallucinations.

The word 'nightmare' actually stems from sleep paralysis. A 'mare,' or demon, was supposed to terrorize people – mostly women – by sitting on their breasts, making it difficult to breathe. Often, the mare was an incubus or succubus who also forced the frightened sleeper into sexual intercourse. The following is a 1763 description of the phenomenon:

> The nightmare generally seizes people sleeping on their backs, and often begins with frightful dreams, which are soon succeeded by a difficult respiration, a violent oppression on the breast, and a total privation of voluntary motion. In this agony they sigh, groan, utter indistinct sounds [until] they escape out of that dreadful torpid state. As soon as they shake off that vast oppression, and are able to move the body, they are affected by strong palpitation, great anxiety, languor, and uneasiness.[54]

David Hufford has written an entire book about sleep paralysis, *The Terror That Comes in the Night*. His 1973 interview with Caroline, a young graduate student, sounds quite similar to the reports of many 'incest survivors.' When Caroline woke up one day, she reports, 'I felt like there was a man next to me with his arm underneath my back, and holding my left arm.' His smell was quite distinct, 'all sweaty and kind of dusty.' When she tried to move, he gripped her arm tighter. 'Now

---

* Two interviews in this book – of Frieda Maybry in Chapter 6 and Leslie Hannegan in Chapter 8 – provide classic examples of sleep paralysis, as does the experience of A. G. Britton related at the end of Chapter 1.

if I move again, he's going to rape me,' she thought. She tried to scream, but she could make no sound. 'Then he was on top of me, and I tried to look up to see who it was or something . . . I could just see this – it looked like a white mask. Like a big white mask.' After several minutes of this horrible experience, Caroline 'felt sort of released, you know. And I – I could sit up, and I got the feeling there was nobody there.'[55] In the 1990s, such experiences are frequently interpreted as 'flashbacks' or 'body memories,' and women are encouraged to visualize a face to fill in the blank mask.

Other 'evidence' of repressed memories also relates to sleep – or its lack. In *The Courage to Heal*, Ellen Bass and Laura Davis quote one typical woman's experience as she obsessed over possible repressed memories: 'I just lost it completely. I wasn't eating. I wasn't sleeping.'[56] Sleep deprivation is a well-established technique used in brain-washing. As sleep expert Alexander Borbely writes, chronic lack of sleep blurs the borderline between sleeping and waking, 'so that the kind of hallucinations that often occur at the moment of falling asleep now begin to invade the waking state as well . . . the floor appears to be covered with spider webs; faces appear and disappear. Auditory illusions also occur.' In addition, 'when sleep deprivation experiments last more than four days, delusions can manifest themselves, in addition to the disturbances of perception. The participants grow increasingly suspicious and begin to believe that things are going on behind their backs.'[57]

FLASHBACKS OR VISIONS?

It is likely, then, that many of the so-called 'flashbacks' reported as repressed memories are the result of sleep deprivation, combined with expectancy. Flashbacks themselves have been widely misunderstood. Even in the case of war veterans, these very real terrors, often triggered by the sound of an explosion, are not the reliving of actual events. Rather, they are *worst-fear* scenarios, as John MacCurdy pointed out in his classic 1918 book, *War Neuroses*.[58] MacCurdy called such moments 'visions,' arguably a more accurate term than flashback. Similarly, psychiatrists treating World War II veterans found that leading patients to dramatically 'relive' fictional events seemed to help them as much as recalling a real trauma. One man who had been in a tank regiment vividly visualized being trapped in a burning tank. 'This had never actually happened, though it must have been a persistent fear of his throughout the campaign,' his doctor noted.[59] Similarly, under the influence of sodium Amytal, a 35-year-old Vietnam combat veteran 'lived out' a feared fantasy of having been captured and tortured by the Viet Cong, though nothing like that had actually happened to him.[60]

An even more interesting war-related case occurred recently. In a Vietnam veteran's support group, Ed recounted how he had watched a buddy's head explode during a firefight. He had relived this and other harrowing memories in therapy. But when one of his group members called Ed's parents for help in staging a surprise birthday party, his mother said, 'What? He's in a veterans' recovery group? But he was rated 4-F. He never was allowed to go to Vietnam!' Even when confronted in the group, however, Ed maintained that his story was true. He had fantasized his 'flashbacks' so successfully that they had become real.[61*62]

BODY MEMORIES AND PANIC ATTACKS

People who are trying to recover repressed memories are often told that 'the body remembers what the mind forgets,' particularly in cases of abuse suffered as a pre-verbal infant. These 'body memories' can take the form of virtually any form of physical ailment, from stomach aches to stiff joints. As I document in Chapter 10, psychosomatic complaints such as these have always been common in Western culture and almost invariably accompany general unhappiness and anxiety. Add to this the 'expectancy effect,' and it isn't surprising that during the 'abreaction' or reliving of an event, a woman might feel terrible pelvic pain, or a man might experience a burning anus.

Those in search of memories often submit to massages by experienced 'body workers,' who can trigger feelings either by light touch or deeper muscle manipulation. 'An area of your body may get hot or feel numb,' Renee Fredrickson assures readers in *Repressed Memories*. 'Powerful emotions may sweep over you, causing you to weep or even cry out.' It is certainly true that people can experience profound, inexplicable

---

* Psychologist Michael Yapko reports a similar case in which a man convinced his wife, therapist, and apparently himself that he was experiencing excruciating flashbacks to his imprisonment in a Vietcong bamboo cage. After he committed suicide, his widow tried to locate his official military record and discovered that he had never been in Vietnam.

emotions while they are being massaged, particularly if they are tense and unhappy in general. When they let down their guards and relax, allowing intimate touch by a stranger, they often do weep. Given the admonition to be on the lookout for any stray sensation, many subjects have no difficulty locating and interpreting various body memories. Fredrickson gives two examples: 'She [Sarah] was undergoing a passive form of body work involving laying on of hands when she had a slowly burgeoning sense of rage at her father for abusing her.' Later on, Sarah discovered that the 'exquisite sensitivity' of her toes was caused by her grandfather having shoved a wood chip under her toenail.[63]

Some 'body memories' take the form of rashes or welts that fit particular memory scenarios. The mind can apparently produce remarkable and sometimes quite specific effects on the body. As I already mentioned, hypnotic suggestion can actually remove warts, while some people can consciously control their pulse rates, respiration, or blood flow.[64] Some observers claim to have documented cases of 'stigmata' – replicating the wounds of Christ – that, if true, indicate how mental concentration can even cause spontaneous bleeding. As Ian Wilson writes in *All In the Mind*, 'the nail-wounds in the hands have varied from simple red spots in some to complete penetrations of the flesh in others, again taking every conceivable shape – oval, round, square, oblong.' These shapes usually correspond to the wounds portrayed on the crucifix before which the stigmatic worships.[65]

One such case involved Elizabeth K., who entered therapy with psychiatrist Alfred Lechler in 1928 when she was 26. Since her early teens, she had suffered from headaches, nausea, paralyses, blackouts, and bowel disorders. By the time she came to see Dr. Lechler, Elizabeth suffered from insomnia and had attempted suicide. She proved to be highly suggestible, with a tendency to take on any medical symptoms she heard about. Lechler hypnotized her, getting her to produce the classic stigmata of Christ. Later, after she had returned to normal consciousness, the psychiatrist asked her to picture blood-stained tears. Within a few hours, blood welled up inside Elizabeth's eyelids and poured down her cheeks.[66*67] In *Michelle Remembers*, Michelle Smith evidently

---

* It is possible, however, that Elizabeth somehow faked these phenomena. As a psychologist pointed out in 1946, one hypnotic subject, eager to show his abilities, 'proved' that he could raise blisters under suggestion. Secret observation through a peep-hole, however, showed him 'deliberately rub the bandage with all his strength so as to irritate the skin beneath. Worse still, some subjects were seen to take a needle [and] thrust it under the bandage.'

possessed similar powers, producing a red rash on her neck that her psychiatrist interpreted as a welt left by the devil's tail.[68]

Nothing so dramatic need account for most 'body memories,' however. One of the most common was recounted by A. G. Britton in her article, 'The Terrible Truth.' She experienced a choking sensation and interpreted that as evidence that her father had forced his penis into her mouth when she was a baby. It turns out, though, that a constricted throat is one nearly universal human reaction to fear and anxiety. In fact, the word 'anxious' derives from the Latin word meaning 'to strangle.'[69] This classic symptom – an inability to swallow and the feeling of being choked – is now one of the diagnostic symptoms for panic disorders. For hundreds of years it was called, among other things, *globus hystericus*, because it felt as though a ball were rising from the abdomen and lodging in the throat.

Many people who fear that they may have been abused suffer repeated panic attacks at unexpected moments and, with their therapists' encouragement, interpret them as repressed memories surging forth from the subconscious. Yet these little-understood episodes are extremely common. As psychologist David Barlow points out in his comprehensive text, *Anxiety and Its Disorders*, 'Anxiety disorders represent the single largest mental health problem in the country, far outstripping depression.' In Western cultures, reports of this affliction are much more common among women than among men, although that is not so in Eastern countries. Recent surveys indicate that 35 per cent of Americans report having experienced panic attacks.[70] Unfortunately, those seeking help for severe anxiety disorders are frequently misdiagnosed, seeing an average of ten doctors or therapists before receiving appropriate help *(See Chapter 13 for resources.*[71]

As listed in the fourth edition of the *Diagnostic and Statistical Manual of Mental Disorders*, familiarly known as the *DSM-IV*, the symptoms experienced during panic attacks (four or more being sufficient by the official definition) sound like a checklist for what trauma therapists interpret as body memories:

(1) palpitations, pounding heart, or accelerated heart rate, (2) sweating, (3) trembling or shaking, (4) sensations of shortness of breath or smothering, (5) feeling of choking, (6) chest pain or discomfort, (7) nausea or abdominal distress, (8) feeling dizzy, unsteady, lightheaded, or faint, (9) derealization (feelings of unreality) or depersonalization (being detached from oneself), (10)

fear of losing control or going crazy, (11) fear of dying, (12) paresthesias (numbness or tingling sensations), (13) chills or hot flushes.[72]

Surprisingly, Barlow reports that 'the overwhelming evidence is that many phobias and the majority of fears are not learned through a traumatic experience.' Instead, panic attacks appear to stem from contemporarily stressful life situations and a fearful mindset – though biological factors and early childhood trauma may contribute to a predisposition to anxiety disorders. Psychologists Aaron Beck and Gary Emery give an example of a typical episode involving a 40-year-old man who, while on the ski slopes, began to feel shortness of breath, profuse perspiration, and faintness. He thought he was having a heart attack. In the midst of this, he had a vivid image of himself lying in a hospital bed with an oxygen mask. It transpired that this man's brother had just died of a heart attack, and he feared the same might happen to him.

Similarly, people who think they may have repressed memories fear that they may be like others they know (or have read about or seen on television). They, too, may be unknowing incest victims who will have flashbacks. For such people, panic attacks are often triggered when they become over-tired or over-stressed and spontaneously envision images of their worst fears, which, in turn, provoke even more anxiety. 'Once the fear reaction has started,' Beck and Emery write, 'it tends to build on itself.' These 'autonomous' images then 'persist without the patient's being able to stop them,' and they seem utterly real, 'as though the traumatic episode were actually occurring *in the present.*'[73]

After the first attack of this inexplicable fear, a vicious cycle can commence in which the very fear of another episode provokes it. This would be particularly likely for a woman who is extremely stressed by the idea that she might have been sexually abused and is minutely aware of every bodily and emotional twinge. As David Barlow notes, 'self-focused attention greatly increases sensitivity to bodily sensations and other aspects of internal experience. Furthermore, this sensitivity ... quickly spreads to other aspects of the self, such as self-evaluative concerns.' Barlow calls this process a 'negative feedback cycle' which leads to a chronic feeling of helplessness, dependence, and self-absorption.[74] As Ann Seagrave and Faison Covington – two women who have overcome their panic attacks – write in *Free from Fears*, 'We can become frightened to such a degree that we learn to monitor every twitch, every ache, and it is in that way that we often scare ourselves needlessly.'[75]

One final point related to panic attacks seems quite puzzling. Attacks are often triggered by deep relaxation exercises such as those which induce hypnosis or guided imagery sessions. In one study, 67 per cent of a group of panic-disorder patients experienced three or more symptoms while listening to a relaxation tape. As David Barlow notes, 'relaxation is surely the strangest of panic provocation procedures.' He hypothesizes that it may be caused by a fear of losing control.[76] Whatever the reason, this finding certainly relates to therapy clients who are led to a 'safe place' during deep relaxation exercises. It contributes to our understanding of why they might experience panic attacks during the process.

The scope of what recovered memory therapists sometimes label 'body memories' is staggering, encompassing virtually every illness or somatic complaint. If you have cancer, asthma, multiple sclerosis, or even AIDS, you may have contracted it because of your undiagnosed repressed memories of sexual abuse. The same applies to tight muscles, stuttering, facial tics, chronic headaches, or diarrhea. Some women have recovered memories (and sued for same) after being jarred in an auto accident. Or 'body memories' can be extraordinarily vague, including the awkward way one moves. One woman's dance instructor diagnosed her as having repressed memories from observing her in practice.[77]

SYMPTOMS: PICKLE AVERSION AND EATING DISORDERS

For many potential 'Survivors,' neither hypnotism nor panic attacks are necessary to believe the unbelievable. *Belief* that they *must* have been molested as children is sometimes enough, without specific 'memories.' In fact, as we have seen in Chapter 1, Ellen Bass and Laura Davis inform their readers that *symptoms* are sufficient to diagnose repressed memories, regardless of whether they are ever visualized. And herein lies an important point: *belief* always precedes *memory*, and is often sufficient unto itself. That is why the therapeutic or self-help process is largely a matter of re-education.

That is why recovered-memory therapist Charles Whitfield often spends over an hour carefully reviewing the criteria for post-traumatic stress disorder with his clients, encouraging them to identify with the symptoms. Not only does this give him a ready-made diagnosis that an insurance company will pay for, but it labels the client a victim of PTSD who *must* seek memories as an explanation. 'Oh, my God, is *this* what it is?' they exclaim. 'Oh, does this explain a lot of things to me now!' It is, as Whitfield tells his audiences, 'like doing a jigsaw puzzle, and you start to put the last piece of the puzzle in there, and now you can see the big picture.'[78] From there, it is a small, almost inevitable step to some form of abuse memory retrieval.

As a species, human beings seem to have a natural desire for explanations. As soon as they can speak, children begin pestering their parents with 'Why? Why? Why?' Often, there is no simple answer, but patients seeking therapy are highly motivated to find specific reasons for their unhappiness so that they can 'fix' it. When therapists tell them that they have all the 'symptoms' of an incest survivor, they can easily believe it. *So that's why my marriage is so difficult, why I yell at my children, why I can't hold a job, why I have low self-esteem, why I feel uncomfortable at family reunions! Now everything falls into place.*

It's an answer that can be adapted to fit almost any question. Holly Ramona, a young California woman whose father successfully sued her therapists, doesn't like pickles, whole bananas, mayonnaise, cream soups, melted cheese, or white sauce. According to Lenore Terr and Holly's therapists, her eating habits are compelling evidence that her father forced oral sex on her as a child, because pickles and bananas are penis-shaped, and mayonnaise, creamy soups, and white sauce resemble semen.[79] Of course, this logic could be used to label most of the children in the United States as incest survivors. I don't like bananas, either, and I don't like cooked okra because it's so slimy, but I do not regard these personal aversions as evidence of childhood molestation.

In addition to her distaste for pickles and bananas, Holly Ramona entered therapy with a full-blown eating disorder. She was bulimic, eating large amounts of food and then vomiting in a terrible binge/ purge cycle. Both bulimia and anorexia – self-starvation – have become epidemic ailments, particularly among young women, in late-20th-century English-speaking countries. The reasons for such eating disorders are complicated, but they clearly have a great deal to do with societal pressure on women to remain abnormally thin. For quite a while, the conventional wisdom held that women with eating disorders had over-protective, over-involved mothers. In the last few years, however, the blame has been shifted from mothers to fathers. Many therapists consider eating disorders a nearly fool-proof symptom of childhood incest. Holly Ramona's therapist told her that 80 per cent of all eating-disorder patients had been sexually abused.

Dr. William C. Rader, a self-styled expert, has written that 'approximately 85 per cent of eating disordered patients have been sexually or physically abused.'[80]* He derived this statistic by surveying patients attending his own 'Rader Institute,' thirteen eating disorder units located in Alabama, California, Florida, Texas, Illinois, Michigan, Missouri, Oklahoma, Washington, and Massachusetts.[81] When I spoke to a psychiatric nurse at a Florida unit, she told me that 90 to 95 per cent of their clients found repressed memories of sexual abuse during their stay.[82] Rader is clearly relying on a self-perpetuating set of statistics, created by his own belief system.

Indeed, many of the inpatient eating disorder units throughout the United States – well over 200 – are virtual memory mills, with incest survivor groups meeting daily.[83] The ads for such institutions make their assumptions clear. 'Shades of Hope is an all addiction treatment center, specializing in the treatment of Eating Disorders, Co-Dependency, and Survivors of Childhood Abuse,' reads one. Another promises: 'At The Meadows our "family of origin" therapy uncovers original childhood traumas which often are at the root of eating disorders.'[84]

Women seeking help for bulimia and anorexia throughout the United Kingdom are also quite likely to be told they harbor repressed memories of sexual abuse. In 1989, the British book *Surviving Child Sexual Abuse* informed readers that 'as many as two-thirds of women with bulimia' had been sexually abused as children.[85] Indeed, *The Courage to Heal* is on the top of the list of books recommended by the British Eating Disorders Association, which describes the recovered memory text as a 'comprehensive and compassionate guide.' The Association literature states that 'child sexual abuse is all too often something that has been experienced by sufferers of eating disorders.' Specialist treatment centres throughout the U. K. treat approximately 1,500 bulimic or anorexic patients annually.[86] It is frightening to consider how many leave such centers believing that they are incest Survivors. Indeed, it seems only a

---

* Dr. Rader's explanations for why incest survivors develop eating disorders are illuminating. 'For compulsive overeaters, fatty tissue becomes a protective layer.' On the other hand, 'anorexics may appear more like adolescent males than mature, sexually desirable women,' thus avoiding their sexuality. 'For bulimics, vomiting can become the mechanism of release for anger and pain. At times, they will actually shout out the name of their perpetrator as they vomit.'

matter of time before some therapist attempts to persuade Princess Diana, certainly the most public British bulimic, that she was a sex abuse victim.[87]

In one high-profile British case, 22-year-old Anna Hunter sought help for her anorexia in 1991 with psychiatrist Robin Farquharson of the Hadrian Clinic at Newcastle General Hospital. After the first session, he wrote 'Sexual abuse?' in her notes, which she subsequently saw. He also gave her *The Courage to Heal* and asked her to keep a dream journal. Within months, Hunter had come to believe she had been molested with screwdrivers, chisels, and penises in a satanic cult, as well as having been tied to a cross in the garage and having the blood of slaughtered kittens daubed on her. Though Hunter has now realized that none of these 'memories' were true, she continues to suffer mental problems in the wake of her therapy.[88]

Yet there is no scientific evidence that eating disorders stem from childhood molestation, as Harvard psychiatrists Harrison Pope and James Hudson, specialists in the field, have repeatedly stressed. 'Current evidence does not support the hypothesis that childhood sexual abuse is a risk factor for bulimia nervosa,' they wrote in a 1992 article in the *American Journal of Psychiatry*. There are 'no differences in the prevalence of childhood sexual abuse between bulimic patients and the general population.'[89]

Despite such findings, thousands of vulnerable women desperate for help with their eating disorders continue to search for repressed memories, and they are encouraged by articles such as one appearing in *The Scotsman* late in 1995. 'Symbolic Rejection of Food Has a More Sinister Meaning,' the headline informed readers. Author Sarah Nelson repeated the dogma that women with eating disorders may be unconsciously 'making themselves unattractive to abusers, and safe from pregnancy,' or that their disorders may be caused by revulsion at having been forced to eat grotesque items in ritual abuse cults. She quoted Sue Hutchinson, director of SAFE, a Survivor organization: 'I actually had to learn the difference between abusive and non-abusive food.' Hutchinson has recovered memories of having to drink urine spiced with Andrews' liver salts as a child.[90]

The misguided diagnosis of repressed memories is particularly unfortunate in these cases, since many patients with eating disorders respond to conventional medical treatment with anti-serotonin uptake drugs such as Prozac. In a 1995 article, Susan McElroy and Paul Keck describe three case studies of women with eating or obsessive-compulsive disorders, all of whom initially believed that they harbored repressed memories. All three responded quickly to medical treatment.[91]

I will end with a cautionary tale recounted by psychologist Kay Thompson. A female client sought therapy for help with a dental gag reflex which prevented dentists from working on her. Under hypnosis, she revealed that the gagging started soon after she received a tonsillectomy when she was seven years old. Having located the psychic root of the problem, the hypnotist suggested that it would no longer bother her and, indeed, the symptoms disappeared. When she told her family doctor about this miraculous cure, however, he told her she had never had her tonsils removed.[92] Similarly, several young women with intact hymens have 'remembered' multiple childhood rapes.[93] The moral: it is all too easy to identify *the* root cause for a current symptom, even though it may be incorrect. There is no way to determine simple causality for human behavior.

DRUGS

In conjunction with suggestive therapy, drugs can significantly increase the likelihood of illusory incest memories. Even without such overt suggestion, physicians and therapists have long recognized that strong sedative compounds can lead to false accusations. 'When my father went to medical school in the early 1930s,' psychiatrist Harrison Pope says, 'he was admonished never to administer nitrous oxide or other anesthetic agents without a chaperone in the room because of the risk a female patient might wake up and claim that she had been sexually abused.' Recently, a number of British doctors have been accused of abuse by women given midazolam (Versed), even though there were several witnesses in the room who saw no such behavior.[94] Considering the substantial doses of mind- and mood-altering drugs that many depressed people are given nowadays, it is not surprising that they are more suggestible. Many women I interviewed reported that they were 'walking zombies' because of the multiple drugs they were taking while in therapy or on a psychiatric ward.

The most widely used 'memory aid' drugs intentionally used by recovered memory therapists are barbiturates, notably sodium Amytal. American psychiatrist Eric Lindemann introduced sodium pentothal and other barbiturates into psychology in the 1930s. Because Lindemann considered his patients *unable* to refuse to answer questions while drugged, he believed they could not lie. Hence, the drugs became known as 'truth serum,' and the popular press spread this misinformation quickly. 'Narco-synthesis' and 'narco-analysis' were the new pseudo-scientific buzzwords for abreactive sessions using the drugs.[95]

In fact, Amytal interviews are even *more* likely than simple hypnosis to produce confabulations. The barbiturates do not magically enhance memory. Like hypnosis, they simply render the subject more relaxed and suggestible. According to psychiatrist August Piper, Jr., Amytal produces 'slurred speech, drowsiness, a feeling of warmth, distorted memory, and an altered time-sense.' In other words, it creates a state 'similar to alcohol intoxication.' Many therapists continue to tell their clients that the drugs actually do promote only true memories, however. As a consequence, a 1991 Ohio jury convicted a psychiatrist of malpractice for injecting a patient over 140 times with 'truth serum' to help uncover her repressed memories.[96]

COGNITIVE DISSONANCE AND GROUP CONTAGION

All of the methods discussed thus far can contribute to false belief in sexual abuse, but all of them are reinforced and amplified by the general social context. As Jerome Frank writes in the introduction to *Persuasion and Healing*, 'man is a domestic creature, with infinite social and cultural involvements. He is continually and crucially influencing others and being influenced by others.'[97] A full understanding of the memory manipulation process requires examination of such interpersonal pressures.

In 1957, Leon Festinger published *A Theory of Cognitive Dissonance*, which offered an intriguing explanation of how and why people can radically change their opinions. Normally, we maintain an internally consistent world-view. When we experience some kind of disequilibrium – when one of our central beliefs is somehow challenged – it results in an internal conflict that Festinger termed 'cognitive dissonance.' The more important and dramatic the conflict, the greater the magnitude of the dissonance. When we suffer such massive internal tension, we must come down on one side or the other, or go insane.

Certainly, there could be no greater cognitive dissonance than that produced by the Incest Survivor Movement. A woman is suddenly asked to believe that her father, previously regarded as someone who loved and protected her, raped her throughout her childhood. In *The Courage to Heal*, Ellen Bass and Laura Davis document the intolerable confusion and upheaval this causes. 'The hardest thing was accepting the fact that someone I loved and cherished – my father – could have violated me so deeply,' one woman told them. Another said, 'It's like you're dissolving and there's nothing to hold on to.' A third confessed that 'trying to fit the new reality into the shattered framework of the old was enough to catapult me into total crisis. I felt my whole foundation had been stolen from me.' Recall the story of Emily, already recounted in Chapter 1. 'Every time Emily spoke to her parents she became ill – the conflict between what she knew inside and what they presented was too great.' Her solution was to cut off all contact with her parents and seek reassurance from her therapist.[98]

In order to produce the initial dissonance, of course, one has to accept the idea that has been seeded in one's mind. Festinger points out that if the seed-bearer is 'seen as expert or very knowledgeable about such matters, the dissonance between knowledge of his contrary opinion and one's own opinion will be greater.' Once a situation of intolerable internal conflict exists, the sufferer is under intense pressure to choose one side or the other. Something has to give.

'When dissonance is present,' Festinger adds, 'in addition to trying to reduce it, the person will actively avoid situations and information which would likely increase the dissonance.' Simultaneously, she will seek out those who reinforce her new belief system. This insight helps to explain why people with newly found memories cut off all old friends who express even the mildest doubts. Festinger points out a paradoxical truth – the greater the underlying dissonance, the more confidence a person must feel in the decision to opt for a new world view, and the less likely she will be to reverse that decision.[99] Once you become an Incest Survivor, in other words, it becomes unbearable to consider that you might be wrong. You are stuck with your new identity. To turn back would renew the confusion.

In his classic 1984 text, *Influence*, social psychologist Robert Cialdini makes a similar point. 'Once we have made a choice or taken a stand, we will encounter personal and interpersonal pressures to behave consistently with that commitment. Those pressures will cause us to respond in ways that justify our earlier decision.'[100] One retractor's revealing comment in a letter to her father illustrates this principle. 'Right after I brought the lie [the accusation] into the open, I began to doubt its truth. But I couldn't believe that I would do such a thing. I couldn't believe I was capable of making up such a lie, believing it, and then taking it to the lengths I did.'[101]

'The social group is at once a major source of cognitive dissonance for the individual,' Festinger wrote, 'and a major vehicle for eliminating and reducing the dissonance.' Bass and Davis repeatedly emphasize how important such groups are. 'Being in a group with other survivors can be a powerful way to vanquish shame. When you hear other women talk about their abuse and are not disgusted, and when you see those same women listen to your story with respect, you begin to see yourself as a proud survivor.'[102] This social reinforcement is key to the Incest Survivor Movement. 'Social support is particularly easy to obtain when a rather large number of persons who associate together are all in the same situation,' Festinger notes. 'If everyone believes it, it most certainly must be true.'[103]

In *Motel Nirvana*, her 1995 exploration of American New Age beliefs, British author Melanie McGrath makes an incisive observation about how *anyone* could be swayed within a restricted group setting:

> I don't think anyone is immune to implausible beliefs, however rational and wilful they think themselves to be. It is an easy matter to deny everything you thought you knew and to believe its contradiction rather than to live out your days in bottomless isolation. Only the most rare of individuals will stand up for a belief when all around are declaring its opposite, for most of us feel more anxious to be at ease with each other than we do with ourselves.[104]

It is truly remarkable how suggestible people become in groups, as Solomon Asch demonstrated in a series of 1956 experiments. Eight college students, assembled in a group, were shown a simple line, then asked to specify which of three alternative lines were the same length. Although the answer was obvious, seven of the students, who were coached ahead of time, answered incorrectly. The real subject of the experiment always reported next to last. Seventy-five per cent of these subjects gave an incorrect answer at least once, although when they performed the test alone, they *always* chose the correct response. 'At first I thought I had the wrong instructions,' one student said, 'then that something was wrong with my eyes and my head.'[105]

Near the end of his rather dry book, Festinger relates a fascinating story about a small sect of people who believed that alien 'Guardians' from outer space would arrive at a specific time to whisk them off to another planet just before a huge flood. Prior to this predicted cataclysm, the sect members avoided publicity while quietly preparing for their departure. After the flying saucer and flood repeatedly failed to appear, they reacted in an unexpected manner.

'A message arrived from God which, in effect, said that He had saved the world and stayed the flood because of this group and the light and strength they had spread throughout the world that night.' As a result, they now became avid publicity seekers, announcing their epiphany. Festinger explains this illogical behavior as a predictable reaction to increased cognitive dissonance. To preserve their threatened belief system, the sect members became even more dogmatic and sought to proselytize.[106]

This insight may help to explain why women who have recovered repressed 'memories' feel compelled to tell the world about them, while real incest victims, who have always remembered their abuse, generally do not. It also predicts that, in the face of increased skepticism, the Survivor Movement will become more vocal and strident.

Frederic Bartlett made similar observations in 1932. 'The organized group functions in a unique and unitary manner in determining and directing the lives of its individual members,' he wrote, then quoted a bemused British statesman: 'I may seem to know a man through and through, and still I would not dare to say the first thing about what he will do in a group.' Moreover, Bartlett observed that when a social movement feels itself threatened, 'social remembering is very apt to take on a constructive and inventive character, either wittingly or unwittingly. Its manner then tends to become assertive, rather dogmatic and confident, and recall will probably be accompanied by excitement and emotion.'[107]

Not surprisingly, many people have their first flashbacks and abreactions in the stimulating atmosphere of the group. When one woman suddenly cries out, falls to the floor, and acts as if she is being attacked, she provides not only a role model, but a powerful stimulus to others. In many groups, members either consciously or unconsciously strive to outdo one another. The emotion is contagious, something like the atmosphere of an old-time revival meeting. Rather than crying out 'Praise the Lord!', however, these women are more likely to scream 'Keep away from me! I hate you! I hate you!'

THE CONTEXTS OF INSANITY

In conclusion: A vicious cycle of social influence, combined with a widespread belief in massive repression of sexual abuse memories, has produced an epidemic of Survivors. In the current situation, it is sometimes difficult to ascertain *who* is fulfilling *whose* expectations. A woman enters therapy, already afraid that her problems may stem from repressed memories. Her therapist plays into those fears, and between the two of them, they find 'evidence' in the form of dreams, flashbacks, body memories, or eating disorders. They see dysfunction everywhere, and when the client sinks into a hypnotic trance, she pictures horrifying events from her childhood.

Once even the smallest image is visualized, the process of *memory rehearsal* commences, piecing the puzzle bits into a coherent narrative. As Robert Cialdini points out in *Influence*, getting someone to commit new beliefs to writing can be a powerful reinforcement. 'As a commitment device, a written declaration has some great advantages.' After all, 'there it was in his own handwriting, an irrevocably documented act driving him to make his beliefs and his self-image consistent with what he had undeniably done.'[108]

As we have seen, some therapists encourage clients to run mental video tapes of their new-found 'memories' until they seem real. Sometimes this process can become quite literal. In one remarkable article that appeared in *Child Abuse & Neglect* in 1992, several therapists explained how, in 27 cases, they had made a 'videotaped disclosure' of their clients who had recovered memories, to act as a reinforcement. 'Several viewings of the tape may be required before the patient is able to accept the tape as accurate,' they explain.[109]

Recovered-memory therapists usually cite two reasons for their belief in the process: overwhelming affect and convincingly detailed accounts. Unfortunately, powerful emotions are not a guarantee of accurate memories. Anyone who has ever become engrossed in a thriller or dramatic movie knows how easily our emotions can be aroused, even when we *know* intellectually that it is fiction. Similarly, detailed narratives do not necessarily translate to verity. Indeed, some memory experts doubt the accuracy of 20-year-old memories that are recalled in such detail, since they are *more* likely to be confabulations.[110]

The extent to which *expectation* and *context* can determine how professionals view someone was made manifest in a classic experiment conducted by Stanford psychology and law professor D. L. Rosenhan, published in 1973 in *Science* with the compelling title, 'On Being Sane in Insane Places.'[111] Rosenhan sent eight subjects to 12 in-patient psychiatric wards around the United States, where, during admission, they complained of hearing voices that said 'empty,' 'hollow,' and 'thud.' In reality, the subjects were a graduate student in psychology, a pediatrician, a psychiatrist, a painter, a housewife, and three psychologists. Aside from making up their voices and giving false names and occupations, the subjects did not change their actual personal histories or circumstances. As soon as they were admitted, they ceased simulating any symptoms whatsoever.

'The pseudopatient spoke to patients and staff as he might ordinarily,' Rosenhan noted. 'Because there is uncommonly little to do on a psychiatric ward, he attempted to engage others in conversation. When asked by staff how he was feeling, he indicated that he was fine.' All the subjects also wrote down their observations of the ward, patients, and staff.

None of the pseudopatients was detected. Eventually, each was released with a diagnosis of 'schizophrenia in remission,' having been kept anywhere from a week to nearly two months. Many of their fellow patients detected the ruse. 'You're not crazy,' they would say. 'You're a journalist or a professor. You're checking up on the hospital.' The staff, however, was not so astute. 'Patient engages in writing behavior' was the repeated comment on one patient's chart. Another subject accurately recounted his life history, in which, during early childhood, he had a close relationship with his mother, but felt remote from his father. As a teenager, he had become good friends with his father, while his relationship with his mother cooled somewhat. The hospital case summary for him read, 'This white 39-year-old male ... manifests a long history of considerable ambivalence in close relationships.'

As Rosenhan observed, 'having once been labeled schizophrenic, there is nothing the pseudopatient can do to overcome the tag. The tag profoundly colors others' perceptions of him and his behavior ... A psychiatric label has a life and an influence of its own.' As readers will see in the following chapter, Rosenhan's subjects were lucky they did not enter a dissociative disorders unit at a private psychiatric hospital 20 years later. They would have been diagnosed as possessing multiple personalities and kept on the ward indefinitely, not just for two months.

Even in the milder cases of 'recovered memory,' however, Rosenhan's experiment offers an instructive example. A CNN television reporter – presumably free of childhood sexual abuse – took a hidden camera into a 1993 counseling session with a therapist known to have convinced at least six other women that they were Survivors. The reporter said that she had been 'kind of depressed' for a few months, and that her marital sex life had worsened. At the end of the *first session*, the therapist suggested that she might have been sexually abused as a child. When the reporter said she had no such memories, the therapist stated that *many* women completely forget incest. '*They have no idea, in fact. I mean, what you've presented to me, Lee-Anne, is so classic that I'm just sitting here blown away, actually.*'[112]*[113] Once a therapist labels someone an Incest Survivor, everything the client says is perceived as evidence to validate the diagnosis. And the client, having accepted the possibility that the label might be accurate, quickly falls into the trap of seeing the same life problems as symptoms of a childhood full of sexual abuse. Once that belief system is in place, 'memories' are usually not far behind.

---

* One concerned younger sister hired a private investigator to make an appointment with her accusing sister's therapist. Though Ruth, the investigator, told the therapist that she had been rear-ended in an auto accident, the therapist led her through guided imagery to believe she had been sexually abused and repressed the memories. At one point, Ruth asked, 'How do we know, when the memories come . . . that it's not our imagination or something?' The therapist answered, 'Why would you image this, of all things? If it were your imagination, you'd be imaging how warm and loving he was . . . I have a therapist friend who says that the only proof she needs to know that something happened is if you think it might have.'

CHAPTER FOUR

Multiple Personalities and Satanic Cults

> [Jesus] said to him, 'Come out of the man, you unclean spirit!' And Jesus asked him, 'What is your name?' He replied, 'My name is Legion; for we are many.' And he begged him not to send them out . . .
>
> Gospel of St. Mark 5:8–10

> I felt a Cleavage in my Mind –
> As if my Brain had split –
> I tried to match it – Seam by Seam –
> But could not make them fit.
>
> EMILY DICKINSON

One of the most intriguing and controversial products of hypnotic suggestion is a belief that some people harbor multiple internal personalities – an idea that became popular around the turn of the century. (*For the early history of this phenomenon, see Chapter 10.*) Just as past-life regressions yield 'secondary role enactments,' a person with multiple personality disorder (MPD) can perform as an entire ensemble in *this* life.

But many critics have persuasively argued that *the phenomenon of multiple personality is almost invariably an artifact of therapy, produced by the therapist's expectations and the suggestible, vulnerable, attention-seeking client.**

This does not mean that the therapist intentionally creates the condition, nor does it mean that the client suffering from MPD is consciously acting fraudulently. Because the modern proliferation of multiples is so intimately connected with the hunt for repressed memories of sexual abuse, a brief review of its modern rise is in order.

---

* MPD may exist independent of cultural influences, but if so, it is extremely rare. Whether or not there have been isolated instances of true MPD is outside the scope of this book.

The diagnosis of multiple personality disorder was extremely infrequent until the cases of Eve White (a pseudonym for Christine Sizemore) and Sybil, both of which spawned best-selling books and movies. These two cases have exerted enormous influence, providing models for thousands of others that have come in their wake.

Psychiatrist Corbett Thigpen, co-author of *The Three Faces of Eve* (1957) at first found Eve White to be rather boring – a 'neat, colorless young woman.' She came to him because of terrible headaches, apparently caused by intolerable tension related to her failing marriage, exacerbated by her unwillingness to raise her daughter Bonnie in her husband's Catholic faith because she herself was a Baptist. Mrs. White's therapy was clearly important to her, as she had to drive 100 miles to meet with Thigpen. Her husband Ralph characterized her as 'too good' but possessing a 'little erratic streak.'

After several sessions, Thigpen suggested hypnosis in order to help analyze a dream. Soon after that, Mrs. White apparently experienced amnesia following a huge fight with her husband. Thigpen suggested to her that 'unacceptable events are sometimes unconsciously repressed from memory or involuntarily dissociated from awareness,' and this seemed to make her feel better. Soon afterward, during a session, Mrs. White appeared 'momentarily dazed,' looked blank, then transformed her entire appearance. 'There was a quick reckless smile. In a bright unfamiliar voice that sparkled, the woman said, "Hi, there, Doc!"' After some confusing conversation, Thigpen asked, 'Who *are* you?' and she answered, 'Eve Black,' her maiden name.[1]

Eve Black was everything Eve White was not. She was irrepressible, naughty, sensual, spontaneous. In many ways, she was a duplicate of Morton Prince's 'Sally Beauchamp,' the lively alternate personality (known as an 'alter') in that famous 1905 case.* Dr. Thigpen was clearly taken with Eve Black, noting 'how attractive those legs were.' Suddenly this boring patient was a lot more interesting. The idea that several entirely separate personalities could co-exist inside one brain or body has always intrigued not only psychiatrists, but the general public. Soon afterward, a third alter, 'Jane,' appeared as a balanced, intelligent midpoint between the two Eves. By the end of the therapy, however, all of the personalities appeared to have integrated, and all was well.

---

* See Chapter 10 for a detailed description.

SYBIL AND HER TRAUMATIZED ALTERS

In September of 1954, a few months after Thigpen and Cleckley published 'A Case of Multiple Personality' in the *Journal of Abnormal and Social Psychology*,[2] Sybil Dorsett (a pseudonym) moved to New York City and commenced psychotherapy with Dr. Cornelia Wilbur. After three months, Wilbur met Peggy Baldwin, a disturbed child alter, and diagnosed Sybil as a multiple personality. Over the next 11 years, in over 2,300 sessions, Wilbur identified 16 different alters before triumphantly integrating them all. In 1973, Flora Rheta Schreiber, a literature professor, actress, and free-lance writer, published *Sybil* in a dramatic novelized form. That book, along with the subsequent movie, has provided a template for the modern epidemic of MPD diagnoses, including the idea that grotesque childhood sexual and physical abuse causes 'dissociation' of various alters. Sybil's tortures primarily featured enemas that she was forced to hold while her mother played piano concertos, but the sadistic parent also enjoyed pushing spoons and other items up her child's vagina, making Sybil watch sexual intercourse, and hoisting her up to hang helplessly from a pulley.[3]*

Recently, however, Dr. Herbert Spiegel, a psychiatrist intimately familiar with Sybil's case, has come forward to question her MPD diagnosis. Spiegel isn't just your run-of-the-mill expert. He first identified highly hypnotizable people and has specialized in dissociative disorders.**[4] Schreiber thanked Spiegel in her acknowledgments, noting tersely that he called the patient 'a brilliant hysteric.'[5] In a recent phone conversation, Herbert Spiegel told me that Cornelia Wilbur had brought Sybil to him for consultation early in her therapy. He had

---

* Eve White wasn't nearly as satisfactory as Sybil in terms of childhood abuse. Her parents seemed to be fairly normal, and her major childhood traumas – seeing a drowned man at two, touching her dead grandmother's face at five – weren't sexual.

** His son David Spiegel, a Stanford psychiatrist, pushed through a change in the MPD diagnostic category for the *DSM-IV*, calling it Dissociative Identity Disorder in an attempt to steer away from the idea of separate personalities. Herbert Spiegel himself has not been immune to questionable claims stemming from hypnotic regression. In 1976, he wrote the foreword to *The Control of Candy Jones*, the story of how a former fashion model's disk-jockey husband hypnotized her so that she could 'remember' how she was programmed by the CIA as a double personality. Spiegel called the book 'fascinating and compelling.' To his credit, he did note in the foreword that 'Without external confirmation of data, the possibility of stress-hallucination is not ruled out.'

diagnosed her as highly hypnotizable. Whenever Wilbur had to leave town, Spiegel served as Sybil's temporary therapist. In addition, Sybil visited his Columbia University classes annually for a hypnotism demonstration, and she participated in his study of age regression.

'When Sybil came to therapy with me,' Spiegel says, 'and we were discussing some phase of her life, she asked me, "Do you want me to be Peggy, or can I just tell you?" That took me aback, and I asked her what she meant. "Well, when I'm with Dr. Wilbur, she wants me to be Peggy." I told her that if it made her more comfortable to be Peggy, that was fine, but otherwise it wasn't necessary. She seemed relieved and chose not to assume different personalities when she was with me.'

Later, Flora Schreiber approached Spiegel to ask if he would co-author the book, which initially intrigued him. But when he found that they were planning to call her a multiple personality, he objected. Schreiber explained that the publisher was interested only in this sensational approach. When Spiegel told her he wanted no part of such a venture, 'she got in a huff and walked out.' At subsequent psychiatric conferences, Wilbur refused to speak to him.[6]

Cornelia Wilbur was also instrumental in diagnosing Jonah, another well-known multiple. In 1970, Jonah, a 27-year-old black man, entered the University of Kentucky Medical Center after attacking his wife with a butcher knife and beating her. As he did so, he claimed to be 'Usoffa Abdulla, Son of Omega.' Under hypnosis with Dr. Wilbur, Jonah soon revealed that he had two other alter personalities aside from the violent Usoffa: 'Sammy,' a rational lawyer/mediator, and 'King Young,' a seductive lover. Although Jonah was characterized as a 'relatively unsophisticated person from a lower socioeconomic group,' he was certainly highly imaginative and understood how to keep the attention of five psychiatrists.*[7] He apparently enjoyed frightening them as well, since he announced that he felt another alter brewing that would be 'five times worse than Usoffa' and 'would probably be somewhere in between dynamite, electricity, and nitroglycerine.' This fourth alter failed to materialize, much to the relief of the psychiatrists.[8]

The fascinated doctors administered several batteries of personality tests, EEGs, and the like, claiming that these constituted a 'controlled

---

* The principal author of the Jonah study, Dr. Arnold Ludwig, had long been fascinated by 'altered states of consciousness.' In 1966, Ludwig wrote an article on the subject in which he revealed that, while taking LSD 'for experimental purposes,' he had needed to relieve himself. Standing at the urinal, he read a sign, 'Please Flush After Using,' and realized that the words conveyed 'profound meaning.'

comparison' of the alters, even though, their study consisted of one person. They discovered that Jonah's various alters performed distinctly on emotional material, but that the responses were quite similar for neutral material. This outcome should surprise no one, since role playing would produce just such a result. It should also not come as a shock that the tests identified Jonah as a paranoid schizophrenic. Nonetheless, the five psychiatrists asserted that 'the internal consistency of the individual profiles is remarkable and argues against the possibility of faking.'

At least, however, they recognized that the MPD role allowed Jonah to 'express taboo feelings without having to assume responsibility for them.' Indeed, such was the alters' appeal that they were loath to be 'integrated' and agreed to join forces only on a trial basis, provided they got 'equal representation' alongside Jonah, the core personality. Consequently, they compromised on a new name, 'Jusky,' an acronym for Jonah-Usoffa-Sammy-King-Young. The psychiatrists gave the newly constituted Jusky their battery of tests. 'Unfortunately,' they concluded, 'some of the results indicate that this new identity may be psychiatrically "sicker" than any of the others.'

RALPH ALLISON'S NEW FRONTIER

Throughout the 1970s, Cornelia Wilbur was the acknowledged authority on MPD because of her professional publications as well as the popular novel about Sybil. During the decade, a growing number of other psychotherapists became interested in multiple personalities. California psychiatrist Ralph Allison provided an early networking tool through his newsletter, *Memos in Multiplicity*.

In 1980, Allison published *Minds in Many Pieces*, the first popular professional book on multiple personalities. His account of how he first 'discovered' that a patient named Janette suffered from MPD is extremely revealing.

A 29-year-old housewife, Janette was chronically depressed and unhappily married. Her mother had been 'a bossy hypochondriac, always whining about imagined ailments.' Following a suicide attempt by Janette, Allison had her committed to a psychiatric ward, where he asked Katherine, a resident psychologist, to evaluate her. That night, Katherine called Dr. Allison and informed him that Janette was a 'classic case' of MPD, 'another *Three Faces of Eve*.'

The following day, after a sleepless night, the nervous Dr. Allison informed Janette that 'the psychologist who saw you yesterday says there's someone else here with you.' Janette looked puzzled. 'What I mean is, there's someone inside your head – someone else sharing your body.' Still no response. 'I want to meet the other person. I think I can if you'll give me a little cooperation.' He asked her to close her eyes and relax. Then, in a 'commanding, forceful voice,' Allison intoned: 'Now I want to talk to whoever or whatever spoke to the psychologist last night. Come out by the time I count to three. One . . . Two . . . Three!' And with that, Janette opened her eyes and, in a loud, grating voice, said, 'Okay, doc, what do you want? And God, it's good to get rid of that piss-ass Janette.'[9]

Thrilled, Allison observed that 'it was like something out of a movie. It was Joanne Woodward changing from Eve White to Eve Black in *The Three Faces of Eve*.' Exactly. Although it is likely that Janette, too, had seen the movie, it did not occur to Allison that he may have *cued* his patient into multiplicity. From that humble beginning, he was off and running. Later, through hypnosis, he had Janette 'remember' a rape by a schoolyard bully. But that was just the beginning. 'We identified traumas through the use of hypnosis and other techniques. Often one memory led to another and we delved deeper and deeper into her past.'[10]

Once Allison learned how to look for multiplicity, he began to find it in more patients, including Carrie – a beautiful, tall redhead with a history of severe depression and mood disorders. 'I had an odd feeling that this young woman was going to play a unique role in my life. She would influence my work,' he noted.

Allison introduced Carrie to Janette, and soon his first MPD patient was counseling his second. 'Debra,' Carrie's first alter, called Allison her 'Daddy' and Janette 'Mommy.'

Dr. Allison discussed the matter with a parapsychology instructor, who sensed that the spirit of an evil deceased drug addict named Bonnie had invaded Carrie's body. Allison apparently believed this assertion and subsequently carried out a formal exorcism, which he claimed was a success. This didn't prevent Carrie from developing other alters, however, and it didn't stop her from committing suicide the day after he visited her in the hospital*[11] – she had been brought there in restraints

---

* Carrie's husband unsuccessfully sued Dr. Allison for malpractice following his wife's suicide, claiming Allison had prescribed the pills that killed her. Allison not only denies supplying the pills, but says that she was no longer officially his patient at that point. She did, however, come to visit him in his office on the day she killed herself.

after a new 'alter' violently attacked Allison, screaming 'Goddamn-motherfuckingbastardIhateyou.' Even her death did not keep Allison from proclaiming his treatment to be successful. 'I don't always like being a loner,' he wrote in his chapter about Carrie. 'It hurts to know that I am ridiculed as a "fool" by people who don't dispute my successes, but only my methods.'[12]

In *Minds in Many Pieces*, Allison expressed a belief that he had discovered a new, exciting form of therapy. He likened his probing of the mind's inner mysteries to the space program and referred to himself as 'an explorer of this second "frontier."'[13] Despite appearances that he was creating the very disorder he was supposed to cure, his book has exerted an enormous influence, providing models for the 'inner-self helper,' a kind of guardian angel alter, and the 'dark alters' or demons who need to be exorcised.*[14]

The idea of demonic possession, widely believed until the end of the 17th century, appears to have maintained a fairly strong hold even in modern times. With the publication of *The Exorcist* (1971) and its inevitable movie (1973), popular interest in the occult burgeoned. Before that, in the mid-'50s, Thigpen and Cleckley received several suggestions that Eve White might have been possessed by 'discarnate spirits.' Other correspondents, claiming personal experience with demonic possession, volunteered to 'cast out the indwelling fiend they were sure resided in the body of our patient.'[15]

Although Thigpen made fun of such notions, many post-Allison therapists have taken them seriously. *Michelle Remembers*, the recovered memories book about satanic abuse (*see Chapter 1*) appeared in 1980, and since then, Satan has been given his share of blame for the phenomenon of multiplicity. To lend an air of science, however, demons are often called 'introjects.'[16] Psychiatrist M. Scott Peck, who charmed those in search of pop spirituality with *The Road Less Traveled* (1978), followed it with *People of the Lie* in 1983, in which he espoused a firm belief in pure evil and the efficacy of exorcism. 'The diagnosis of possession is not an easy one to make,' however, because 'the demonic hides within and behind the person. For the exorcism to occur, ... the demonic must be uncovered and brought into the open.' To accomplish this, an exorcist must make direct contact with the demons. 'When the demonic

---

* It should be noted that Ralph Allison never became part of the MPD 'establishment' and has, in recent years, taken a firm stand against the hunt for satanic ritual abuse. He has not, however, changed his mind about MPD and has been attempting to have his book reissued in paperback.

finally spoke clearly in one case,' Peck wrote, 'an expression appeared on the patient's face that could be described only as Satanic.' That proved that the patient was possessed, even to Peck, who considered himself 'a hardheaded scientist.'*[17]

JAMES FRIESEN'S MULTIPLE DEMONS

The influences of Ralph Allison and Scott Peck came together in 1991 in James Friesen's *Uncovering the Mystery of MPD*, the most popular book about MPD to be written for a Christian audience. Friesen, a Californian Ph.D. psychologist and minister, was already engaged in 'spiritual warfare' against the invisible powers of evil when he discovered multiple personality disorder. He trained himself primarily by listening to a tape about MPD and by reading the works of Allison and Peck.

Friesen's book makes it quite clear how he came to believe that most of his clients contained unrecognized alters, and why he insisted that his diagnosis was correct, even in the face of considerable resistance. 'Every life experience must be stored and filed somewhere,' he writes, 'and no event can be erased. The closest a brain can come to erasing a memory is to become amnesic to what just happened. That involves creating an alternate personality for the occasion.' Because it is the alter who remembers the abuse, the memories seem doubtful to most clients at first. 'When dissociated memories start to surface during treatment, they *always* seem unreal. The clients have a hard time accepting the reality of the memory, because it does not seem like it happened to them.'

One client, whom he calls Helen, told one of her friends proudly that Friesen was 'fascinated with me,' though she was skeptical of this MPD business. 'She had not yet found out about the awful things that must have happened to her as a young child,' Friesen explains. 'One of the benefits of dissociation is that the dissociator grows up with healthy alters who know nothing about the abuse. Those alters are the ones who come to therapy, believing they have had a simple childhood. They go through a lot of denial when the truth breaks through the amnesia.'

---

* Peck came to believe in evil patients after 400 sessions with a patient named Charlene. The therapist was frustrated because 'she totally failed to be affected by it.' Rather than blaming himself, Peck concluded that there was a simple reason: she was evil. 'Charlene's desire . . . to toy with me, to utterly control our relationship, knew no bounds.'

Indeed, 'Helen's host alter fought very hard to maintain the posture that she had gone through a normal childhood, and that her family was a good one.' The insightful Dr. Friesen was eventually able to overcome her resistance and convince Helen of her multiplicity. She later attempted suicide several times and was repeatedly hospitalized. Since 'practically all MPD clients have periods of suicidality,' the therapist observes, 'it may be necessary to protect the life of the client with brief hospitalization.'

It is little wonder that one of Friesen's patients told him, 'I don't know what I'm doing here, Jim. I've been seeing you for more than a year, and my life is not getting easier. I didn't come here to feel worse! I know you keep saying that all feelings are important, but I'm tired of despair.' Another said, 'You didn't tell me it would be this painful. This pain will never stop! I will never get over it. It would be better if you would just let me die.' In the face of such anguished outbursts, Friesen staunchly maintained his belief in MPD and his therapeutic approach.

Part of that approach was to encourage clients to cut off contact with accused family members and to throw away letters from them without opening them. When confused patients ('certain alters') complained that this appeared un-Christian, Friesen quoted scripture to them, noting that Jesus had said, 'Anyone who loves his father or mother more than me is not worthy of me.' Thus, he explained, 'The Christian thing to do is to . . . let go of "family members" who are unsafe. After all, family is only "family" in the Christian sense of the word when it adheres to Christian principles.'

Jesus has proven to be quite an ally for the therapist. In conducting guided imagery sessions, Friesen encourages clients to create a 'safe place where the hurting alters can go for recovery.' Generally, he recommends a meadow with a gently flowing brook and a warm breeze. 'For Christians, it is good to have Jesus waiting there to help in any way He sees fit.' Leaving the meadow, he conducts his client through an imaginary house, 'with a room for each of your alters, and a conference room right by the front door.' Then they go into the 'screening room,' a private mental theater where they can watch abuse memories unfold.

Soon, Friesen's MPD patients were seeing bizarre, hooded figures on their mental screens. They began telling Friesen about satanic ritual abuse. Fran recalled being placed by her mother in a casket, lowered into the ground, and hearing dirt piled on top. 'I couldn't breathe,' she remembered. 'I've had claustrophobia all my life and [now I know] that is why.' At various times during her therapy, she had trouble coming up with new stories. 'There were times with my therapist that I just knew the enemy was trying to keep a memory from me, but we would pray and it would be broken.' Finally, she remembered being raped by a demon during a ritual. 'It was an extremely violent instance of incubus,' Friesen explains.

Despite the number of babies sacrificed during the cult activities, no one could ever find any remains. Such lack of evidence didn't faze Friesen. 'The perfect way to discredit the children's testimony is to exhume the remains later, after the children have watched them buried! Who would believe a child's story when he says he knows exactly where the baby is buried, but no baby is found at the site?' Satanic abuse perpetrators are, he concluded, 'masters at cover-up.'

Even patients who had progressed to satanic abuse memories had a hard time believing them, however. 'Those memories in the church basement are crazy!' a client named Carla told Friesen. 'They couldn't have happened to me ... I am willing to go through whatever it takes to get the different personalities in me to work together, but those things didn't happen to me! My family is not like that – they couldn't possibly have done that. Maybe my mind is just playing tricks on me. Do you think that could happen, Doctor Friesen? Am I making it all up?' Of course, Friesen assured Carla that she could *not* be making it up. It was all true.

Eventually, after reading *People of the Lie* by M. Scott Peck, Friesen realized that some of his worst MPD/SRA clients contained not just alters, but actual demons, and he began to exorcise them.*[18] This was a delicate matter, he cautioned, because it wouldn't do to cast out an indigenous alter. You can tell if it's a demon by the guttural tone of the voice, foaming at the mouth, and general nastiness.

As a model, Friesen relates his exorcism of a demon named 'Fracture' from his client, Rosie. 'In the name of Jesus, all spirits are bound, mute and immobile. You cannot influence Rosie in any way. You cannot hurt

---

* While giving a speech in Kansas in 1995, I met Kathleen Knott, who allegedly was identified as having MPD with introject demons by her therapist at Prairie View, Inc., in Newton, Kansas. Four exorcisms failed to heal her. She is now suing Prairie View and seeking an injunction to prevent the institution from allowing further exorcisms. Prairie View has strongly denied her allegations and maintain that its primary interest is the safety, security and efficacious treatment of the patient. In another case, California retractor Kimberly Mark was taken to Idaho so that 'Entity Extractors' could excise the monsters supposedly inhabiting her body.

her on the way out, and you will be able to respond only if spoken to in the name of Jesus.' Then, after finding the name of the demon, along with how and why he entered Rosie, he simply said, 'In the name of Jesus, you must leave.' Just for good measure, he then did some house-cleaning and ordered any other stray demons to depart as well.

Lest anyone be concerned that his approach is a bit radical, Friesen explains that the 'scientific method does not automatically deny that there is a spirit world.' Following the lead of Scott Peck, he reassures the reader: 'I take a "pure" scientific approach – I want to be open to all the data, without fitting them into a narrow framework.'[19]

It isn't surprising that demonic possession should be identified with multiple-personality disorder. They are different faces of the same essential phenomenon, as Nicholas Spanos, Michael Kenny, and several other observers have noted.[20] In each case, a person is convinced that he or she possesses indwelling alternate personalities, often unaware of one another, each with a distinct name and birth date. In either case, it takes an expert – a priest or a therapist – to identify the disorder, to call out the demons or alters, and to converse with them. Finally, this same expert must 'cure' the disorder, often at great personal risk, by dispensing with the demons and restoring the subject to wholeness and health. As one of Scott Peck's patients commented, 'All psychotherapy is a kind of exorcism,' and the reverse is true as well.[21]*

DIAGNOSING THE ELUSIVE MULTIPLE

At the 1977 annual meeting of the American Psychiatric Association, Cornelia Wilbur chaired the first organized panel on MPD and invited Ralph Allison to present his views. Allison brought along Henry Hawksworth – an MPD patient who later wrote his own book – as a surprise guest. Subsequently, Allison was asked to chair the panel the next year.[22]

Soon, however, the California psychiatrist was eased out of power by younger colleagues, including Bennett Braun and Richard Kluft, who were determined to lend an air of scientific credibility to the diagnosis. Allison, with his shamanistic belief in demons, proved to be an embarrassment and was effectively shut out of the movement.[23]

* For the historical background on the switch from demonology to hypnotism and MPD, see Chapter 10.

By the mid-'80s, under the influence of Kluft and company, an entire MPD industry had arisen, with its own societies, authorities, specialized journals and newsletters. Because of Eve, Sybil, Ralph Allison, and other interested therapists, multiple personality was included in 1980 in the third edition of the American Psychiatric Association's *Diagnostic and Statistical Manual of Mental Disorders* (*DSM*), which meant that an MPD diagnosis could draw insurance payments. In the early 1980s, a core group of therapists – Bennett Braun, Richard Kluft, Eugene Bliss, George Greaves, David Caul, Colin Ross, and Frank Putnam – cranked out articles on MPD. Several prestigious psychological journals published special issues devoted to the topic. In 1984, the International Society for the Study of Multiple Personality & Dissociation was founded.[24] In the late 1980s, more popular books and professional articles on multiplicity poured forth.[25]

In 1989, psychiatrist Frank Putnam, who works at the National Institute of Mental Health, published *Diagnosis and Treatment of Multiple Personality Disorder*, intended as a textbook 'for therapists unfamiliar with dissociative disorders.'[26] Putnam asserts that the initial diagnosis is often 'difficult and anxiety-provoking for both therapist and patient.' Why this should be so soon becomes clear. Few of those who suffer from MPD realize that they harbor any internal personalities *until* the therapist seeks them out. To complicate things further, the alters are wily creatures. 'The personality system may be actively eluding diagnosis,' Putnam writes.

'The trick,' he continues, 'is to recognize and follow up [any] manifestations of MPD.' It is important to 'maintain a high index of suspicion regarding the possibility of covert switching occurring during sessions.' Any mood changes, momentary silences, physical shifts, facial tics, or inability to remember past events should be taken as clues to multiplicity. 'A clinician will not find MPD if he or she is not willing to look for it.' But one must also be willing to wait, usually six months or more, before spotting MPD in a particular patient. That way, the therapist establishes trust, rapport and knowledge of the person's background. During this time, patients should keep diaries in which different handwriting or moods might indicate MPD.

Putnam describes the crucial initial contact with an alter. 'My first approach is one of indirect inquiry. I broach the subject gently, often first asking the patient whether he or she has ever felt like more than one person.' He follows up with other inquiries, such as 'Do you ever feel as if you are not alone, as if there is someone else or some other part watching you?' Or, 'Do you ever feel as if there is some other part of yourself that comes out and does or says things that you would not do or say?' Once the psychiatrist finally gets a positive response, he latches onto it. 'In particular, I am looking for either a name or an attribute, function, or description that I can use as a label to elicit this other part directly.' A proper name such as Helen is preferable, but Putnam will accept 'the angry one' or 'the little girl.'

Regardless of the label, at this point the therapist should inquire, 'Can this other part come out and talk with me?' Quite often, Putnam cautions, 'the alter does not pop out the first time the therapist asks. It is often necessary to repeat the request several times.' Hypnotism or sodium Amytal are often useful. 'Even if the patient is showing evidence of significant distress with this request, I would urge persistence.' Some patients, when repeatedly pushed to produce a balky alter, report 'feeling smothered, having a sense of terrible internal pressure.' These are signs 'highly suggestive of dissociative pathology,' Putnam asserts. Sometimes, in order to elicit an alter, an extended interview lasting three hours or longer is useful. 'It may be necessary to spend a large part of the day with some highly secretive MPD patients,' he cautions. 'During this interview, which is exhausting and stressful for both parties, it is important to continue to probe aggressively.'*[27]

By this time, I hope that the reader is as appalled as I am. No wonder the patients feel smothered! Here is Dr. Putnam, or any zealous therapist like him, apparently practically interrogating his own patients. He will not take 'No' for an answer.**[28] Even relatively normal people would probably buckle under such pressure and produce alters. How much more likely that a vulnerable patient, who has approached a therapist in hopes of understanding his or her unhappiness, would succumb?

Putnam would prefer to elicit alters without resorting to hypnosis,

* Putnam's approach is mild compared to MPD specialist Richard Kluft, who often will not let patients take breaks or avert their faces during his lengthy interviews. 'In one recent case of singular difficulty,' he says, 'the first sign of dissociation was noted in the sixth hour, and a definitive spontaneous switching of personalities occurred in the eighth hour.' Scott Peck's exorcisms sometimes last 12 hours. Another therapist pushes his thumb against a client's forehead while demanding that an alter appear, an approach similar to Sigmund Freud's 'pressure method' (discussed in Chapter 10).
** The ego of some MPD specialists appears to be matched only by their inability to hear their clients. Dr. Eugene Bliss reports that he intentionally induced a new personality and christened it 'Dr. Bliss' in hopes that the alter could help in therapy. 'Unfortunately, he was not helpful but instead would complain that the region was both overcrowded and unmanageable.' The therapist did not get the message.

but often he finds it necessary. He begins by producing a 'benign trance experience,' which turns out to be the creation of the by-now-familiar 'safe and pleasant place.' From there, he age-regresses patients, hoping to find traumas and the alters they produced. 'It is important to identify a "target" beforehand and to direct the age regression back to that point in time.' Once there, 'the act of remembering will produce a florid abreaction that can cause considerable distress for both patient and therapist. Revivification, the experience of vividly reliving an event, is in some ways more traumatic than the original experience.'

Like Ellen Bass and Renee Fredrickson, Putnam encourages his hypnotic patients to visualize their past abuse on a mental movie screen. 'Events seen on this screen can be slowed down, speeded up, reversed, or frozen by suggestion as needed . . . The patient can also be instructed to zoom in on details, or zoom back and pan for a larger perspective.' Having gotten the hang of this internal movie-making, most MPD candidates really take to the process. 'Once uncovering work has begun to open the closed doors,' Putnam writes, 'the patient will have increased difficulty in keeping painful material out of conscious awareness. This process seems to gather a momentum of its own.'[29]*[30]

Indeed, with practice, most MPD patients no longer require hypnotic inductions. Therapists can simply say, 'I'd like to talk to Sherry now,' and she will instantly appear. Specialist Richard Kluft uses an economy of style when he wishes to make a particularly important announcement. 'Everybody listen!' he demands. His audience is likely to include some standard types: a few traumatized inner children, a suicidal depressive, a protector, a prostitute, and perhaps a demon or two. Indeed, Kluft holds the dubious distinction of having identified 4,500 alters within one patient, a world's record.[31]

---

* To his credit, Frank Putnam has recently expressed doubts about many MPD diagnoses, criticizing the vague criteria for the condition, stating that inpatient treatment often worsens the condition, and stressing that hypnosis and sodium Amytal can produce confabulations. In a personal 1994 communication to me, he wrote: 'Outside corroboration is absolutely necessary before one undertakes any kind of action outside of the therapy based on such memories. When my book was written, people were not suing their parents for alleged abuse.' Putnam has not, however, retracted any of the material in his 1989 textbook. Psychiatric anthropologist Sherrill Mulhern, who knows all of the major MPD specialists well, believes that Putnam's book reflects not only his own theories, but those of other MPD gurus, particularly Richard Kluft. Kluft is the acknowledged master of the 'scientific' presentation of MPD, writing about the 'polysymptomatic pleomorphic presentation of MPD' – by which he apparently means that he can interpret virtually any behavior as evidence of possible MPD.

'The alters are typically stock characters, with bizarre but completely unimaginative character traits, each one a stereotype,' writes philosopher Ian Hacking. 'Persona-switching now happens much more suddenly and instantaneously than in the past. There is no need for a trance or sleep period between alters. The model is "zapping," of switching channels on television.'[32] Another skeptic, psychiatrist Michael Simpson, complains of 'flesh-creepingly embarrassing performances' he has witnessed that do not appear to be genuine personalities but amount to mere 'amateur theatrics.'[33]

To maintain their therapists' attention, some MPDs have gone overboard with their alters. George Ganaway, an Atlanta psychiatrist who is among the few skeptical specialists in dissociative disorders, writes that he personally has encountered 'demons, angels, sages, lobsters, chickens, tigers, a gorilla, a unicorn, and "God",' to name only a few. 'The inscapes in which they exist,' he adds, 'have ranged from labyrinthine tunnels and mazes to castles in enchanted forests, high-rise office buildings, and even a separate galaxy.'[34]

Once diagnosed, most MPD patients are encouraged to attend group sessions with their fellow multiples. At various inpatient units around the country, they have no choice. Here, the group process works its wonders, with an ever-escalating level of alter-switching, trauma-reliving, attention-seeking one-upmanship. Ganaway facetiously calls such dramatic displays *status abreacticus*, as the patient ' "relives" for the therapist's fascination and approval an increasingly expansive repertoire of what both grow to believe are factual trauma memories.'[35] Paul McHugh, head of psychiatry at Johns Hopkins, believes that getting MPD patients away from contagious group settings should be an important part of any cure; he suggests 'isolation [and] counter suggestion.'[36]

Of course, suggesting to identified patients that they are not multiples would be abhorrent to Frank Putnam. At some point, he warns, patients will 'deny that the MPD is active or even that it ever existed. They may seek to disprove that they are or ever were multiples, and even say that they faked it or made it up.'[37] The therapist must accept none of these excuses, he states. This follows the model of Dr. Wilbur, who ignored Sybil when her patient wrote: 'I am not going to tell you there isn't anything wrong. We both know there is. But it is not what I have led you to believe. I do not have any multiple personalities. I don't even have a "double" to help me out. I am all of them.'[38]

MANUFACTURING MPD

Usually, it doesn't take all the pressure Putnam exerts to produce a multiple personality case, as psychologist Nicholas Spanos has shown in a series of experiments. Spanos became intrigued with the case of Kenneth Bianchi, the 'Hillside Strangler,' who was diagnosed in 1979 as a multiple personality by therapist John Watkins. It wasn't Bianchi who had murdered all those women; it was his vicious alter, Steve Walker, according to Watkins. Ralph Allison, who was called in as a consultant, agreed.[39]*[40] Spanos read a transcript of Watkins' interview with a hypnotized Bianchi. 'I've talked a bit to Ken but I think that perhaps there might be another part of Ken that I haven't talked to.' He paused. 'Part, would you come and lift Ken's hand to indicate to me that you are here.' The hand lifted.** 'Would you talk to me, Part, by saying, "I'm here."' Bianchi obliged him.

Having summoned this Part, Watkins then engaged in the following dialogue:

> Part, are you the same as Ken or are you different in any way?
> *I'm not him.*
> You're not him. Who are you? Do you have a name?
> *I'm not Ken.*
> You're not him? Okay. Who are you? Tell me about yourself. Do you have a name I can call you by?
> *Steve. You can call me Steve.*[41]

After the hypnotic session, Bianchi purportedly could not remember anything about Steve.

In 1985, Spanos decided to replicate this conversation as nearly as possible with a test group of college students, each of whom was asked to play the role of an accused murderer under hypnosis. The students were *not* told anything about multiple personalities. Yet 81 per cent of

---

* Several years later, Allison changed his mind when new evidence cast doubt on the truth of many of Bianchi's claims.

** Such hypnotic instruction – to raise a hand or finger to signify 'yes' or 'no' – is called 'ideomotor signaling' and is widely practiced by hypnotherapists, despite the obvious hazards of leading the patient.

the participants adopted different names and referred to their primary identities in the third person, and 63 per cent displayed spontaneous amnesia for the hypnotic session after it was finished.[42] Spanos concluded that the amnesia and MPD were an unconscious fraud, a 'strategic enactment' to fulfill a role. 'The displays of forgetting exhibited by these patients are selective and context dependent.' Finally, he concluded, 'these findings indicate that the multiple personality role was viewed by subjects as a credible vehicle for negotiating a difficult personal dilemma.'

The following year, Spanos replicated his experiment, adding an age-regression component based on the Bianchi interviews. Not surprisingly, those treated like Bianchi 'recalled' traumatic early childhoods that caused them to split off their alters. 'My parents hate me,' one subject reported. 'Sometimes they start slapping me around.' The subjects seemed to realize instinctively that this traumatic background would 'explain' why they were multiples. Their psychopathology provided a means of 'disavowing responsibility for past difficulties and for antici-pated failures.' Spanos concluded that 'people who adopt this role often become convinced by their own enactments and by the legitimation they receive from significant others. In this manner such individuals come to believe sincerely that they possess secondary identities that periodically "take over."'[43]

Some critics feel that *all* MPD involves role-enactment, which is an extreme position. Yet consider that multiple personalities are almost entirely a product of a small cadre of North American therapists. The phenomenon does not exist at all in many cultures, although belief in demon possession is certainly widespread. This observation led British psychologist Ray Aldridge-Morris to call MPD 'an exercise in deception' in his comprehensive 1989 book on the subject. 'My initial impetus to write this monograph,' he notes, 'was the dramatic incidence of multiple personality syndrome in the United States relative to its virtual absence elsewhere in the world. An extensive canvass of psychologists and psychiatrists in Great Britain produced not a single, unequivocal case.'[44]

The British Invasion

Since Aldridge-Morris wrote those words in 1989, MPD has indeed made inroads with British therapists and patients, thanks to help from American 'experts' and the importation of books such as *Suffer the Child*, in which 'Jenny developed multiple personalities in order to survive,' according to the Nightingale Books catalog.[45]

The 1992 publication of *The Filthy Lie* by Hellmut Karle, a psychologist at Guy's Hospital in London, gave a tremendous boost to recovered memory, hypnosis, and MPD in England. It tells the dramatic story of Meggie Collins, a depressed, obese middle-aged woman. At first, Karle hypnotized her in an attempt to help her lose weight. Then, after the session, she supposedly told him, 'When I was a little girl, my father interfered with me.' When he asked her about this revelation later, she repeatedly denied that incest had occurred or that she had said such a thing.* He 'persistently pressed her to say more,' and eventually she agreed. He explained that 'the memories of experiences which were severely frightening to a child can become separated off from the central memory of the adult, but persist within the mind rather like an embedded foreign body – a septic splinter in your psychic finger.' Over the next two years, Karle helped Collins to unearth memories of gang orgies and abuse by various perpetrators. He also located two internal 'alters' named Little Meggie, an eight-year-old, and Big Meggie, twenty. To do so, he frequently hypnotized Collins, encouraging a mental video-screen projection of abuse memories.

The book offers a compelling case study of a *folie à deux* in which doctor and patient collude to produce an iatrogenic illness. Karle's approach was, by his own admission, 'more like voyeurism than proper inquiry.' The resultant process produced in Collins a 'state of continual, unremitting and intense inner turmoil,' as she became 'determined to unearth all the memories that had been blocked or buried.' It occurred to Karle that perhaps his approach was 'encouraging her to manufacture further horrors in order to engage my continuing interest,' but that did not stop the misguided process, nor prevent him from suggesting she enroll as a full-time patient so that she could 'be relieved of her daily responsibilities.'

The therapist's fascination with his client deepened when he diagnosed her with MPD, and he decided to write a book about her. 'I found myself almost pursuing her now, almost indeed courting her.'

---

* It is quite possible, in fact, that Karle misinterpreted what she said. Collins may have said something about her resentment over her father's interference in her life. It is significant that at that point, Karle cut off the conversation. 'Very conscious of the ears I believed to be pricking up around the ward, I suggested that we leave further discussion until she had been discharged.'

Later, when Collins did not evince sufficient hatred of her mother, Karle became exasperated with her. 'The aggressive and invasive manner in which I pressed Mrs. Collins at this time,' he writes, 'came very close to being an assault on her.' Finally, the patient learned how to please her therapist by giving vent to 'her violent and completely unrestrained rage' at her supposed abusers. 'I almost hugged myself with delight,' he recounts. 'She was simply magnificent as she raged around the room.'

The Filthy Lie is a remarkably honest book. Karle admits that his client's dependence upon him was 'quite explicit and at times felt really oppressive.' He found this dependence both 'rewarding and irksome.' He gloried in his heroic savior role, but he also lost considerable sleep and endangered his own health. Karle also admits that his colleagues universally pooh-poohed the MPD diagnosis. 'They tended to interpret what was happening between Mrs. Collins and myself as histrionic manipulation by her,' he writes, 'and considered that I was at least in part colluding with the maintenance of her condition.' Such, indeed, appears to have been the case. Meggie Collins herself observed near the end of her therapy that 'I've planned, I've worked, I've tried to be a good mother and wife, but nothing ever worked.' The diagnosis by a consultant psychiatrist during one of her hospital stays seems accurate. He noted that the patient was 'depressed, having difficulties in coping with life, and lonely.'[46]

Despite these fairly obvious conclusions, the book has been hailed as 'proof' of repressed memories and multiple personality disorder. 'In Britain,' noted one reviewer recently, 'where MPD has made slow but predictable progress, The Filthy Lie has been recommended as gospel for recovered memory and MPD enthusiasts – not least because it has the imprimatur of being both British and by a respected psychologist.'[47]

The year following publication of Karle's book, Ray Aldridge-Morris conducted a survey of British psychotherapists in an attempt to assess the prevalence of MPD diagnoses in the United Kingdom. He sent an anonymous questionnaire to 680 therapists, only 140 of whom responded. Of these, 15 (11 per cent) had diagnosed and treated multiple personality disorder, reporting a total of 53 cases. Two respondents had seen the vast majority of the cases – one diagnosing 20 clients, the other 10, with the others seeing between one and three MPDs.[48] Thus it appears that by 1993, a disturbing number of British therapists were diagnosing MPD, with a very small minority providing the majority of the cases.

A year later, in 1994, a chapter of the American-based International

Society for the Study of Dissociation was formed in Great Britain. The same year, the British book *Treating Survivors of Satanist Abuse* was filled with credulous information about MPD, including a chapter by Ashley Conway, a psychologist at Charing Cross Hospital who, ironically, warned that hypnosis should be used cautiously, since 'secondary or multiple personalities may emerge at this time.' The volume also included a chapter by American psychiatrist Sandra Bloom, who found herself 'profoundly shocked' when she first discovered a five-year-old alter. Now, however, the phenomenon is old hat to her, since MPD patients comprise 25 per cent of the in-patient population in her Philadelphia hospital, and a quarter of those were supposedly ritually abused. Bloom, whose dissociative disorders unit is known as 'The Sanctuary,' has had a major impact as a consultant in England. At a 1995 conference in Kensington, London, she told a British journalist, 'You should have centers like this [The Sanctuary] all over Britain.' She repeated stock recovered memory beliefs about body memories and flashbacks. 'They relive the original trauma, consciously and shockingly. It is a terrible thing to witness. They scream and struggle and retch. Nobody could doubt the reality of the appalling things these patients are going through.'[49]

The hunt for ritual abuse cases involving young children (documented in Chapter 9) also indirectly spawned an interest in multiple personality cases. British evangelical Christian ex-nurse Maureen Davies, prominent in the U.K. ritual abuse scares of the 1980s, visited the United States in 1990, where she discovered the link between MPD and adult ritual abuse Survivors. 'Nobody believes the children,' she announced upon her return. '[So now] we're going on the adult survivors.' She does so through her Beacon Foundation.[50]

Skeptical Inquirers

Despite such spreading belief in MPD, Canadian psychiatrist Harold Merskey, who published an extensive historical review of the syndrome in 1992, concluded: 'No case has been found here in which MPD, as now conceived, is proven to have emerged through unconscious processes without any shaping or preparation by external factors such as physicians or the media ... It is likely that MPD never occurs as a spontaneous persistent natural event in adults.' Rather, Merskey asserts, 'suggestion, social encouragement, preparation by expectation, and the reward of attention can produce and sustain a second personality.'[51]

Anthropologist Michael Kenny echoes Merskey in his book on the subject: 'Multiple personality is a socially created artifact, not the natural product of some deterministic psychological process.' It is rather a useful 'idiom of distress' for our times.[52]

South African psychiatrist Michael Simpson agrees. According to Simpson, MPD is invariably produced by input from 'the media, enthused therapists, amateur zealots, other marketers and profiteers, and strong cultural priming.' He notes that many MPD patients have claimed supernatural or psychic powers such as ESP, clairvoyance, reincarnation, astral travel, and poltergeists. 'This suggests the possibility of similar origins for all these experiences,' he notes drily, then quotes a patient who explained: 'My therapist educated me, so by the time we decided I had MPD, I knew a lot.'[53]

American psychiatrist August Piper, Jr., takes a similarly jaundiced view of MPD diagnosis. 'Few limits exist to the number of "personalities" one may unearth,' he observes. 'The number is bounded only by the interviewer's energy and zeal in searching, and by the interviewer's subjective sense of what constitutes a "personality." '[54]

The World Health Organization has also maintained a healthy skepticism regarding the diagnosis, noting in its 1992 classification system that 'this disorder is rare, and controversy exists about the extent to which it is iatrogenic or culture-specific.'[55]

Finally, Johns Hopkins psychiatrist Paul McHugh states flatly: 'MPD is an iatrogenic [doctor-induced] behavioral syndrome, promoted by suggestion and maintained by clinical attention, social consequences, and group loyalties.'[56*57]

If that is so, how do we account for a case like Eve (Christine Costner Sizemore)? She appears to have taken Dr. Thigpen completely by surprise, and her 'split' occurred before the current vogue. Thigpen probably cued his patient without being aware of it. He had read Morton Prince's description of Christine Beauchamp. Before 'Eve Black' appeared, Thigpen had already hypnotized her at least once and had

---

* Ever since Morton Prince, MPD specialists have attempted to prove that an individual in different 'alter' states displays different physiological functions, becoming, in effect, a different person. Alters within the same person are supposed to have different allergies, eyesight, and handwriting – all anecdotal reports. Frank Putnam and others have conducted experiments that indicate different brain wave patterns (EEGs or evoked visual potential) among alters. Although interesting, none of the experiments proves the existence of MPD, as psychiatrist Carol North points out in her excellent summary of the physiological studies: 'No laboratory measurement has been developed that can differentiate MPD from other disorders.'

explained the concepts of repression and dissociation. We have only his retrospective account, which is highly colored by his assumption that he did *not* cue her. It is quite possible that he loaned her his copy of Prince's *Dissociation of a Personality* or told her about it, or that she was familiar with the concept of multiple personality in some other way.*[58]

Regardless of how Chris Sizemore initially became a multiple, she thrived on the role and has made it a life-time occupation. At the conclusion of *The Three Faces of Eve*, we are led to believe that her alters were well integrated. Far from it. In the ensuing years, at the urging of her new therapist, she developed a total of 22 personalities with names such as Purple Lady, Retrace Lady, and Strawberry Girl. She has published two additional books about her dramatic experiences, in which she name-drops mercilessly, brags about her accomplishments, and laments her inability ever to meet Sybil, her main competition. She has experienced, as she writes in a revealing passage, 'a lifetime of *continual expectancy*.'[59]

DISSOCIATIVE DISORDER UNITS:
TERROR IN THE MPD MILLS

Why would a trained professional, whose goal is to help afflicted patients regain mental health, instead push them further toward the brink of complete terror and disintegration?

Sheppard Pratt, a large psychiatric hospital in a northern suburb of Baltimore, provides an example of just how this can happen. Since psychiatrist Richard Loewenstein, an MPD specialist, appeared there in 1987, the number of MPD diagnoses has skyrocketed – not surprising, given Loewenstein's mindset, as revealed in a 1991 paper. 'Dissociation and MPD are primarily hidden phenomena,' he writes. 'Patients may deny, minimize, or rationalize their presence.' Experienced diagnosticians must, he asserts, be alert to 'subtle facial or body shifts by the dissociating patient during the interview.' He advises clinicians to search

---

* Harold Merskey points out another interesting aspect of the case. Rather than 'Eve Black,' the actual name of the first 'alter' was really Chris Costner, her maiden name. Since she was experiencing marital strife and couldn't allow herself to express it, it's quite possible that this role gave her an outlet. 'It was an affirmation of a previous [real] single state which the patient regretted leaving,' Merskey hypothesizes.

for changes from session to session in 'style of clothing, hair, makeup, eyeglasses, posture, level of motor activity, jewelry, handedness, taste and habits,' all of which can be 'very subtle.'[60]

Psychiatrist Donald Ross, the training director for new residents at Sheppard Pratt, is disturbed by Loewenstein's influence, which he perceives as producing young 'true believers' in the MPD diagnosis. The process begins, Ross posits, when patients with 'insecure self-identity and permeable ego boundaries' appear in the hospital ward. 'They present us a therapeutic dilemma we find overwhelming. We want to help. We also want to diminish our anxiety.' Up until now, no adequate theory or treatment has appeared to make much difference. 'The conceptual framework of trauma theory, with its emphasis on dissociation and the use of . . . hypnosis, offers some promise of helping our patients and reducing our anxiety.' It seems to work. 'It gives the patients a dramatic language to express their identity diffusion and their massive internal conflicts or "parts." Besides, it engages us in a way that is exciting and reinforcing.'

With time, this new approach catches fire, as Ross has seen. 'A group knowledge of MPD begins to circulate among the patients and, like a contagion of sorts, it multiplies. We see dissociative phenomena more readily . . . The therapeutic techniques used – hypnosis, regression, and abreaction – give us a sense that we are doing something and that therapy is moving in an understandable direction.'[61] Over a hundred years ago, Sigmund Freud succumbed to the same kind of temptation, as he later confessed: 'There was something positively seductive in working with hypnotism. For the first time there was a sense of having overcome one's helplessness; and it was highly flattering to enjoy the reputation of being a miracle-worker.'[62]

Unfortunately, the results of such 'miracles' at Sheppard Pratt are devastating for people such as Donna Smith and her family, whose story has been documented in *Esquire* and on the American television show *20/20*.[63] Primed by a therapist, Smith had already retrieved extensive 'repressed memories' of paternal incest by the time she was committed to Sheppard Pratt just short of her 18th birthday. The in-take psychologist spotted six alters during the initial interview. During her 19-month hospital stay, Smith was heavily drugged, frequently held in restraints, hypnotized over 60 times, and attempted suicide twice. In the process, she found 65 new personalities along with memories that her mother had inserted various objects into her vagina before she was eight years old. When other alters claimed that Smith's parents had also abused her two younger brothers, the police came to their home and hauled the terrified boys away in handcuffs to 'protect' them.*

Another former Sheppard Pratt patient, who prefers to remain anonymous, never completely fell for the MPD diagnosis, although he says that his therapist at Sheppard Pratt certainly tried her best to turn him into a multiple. 'I was harangued by her for not having names for emotional aspects that she felt were alters,' he told me. 'I kept telling her I was uncomfortable with the whole context of "alters" and naming them, and she stated that in order for us to have a working relationship, we needed alters with names. At times I found myself desperate to have them just to please her.'[64]

Part of the problem at Sheppard Pratt, of course, is inherent to any totalistic institution in which people are cut off from any other reality. As sociologist Erving Goffman observed in his classic 1961 book, *Asylums*, 'their encompassing or total character is symbolized by the barrier to social intercourse with the outside.' Typically, Goffman wrote, an inmate's indoctrination begins with 'a series of abasements, degradations, humiliations, and profanations of self. [The] self is systematically, if often unintentionally, mortified.'[65]

It is not surprising, then, that Sheppard Pratt is not an isolated example. Bennett Braun's dissociative disorders unit at Rush Presbyterian-St. Luke's in Skokie, Illinois, is apparently also fertile ground for MPD contagion. Pat Burgus, once Braun's prize patient, along with several other former patients, is suing Braun and his colleague Roberta Sachs for abusive therapy. Her life was nearly destroyed by the process. She became convinced that she had been a high priestess in a satanic cult. Not only that, but her two sons, then four and five, were also diagnosed as MPD cult members and were hospitalized for nearly three years. The children were given stickers as a reward for coming up with grotesque fantasies. The Burgus family tragedy, which cost an insurance company $3 million, is told in detail in 'Therapy of a High Priestess,' a chapter in Richard Ofshe and Ethan Watters' compelling 1994 book, *Making Monsters*, and in the 1995 *Frontline* documentary, 'The Search for Satan.'[66]

Braun was clearly fascinated and moved by his clients' bizarre revelations. Sometimes he would cry along with Burgus. Other times, he

---

* Fortunately, the Smith story has a happy ending. After reading the *Esquire* article, Donna Smith began to question her MPD diagnosis and her memories of abuse. She has now reconciled with her parents, whom she no longer accuses of abuse, and is suing her former therapists.

apparently became sexually aroused during her lurid descriptions of sexual assaults, according to Burghs. With the encouragement of Braun and Sachs, Burgus eventually came up with memories of lit torches being pushed inside her, being buried for days on end, and having to eat the body parts of two thousand people a year. While they ate dinner one night in the hospital, Braun asked Burgus if the cottage cheese reminded her of anything, then wondered aloud whether she had ever opened a human brain. He believed that flowers sent to patients in his unit were really dangerous triggers. 'Red roses or white baby's breath means bloody suicide. Pink roses mean hanging,' he told other therapists in a 1992 presentation.[67]

And Bennett Braun is not just any psychiatrist. He has been the acknowledged leader in the diagnosis of multiple personality in the United States, the expert's expert. Typical of the cutting-edge MPD gurus, Braun prides himself on his courage and adventurous spirit, testing the frontiers of human experience. He enjoys skydiving, technical rock climbing, scuba diving, and horseback riding. He once tried fire walking. He appears to get a kind of paranoid thrill from his belief in widespread satanic cults. 'About 20 patients have told me they were sent to kill me,' he told one reporter.[68]

Another alarming example of MPD treatment in Texas was revealed in an article by Sally McDonald in the *Journal of Psychosocial Nursing*.[69] Psychiatric nurse McDonald discusses how MPD specialist Judith Peterson, called 'Dr. M.' in the article, came to Houston's Spring Shadows Glen Hospital in 1990 to head the new dissociative disorders unit. McDonald's article makes startling assertions. Completely supported by new medical director Dr. Richard Seward, and by the hospital administration – because her patients brought in $15,600 a day – Peterson instituted a virtual reign of terror on the ward, according to McDonald. Peterson subscribed to Bennett Braun's methodology, hypnotizing patients and convincing them to relive supposedly forgotten traumas. She believed that virtually every patient harbored multiple personalities formed during satanic cult abuse. 'One young patient was placed in nine-point mechanical restraints for three days,' McDonald writes, 'not because he was a threat to himself or others . . . but because those three days coincided with some satanic event.'*[70]

* Satanic cult 'experts' have identified festival days throughout the year. One inventive list from a Survivor organization provides detailed descriptions. A sampling from September: 'Sept. 7: Marriage to the Beast Satan, Sacrifice/Dismemberment. Female child under the age of 21. Sept. 20: Midnight Host, Dismemberment. Hands planted. Sept. 22: Feast Day, Fall/Autumn Equinox. Orgies.'

Twelve nurses fled the unit within a year and a half, but no one dared confront Dr. Peterson directly until she diagnosed a 'bright, articulate, preadolescent' girl, an honors student, as having been involved in a satanic cult. Confined to one room, the girl was denied access to her parents. In weekly staff meetings, nurses begged for a less restrictive environment, asking that the child be given 'freedom of movement, peer interaction, fresh air, exercise, and a bed to sleep in,' but Peterson refused. The girl became pale, thin, and dispirited. 'These nurses knew they were the only advocates this girl had,' McDonald writes. 'Alone she was unable to object to what her doctor and therapist thought "best" for her.'

When insurance companies began to question why it was only Peterson and Seward who ever recorded 'altered states' or 'violent behavior' on the patients' charts, the nurses were pressured to write up such behavior, McDonald asserts, even though they had never observed it. Nurses were intimidated, constantly written up for non-existent violations. Peterson 'threatened lawsuits so frequently that the nurses were afraid to counter her demands; they spoke in whispers in hallways because she taped their conversations.' When the nurse manager sat in on 'abreactive sessions,' she was horrified by the 'coercive, leading nature of these therapy sessions.'

Mothers who had hypnotic memories of cult involvement were coerced into getting divorced and giving up their children, McDonald writes. 'Nurses advised these distraught couples to seek legal counsel, especially before signing divorce papers, but the patients were too fragile to pursue outside opinions, and too frightened of incurring the wrath of their therapist, Dr. M. They believed [as she told them in sessions under hypnosis] that she was the expert, and only she could successfully cure them.'

In a 1993 *Houston Chronicle* article, journalist Mark Smith quoted several former patients who are suing Judith Peterson. Lucy Abney, 45, who sought treatment for depression, spent nearly a year (and over $300,000) at Spring Shadows Glen and came out with more than 100 alters and vivid memories of ritual abuse. Her two daughters are in state custody. As an example of the paranoia rampant on the hospital ward, Abney described how her husband was turned away when he tried to give her a carnation. Patients were warned that items such as flowers could trigger alter personalities.[71]

According to several former patients and nurses, Judith Peterson specialized in convincing mothers that they had abused their children, who were also supposedly cult members. Then the children would also be admitted to the hospital. In an anonymous interview, a former nurse on the dissociative disorders unit told me that five families entered the hospital in this manner. Of those, three mothers ended up divorced and losing all contact with their children.[72]

Kathryn Schwiderski and her three children were all patients of Judith Peterson at another Houston hospital and came to believe that their entire family had taken part in a satanic cult. Their collective therapy and hospitalization cost over $2 million. In a 1990 presentation at a national MPD conference, Peterson described a family suspiciously similar to the Schwiderskis (without using their names), including details about 'human sacrifice, cannibalism, black hole, shock to create alters (other personalities), marriage to Satan, buried alive, birth of Satan's child, internal booby traps, forced impregnation, and sacrifice of own child.' While most of the family members no longer believe in these 'memories,' 22-year-old Kelly Schwiderski remains convinced that she killed three babies in a 'fetus factory' in Colorado.[73]

I interviewed one of Judith Peterson's former patients, who verified much of what McDonald and Smith wrote.[74] Because she insisted on anonymity – out of fear that Peterson will sue her – I will call her Angela. During her private sessions with Peterson, Angela found her 'charming, even bewitching. She had an air about her of insight and caring. In my first session, she was all ears and supportive emotion. It felt good to have someone who was so attentive to every word that I spoke, every movement that I made.' Soon Peterson convinced Angela that she should enter the hospital, where she could see her more often.

Once admitted, Angela says she couldn't get out. Peterson became 'a monster – harsh, hostile, interrogating, guilt-imputing, accusatory,' according to Angela. The therapist and her staff tried to convince Angela that she harbored multiple personalities and had been in a satanic cult. She was heavily drugged. 'Dr. Peterson told me my anger came from a cult alter trying to come out, and that physical problems I was having were body memories.' Peterson's patients weren't allowed to use the telephone unmonitored, Angela told me. Their mail was censored. Only approved visitors were allowed, and those few were closely watched. 'If we weren't cooperative – revealing new alters, talking about Satanism – or were resistant to what we were told about ourselves or our families, we weren't considered "safe" and often were restricted to the central lobby.'

Angela likens the treatment to attempts to break prisoners of war. 'They had a board with all the patients' names,' she told me, 'and every one had an "S" after it for suicide precaution – not because we were really going to kill ourselves, but because that kept our insurance payments flowing.' Finally, Angela escaped when her insurance ran out. 'At first, Dr. Peterson was like my angel from heaven, but instead she took me to hell, and I've been struggling to get out ever since.'

Another former patient, Mary Shanley (her real name), echoes much of Angela's experience.[75] As a 39-year-old first grade teacher, she entered an inpatient unit under Bennett Braun's supervision in the Chicago area early in 1990. She disliked Braun intensely. 'He thinks he's God,' she told me, 'and you'd better think so, too.' But Shanley admired Roberta Sachs, her psychologist. Under Sachs' tutelage, Shanley came to believe that her mother had been the high priestess in a satanic cult, and that she, Mary, was being groomed for the position. 'I remembered going to rituals and witnessing sacrifices. I had a baby at age 13, supposedly, and that child was sacrificed. I totally believed all of this. I would have spontaneous abreactions, partly because I was so heavily medicated. I was on Inderal, Xanax, Prozac, Klonopin, Halcion, and several other drugs, all at once. No wonder I was dissociating.'

After eleven months, Shanley finally got out of the hospital for three months. Then Roberta Sachs called her and asked if she would consult with psychologist Corydon Hammond, who was coming to town to give a workshop. After a hypnotic session during which Hammond tried to get Shanley to name Greek letters and identify a Dr. Green, he announced that she was so highly programmed and resistant that she was not treatable. Her nine-year-old son, however, might still be saved if he was treated in time. Otherwise, the cult would kill him. Shanley's husband believed Hammond, and a week or two later Mary Shanley was taken to the airport, not knowing her destination.

She arrived in Houston in May of 1991 to enter Spring Shadows Glen under the care of Judith Peterson. 'When I first met Dr. Peterson, I thought she had this beautiful smile, and she spoke so softly and gently. She's tall and thin, sort of like a china doll, with a porcelain complexion and bright red hair. She's very striking.' Once inside the hospital, however, Shanley found Peterson to be precisely the opposite of her first impression. 'She was known on the ward as the red-headed bitch,' Shanley told me. 'She did not like me at all and made no bones about it.' After Shanley called a mental health advocacy hotline to complain, she found herself accompanied 'one-on-one' for 24 hours a day by a technician. 'I was locked out of my room and kept in the central lobby. I wasn't allowed to use the telephone or to go outside. That's when I took up smoking, so that I could at least go outside briefly. I slept on the floor or on a couch. After I hurt my back in abreactive sessions, they let me drag my mattress out.'

Part of Shanley's problem was her honesty. Even though she believed that she had been in a cult and possessed internal alters, she would not make them up on cue to please Dr. Peterson. When she would not perform properly during an abreactive session, she would be kept in restraints for up to nine hours until she said what Peterson wanted to hear. 'A lot of the times, the tech and I would discuss what answer she might want.' Sometimes, the psychodramatist and another psychiatrist would sit on either side of Shanley during sessions. 'If Dr. Peterson asked a question and I couldn't answer, they would talk back and forth, representing my alters, literally talking over my head.'

Most of Peterson's efforts concentrated on eliciting information regarding Shanley's son, who was going though a similar abreactive process back in Chicago with Roberta Sachs. Peterson would fax new information to her colleague in Illinois. 'It would work the other way, too,' Shanley says. 'Dr. Peterson told me how my son acted out how he could cut a human heart out of a living body. I thought, there's no way he could imagine that. And I thought, he doesn't lie, I know he's not a liar. So I believed it all.'

After over two years in Spring Shadows Glen, Mary Shanley finally got out in 1993. She has lost her husband and child, who still believe in the satanic cults. She has lost her home and her 20-year teaching career. 'I have absolutely nothing. I don't even have enough clothes to wear to my work in a department store.' She can't teach or hold a federal job because she is on a list of suspected child molesters.

There is hope, however. In 1995, Shanley's horror story was featured in a *Frontline* documentary, 'The Search for Satan,' making it painfully clear that she was a victim of terrible therapy.[76] Two lawyers – Zachary Bravos of Wheaton, Illinois, and Skip Simpson of Dallas, Texas – are representing Shanley and several other patients in suits against Judith Peterson, Roberta Sachs, Bennett Braun, and others. Because of their willingness to take her case, Shanley feels some hope for the future.

*   *   *

By the end of 1992, nurse Sally McDonald had been shifted from the adolescent unit to another department in the hospital because she kept calling Peterson unethical, and the head nurse of the dissociative disorders unit had also been forced out of her position for 'insubordination.' Morale on the dissociative disorders unit had sunk to an all-time low, according to McDonald. Although nurses repeatedly protested to hospital administrators, nothing happened. Then, in the last week of February, 1993, Medicare officials arrived for a routine hospital inspection.*[77] Within hours, they brought in Texas health authorities, and on March 19, the dissociative unit was closed. Two patients walked outside for the first time in two years. Since then, former patients have begun to talk to the media about their experiences, and at least seven are suing. Judith Peterson no longer works at Spring Shadows Glen, but *she* has sued the hospital, McDonald, and another nurse for slander and libel, and she plans countersuits against several patients. She continues to practice as a private therapist.[78] Richard Seward now works with prisoners, but he remains on call at the hospital.[79]

The charismatic Dr. Peterson has her champions, however. I interviewed 23-year-old Christy Steck, an MPD patient who has been seeing Peterson for four years, and who spent most of 1992 in the dissociative disorders unit at Spring Shadows Glen. Steck has always had stomach problems and other vague physical complaints, which she now blames on her biological mother, since recovering memories of her mother and grandfather abusing her in a satanic cult. Her first flashback to ritual abuse occurred while she was watching the horror movie, *Friday the Thirteenth*. With her therapist's help, Steck has been able to identify alters named Tyrant, Tricia, Angela, Whore, and Fucking Bitch. The last two are 'real deep parts that answer to whistles, clickers, and metronomes,' Steck told me. They are the ones programmed to be sex slaves in pornography and prostitution. She has spots on her body that look like 'just birthmarks,' she said, but in reality they are tattoos and scars from electroshock torture.

---

* The abusive treatment of patients in dissociative disorders units is part of a larger problem documented by journalist Joe Sharkey in his 1994 book, *Bedlam: Greed, Profiteering, and Fraud in a Mental Health System Gone Crazy*. Sharkey describes how private psychiatric hospitals have paid clergymen, school counselors, and other 'bounty hunters' for referrals, while using hard-sell advertising tactics to attract new patients. His book includes numerous horror stories, including that of one 13-year-old boy whose insurance paid for 41 group therapy sessions in one day. Curiously, Sharkey does not even mention multiple personality disorder, ritual abuse, or repressed memories.

'Dr. Peterson is so sincere and genuine, also strong-willed and dedicated,' Steck told me. 'When she first met me, she shook my hand and looked into my eyes. I saw the most caring, genuine person I've ever met. She kept holding my hand and said she'd always be there for me, no matter what I said.' Peterson confirmed that Steck was not only an MPD, but a *special* kind. While in the dissociative disorders unit, Steck voluntarily entered restraints during abreactive sessions. 'I have violent seizures from remembering electroshock, and I have violent alters programmed to kill whoever is hearing this. That's why they put me in restraints. Otherwise, I would try to hurt myself or Dr. Peterson.'

Steck calls Peterson her 'savior' and insists that she has 'always given me the freedom to choose my own path.' The therapist often asks her, 'Okay, do you want to go back to the cult, or do you want to work? If you're not going to talk, why should I bother to work with you?' Steck calls Peterson 'tough but caring,' and says that the therapist has never really pressured her. 'She gives people a choice of what to believe. She never says, "I believe that's what happened." She says, "It's up to you to figure out what happened."'

When Steck's insurance had almost run out, Bennett Braun flew in from Rush Presbyterian in Chicago to evaluate her. Braun's 500-page report, which discussed her abuse and suicide attempts in detail, allowed the doctors to declare Steck a 'catastrophic case,' so that a special rider on her insurance kicked in to continue to pay for treatment. Later, Richard Loewenstein came from Sheppard Pratt to confirm the diagnosis.

Now, Christy Steck sees Judith Peterson two or three times a week. 'I'm doing better than I ever have in my whole life,' she told me. 'But I can't be left alone yet. I can't really work, but I clean a couple of houses for people I know well. They stay there while I work. It's just a matter of working through this programming to where I'm not accessible to the cult. The more I see that I've been programmed and brainwashed, the more I can work with it. If I don't see it, I won't get well.' She predicts that she will need another four years of 'intensive therapy,' after which she will probably need a weekly check-up. 'I hope some day I'll be integrated.'[80]

Finally, I interviewed Judith Peterson, and I came to understand how all three of her patients are probably telling the truth. Peterson denies McDonald's accusations. 'The lady spelled her own name correctly;

almost everything else in that article is a lie,' she told me.* She denies that any phone calls were monitored, that patients were held against their will, that they were kept until their insurance ran out. She points out that McDonald never worked on the dissociative disorders unit, but only on the adolescent unit.[81]

As for the preadolescent girl who concerned McDonald so much, Peterson asserts that she was a 'very acute' case of MPD who tried to crash through a plate glass door in order to escape, and who repeatedly attacked Peterson, once with the broken shards of a compact mirror. 'Not infrequently, I've been knocked across the room by violent alters,' she told me. Yes, some patients had to be restricted to the central lobby near the nursing station, so they could be watched, but that was only to keep them from hurting themselves or others.

Peterson says that she no longer uses the term 'abreactive sessions,' preferring to speak of 'memory processing.' Before each session, she asks patients to write down their new memories, which may have come through flashbacks, journaling, artwork, dreams, or body memories. Then, after placing them in a 'light hypnotic state,' she encourages them to go through each memory to 'deal with the feelings' and perform 'cognitive restructuring.'** These sessions clearly get quite intense, with patients purportedly reliving torture and electric shock treatment. 'They have pseudo-grand mal seizures,' Peterson told me.

She is no longer so sure that her patients were actually involved in satanic ritual abuse cults. Rather, the ritual abuse may have been used 'as a screen and creator of terror. Underneath it, in terms of complex alter layers, is organized crime.' In other words, she believes that criminal gangs intentionally terrified her patients, often making them mistakenly *believe* that murders had taken place. 'They have ways of tricking

---

* When I told her that Peterson said she had lied, Sally McDonald laughed. 'I was really careful that anything I wrote was the absolute truth and could be verified. There was much, much more that was deleted. What you read was a watered down version.' She told me of an abreactive session during which Peterson asked a child questions, and one of Peterson's associates answered for her. The child never said a word. At the end, Peterson praised the child, saying 'You really worked well this session.' Asked why the patient had not answered for herself, Peterson allegedly said, 'Her alters were mute.' Another anonymous nurse told me that until a Texas 'patients' rights' bill was passed in 1992, dissociative disorder patients could not use the phone, receive mail, or see their families at all. 'They were not allowed off the unit. They lived totally in a closed society, dependent on the whim of the therapist and the M.D. overseeing the unit.'

** For a full written description, see Sachs and Peterson, *Processing Memories Retrieved by Trauma Victims and Survivors: A Primer for Therapists* (1994).

people; they're given drugs, and they're terrified and confused.' The crime groups do this in order to produce 'synthetic alters' who will act in pornographic films or become prostitutes. Other patients, she thinks, were thus treated by the Ku Klux Klan.

Of course, Peterson cannot tell for sure whether these memories are accurate. 'My patients tell me very bizarre stories.' She simply listens. 'I'm a guide, asking "What happened next?" I don't lead them.' Yes, she has heard stories of murdered babies. 'It doesn't particularly matter if it's true or not. I wasn't there. The dilemma of true or not true is up to them.' Of one thing she is certain, though: 'These people don't make up the terror; that's pretty hard to do. They also don't make up the electric shocks. They have body memories of them.' That accounts for the pseudo-seizures.

Judith Peterson, now 48, seems genuinely outraged that her integrity has been impugned. She has always considered herself an altruistic, idealistic person trying to help the world. She began her career working with migrant workers and Head Start children and parents. She considered going into the Peace Corps. She has only tried to help those who come to her 'depressed, anxious, overwhelmed.' In her workshops, she says, she even warns against the dangers of telling patients during an initial session that they must have been sexually abused. 'Yet here I am so viciously attacked,' she laments. She explains her former patients' dissatisfaction by referring to their mental condition. 'Basically, these patients are sociopathic. They have their own reasons for targeting me,' she says darkly.

Peterson sent me a revealing article she recently published in *Treating Abuse Today*, in which she compares her plight with that of her abused patients, coping with 'existential crises at a depth I never thought imaginable.' She complains, 'Those I tried to help sadistically turned on the very person who reached out to help.' This article eloquently expresses Peterson's experiences and beliefs:

> I've spent timeless moments, hours, days and years listening to those with souls that were shattered. I moved from being a therapist who thought incest was the worst thing imaginable, to hearing of abuses so unimaginable that I walked out of therapy sessions stunned . . . Sometimes I would just cry over the range and extent of human cruelty. There are no words to express what I have felt as I have heard people describe everything from having a broom handle stuffed up their anus to having their teeth electrically

shocked. I have listened to a mother describe how she tied her small child to the bars of a crib before putting something in every orifice of the body – a rag already in the mouth to prevent screaming. I've listened to descriptions of electroshock on a baby and the baby's seizures.[82]

Despite Peterson's willingness to share the pain of mothers' 'horror of damaging those they love,' however, some of these same mothers have now turned on her. 'The shame and guilt were then transferred to me, the therapist. Kill the messenger. Lie. This client relived the trauma by victimizing me. Suddenly, the therapist is the victim.'[83]

Peterson is stung by allegations that she separates families and encourages Child Protective Services (CPS) to take her patients' children away. 'I've found something new in our field,' she told me. 'There's a high degree of mothers who have perpetrated their children.' When she discovers this during therapy sessions, she is mandated by law to inform social services. 'It's almost impossible to persuade CPS to let children stay with their families under such circumstances. The CPS people are, unfortunately, mostly incompetent and overworked.'

I came away from my interview with Judith Peterson thinking that she was intelligent, assertive and quite possibly insane. She does not think that she is leading her patients. She completely believes that they are inhabited by violent, dangerous internal personalities, that they are a danger to themselves and their families, and that she is striving to heal the wounds of terrible past trauma. She cannot admit the possibility that the terror they are experiencing might be an artifact of her therapy rather than symptoms of past abuse.

The stories about Judith Peterson told in these pages only skim the surface. As more of her clients begin to speak publicly, the incredible paranoia she inspired – and the destruction of families – becomes clearer. In 1995, Houston journalist Bonnie Gangelhoff wrote a devastating article on Peterson called 'Devilish Diagnosis.' One former Peterson client told Gangelhoff, 'Every day was total chaos ... You could be talking to someone and suddenly they would switch personalities. I started doing it, too. It all started to seem so normal.' The husband of a former client revealed that Peterson told him that 'people could control my wife by transmitting sequences of phone tones to her over the telephone.' Peterson herself wrote to the Texas licensing board, complaining that 'an alter was programmed to knife me in my office.'[84]

DISSOCIATION AND THE ABSENT-MINDED PROFESSOR

While most therapists tell their clients that they hold *repressed* memories, MPD specialists rely on the subtler notion of *dissociation*. The concept of dissociation was invented by Pierre Janet, who, in his old age, warned: 'Beware, it is only an idea that I express. It is an hypothesis for your research.'[85] Yet precious little controlled scientific research has followed. Recently, psychiatrist Fred Frankel objected to the broad, indiscriminate use of the term 'dissociation,' complaining of the 'large number of vague concepts' it appears to cover, and comparing it to the all-inclusive 'hysteria' of the last century.[86]

According to one definition of dissociation, it is 'a psychophysiological process whereby information – incoming, stored, or outgoing – is actively deflected from integration with its usual or expected associations.'[87] That's a windy way of explaining the process of daydreaming, spacing out, and losing track of normal consciousness.

If that's what dissociation is, most of us experience it at times. 'Highway hypnosis' is one widespread type of dissociation, in which a driver on a familiar stretch of road or an interstate suddenly snaps to, arriving at a destination or landmark without remembering the drive at all. This is the sort of 'lost time' experience that MPDs are supposed to experience frequently. There's no question that the phenomenon exists. I have even been able to time it. I often listen to books-on-tape while taking long trips. My thoughts sometimes drift onto other matters, and I suddenly realize that I've been listening without hearing. I can rewind the tape and find the exact point where my mind took off.

But is it necessary to use this concept of 'dissociation,' with its assumption of a solitary, normal mind from which something splits? I don't think so. We can often think consciously about several things at once, but there is a limit. When we concentrate on one particular strand of thought, we aren't necessarily splitting *from* anything. We are simply *paying more attention* to one thing than the other. Rather than dissociation, I would coin the term 'kaleidoscope thinking.' In our constantly churning minds, different thoughts roll into view, coalesce, then disappear. Some of us are better than others at blocking out everything except what we're thinking about. That's the very definition of the absent-minded professor.

While taking a morning shower, I sometimes become so preoccupied with planning my day that I forget whether I already shampooed or not. I'm sure that I've washed my hair twice plenty of times. But it isn't this normal type of dissociation that concerns trauma therapists. Rather, it is what they believe to be a capacity to 'space out,' to numb our feelings, to enter a self-induced trance state, to split off one portion of the mind from another in order to endure otherwise unendurable abuse. Again, there is experiential validation for this phenomenon on a limited basis. We *do* tend to go numb or experience a feeling of unreality when we are threatened, frightened, or wounded. In extreme cases, people sometimes go into physical and psychological shock. They wander aimlessly in a 'fugue state' and sometimes present themselves as having amnesia immediately afterward.

As I mentioned in Chapter 2, some authorities question whether true psychological amnesia actually exists. But in any event, there is *no* scientific proof of massive 'dissociation' in the sense that it is used by some trauma therapists.[88] It is a hypothesis that has been taken for granted, but, as with repression, we are left in the realm of *belief* rather than *proof.*

Certainly, people have the capacity to 'take their minds away' from a horrible event, but that does not mean that they can 'dissociate' memory of the event completely. As a child, I hated and dreaded having my teeth drilled on. My dentist must have known something about the value of dissociation, since he had mounted a blown-up color photo of a bucolic summer lakeside scene on the wall. I would concentrate on that picture, placing myself beneath a particular tree by the lake, taking myself away from the pain in my tooth. But I was always perfectly aware that the dentist was at work, and I never stumbled out of his office wondering where I had been.

Similarly, if a father is raping his daughter, she might very well concentrate on a crack in the ceiling, numb her feelings, or try to think about her favorite cartoon. It might help her to endure the event. She might even separate her role as victim from the rest of her self-image. But she would not forget what was happening. And it seems far-fetched to assume that she would invent a cast of internal personalities that rival a Tolstoy novel in their complexity.

How, then, can we account for the fact that many people truly *experience* multiple personalities? In a sense, we are all MPDs. Each of us acts different roles every day, assuming radically different personalities as we do so. With a boss, we are the employee – outwardly respectful, perhaps, but sometimes frustrated. With a spouse, we might be romantic one moment, the exasperated mate the next. With a child, we may be a nurturing or frustrated authority figure. 'A person might see herself or himself as *authoritative* in the role of employer, *submissive* in the role of daughter or son, *companionable* in the role of wife or husband,' writes psychologist Peter Gray.[89] Through it all, each of us maintains a unique sense of identity, but that is often simply a social construct, an illusion.

At times of crisis in our lives, many of us become uncertain of ourselves and our identities. 'There are unavoidable transitions in any life in which the content of selfhood is in flux,' writes anthropologist Michael Kenny, such as 'becoming an adult, finding a place in the world, marriage, having children, facing death.'[90] Most societies offer formal rites of passage to ease these transitions, but in modern America, our roles and identities are more amorphous, and the transitions are more difficult. We suffer 'identity crises' during which we are much more vulnerable to manipulation because we don't really know who we are, and we desperately desire a firm identity, an explanation for our predicament. It is just at such a crucial crossroad that the therapist comes along with his MPD diagnosis, calling out 'parts' of us and labeling them.

Rather than helping a person to develop a better self-concept, the MPD specialist does the opposite. There can be no 'self'-esteem without a unitary self. These therapists encourage – indeed, command – their patients to shatter psychically. 'When the organization of the self-concept is threatened,' one psychologist wrote in 1973, 'the individual experiences anxiety, and attempts to defend himself against the threat. If the defense is unsuccessful, stress mounts and is followed ultimately by total disorganization.'[91]

GRADE FIVES, TEMPORAL LOBE SPIKES, AND PERSONALITY

Because of media saturation, the MPD role is as well known today as the demoniac's behavior was in 1600. 'People can learn the components of the multiple personality role from a variety of quite different sources (e.g., movies, books, gossip),' Nicholas Spanos noted in 1986.[92] Since then, the MPD myth has spread even more widely. By 1991, MPD specialist Richard Kluft could write that 'many MPD patients have informed themselves about their condition from the broadcast media and lay and professional literature.' He added that a 'significant minority' are such voracious readers and researchers that they develop a 'broader knowledge base' than their therapists![93]

Not only that, but the role has become more attractive with time. Those who harbor a hundred or more alters now object to their malady being termed a *disorder*. Rather, it is a distinction, or a miracle. While MPD may have commenced because of overwhelming trauma, it has released entertaining alters to cope with it. They are interesting, creative personae who allow the MPD Survivor to use the royal 'we' and to take part in endless internal dramas. 'I can't imagine being a singleton,' one MPD Survivor told me. 'How boring that would be!'*[94]

She must have read *When Rabbit Howls* (1987), written 'by The Troops for Trudi Chase.' Chase, a commercial artist, real estate agent and sometime legal secretary in her 40s, 'went to sleep' at the age of two, when her stepfather allegedly raped her. The 'Troops' are her 92 alters, including such personalities as Rabbit, Miss Wonderful, Elvira, Lamb Chop, Ean, Mean Joe Green, Sister Mary Catherine, Nails, the Zombie, and the Interpreter.**[95] Of course, Chase was completely unaware of this menagerie until she entered therapy with Robert A. Phillips, Jr., a Ph.D. clinical psychologist who wrote the introduction and epilogue to her book. Before discovering her multiplicity, Chase 'had tried unsuccessfully to discover a medical reason for her temper tantrums, periodic blackouts, and a feeling of continual "dizziness,"' Phillips reveals. By book's end, the Troops and Dr. Phillips come to a mutual decision to 'maintain multiplicity.' As a result, 'communication among the Troop members has been enhanced, and there is evidence of increased ability to cooperate and work together.'[96]

The MPD role tends to attract extremely creative, suggestible clients with a craving for attention. Most are highly hypnotizable, among the 10 per cent of the population psychiatrist Herbert Spiegel has called 'Grade Fives,' on a scale from one to four. These Fives have an uncanny ability to sense what behavior may intrigue a therapist, and they fulfill all

---

* As I pointed out in Chapter 1, those who believe they have multiple personalities have found all kinds of creative outlets through print, paint, or song. Multiples produce their own newsletter and have even written an anthology called *Multiple Personality Disorder from the Inside Out* (1991), in which alters take turn addressing the reader. 'It's Gregory writing this for everybody inside,' a typical entry by Cindy B. commences. But then Gregory is interrupted. 'Somebody else inside wants to add that it is very confusing and scary being a multiple . . .'

** Some multiples now claim to house *hundreds* of alters, but that's nothing compared to a 16-year-old girl who, in 1583, was found to contain 12,652 living demons.

174

expectations. That does not mean that they are easy patients, however. Rather, they must up the ante in order to maintain dramatic attention. As soon as one alter appears to be integrated, another will pop out. Then, just when a whole system seems to be settled, another whole layer is uncovered, and more alters pour forth from the mental shrubbery.

Consequently, MPD patients rarely get better. They enter a cycle of extended abreaction and misery which sometimes ends in suicide. This may seem a paradox. Didn't I just say that patients revel in the attention? And isn't this all just role-playing? Yes and no.

Take the example of Canadian Roma Hart, who, feeling over-stressed in 1986, went to apply for unemployment insurance. She needed a psychiatrist to sign the requisite form and went to see Dr. Colin Ross, who promptly diagnosed her as having multiple personalities. Hart, whose background included extensive theatrical experience, decided to go along with it so that she could get her unemployment checks. 'If I became bored, I would pretend to switch personalities just for the hell of it. No one could put any demands on me any more and sympathy was just a phone call away.'[97]

But an odd thing happened. Roma Hart began to believe her own play-acting. She became completely dependent on Dr. Ross, who put her on large doses of mind-altering drugs such as Halcyon. She attempted suicide. She wound up in a locked hospital unit. When she got out, she joined an MPD support group, where Dr. Ross told them all how special they were. 'We were more creative, more sensitive, and better able to adjust in difficult situations,' Hart recalls. 'Being diagnosed as an MPD was practically an honor!'

In the groups, a strange competition commenced. 'One thing I can tell you about MPD patients,' Hart writes, 'is that they're competitive. If one recalls an animal personality, then the rest soon will. If one recalls a baby personality, then you better order a case of baby food.'

Eventually, by the summer of 1991, Roma Hart's life had become so chaotic that she left Colin Ross, who informed her that she had 'failed therapy,' that she would never make it. There's much reason for hope that Hart *will* make it, but her life continues to be a struggle. Even though she knows intellectually that all her satanic abuse memories were false, she cannot completely shake them. 'My parents came for my one-year-old's birthday,' she told me late in 1995, 'and that night I had nightmares about them being in a cult and trying to hurt my baby. I woke up and thought, "Maybe it was true. Maybe I'm just in denial." But of course I know it isn't.' Hart is currently suing Colin Ross.

In the case of Roma Hart – and many other MPD patients – role-playing becomes reality, and the attention-seeking lurches into self-destructive behavior. The syndrome is no longer a game, and the wounded players, expert dramatists, enact tragic parts. I recently heard the story of a Latin American soap opera star who became so absorbed in his role that, in real life, he murdered the actress who had jilted him on TV. The same sort of thing happens with MPD Survivors, for whom the acting becomes reality; only in their case, the violence is usually directed at themselves.

Exactly what are the characteristics Spiegel identified in his Grade Fives? Curiously, there is a physical symptom, the 'high eye-roll' in which someone can look up so far that only the whites of the eyes are showing.*[98] Spiegel also claims that Grade Fives exhibit 'readiness to trust; a relative suspension of critical judgment; an ease of affiliation with new experiences; a telescoped time sense; an easy acceptance of logical incongruities.' He thinks that they possess a capacity for intense concentration, 'overall tractability [and] role-confusion, [with] a subtle sense of inferiority.'[99] In other words, they are the perfect subjects to become multiple personalities.

Spiegel isn't sure how to account for the high eye-roll.**[100] 'Our best hypothesis to date is that the reticular activating system is like a switchboard that coordinates the deep part of the brain with upper and lower parts. Some people are wired in a tight way, others in a loose way, and the majority in between. Those with loose wiring have high eye rolls. If you think about it, it makes sense. The eyes are really a direct extension of the brain.'[101]

---

* In their 1978 book, *Trance and Treatment*, Herbert and David Spiegel carefully described how to observe this mysterious indication of hypnotizability. 'Accurately rating eye-roll signs takes a great deal of practice,' they wrote. 'You may not feel confident in judging them until you have seen fifty to a hundred.' In a recent interview, Herbert Spiegel told me, 'You develop a greater ability to observe it once you know what you're looking for.' In other words, this 'sign' calls for the same sort of attention to 'subtle' details that MPD specialists are fond of talking about. As a consequence, some skepticism about the high eye-roll may be in order. On the other hand, as Richard Webster points out in his 1995 book, *Why Freud Was Wrong*, an upward gaze has been associated with trance phenomenon since the 19th century.

** No one really knows how the 'reticular activating system' works. As a 1990 science encyclopedia explains, the reticulum is a mass of fibers ascending from the brain stem and branching into every part of the brain. It appears to modulate 'sleep, wakefulness, attention, and other aspects of consciousness, as well as effects on muscular coordination, vascular tone, [and] blood pressure.' The system is a 'fascinating regulatory mechanism, at present only dimly perceived.'

It is possible, though quite hypothetical at this point, that abnormally high electrical activity in the temporal lobe of the brain may have something to do with the high eye-roll as well as the Grade Five syndrome. Experimental psychologist Michael Persinger has published an intriguing series of papers on temporal lobe EEGs (electroencephalographs). He believes that there is a continuum of temporal lobe activity within the population, ranging from very low to those diagnosed as having temporal lobe epilepsy. Regardless of whether they experience real seizures, those with high electrical activity display an interesting set of phenomena, according to Persinger: 'visual hallucinations, the sense of a presence, mystical (paranormal) experiences, unusual smells, anomalous voices or sounds, vestibular movements, and anxiety.' Over time, such people often display 'stereotyped thinking, a sense of personal destiny or uniqueness, elaborate delusions, and excessive interests in religious or philosophical topics.' Persinger's studies indicate that about a third of the population displays 'temporal lobe signs.'[102] Because nearly 10 per cent of the population experiences a seizure at least once, these findings aren't surprising.[103]

Some authors, including Persinger himself, have concluded that abnormal temporal lobe activity is responsible for many mystical experiences.[104] While these experiences can produce a feeling of euphoria and unity with the universe, however, they can also result in intense anxiety, terror, and delusions.*[105] All of this takes us back to Wilder Penfield's surgical probing of the temporal lobe. The 'memories' he elicited from his patients were, as we have seen in Chapter 2, probably hallucinations, but the implication of the temporal lobe is nevertheless intriguing. During my research for this book, I ran into several cases in which the accusing offspring had been diagnosed with temporal lobe epilepsy. Similarly, Frank Putnam reports 'a higher-than-expected apparent incidence of abnormal EEG findings in MPD patients ... and [a]

---

* More recently, Persinger has conducted experiments that he believes indicate that women are biologically more prone to elevated temporal lobe activity than men, which he thinks may explain why more women than men recover illusory memories of abuse. His experiment consisted of putting modified motorcycle helmets on subjects wearing opaque goggles inside an acoustic chamber, while a magnetic field pulsed through their brains. His 'working assumption' for the experiments was that this amplified 'internal neuro-electrical noise,' or thoughts. More women reported 'fear or phobic experiences' in these circumstances. I question whether these results indicate much about temporal lobe activity *or* innate gender differences. Rather, they may indicate that women are more fearful in our society, for good reasons.

disproportionately high number of case reports of MPD and concurrent epilepsy.'[106]

Case reports of temporal lobe epileptics often bear a striking resemblance to those of repressed memory incest survivors:

> TF, a 29-year-old married woman, presented with a chief complaint of uncontrollable depression for which she could see no precipitating event. Her symptoms included difficulty falling asleep . . . nightmares . . . loss of weight, extreme tenseness, anxiety, and occasional panic attacks. She alternated between global hyposexuality [no interest in sex] and driven promiscuous hypersexuality.[107]

This patient, as well as many others, responded well to carbamazephine (Tegretol), the current drug of choice for temporal-lobe epileptics.

Epileptic researcher David Bear has suggested that a cluster of 18 personality traits identifies temporal lobe epileptics (TLEs); his findings have been replicated by several other researchers.*[108] Among other things, Bear believes that TLEs are frequently irritable, angry, aggressive, depressed, and paranoid, with sudden mood shifts. They are singularly humorless and often believe they have profound personal destinies. They tend to be dependent and 'clingy' upon figures of authority. They often feel compelled to write long autobiographical passages. In addition, they commonly complain of 'amnestic gaps' before, during, or after seizures, along with other subtler memory disturbances. Their sex drives are often impaired, but sometimes they become oversexed instead. They sometimes experience 'conflict regarding sexual preference.' Just before TLE seizures, they routinely get feelings of *déjà vu*, smell something odd, and sense impending doom.[109]

There are, however, positive sides to high temporal lobe electrical activity, including creativity and charisma. An impressive array of famous historical figures were supposedly epileptics of one sort or another, including Alexander the Great, Lord Byron, Buddha, Julius Caesar, Dante, Charles Dickens, Feodor Dostoyevsky, Mohammed, Napoleon Bonaparte, Isaac Newton, Blaise Pascal, Pythagoras, Socrates, St. Paul, Ludwig van Beethoven, and Vincent van Gogh.[110]

---

* Bear's concept of an 'epileptic personality' is still controversial, primarily because epileptics have been socially stigmatized for centuries. Some researchers want to 'protect' patients from further prejudice by minimizing the relationship between epilepsy and behavior.

In some cases of supposed multiple personality, it seems painfully evident that the eager clinician has misdiagnosed a client with real physical ailments. One clinical psychologist, for instance, recently wrote of a 47-year-old Vietnam veteran who entered his office leaning on a cane. 'He had a history of seizure disorders, right hemiparesis, right hemisensory loss, and right visual field defect arising from a suspected arterial venous malformation in the basal ganglia region of his brain.' Further, the patient's memory was impaired due to a 'closed head injury from ten years previously' and a subsequent fall off a ladder. Despite these clear organic problems, the psychologist proceeded to 'discover' various alter personalities and hidden traumas to explain his memory gaps. 'Later in therapy, it became clear that he had suffered early childhood sexual, physical, and psychological abuse by his father and siblings. He was repeatedly tortured, thrown out of a second floor window, sodomized, and used as an object for sadistic gratification.'[111]

Such cases are disturbing, but not the norm. Because I am fascinated by the possibility of some physiological explanation for those who most readily retrieve repressed memories and play the MPD role, I have dwelt at some length on possible organic problems, particularly temporal lobe EEGs, which may or may not have anything to do with recovered memories. I want to emphasize, however, that *I do not think people have to be 'Grade Fives' or exhibit high temporal lobe activity in order to be convinced that they are incest survivors or harbor multiple personalities. Such beliefs can be instilled in anyone, given the right circumstances and mindset.*

SATAN'S MINIONS

An astonishing number of repressed memories involve some form of group ritual abuse, usually with an explicitly satanic component.*[112] A high percentage of such ritual survivors believe that they split off internal alters as a result of this dreadful experience.

---

* *The Courage to Heal* offers a short course in ritual abuse memory, using 'Annette' as a role model. 'From infancy, Annette was abused in rituals that included sexual abuse, torture, murder, pornography, and systematic brainwashing through drugs and electric shock.' Of course, she forgot all of this until she was 48. 'I was what they called a "breeder,"' Annette explains. 'I was less than twelve years old. They overpowered me and got me pregnant and then they took my babies. They killed them right in front of me.'

The events usually unfold as follows. First, a young woman enters therapy for depression or some other complaint. Her therapist encourages her to see her family as dysfunctional, and herself as the victim of 'emotional incest.' Soon, she reads self-help recovery books and retrieves memories of physical incest by one family member. Then, as her memories flow more easily, she names other perpetrators. Finally, she recalls ritual abuse, is diagnosed with MPD, and often winds up heavily drugged and suicidal in a psychiatric ward.

Other writers have already convincingly demolished the notion that such cults actually exist,*[113] although nothing will ever sway those with an invested belief in them. People who can believe that a child's heart was surgically removed and replaced with an animal's ticker during ritual abuse, and who refuse to accept physical evidence disproving such an event, are not likely to accept logical arguments either.[114]

After years spent trying to track down such cases, FBI investigator Kenneth Lanning concluded that 'there is little or no evidence [for] large-scale baby breeding, human sacrifice, and organized satanic conspiracies. Now it is up to mental health professionals, not law enforcement, to explain why victims are alleging things that don't seem to have happened.'[115] At least five well-researched books** have already been published on this 'contemporary legend,' and they have all reached the same conclusion: this is a hoax, a fraud, a paranoid delusion fomented by the media, credulous therapists, distraught patients, pressured preschoolers, fearful parents, and over-excited policemen.

Two major studies – one American, one British – came to the same conclusion in 1994. Funded with $750,000 by the U.S. government, Gail Goodman and her team examined thousands of purported cases of satanic ritual abuse and failed to find any evidence for stereotypical multi-generational cults that sexually abuse children. All

---

* There are three types of 'satanic' or ritual activities that actually do exist: (1) Harmless organized religions led by flamboyant characters such as Anton La Vey, the former circus musician who heads the Church of Satan. (2) Teenagers and others who, as part of societal rebellion, dabble in the occult, draw pentagrams, and perhaps sacrifice a stray cat. (3) Aberrant psychopaths such as the Matamoros murderers, who act out the myths they read about or see in movies. Folklorists call this copy-cat process 'legend ostension.' Given the seemingly limitless human capacity for evil, it is not surprising that someone would act out an evil myth.

** The books are: *Satan Wants You*, by Arthur Lyons (1988); *In Pursuit of Satan*, by Robert D. Hicks (1991); *The Satanism Scare* edited by James T. Richardson (1991); *Satanic Panic* by Jeffrey Victor (1993), *Satan's Silence*, by Debbie Nathan and Michael Snedeker (1995).

they found were 'a few "borderline" cases, typically involving a lone individual or two people whose abuse of children involved satanic themes.'*[116]

A similar study conducted by Jean La Fontaine in Great Britain took a close look at over 200 claims of satanic ritual abuse. Again, no evidence emerged to support the notion of widespread intergenerational sex abuse cults. La Fontaine found only three cases with any firm evidence. 'The three substantiated cases are not instances of Satanism or witchcraft,' she concluded. 'They are also significantly different from the other cases in the study. They show a single perpetrator of abuse claiming spiritual powers.' She explained the mythical ritual abuse cases as a sociological phenomenon. 'A belief in evil cults is convincing because it draws on powerful cultural axioms.'[117]

Why do so many well-trained therapists believe in satanic cults? They will tell you that their clients couldn't make up these gory details or display such terror if the stories weren't true. They will say that their clients knew nothing about ritual abuse, yet they came up with the same breeding strategies, sacrificed babies, blood-letting, rape, and murder that others across the country – around the world – have reported. Witch-hunters in 1670 made much the same observation, citing 'so much agreement and conformity between the different cases' as proof of witchcraft.[118] Of course, that's the way folklore legends work, as sociologist Jeffrey Victor has masterfully documented in his book, *Satanic Panic*. The stories float on the airwaves and bubble in the rumor mills. Just as someone transported back to a past life doesn't remember where she originally learned about a particular epoch, many ritual abuse survivors honestly believe that they never saw a movie, read a book, listened to a talk show, or overheard a conversation that provided the details they bring forth in a hypnotic session.

Even if they never *did* see such a movie or hear a talk show, the therapists can cue them inadvertently, particularly using the 'ideomotor method' in which a hypnotized subject merely raises a finger to indicate

---

* Far more disturbing were the cases of 'religion-related abuse' documented in the Goodman study. 'My client was a 14-year-old boy whose eyeball had been plucked out of his head in an exorcism ceremony,' one therapist wrote. 'The father performed an exorcism on his children by dismembering and then boiling them. Evidence? The children were dead,' wrote another. One mother who thought her 12-year-old boy was possessed by the devil first had sex with him, then decapitated him. Goodman's conclusion seems rather mild under the circumstances: 'Religious beliefs can at times foster, encourage, and justify abusive behavior.'

a positive response to a leading question. 'Familiarize yourself with signals and symptoms of ritualized abuse,' one psychologist advises in a handout. He goes on to explain that 'survivors of ritualized abuse *have many special needs*' and must be seen beyond the normal hour limit. 'If you are uncomfortable with the reality of ritual abuse, then you should not be treating survivors of ritual abuse,' he asserts.[119] Following this advice has a mutually reinforcing effect in which both patient and therapist feel *special*.

The moral panic*[120] over satanic cults has produced a curious partnership between some left-wing radical feminists and selected right-wing Christian fundamentalists. Members of both groups believe that there is an international conspiracy of sexual abusers who brutalize children, use them in violent child pornography, then murder and eat them. Cult members, they assure anyone who will listen, include the pillars of society – doctors, lawyers, bankers, policemen. The perpetrators are cunning beyond belief in hiding their revolting activities. To indoctrinate children, cult leaders routinely use electric shock, isolation in closets, mind-altering drugs, and starvation. In addition, according to a pamphlet from VOICES in Action, a Chicago-based Survivor group, brainwashing includes the 'Black Hole' experience, in which members are 'suspended head first into a dark deep pit, the pit containing human/animal parts, blood, rats, snakes, spiders, for up to 24 hours.' Sometimes a child is given a 're-birthing ritual' in which he or she is inserted into a cow's abdominal cavity for a while, then pulled out by the high priest.[121]

In 1988, Lauren Stratford published *Satan's Underground*, which continues to exert a wide influence, despite Stratford's story having been thoroughly discredited by journalists for the Christian publication, *Cornerstone*.**[122] In the book's foreword, Christian author Johanna

---

* In his classic 1972 book, *Folk Devils and Moral Panics*, sociologist Stanley Cohen defined the term 'moral panic' as a period in which a group or phenomenon is regarded as 'a threat to societal values and interests; its nature is presented in a stylized and stereotypical fashion by the mass media; the moral barricades are manned by editors, bishops, politicians and other right-thinking people; socially accredited experts pronounce their diagnoses and solutions.'
** 'Lauren Stratford' was in reality Laurel Willson, who, although she was clearly a very troubled individual, was apparently not a victim of satanic cults. The portrait that emerges from the meticulously researched *Cornerstone* article is of a sad, manipulative, attention-seeking individual. Similarly, in *Selling Satan* (1993), investigative reporters have demolished the story of Mike Warnke, who has claimed for years to have been a high priest in a satanic cult.

Michaelsen admitted that the story was 'beyond belief,' but explained 'that attitude is precisely what Satanists are counting on.' After all, 'it was only a few short years ago that we had a problem believing that incest was rampant.' Michaelsen was not dismayed by the complete lack of evidence of this widespread cult activity. 'If there is one thing that cult Satanists do well, it's cover their tracks.' Thus, she reasoned, 'animals are indeed killed and buried, but are later dug up and disposed elsewhere.' No satanic child pornography had surfaced because it is 'carefully kept in vaults of private collectors.' And so on. There's no question: 'Satanism is on the rise.'[123]

In the book itself, Stratford described how her sadistic mother allowed her to be raped by a group of tramps in the basement. That experience was just training for her teenage and young adult experience in a satanic cult dominated by the evil Victor. The cult members drank a brew of blood, wine, and urine and then gang-raped her. 'With each vulgar act, my will to resist lessened,' she wrote. Later, she witnessed many other terrible events. 'They ordered acts of sexual perversion that went far beyond the descriptions of lewd, perverse, and vile. They ordered the literal sacrifice of animals and even humans – both willing and unwilling victims.' She watched 'the ultimate sacrifice of a baby – skinned while still alive.'

In order to break her, the cult members put Stratford into a barrel and threw dead babies on top of her. Then she became Victor's personal mistress. Only when the cult tired of her and she had a nervous break-down does the reader learn, on page 120, that she had *entirely repressed all of these memories*, which came back with the help of guided imagery and Jesus. Eventually, she recalled how she had borne three children – Joey, Carly, and Lindy – all of whom were sacrificed to Satan. 'What happened to Joey is even now happening to babies, children, and teen-agers across the country,' Stratford wrote. 'Believe the unbelievable!' In the end, however, she was healed by meeting Johanna Michaelsen – the author of the book's foreword – who told her that while they were praying together, 'I saw Jesus standing with His nail-scarred hands outstretched toward you.'[124]

Great Britain had its equivalent to Lauren Stratford in the pseudony-mous 'Hannah,' whose real name was Caroline Marchant. Hannah com-mitted suicide, leaving a ritual abuse memoir that echoed much of Stratford's book. She claimed that she had been a 'brood mare' for a satanic cult, which she entered at the age of thirteen. In March of 1990, the *Sunday Mirror* reported her story as factual under the headline, 'I

Sacrificed My Babies to Satan: From Sex Orgy to Death at the Hands of the Devil's Disciples.' Although a detailed story in the *Independent* soon debunked the lurid tales, it entered British ritual abuse folklore, particularly among fundamentalist Christians.[125]

Modern rumors of satanic cults represent nothing new, but follow a long tradition in Western culture, as Norman Cohn meticulously documented in his 1975 book, *Europe's Inner Demons*. Beginning in the second century, early Christians were accused of 'holding meetings at which babies or small children were ritually slaughtered, and feasts at which the remains of these victims were ritually devoured; also of holding erotic orgies at which every form of intercourse, including incest between parents and children, was freely practiced; also of worshipping a strange divinity in the form of an animal.'[126]

The Christians outlived these defamations, only to use them on the Jews, who were supposed to have drunk Christian children's blood in their synagogues and carried on in other disgusting ways.[127] The Catholic hierarchy and various monarchs spread similar rumors about any splinter sects, such as the Waldensians and the Templars. Belief in organized satanic orgies flowered in the 16th and 17th centuries during the Great Witch Craze. Throughout the centuries, as Cohn described it, 'the essence of the fantasy was that there existed, somewhere in the midst of the great society, another society, small and clandestine, which not only threatened the existence of the great society but was also addicted to practices which were felt to be wholly abominable, in the literal sense of anti-human.' It was usually the intelligentsia who fomented these conspiracy theories and led the quest for satanic abusers.[128]

In our own time, that generalization holds true. Ph.D. clinical psychologists and psychiatrists – trained as physicians and then mind-healers – are the primary agents to spread authoritative stories of ritualistic abuse and conspiracy. Psychiatrist Bennett Braun explains that 'we are working with a national-international type organization that's got a structure somewhat similar to the communist cell structure.' He asserts that cult members are 'trained to self-destruct' if they remember too much.[129]

Corydon Hammond, the former president of the American Society for Clinical Hypnosis, is widely respected by his peers and has edited a scholarly 1990 volume entitled *Handbook of Hypnotic Suggestions and Metaphors*. 'Dr. Hammond is a master clinician of unusual breadth and talent who has become one of the giants in the field of clinical hypnosis,' wrote a colleague in that book's foreword.[130]* In recent years, Hammond has traveled throughout the United States, giving workshops on ritual abuse. He dismisses those who are 'such intellectualizers and skeptics that they'll doubt everything.' Alternatively, those casting doubt might be cult members themselves, he asserts. He describes 'very organized groups with interstate communication and who use a very, very systematic brainwashing.'

Hammond states that the cult members learned these brainwashing techniques from sadistic Nazi scientists secretly brought to this country by the CIA to conduct mind-control experiments. Drawing on a long tradition of anti-Semitic rumors, he also asserts that a Jewish teenager named Greenbaum learned the Nazi secrets and now, as a Dr. Green, is coaching cults in the United States. 'I know of cases,' Hammond asserts, 'where the Mafia likes to use cult people as hit people because they can have one personality who will come out and . . . perform a cult blood-cleaning and have no emotions about it, come back and everybody has amnesia for it.' To train children in strict obedience, the cults may apply electrodes to a little girl's head and inside her vagina. 'Perhaps a finger might be cut off and hung around their neck on a chain as a symbol to them they had better be obedient. They may be given drugs.'[131]

Psychiatrist Colin Ross, who wrote an influential 1989 textbook on MPD, agrees with Hammond. In fact, in his proposal for a book to be titled *CIA Mind Control*, Ross discloses that the U.S. Central Intelligence Agency has been turning children into Manchurian candidates since the 1940s.**[132] 'These individuals were systematically abused in laboratory

* In the *Handbook*, Hammond recommends asking hypnotized MPD clients to raise their fingers in response to the question, 'Is anyone inside afraid of . . . ?' His list includes words that are supposedly indicative of a ritual abuse background, including *stars*, *fire*, *knives*, *blood*, *being photographed*, *dying*, *candles*, *feces*, *animals being hurt*, *robes*, *a certain color*, *eating certain things*, *digging in the dirt*, *Halloween*, *the equinox*, and *people in a circle*.
** During the Cold War era of the 1950s and 1960s, the CIA did, in fact, experiment with hypnosis, Amytal, LSD and other mind-altering drugs in an attempt to create an unconscious killing machine or find a way to extract information from spies. As John Marks documented in his 1979 book, *The Search for the 'Manchurian Candidate': The CIA and Mind Control*, the unethical secret experiments were complete failures, characterized by 'bumbling and pure craziness.' Therapists such as Colin Ross and Corydon Hammond have taken bits and pieces from Marks' book (such as his discovery that the Nazis tried out similar unsuccessful experiments) and have recycled the myth of 'mind control.' *The Manchurian Candidate* was a popular 1959 book and 1962 film starring Frank Sinatra, popularizing the myth that someone could be 'programmed' to become a killing machine when properly 'triggered.'

and experimental settings,' he writes. They used 'drugs including halluc-inogens, sensory deprivation, flotation tanks, electric shock, enforced memorization and other techniques. The programming involved the deliberate creation of multiple personality disorder with specific letter, number and other access codes for contacting alter personalities.'[133] In 1993, Ross reiterated his claims to a television journalist, explaining that the 'political strategy' to counter his revelations was to assert that 'it's all created in therapy, it's fantasy, it's not real.'[134]

The paranoia over 'mind control' and satanic ritual abuse takes advantage of the modern fear of impersonal and seemingly all-powerful technology. Ever since the 1950s, when a con artist claimed that he could increase the consumption of popcorn and Coca-Cola by flashing 'subliminal messages' on a movie screen, Americans have believed that their minds could be controlled by nefarious authorities without their knowledge.[135] More recently, therapists such as E. Sue Blume have seized 'virtual reality' technology as an explanation of alien abduction memories. They were *really* just fooled by satanic cults, according to Blume:

> These groups often employ sophisticated and elaborate special effects and computer-generated 'virtual reality' to make people think that they have experienced things which have not really occurred. For example, a victim will 'remember' being abducted by aliens to their ships, where 'medical experiments' were performed.[136]

Despite the lack of any physical evidence that satanic cults exist, and many well-researched books debunking them, many therapists continue to tell stories about ritual abuse. An entire 1994 issue of the *Journal of Psychohistory* was devoted to the topic, with the overwhelming majority of the articles exhorting us to believe, believe. In this issue, one Albany, New York, psychiatrist explains how cult members 'injected blood from a chalice into all her [his patient's] orifices and raped her six times each. A mother cat and her kittens were shot with a pistol and were buried with my patient in a coffin-like box. She was then removed, thrown into a lake, cleaned up and brought home.'[137] And, of course, she remembered nothing about all this until she entered therapy.

Also in 1994, in England, Tavistock Clinic consultant psychotherapist Valerie Sinason edited *Treating Survivors of Satanist Abuse*, including accounts from 38 professionals, mostly British. As in the United States, belief in ritual abuse was spread through a network of 'experts,' most of whom belonged to RAINS, the Ritual Abuse Information and Network Support, founded in 1989 with five members. The hysteria over ritual abuse spread rapidly, particularly after three British books came out: *Dance With the Devil*, by Audrey Harper (1990), *Children for the Devil: Ritual Abuse, and Satanic Crime*, by Tim Tate (1991), and *Blasphemous Rumours*, by Andrew Boyd (1991). In February of 1992, Channel 4 aired *Beyond Belief*, a show featuring adult Survivors who had recovered ritual abuse memories, some through Christian 'deliverance ministry.' An 0800-number 'helpline' available after the show received 191 calls, with thousands more failing to get through. Clearly, by that time, many British men and women had recalled abuse memories or were concerned about them. By the summer of 1993, RAIN claimed 150 members, all professionals working with purported ritual abuse victims.[138]

In *Treating Survivors of Satanist Abuse*, RAIN founder and psychiatrist Joan Coleman related horrific recovered memory stories. 'One survivor described being left alone, naked and cold, at the age of 4,' she wrote, 'for three weeks in an underground room, while her mother went abroad. Her only company was the corpse of a woman she had seen killed.' Given water but no food (she was expected to dine on the cadaver), the little girl was 'finally taken out by her father, who then sodomized her.'[139]

In 'The Impact of Evil,' another chapter of the 1994 book, British consultant clinical psychologist Phil Mollon told the dreadful tales of two ritual abuse clients. During four years of therapy, Helen, a 40-year-old schoolteacher, recalled (among other things) witnessing a man's throat being slit, after which cult members drank his blood from a ceremonial bowl. Mollon's reaction to her stories was 'shock, disbelief, horror, dread and terror – including fear for my own safety.' He anticipated skeptics who might think the memories untrue. 'To counter such doubts, I can say that subsequent communications have provided a full and coherent picture of the ritual context of Helen's abuse.'

For five years, Mollon also saw Mary, an Irish divorcee, during which time she developed multiple personality disorder, discovering 'Hazel and her gang' within her, created to 'ensure that she did not remember or reveal secrets of her childhood.' Numerous traumatized child alters also wailed within. Hazel did not, of course, prevail. With Mollon's help, Mary recalled her father, dressed as Satan, raping her during a ritual abuse ceremony. As a 'last resort,' he suggested that she undergo a 'drug-assisted abreaction' (presumably a sodium Amytal session), during which Mary did indeed spill out more tales of abuse. 'Many further scenes of horror, macabre, obscene and criminal in the extreme, have since emerged,' the therapist informed his readers. Might not Mary be hallucinating? 'She does not feel to me to be paranoid,' Mollon noted. 'She comes across as a warm and caring person, coherent and rational.'

'Neither patient nor therapist want to believe what is being communicated,' Mollon emphasized. 'Both parties have to overcome their inner resistance in order to recover the lost experiences.' In closing, Mollon stressed that therapists must 'maintain an open mind about what is real and what is phantasy,' but it is quite clear where his beliefs lay. Besides, he wrote grandly, 'I would rather risk being deluded by my patients – rather risk appearing a fool – than risk abandoning the terrified traumatized child within.'[140]

Fortunately, the widespread search for MPD and ritual abuse in Great Britain appears to have been effectively stymied by early warnings from the media and the British False Memory Society. Phil Mollon, for instance, has backed off from his ritual abuse beliefs and, late in 1995, published a relatively reasonable article, along with a set of guidelines, on the hazards of recovered memory therapy.[141]

In the United States, however, specialists such as Bennett Braun, Corydon Hammond and Colin Ross have received enormous support from books, articles, and conferences where the myths of satanic cults are repeated and elaborated.*[142] In the final analysis, such therapists believe in the cults because they *want* to believe. The sessions in which menacing, evil alters appear provide the same thrill which exorcists experienced hundreds of years ago. It is challenging, exciting, frightening work – a far cry from the humdrum existence of the routine mental health professional who listens to a boring litany of drab complaints all day long. Yes, it's difficult work – dangerous, in fact, because the cult members may even try to assassinate the therapist. But for the intrepid mind explorer, savior of souls, healer of splintered selves, it is all worthwhile.

---

* It is impossible to exaggerate the level of paranoia exhibited by ritual abuse believers. At the end of 1992, for instance, members of the Los Angeles Ritual Abuse Task Force claimed that Satanists were poisoning them with a toxic pesticide pumped into their offices, homes, and cars. Catherine Gould, a clinical psychologist on the task force, told a reporter that the gas had given her blurred vision and faulty memory. Gould should go back and read a 1945 article in the *Journal of Abnormal and Social Psychology* entitled 'The "Phantom Anesthetist" of Mattoon: A Field Study of Mass Hysteria,' which reveals how citizens in Mattoon, Illinois, became convinced that a mad gasser was pumping a spray gun into their homes.

A WARNING FROM THIGPEN AND CLECKLEY

Ten years ago, when the great MPD hunt was just heating up, Corbett Thigpen and Hervey Cleckley, who started the ball rolling in 1957 with *The Three Faces of Eve*, saw what was coming and tried, in vain, to stop it. 'Over the last 25 years we have had sent to us hundreds of patients, many of whom were either referred to us by therapists who had already diagnosed them as having the disorder, or who came to us for treatment based upon their desire or belief that they had the illness.' Of these, they concluded that perhaps one was genuine. One woman phoned and 'went so far as to have each personality introduce itself and speak in a different voice,' while another changed her handwriting from one paragraph to the other.

'It seems that in very recent years,' the psychiatrists lamented, 'there has been even a further increase in the number of persons seeking to be diagnosed as multiple personalities – some patients move from therapist to therapist until "achieving" the diagnosis.' In addition, the psychiatrists noted 'a competition to see who can have the greatest number of alter personalities.' They objected to Billy Milligan's feigning MPD to get out of a rape conviction, adding that 'sexual child abuse . . . can hardly be used as the core criterion for diagnosing multiple personality disorder.'*[143] Finally, they concluded: 'Everyone changes nearly all the time, and extreme swings of behavior and feelings are hardly unique to multiple personality disorder.'[144]

---

* In 1977, police arrested 22-year-old Billy Milligan for multiple rape. The talented artist also turned out to be a marvelous actor and con artist who convinced a jury and author Daniel Keyes that he possessed wonderfully diverse alter personalities, including a diffident Brit and a sinister Slav. Luckily for Keyes, who wrote the best-selling *The Minds of Billy Milligan* (1981), Milligan magically 'fused' in order to tell him his story, which included allegations that his sodomizing stepfather buried him alive, leaving a pipe over the boy's face for air, into which the sadist then urinated.

A Note on the Interviews

I conducted the interviews that follow in Chapters 5–8, throughout the United States, Canada and England from 1992 to 1995, in person or by telephone. I found subjects through numerous means – by contacting organizations such as Survivors of Incest Anonymous, the False Memory Syndrome Foundation, or the British False Memory Society, by reading newspapers and watching television, by browsing through yellow pages in telephone books, and, quite often, by word-of-mouth, referral, or pure serendipity. Because the repressed-memory phenomenon has affected so many people in this country, it was not difficult to find a cross-section of stories.

I told people that I was writing a book about the repressed memory debate and that the heart of the book would consist of interviews with those on all sides of the issue. In every case except one, I sent the transcript to each interview subject for approval, change, or amendment. (In the single exception to that rule, the massage therapist specifically assured me that he did not need to see the interview.) I explained that I would use fictitious names unless they preferred using their real names, and that the interviews would be edited, but that they would feature verbatim voices and opinions.

To remove my questions from the transcripts, I sometimes had to paraphrase a sentence. For example, I might have asked, 'How did you feel about your parents before your memories came back?' In the printed interview, that becomes, 'How did I feel about my parents before I recovered my memories? Well, I knew I never felt loved . . .' Aside from such minor adjustments, all words here were spoken by the subjects. I cut extraneous background information, using it to write the italicized introductions. Since most conversations jumped from one idea or time reference to another, I also rearranged portions of the interviews to promote a smooth flow. These are standard journalistic techniques pioneered largely by Studs Terkel, whom I consider a mentor.

CHAPTER FIVE

The Therapists

> We are especially prone to make mistakes when dealing with a domain in which we are expert. Knowing a lot about the self and a little about the other person is a recipe for a radical misreading of personality ... This means that an expert is not open-minded about himself or about other people, and is less open-minded as the information available declines in quality.
>
> JEREMY CAMPBELL, *The Improbable Machine*[1]

INTERVIEWS IN THIS CHAPTER:

SAM HOLDEN, *Christian counselor*
PETER JONES, *physician/hypnotherapist*
JANET GRIFFIN, *M.S.W.*
HORACE STONE, *minister/counselor*
LESLIE WATKINS, *Ph.D., clinical psychologist*
DELIA WADSWORTH, *consultant psychiatrist*
JASON RANSOM, *body worker*
HAMISH PITCEATHLY, *primary cause analyst*
KATHERINE HYLANDER, *past-life hypnotherapist*
SALLY BIXBY, *psychotherapist*
ROBIN NEWSOME, *retractor therapist*

If I had met the following therapists at a party and the subject of repressed memories had never come up, I would have thought they were interesting, vital, caring people. And, in their own ways, they are. Yet all of them, except Sally Bixby and (now) Robin Newsome, are busily helping their clients unearth memories, most of which I believe are illusory. They repeat the same clichés that we've already encountered in Chapter 1, speaking with great assurance about repression, dissociation, inner children, body memories, and intergenerational abuse. They explain how they help their patients overcome the inevitable denial following their returned memories. They speak soothingly of safety and healing, while promoting what some would take for mental tortures.

The voices represented here are by no means unusual or extreme. I conducted many more interviews than those you will read here, some far more outrageous. These therapists are representative of those whose speciality is repressed-memory extraction. They attend the same continuing-education conferences, read the same books, consult with one another, and develop their own pet variations and theories. The vast majority of American and British therapists believe in the reality of repressed memories, as several recent surveys have demonstrated. A sizeable minority – perhaps 25 per cent – *specialize* in incest memory retrieval.[2] With few exceptions, those who doubt the validity of memory extraction techniques keep their opinions to themselves. Indeed, perhaps the most disturbing voice in this chapter belongs to Sally Bixby, who knows exactly what her colleagues are doing but is afraid to speak out. 'I'd be tarred, feathered, and ridden out of town on a rail,' she told me. 'If you can tell me how to make a living afterwards, I'll be glad to go on the record.'

Included here are a psychiatrist, Ph.D. psychologist, and a psychotherapist with a masters in social work, as well as those with little formal training, including a general-practitioner-turned-hypnotist, a 'primary cause' analyst, a body worker (massage therapist) and a past-life hypnotherapist. Generally speaking, one would expect that the less formal education, and the more 'far-out' the approach, the greater the danger of misdiagnosis. To a *very limited degree*, this may be true.

As a group, psychiatrists, indoctrinated in the much-maligned 'medical model,' appear to be the least eager to find hidden memories. As we will hear from a few retractors in Chapter 8, some psychiatrists literally saved their lives. On the other hand, because they can prescribe medicine and sign off on insurance forms, these psychiatrists often head large mental health clinics, where they sometimes lose touch with therapy administered by the social workers working under their nominal supervision. In addition, *many psychiatrists are directly implicated* in this disaster, as the interview with Delia Wadsworth indicates. Indeed, because MPD is considered a more exotic 'disease,' it appeals to some psychiatrists, who of course have medical training.

Doctoral-level clinical psychologists tend to be much worse, in large part because their training, over the last few decades, has only marginally stressed scientific research. Rather, they are encouraged to exercise their 'clinical intuition' to discover the subtle causes of their clients' symptoms. Steeped in neo-Freudian dogma, they are primed to uncover repressed memories.

The most zealous memory extractors, however, appear to be those with masters degrees or less. I interviewed a terrifying young man, for instance, who possessed only a bachelor's degree and a summer's experience at a recovery movement retreat center. He used automatic writing, visualization, and body work to help 70 per cent of his clients find memories of abuse. His command of the jargon was in no way inferior to that of the Ph.D.s. 'I'm very careful not to lead my patients even when I know unequivocally they are secret incest survivors. I don't plant memories. I let them figure it out.'

Essentially, the level of training does not seem to make that much difference. Much of the interview with Hamish Pitceathly, the British historian-turned-therapist who espouses the disturbing fringe therapy called 'primary cause analysis,' could as easily have come from the mouth of well-respected consultant psychiatrist Delia Wadsworth.

Even Katherine Hylander, the past life tour guide, spouts the familiar rhetoric. So does the older woman I interviewed who 'channels' Krishna and Jesus Christ through automatic writing – which reveals long-forgotten incest, of course. *Educational level does not really appear to make a substantial difference in this process.* What is vital for successful trauma therapists, regardless of any particular philosophy or approach, is the *expectation* that their clients will remember abuse (or, in the case of the channeler, that Krishna will prompt her to write about it).

In the past few years, more and more clients have brought that expectation into therapy with them, as Janet Griffin observes in her interview. They arrive *demanding* to retrieve memories, already having the *feeling* that they were molested as children. They've already seen *Oprah, Donahue*, and *Kilroy*, already read *The Courage to Heal*. With such well-primed repressed memory candidates, therapists can easily believe that they are not leading clients.

Most of the therapists I interviewed told me that a *few* of their colleagues were probably eliciting false memories, because they were pushing their patients far too hard. But they themselves *never* used suggestive or leading techniques, of course. They would tell me this just after revealing in detail how they led clients into such beliefs and then insisted upon their maintaining them.

It is remarkable how many therapists believe in ritual abuse, with its human sacrifice, blood, and multiple sadists. Most of the therapists interviewed here believe (or once believed) that satanic cults are thriving in their particular part of the world. The 'Christian' counselors appear to be among the worst offenders, which I find particularly distressing. When a parishioner approaches her pastor for counseling, she should not have to worry that he might try to convince her that her parents and their friends were monsters.

It has long been recognized that some psychotherapists enter their profession in order to heal their own neuroses, as Sam Holden's story demonstrates. Some therapists are clearly disturbed and engage in forms of sexual abuse themselves, as in the case of a London 'body therapist' who forced his client to lie on her back while he sat on top of her and suggested abuse memories.[3] Some trauma therapists were themselves incest victims who bring their own agendas to each session. More frequently, they have recovered their own 'repressed memories.'*[4] I believe it is a mistake, however, to emphasize the therapists-with-their-own-issues aspect of this phenomenon. Those quoted here do indeed have an agenda, but it isn't a particularly *personal* crusade. Rather, it is a dogma learned from books, tapes, fellow therapists, and seminars.

Nor is it my sense that female therapists elicit memories more frequently than their male peers. While women recover the majority of the incest memories, both genders participate in promoting the process. (More female therapists help clients recall repressed memories simply because more women than men currently become counselors.)**[5]

* An alarming 1994 survey of therapists indicated that 21.8 per cent remembered being sexually abused as children. Of those, *52.7 per cent reported having forgotten some or all of the abuse.* In other words, over half of them had recovered 'memories' of abuse themselves. In *The Healing Woman*, many of the testimonials are written by Survivors who are also therapists or psychics. I interviewed one staff member at an eating disorders facility who had originally gone there as a patient. While there, she recovered memories of incest during 'Survivors' Week.' Now she helps others retrieve *their* memories. Sometimes the procedure can work in the reverse direction, however. One psychiatrist tired of his MPD patient calling him at home every night, so he asked his teenage son to talk to her instead. After a year of such phone conversations, the son entered a mental hospital thinking that he, too, harbored multiple personalities.

** Increasingly, therapy is being taken over by women, who have always dominated social work. The M.S.W. is now the primary degree held by clinicians. In 1976, women constituted just over 31 per cent of all Ph.D. recipients in clinical psychology. By 1990, they made up over 58 per cent. 'Due to the feminization of psychotherapy,' Ilene Philipson observes in her 1993 book, *On the Shoulders of Women*, 'the experience of examining one's inner life by working with a caring and authoritative male therapist is becoming less common and may soon be anachronous. Men who ideally could serve as benign, caring, and attentive figures of authority – a role increasingly left vacant in families today – represent a small minority in most clinical training programs.'

Even though 'feminist' therapists have been accused of conducting a warlock hunt against fathers, it is obvious from these interviews that *mothers* are also on their hit lists – see Leslie Watkins' observations on mothers who try to drown their infants.

I was particularly disturbed by the tendency of most therapists to absolve themselves of any responsibility.* Almost all of them assert that it doesn't matter whether the memories are literally true or not. The memories represent the 'internal truth' for the client, and it isn't the therapist's job to search out the facts. It doesn't disturb them that their clients nearly go crazy thinking such awful things, or that the 'memories' often result in shattered families and lawsuits.

The reason such therapists are not disturbed is that they genuinely *believe* that they are not leading their clients and that all the suffering they induce is a necessary adjunct of the 'healing' process. Given their entrenched belief in recovered memories, they are perfectly capable of rationalizing away the palpable pain and bewilderment of the accused parents whose protestations of innocence appear so genuine because they, too, repressed all memory of what they did, as Delia Wadsworth and Hamish Pitceathly explain.

These therapists regard their task as one of step-by-step education – or, better, indoctrination. Thus, when Hamish Pitceathly says, 'I spend a lot of time emphasizing that *they* are in control of this whole procedure, it's *their* analysis, not mine,' he probably believes it. Such clients, reassured that 'the memories are their memories, the feelings are their feelings,' also come to believe it.

Finally, I urge readers to attend to the subtle and not-so-subtle ways that these therapists encourage their patients to redefine their pasts – or, as Janet Griffin phrases it, 'expand the problem space.'

If they always remembered abuse, that isn't enough. They must remember more! Ever vigilant to spot symptoms that might indicate abuse, therapists unwittingly create the very problems they seek to heal. As Leslie Watkins observes, 'You start to see things when you realize that they might be there.'

* Not only do therapists disclaim responsibility for harming clients, they often *blame* them for everything. Thus when Sam Holden feels like hitting them, it's not because he has a problem, but because they subtly invite abuse. Katherine Hylander thinks that her clients *deserve* their traumas to atone for the sins of their past lives. And Leslie Watkins, who wants her clients to remain utterly dependent upon her, interprets their excitement over a new relationship as *attempts to 'derail' therapy*, informing them they are delaying the recovery process.

I close this chapter with a hopeful and revealing interview with Robin Newsome, a therapist who once led her clients into believing their 'repressed memories' and who now realizes what harm she was doing. She provides a wonderful role model for other therapists who have the courage to admit that they were wrong, and the compassion and wisdom to help reunite the very families that they once tore asunder.

SAM HOLDEN, CHRISTIAN COUNSELOR

Sam Holden, a slightly built, soft-spoken man of 35, bills himself as a 'Christian counselor,' in part because he served as a fundamentalist minister for ten years, as did his father before him. Holden was remarkably open about his own personal problems and his therapeutic methodology. 'I really wished I was a girl,' he told me. 'At the age of six, I realized I would never turn into a girl, and it disappointed me. I think it's because I felt so rejected at birth, when my mother's breast milk gave out and she switched me to a bottle.' He received his masters in counseling through an innovative program that allowed minimal classroom time and substantial correspondence through the mail. He practices in Los Angeles.

In addition to memory retrieval, Holden was involved in a child sex abuse case in which a father, convicted of sodomizing his sons, was sent to prison. The case commenced when the wife went for a counseling session with Holden. When she described her concern about her children's sexual acting out, Holden deduced that the husband was a pedophile and gave her two hours to get a restraining order before he turned the case over to the social service agency. From there, the case escalated, the children were subjected to repeated, coercive interviews, and a case was built.

'When I first saw John Bradshaw's *Homecoming* video series, he had a man imagine he was holding a younger version of himself on his lap. He said, "Tell him you'll be there for him," and the man started crying. He couldn't do it. So I imagined my two-year-old self, and the first thing that flashed into my mind was pushing him onto the floor and kicking him. That was a piece of me I couldn't accept. I didn't like the temper tantrums, the part that was always getting spanked. I went on to heal that part of my life.

Yes, inner child work has helped me a lot. I combine it with faith work as well. I ask people to imagine their Higher Power coming and talking to the child.

I was very confused about sexuality when I hit puberty. Many classmates informed me that I was gay, harassed me on a daily basis, called me a fag or a fairy. Mostly they would imitate me. It hurt a lot. I became very depressed for years. I didn't become suicidal, but I wished I was dead. I spent a lot of time praying.

After I hit puberty, I had fantasies of cross-dressing. I was curious about other males and their sexuality. I had strong homosexual tendencies, which upset me a lot. My parents tell me that they never noticed I was effeminate, but every single classmate noticed it.

I was socially adept in structured situations, was the president of the drama club and debating team and did well in school. But I took part in no sports.

I went to a small fundamentalist college, where I started to date. It made me feel more masculine. The girls I dated liked me, because I wasn't so threatening. I eventually married someone who appreciated not being threatened. No, that's not a great reason to marry someone. When I really got into the recovery process and started to become more masculine, she felt scared. She said she didn't like my voice, it frightened her.

For a long time as an adult, I had exhibitionistic tendencies. I was really captivated by nudity, and I would find some woods where I could be naked. I almost got caught several times. There's an addictive nature to it. I think it had to do with a lot of repressed anger coming out. I was one of the nicest people you'd meet, almost saccharine; some people couldn't stand it.

I was also sexually attracted to boys. I did grooming behavior, trying to get close to them and see them naked. I once went skinny dipping with a group of boys. I had clear boundaries against molesting and didn't act on anything, but it really upset me.

I eventually grew out of my denomination. I don't consider myself a fundamentalist any more. Being a therapist is a lot less stressful than the ministry. When I was a minister, I used to have somatic complaints, pinched nerves, a numb right arm. Besides, I'm more well-respected as a therapist.

I started to deal with sex abuse about eight years ago, when some of my parishioners came to me with their problems. I received my training mostly by reading and talking with other therapists. At first, I used free association and guided imagery, but now I use hypnotic age regression to get at repressed memories. I learned it from the Bradshaw videos. I never called it hypnosis until a few months ago when I described it to other counselors and they said, "Yep, that's hypnotism, all right." About 80 per cent of my current clients have been sexually abused.

I'll describe the hypnotic process. I usually ask a person to uncross their legs, put their hands by their sides, and take a few deep breaths. Then I say, "Imagine walking down a flight of stairs. Remember that as an infant, you practiced holding on and letting go, holding on and letting go, until you knew just when to let go and when to hold on. As a toddler, you practiced running away and coming back, running away and coming back, until you had just enough distance. Those skills will help you in this meditation. If you encounter something scary, you can run upstairs and open your eyes any time; you don't need my permission. When you get to the bottom of the stairs, imagine walking along a corridor with doors on either side. They may be multicolored or all one color. Behind each door is a memory or an age. Find the door that you need to look at today. When you find the door, say 'Aha.' When you are ready, open the door and walk through."

If they are worried about having been sexually abused, I'll ask, "Do you want to open the door, or look through the window?" That way, it feels safer. "Look around for yourself as a young person. Tell me when you can see yourself. For a few moments, I want you to become that little person, see what they see, hear what they hear, and feel what you feel." Notice that I shift from saying *they* to *you*.

"Now tell me what's going on." I ask what they are wearing, how old they are, and who's with them, if they don't come up with that on their own. If nothing is happening and they are all alone, I say, "Someone is coming down the hallway and entering the room. Who is it, and what do they do?" Usually, though, as soon as they walk into the room, they are in the place where they were sexually abused.

I can't give you specific case histories, but I'll describe composite semi-hypothetical clients. Let's say Ralph comes into therapy feeling depressed and isolated. He's had sex only a few times, and it was a very anxious experience for him. When we do memory work, he sees himself in a city park near his home. Three men jump on top of him, throw him to the ground, yank his pants down, and anally rape him. He cries, asking them to stop, stop, but they all rape him. In later sessions, he remembers more about this scene, how one man forced him to perform oral sex and then ejaculated on his face.

Ralph might also do memory retrievals at home. I often teach my clients to do this process on their own. He tells me he remembers one of the men who raped him was his private school teacher, who drugged him and took him to an apartment in the city, where he was raped, then given candy and a Coke in the kitchen. Then he was told to perform sex acts in front of a camera with lights. Ralph was eight at the time. All of this was filmed. That's pretty common with many pedophiles. He remembers numbness around the mouth from the drug.

Typically, Ralph might not be sure any of these memories are true. "I believe you," I tell him. "Everyone questions whether these memories are real." I used to tell clients that it's normal to need validation, that they're in denial. Now I just tell them that they will know whether the memories are true or not eventually. I tell Ralph, "If they aren't true, it's okay, let's just work on your depression." I used to tell people it didn't matter if it was true or not, but I've stopped saying that. It does matter, I think. But it's getting away from therapy to try to verify and play detective. That would be like the therapist saying to the client, "I don't trust you."

I also do some dream work. Many clients dream about the rapes, and sometimes they have flashbacks, body memories. I had a client once whose shoulder popped out of its socket. It was the arm that had been pulled up behind her back during a rape.

I've had multiple personality disorders. Actually, they were more of a simple dissociative disorder, but they have names for different pieces of themselves, and each has a different age. Most can't control who comes out, and people can tell they act differently at different times. Usually, these multiples were severely, sadistically abused by one or both parents, often just the mother. It comes out in age regression work. I sometimes suggest to people that it would be good to cut off from their abusive parents. In their present life, if they can stand up to them, it would be much better than cutting off relations, though.

Many clients remember multiple perpetrators, maybe including their father, uncle, the next-door-neighbor, and a cousin – all separate instances, and not all of them necessarily successful molestations. Why would someone be subjected to so many perpetrators? People can sense when someone is vulnerable. In fact, sometimes when I'm sitting with a client, I will have the urge to beat up on them. Why? They're giving out a message that they expect to be beaten up at every turn.

I do think that preverbal memories come back. Some clients remember back to six months old, when their fathers may have taken them out of their cribs and molested them. One of my clients remembers being dropped on the floor after being molested and dislocating her hip. That memory came back to her at home, in a meditation she did on her own.

Some of my clients were abused as part of satanic ritual abuse. Oh, yes, I'm quite sure satanic cults exist. In fact, there's an active cult that the police know all about near here.

Memories come back only when they are ready to come back. Often, they are triggered when someone's child reaches the same age they were at the time of the abuse. If they aren't prepared to face them, they might find dragons in the hypnotic hallway or a locked gate, so they can't even get to the doors. Those memories are too dangerous to deal with yet. I've tried to push people to get memories, and they won't do it if they're not ready. They just open their eyes and say, "That didn't happen. I just made that up."

I do sometimes recommend bringing parents into therapy, but I've never done it in a sex abuse case. I encourage clients to confront perpetrators in an assertive manner. We fantasize aggression, but they should just be assertive in reality. An in-person confrontation is best, but a letter is okay. I will help them with the letter, asking them to rewrite it after we go over it, encouraging them to be more specific about the accusations, what they want from the perpetrator, etc. With each person, what they want is different: an apology, commitment for the perpetrator to go to therapy, or money to go to their own therapy.

There's another, more subtle form of abuse called emotional incest. They show the same symptoms as other incest victims, sometimes worse. I believe that all gay people were emotionally incested and show severe symptoms. These cases can involve parents who were either too close or too distant. In my case, I was my Mom's best friend. Also, just looking at your daughter lustfully or barging unannounced into the bathroom is incest.

I agree with *The Courage to Heal* that if you think you were abused, then you *were*. People have been told that they can't trust how they feel or trust their memories. You know, "Don't tell me I hit you! I didn't hit you." Or, "I never promised you we'd go to the store." So to counterbalance that, they need to hear, "I believe you, I believe you one hundred times over."

Yes, this sort of therapy is fascinating in a bizarre sort of way. I often worry about whether I'm a voyeur. The answer is yes, in a sense, but as long as I know it, I can do good therapy.

I do worry sometimes about whether these memories are all true. I'm very careful not to use leading or directive techniques. Still, I have to wrestle with my conscience. Am I helping them make this up? But then I think about people like Jeffrey Dahmer, the mass murderer. I know that psychopaths like that exist, and all their victims aren't killed. They grow up. These things do happen. So I just sit and listen.'

PETER JONES, PHYSICIAN/HYPNOTHERAPIST

Dr. Peter Jones, a Birmingham physician in general practice for over two decades in the U.K., has also become a specialist in hypnosis over the past few years, training with the British Society for Medical and Dental Hypnosis for two weekends, and subsequently taking advanced courses and workshops. He now lectures on the subject and conducts private hypnotherapy. In much of his work, he uses hypnosis for stress management, weight loss, and smoking cessation, but he has also used it in 'age regression' sessions to recover hidden memories of sexual abuse. Here he describes one such case.

'To regress clients, I put them in trance and ask them to go to that time and place which their subconscious mind thinks is important. I *never* use leading phrases or ask them to go to a specific time when a specific thing was happening to them. I am extremely careful not to give verbal cues, and so my verbalizations are probably limited to a non-specific "mmm..."

The case I am going to tell you about involves regression therapy with Cheryl, who was 32 years old. She had always remembered that she had been sexually abused by her father when she was a child. She remembered some things but wanted to know more details and asked that she be regressed and notes taken or a tape recording made so that she would know every detail.

Her father had been accused of sexual abuse of her best friend when they were about eight years old. She had been interviewed then but could not give any corroborating evidence, so the case was dropped by the police. Soon after this, her mother left the marriage, abandoning her and her older brother with their father. After this, he abused her regularly and used to beat up her brother in front of her, telling her that she too would be beaten up if she did not do as she was told. She ran away on many occasions to her mother, but she was always taken back to her father. Eventually, she went to live with her mother.

I engaged in regression therapy with Cheryl shortly after her father's death. She said she felt someone else had also been involved in the abuse.

She had watched a television program about false memory syndrome, so she knew those issues. I assured her that I would be scrupulously careful not to implant false memories and said I wanted a witness present during the regression therapy. I chose to use a Community Psychiatric Nurse for this purpose. She saw Cheryl on her own for three sessions, then we all met for an hour on her premises to do the regression therapy.

Before the session, in Cheryl's presence, I asked the nurse to watch very carefully that I did not ask any leading questions or put in any false ideas. Cheryl entered trance easily. I asked if there was a time and place where her subconscious mind felt she should go in order to help her. I then checked by ideomotor signaling, which comes from the subconscious part of the brain, that it was safe to re-live this experience. She indicated that it was.

During this session, she described an occasion when a group of men visited her home, and she was taken into a room in the house – she didn't say where, but it sounded like a cellar or attic. Black candles were lit in black candlesticks, and there was a symbol like superimposed triangles painted on the floor. She was undressed and then held down over this symbol by the group, who formed a circle.

While in trance, she assumed a position with her arms above her and her legs apart. While crying, she struggled in this position, but the remarkable thing was that her wrists and ankles stayed in the same position as if held there. She then cried out, "Don't, Daddy, you're hurting me." I asked where she was hurting and she said, "My bottom."

The sobbing settled down, and I asked her to go in her mind to a safe place where she was secure, and told her that the painful memories were now dealt with and would not trouble her again. I then taught her self-hypnosis and then reversed the trance. She was not too distressed prior to leaving and said she would return the following week. Being involved in her disclosure of such events was extremely distressing to me. She had mentioned sexual abuse prior to the therapy but had not mentioned satanic abuse, and I believe did not know any of the details. She said that the same group of men used to visit her house quite frequently. She did not know any of their identities, but she felt that one was a solicitor.

During the second session, she described an incident in a farmhouse set in the middle of a field, where she went with her brother. He was told to wait outside while she and her father went in. There was a group of people in a circle in the large kitchen. She was told to sit on a man's knee and he "played with her bottom," as she put it. They then all went into another room, and a carpet was rolled back to reveal a symbol similar to the one she had described before. She was again undressed and held down over this sign. A door opened, and a man came in wearing a cloak and a long red mask. She again described what was clearly rape.

On the third occasion, she said she was much better and did not need further therapy. She said she always remembered her distress after coming out of this farmhouse but could never remember what had caused it. She also said that a friend had a long mask on the wall, and she became extremely distressed whenever she saw the mask. She had always wondered why she reacted in this way to what was only an inanimate object. Now, of course, she understood fully.

This case made a great impression on me, and I was pleased that it was sorted out very successfully in two treatment sessions and one review. The psychiatric nurse with whom I worked was amazed. She has considerable experience in satanic abuse and said the normal experience was that after 18 months of counseling, one would be left with someone who was still very scarred and who would not function well socially. Here we had a lady who "got her act together" very successfully.

What worries me is non-professional people who use hypnosis after what is in some cases totally inadequate training. In some cases, they believe that every person has some extremely distressing event which is the root of their problems. Hence they persevere in fishing for what is in some cases not there.

On the other hand, I totally believe Cheryl's story. I do not feel she could have faked her struggling movements while in trance.'

JANET GRIFFIN, M.S.W.

Janet Griffin, who received her master's in social work in 1982, prides herself on having pioneered incest therapy in the early 1980s. She practices in Illinois. 'I had to figure out a speciality that was compelling to me and also a marketable expertise. At that time, few people knew about sex abuse. It was easy to do a literature search and teach myself everything within a year.' Throughout our interview, she revealed her impressive scholarship, suggesting books by Sandra Butler, Judith Herman, Charles Figley, and other background reading. Her comfortable office contains not only bookcases but pillows and stuffed animals.

'I am a clinical social worker in private practice. I make my living providing counseling primarily to adults, both men and women, of whom 95 per cent are sex abuse victims. My clients are probably not completely representative as a cross section of incest victims. Because I'm a woman, I tend to get more women, and because of the middle-class setting of this private practice, I see more people who are covered by insurance. They tend to be high-functioning clients who hold down jobs – not the chronically mentally ill.

Five or six years ago, people would come to see me, presenting with depression, anxiety, and so forth. Nowadays they often self-identify as incest survivors, because of watching *Oprah* or whatever. I'm well-known as a sex abuse therapist, so there's a referral network leading to me. My average client? I had a group once in which all seven women had recovered repressed memories at 38 years of age. They were high-functioning, were married and had children. One was a lesbian, the same rate as in the general population. Since accommodation to trauma taught them how to take care of other people, they tend to be care-givers such as day-care workers, social workers, nurses, doctors, or teachers. That's a stereotype, of course, but accurate as a composite.

On the high-functioning end, they come in for depression. With lesser function, they arrive in a state of high anxiety. In the more desperate cases, they will come in with dissociative disorders, some with multiple personalities. But all trauma victims dissociate one way or another. As you progress down through worse trauma, the greater the dissociation, the more problems you have – until you go to multiple personality disorder, and then you can look high-functioning again, because that superior, elaborate coping mechanism can look very high-functioning. MPDs have families, hold down professional jobs, function fine in public.

I really admire Judith Herman's latest work, *Trauma and Recovery*, in which she correctly recognizes that all trauma victims have post-traumatic stress disorder [PTSD], first identified in Vietnam veterans. The same theory applies to incest and Holocaust survivors, battered women, rape victims. Herman puts it in the proper political context.

I follow Herman's philosophy. There are three components of good therapy: (1) establishing safety, (2) remembering, looking back, mourning, grieving, and (3) reconnecting with people and the world. Survivors have to revisit the time of their trauma and re-evaluate it from their current position as an adult.

Survivors never really forget the trauma. It gets dissociated off. The child's ego can't hold the reality of sexual abuse and the demands of living every day. So call it something else, pretend it didn't happen, leave the body. There are lots of ways to make it not be happening. But it leaves footprints in the snow of everyday living, though the symptoms need not be dramatic.

I always begin therapy with an assessment interview in which people tell their stories about important events in their lives. They might remember a sexual incident but minimize it. "Oh, yes, my cousin molested me, but it doesn't matter." When they come in with depression or anxiety, they will often be in denial or minimizing. "Well, yeah, there was this uncle, but I never told anybody, it's all in the past, it's not that important." I have to respect what they say, but at the same time expand the problem space. I ask about the context of the abuse. I ask them, "How could that have happened? Where were your father, mother, sister?" As the problem space expands, the reality of the neglectful, aggressive environment becomes clear. It's important to get the patient to describe the experience, but the goal is not to determine the truth, but to witness the patient's experience and carry it forward so that they can see it more clearly and re-evaluate it. I rely on the client's strong feelings and ability to discharge emotions.

My standard technique for unlocking repressed memories is to use guided imagery. I teach a patient how to close her eyes and imagine a safe place. We spend a number of sessions constructing that safe place. It's a standard meditative technique. Then, from that place, they can do their remembering. That way, they don't just sit and chit-chat with me; I get to see it and hear about it as it's re-lived. Every client develops a different safe place. For some, it's a beach or pond, with no one else around. Others will construct a container, a bunker, a huge cement building, a toxic waste site where no one can go in except them. They choose when to go in and out.

Then we go in and remember. I cue a person, giving them a choice. "This is all about when you were little, and everything about your grandfather is in there. You choose. Let's shine the flashlight on the scene." A lot of people carry imaginary flashlights with them. I'll ask them to describe their grandfather, and some will say, "I can't." I'll suggest starting with his feet, and they will in fact begin to describe him. "Where are you?" I'll ask. "What time of year is it? What are you wearing, what do you see? Can you smell anything?"

Another quite fascinating aspect of this work is that people come in with physical symptoms which relate to their abuse – constant headaches and migraines, G.I. distress, pelvic pain, stomach aches. So we go to the safe place, then go to the stomach ache. And a client might remember being punched in the stomach, or violently penetrated, or hit on the head. The body holds the memory. The body holds all memories.

Everything that ever happened to you is probably preserved in your brain somewhere. Some of the most difficult work with sexual trauma victims is working with those who were abused before they had words – preverbal, infant abuse. They have to go back and re-live the experience, and I have to validate it even when there are no words or pictures. I have to accept what they say, their experience.

That brings us to another level of therapy, that part about accepting the client's truth. We have to accept it whether it existed in objective reality or not. How is that truth playing out in the client's life? It's the *dynamic* past, not the *content* past, that is important. If somebody thinks they were orally penetrated at nine months old and objects were inserted in her vagina, then if they have a gag reflex and can't eat solid food and can't enjoy sexual contact with their partner, it seems reasonable to look back, accept the story, expand it, and explore it with that person. Yes, if that happened, it would cause incredible pain. Now how can you claim your own body and your own sexuality?

There's an even greater difficulty with the preverbal abuse victim, because it's a matter of claiming the body for the first time, not *re*-claiming it. Let's say you're the victim of a fire. In that case, there's a pre-trauma existence, you can remember what it was like before the fire. The task of the therapist is to get you to discharge the trauma and return to the prior level of okay functioning. But with a child who *never* achieved full developmental growth, who was abused as an infant, you have to go back and "regrow" the person, help them reinvent themselves because they have no baseline. A lot of that is done by nonverbal work. I encourage them to do body work – massage, dance, finger-painting, drawing, physical nonverbal ways to get to know the body.

One therapist I know tells the story of reclaiming one square inch of the body at a time. She tells people to find an acceptable part of the body. It's actually sometimes quite difficult. If you can't find even one square inch, you're in deep trouble! Women often find it behind their knees or on their hands or in their hair. Every week, you pay attention to that square inch, like it, admire it, buy it a present. One woman bought pieces of fabric, one square inch at a time, and eventually could look at all parts of her body and see curves. It's sort of like putting together a patchwork quilt.

The most horrific cases involve ritual abuse. Sometimes, the father impregnates the daughter, then takes her infant for sacrifice during a cult ritual. I know that the FBI has conducted an investigation and found no evidence of this. So much for the FBI! Look at how well they did at Waco with David Koresh. Just because they can't find bones doesn't prove it doesn't happen.

There's another insidious form of incest called covert or emotional incest. Those survivors deserve to be validated just as much as clients who have been touched. This involves the way the father looks at his daughter, his comments about her growing breasts, or barging into her bedroom without knocking. Sometimes, victims of covert incest can be the most difficult clients. One woman was watched her entire life by her father and brothers, who had drilled a peephole into the bathroom. She eventually came to know it. Then, whether they were watched or fondled inappropriately, they have to go downstairs and sit at the breakfast table as if nothing happened. And they wonder why women get eating disorders! How can you have a good relation to food when a lie as big as an elephant is sitting in the middle of the dining table? We know what Dad did last night, but we're not going to talk about it.

I tell my patients, "There are dinosaurs, dragons out there. Everyone needs to be able to go to the back of their cave and rest, lie down in a safe place. But if there's a sexual predator in the house, you can't ever do that. When you're 5 or 14, you know you can't ever put it down, and it has a grinding effect on your mental health. So of course you have sleep disturbances, you've never been able to rest."

Once the memory recovery process starts, the memories don't come back like cars on a train in perfect order; they don't come back like snapshots. You may not get a picture, but you know you hated that bedroom at camp; that counts. Things come back to you out of order, not ideographically as a picture. Sensations and smells are important. You get a feeling, but you can't quite name it. I actually have pages of words to describe different emotions. Emotions come from the body, not from the mind, but patients don't know that. I have to explain it to them. A lot of trauma therapy is teaching.

There's this raging debate now about whether some of these are false memories. I attended a conference last year on memory sponsored by a society for MPD. It was very scientific, full of neurologists. From a forensic standpoint, we don't know much about memory. I can't really address that. The purpose of trauma therapy is witnessing and validating the individual experience and the dynamics around it, not so much the specific content. There is a tie to your current life. I mean, you're not walking along having a trouble-free life. Say your grandfather sodomized you as a child. You've been constipated all your life, can't stand anyone to touch your anus. You have this secret no-touch zone. You have some discomfort around this grandfather. You get migraines when you go home for the holidays. You're in constant upheaval with your superiors at work. All of this is not a surprise, it's not just out of the blue.

Let me tell you, I never met anybody who tried to be a survivor on purpose. There's precious little to be gained by being in this club. Most of the people you see on *Oprah* who describe this dynamic are in therapy and taking responsibility for their current lives, not using it as an excuse. Who would want to put themselves through this pain, or think their father did this to them? I've never seen a confabulation in my practice.

It would be interesting to compare parents who have joined the FMS Foundation and imprisoned sex offenders. Sex offenders will often pass lie-detector tests. They are so into denial. And believe me, you have to be really bad to get convicted. The numbers who walk are incredible. Those guys still sit in jail and say they didn't do it. The level of pathology that sex offenders can gather is incredible. So for some parents, it must be comforting to join a club like the FMS Foundation, which tells you, "No, your family is fine, this pebble your child threw means nothing."

Is it possible that the parents in the FMS Foundation really did abuse their children but repressed or dissociated and don't remember? I don't think so. I don't believe that the sex offender dissociates. He minimizes and denies, but he remembers, all right. Yes, it's possible but extremely unlikely that someone would make up stories of abuse. Well, maybe this woman just hates her parents, wants them to leave her alone because they're intrusive assholes.

How clients want to handle confronting parents is up to them. *The Courage to Heal* has a good section on how to write a letter to them. I use that for clarification, not confrontation necessarily.

Some people benefit from writing a letter, even if they don't mail it. It puts the trauma outside them, gives them another dimension of their reality to see it on paper. I will help them write the letter, work on different drafts, clarify what they want to have happen. *Do I want my father to apologize, Mom to admit she knew? Do you want money? Never to talk to them again?* They decide what they want, then work through all possible responses they might get. We practice it over and over. What if your parents call you up? What if Dad calls and yells at you? What if he says he's sorry? It often takes six months to prepare for this, to finally mail the letter. Some clients prepare and prepare and prepare, make piles of 3 x 5 cards, as if for a court situation. You have to prepare them for when the dragon wins. They tell you you're a liar, that they are disowning you. They try to get the jump on your power.

If they say, "We don't know what you're talking about," it's the same as saying, "You're lying or hallucinating." So you prepare someone for that. The purpose of therapy is to validate the person's experience. If Mary Jane works on therapy for a year, knows her truth, wants to write that letter, wants an apology, and is prepared that she won't get it, then she will work through her grief and loss in therapy. Ultimately, she may never get the validation she wants.'

HORACE STONE, MINISTER/COUNSELOR

Reverend Horace Stone, a Methodist minister in an Indiana city, has worked with incest survivors for 20 years. A graduate of a prestigious divinity school, he speaks knowledgeably about Freud, genograms, and dissociative states. He is a firm believer in the reality of satanic ritual abuse and leads a group for incest survivors.

'Of many dozens of people I've worked with who claim they were sexually abused, I have found virtually no one in which it was not so. They don't come to a minister to make a court case. They say, "Why am I so depressed?" A clergyman is in an interesting position. God and the priest are the "father," and in a large number of abuse cases, the perpetrating parent has said, "God and I are right, and once you've been sexually abused, you're worthless, God wouldn't love you anyway, because you're a slut." So many of the people I see have low self-esteem and feel that God wouldn't accept them.

Half of the women don't remember until they're 30. They try to run faster, thinking, "If only I do it better, right, faster, then I'll be okay." Then they run out of better, right, faster, and they crash. That's when I see them. They have hit a spiritual bankruptcy, also physical and emotional. Why are they so compulsive, trying to be super-Mom, why are they so fearful of God? As we deal with fears and issues, flashbacks often start happening, in dreams, in day-to-day encounters, when they're in an awkward situation. When they come to see me for the first time, they're nervous. I always let them sit by the door, so they can escape. A bolting response is very common. They don't know why they are claustrophobic, fear being trapped, can't sit between people in church pews.

Then they realize that something awful happened to them. It starts with little bits of memory, body memories, perhaps pain in the genital area, or choking. Sometimes a texture puts them off. Some people can't take anything that resembles semen – whipped cream, ice cream – and they don't know why. The conscious mind has just pushed the memories off to the side. When they do remember the abuse, it is with horror and a lot of self-blame. I say, "It's not your fault, children are not the cause of abuse. You had no choice, you were dependent on your parents for your very survival."

Then there's a period of anger against their parents. It often takes a long time before they approach the parents, who usually deny it at first. Given a chance to struggle with this and to see the damage they've done, a fairly high percentage of parents will eventually admit it. Reconciliation won't usually come if the parents deny it. In most cases, the children previously thought they had a wonderful childhood, a fiction they had to piece together to repress the memories.

Now many therapists are asking, "Is there any chance your parents abused you?" First, the answer is "No!" But a few weeks later, they rethink it, they have permission. Until now, our medical, legal, and psychological systems have all been biased against people remembering.

Another interesting area is abuse by the mother. We talked about it in the survivors' group last week. It's easier to recognize the male perpetrator. Frequently, the mother and father know what the other was doing. Typically, the mother says, "I knew my husband was going to our daughter's room at night, and I wondered what was wrong with me, but she could have locked the door, so I knew nothing was going on." That's denial, not really wanting to know. A woman in the group had been angry at her father for the last two years, and now she realizes that her mother was behind it. The father *and* mother physically and sexually abused her.

My group isn't a therapy session, but a support group for people of faith, struggling with day-to-day issues.

Yes, I am sure there might be a few false memories, if someone asked leading questions. I don't do that. We all have skewed memories. We all bring our own framework, our own set of binoculars. What would seem abusive to one person might not to another. But I believe the survivors' stories because denial has been so key already in their life. I will believe them and keep working on what happened. The memories continue to be amplified.

In many cases, the stuff that was done is so horrendous that it cannot be understood. I deal with many ritual abuse survivors, and many of them are multiple personality disorders. There's well over a 90 per cent correlation between MPD and sex abuse. Same with uncontrolled weight swings, bulimia and overeating, anorexia. Why does a woman weigh 350 pounds? Because she's safe.

The MPD people in my group talk about struggling with this or that personality, but they usually stay in their core alter for the group. One gal says that Stephen is the only one of her personalities who can drive safely. She has to call forth Stephen to drive her home at the end of the meeting, or we have to drive her home. These people look like anyone else and function in society quite nicely. You'd never know they were MPD.

My information is that there's a satanic cult locally here. I can verify that, I've been working with people from that area. They have terrible memories: torture, sex slaves. They hang little girls up by leather garments and you choose which one you want to fuck around with, then hang them back up on the wall. Murdering of children is common. On certain days of the year, a child must be sacrificed. The amount of physical torture is incredible, you'd think they would have permanent scars. Splinters under the nails, electric shocks to the genitals, slicing open a pregnant woman, taking out the baby, burning it.

People tend to remember this grotesque abuse last, after they have retrieved other memories. Often, the cult members would take a favorite pet of the child and torture it to death, then skin it. They'd say to the child, "You're next. Do you want to give in or not?" They take anything of value and destroy it to gain psychological power over a child. When she was three, one girl tried to tell her mother how she was initiated into the cult. Her mother slapped her, told her it wasn't true, just in her imagination. Her father dunked her under the water next day until she choked and passed out. He said, "Little girls drown very easily in bathtubs. Don't tell anyone what happens between us, or I'll drown you." Oh, yes, both of her parents were involved in the cult. She never thought her mother was at these events, but that memory is just coming out now.

In regard to cult abuse, there is extraordinary paranoia, for good reason. They have been warned, "If you ever have children and speak about this, your children will disappear." That's what you should do *[referring to me, the interviewer].* Go undercover into a satanic cult to validate it. They're so good at burning up the bones, the police have not been able to find anything. They cover their tracks so well.

In my sermons, I do talk about dysfunctional, abusive families and the need for abuse to stop. As a result, many people come to me as a safe person to help with these issues. I've written newspaper articles saying that the silence surrounding abuse must be broken. My job is to affirm people in their work as they struggle to figure out who they are. It's very much a faith journey.'

LESLIE WATKINS, PH.D., CLINICAL PSYCHOLOGIST

Leslie Watkins, 42, is frustrated with many of her Georgia peers. Having written her dissertation on hypnosis, she complains that some clinical psychologists are afraid of that memory-retrieval tool. 'It's ironic that mostly social workers and those with masters in counseling are doing this important work. Psychologists have this elitist attitude that doesn't allow them to get mud on their boots, dealing with these difficult cases.' Watkins estimates that 80 per cent of her current clients, most of whom are women, were sexually abused. 'And if you include people who have symptoms but no memory yet, it's probably 90 per cent.'

'It takes a long time before a person has a memory in therapy, usually over a year. I'll give you an example. Tracy, a nurse in her late 20s, came to see me because of anxiety. She wasn't able to find good relationships. At one time, she'd been married to an abusive alcoholic. Once she felt safe enough in therapy, she began to have flashbacks and intrusive visions while she was driving her car. In her first memories, she discovered that her father, a minister, had sexually abused her. As the memories developed, she recalled observing her father engaged in ritualistic killing. At one point, her life was nearly sacrificed.

How do we know if the memories are real? We use our gut reactions at times. Besides, if it takes years in therapy, that's a good indication they are real memories. I consider the vividness, clarity, and specificity of the memory. You know, like "I was wearing a red striped T-shirt, the sun was coming in the window, my father wore tennis shoes." Some people actually smell the smells, hear the words that were spoken to them. Sometimes they feel searing pain in their genitals. They shake and cry, saying "Oh, NO!" They can remember all of it at once, or in segments. Sometimes they tell me the most horrible atrocities in unemotional tones. You know, one tear trickles down as they describe the killing of children. My goal as a therapist is to get all those pieces of emotion and memory together.

I think of myself as being like a police investigator. A person comes in with current problems regarding weight, body image, fear of small spaces. She may hate to put a scarf around her neck and has a sexual dysfunction – that could be either heightened appetite, numbing, or intrusive fantasies during sex. These symptoms present evidence of a crime. I go back and piece together the evidence. That's why therapists should see symptoms. What does it mean when a woman runs when she sees her father? When she can't give oral sex without throwing up? I have a mental image of a map. If a person tells me they have a severe fear of genital intrusion and can't go to a gynecologist, it fills in my map a little bit. I may tell them, "This sometimes means something has happened, but it's not sufficient to draw conclusions. Let's put a pot on the back of the stove, and put these things in it, and see if it makes a soup."

Emotional incest can be as bad as physical sexual abuse. I think about it in terms of appropriate boundaries. A four-year-old might hear Mommy or Daddy talking about financial worries or their sex life, topics the child shouldn't be privy to. That sets the child up to be responsible for the parent. You might hear Dad talking about not getting enough sex from Mom. A parent who beats or rapes his children, everyone agrees that's terrible, but emotional incest is harder. Gloria Steinem talks about the crime that's hard to nail down, a passive kind of thing, where Mother never speaks to you.

It's remarkable how common physical incest is, though. Many times, I'll think a client won't have a history of abuse. Then she'll have a dream of someone on top of her, she can't breathe, and I think, "Oh, gee, here we go again."

Following the memory, there's almost always denial. "I don't believe this; this didn't happen." I can only think of one time a woman remembered during a session and didn't deny it. When they deny it, I tell them, "It's understandable; who would want to believe it? It's hard to believe. If it's true, it will become more clear as more evidence comes up." Also, you can see a drop in symptoms. A woman who hasn't been able to go get a Pap smear for ten years remembers a rape by her father, and then she can get the Pap smear without anxiety. She may stop starving herself, will drink less. Then you say, "Yeah, those memories were real."

I don't always have to hypnotize people formally. I have some people who just come in and dissociate. They're gone. I tell them they can go with it or bring themselves back to the room. They have a choice; it's very important to recognize that. Judith Herman has a good description of dissociation in *Trauma and Recovery* – a dazed look, with eyes either open or shut. I have one man who likes to lie on the couch and remember his mother touching him inappropriately, tears running down his face. It felt good to him. He remembers it fondly. But it has created problems in his life. It wasn't necessarily confusing at the time of the abuse. The adult outcome is what makes it abusive or not. If an adult grows up and thinks his meaning in life is to be a sexual stud, he's got a problem. Otherwise, there's no reason to look for memories. Everyone has some kind of stuff, times when they were neglected or spoken to in bad ways.

Once the memories come up, if it's the father who did it, it's not a good idea to seek confirmation from the mother. If she was abused herself as a child, she probably chose an abuser for a husband unconsciously. She will be in denial of the abuse. It serves a family function; she doesn't have to have sex. Therefore, just because the wife says, "Oh, I know he couldn't have done it," that doesn't mean much.

Besides, many of the perpetrators were in severely dissociated states when they were abusing, and they themselves don't remember it. So they can sincerely protest their own innocence. If Dad is being accused, he should go to therapy and try to get memories. If he's really concerned, he'll try to remember. Many perpetrators look perfectly normal. You'd be shocked by the number of public figures who have abused children. Not many perpetrators knock on your door and say, "Please help me."

Sometimes, when the memories are too difficult to face, women will unconsciously try to derail the therapy process. They've remembered Dad, read the books, and are doing well. But darn if we didn't see something, a funny little dream or two, or a fantasy, or a drawing, and *Mom* might be involved, too! The next thing you know, something outside therapy makes them pay total attention to it. They go out and fall in love, right then. Sometimes I tell people, "Look, this might delay things for a year."

People don't realize how frequently mothers are perpetrators. I have five patients whose mothers tried to drown them. That goes on a lot with new mothers with post-partum depression. Also, if a mother had *her* mother do it to her, she might repeat it, in an alternate psychological state of dissociation. Sex abuse is often intergenerational.

I've heard some pretty unbelievable memories around ritual abuse involving dead babies. I don't have direct knowledge, but I believe it's going on. I have people who have very clear memories of incredible atrocities. Sexual abuse is part of it, but it also involves human and animal sacrifice. Usually, the first memories are of sex abuse and are more tame, so to speak, and they happened in the bedroom at home with one person. Later, they remember a crew of people at an altar site. It's a gradual process. The client gets peeks at things and closes the door really quickly, like, "Oh my God, what was that I saw?"

After a conference last year on the subject, I started to use art therapy with clients. I ask people to draw at home on large paper with crayons and not to throw anything out. I ask them to draw a picture of themselves, but not to make it accurate. Sometimes I get fragments of the abuse scene. When people do drawings and show blood, it's not just virginal blood sometimes, but blood from cult abuse.

There are a lot of valid ways to help people remember their abuse. My fantasy is to have a treatment facility with a psychologist, psychiatric nurse, art therapist, physician, movement therapist, expression therapist, and body worker, all working together. As it is now, too many survivors who are desperate for help go to palm readers, tea leaf examiners, crystal gazers, Tarot card specialists, body workers, Rolfers, acupuncturists, herbalists, everything there is, and they can get confusing and contradictory input. Professionals should be working together.

I've gone to three conferences on multiple personality disorders and have another one lined up. I'm not an expert on MPD, but I'm in the learning curve. I'm open to the idea now. When someone says, "There's a voice in my head that won't talk," I ask them if it is an embodiment next to them, or inside them? "Could we meet this part of you?" I ask. We all have parts of ourselves. If you take away this notion that MPD is weird, it's just like the child within. If it develops into a full-blown person, it might receive a name. All alters come into being for a constructive purpose, to help get through the trauma. But they're outmoded in adulthood.

One of the alters might still be in cults, another says it will die if it tells its story. It takes a lot of trust. You have to get all of the alters on board, meet them, get to know them, get them to appreciate each other. Each may hold separate functions and memories. Some people have over 100 alters, they say. But I'm really new at this, just starting to ferret it out in my practice. You start to see things when you realize that they might be there.'

DELIA WADSWORTH, CONSULTANT PSYCHIATRIST

Delia Wadsworth, 62, is a British consultant psychiatrist who describes her therapeutic approach as 'psychodynamic and eclectic.' Although she finds Freud's insights extremely useful, she cannot forgive him for rejecting his seduction theory and instead formulating the whole Oedipal theory, much of which she characterizes as 'complete bunk.' For several years, she has led therapeutic groups, along with a male therapist, for female sexual abuse victims, many of whom did not recall their abuse until recently. She is also in private practice. I interviewed her in her comfortable country home in the Lake District.

'I saw my first patient who disclosed sexual abuse around 1980. I didn't realize its extent, however, until 1984, when I had to give a lecture on the subject. So I read up on the Americans, who were ahead of us by about ten years. My eyes were beginning to be opened. By 1986, we were getting so many sex abuse referrals at my clinic that we decided to run a group. Although we never kept such records, I would guess that about half had *always* remembered their abuse, while half had not.

How do I explain repression or dissociation? The analysts believe that the immense trauma to a young child is so devastating. "Here is someone who should be protecting me and is abusing me instead. How do I reconcile this?" It's so mind-blowing that they repress or even develop multiple personality disorder. The MPDs have usually been badly abused. I have only had one client I thought was perhaps an MPD. I may have missed some, I suppose. Anything is possible.

Various key life events make their memories come back. These include childbirth, or their daughter reaching the age at which they were first abused, or their son becoming pubertal and therefore threatening. Or they may have watched a television program, such as the one by Esther Rantzen, who did a program on child sexual abuse. Some women watched and suddenly a memory came up.

You must understand that when memories come up, they don't come very clearly. They erupt from the subconscious, often in fragments and images.

In my assessment interview for each person joining the group, I have to discover exactly what has happened to them. If they cannot bring themselves to put into words what happened, I go through the known forms of passive and active abuse in a matter-of-fact, practical way. I ask in detail, inquiring, if it seems appropriate, about desecration of the body by semen, urine, or feces. They sometimes only nod their heads. They won't say the words. Sometimes they suddenly say "Rape" or "Father" and are excited that they have actually said it. They are thrilled that the block is over. One woman started telling me, then hit her head and went sort of psychotic. That was sort of a body memory.

I try to introduce them into the group as soon as possible after this difficult interview, since they may fail to attend if there is too long a wait.

It is important not to lead patients. For instance, I don't use hypnosis at all in psychiatry. I think the patient feels you are in control if you hypnotize them, and that is not good. The purpose of psychotherapy is for people to become more responsible for themselves. I think people can unlock their unconscious quite well in ordinary analysis, at their own pace. Nature decides for them, and I wouldn't push it. I wouldn't tell anyone I suspected they were abused, even if I did.

I do ask practically every patient I see, "Were you at any time, did you experience any sort of abuse as a child? Did anyone approach you too closely and you found it difficult?" I give them the opportunity. But I don't press and dwell on it. People just remember things, they float up during therapy. Therapy is a very close and intimate relationship. They perhaps begin to trust more. Often, an apparently unimportant event leads to something important.

There are various things that make me wonder whether a patient might have been sexually abused. If they can't remember their childhood at all up until a certain age, or if they were happy until a particular point in time, or if they acted up as adolescents, stealing, shoplifting, being promiscuous, overdosing. Such adolescent behavior makes one wonder.

Dreams can be clues as well. Usually, dreams of actual abuse come up only after patients have consciously remembered their abuse. Before that, they may dream of knives, spiders, snakes – hidden, masked dreams. That's one of the things that makes one wonder that perhaps they were abused.

There are four classic symptoms of sexual abuse: 1) very low self-image, 2) obsessive ruminations and flashbacks, 3) disabling mistrust of men and sometimes of women, and 4) sexual dysfunction of some sort. Other symptoms? Eating disorders make me just wonder, but the research now shows that up to 50 per cent of the psychiatric population has been abused in one way or another, so it isn't surprising that a high proportion of patients with eating disorders have a history of sexual abuse. Also, those who were sexually abused as children may now live with abusive partners. They are repeatedly abused, are endless doormats. It's all part of being a victim.

Other incest survivors may react with a startled response when people come up behind them. Some refuse to be examined by doctors, hate gynecological exams, anything like that. There are children who don't like their throat looked at or who greatly fear going to the dentist. You just wonder if they might have been orally abused.

None of these signs is definitive, of course. A good therapist is like a doctor who thinks it's probably a mild infection, but it could also be cancer. So at the back of your mind, you think, am I missing something more important?

I tell therapists I'm supervising, when they describe a patient to me, "I just wonder if she was sexually abused. Just bear it in mind as a possibility." But I don't encourage them to tell the patient. No, when I supervise new therapists, I don't sit in on a session. They come once a week and talk about the content of a session. We discuss it and try to hear the hidden meaning in what their clients told them.

When patients have said, "I think my father abused me," they say it spontaneously. If up until then they haven't said it, sometimes they haven't wanted to admit it to themselves. Sometimes they have known it all along in a way but were just in denial.

Particularly when the father is the perpetrator, people don't want to admit the abuse. They may say one week, "I realize my father abused me." Even in the same session, they'll then say, "No, it was just a bad dream, I made it up." They will deny it because they don't want to admit it. I will then say to them, "I wonder if you *really* made it up."

Memories have floated up over the years we've run our group, and former group members have sometimes written to me afterwards, saying, "I was much better, but now another memory has come up, and I need more help." The way to treat victims is for them to share it so that they can process the memories. Once you have remembered the trauma and shared it with someone and have experienced the emotions you suppressed at the time, you can lay it aside. It doesn't have the same intensity and terror. But you may not have completed it all; another memory may float up later. It's very sad. You think you're so much better, then something more comes up.

The earliest I've had someone remember is abuse when they were two or three. On the whole, they think it started around five or six. As memories come back, they seem to remember it earlier and earlier. "I remember that room," they'll say, or "I always think about that room." They go back to the room and remember something nasty happened in it but they're not sure quite what.

I've had patients who are determined to get to the bottom of it, who want desperately to know if they were abused. They want me to take them back and put it behind them. I tell them, "We've tried to go back and we haven't succeeded. You're improving anyway. We'll never know. We've at least confronted the fact that it could have happened."

I think it's wrong that in the States, many therapists encourage patients to take destructive action. It's very bad for anybody to set out to destroy another person in any way. It's untherapeutic. I do encourage the expression of rage or fury in a group. That's healthy. And I'll discuss with them if they want to confront the perpetrator, whether they might get terribly hurt by his denial or whether it might be a good thing, but I won't advise in any way.

Most often, people have to decide whether to go again to see the perpetrator. They may dread being left in a room with him, even though he may now be an old man. I say, "Why do you go and see your parents if you don't want to?" My patients answer, "Because they expect it." I say, "Have they any right to expect it? Surely, it's time not to be the little girl any more, and do what *you* want. You have to distance yourself emotionally from your parents and form your own views about right and wrong and what you need to do."

That approach goes right through my therapy for all patients, not just those who were sexually abused. *You* make the decisions. It's a growing up. A lot of us never really do it.

Primarily, I take a cognitive approach to memory. I just talk with people. I think there is a need for the experiences to be put into words. Verbalization seems to remove some of the terror attached to what was often a preverbal experience or one for which the child could find no words. It's important for patients to write. We've had poems that come straight out of their unconscious, and they don't know what they mean quite. Looking back, they say, "Of course! *That's* what they mean." Art work can also be useful.

I'll also encourage patients who have recalled abuse by their father to be careful about their own children. My common law duty would require me to say, "It's something you should think about, whether to allow your father to be around your children or not."

Many who have confronted their fathers are pleased to have done it, even if their fathers don't acknowledge the abuse. But the worst pain is that their mothers didn't protect them. They say, "Surely, she knew. Surely, she heard my screams."

Some go and talk to their mothers about it. The mothers usually don't want to know, and I can understand that. I believe that victims suppress the memory in a dissociative process. I think that perpetrators may also suppress it. They don't remember it either.

You ask why I believe the parents can also repress the memory. Have you ever been to meetings of the False Memory Society with these accused parents? The pain there is palpable, isn't it? There must be an element of suppression there. It's the only thing that makes sense to me. Otherwise, why would they appear to be in such bewildered pain?

I get very frustrated with the academics who defend this idea of a false memory syndrome. They talk about their research on memory, but they don't know about the human emotions connected with this. I'm not saying that what they say is nonsense, but it doesn't address the problem of sexual abuse, of repressed memories that float back up. It's so hard to connect these dry academic studies with my clients who may be cowering on the floor, screaming.

I think that this FMS thing will evaporate. It's nonsense, I don't take it too seriously. Reputable, good therapists don't produce false memories. I expect some therapists do bad things, but very few.

Everything adds up as therapy continues and memories float into consciousness. You can't do good therapy unless you trust the patient to try to tell the truth. In therapy, it doesn't matter whether it's verifiably true. One's aim is to get the patient better. I know when someone is telling the truth. I can just tell. It's experiential. I usually can't *prove* that they're telling the truth. Sometimes you get corroborative evidence, such as scars from the abuse. Sometimes other siblings confirm the abuse.

One instance of a returning memory is someone who came to me in 1991 who had suddenly remembered just after her father's death. We worked on that and she got a bit better. Then she came and remembered a piece of material of a dress she wore as a child. She was very disturbed but couldn't figure out why. She was very frightened. Finally, she recalled that she had to take off her dress when she was abused by her father, and that there had been other children present. Then she remembered other men, the fathers of these children. Then she remembered it all. This was a group rape of young children, when she was four years old. Eventually, these memories came to include elements of group ritual abuse.

It's difficult to counter claims that satanic ritual abuse doesn't exist. The critics ask for evidence, for the bodies of murdered babies. One wonders why there isn't any evidence. I am not an expert on such matters. It is the social workers and church counselors who have the most experience with ritual abuse survivors. They claim that the lack of evidence can be explained by cult members in high places very cleverly hiding it. They believe that there are doctors, lawyers, politicians, and mortuary attendants involved. A good book on the subject is *Treating Survivors of Satanist Abuse*, edited by Valerie Sinason of the Tavistock Clinic.

Over the years, there has been a progression for me. I first noticed just abuse, incest. Then I noticed some torture. Halfway through I discovered that there was desecration, urine, feces, semen, then ritual abuse. I've grown to understand it more now. At the beginning, I didn't know about a lot of things that went on. The patient can't tell you until you're ready to accept it. People now tell me quickly what they wouldn't have before. I think it's because I'm ready to pick it up now.

The group process can be highly stressful. Members find the exposure of feelings in the group painful, sometimes dreading each session, yet forcing themselves to attend. They usually go through a period where they are worse, with sleeplessness, nightmares, sobbing, an inability to concentrate on housework, jobs, or relationships because of flashbacks and memories, but we warn them that things will get worse before they get better. Others in the group say, "Stick it out, you'll get better." Sometimes people have to be admitted to hospital for a week or two. A few have left the group in angry protest.

But on the whole, if people stick it out, they get better, their depression lifts, and they become much more assertive. At times, my male co-therapist feels isolated and silent, ashamed to be a man, making it impossible for him to actively lead the group. I have to take the main facilitator role. I try to establish myself as the "caring mother" so that I can explore whether all men are in fact as dangerous as their perpetrators were and to suggest that perhaps men are human beings, too, like women, and can be hurt.

I've been contacting former group members to document their progress. On the whole, people in my group have accomplished important life tasks, left their abusive husbands, made positive steps forward. I've had some lovely comments from former group members. "I've met a man, and dare I say I'm in love for the first time?" Or "I managed to pass my driving test, even with a male instructor." Or "I've had my first grandchild. I didn't think I would be alive to see this day."

Of course, some said, "It was all doom and gloom and I came away from each session worse than when I came in." One just wrote back, "Fuck off."

Most clients, however, said it was marvelous to be believed. They were not isolated any more. Everyone there had been abused, so they felt safe in the group. "It's like a cocoon in here," one patient told me. "Everyone understands." Another said that her mind was much clearer and less confused. "It's as though we'd done our dirty washing, it's all come out clean, and now it's nicely ironed and folded and put back in our heads."

Yes, it is so disturbing and strange, isn't it? Here we are in this beautiful, civilized country that looks so peaceful. Yet sexual abuse and satanic ritual abuse go right across the board, through all social classes. I am always shocked by each new revelation, although I am no longer surprised.'

JASON RANSOM, BODY WORKER

In his early forties, tanned, trim Jason Ransom looks extraordinarily fit, and he is. 'I'm really active, play every sport I can, and love being outside,' one of the reasons he lives in New Mexico. Originally trained as a masseur, he now prefers the designation 'body worker,' since his therapeutic touch has moved beyond simple muscle manipulation. Since the late 1980s, when a client first recalled sexual abuse during a session, more and more memories have emerged under the tutelage of his expert hands. 'I have a reputation now for working with survivors, who make up half of my patient load.'

'I believe it's clearly possible that people can stimulate false memories. On the other hand, I'm worried that long-forgotten trauma might get written off as false memory. Both can occur, in other words. It's quite possible to suppress the memory of that type of trauma, which will only return when the person returns to the same state, whether emotional or physical. We call these state-dependent memories. When you're in a highly psychologically disturbed state, information gets encoded into the brain and body at a certain level or frequency. Think of it like a radio band. The only way to tune in the station is to get that frequency, and then, *voilà*, the information comes back.

The memories are encoded on an unconscious level in the brain, and at a cellular level in the body. There's a communication system between the two that we're just beginning to understand. Sometimes the memory is stored in a tense part of the body, part of the musculature locked into an armoring protective pattern. Sometimes it's stored in an area of chronic injury, such as the low back, neck, or knee. But it can be any physical location. The body stores it, on hold, sort of like an Individual Retirement Account, ready to come out when the person is old enough.

I'm not really focused on helping people get specific memories. That's not the point to me. I want people to enjoy their bodies again, to relish in their advantages and thrills. After they get their memories out, they don't have to store them in their bodies any more. They can play sports again, garden, go bowling or fishing or whatever they've had to put away, because they thought they couldn't risk it.

I had one male client with a deep core muscle problem in his lower back, which he had strained playing football in college. In a sense, we were going back in time through massage. He started saying that he felt anxious, scared, nervous when I touched him there. He had this horrible feeling that he had been abused, and his mind kicked in to determine who it could have been. I asked if he saw an image. He just felt this presence and saw blackness. I said, "Look into that," and he saw his father's face. During times like that, I still maintain contact, but I am not actively massaging. If I just stopped or withdrew, it would give the message that this was not okay to talk about.

A lot of therapists looking for repressed memories encourage their clients to fill in memory gaps, to put together a movie or script. I disagree with that, because mountains can be made out of molehills. These are serious accusations. But where there's smoke, there's fire. *Something* is going on with that client, who is psychologically distressed and has physical symptoms. But to sever relations with family, that's a terrible cost, and I don't advocate it. It really irritates me that a lot of therapists are on a kind of witch hunt. If you're screwed up, had a bad childhood, can't maintain a job or relationship, then you were automatically sexually abused. I hate that kind of interpretation, that sex abuse is the cause of every symptom. It keeps people from taking responsibility for their lives.

At the same time, we know that abuse does occur, much more frequently than anyone knew. So how do you balance it out? There's no clear way to do it. Yes, it is quite possible to be raped once a week for years and not recall it. I go back to that state-bound idea. Information is locked away in a certain compartment, and it doesn't come out until it's triggered.

Repressed memories are part of a larger pattern I see in most of my clients, who feel uncomfortable, disconnected and dissociated from their bodies. They live from the neck up, where everything is cognitive and analytical. So only part of what I do is to help retrieve memories. The bigger part is body image stuff, to help the client come to an acceptance of the body, to make wise choices about how to take care of the body in the future.

I have one current client who has retrieved memories of being sexually and ritually abused. She was working with a female therapist and already had an idea that some things had happened when she came to me. She started to retrieve memories at a rapid rate. For instance, I would pull her arm back to work on the triceps, and she would resist every time at that part of the massage. It turns out that during ritual abuse, she had witnessed another victim's arm being lifted in a similar fashion and severed at the shoulder, which explained her fear. When she was four, she remembered witnessing a girl her age being molested, killed, and dismembered. A lot of times, she wakes up at three in the morning and realizes, "Oh, my God, I know what that's about now!"

Similarly, in working with her hands, I put lotion on them. She felt that was creepy and had an image of blood being poured on her. Once she got the memory, then it felt fine to massage her fingers and hands. That's what we mean about being free of muscle memory. Now she gets her hand and body back. The last two weeks have been great for her. Her world is so bright right now, it makes it all worthwhile. She went through a scary time when she was getting worse instead of better, when she was less able to function, but she's through that now. We held her head above water until she could tread water, and now she can hold her head up and swim strongly.

I don't say, "Yes, this happened." I know that *she* believes it happened, and that's enough. Her well-being is my concern, making sure that she gets over the effects of whatever it was. Whether it was witnessing this ritualistic dismemberment or something else, she's reclaiming her body and power. That's my commitment. I don't verify that it happened, nor do I deny it. I just don't know.

No, I've never felt that I was being used by someone who wanted to get a memory, and that it was false.'

HAMISH PITCEATHLY, PRIMARY CAUSE ANALYST

Until his early retirement in 1993, Hamish Pitceathly [his real name] was a professor of history at the Roehampton Institute of Higher Education. Since the early 1980s, however, he has also practiced as a psychotherapist. Though lacking formal education in psychology, he has read widely in Freud, Jung, Adler, and others. In particular, he is a follower of the late New Zealand therapist James Bennett, who invented the 'primary activation' method. Pitceathly has altered the name somewhat to 'primary cause analysis' (PCA), but his approach is fundamentally the same. He believes that there are 39 basic 'scenes' of sexual abuse, all repressed until recalled under hypnosis in therapy. He presumably uncovered scenes of his own when he undertook a personal analysis with Bennett in 1986. Stung by what he calls 'a hatchet job' in the Sunday Times *('Fanatical Therapists Train Secretly in UK,' May 22, 1994) and a subsequent television documentary, Pitceathly agreed to an extensive interview to set the record straight.*

He belongs to the British Association of Counseling and the National Council of Psychotherapists. The BAC demanded to see his training manual, but Pitceathly refused, and the organization backed down. He has trained some 50 British therapists, but only 30 are currently PCA analysts. Pitceathly sees approximately 50 clients a year.

'Basically, I spend the first session or two just talking with clients, getting to know them. I want to know about their attitude toward themselves. Do they like themselves? Have confidence in themselves? Most people who come in say, "I lack confidence," or "I don't feel I'm reaching my full potential, and something is holding me back." That opens a Pandora's box that runs across a wide spectrum. You begin to find that if they're feeling inadequate in one area, they feel inadequate in a whole range of areas – relationships with siblings, parents, wives, mistresses, husband, their children. A whole range of self-doubts come up, feelings they can't handle of one sort or another.

We all create a framework within which we function until something disturbs it. We sort of manage within it, then something like a divorce happens, and it starts pushing around the frame a bit, putting a bit more guilt on. Some people say, this framework won't do, I must do something about it. This can't go on. But once you start working with them, and they look change in the face, it can be rather frightening. Sometimes it's a bit of a tussle.

After getting acquainted, we spend a session doing a long induction of a traditional kind, which is a gradual body relaxation, followed by a series of exercises. We try to keep the conscious mind occupied, perhaps by writing letters on a mental blackboard. Then we have exercises in communication, so they get used to talking to you while in a suitably relaxed state. I spend a lot of time emphasizing that *they* are in control of this whole procedure, it's *their* analysis, not mine. I'm trying to avoid any unnecessary transference. The memories are their memories, the feelings are their feelings. Then we spend some time building up their sense of confidence in the procedure and what they're going to do and their motivation. We use simple suggestion that they're going to allow themselves to feel physically better, mentally more alert, feel calmer, and develop a better attitude in life.

We ask them to practice self-hypnosis in between whiles. It's quite simple. While they are still in a relaxed state, we give them a few directions, it's a very simple procedure. When they come round, we ask if they remember how to do it, then practice it immediately. Often when they come back for the next session, I just tell them to close their eyes and relax, and that's it. The induction takes only a few minutes, sometimes not even that. They just close their eyes and they can switch themselves into whatever mode we want. I don't like all the hullabaloo that goes on around the word "hypnosis." You're hypnotized a good deal of the time anyway, such as driving on the M1 in a trance and saying, "How the hell did I get here?"

During hypnosis, I look for a general part, maybe the part responsible for their feeling inadequate, or for feelings of rejection. For every event that has a negative significance, which we can't resolve at the time, which we therefore have to repress, we create a defense mechanism for which a part of us is responsible. I try to get that "part" to respond. And when it is ready to do so, I ask it a yes/no question. The part responds with an ideomotor signal, one finger for "yes," another for "no." We establish how old the whole person was when that part came into being. Did it come into being when the whole person was a child? Was the whole person younger than 10? Most parts, I find, are already established by the time we're five. Some are sort of put in storage as it were and triggered off by something at one stage or another. Sometimes they even precipitate events in order to operate.

I don't use ideomotor signaling for finding out about the scene itself. I simply ask where they are, identify the time and place. I ask, "Was he playing with you?" or "Was he reading the newspaper?" Was the whole person upset by this event? Did he feel afraid? Was it fun? As one begins to touch on the area where feelings might become involved, you ask the part to allow the whole person to experience those feelings, to make contact with himself by whatever way is convenient to him, either by visualization, by feeling himself back there, and so on. I'll say, "Tell me if you're seeing anything or feeling anything." Sometimes they remember it with very little emotion – with a bald and emotionless statement.

Some people will go back and will behave as if they are really right back there. I emphasize, "You are going back as an adult sitting in this chair." This "child within" is a marvelous metaphor, but that's all it is. You're asking for a lot of emotional mess with that concept. I prefer to work with an adult, even if he chooses to re-enact childhood. I treat them as adults all the time.

We stay in it, go through it, get them, once they've been through the entire scene, to try to find the point at which they repressed it. Bennett emphasized that the process of repression – to change it from simple amnesia to full repression – requires collapse (sleep, in other words) and dream. One of the major functions of dreams is to repress something, to change one reality into another symbolic representation. We have people remember the dream, because it completes the process. The dream won't be any use any more to them, so they will stop having it.

I don't want to go into detail about all of the scenes, but I will give you a few examples, such as a little boy whose father forces him into oral sex. Oral rape of a male could relate to the development of all kinds of characteristic behaviors, such as a feeling of being put down. After all, that's what's happening to him, being controlled and put in his place. He's also often made to feel responsible for what happens because such acts are often preceded by something which is quite pleasurable. Then the child gets hurt and withdraws from the pleasurable contact.

This causes the father to go to the next stage. He loses his temper or detaches, dissociates. The word "dissociation" caught on in the late 1980s. Bennett called it detachment. So the individual detaches from conscious responsibility, then performs something automatically. Often, the child has learned to detach by this time, too. Sometimes the child recognizes when the parent has detached and therefore it detaches as a sort of safety guard. It then doesn't feel it so badly, and then represses it. And the adult represses it too.

There's a sort of intergenerational thing about this. Let's say some-thing happened to you when you were three, you were orally raped. You bury that, along with all memories of the circumstances. But it's built into it. You have reactions to authority figures, plus a desire to get even. You may become a driver on the road who wants to beat up everyone else on the road, pass everyone, a general road raider as they call it. Then you get to adulthood and marry and have your own child. Then lo and behold, when your child is three, you see your child playing exactly the same game that you were playing when you were three, on the sitting room floor, and that tricks your mind back into the same situation that you experienced. Now the person you see playing on the floor is not your child, you now see yourself at that age.

Then you see the child not as a child at all, but as your father who did it to you. So you are then driven to do it back to him. The person you think you're doing it to is not your child, but your father. It's automatic behavior. You think you're doing it to your father, but in fact you're doing it to the next generation, and you're making sure it's passed on to the next generation after that. When you've done it, you will then walk out of the room, and you will go and lie down and go to sleep and have a dream, and you will repress it. And the dream you will have will be either the same as the dream you had when you were three or a very similar one. That's the basic theory. And I'm afraid we've dug up many many many "passing-on" scenes of that kind.

Now the principle of "passing on" is well known with conscious sex abusers. It's commonplace to say, "Oh, they suffered sex abuse them-selves as children." We're just taking it a stage further. The subconscious scene has to be acted out with a kind of appalling logic. This gets uncovered under hypnosis. Some people may recall passing-on scenes from later in life. Some have to do with puberty, adolescence, or even post-marital activities. A parent sometimes establishes hold over a grown child by performing a sexual scene even after marriage.

My brother, who lives in New Zealand and also practices PCA, told me of a woman who used to take her child to school and would then have no memory until she found herself in a car park looking out at the sea around 11 a.m. Analysis showed that in fact she was going home to her father, having a sexual relationship with him on an automatic basis, then leaving him until she found herself in the car park. Once she recalled it, she stopped doing it. He was equally unconscious, so there was no point in confronting him. That's why our therapy avoids all confrontation between children and parents. It's non-productive.

They are liable to confront someone who has no memory whatsoever either, and they're not going to get it unless they too are prepared to go through the proper kind of therapy.

Most people have some sort of scene such as this in their past. Yes, this is clearly very important information. I have been worried about the right time to come forward with it. I am preparing not just one book but perhaps several, full of case histories, including verbatim transcripts. I've been at it for over a decade now, and as a result of the *Sunday Times* article, and all the other crap that came out, I went into sort of automatic mode and couldn't take any more. It destroyed my practice for a while. But that doesn't matter. It's taken off again now.

One of the earliest scenes usually occurs between birth and six months old. The mother holds up the child by one leg and presses the child's head against her genitals. This can have a large number of effects. The most important is distrust, because after all, at that stage, the infant feels the mother is the entire source of sustenance. Suddenly the whole world gets turned upside down quite literally and metaphorically, and the damned thing is nearly asphyxiated – and in some cases *is* asphyxiated. Then you get a built-in distrust which begins to affect virtually everything it does thereafter in life. Others might develop a fear of heights, or claustrophobia. Also, some type of autistic reactions can probably be taken back to this kind of thing.

This often leads to a second scene when the child is a little older. The mother can't hold it up by one leg any more, but she can sit on the damned thing on the ground. The mother is involving her own sexual organs, sitting on his face. By that age, the child is much bigger and can always breath.

She rubbishes the child. She beats it up basically. There's no sexual gratification for her. She is too angry. The best way of making yourself angry and frustrated at the same time is to use the sexual drive and frustrate it, which is what seems to happen.

Funnily enough, the most important part of that scene is not so much the physical discomfort, which is bad enough, but the verbalization that goes on with it, which usually contains statements like, "You're no bloody good, I can do it better myself. You're useless, just like your father. You'll never be any good to anyone." You can see that if this sort of material goes into the subconscious of that child, it lays a foundation for all sorts of debasing thereafter, such as an inability to form good relationships. She makes herself more and more and more angry and gets to the point where she hits or kicks the child.

These things tend to end once the child's resistance ends. If a child puts up a fight, she will fight harder, and she will win, of course. What appears to happen in the very early scene, the child learns detachment by blacking out in the earliest scenes. Having learned how to black out, by the time the second one occurs, subconsciously it remembers that when it blacked out, it all ended. So in this case, it just detaches and goes within. It can't black out because it can still breathe, but psychologically it can make a dissociation or detachment, and at that point, it all ends.

I see this sort of thing over and over again in my practice. We stand accused, of course, by those who don't want to know anything about it, of implanting ideas in people's minds, but I'm afraid we don't. I would fight that one right the way down the line. Actually, we waste an awful lot of patients' time making sure we are not leading them. There's no reason why you shouldn't have a damned good idea what's there simply on the basis of your own experience of the type of material the patients give you.

I mean, if I go to a doctor, and I say, "Look, doctor, I've got a bloody awful headache," I would expect him to give me some kind of diagnosis. After appropriate tests, I would expect him to say, "You may have a tumor," or "You may just have a hangover." Similarly, someone comes along to me and says, "I have this whole range of feelings." A symptom is a symptom but once you start putting symptoms together with many others, you can begin to suspect. So in fact, I would regard myself as incompetent and irresponsible if I did *not* look out for things and satisfy myself that they weren't there.

If I start looking to see if a particular event is there, I will camouflage my activities until I'm almost black all over, as it were. But Bennett would go about it in a much more direct way. I have used his ways in the past, and with those with whom you establish a resonance, the scene will come out, even though the approach itself describes nothing. On the other hand, those for whom there is no resonance bring up nothing. In principle, yes, you could ask directly if the mother held the child up by the leg, and if there were no resonance, they would simply say "No." I would only do this with someone I had worked with for some time.

Say we've already taken out a fair number of scenes, in which case, that client has trust in me, and I have trust in that client. I will get them relaxed and say something like, "I want to look and see if something happened to you below the age of 10. Perhaps you were ill and at home. Let's just imagine that you're in bed, and your mother's come to look after you and give you a bowl of soup and wipe your face." That may not be the right scene at all, but I'm afraid if that's what I'm looking for, usually it is. But someone may say, "No, no, it's not there at all, I'm on the settee, I've been allowed to get up and watch television." And they'll take it on from there. Or they may say, "No, I'm afraid there's nothing there at all." And by that time, we have enough knowledge of each other, I'll say, "OK, fine, leave it." But at least I've checked it out.

The topic of false memory comes up. People want to talk about it, so we talk about it a bit. I don't accept the automatic assumption that any material brought up in hypnosis is false. I keep an open mind. I must admit, on some occasions I wonder whether what I'm hearing is necessarily actually totally true. I adopt a pragmatic attitude. I mean, if, if, IF, IF, with a big if, it turns out to be fantasy, well then it's just as well the fantasy's brought out, isn't it? Because it's clearly being used for some purpose or another. But on the whole, I've never myself in the end found any reason to doubt the stories people tell me.'

KATHERINE HYLANDER, PAST-LIFE HYPNOTHERAPIST

In 1990, Katherine Hylander was hypnotized for the first time by her dentist when she underwent oral surgery. 'I had no pain and was completely transported into another consciousness,' she recalls. Unfulfilled at her job as a computer payroll manager for a large California bank, Hylander pursued training in hypnotherapy over the next year and, by the end of 1991, she wasn't altogether upset when her position at the bank was cut. Since then, she has been a full-time hypnotherapist. In 1992, she accidentally hit upon her speciality: past-life regressions. Hylander also helps clients uncover UFO abductions, spirit possessions, and repressed memories of sexual abuse in this life. Lately, she has progressed some clients into the future, which can be frightening – particularly when they see California covered by the ocean.

'I had heard so much about past lives, but then it happened spontaneously in a 1992 session. I had a client coming for hypnotherapy to build her self-esteem. She was a prober who wanted to understand the mysteries of life, to know why she was here on this earth. She wanted to learn about her earliest feelings. I had her visualize a one-handed clock, letting it count down backwards. I got down to three, and she kept saying "More, more." We got to where she was a newborn baby.

233

She still wanted to go further back, so I said, "Okay, you're in the womb." She experienced her mother's feelings and emotions. As the youngest of seven, she wanted to make sure her mother wanted her. It was beautiful, because her mother *did* want her.

One day, she came holding her jaw, with a painful neuralgia in her face for no apparent physiological reason. When she was under hypnosis, I instinctively said, "Go way back, find out where that pain came from." She suddenly found herself being attacked by peasants somewhere. I didn't understand. I said, "Is this San Francisco?" She just said, "No!" like I was stupid. These peasants were angry at her because she had this wonderful spirituality, and they accused her of being different. They stoned her to death, and the last thing she remembered was being hit in the face. She said they were speaking this funny language. I think this was some time in the Middle Ages in Europe.

Since then, I've done more and more past-life regressions. I'm not out to prove anything by it. I'm nonjudgmental. I tell people they may not have a past-life regression. The issues may be from this lifetime, from this childhood. You see, a lot of patterns are repeated, either from this life or past lives.

Repressed memories are a major cause of suffering for my clients. I see it every day, in about 90 per cent of the people who come to see me. They often feel depressed, with a general malaise. They might cry for no reason. Oh, they may take Prozac, but that just treats the symptom without touching the underlying problem.

We must find the root, the origin of the problem. Memories can fester if they are not dealt with. I see so many wounded children inside my clients. They may have been sexually abused, raped, or totally ignored, which may be even worse.

There are quite a few physical symptoms that result from trauma in a past life. I really believe that all illness is psychosomatic. For instance, asthma may be the result of smoke inhalation in another life. An allergy to wheat may stem from a rape in a wheat field, or arthritis from being stretched on a rack during the Inquisition.

I'll give you some specific case histories. One 42-year-old divorced woman came with generalized sadness, but she couldn't put her finger on just what she was suffering from. She felt major anxiety every evening around dusk, just when she was going home from work. If she happened to be with a man around that time of day, she felt a tremendous fear of sexual contact. She asked me, "Am I crazy?" So I hypnotized her. She didn't think I would be able to, because she couldn't relax. The people who say that are usually my best subjects. I regressed her to a past life, and she gave very vivid commentary. "I'm in Mexico, I'm eight years old, I'm wearing a white dress. I have no shoes on, but I'm very pretty, very dark." She described the room where she lived with her family.

Suddenly she was tense. "Oh, oh. He's coming home now. My father. I don't like him." I asked her why, and she said she didn't want to talk about it. But then she relived the terror. Every night when he came home from the fields, he went into her room, closed the door, and raped her on her bed. I said, "Do you know what time it is?" She answered, "Yes, dusk." I told her then that it was time to let go of that memory and get on with her life. I progressed her to a time when she was happy, at 18, and in love. But then she got pregnant and died in childbirth. After her death, she experienced a feeling of peace and spoke with her spirit guides. I asked if there was anything else she wanted to find out. "Yes, I want to go back to that little girl and wash her, cleanse her. I always feel dirty and don't know why." So I helped her to go back and gave her as much time with that little girl as she needed. I told her to tell the girl that she'd come from the future to heal her.

I do that a lot now in regular regression, healing the wounded inner children, picking them up, putting them in the heart center, stroking them, just letting them know that they're wonderful, clean, good. They've never been told that. A child who's been abused feels worthless, not respected. I take my clients to different stages of their childhood. We might go to a beautiful garden and bring their abuser there to tell him how they feel. But I always come out on a positive note. "Look at me, I'm stronger than you are," they tell the abuser.

Another 34-year-old woman came to me with a myriad of problems. The first thing she mentioned was this phobia she had about her husband's hands. Her marriage wasn't going well, but every time she tried to leave him, she kept getting this vision of his hands, and it stopped her somehow. So we went to regression. In a past life, she had also been married to this same man. I find that's fairly common, that the same group of people often interacts throughout different lives, which can account for why you have such a strong immediate reaction to someone you meet for the first time. In this past life, her husband wouldn't give her any space and wouldn't allow her to leave. She started screaming. She smelled something terrible. Her eyes and nose started running, and she had trouble breathing. His hands were covering her mouth. "My God!" she said. "He's a doctor! He's putting ether on me!" Eventually, in that life, he strangled her.

While she was still under hypnosis, I regressed her to another life. "Dear God! I've done it again!" she cried. "I'm married to the same son-of-a-bitch! He's blinded me! I have psychic abilities and he doesn't believe in them." She was going so fast, I didn't have time to ask any questions. Between lives, though, she said, was the most beautiful experience. "I'll never fear death again."

She taped the whole session, and afterward, she said, "Wait till he hears this. My husband is against anything New Age or psychic." She felt that she was very psychic, but her husband always ridiculed her. When he found out she was coming to see me, he said, "You're crazy. Don't waste money on that hocus-pocus." But just before she left, he said, "If you like it, make an appointment for me." So maybe there's a chance for reconciliation. I told her not to go home and tell him everything, but to give him the information in spoonfuls, to say something like, "You know, honey, I like to confide in you, but sometimes I feel a little threatened. There's something new I've just learned . . ."

The whole object here is to be healed, not to heap blame. There's really no injustice. We're required to experience everything to learn. It's a natural evolution of the soul. I think we choose our parents and our circumstances. If you experience terrible abuse, maybe it's because in a past life, you've been a horrific person, and you need to know what it feels like to be abused in this life. Once you learn the lesson, you can truly forgive. I don't believe in retribution. This planet is a great big classroom. Once we're perfect, we won't have to come back. Suffering is here, not on the other plane of existence.

I'll give you one final case study about a young Indian girl, about 24, who discovered repressed memories from this life. Her parents brought her to America from India at a very young age. When she came to me, she was very troubled and said she hated San Francisco but didn't know why. "I feel it's dead here, I can't get out, my parents won't let me go." She lived a very cloistered existence. I hypnotized her and said, "Go to the subconscious origins of this tremendous fear and hate." I've found that the subconscious is very literal. You have to give it explicit instructions. But I'm very careful not to lead anyone. I don't say things like, "Go to a time you were raped."

This girl said, "I'm standing at a bus stop, coming home from school. I'm nine years old. A man dressed in black is watching me. He has his collar up." She walked home down a wooded street, but she felt he was following her. She went up to her bedroom and was doing her home-work. It was daytime, and she was alone in the house. "I'm afraid, I'm so afraid." So I asked her to lift herself out of it, to become just a witness. "That man from the bus stop, he's in my room. He puts me on the bed, he's taking my clothes off. I'm quiet, I'm numb." He raped her, then nonchalantly put his clothes on and left her lying there. It turns out he was the family doctor who lived on the same street. "I didn't tell my parents, they would never believe me," she said. So she repressed it.

I told her, "It's not that you hate San Francisco, but what happened here." In other sessions, we found that during her annual check-up, he raped her in his doctor's office once a year until she was 16, with her mother in the waiting room. This is a very well-behaved, proper young lady. I asked her if she wanted to be angry. I told her she could shout and call him every name under the sun. She said mildly, "You were a very bad person, and I'm telling you now I'm really angry." I'm working with her on a weekly basis. She's got a new job and is moving to a different city. She doesn't want to confront the doctor in real life. She won't tell her parents, even today. They would only call her a liar.

Some of my clients were abducted by aliens and taken to UFOs in the middle of the night. It's utterly horrifying for them, a real violation. There's a ten-point checklist which cues me to look out for these cases. That includes things like missing time at night, nightmares about UFOs or vampires. Very often, people who have been abducted will wake up at the same time every night. The subconscious remembers everything; it's trying to protect itself. Some people are so vigilant and don't know why. They wake up and can't sleep until dawn. Sometimes they experi-ence bodily sensations, tingling, paralysis, or pain. Some have mysterious marks on their bodies, bruises, scars, when they wake up. I've seen these. A lot of UFO abductees tell me they had ear problems as a child, which is a sign of an implant which can't be detected by our science. The aliens put them in to observe us.

Another sign is if someone reacts violently to the subject of UFO abductions. The other day, I was giving a public speech. As soon as I started talking about UFO cases, one woman just shot out of her chair and ran out of the room. I almost stopped the speech to run after her, because I'm sure that she was taken up by a UFO and needs to face it.

Everyone can be regressed, if they don't block the process. Well, almost everybody. A few people have told me under hypnosis that they are from another galaxy and can't be regressed. But for most people, you have to chip gently away at their armor, their defense mechanisms. I give them the chisel and let them do it under hypnosis. I must be gentle and respectful. If they are ready, they'll be regressed. No, they don't have any trouble getting back – no one's ever been left in a past life!

I love what I do, but I don't let my ego swell over it. I'm just a facilitator. I don't profess to heal anyone. I'm an instrument.'

SALLY BIXBY, PSYCHOTHERAPIST

Sally Bixby, 50, who holds a master's degree in counseling, is a therapist in a large Colorado city. Although she is extremely skeptical of the search for repressed memories, she will not go public with her concerns. 'I'd be tarred, feathered, and ridden out of town on a rail,' she explains. 'If you can tell me how to make a living afterwards, I'll be glad to go on the record.' So, as with the other therapists here, her name has been changed.

'More and more is being written to indicate that memory is not the infallible resource that people thought it was. Like eyewitness accounts, memory is open to suggestion. What I see and interpret can be very different from what you see. We're subjective beings, and we tend to attach meaning to what we see, which results in skewed memories.

The whole notion that people can forget massive trauma entirely, and then it comes back later, is also being challenged. Those who suffer post-traumatic stress disorder, such as Vietnam veterans, never forget what happened to them. Their difficulty is *not* being able to forget.

I can see how, given the right encouragement, people could mix together real feelings and incidents from their childhoods with invented abuse memories. Being a child is difficult. You're small, defenseless, and you don't know how to interpret things. A lot of things appear frightening. Your father's face near you can be scary, and the smell of his aftershave may indeed bring back a memory of that fear.

For instance, I have a very clear memory which I never "repressed." When I was four, I had my tonsils out. I was convinced that I had been a bad girl, and they were going to kill me. They rolled me into this operating room, and there were guys with white robes and what looked like jars of blood, and they put this thing over my face. I thought they were going to smother me. I was terrified. When I came to, I realized

I was okay. If I didn't know any better and went to the right therapist, this memory could be turned into a satanic cult ritual.

That sort of therapy does a real disservice to people on a number of levels. It provides a simple explanation for all the troubles they have in their life. You know, "This awful thing happened to me, and that's why I have so many problems. It's not my fault. I can't help it." As a matter of fact, there is evidence that people can be terribly abused and still function quite well in their lives. Humans are more resilient than we give them credit for. But now there's this idea that damage in your childhood creates these insurmountable problems for the rest of your life. I've just been reading this *Vanity Fair* interview with Roseanne Arnold, and she says every day is hell for her because she was so traumatized. I'm sure she honestly believes it, but she's a perfect example of this whole thing.

I'm not trying to minimize real abuse or its effects. There is clearly incest and abuse, and these people have real stories to tell and difficulties to overcome. But I don't think they ever forget it.

The work of Murray Bowen, who pioneered in family systems therapy, has influenced me a great deal. He tried to stick to observable facts instead of subjective interpretation, and he studied animal behavior. People are not all that different from animals. We *are* animals. A lot of Freud's theories set us apart, but we're more alike than unlike. Bowen said that the degree to which people individuate and become their own person, separate from their parents, has a lot to do with how well they will function in life. How a person fares at any given time is a function of the amount of anxiety they feel and their level of individuation. That's one reason so many of the women are accusing their parents – they were probably *too close* to them. This is a way to separate, but all they're really doing is transferring that dependence to their therapist.

I get a lot of people walking in the door who are very pop-psychology-wise. They'll announce, "I have co-dependent issues," or "I'm an ACOA," or "I think I was sexually abused." The first thing I do is to get clear what they mean by that term. I want them to think for themselves in more detail instead of grabbing onto some label that will give them an easy answer. We're all co-dependent. It's not bad; it's just a fact of life. Anyone could relate to the list of symptoms, just as with supposed repressed memories of sex abuse. They are symptoms of human experience. If you have those symptoms, it means you're human, and you should rejoice.

I tell clients right out front that I have no answers and I can't cure them. I try to dispel the notion that I'm God or some expert. Some of them never come back to see me again. Others catch on, and it helps them function more clearly. If I'm doing my job, I help people manage themselves in their lives a little differently, so they can function better. I use here-and-now cognitive work. Sure, I do a family history because it tells me something about the system they come from, what they have to deal with, but really, we're not trying to heal past wounds or get in touch with feelings.

I see a lot of people who are angry at their parents. I don't try to tell them not to be angry, but I do ask them to look carefully at their own role. People tend to blame others and absolve themselves of any part in what happened. Certainly a small child who is terribly abused has no responsibility for it, but as you grow older, that's not so true. It's an interpersonal dynamic. This label of "emotional incest" is dangerous, because it encourages such anger and blame. There's some truth to the basic idea sometimes, but we should look at it without blaming, just looking for information and how to function better in your life.

For those reasons, I rarely suggest bringing parents into therapy. There's no point in telling them how pissed off you are. If I make it clear that we're not bringing them in to unload on them, then I can do it. A lot of what I work on is reactivity. Can you be in the same room with someone and not necessarily react? When even one person in a relationship can manage their reactivity, it can change the relationship.

This whole idea that we must unburden ourselves immediately of any feelings we have bottled up is wrong, I think. I went to a workshop a few years ago with an old-school therapist who told us, "If you're a therapist who goes after the feelings, you're like a surgeon who operates because he likes to see blood flowing." As some part of personal growth, you'll get feelings, but that's not the important point. The aim is to know what your feelings are, but not be ruled by them.

It would be interesting to trace all the threads that have led to this rage to uncover repressed memories of incest. I think it's ironic that this started out as part of the women's movement to empower women, but now it is disempowering them, putting them in the role of victim. Somehow, confronting parents and cutting off from them, suing them, is supposed to help. I think it just creates more anxiety and makes women less able to function independently.

I don't usually get patients who try to retrieve memories, because that's not what I'm known for. But I did have one client, Stephanie, with a lifelong history of mental illness, who has spent a good deal of time in institutions, where she was always diagnosed as schizophrenic. A few years ago, she went to the Pines Retreat Center, where they diagnosed her as a multiple personality disorder and she began to retrieve memories of incest. I didn't know anything about MPD, and so I attended some conferences on it. At first, I embraced the idea fully, but now I'm beginning to question it. We all have multiple personalities. For some people who don't have a firm center, those personalities can get fragmented.

At this point, I don't challenge that Stephanie has MPD, but I don't spend much time talking to her different personalities, looking for more memories, or talking about them. I've also found out that the Pines Retreat specializes in diagnosing MPD and eliciting repressed memories, and some insurance companies won't pay for people to go there any more.

No, I don't use any form of hypnotism or guided imagery to help retrieve memories. When I first started my practice ten years ago, I used a lot of creative visualization for anxiety reduction. But I got scared off when I had one extremely agitated client who couldn't sit still during a session. I thought I would try relaxation techniques. But it just made her more upset. It triggered all her anxieties about safety.

I'm not too sure what hypnotism really is. There are people who say that whenever you sit down with somebody, in a sense you're hypnotizing them. It's fairly well documented that people with dissociational disorders are very hypnotizable, which could explain why they are so open to suggestion.

I don't challenge my patients' memories. I would not try to convince them that their repressed memories were true or not true. But I wouldn't focus on the memories. If they have cut off from their parents, I tell them it would make a world of difference to them if they could learn to be with that parent and not automatically react. I think people will come to question the "memories" on their own if there's a seed of doubt. I don't need to plant the seed. If they come to me in the first place, it's probably because they instinctively are calmer and willing to question.

What would happen if you took this interview and published it with my real name in the local paper? Oh, my God! I don't even want to think about it. A number of people might say, "Wow, she's really brave to say that," and they would secretly agree. Others would see it as heresy, as being abusive to clients, not validating or hearing them. I might lose my referral base. I would also worry that some of the clients I work with would say, "Oh, wow, she thinks I'm just making this all up."'

ROBIN NEWSOME, RETRACTOR THERAPIST

Texan Robin Newsome, 49, is a soft-spoken, gentle woman. She became a devout Christian her junior year in college when she joined a Christian campus organization. After graduating with a degree in early childhood education, she married and had two children. In 1982, she returned to school for a master's in counseling, where she embraced Gestalt therapy and encountered her first case of recovered memory.

'One of my first courses was called "Anger Therapy." It met every day for three weeks. After a short lecture, we'd meet in small groups with a therapist. This was a very intense, emotional experience. After a round of checking in, each group member was asked whether they wanted to "work" or not on any particular day. That meant doing a two-chair visualization, where you imagined the person you were angry at to be in the chair across from you, and you vented your anger, using a bataaka bat to hit a foam pad. This was supposed to get out your unresolved anger. This was a whole new world to me. I felt like Alice falling down the rabbit hole with this stuff. Here I was in my placid little world, and this was like entering a subterranean world I never knew existed.

One Friday, a woman in the group told us she had an image of herself being sexually abused when she was two years old. She said, "I know I was abused by someone, but I can't see who it is." On Monday, she told us with tremendous sorrow that she had realized that it was her older brother. The therapist had her "put him in the chair," but instead of using the bat, she said she wanted to rip his head off. The therapist handed her some magazines and told her to have at it. She started screaming at the top of her lungs at her brother, crying and ripping magazines. Everything was going well until she grabbed one of the therapist's favorite *Smithsonians*, and the therapist yelled for her to stop and not rip that one. This woman completely shifted gears. She very politely said, "Oh, I'm sorry," and put it down. Then, with a vengeance, she grabbed another magazine and went back to ripping and tearing.

At the time, I interpreted this to mean that she had control over her anger. I had wondered if people would get so angry during these exercises that they might just lose it completely. This woman's ability to stop herself so quickly showed me that people weren't really losing total control. In fact, this incident made the therapy feel more like a play with a therapist/director who had just yelled, "Cut!"

Still, I had no reason to doubt that she had been abused – her tears, her sorrow, her anguish, her rage, her sense of betrayal were painful to witness. I remember being so angry at the thought that anyone could do such a thing to a small, helpless child. The fact that she had remembered her relationship with her brother as being happy prior to this memory seemed irrelevant. Obviously, her mind had shielded her from the awful truth. No one even remotely thought to question the memory of a two-year-old. Also, the idea was that young children had trouble giving words to their abuse, because they were in a preverbal state. So there was just this nameless rage buried there all these years.

Throughout my courses, there was a lot of talk about "body memories." We were taught that anger was stored in the body. During times of anger or stress, you could identify your "stress organ." Mine is in my neck muscles. This woman stored her anger in her jaw. I found this concept very useful. During guided imagery, I would ask clients to recall a specific memory and ask them where they felt it, in what part of the body. When they finished their anger work, the tension would usually be gone, which I took as an indication that they had worked through that emotion.

Another woman in our group had come from an unhappy, dysfunctional home. Our instructor led her in a guided visualization and helped her create a new family for herself. At the therapist's suggestion, she re-invented her childhood, which included growing up in a different state, in a new house with a new, improved family. It seemed to be helpful to her, and everyone in the group praised her. I wondered at the time what she planned to do with her real family – the one she still had to deal with. But then, I was just a student and the therapist was the expert.

I also remember one woman who had polio when she was young. The therapist asked her what the *purpose* of the polio was. The idea was that your body and mind collaborate, and that nothing that happens is simply circumstantial. Initially, this feels like an insight and explanation for something that seems so unfair and irrational. In this case, the implication was that she was being sexually abused by her father, so she developed polio in order to escape to the hospital.

At the time, I really admired this therapist who led my groups. She was bold, outspoken, and fearless – a really good role model for mousy little me. She seemed invincible and infallible. She was very much in control of the group, always starting and ending on time. She had people sharing their deepest secrets and unleashing their rage from day one. I'd never seen anything like it. Then, after people had bared their souls, she would be very tender and caring, like the Mom we had always wanted. But at precisely 12 noon, the warmth would end. I always had the feeling that if I saw her in the grocery store, she wouldn't give me the time of day. She was someone I both admired and feared.

Probably because I had not been very open with my true feelings before, I really took to Gestalt therapy. It was very freeing for me. I saw it work, and I still believe it can be very helpful to people. One of my first attempts at Gestalt therapy was a piece of work I did with a woman at my church who was still grieving over a miscarriage. She did a beautiful piece of grief work over the loss of her unborn child. That was one of the most amazing things I have witnessed. I saw her almost transform in my presence. She was able to find peace in her miscarriage and let go of some aspects of it.

Once I graduated with my master's in 1986, I began to counsel people with a variety of issues, but I also developed a sub-speciality in sexual abuse. In 1990, I ran a sexual abuse group that lasted nine months. While most of the women in the group had always remembered their abuse, there were a few who had vague images or just a gut feeling that they had been abused. I remember conducting a guided imagery session with one such woman. I had her close her eyes, get comfortable, and find the tension in her body. I said to her, "How old are you in this memory?" She was about four. I would ask other questions, like, "Do you know where you are? Do you feel like you're inside or out-of-doors?" In my own mind, I did not see this as leading at all. They seemed like innocuous questions. Later, I realized that this was almost like playing scrabble with someone and putting in a little word that suddenly opens up a whole new section of the board. I was helping her to take that little image and let it flow into a specific place. I was actually helping her fill in the details.

She said, "I feel like I'm being smothered. Something's in my face, and I don't know what." I took a pillow and gently put it on her face to simulate the experience. She sat with it for a while, then suddenly she started crying. She said, "I see it now." It was her babysitter abusing her. She remembered a nude woman forcing her to have oral sex. At that point, she sort of emotionally closed down and couldn't go any further with it. I said, "When you're ready, you can open your eyes. How is your stomach now?" It felt a little better, she said. Then I told her, "I'm really proud of you – you worked really hard." Others in the group also gave her feedback, such as, "What you remembered was really helpful to me, because it helped me be in touch with what it was like to be little and to remember what happened to me."

I wouldn't have said I was doing hypnosis at all. I tended to think of hypnosis as induced by a swinging watch chain. This was just guided imagery. I thought I was getting into the subconscious. We had been taught in our anger therapy class that you stored memories in your body. No one explained exactly how that was done. I just took it for granted. Another thing we learned was that claustrophobia often indicated a person had had oral sex forced on them. It made a certain amount of sense.

Unfortunately, this client with the babysitter memory never really got better. Few of my recovered memory clients ever improved. This person was always terrifically angry, and the work we did never seemed to help her. In fact, I would say that the sexual abuse group made her worse, and it just distracted her from her real issues – her daughter, her troubled marriage, and a stressful job situation.

Still, I completely believed in the memories I was hearing in my therapy sessions. My first doubts began with Sally, whose story continues to haunt me, especially because it is on-going. Sally is in her mid 30s, and she came to see me almost four years ago, wanting help with her compulsive eating. Later, she told me that her father had been an alcoholic, and we began to focus on her dysfunctional family. One day, Sally came to see me after getting the image of a little girl sitting in a pool of blood. All the details of when, where and who were unclear. I had her close her eyes and led her through guided imagery, asking my typical questions: "How old are you? What are you wearing? What time of year is it? What happens next?" With my prompting, she began to retrieve little bits of memory. In the end, she saw her father penetrating her when she was three.

At the end of the session, Sally asked, "Can this possibly be true?" She had always felt so close to her Dad. His drinking had always made him a happy drunk, and she was actually closer to him than her Mom. She had no memory of him sexually abusing her before this image. I gave her the classic line: "Sally, there would be no way for you to have invented this much detail unless it really happened."

After that first memory, she started having others. They would come to her during the week, and she would come to each session more and more depressed. She also had terrible insomnia and pelvic pain, which I explained to her as body memories. They were further proof that her memories were true.

By this time, I had witnessed many clients recovering repressed memories, and I totally believed them. If you saw the emotion, you would have no reason to doubt. The images were punctuated over and over again by the anguish, tears, contorted face, clenched fists, and rage that was expressed in hitting and kicking and ripping and gnashing of teeth. And there was always the pleading question, "How could he do this to me?" It would have been incomprehensible to think that the person just came up with it to play act. They weren't play acting. We honestly believed the images that came into their heads were the horrifying records of real events.

When Sally first came to see me, she was a relatively functional person. Home schooling is very popular here, and she had been home schooling her two boys for a couple of years. But after she started to get the abuse memories, she became so emotionally fragile that she decided to put her sons in public school. Sally would have horrible nightmares and days of sitting in a dark room just staring at the wall. She couldn't do her housework, so her husband had to do his work and then come home and do hers.

Sally's husband was very supportive of her, yet there were times he would get really frustrated, watching his wife slip away before his eyes. They had no sex life because she wouldn't let him touch her. He would vacillate between being understanding and being really angry.

Meanwhile, Sally decided to confront her Dad. I would say to clients, "One of the issues facing you is whether to confront the perpetrator or not." If a person decided to confront, we talked about how to do it, how to craft a letter, or, if they were going to confront in person, we would role-play. We always planned how they would react if the perpetrator denied what happened, what boundaries should be set. Sally wrote her father a letter. He called her and completely denied everything, but we took that as evidence that he was in denial.

After confronting her Dad, Sally seemed to get a little better, but it wasn't long before she started having more images, and another round of memories would begin. Just when we would start to work on current issues, like her troubled marriage or the problem she was having with her youngest son, boom! There would be another image.

Then one day, she came to me and said, "I had this image that involved my mother." She closed her eyes, and we went back to a time when she was a little girl living in Iowa, in this sleepy little Midwestern town. She remembered that her mother had a miscarriage. Sally was seven years old, and she found her mother in the kitchen dismembering the fetus with a knife on a chopping block. When her mother saw her, she made her help. Sally remembered severing a tiny leg, and then she had to fry it and eat it.

I was horrified. During the week after this session, I began to realize I was having a hard time believing this memory. I told myself that it was so horrible that I probably just didn't *want* to believe it. That year, I had attended a presentation at a local Baptist church, where a patient described her experience in a multi-generational satanic ritual abuse [SRA] cult, so I was somewhat familiar with this type of story. She had been locked in a rat-infested basement with other children. They had been drugged and programmed to cut themselves if they ever told. She described how she had repressed all of this and recalled it in therapy. Her therapist, a counselor at the church, was a man who seemed very caring, very professional. I bought this presentation hook, line, and sinker.

So now, when I was having trouble believing the memory, I put the blame on myself. I realized that I had to tell Sally and, even worse, I realized that I could no longer do therapy with her. We had built up such trust, and I was really worried about Sally's reaction. She had begun cutting herself by that point. I had been taught that it would be a thousand years in purgatory to doubt the memory of a client. Nonetheless, I knew that I could not be effective in Sally's recovery as long as I harbored doubts. Furthermore, we had crossed into the uncharted territory of SRA, and I felt that I was no longer qualified to treat Sally. I referred her to an expert, the counselor at the Baptist church.

I later learned that after the first week or two of her new therapy, her counselor suggested that she might have multiple personality disorder [MPD]. By her fourth session, she had discovered three personalities. From that point on, she developed more and more. I understand that she now has 35 or so. She has been hospitalized at least five times. She has overdosed and cut herself again and again. After three years of weekly and sometimes twice-weekly therapy with a counselor and a psychiatrist, she shows no sign of improvement. Her marriage is now on the brink of divorce, and her two sons are tired of their Mom being so crazy. They are frightened of her and for her. I get the feeling that they feel responsible for keeping her alive. Her new counselor told Sally that things would have to get worse before they got better. He sure was right about that!

A couple of months later, a woman named Rebecca came to see me. She was having images of ceremonial-type murders. In this case, there was a corroborating witness who had instigated an investigation against her parents. This involved a real unsolved murder from many years ago, and the police were called in. I thought, "Here's an example of SRA really happening." Before, I had queasy feelings, but here were the police giving credence to it. Again, I referred this client to the so-called experts, this time to a residential treatment center in New Mexico called Cottonwood, where they specialized in the treatment of SRA victims. The main focus was on recovering repressed memories. In group, they would share any thoughts or dreams, and if a person had a memory, they were highly praised for it. The worst thing you could say was, "I don't know if this is true or not."

Rebecca got much worse instead of better. She told me later that the images never felt quite like her other memories, and she continued to question their validity. She also found out that the corroborating "evidence" of her friend consisted of recovered memories she had retrieved in therapy. After the police investigation failed to turn up any physical evidence to support the accusations, she decided to take a break from all the stress of therapy and make an attempt to get back some kind of normal life with her husband and young children. As time passed, she noticed that she felt better. The nightmares stopped, her symptoms abated, and her thoughts cleared. In fact, she began to seriously question whether any of her repressed memories were true. She missed her family but was uncertain how to reconcile with them, particularly with her father. Finally, when Rebecca became seriously ill herself, she called on her mother for help.

By this time, Rebecca's parents had discovered the False Memory Syndrome Foundation and had tried to get some FMS literature to me through my pastor. He gave it to me to read. I took one look at it, and the tone seemed very anti-therapist. I said, "This sounds like nonsense, like perpetrators trying to invent a safe haven." I didn't pay much attention to it.

Rebecca went through her surgery, and her parents were very loving and supportive – pretty amazing, since she had accused her Dad of murder. She finally allowed them to see her children, whom they had not seen in over a year. In the past few months, I have met her parents and tried to make amends for the damage I caused their family. They have been incredibly kind and forgiving.

After her surgery, Rebecca started reading the FMS material and realized that she fit the pattern of the repressed memory victim to a T. Instead of merely doubting her abuse memories, she began to denounce them. In early 1993, she came to me with the article about Paul Ingram from *The New Yorker*. That article was a turning point for me. As I read it, I kept thinking of my experience with Sally and how she had not gotten better, but worse. She had gone from mere hell to sheer hell.

I began to think maybe there was such a thing as false memory. I wondered why the Vietnam vet doesn't forget being in Vietnam, or the Chowchilla children being buried in a bus, or the Holocaust survivors. Why don't flood victims forget? The problem with real victims of trauma seems just the reverse – they can't forget about those experiences. Does the mind work like a movie camera, recording every detail of an event? How early can memories be retrieved? How can people remember back to six months old? One of my clients had recalled being sexually abused in her crib by her grandfather. Where is the science to give credence to a belief like that? Or for that matter, do women in their teens forget incidents of repeated abuse? One incident might be forgotten, but repeated acts of torture, how do they get repressed? And why was it only sexual abuse that was blocked from memory? Why not physical abuse?

I had just re-read *The Crucible* about the Salem witch trials, and I began to see parallels. The same flimsy "evidence" that condemned innocent people to die in Salem was now being used to accuse and sometimes even charge parents of crimes, the only evidence being a repressed memory. I realized that I had never once questioned the idea of repressed memory. It was a presupposition that had been laid down in my profession as a foundation, and I had just stepped out onto it without questioning whether it was a solid foundation on which to build beliefs. I began to read snippets of the FMSF literature, which was based on scientific research in the field of memory and hypnosis. I realized that I needed to rethink many of my fundamental assumptions.

In the fall of 1993, I attended my first local FMSF meeting. I wasn't sure what to expect. These were the accused, after all. I remembered all that I had learned about how all perpetrators are in denial. I expected a room full of defensive parents. What I found instead was a group of sad and shocked parents who asked the same question their daughters asked: "How could she do this to me?" I had been so supportive of women and their repressed memories, but I had never once considered what that experience was like for the parents. Now I heard how absolutely ludicrous it sounded. One elderly couple introduced themselves, and the wife told me that their daughter had accused her husband of murdering three people. Another woman had been accused of being in a satanic cult that had used babies for sacrifices. This woman in a pink polyester suit was supposed to be a high priestess. The pain in these parents' faces was so obvious. And the unique thread was that their daughters had gone to therapy. I didn't feel very proud of myself or my profession that day.

I think that if I had been counseling *only* sex abuse cases, or if I had pressed my clients further when they denied being sexually abused, or if I had used "symptom lists" on clients, I probably would never have gone to that FMSF meeting. I think that there is a point of no return with repressed memory therapy, where admitting what you have done to clients would be too terrible to ever face. Fortunately, I had not yet reached that point. Still, I left that meeting with a tremendous discomfort, realizing that I had clients who had cut off all relationship with parents who would have looked exactly like these people and would be in as much shock and disbelief. I felt like the sorcerer's apprentice.

After that FMSF meeting, I would frequently wake up in the middle of the night in terror and anguish, thinking about clients who fit the pattern for False Memory Syndrome. Sometimes I worried about being sued. A number of the parents I had met were eager to sue their child's therapist. Most of the time, though, I just thought about those mothers and fathers who wanted their children back. Most of them hadn't talked to their children in at least two years, often longer.

There was one client who kept coming to mind. She had occasionally voiced doubts about her memories – they had always been very vague, and I had secretly wondered if she hadn't jumped to a false conclusion when she accused her Dad. The next time she came in, I asked if she would like me to attempt mediation with her father, and she was open to the idea. He must have been stunned when I identified myself as his daughter's therapist. He told me that he was so hurt that he never wanted to speak to her again. But he also told me, "You know, my daughter really was sexually abused by a babysitter when she was five," which coincided with the age she had memories of being abused. I told him a little bit about FMS and that his daughter had not maliciously accused him. I gently pressed the issue and found that he really did want to reunite with his daughter. Finally, after a good deal of trepidation, she called him. Now they are on the path to making peace with one another.

Since then, I have been going back to former clients, one by one, trying to undo the damage. I will meet with them and ask them to read over some FMSF material. "Even if it turns out that your repressed memories are true," I say, "you should know that information questioning them is out there. I want you to read it, and then we'll talk." Some clients, like the woman who thought her grandfather had abused her in the crib, have retracted with evident relief. Others have re-established some sort of relationship with their parents, but they haven't taken back the allegations. One just shrugged and told me, "I guess we'll never know whether these memories are true or false." That attitude really disturbs me. And Sally won't hear what I have to say yet, but some day, I hope she will retract.

I have also changed the way I practice sex abuse therapy. I only work with clients who have long-standing memories. Now I never ask if a client has been sexually abused. I leave it up to clients to present their own issues. And I no longer refer anyone to experts on satanic ritual abuse, since there *are* no real experts. There may really be groups of people dabbling in ritual abuse, but I do not believe in multi-generational everyone-in-town-is-involved SRA cults. The FBI and police forces around the country have found no evidence to support their existence.

It is very disturbing to me that many who consider themselves Christian counselors are among those searching for repressed memories, particularly of SRA. Christians believe in the concept of an evil force called Satan. Ritual abuse gives credence to that kind of evil, a personal Satan with attendant spirits. It gives that spiritual dimension to the counseling. One counselor I know tells clients to ask God to tell them if they were sexually abused. God is supposed to reveal their abuse in response to their prayers. This makes God Himself an accessory to this dubious practice of retrieving memories. In the name of God, thousands of families are being split apart.

I believe that therapists constitute a new priesthood. I think we all have been sold a bill of goods that human misery can be attributed solely to traumatic childhood events. I'm often struck by people who have relatively normal lives who experience the same kind of misery. I am not minimizing the effects of trauma, but as Jesus said, "In this life, you will have tribulation."

Another saying of Jesus also has great resonance for me now. He said, "Perfect love casts out all fear." That's true, but I think the reverse is also true, that perfect fear casts out all love. That is what happens in recovered memory therapy.

I recently got a call from an elderly gentleman who had heard about my efforts to reconcile families. He wanted to talk to someone who would understand his story. He's 84 years old and had just lost his wife of 56 years. Five years ago, their only daughter had written them a letter accusing him of sexually abusing her and vowing never to speak to them again unless he confessed. He denied the charge and hasn't heard from her since. Other family members have told him that she now believes she has multiple personalities.

When I told him that there was a support organization for accused parents, he was really surprised. He and his wife had thought they were the only ones. But he saw no point in attending an FMSF meeting. At his advanced age, he didn't expect ever to see his daughter again. Before he left, I said, "I have a prayer for these lost daughters. Can I share it with you?" He agreed, and I began quoting from Luke 15, the Parable of the Prodigal Son. "I will arise and go to my father and will say unto him, 'Father, I have sinned against heaven and before thee.' " Obviously recognizing the story, he stood and continued: "But when he was yet a great way off, his father saw him and had compassion and ran and fell on his neck and kissed him." We finished together. "For this my son was dead and is alive again. He was lost and is found." Together, we found a small glimmer of hope in that moment, enveloped in an awful lot of charity. We both cried. I wished him God speed, and then he left.'

CHAPTER SIX

The Survivors

What seems to Be, Is, To those to whom
It seems to Be, & is productive of the most dreadful
Consequences . . . even of
Torments, Despair, Eternal Death.

WILLIAM BLAKE[1]

First she sees her hypnotist,
Then she rushes to her psychiatrist,
Sees her acupuncturist,
You know she's got to, got to get fixed.

CARLY SIMON, 'Floundering'

INTERVIEWS IN THIS CHAPTER:

VIRGINIA HUDSON, *incest survivor (letter)*
ANNE SOMERVILLE, *incest survivor*
SUSAN RAMSEY, *incest survivor*
DIANE SCHULTZ, *incest survivor*
FRIEDA MAYBRY, *ritual-abuse survivor*
PHILIPPA LAWRENCE, *incest survivor/therapist*
PATRICIA DELANEY, *survivor and lawyer*
ANGELA BERGERON, *multiple-personality survivor*
MELINDA COUTURE, *sexual-abuse survivor, wife of accused father*
SALLY HAMPSHIRE, *incest survivor who has always remembered*

When listening to self-described incest survivors, it is difficult to distinguish fact from fiction, real memories from illusions. Generally speaking, I believe people when they tell me about abuse they have always remembered, while I have come to doubt memories of long-term abuse that have been 'recovered' many years later. Consequently, I suspect that Sally Hampshire's account of incest, the last one in this chapter, is accurate. I also think that Philippa Lawrence's disturbed mother probably really did fondle her when she was 12.

One of these stories illustrates the difficulty of defining 'repression.' There are gray areas, such as Melinda Couture's explanation of how she suddenly recalled her brother-in-law's attempt to feel her breasts when she was 12. This is the sort of one-time event that can indeed be forgotten and then remembered, a process far different from 'massive repression.'

In my opinion, most of the other 'memories' recounted here are probably well-rehearsed confabulations, though that does not diminish the pain they represent.*

Even when Susan Ramsey, the first person interviewed in this chapter, says that she *always* knew that her father was an alcoholic, a 'nasty, mean, cruel drunk,' I'm not sure how much credence to give her words. He probably really did drink too much, and I suspect that he was a far-from-perfect parent. But when pressed to describe the verbal abuse he heaped on her, she said that he called her a 'lazy no-good young-'un,' well within the realm of things that a parent might blurt out in a moment of exasperation. She also fondly recalls sitting on his lap listening to the radio, or him comforting her when she was sick. Consequently, readers should bear in mind that extremely negative versions of the past may be exaggerated by current attitudes.** Of course, not all Survivors had happy or normal childhoods. Few people would describe their early years in such terms without qualification. But troubled childhoods do not necessarily stem from years of hidden incest.

Assuming that the recovered memories of abuse are illusory, how did they come about? Who is to blame? Are therapists primarily responsible for leading people to believe in fictional incest? I would answer with a qualified yes, though there is a mutual influence here, embedded in a cultural context that encourages the hunt for repressed memories. With-

---

* The following interviews may not be altogether representative of those who have recovered abuse memories because: (1) All of them are women. About 10 per cent of Survivors are male. There are stories involving male Survivors in Chapters 7 and 8. (2) Most of these are interviews with middle-aged women, many of whom recall ritual abuse. As will become clear in subsequent chapters, there are many younger Survivors who recall simple incest, but I could not find many who would talk with me on the record.

** Similarly, I don't necessarily take Survivors at their word when they tell me they cannot recall whole years of their childhoods. When you catch them with their guards down, they will tell you particular incidents from those lost years. Few people remember their youth in much detail, so it's easy for therapists to convince clients that they have amnesia for vast chunks of time.

out therapists 'validating' and encouraging belief, most of those speaking here would not have visualized incest. Susan Ramsey expresses grave doubts about her memories, but her therapist convinces her that they are essentially true, and that he has not led her in any way. Similarly, Diane Schultz relies on her counselor, though she secretly worries that she may have been brainwashed. Frieda Maybry prides herself on seeking only peer 'co-counselors,' but they serve the same function as a therapist.

The dependency that many of these women exhibit toward their therapists is intense, and the professionals often appear to encourage it. 'If Hugh moved away right now, I'd be dead,' Angela Bergeron asserts, while Susan Ramsey admits that she is extremely dependent on Randall Cummings and wishes for a sexual relationship with him.

On the other hand, most of the self-identified Survivors seem to take some comfort in their victimhood in a process psychologists term 'secondary gain.' Being a Survivor makes them feel special, brings them sympathy and attention, and explains all of their problems. They don't have to worry about failed marriages or relationships, which aren't their fault. They were irretrievably wounded as children and cannot function properly as a result.

Some women have recovered their 'memories' without the help of a therapist at all. Even if they had never read a book on the subject or gone to therapy, by the early 1990s, virtually every woman in our society with a problem had at least briefly pondered, 'I wonder whether this problem stems from repressed memories of sexual abuse?' All too many then sought out *The Courage to Heal* or another similar book. Only then did they enter therapy, having already 'remembered' abuse, or *demanding* to retrieve memories. Such Survivors are then convinced that they were never led into such beliefs, and that their memories must therefore be accurate.

The memory-retrieval process also provides drama, mystery, and excitement, as quotes from *The Courage to Heal* make abundantly clear. One woman in the book realizes that she is 'addicted to my own sense of drama and adrenaline.' Another says, 'Whenever my life would calm down, I would start wishing for something major to happen so I could feel at home.'[2]*[3] Consequently, Survivors must take a share of responsibility

---

* Psychologist Joy Davidson has written an interesting book called *The Agony of It All: The Drive for Drama and Excitement in Women's Lives* (1988). Davidson believes that human beings have an innate need for challenge and thrills, but that women in Western societies have been denied healthy outlets. 'For women,' she writes, 'drama-seeking extends from restrictive, sex-biased conditioning imposed by both society and family . . . Women often learn to create drama as the *primary* means of satisfying their sensation-seeking needs.'

for their mistaken beliefs. So must the authors of recovery self-help books, as well as support-group members who egg one another on. 'I am addicted to groups,' one Survivor admitted in *The Courage to Heal*. 'I am a sponge. Put me somewhere where people are nice to me, and I'll learn their whole scene.'[4] Or, as Diane Schultz, in her interview here, observes of members of her Survivor group: 'They believed me more than *I* believed me.'

Do those who eventually recall memories have anything in common? Yes. They are all experiencing stress and uncertainty in their lives, or they wouldn't be seeking therapy. Many women are feeling trapped by motherhood or marriage. Some seek therapy in the wake of postpartum depression or miscarriages. Others struggle with the transition from adolescence to adulthood. Aside from approaching a vulnerable point in their lives, however, they do not necessarily have much in common, other than a therapist with a particular mindset, or simply being a self-doubting woman at a particular time in history.

The median age of women recovering 'memories' appears to be around the age of 30, though the age range has widened as recovered-memory therapy and books espousing it have become more popular. Girls as young as 12 are recovering memories. Even preschoolers have been told by therapists that they must have repressed memories of sexual abuse. At the same time, therapists have been recruiting in nursing homes. One 1994 article advised that 'psychologically fragile' elderly women, particularly widows, should be helped to recall the incest of their youth. Another MPD specialist agrees, but he warns against doing abreactive work with octogenarians. 'One of my multiples had a stroke during an abreaction.'[5]

While there is no necessary common thread among Survivors, there are several interesting subsets. A number of accusers are very suggestible and hypnotizable, as I mentioned in Chapter 4. Many such Survivors are also quite dramatic, creative, and imaginative. 'I can work myself into a state of sobbing over something in a fantasy,' one Survivor acknowledged in *The Courage to Heal*.[6] They play roles well, consciously or otherwise. A surprising number are either professional or amateur actors. Many Survivors have always read mystery, fantasy, or horror stories. They enjoy solving puzzles or envisioning other worlds and possibilities. Often, they sing professionally or exhibit artistic talent.*

* Most parents actively encouraged this creativity. When my children were little, for instance, I would put on different kinds of music – classical, rock, or folk – and they would take turns conducting with their hands over a candle, the only light in the room, while looking up ecstatically at the huge shadowy choreography they created on the ceiling. How was I to know in those long-ago, innocent days that the shadows they created on the ceiling would one day become reality for them?

Many Survivors also seem to be among the helpers of the world, easily empathizing with those who suffer. They often enter the helping professions, becoming teachers, nurses, or counselors.

A majority who come to believe in their 'recovered memories' are high-achievers who did quite well in school and may have advanced degrees. Just as they were good students in school, they make excellent therapy clients, dutifully reading recovery books, filling out workbooks, and performing other homework assignments.

Other Survivors were probably *too close* to their parents. While their friends rebelled as teenagers, they continued to consider their parents to be best friends. These overly dependent adult children, who have difficulty individuating from their parents, often have a love/hate relationship with them. They long to break away, but can't seem to do it. The incest memories allow them to do so, but they do not really stand on their own. Instead, they transfer their dependence to their therapists. Psychiatrist George Ganaway speaks of such a case: 'An unmarried 25-year-old woman . . . has unresolved early separation and individuation conflicts with her parents, leaving her with a feeling of hostile dependence on them.' Although she is a high achiever, she has a 'constant need for approval and validation from others.' The therapist becomes a substitute parental figure, 'all-accepting, all-believing and all-approving.'[7]*[8]

Another subset consists of 'lifers' who have bounced from one diagnosis, therapist, or movement to another for most of their lives. 'I've been mentally disturbed all my life,' one such woman told Ellen Bass.[9] Many of them have always suffered from assorted mysterious bodily ailments. Adopting the Survivor persona is simply the latest in a series of explanations for these maladies.

Finally, and perhaps most tragic, there are undoubtedly those who have real disorders such as manic-depression (bipolar disorder), anxiety disorders, obsessive-compulsive disorder, clinical depression, or epilepsy that go undiagnosed. Indeed, the conditions are exacerbated by the acting out that is demanded by the Survivor role.**[10]

* In *Anxiety Disorders and Phobias*, Aaron Beck and Gary Emery discuss cases in which a '*lifelong* pattern of separation fears and dependency' can lead to agoraphobia (fear of leaving the house) and panic attacks. As we have seen in Chapter 3, such anxious symptoms are often interpreted as flashbacks or body memories. In such cases, Beck and Emery write, there is 'the increasing expectation that the individual take on the demands of adulthood or parenthood and at the same time function more independently. Birth of a child, loss of a caregiver through separation or death, increased demands at home or at work, all may precipitate agoraphobic symptoms.'
** Harvard Medical School researchers have reported three cases in which patients saw vivid intrusive obsessional images and were convinced that these represented flashbacks

I cannot overemphasize the strong motivation that impels people to discover hidden memories, once the idea is planted. They yearn for an explanation for their current despair, and they become dogged in their pursuit of the mystery. 'My therapist told me to read *The Courage to Heal*,' one woman told me. 'I opened the book to the first page, and three hours later, I looked up, sobbing. I was totally consumed by this book. I couldn't read enough, find out enough, couldn't let it go. Everything was leading me down this road. My therapists weren't necessarily saying "Confront your parents," but society and books and my need to be healthy were driving me. I was absolutely driven.'

One of the most compelling aspects of the memory retrieval process is how it provides answers. When a particular memory 'explains' something from that past, it is particularly convincing. Thus, Philippa Lawrence now understands why she was so upset as a child by a horror film. (Never mind, of course, that such a reaction is normal, or that her 'memory' might be *based* in part on the film rather than the other way around.) Everything then 'links up,' as she puts it. 'So *that's* why.' Everything now made 'complete sense.'

Once someone is sucked into the recovered memory vortex, it is clearly difficult to get out. 'There is an identity in being a committed survivor of sexual abuse,' Bass and Davis accurately observe in *The Courage to Heal*. 'It can be hard to give up.'[11] More and more memories surface, along with diverse perpetrators. Once a confrontation takes place, it is hard to back away. Besides, admitting you were wrong would involve losing all your new friends and your all-important therapist. The shame and guilt from admitting false accusations would be overwhelming. Also, people have an innate resistance to cutting their losses, once they've made a major investment. 'The memories might not be totally accurate,' Diane Schultz allows in her interview here, 'but what purpose would it serve me to spend so much time, energy, and money to blame my father for something he didn't do?' Therefore, according to this circular logic, he must have committed incest on her.

It seems painfully obvious in some cases that these 'memories' do not seem real, even to those who remember them. One woman I interviewed (not included here) has never managed to retrieve *any* memories, though she is still sure she is a Survivor. In other cases, always-remembered normal events of childhood are re-interpreted as abusive. Thus, Anne

---

to abuse. When given appropriate medication (serotonin reuptake antagonists), all three stopped having their 'flashbacks.'

Somerville's father once asked for a kiss with the rest of the family around, and she now 'knows' that he wanted to go further. 'I had always remembered that. Once I had the hypnotherapy, it was something I zeroed in on.' Indeed.

Another Survivor I spoke with strove in vain to recall real incest, but settled for memories of *emotional* incest. 'I've concluded that you never overtly molested me,' she told her father recently, 'but you did violate some very important boundaries. You hugged me too long, looked at me too fondly.' I suspect that this nagging uncertainty may be what prevents some children from directly accusing their parents or telling them precisely what they are supposed to have done.

The saddest feature of the 'therapeutic' process is the frightful amount of pain it unnecessarily inflicts upon unwary clients. They often go through awful depressions, suicide attempts, and hospitalizations. They lose their families, their jobs, their relationships. Yet somehow, they convince themselves that they are getting better. Relatively speaking, over the short term, they eventually *do* get better. Few people can keep themselves in such a state of turmoil indefinitely, and when Survivors adjust to their new status and begin to feel relatively calm, they often perceive that they have made great strides. Compared to how they functioned when *entering* therapy, however, most are worse off.

There are undoubtedly those who genuinely benefit from recovered-memory therapy. Their long-term depression lifts. They feel energized. They are able to enjoy sex. They feel renewed purpose in life and enjoy the righteous anger of the Survivor. Because they feel better having an explanation for all their previous troubles, they are sure that their memories must be accurate. Why else would they have improved? The answer is that *any* explanation for life's troubles can have a placebo effect. Unfortunately, their newfound purpose comes at the expense of grieving families, devastated by false accusations. And, however fulfilling their lives may be, they have been deprived of the support and comfort of their families.

VIRGINIA HUDSON, INCEST SURVIVOR

I did not interview Virginia Hudson, 45, a New Jersey preschool teacher. Her 74-year-old father gave me a copy of her 1992 letter to him, which she handed to him in person at a therapy session at a Christian counseling center. (He

denies all of the charges and says that, to his knowledge, Virginia never had
an abortion as a teenager.) I have reproduced portions of the letter, conveying
the flavor of many such messages.

'Dear Dad,

This is so hard for me to write. Please try to listen to it without attacking what I have written.

In the past, I always thought the world of you, Dad – that's certainly no secret to anyone in our family and I, also, thought I was so precious and special to you. Lately, though, my heart was greatly grieved and saddened when I started remembering what my childhood and relationship with you was really like. Unfortunately, my reality today bears little resemblance to the fantasy I had built in my mind over the years.

The truth is that you were incesting me from infancy through the age of 15. My adoration of you masked my submission to the horrifying events that were happening to me. Your violence toward me was so terrifying that I tried to forget what was going on even as it was happening. It is no wonder that it has taken until this past year to open myself up to remembering these things that happened to me 30 to 40 years ago.

In case your mind has drawn a veil over this span of time, I will try to refresh your memory about those years. When I was an infant, you began violating me by sticking your finger in my vagina. By the time I was three, you were telling me how wonderful I was, how I was Daddy's little girl and how much you loved me. You then claimed to express that love by playing this "game" you called "Doggy." Doggy was painful, terrorizing and in reality was anal sex. By the time I was five you coerced me into oral sex.

When I was in my early teens, you had intercourse with me. At the age when I should have been rejoicing over my blossoming femininity, I was ashamed of my body, petrified that I was continuing to grow more into a woman (which I thought spelled more abuse) and cursing the fact that I was alive at all. You robbed me of so much of the joy of my femininity.

At 14, you brought me to a doctor to have an abortion. You did not have the decency to tell me why we were going to the doctor. This is the hardest reality for me to accept. What you continued to do to me over the years is despicable, but I have no words for the mourning I have experienced because you took this life being formed in me.

As an adult in Christ, I can now protect and care for myself. You will not violate me again. I will not go back to living a fantasy and a lie and from now on, I am going to continue to speak the truth as best I know it.

What I would like from you, Dad, is an admission of the truth in what I have stated. I want you to ask me to forgive you. I have said all that was in my heart to say. It is now your choice as to what to do with this.

Sincerely,
Virginia '

ANNE SOMERVILLE, INCEST SURVIVOR

In 1988, when she was 28, Anne Somerville of Dorset in England had terrible headaches – not terribly surprising, given her stressful life circumstances. Her parents' marriage had ended in a bitter divorce. She was a nurse in an intensive care unit. She had a two-year-old daughter. 'I didn't know how to love her or give her what she needed. I felt inadequate as a mother.' In addition, she had had a clandestine affair, and her lover died after a long-term hospitalization following a car accident, four months into her pregnancy. Her husband complained that she woke him up by grinding her teeth. Visits to her dentist and doctor failed to help. Then Anne read an ad in the newspaper about Harold Johnson, a local hypnotist who could help with stress and headaches. She made an appointment.

'Harold told me what he could do and how. He would sit me in a chair. It was very simple. He would just count down, tell me to relax my limbs and close my eyes. Talking about "hypnotic states" sounds far-fetched, but it's actually quite natural. You're well aware of what he says, what you say, and what you're doing. It doesn't seem like a big deal. I knew I was hypnotized, though. It did feel different. I was a lot more relaxed, but at the same time I was in full control.

He took me back through my childhood, and certain pictures would appear in my mind. Harold told me that my headaches came from some forgotten childhood trauma. We lock things away, and there's a lot we don't remember because it's too painful.

During the first session, I was around 11, standing on the landing upstairs. It was very, very real, as if I were really there and wasn't a 28-year-old any more. I felt all the feelings I felt as a child, helpless and frightened. I could hear a belt going back and forth. When my father couldn't find out what was wrong, he would beat all three of my younger brothers. I wanted to do something to help, but I couldn't. That's something I have always remembered. It was very disturbing, though. When I came out of it, I was quite upset. Harold reassured me that it was quite normal and helpful.

During another session, he took me right back to my birth. I found that amazing. The only thing I was aware of was an aura, and I could smell very strong urine, as if I were a baby lying in a pool of urine, an ammonia smell. I don't know if it was birth or maybe a baby lying in a cot. It seemed very, very real.

I went to nine or ten sessions, but the only other one that sticks in my mind is the ultimate one. He carried on regressing me, saying, "Where are you now?" In my parents' bedroom. He said, "Have you got any clothes on?" I said, yes, I had my pajamas on. I was able to describe the room exactly, including the position of the furniture. I was about seven. The next minute, he said, "Where are you now?" I said I was on the bed. Suddenly, I was screaming and crying, "No, no, no!" And I just wanted to come out of that session. I could see my father's face above me. I was lying flat on my back, being held down by him, and his face was on my face.

He said, "Do you want to go on?" And I said, "No." He brought me back out, and I sobbed for a long time. He asked me about the emotions I felt. He told me to beat a cushion, and I did, though it made me rather self-conscious. Harold stressed to me that I shouldn't have bad feelings towards my father, because my father didn't remember either. Harold said that repressed memories were very common. He said one in five women were sexually abused by their fathers.

I didn't want to find out what happened next, though I did have one last session with Harold's wife. I didn't want to have a session with a man again. His wife also did hypnotherapy, but she didn't get anywhere with me.

I was very upset by all of this. I turned to a brother I was close to, and he said I was lying and that my father wouldn't have done that sort of thing. I decided not to say anything to my mother. She asked me what was wrong. I just looked at her, and she looked at me, and she said, "My God, what's he done?" She knew I had a lot of anger at my father. So I told her what I'd seen. A little later, she said, "I could believe he did that to you." They had been divorced a few years at that point.

I finally confronted my father. I went to see him at his home, in his environment, which was wrong. I was fluttery and stumbly, very nervous and uptight. I wanted to find out, I wanted an answer. I wanted to get back at him and make him pay for what he'd done. I wanted to tape his confession and take him to court and sue him for all he had. Yes, at this point I had read a lot of healing books. They were very helpful.

He said, "What do you want? Spit it out." I said, "It's about, about my childhood. It's about abuse." He said, "Who told you this?" This was before I told him any details. He just assumed that's what it was about. I felt that indicated he was guilty. I cut off all contact with him for seven years.

I went to see a psychiatrist a few months after my hypnosis sessions, and the psychiatrist suggested that maybe I hadn't been raped after all. Perhaps I had only been groomed towards it. So what I remembered in hypnosis was as far as it went. That was a great relief to me in some ways.

I just got together with my father again last year. We don't talk about the abuse memories. He didn't try to approach me directly, but he told my mother he was very upset and wanted to see me. I'm having a much better relationship with him now. I relate better with him than I do with my mother. He's more steady. My mother can be nice one minute and then angry the next. You see, I love my father very much, even though he was a Jekyll and Hyde. He could be a very charming man. He did have a horrible temper, though, and he would beat my mother. His eyes would glaze over and there was no feeling in them. He never beat me. When I look back on what I discovered in hypnotherapy, I feel he must have felt guilty about the sexual abuse, which is why he did not hit me.

I still think hypnosis can be quite useful. We need to face up and be objective about what happened to us. The actual situation was so real to me, his face above me and the feelings I had. As a child, you don't have the verbal language, but you know it's wrong, it's not a game.

I had a lot of sexual feelings as a child. I wanted to express those feelings with my brothers, and it confused me. When I was eight or so, I played doctor with my brothers. Nobody ever talks about it, but it might not be all that unusual.

There was another situation with my father that felt wrong as well. I went to say good night, and he said, "Give me a kiss." So I gave him a peck on the cheek. He said, "Give me a proper kiss." It was the tone, you know. My brothers were around and my mother was in the kitchen, so he couldn't follow through. I had always remembered that. Once I had the hypnotherapy, it was something I zeroed in on.

I can't remember if the hypnotherapy made my headaches go away. I still get headaches now, but not as many. I find other ways of controlling my stress. I meditate, and that's more helpful than anything else.'

SUSAN RAMSEY, INCEST SURVIVOR

Susan Ramsey, a New York social worker, looks younger than her age of 51. After agreeing to talk with me about how her repressed memories came back, she called with second thoughts. 'There is some stuff I have a very difficult time talking about,' she explained. 'Maybe I could just write it down.' That was fine with me, so she wrote the following and handed it to me just before our interview:

> *I have memories of being abused by my mother, my father and my maternal grandmother. I also believe I was abused by a family doctor and some uncles, but that is really too vague to go into. My parents abused me both separately and together. The abuse from my mother was her fondling me and making me fondle her breasts and genitals. My father was an alcoholic and when he abused me alone, he was drunk. He fondled me and forced me to do oral sex on him. Eventually he raped me. He came into my room at night and it was totally dark except the light of the cigarette he was smoking. He used the cigarette to threaten me with [burning] if I didn't do what he wanted. What the two of them did to me together was to force enemas on me and make me hold them. The cramps were severe and then when they finally let me go to the bathroom they made fun of me as I rushed off. Sometimes they sexually stimulated me (manually) while making me hold the enemas. After I came back from the bathroom, they would make me watch while they had sex. Humiliation and shame were a big part of it as was pain. I repressed all of these memories.*

'I'm the oldest of three children. I have a brother two years younger than me and a sister seven years younger. I'm not really that close to my siblings. I've only spoken to my sister about my abuse. I didn't really plan to tell her, but it just came out. She feels she might have been abused, too, but she hasn't had any memories yet. She was in therapy, but she kind of stopped connecting with me about this. My therapist thinks she got scared and backed off.

I always knew that my father was an alcoholic. I've been depressed and in therapy most of my adult life, but I never dealt with abuse issues. The first inkling I had was when I was in group therapy for ACOAs [Adult Children of Alcoholics], and the therapist said she sensed that I had been sexually abused. My reaction was to say, "I don't know." I didn't say it was ridiculous, I just didn't know. This was about ten years ago.

I was seeing a psychiatrist, but he never really involved himself in my childhood. I was in an unhealthy marriage, my two kids were driving me nuts, and he was just trying to keep me together in my present life. Eventually, things settled down, I seemed to be able to cope, and I wanted to do some deeper recovery work. But he was no use. I terminated with him after 12 years. The subject of sex abuse never even came up with him – it's kind of surprising, but it didn't.

About three years ago, I found Randall Cummings, a therapist who specializes in trauma. I started doing inner child work with him. I had already seen Bradshaw videos and read some of his books. Then Randall and I started doing age regressions in therapy. No, it's not hypnotism, just relaxation exercises. You spend time breathing and relaxing, going back to remember the house you lived in and the neighborhood, seeing the child you were, then you become her. I was dealing with being a toddler at the time, and during age regression, I first remembered the abuse.

I pictured this child, you know, and I have real photos of me which helped. I let myself be her and feel her, and once that happened, he would ask questions like, "How old are you today? What does it feel like to be three?" And I would say, most of the time, "It doesn't feel too good. Things are happening I don't like." He never said, "Do your mother or father touch you or do things you don't like?" He just let the process flow. That's kind of validating, that it just came from me. After the first memories started coming, I asked if he knew this would happen. He said he didn't know, but he wasn't surprised. He said he didn't want to force things.

I was doing age regressions regularly in therapy for a long time, and I kept getting memories. Now I know that I was abused from the time I was in my crib at six months or younger, up until I was 18 and left for college.

The other thing Randall taught me was to do inner child meditations on my own. I do them every day. I get in touch with my inner child, learning to nurture and care for her. I let her know that I love her in spite of what happens. When she's scared about things, I listen. The child within is really my feelings. I never knew what I was feeling before, ever. Now I've stopped being depressed. I'm doing a lot of grieving for losses of childhood, but I'm not depressed so much. Anger is still really hard for me. I'll start to get in touch with it, then push it away. It's starting to come up, and there's a lot of it there.

The only one of my abusers alive is my mother, who's 75. I first told her, "I don't want to talk to you for a while." Since then, I've gotten back into contact. I have to call her, though; she isn't allowed to call me. I didn't tell her why at the beginning. Eventually, I told her I was sexually abused, but I wouldn't say who did it. She kept hounding me. Finally, I told her it was several people, that she and my father were two of them, and that I couldn't discuss it with her. Now she's dropped it. We don't discuss it any more.

During those months when I wouldn't allow communication, she abided by it for the most part. I had called to tell her this from my therapist's office, and when I got home, there was a message on my machine. She wondered how long this would last, and wanted to know if she could talk to my therapist about it. I was a little annoyed by that. I didn't respond. I didn't feel it would serve any purpose for her to talk to Randall. I think she's probably blocked it out like I did.

What did I think of my parents before I knew about the abuse? Dad was a nasty, mean, cruel drunk. When he was sober, he was a pretty nice guy. We had some good times, though not many. I remember sitting on his lap on Sunday nights listening to the radio. When I was little, I was sick a lot, and my mother was always very, very busy, with no time for kids. Dad would come and sit on my bed and talk to me.

By the time I hit adolescence, I didn't want anything to do with him, though. He could be physically abusive when he was drunk. He once threatened to kill us all. He was also verbally abusive, repeatedly calling me a "lazy no-good young-un." I am still convinced I'm lazy. He criticized everything I did. I didn't wash the dishes right, didn't help my mother enough, sat and read books all afternoon. I would be careful not to do that thing again, but the next time it would be a different list. I couldn't please him.

I felt safe around Mom, thought I really loved her, and I would get really scared if I thought anything would happen to her. I was very dependent on her, even asking her what to wear in the morning until I left for college.

I think I'm overweight as a direct result of trying to use food to make my feelings go away. I've been overweight since second grade. It could also be a way to deny my sexuality, to hide it behind all this fat.

I've been in Survivors of Incest Anonymous [SIA] for almost two years now. It's been good. Some people have flashbacks during the meetings, but that hasn't happened to me. I've been triggered, though, by what someone said. After one meeting, I remembered my parents telling my younger siblings that they were going to do to them what they did to me when I went to college. They had my brother and sister watch them having sex with me when I was 18. I don't think they remember it. My sister doesn't.

I know it's hard to believe that an 18-year-old could block out a memory like that. You just split, you can't stand what's going on, your mind takes off and lets your body stay there. The body is what remembers, not the mind. When you feel ready to hear and believe, it comes back. I think that's how I've heard it explained [*laughs*].

I subscribe to *Changes Magazine*, and there was an article in there that was somewhat disturbing to me. It was about how some of these memories might be false. It's hard when you don't have physical evidence to accept them. You don't really want to accept them anyway. Some of these people who think these are false memories are appearing on talk shows, and my mother might see them and think, "Oh, this is what's wrong with my daughter." It would validate her point of view. She'll say, "Oh, she'll snap out of it one day." I was reassured because Randall didn't use leading questions in my case.

I've asked Randall, "Am I wrong? Could I be making this all up?" His attitude is, "Whether the details are accurate or not, it's extremely evident to me that you were a severely wounded child. Something happened. I strongly suspect that most of what you remember is true." In his mind, it's irrelevant whether the details are true or not. I don't agree, though. I don't want to go around saying this stuff unless it's true. When I first had these memories, I doubted and vacillated a lot.

But I agree with Randall that there's something wrong, there are major problems in my personality, and they didn't just happen on their own. So something happened. I didn't get my basic emotional needs met as a child, that's for definite sure. My relationship with Randall demonstrates that. I'm very dependent on him, I feel very needy and worthless without him, and I want him to have more than a professional relationship with me. I want him to be my Daddy. Lately I've been starting to have sexual feelings toward him.

I have a teddy bear named Serenity who helps me. I used to take him with me to SIA meetings, and I still do when the mood strikes me. Sometimes I'll cuddle with the bear on my bed, but I don't sleep with him every night.'

DIANE SCHULTZ, INCEST SURVIVOR

Diane Schultz, a North Carolina accountant, appears to be the opposite of overweight Susan Ramsey. Schultz is small, even petite, and quite attractive by American norms. Yet she too blames her eating disorder – bulimia – on long-forgotten incest. She first entered therapy for marital counseling when she was 27, but she was soon seeing therapist Sondra Atkins individually and getting divorced. Three years later, she went to the Healing Heart, described in its brochure as 'a safe, nurturing environment,' for an intensive two-week workshop intended to address 'childhood issues and adult dysfunctional behaviors.' During guided imagery at Healing Heart, she regressed to her birth, where she suffered 'prenatal suffocation syndrome.' During similar regressions, other participants remembered sexual abuse. Soon after coming back from the workshop, Schultz commenced the difficult work of retrieving her incest memories, a particularly painful process for her, because she had previously recalled her childhood quite fondly.

'When I was 30, after I returned from the Healing Heart, I thought, "Maybe that happened to me, too." I had similar symptoms: eating disorders, relationship difficulties, a dysfunctional family, my sexual acting out. As soon as I acknowledged that fact, I started having dreams, physical body memories, feelings, sensations, and visual images, like unclear snapshot photos. They just wouldn't leave me alone or go away.

I would dream about my father raping me, but I would at first minimize and deny it. I dreamed about my mother sexually violating me also; she had a penis and would sometimes anally penetrate me. It could have been her finger in reality, any sort of phallic thing. The idea of my mother being sexual with me is the point.

Eventually, I had dreams about a particular canoe trip my father took me on with my uncle and his best friend, when I was 16. My dreams indicated that I was drugged at the time, and raped, at least by my father and uncle. I would do art therapy, and pictures would come up about it. I would take the pictures to my survivor group and have physical memories there. My tongue would get numb like I was on drugs, and I could feel myself being penetrated both orally and vaginally. I would have these sensations right there. One of the benefits of such a support group is that someone has witnessed it. To be honest with you, they believed me more than *I* believed me. There are some things you just cannot make up, they told me.

As the memories came up, I was physically and emotionally drained. Sondra Atkins, my therapist, diagnosed me with post-traumatic stress disorder, and I took a four-month leave from work. I was an accountant, and I couldn't add two and two together to get four. I couldn't carry out everyday responsibilities.

Sondra just kept saying she believed me. The False Memory Syndrome Foundation and my father say that these memories are the product of man-hating therapists, but Sondra doesn't hate men. She's married, has kids, and is a pillar of the community. Still, I've worried about this myself. Did Sondra brainwash me? She said she believed me, that there was an end to all the pain, and she encouraged me to find ways to nurture myself, to take care of myself, and she trusted my inner wisdom.

Eventually, I realized that I was molested from infancy until 16. My mother abused me when I was in my crib, until I was four. My father did it the whole time.

When I would have the dreams, sometimes I would feel bad and washed out afterward, but sometimes I wouldn't feel much at all. But then I'd go to therapy, and I'd start having convulsions – sobbing, crying and gagging. I couldn't scream loud enough, and that's when the dreams would come to life as memories in fact. I would experience the grief, the terror, and I would shake. I'm shaking right now. This is difficult to talk about. Sondra would have to constrain me to keep my skin on, to keep me from exploding, to keep my heart from breaking, which it is.

Sondra uses what she calls the psychomotor method. She says that the body remembers more than the mind does. I would have tension in my jaw, and Sondra would come and hold my jaw, saying, "Feel it! Exaggerate it!" and she'd ask what I was seeing. It would accelerate to gagging and the feeling of a penis in my mouth, then mental images, the pubic hair and skin and legs. And it all starts, the feelings, terror, shock, confusion, and rage, rage, rage, *rage*. Sometimes I would take a tennis racket and hit the pillow, bite things, release the rage.

I also have memories in my shoulder, where I was held down. Sondra would push on it, and I would feel like being held down. I'd see my mother on the right, my father on the left.

The memories come slowly, as a progression, like one when I was a baby, involving my mother. I took a nap one afternoon and dreamed that one of my best friends and I were masturbating each other. I woke up with the sensation that I had used my entire right hand to mastur-bate her. And I had the desire to wash the hand, or just wring it, pull it off. Then the memory came later, where I see the crib, the gate is halfway down, and I see the bars, and my mother from the belly button to mid-thigh, and she's using my right hand to masturbate with. It took several months to put the pieces together. I call them con-fetti memories. It's like my life was a sheet of whole paper, and it has been shredded into tiny pieces, and I put it together one piece at a time.

Sometimes Sondra asks me to draw or write with my left hand, to contact my unconscious better. See, here's a picture, and I wrote this with my left hand: "It's true, you will know, I know. I'm inside. Listen to me, I'm inside." That was my inner child writing.

During this leave of absence, I was seeing Sondra three times a week. I had to learn to trust her. The most intimate people in my life had been violating me. I still struggle with that. For 30 years, it wasn't safe. Finally, I could trust Sondra enough to let down my guard, and to trust my friends in the survivor group.

I've told a lot of people about my abuse now, and they sometimes ask, "How could you forget all of this?" But these were my parents. I had to greet them every morning, eat with them, day in and day out, and I had to forget in order to be with them. I had no place to go, and no words to articulate the abuse as an infant.

I've had to let go of the myth of what I thought my childhood was like. It was like bursting a beautiful bubble, and it's very difficult to do. My mother was a beautiful woman. She died before I had my memories. My father is a plastic surgeon. We used to travel a lot. We'd hike and horseback ride in the summer, and we'd ski in the winter, all as a family. There wasn't much yelling or screaming, no anger expressed. There was no punishment. They were very permissive. They used to go skinny dipping with us, even when I was a teenager. We'd light up joints first. I was so self-conscious, I'd go over to the side to get undressed. I never thought of that as abusive, didn't think of drugs as being wrong. I thought I had cool parents.

I liked the hiking, the family thing. My parents were young at heart. Here are some pictures.

[*Schultz shows me family photos of a handsome family. There she is with her younger brother Kevin, her father pulling his ears playfully, the whole family aboard their sailboat.*]

After my leave of absence, I confronted my father. This was all in letters. I didn't want to do it on the phone or in person. I wanted to have everything in black and white. So I wrote him a letter, told him what I remembered, and gave him a list of my symptoms. He wrote back and said that it never happened, it was all in my fantasy, that I was bulimic because it was fashionable, and that the sex abuse was made up by a man-hating therapist. He said he was a good father and didn't do anything wrong. I wrote back and said I didn't want to close the door entirely, but I wanted to sever the relationship for the time being. That was a year ago. He wrote back to get the last hit, saying that I was right, it was best not to communicate as long as I felt that way.

I do know he loves me, and he did the best he could. He may not remember the abuse himself. He may have been in a trance state. I still love him, still miss him, but I'm very hurt and angry. That's another reason this is so crazy. How could I love him after what he did? But I still do, because he's my father.

The memories might not be totally accurate, but what purpose would it serve me to spend so much time, energy and money to blame my father for something he didn't do? I've spent about $60,000 in the last six years on the retreat, the therapy, a hospitalization, the leave, doctor's bills, massage therapy, art therapy, all inclusive, and that's not taking into account the loss of not knowing what to do with my life.

Still, I'm much better now. I stay present more. I used to dissociate a lot. I would be in the middle of a business meeting and lose track of the conversation. I see people more clearly for who they are now. I think there are still some memories to be had. I'm at a plateau, at a stairstep. Maybe there will be more vivid memories of my parents. They get clearer every time. I get more details, more feelings. The whole process of healing has been a spiritual one. I thought God had forsaken me. I have become more spiritual and believe in a power higher than myself. We need to learn the lessons we're here to learn.'

FRIEDA MAYBRY, RITUAL ABUSE SURVIVOR

Frieda Maybry, 54, tends to the poor, who often find her at home in a lower-class Chicago neighborhood. She can afford such time and kindness because she lives on total disability resulting from the purported ravages of ritual abuse by her father and his fellow Masons, which she recalled relatively recently. Prior to that, she had spent a great deal of her life in therapy or New Age movements, searching for answers and solace. 'As a child, I had frequent bronchitis, colds, flus, allergies, headaches, G.I. tract indigestion. I had hemorrhoids by the age of ten, and a lot of nervous habits and tension – little twitches and things.' Her parents were divorced when she was 14; her mother died three years later. She recalls her mother as loving and supportive, while she describes her father, also now deceased, as cold, non-verbal, and frightening. Now she feels she finally has the answer for her various physical and mental ailments. Frieda is sure that her memories, first retrieved while she was in graduate school in her late 40s, are accurate, because she recovered them with her peers rather than with a professional therapist.

'I began remembering sexual abuse seven years ago in 1987. I had no idea that I had been sexually abused, although several therapists had suggested to me that it seemed a high likelihood, especially since I had absolutely no memories before the age of seven.

I took a weekend workshop with a self-help group called Re-Evaluation Co-Counseling, RC for short, in which people learn how to counsel each other. They use very basic non-intrusive, non-directive techniques. Once you learn how to do that with the group, you exchange time. I get an hour, the other person gets an hour, and we don't have to pay. Being a peer relationship, it's not a situation where a professional has power over you and you're coming to be fixed.

About two months later, there was an advanced course, which happened to be on early sexual memories. All 11 of us from the original class attended. The leader gave us a lot of information about sexual development, family problems around sexual behavior, and child sexual abuse. She taught us how to approach this in counseling if any of us had material around this issue. She also talked about what to do if we didn't remember that this had happened to us, but we suspected it might have. She gave about six indicators that would indicate likely incest. Every one of them was remarkably true for me except one, and that was that you remembered.

So during a counseling session, I tried what she suggested. You just sit face to face with your co-counselor, put your hands together and push against each other, palm to palm. You're not trying to overcome each other, just put a lot of pressure. And then, you move around a bit with it and notice what feelings come up in whoever is being the client. If it feels like you want to push more, let some aggression come out, you go with it, and say whatever you feel like. You might say, "No," or do some yelling or whatever, all within the parameters of being safe and careful.

When I did that, immediately *very* strong feelings came up. Not a real memory, but I broke into really heavy sobbing. I pushed very hard and started saying "No, No, NO, NO, NO!" and it went into desperate feelings and crying. The theory of co-counseling is that memories bring with them all the emotions that were there during the event, and those emotions need to be felt and gotten out for healing. So it doesn't really matter whether you get the memory or not. If you keep working on it, over time, whatever memory might be there will come up.

Then I had an experience which had happened a few times before, but not for years. I woke up suddenly in the middle of the night. My eyes would just be open, and I would be frozen in terror in my bed, stiff. I couldn't even breathe. And I would be looking up at the silhouette of a dark figure reaching down to get me. It was really as if there were someone right there, but I couldn't move. Eventually the figure would fade completely. I would finally be able to get a breath, and I would really have to work at making myself move a finger, a hand, and finally be able to reach for a light and turn one on and sit up.

Well, I had never understood this, but now I connected it with the possibility of sexual abuse, like maybe somebody came and got me in my bed at night. So I wrote in my journal about that, and I really started working on these memories. I was using money I'd inherited to live on and was going to write my thesis. Instead, there were these memories and distress, crying, depression, anxiety, and just incredible turmoil. I started co-counseling at least three times a week. I did a lot of journaling and reading books. *The Courage to Heal* was the first one I got. It was brand new then and was considered *the* book to get.

I had this terror every time in counseling. I would try to address that figure in the night. I would freeze again, go into panic, and would physically jerk away and say, "No, No, I *can't!*" I literally couldn't face it. One co-counselor suggested real gently, "Can you imagine a situation where you could bring love into this scene, where you could feel safe?"

I couldn't, but one day I was driving along, and it suddenly popped into my mind what an amazing thing it was that my brain could reproduce this phenomenon so totally real that I believed that there was somebody standing beside my bed now, when here I was 48 years old and this had happened when I was a kid, and I didn't even remember it. What amazing creatures we are, what strange brains we have, that we are capable of such a thing! [*laughs*] I was actually kind of chuckling out loud, in awe of the human capacity. I thought, "Boy, I'm *glad* people are made like this, I'm so thankful that we have this ability to make us heal. And I realized it was something close to love I was feeling. I was loving myself, my ability to do that. I thought, "Oh! This is a little way to put love into that scene."

I've always been a very spiritually focused person. I've attended various religious groups, then explored Eastern philosophies and New Age things and whatever I felt drawn to at the time. I was attending a New Age meeting around then, and after it broke up, while people were socializing, there was this woman who frequently got messages from this Spirit Being friend of hers, Shepti. She was talking to somebody else with her back to me, when she suddenly whirled around and said, "Frieda! Shepti just told me to tell you that there's a gate. I don't know what that means, but that's what he said. There's a gate."

So the next time I went to a counseling session, I said I had discovered I could bring love into this terrifying fantasy. But I still had trouble and turned away, "No, No, I can't." Then what popped into my head was a gate, this really big heavy wooden old-fashioned gate, and I was standing uphill from it and felt really safe. And on the other side of the gate was the silhouetted figure. This was just a device to make me feel safe. I noticed there was a little girl who was me at the age of five, right up on my side of the gate on tiptoe, trying to peek over and see who was there.

So I asked, "Who are you?" I didn't get any words. A little more light came, but I still couldn't tell for sure. Still, I felt like the silhouette was probably my father. And this was the first time I had any clue as to who might have sexually abused me. I had imagined a cousin, an uncle, or several other people. It wasn't like I was necessarily expecting it to be my father, although intellectually I had figured out that he had the best access to me at night. Plus, I had all these negative feelings toward him.

All this was with my eyes closed. There was another man next to my father, and they were holding hands, and it became a little bit lighter.

"Why did you do that to me?" I asked. And my father's face and voice were on the edge of crying as he said, "I loved him," with great feeling. I already suspected that my father had been gay before he married. I had already had a flashback to when he and his lover were both present, and I was being sexually abused, with a penis in my mouth. It was brief, just a flash, but I knew it was two of them. I think I was between three and six months old then. I looked very much like a photograph of me as a baby.

Anyway, during this gate episode, I felt my own anger well up, and I pointed my finger and said, "Well, I don't care, even if you did love him, you shouldn't have done that to me. Now you two go off and talk about it!" And I saw them in my mind turn around and go away. Then the little girl at the gate ran to me, and as I picked her up, she turned from a five year old into an infant. And I cradled her in my arms. Then I did what I read in a book somewhere, that you imagine your own child-self going inside of your adult body and belonging in there. So I imagined it and felt like it really happened. And I felt like I could just hold my hands over my tummy, and it felt like I was cradling my baby inside.

From then on, for several weeks, a lot happened, dialoging with my father over the whole thing. [*Her father was already dead.*] It was just like *the* breakthrough. And after that, there was healing after healing, which would take a long time to describe.

About two years later, I thought I was just about finished with the memories, when I attended a seminar given by Ellen Bass, the author of *The Courage to Heal*. When I got there, I realized I was totally numbed out emotionally. My affect just was not there, so I knew that was an important sign. I always knew that when an emotion twinged at whatever somebody was saying, it probably had something to do with me, and I should pay attention to that. But that day, there were no emotions to go on. So I thought, well, I'll make a note in the margin of my journal whenever I have a *physical* discomfort. I made one mark in the morning when I had a real brief little twinge, then another one in the early afternoon. Late in the day, it happened again. And that third time, she had just done a ten minute talk about ritual abuse. Without gory details, she presented just the minimal facts, but just the idea that babies were sacrificed was so horrible the room was in shock.

And it was during that time that I put this note in the margin about physical discomfort. And I went back and looked, and the other two times were the only other times in the whole seminar when she'd even mentioned ritual abuse. And I thought, "Oh, no, *oh, no!* I can't deal with this, this can't be my story." I mean, I didn't want this to be anything to do with me. And I had zero memories and no reason to believe it would be so. But I had to face the fact that it was there in my notes, three times that day.

I had an appointment the next morning with a co-counselor, and right away I started crying, the hardest crying I'd ever done in my whole life. This was so incredible, I was amazed that my co-counselor wasn't terrified, the way I was behaving. The noises I was making and the bending over and the – I didn't actually retch, but it was close to it. I wasn't saying anything, just "No, No, it can't be, not that, no!" And finally, "No, No, not babies, it can't be, *not babies!*" Finally, I was just exhausted. An emotional discharge played itself out. Then we talked about it. I had very little in terms of data, but an undeniable strong knowing. Yes, there were babies, and yes, they were killed.

[Frieda eventually recalled gory details of abuse by the Masons in their Temple. She could never identify any of the faces, however. She just 'knew' that her father was one of them. She recalled most of the scenes by visualizing them during counseling sessions, but she had one flashback at night.]

That night I got into bed, not feeling good, restless, couldn't sleep. I lay on one side, then turned over, and when I did, I found myself looking at a ritual abuse scene, right there in front of my face. I was standing at the side of a sacrifice table with my eyes and face about six inches from a neck that had just been sliced, and the fresh blood was running down off the table, being captured in this silver goblet. The scene was so real, the blood was so bright, it was like I could smell the blood. And all I did was turn over in bed!

My memories of ritual abuse go from around six months old till when I was seven. In the earliest one, I was naked on a cold, hard floor like cement, and there were men standing around me in a circle, and they peed on me, and it was just humiliation like I could hardly believe, and I didn't expect it.

One of the worst memories I have is of being buried alive, and the sacrifice that preceded it. The basic message of the sacrifice was proving that love has no power at all. I was about five. They murdered a baby, then they cut off his mother's arm. I don't know what happened after that, because they buried me alive, put me in a coffin. When they dug me up, I was completely blue and stiff, yet I wasn't quite dead. Getting that particular memory up has been one of the hardest parts of my recovery. It's taken me more than a year to get the pieces I have.

I don't really know if I'll ever be finished with this process, where I'll know I've gotten all the memories, where I won't be just "in recovery" but "recovered." I've made another big transition just in the last few months. I've gone from victim to survivor, and now I feel like – for lack of a better word – a warrior. I don't like the war imagery, but it's the only word I know that adequately conveys the sense of being a fighter, not just for myself but for all children everywhere. Just in the last few months, I've been feeling healed enough that I feel more capable of carrying on this work. I will have the coping skills that I learned to survive – all the dissociating skills that I learned during the abuse years. I will have those available to me for conscious use when I need them.

Oh, yes, the flashbacks and memories have been very real. I don't have any doubt, that was me, and that happened to me. It's *so* real, and I'm in it. There's just no way I can doubt that it's a real memory.'

PHILIPPA LAWRENCE, INCEST SURVIVOR/THERAPIST

In 1980, Philippa Lawrence, a hairdresser, took a course in London on bioenergetics with one of its inventors, the Greek John Pierrakos [his real name], who combined 'basic Reichian therapy with the insights of modern physics,' according to one of his book jackets. 'He could read bodies like some people can read palms,' Lawrence explained. He told her very little, other than to look more closely at her relationship with her parents, despite her assertion that she 'owed them everything.' Inspired by the course, Lawrence quit her hairdressing job to teach yoga and alternative therapies. She has practiced a number of them herself, including 'rebirthing,' a process in which one hyperventilates for forty minutes and then attempts to recall one's birth. In 1987 or 1988, while studying at the Chiron Center for Holistic Psychotherapy [real name] in London and attending private therapy sessions, she recovered her first memory of sexual abuse.

I had always remembered my mother abusing me when I was 12 years old. It never occurred to me to tell anybody. I used to have to sleep with her, to take care of her. She had six nervous breakdowns, and she used her inability to cope to make everyone look after her. I was her partner when Dad was working nights. I woke up in the middle of the night very aroused, and she was masturbating me. I just froze, then I pissed myself. Then I started a whole episode of wetting the bed. Yes, my mother is a very disturbed person.

It was during my training at Chiron that my repressed memories came up. At that time, I was also seeing John Mellon, a Gestalt therapist. I did dialogue work with my own body. He would ask me to concentrate on a particular body part and exaggerate it. So if he noticed me moving my hand, for instance, he might ask me to pay attention to that. This stuff comes from the gods, really.

The first time it happened, I was in a therapy session and talking about my mother. It was like a series of flashbacks. You know these strobe lights that make things look like fast jerky slides? It was like that. I'm very visual; I think in pictures. I saw an erect penis, a mouth, and at the same time felt my own mouth. I saw a very tiny female baby's vagina. These were all combined with physical sensations in my body. I would feel a sensation in my vagina, then I would see a baby's vagina. My body was trying to talk to me.

My head felt like it was going to explode. I was very distressed. John didn't interpret; he let me be in control. I said, "Oh, my God, I'm scared I might have been abused as a baby." He didn't say Yes or No. He just asked what I'd seen, what was happening.

After this session, I drove over to Chiron for the training and I threw up. I just could not swallow anything, couldn't put anything past my mouth for a few days. I think now that was because I had been orally raped and was reliving it. At the time, I thought it was my Dad, but I have since concluded it was my Granddad.

Then a few years later in 1989 or so, I was doing a body-and-energy session at Chiron. I felt really good and energetic. I ended up leaping off a stool onto a pool of cushions. It was glorious. Then I sat down and started getting this feeling in the backs of my legs. At first, I thought I had scratched something. It was like a carpet burn. I told my trainee therapist, "This is really weird." I could tell from people's faces that they knew something had come up. The leader said, "Just go with that, see what it is." I had flashbacks. I was in my grandparents' lounge. Then I wanted to start banging my head, the pain was so overwhelming. I didn't want to know. The training therapist just kept saying, "Don't hurt yourself, don't hurt yourself," so I didn't.

In this flashback, my Granddad was sitting in the corner, and I sat on the settee in front of the fire. It was a horsehair settee, very rough. My mother had gone into hospital, and my father had gone to see her. I was 5 years old. I've since verified all of this with my family.

I was playing with myself as kids do, I was sort of playing with my vagina, and my Granddad was very excited. He dragged me off this settee, and I had feelings between my legs of being interfered with. Then my grandmother came in, and she was furious. I got punished for what was happening. She was slapping me between my thighs. I heard words as well, something like, "Silence! You must never do this again. Never tell anybody. You are a terrible girl." That was my clearest memory, and it crystalized a lot for me. It all seemed to link up for me then. We lived at my grandparents' house when I was first born, so I concluded that the previous memory was of my grandfather and not my father.

I also had a dream not long after that about an old man with my grandfather's face, and this leer. I went to see a horror film as a teenager about a ghoul. I had a bizarre reaction. He had this particular look on his face that was terrifying and made me feel peculiar. I didn't understand it at the time. Also, when I was little, I had a screaming fit at a television program, watching a mask that changed from smiling to frowning. "So *that's* why." It made complete sense. So now this clicked into place. The abuse by my grandfather continued from when I was a baby till I was five and he was found out by my grandmother, so that was the end of it.

I supposed it's possible that my father also abused me, but I hope not. I really love my dad. On the other hand, many people who later have memories of their fathers say, "I don't want to know, I don't want to know about my Dad." So I just don't know.

I had one other memory that came first in a dream, then in a body memory. It was about a shop-keeper near my home when I was a little girl. I processed it in a therapy session. I had the sensation of being very near this big belly. I was watching this child being interfered with by this man, and at the same time, it got enmeshed with seeing his fingers and wanting to see them go through the bacon slicer. That was another huge piece of the jigsaw. In therapy, I saw how he slid his hand inside my bathing costume and played with my genitals and also my bottom. I was less than 10. I told my Dad, "Mr. Barker plays with me and Josephine inside our bathing costumes," and he said, "Don't talk such rubbish." Mother would say, "He's a very nice man, Mr. Barker, very good to us." He used to give us credit. I remembered all of this conversation through therapy.

When I remember these things, my head and throat are pounding. I just want to cry and cry and cry. But I think it's good for me. I need to process it. It's natural that it is painful. Who would want to feel or remember that? That's why it's repressed and forgotten. I've actually read this in a book called *The Courage to Heal*. If a child did not go unconscious, the volume of pain would actually destroy them. I read the book long after the memories came back, but I found the book so validating.

Before I got these memories, I had never even heard of flashbacks. I didn't know the words. None of my therapists have pushed or interpreted what I said. I really feel grateful for that; I've made sense of the whole thing myself. I've just been asked the right questions.

What do I think about false memory syndrome? I think it's possible that some people are being misled. But I absolutely know my memories are real; I believe my experience in my therapy more than anything else. I can't even describe the kind of strength it's given me. It's validated my experience. It did happen, and it shouldn't have.

I don't think I've got all the memories out yet. Certain things start to happen when they are about to come. I get a kind of dizzy pressure in the head, and that's been happening recently. And from the very fact that I'm speaking to you, I think there's something ready to surface. I wholeheartedly believe in synchronicity. It's not a coincidence that you called.'

PATRICIA DELANEY, SURVIVOR AND LAWYER

In her professional life, Patricia Delaney, 35, is a hard-nosed corporate lawyer whose aggressive courtroom tactics make her a respected Ohio litigator. To her three sisters, however, she is a vulnerable survivor of childhood sexual abuse. Delaney retrieved her memories through dreams, journaling, and therapy over a year and a half. Although she has not accused either of her parents, she is bitter about her alcoholic mother. 'I'm very resentful of the lack of supervision that allowed this to go on.' Gradually, she has retrieved memories that George, the son of her mother's favorite drinking companion, was her primary abuser. Unlike many Survivors, Delaney did not find The Courage to Heal *particularly useful, but Renee Fredrickson's* Repressed Memories *helped her considerably.*

'I remember watching an Oprah program years ago. At the end of the show, she said, "There are people who have been sexually abused, and there are others who don't know whether they've been abused or not." That kind of sparked something in me.

When my sister got married in 1990, I brought up the subject of sexual abuse over lunch with all my sisters. I had begun to wonder whether my low sex drive and lack of sexual fulfillment might stem from forgotten abuse. But I didn't really pursue it until a year and a half ago, when I started having bad dreams.

The memories started to come back early in 1993. My first dream involved George, who was one of my best friend's older brothers when I was a child. He's about five years older than I am. In my dream, I was in a white bathtub, which ran perpendicular to the entryway, and it was set against the far end of a wall. George was coming at me, moving these long fingers in a haunting sort of way, like Edward Scissorhands. I was curled up in a little ball and trying to hide myself behind my hair. And as a small kid, I didn't have long hair. Then the dream just stopped. I don't remember him touching me; I just see him coming at me.

I had a friend who had remembered sexual abuse, and she referred me to Rhonda, her therapist, who had a master's in counseling, and who had a reputation for incorporating spirituality into her work with survivors. I am a devout Catholic, so that was important to me. I ended up seeing Rhonda for three months, but I was never really at ease with her. I wanted to explore whether anything had happened, and I felt her pushing me to accept that something definitely *had* happened. I would relate to her what I wrote in my journal about my dreams, and she would ask, "What happened next? What happened next?" I felt she was forcing me to find the ending of a story when I didn't have one. At the same time, I really felt sure that *something* had happened.

At first, I suspected absolutely everybody. Originally, I thought maybe it was George's father. He had a heart attack and died in 1993, which triggered some of my memories, I think. Also, my oldest son was just turning seven, the age when I think I was abused.

When I first started getting these memories, my husband was skeptical. He had read about how some therapists might be fostering false memories. I worried about that, too. I kept thinking, "This is all in my head." As an attorney, I felt I had to have some kind of reliable, legally admissible evidence to back me up.

Then one night when I was writing in my journal, I had this incredible feeling that George was right there in the room with me. Everything just started tumbling out faster and faster. I wrote really fast, almost like not writing at all, but reliving it. It came flooding out. I had this vision of being on a bed in George's sister's room on the second floor of their big colonial house in Glencoe, this exclusive Chicago suburb, across the street from our house. I was lying on the bed, and one of George's friends was there. Someone was kneeling, with one leg up. When I wrote in my journal, I would sometimes write with a child's vocabulary, almost speaking like a child. In that memory, I looked up and saw this white fleshy tummy, and a patch of black worms. I assume that was pubic hair, and a penis was being forced into my mouth.

Starting about ten years ago, I've had inexplicable gagging episodes. Now I think they were body memories of oral sex, but I never identified them as such until recently. The gagging sensations would come in the middle of the day, just out of the blue.

After I saw the flash of white tummy and the black worms, I just flew out the window to this peaceful place. I went to this big tree and tiptoed on the most tender, delicate edges of the leaves. That's because I felt very close to God up there. I felt like I had flown into heaven and was safe. I don't remember flying back. I felt light and clean and feminine, almost like Tinkerbell.

I finished writing about one in the morning and was so shaken up that I called my sister Fran and read it to her. She's a therapist who specializes in ACOA [Adult Children of Alcoholics] issues, and she explained that when I felt myself fly out the window I had been dissociating, taking my mind away with a defense mechanism. When Fran said that, I remembered how I would dissociate when I was a kid. I could be walking in the woods with my friends, and I could see my feet, but I just didn't feel like I was there.

I was still uncomfortable with Rhonda, my therapist. I asked her to hypnotize me to make sure of these memories, but she refused, saying that hypnosis was unreliable. I do credit her, though, for suggesting that I go to a woman's group for sexual abuse survivors, which was literally the best thing that could have happened to foster my recovery. We continue to meet, even though we were supposed to stop after ten sessions. We have a wonderful facilitator, Jodie, who was also my individual therapist during the most difficult part of this process.

Another terrible memory had to do with this area on the third floor, a big attic space where George's room was. My best friend, Carol, was George's little sister, and we used to play on the right side of the attic, a wonderful spot. But the left side was like hell. I have this incredible memory of a brown shag carpet and a brown couch on that side of the attic. I remember feeling the rug on my face and feeling this bouncing. And I remember feeling wet, and that I just wanted to sink down into the dirt of the floor, where no one would ever see me again. I call that dirt under the floor in the attic "The Pit." When I told my group about this, I kept telling them that it felt like part of my childhood self.

Part of me wonders whether it was anal sex. One of the things that really bothered me, in terms of not trusting my memories, was that I bled the first time I had intercourse. So I thought, "This must be all in my mind. I couldn't have been raped, it couldn't have happened that way." If it was anal sex, though, that would explain it. The funny thing is, I don't feel like I have to know now.

I was in incredible turmoil, and really paranoid that George would somehow reappear to attack me. I had a difficult time focusing at work. One day, I was getting ready to go into a meeting with the CEO of a major corporation, and I was a complete mess. I told myself, "Patty, you're 35 years old, you're a professional, you know what you're doing. There's a time for looking into this abuse, but now you need to go into that meeting." And I did, but it wasn't easy.

About six months ago, soon after I called my sister at one in the morning, my three sisters and I got together with a therapist to sort out issues raised by our mother's alcoholism. We didn't want it to become an intergenerational problem or harm our relationship with one another. As part of that session, the issue of my abuse came up, how Mom didn't exercise proper supervision. I opened up to all my sisters completely for the first time. I asked for their help in going back to the house in Glencoe where the abuse occurred. I told them I needed to retrieve the abused part of me from The Pit.

It was really hard to tell my sisters about this. I had to wear a blindfold to do it. I wrapped a plastic garbage bag around my head. It helped me focus, and I didn't have to look at anybody. It hid the shame. Then I took off the blindfold and said, "I'm afraid I'm making all of this up." And one sister looked straight at me and said, "Why in the world would you?" And I laughed and thought, "That's right, why would I?"

We put together a plan for me to shake out that demon. My sister Joan, who still lives in Chicago, set up for me to go back to George's room in the attic with her. She told the family that lived there that there were certain things I needed to settle from the past. They were a little reluctant, but they agreed. I chose Joan because she's the rebel of the family, and I thought she could protect me. I felt that George could just jump out at me from anywhere. I would sometimes panic, thinking he knew that I was telling people. I thought he would hire a hit man and kill me. I know it doesn't make much sense, but that's how I felt.

I flew out in the spring of 1994. Joan and I went over to the house one morning, and I had her bring a little bag with a toy rifle in it. I made her wear a sheriff's badge, and I called her "Rambo." I know that's bizarre, but it made me feel much safer. I couldn't have gone into the house without her. I also brought my special childhood doll with me. During the previous year, I had suddenly developed a strange aversion to the doll. My therapist, Jodie, really forced me to look at that. As preparation for going out to Glencoe, I realized that the doll didn't have any clothes on, and her nakedness was the ultimate vulnerability. So when I got to Chicago, Joan and I went out and bought the doll some nice clothes, wrapped in a warm blanket sent by another sister, and I brought her with me.

When we got to the house, I was expecting to feel very angry. I had told Joan I wanted to borrow the gun and shoot around George's room. But I didn't feel the need to do that at all. I just had this incredible feeling of peace come over me. When we got to the attic, I took my doll in my arms, and told her she was safe. She was out of The Pit and would be part of our family. Then I saw the bathroom . . . just like in my dreams, with the entrance and the white tub against the wall. Nothing any therapist could have said would have given me that reassurance. The whole memory scene hinged on the way George was approaching me there. I couldn't have made that up.

What had been driving me until then was the need to know every detail of what had happened to me. Now I knew that something really *had* happened, but I'll never know exactly what. Now I can put it behind me.

When I came home, my husband was wonderful. He told me how proud he was of me, and how courageous I was, instead of saying, "Oh, you poor thing, what you had to go through." He was very reassuring, telling me that I could move ahead with real strength.

After I went back to confront my past in Glencoe, another sister, who happened to be George's real estate agent, abruptly informed him that she would no longer handle his business. He never questioned why, because he *knows*. Now I know he knows. When I first began to get my memories, I really wanted to confront George, but I don't feel the need any more. For one thing, I would still be very scared of him. I feel that I've confronted the issue and have identified the consequences of the abuse. That's all I want. I have all the support I need to keep my feelings under control, because I couldn't do it alone. I applied what I had learned from my ACOA 12-step background – that I was powerless over the situation, and that has helped me to realize that it wasn't my fault, and I don't need to be ashamed of asking for help.

I think this will always be an on-going process. I take a lot of pride in the fact that I'm doing much better, though. Yes, the abuse had specific consequences. But you can either go through life and be a victim and be stuck in that role forever, or you can acknowledge it and grapple with it and use it as a strength and move ahead.

Looking back at the last year and a half, I'd say that the memories came back because I was prepared to deal with them, and because I dealt with them my own way, surrounded by people I loved. I was fed up with the way things were going, and I wanted my sex life to be different. Now, it's much better. I remember going out to lunch with a friend toward the beginning of this process and saying I wasn't really sure about my memories. Much later, she told me, "Patty, I knew it was going to start for you, because you said you were really ready." And I guess I was.'

ANGELA BERGERON, MULTIPLE-PERSONALITY SURVIVOR

Angela Bergeron holds a bachelor's degree in sociology. A slightly built, polite 43-year-old housewife with glasses, she is convinced that she is a survivor of prolonged sexual abuse by her grandfather, who purportedly belonged to a satanic cult. As a result, she believes she developed multiple internal personalities – as many as 40 or more. As she talked about her various 'alters' and their behavior, I was amazed that the violence she described could inhabit such a mild exterior. Halfway through the interview, she explained that the reason she wore a cast on her right arm was that Hugh, the 'network chiropractor' who elicits her memories, had broken her thumb when one of her 'dark alters' tried to attack him during a session. 'That man has put his life on the line to help me,' she immediately added, 'and I couldn't be more grateful.'

'About three years ago, I started having nightmares. I found myself crying and scared, and I didn't know why. My whole daily life was falling apart. I was so nervous I couldn't answer the door or sleep at night. I felt like I wasn't myself, like this wasn't me. It was a feeling of unreality. Sometimes it would be 8 a.m., then 3 p.m., and I really didn't know what had gone on in between. That was scary.

All my life, I'd thought it would be interesting to go to a therapist.

When I found myself putting items from a store into my pocketbook without paying, I knew I was in deep trouble and needed counseling. So I opened the phone book and picked the first name under A, Frank Adams. Frank was terrific, very supportive. He never mentioned abuse, he just let me talk. After two months, I started to have what he called spontaneous regressions. My body would just start doing things in his office like curling up on the floor. I'd scream and convulse, and a lot of times I wasn't even aware of it. It would get real intense and go on for a couple of hours. He always made me the last appointment of the day. Apparently these were what they call body memories.

That went on twice a week for eight months, every single time I'd go, and I'd remember something different. Sometimes I'd just be reliving the trauma. It started to get into ritual abuse memories, right here in Connecticut. This was about torture, brainwashing, electric shock, programming, body sacrifices, blood, children dying, children in cages. I had never heard of this before. I didn't know where it was coming from. I don't watch horror movies and had never read about this kind of stuff. I know that he did not lead me or suggest anything. I had never thought about terms like *incest*. Since then, of course, I've read all those books.

It was my grandfather who brought me to those places. I had always remembered that he exposed himself to me and wanted me to fondle him when I was five. I was born on his birthday, and that made me his, special to him. There was a shed outside his house. I remembered in therapy how my granddad used to keep me in there, one time for five days straight, chained, and there was a wild, hungry raccoon tied in there, just far enough away so he couldn't get to me, but he would lunge at me.

Then it got frightening to Frank, because I wasn't necessarily conscious to myself when I talked to him. He believed it all, but he had a difficult time with the evil concept of it. So one day I got a phone call from him telling me never to come back. It was devastating. This man used to hold me in his lap after those episodes – nothing sexual, but he felt like he needed to heal my inner child. He used to encourage me to make phone calls to him, because I would be shook up the next day. He was a very spiritual person, and I think he became afraid of the demons or devils in me. It got very bad at the end. He said I would try to bite him, snarl, spit at him, my whole voice changed, very dark and sinister. One time, he threw a bucket of water at my head. Many times, he had to slap me really hard. I didn't think it was wrong for him to hit me. If he hit me, it meant he loved me.

[When Frank terminated with Angela, he insisted she go for a month to an in-patient psychiatric facility, where she was diagnosed as MPD. When she got out, she returned to the stairwell of his building, reverting to a childlike state. He found her and called the police. Later, after attending a local conference on ritual abuse, she worked with a local female therapist. 'But I can't work with women therapists,' she explained, so she quit for a while. Then, she hurt her back and found Dr. Hugh Harrington, a network chiropractor.]

I told Hugh during our second session that there were others inside me. He said it wouldn't bother him. Since then, he has met a flood of people because of the depth of his touches. He worked on the nervous system, and it got very intense. He's told me since then that he never saw anything like this before. He started to find dark alters. They've attacked him with glass, knives, scissors, their bare hands. Bless his heart, he's never been afraid. He said once, "It's clear to me you were programmed by a professional cult. I can see it in your body, your cells." One time in his office, I was reliving electric shock treatments from the cult, and they were in regular clusters, 6, 6, 6. There were 18 of them in all, then a big massive one. 666 is the number for the Beast. Oh, there's a lot of really deep programming.

Hugh started realizing he couldn't do enough contacts to clear the body, because it always involved a physical fight. I suggested, "Why don't you just tie me to the stupid table?" So he started doing that, and it has really worked very well, given me a lot of safety. I care so much about him, but he's getting in really deep. They're very strong and can almost rip the restraints off. So now I have my own room at Hugh's office that no one else uses.

There are alters on the light side and on the dark side. Hugh has a relationship with an 18-year-old male named Talbot. He calls on him when I first walk into the office. I've become co-conscious of some of the alters and their voices. I can feel Talbot, who fights to hold back the others. At first, Talbot was thinking of joining the dark alters, but he and Hugh have man-to-man conversations, they both have guts, and they've built a solid relationship. Talbot protects one of the children, 11-year-old Jasmine. Actually, Jasmine created him, an alter of an alter. I can hear Talbot, but he doesn't think he's in the same body as me. He'll scrunch up in a ball, but there's a big booming Talbot voice. Hugh once asked him if he had a penis, and he said, "What the fuck do you think?" *[laughs]* It's very intriguing.

There's a 19-year-old fun-loving alter, Denise, who flirts with everyone. She's having an affair with Talbot. They're making love inside. It's probably the perfect incest, I don't know. [*laughs*]

[*Angela told me that she traveled to Texas last October to a unit specializing in ritual abuse MPDs. 'There were dark alters all over the place, people being restrained, screaming.' She explained that it was 'frightening but validating' to find others like herself, but that she was disconcerted by the fundamentalist approach, which sought to exorcise demons. 'I don't believe in Jesus,' she said. Still, she's confused. 'It's dangerous to exorcise alters, but you may need to do so with demons.' A transpersonal psychiatrist told her last summer that she might have 'low-level discarnate entities,' a fancy phrase for demons who can come in and out of her body. At any rate, she left the Texas unit after a month, just before Halloween, and Hugh insisted that he stay with her for an all-night session to protect her from ritual programming.*]

When I was in Texas, I saw a new alter inside who called himself Doctor Doctor, a little man with a bald head. I told a therapist friend about him, and she drew in her breath. She had just gone to Europe for a ritual abuse conference, and some former Nazis came and explained how they could put themselves into people. They went by three names, and one of them was Doctor Doctor. That was terrifying to me. He's like an introject, goes in and out. Now, my light alter has made a room of light inside. Some Dark Ones are kept there, and Doctor Doctor, too.

It gets really crowded inside. I got really angry once at Hugh when he deliberately created a new alter, Melissa, who was supposed to protect Jasmine in case anything happens to Hugh, to keep her from committing suicide. See, Jasmine calls Hugh all the time at home, and it's disruptive of his family life, so he's told her to stop doing that. When he created Melissa, I felt angry, violated; I wasn't asked. It was a message that I wasn't strong enough. Also, Melissa took up space, she was new, and nobody in there wanted her. And she's powerful, so it was a major adjustment.

Hugh finds out a lot about what's happening from the Center. That's a sort of core alter that's never supposed to talk to people, but Hugh can communicate with it. He explained it's like the Center of my being, an internal self-helper. It told him that when my mother was pregnant, they tortured the embryo, and it caused a split before I was even born. But my Center would make sure every time I was abused that a new split would occur to balance the evil with a good alter. After some really intense sessions, Hugh has to call for the Center to explain the memory. He'll call, "Is there a space?" over and over before there's room for the Center to come.

I think I was abused in the crib, but I don't have specific memories. When I was four, I've had memories of being in a cage with wild, hungry cats and snakes, naked and cold and hungry and terrified. They poked something real hot, like a red hot poker, in the cage. Then when I was five, I was tied upside down and lowered over a fire until it started to singe my hair, then they would put it out. Very frequently, I was tied on some sort of metal table and given electric shocks. They would push as far toward death as they could without killing me. The abuse went on until I was 12, when there was this huge ceremony. I think they stopped when I was 14, but then my grandfather taught me to be bulimic. He didn't want me to be any bigger.

There were sexual orgies all through there. I'd be lying on the altar naked, with my legs spread. The cult members were disguised as demons, and they'd put knives in my vagina, hot sticks and electrodes inside and outside. They'd lick blood and stuff off me, or I had to do that to other people. I had to abuse other children. It was about power, not sexual pleasure. I think my Mom was involved, but I don't remember seeing her there at the cult meetings. Of course, in a lot of the memories I was in a drugged state. I remember injections, a lot of needles. I still have a horror of needles, won't have a blood test.

Nobody could make up this stuff. I told Hugh once, "I think I made this up." He said, "Your body can't make this up. It's always consistent, everyone has their own personality. You'd have to be a genius, you'd make mistakes."

What did I think my childhood was like before these memories surfaced? I thought it wasn't particularly happy or affectionate. My parents didn't hug me. If you got a B, you should have got an A, like that. No one talked to each other. We were pretty dysfunctional. I knew I had been spanked. My father was assistant manager of a grocery store. My Mom didn't work. She was a cold person. Both were high school graduates. They grew up in Hapeville, this rural town, and stayed there. It's a very closed-minded place. My mother is domineering, wiped my father out, squelched anything in him. I feel nothing for my parents. My father is dead. When I told my mother, who is 78, that I was going to a therapist and remembering abuse by her father, she cried and fell apart. She thought mental illness was a secret, didn't want anyone to know it. I've been told not to keep in touch with her for safety reasons. I get callbacks. People in the cult have put in trigger words. If I hear a certain beep on my answering machine, it makes me want to go back to Hapeville. I think, "Gee, I should go home this weekend, got to go by myself." There may be alters in me who are still participating.

My husband, Leonard, is a former Catholic priest. He doesn't want to believe in my multiple personalities. He doesn't talk about it, never asks what I do in therapy. A couple of weeks ago, he said, "Why does your voice always change?" I said, "You know why, Len." He supports me financially, and he loves me, but he doesn't want this to be true. I haven't even told him about the ritual abuse, because I don't think he'd believe me. I didn't marry him, that's the problem. One of my alters did. I have an alter named Donna, she's the Suburban Housewife. She has nothing to do with Hugh. My children are 11 and 13. They know I was hurt as a child, but they live mostly with Donna. When they need me, I switch right away from Jasmine to the adult Donna. They get lots of hugs and affection from her. Often a cult will program a functional alter into you, so no one will ever suspect.

I like to think of what I have as multiple personality *response*, not disorder, or multiple personality "dignity." This word "integration," it terrifies me. I couldn't live without my alters. We're working toward community living, everyone agreeing they can have their time when they need it. They had to fight to survive, but they can find a better job and function now. I can't imagine being integrated, being a singleton.

It does show you the power of the human psyche. Jasmine can leave her body, travel to other worlds, and she has been able to say who is in every room. She walks across the ceiling. She talks about going to the Blue Land, and I have a sense of it. I wonder if, when you switch from one body to another, the body doesn't change chemically? I went for a mammogram a while back, and I switched, and the doctor said, "This can't be the same person," when he saw the x-rays.

Oh, you'd like to talk to Jasmine? Wait a minute.

[*Angela closed her eyes a few moments, then opened them. She snatched off her glasses and then plucked off her earrings. She spoke in a childish voice, timid but flirtatious.*]

I don't wear these glasses. You can't hurt me, because Talbot's right here. I could hear what Angela was saying. I don't like those things [*referring to earrings*]. A lot of people don't think I'm real, but I don't care if they do. It's okay for you to write stuff down, because Angela says it's okay. I have my baby doll and pictures, my blanket, and Bouncy the Bunny. And I have a red light to keep me safe, like blood, when I go to the woods. I love Hugh very much. I go to the Blue Land, where the wind blows a lot, and bells make sounds, and people teach you things without saying a word. Hugh doesn't tie me up – he just ties the Dark Ones.

[*I asked to speak to Angela again.*] You want me to go away? [*She seemed hurt, but was willing to leave. She closed her eyes, then put on her glasses and earrings, wiping her eyes and regaining composure.*]

I'm OK. She's a good kid, she's brave. I heard her.

The experience on Hugh's table is hard to describe. He works on the nervous system, which carries your whole history. When he touches the right nerve, it's so real that it's frightening. These are light, small touches where the spine attaches to the neck, and at the tailbone. He just reads the body. Once he was touching me, and I said, "Hugh, you've got to stop." And he had let go a long time ago, but that spot was just burning, bringing the memory.

I must be up to 30 or 40 alters, maybe. Also, there's a whole second system, probably with just as many in it, but I don't know much about it yet. Let's say we get the ones in this system all calmed down and in order, but there are layers, and another layer might kick in. That's why suicide is a very possible thing. I've had one who just really wants to die. It's a hopeless feeling sometimes, there seems no end to it. But there has to be an end, because why am I doing this otherwise? I think it will be at least another ten years of work, though.

I think I'm a lot healthier now. But when I walk out of a session with Hugh, it's very difficult, because I feel the anguish of a lot of alters inside who've been exposed, had memories. He's insisted I get a therapist, so I work with John now, too, but I don't really trust him. I resist John, though he's a nice guy. It sometimes feels like Hugh is trying to give me away to John.

I asked Hugh once, why does he do it. "Because I can," he said. I like that. He once told me he didn't have any limits. I think if Hugh moved away right now, I'd be dead.'

MELINDA COUTURE, SEXUAL ABUSE SURVIVOR AND WIFE OF ACCUSED FATHER

I heard this story quite by accident, while interviewing Melinda Couture, 59, the wife of an accused father. During the course of our conversation, she told me how, before the accusations came out, her daughter had told her to read The Courage to Heal. *'I thought maybe she wanted me to read it because*

I had been molested as a child.' Then Couture told me the following story, an interesting account of the spontaneous return of a long-forgotten memory.

'I was in therapy in the early 1960s, when a lot of issues had come up for me. Sometimes I would go home from a session and write about things to get them in perspective. I was home writing, when I remembered this incident and was just blown away. I told my psychiatrist, and he kind of nodded. He didn't seem too alarmed by it.

The incident happened in the '40s when I was 12. There weren't any sex abuse hotlines in those days, and it wasn't something you talked about. I told no one. I remember thinking about it a long time. I almost told my best friend, but then thought, "Nah, we'd have an argument and she'd blab." It was my 22-year-old brother-in-law who molested me. He had been drinking, and my sister had left the house briefly. It was a Saturday afternoon, and I was washing dishes at the sink. He sidled up to me and started asking if I knew what breasts were for. I felt very uncomfortable, but I told him, "Yes, they're for nursing babies."

He continued this suggestive, inappropriate questioning. I was dumbfounded. If I could have gotten angry and swatted him with a dishrag, it would have been okay. But I froze into a kind of compliance. He was saying, "Boys want to pet, but don't let them do *this*," as he gave me a free home demonstration, reaching up underneath my shirt to touch my breast. It probably lasted only a few minutes at the most. I heard a door slam, and everything stopped. I was so thankful. It never happened again. For another 15 years, until I was 27, I forgot about it until that night when it suddenly came back to me. I thought, "How the hell could I have forgotten that?"

It wasn't all that traumatic. He didn't reach between my legs or anything. That one incident happened, and I forgot it, but I never forgot the verbal harassment from the same person that went on constantly. He was a real boor and later turned out to be an alcoholic. It was like he was always trying to get a rise out of everybody. He thought he was so clever. He did the same sort of verbal stuff to my younger sister. She'd get more angry; I would just get annoyed.'

SALLY HAMPSHIRE, INCEST SURVIVOR WHO HAS
ALWAYS REMEMBERED

Sally Hampshire, 49, has always remembered how her father molested her. She does not come down firmly on one side or the other of the repressed-memory debate, though she does believe that false memories can be induced. At the same time, she has read many of the self-help books and absorbed their jargon. She isn't certain, for instance, that her father didn't molest her 'preverbally;' she complains of violated 'boundaries,' and she speaks of 'dissociating' during the abuse. Nonetheless, like many others who have always known they were incest victims, she has neither nurtured her rage nor defined her life solely in terms of sexual abuse, as painful and confusing as it is for her. She has even made an attempt to establish a healthy relationship with her father.

'Sure, there were good parts to my childhood. I was close to my siblings. My mother never spanked us, never yelled at us. She was not a doormat, but she had been raised in a Pentecostal home, only becoming a Presbyterian when she married my father. So she had this deeply ingrained Biblical idea that the male is the head of the house and the authority in all things. But Mom was a lot of fun, outgoing, active. She also had a lot of problems with her weight, up and down, up and down, with very dysfunctional eating habits.

My father did not physically abuse us. I do have one memory of Dad losing his temper and tearing into my brother, but that kind of stuff didn't happen often. I was always aware that he emotionally picked on my older sister and younger brother, but he hardly did it to me. I was his favorite. Dad told me last summer that he had hesitated to marry my mother because of her volatile, chaotic family, and he was afraid it was genetic. He thought my brother and sister had more of that personality, so he constantly corrected and badgered them.

I got most of my nurturing from my father. He held and cuddled me. When he bathed me, I remember complaining about the way he washed my genitals when I was five or six. I think my father began to manipulate me early in life, handling me very sensually. It wasn't until about ten that it dawned on me that this might be something wrong. My breasts began to form. He'd put his hand under my shirt and pretend to be tickling me, and he'd touch my budding breast and say, "Oh, my goodness, what's this?" That's the first real abuse I consciously remember.

He insisted that it was okay to walk into my bedroom or bathroom any time he wanted, and I hated that. I had no privacy. His excuse was that this was perfectly normal, that too much modesty was a negative thing. This was a very vivid part of my childhood, no respect for my boundaries.

My sister and I shared a room. He fondled her, too. We had twin beds, with two desks in between. He'd talk to me gently and stroke my breasts as he spoke to me. Eventually he sucked on them. This was in the dark. My sister and I didn't ever talk about it until we were both married. I was 14 when he first fingered me. I just froze. What you do is, you know internally that this is wrong, yet it's your father, and he told me, "This is what fathers do to teach their children about sex." As time went on, it was like, "You and I have such a special love," that was my father's favorite line. My sister had a more assertive, aggressive personality and could put him off more. I was the caretaker, took care of the emotional needs in the family.

The abuse was very confusing to me. He never exposed himself or asked me to touch him. He only attempted to give me pleasure. I didn't even realize until much later that I got off easy compared to many other incest victims. I was ashamed for years to tell my story. I would dissociate, zone out, I would try to shut my body down. I knew that my body was responding and it felt good, and I felt it shouldn't be responding.

Dad would continue to come into my bedroom, but the older I got, the more careful he got about it. He would walk into the bathroom while I was bathing, when no one else was home. He only touched me at night, though. I didn't really recognize the consequences until I got married. Sometimes at night, when my husband reaches out to me, I jump. When he touches me in certain ways, I freeze. I kept talking myself through it, and I found relief by drinking.

When I was in college, at age 19, I had a serious boyfriend, Jack, and I decided I wanted to lose my virginity to him. We went to a romantic, secluded cabin, and we got hot and heavy, and suddenly he jumped up and said, "No, we can't do this!" He was a good Catholic. Then he said it was getting too serious and we had to break up. I was devastated. When I went home, it happened that only my father was there. Dad was very sensual, lovey-dovey, non-sexual but very erotic, even his hugging. I told him about Jack, and he was very sympathetic, pulled me onto his lap in a chair to comfort me. He didn't try to molest me, he just came across as caring, concerned, and thoughtful.

The next morning, I woke up and he heard me stirring and called out, "Why don't you come crawl in bed with me?" I hesitated, then went and got in bed. He hugged me and stroked me sexually. He had an erection. That was the first time I was physically aware of it. I was getting very aroused and thought, "I have to get out of here." I went back to my room and masturbated, which I always did after he fondled me. I thought, "This is sick."

It began to dawn on me that if I didn't get away from him, I would begin to initiate. A year later, my mother joined a fundamentalist cult, and my father was overseas, but he was coming back for Christmas. I was so scared and terrified, I thought I was becoming demon-possessed. Certain things the minister said stirred things up. On Christmas Eve, I went to talk to the minister and his wife, and I told them about my father. I was shaking all over and trembling. I could hardly talk. They were very sympathetic and asked if my mother knew this. I said no. They said, "You need to go home and tell your mother." I said, "I can't, she'll divorce him."

But I did tell my mother. She looked at me and said, "Oh, my God, I suspected something like this." I felt the whole world drop out from under me. She had known and not protected me! My God, I thought, she has abandoned me also. Betrayed me. It was like I was outside up above the house in the dark night, looking down at myself talking to her in the bedroom. Talk about numb! I went numb for about ten years.

My mother never talked about the abuse after that night. But she moved into my bedroom and arranged for me to move into someone else's house when he came home, and she divorced him. I had to bury my feelings of guilt for breaking up the family.

I wanted to have a healthy relationship with my father, but for years I didn't see him, and I only wrote polite letters, telling him what my children were doing, stuff like that. Finally, I went to see him and said, "Dad, I have to talk to you about the past. I have to know why, when we had such a good relationship, when you were such a good father, why did you do that?" He said, "You know, sometimes people just happen to be born father and daughter, but the love transcends it." I was just sitting there with my mouth hanging open. He said, "I never meant to harm you." He was sorry, but he was still making excuses. He couldn't say, "I abused you, that was incest." I was just sitting there bawling.

But I finally felt in control. Until I confronted him, there was a part of me that was afraid of him. That's the complexity of an incestuous relationship. It was so sensual, and he was the source of the nurturing and cuddling I knew. I said, "Dad, can you imagine the friendship we could have had if you hadn't brought sex into it?" It was a breakthrough for me. I've never been afraid again that I would ever give in to him.

Since then, we've grown closer over the years as I continued to probe him. The irony is that I can talk to my father about anything. I have had to learn what's inappropriate, that it's not okay to talk about my sex life with him. Three years ago, he made a comment when he saw me in a bathing suit. He said, "I always liked you in a bikini." I felt this rage rise up in me. I've always been clearheaded with him, cool and calm. When I got home, I typed a six-page letter, saying "Don't you ever, ever make a statement like that to me again. It shows you still don't understand the whole framework of our relationship." He called me and apologized and said, "I guess I really don't understand yet when I'm being inappropriate." He was sincere, but his self-awareness only goes so far.'

CHAPTER SEVEN

The Accused

I know thou wilt not hold me innocent.
I shall be condemned;
why then do I labor in vain?
If I wash myself with snow,
and cleanse my hands with lye,
Yet thou wilt plunge me into a pit,
and my own clothes will abhor me.

The Book of Job (9:28–31)

INTERVIEWS IN THIS CHAPTER:

HANK AND ARLENE SCHMIDT, *accused parents, and* FRANK SCHMIDT, their son
PHILIP MARSDEN, *accused father*
BOB SCULLEY, *accused father*
JULIA HAPGOOD, *wife of accused*
DR. AARON GOLDBERG, *accused father*
HAROLD BRIGHTWELL, *accused father*
JOE SIMMONS, *accused father*
GLORIA HARMON, *accused mother*
BART STAFFORD, *accused sibling*

It's difficult to convey the horror of being falsely accused. As Franz Kafka's character Joseph K. discovered in *The Trial*, condemned but innocent people begin to believe they must have done something wrong, especially if the particulars are never specified.[1] Almost all of the accused parents represented in this chapter have, at one point or another, questioned their own innocence. After all, it is their own beloved children who are arrayed against them. Like Paul Ingram, the policeman whose tragic story is recounted in Lawrence Wright's book, *Remembering Satan* (1994), they think, 'My girls know me. They wouldn't lie about something like this.'² Some, like Ingram, fall under the sway of zealous therapists/interrogators and confess to crimes that they never committed.*³ In this chapter, for instance, Joe Simmons explains how he came to believe that he had been the high priest in a satanic cult that abused his son Johnny. Fortunately, most parents eventually conclude that they did not overtly sexually abuse their children.

Yet when you've been attacked so ferociously, when you've been called a perpetrator and told that you stole your children's innocence, robbed them of their childhood, you begin to believe it on some level. You must have done *something* pretty bad. As Joe Simmons observes, 'One minute, I was a responsible member of the community, trying to be a good father, and the next I'm like Charles Manson.'

When 'crunch time' arrives, accused older brother Bart Stafford observes, people often find that their friends and even family members turn on them. I have also had this experience, to a limited degree, but I think I understand it.** People don't want to believe that a completely innocent person could be accused of such an awful crime by his or her children. If that were true, it could happen to anyone – it could happen to *them*. Thus, we observe a variation of the familiar blame-the-victim scenario. Job's friends, his supposed 'comforters,' enacted this drama long ago. Eliphaz asks Job, 'Think now, who that was innocent ever perished? Or where were the upright cut off?' Job understands what he really means. 'You see my calamity,' he tells Eliphaz, 'and are afraid.'⁴

Yet *anyone could be accused of incest without any foundation in fact*, given the proper circumstances. As recovered memory critic Richard Ofshe has observed, it's something like the random attacks during World War

---

* As a result, Ingram is currently jailed for acts that he clearly did not commit. Surprisingly, false confessions aren't rare, as Gisli Gudjonsson points out in *The Psychology of Interrogations, Confessions, and Testimony* (1992). Many occur when 'suspects come to believe during police interviewing that they have committed the crime they are accused of, even though they have no actual memory of having committed the crime.' Richard Ofshe, the psychologist who proved that Paul Ingram was fantasizing his own guilt, has also written an interesting paper on how suspects' self-doubt and confusion can lead to false confessions.

** I have heard various rationalizations from friends and family, including: (1) Of course we know that you didn't commit *incest*, but you must have done something pretty inappropriate with your daughters. It's a good thing you're in therapy to figure it out. (2) You haven't *really* been accused of anything outright. Maybe this enforced separation is just a normal part of growing up and moving away. It's just a phase. (3) Why are you obsessing over this? They're adults now, and you wouldn't be seeing much of them anyway. (4) All suffering is part of the spiritual plan. Look how you've grown through this experience!

II in which German 'doodlebugs' randomly dropped out of the sky onto British households. The one characteristic shared by the majority of accused parents is that they are – disproportionate to the overall population – mostly middle to upper-class educated Caucasians with the initial ability and willingness to pay for their children's therapy.*⁵ Aside from that, they do not appear to have a great deal in common. At the FMS Foundation and British FMS meetings, octogenarians who never spoke about sex with their children sit next to accused parents in their 40s or 50s whose parenting philosophies were completely different. Some were exceptionally close to their children; others were emotionally or physically distant. Some were strict with their children, others permissive. Many remain in intact, secure marriages; others are either long-divorced or tolerate poor relationships. The only common denominator appears to be a troubled child who seeks therapy.

A third of the parents who have contacted the FMS Foundation never learn exactly what their children think they did. Others find out the precise allegations by word-of-mouth or, like the Hapgoods, by snooping. I can testify that not knowing what you're supposed to have done is maddening, for any number of reasons. You're left guessing, wondering whether it's something really awful or only a hug or a look misinterpreted as 'emotional incest.' It can actually be a relief to know the worst, to be accused of satanic ritual abuse. At least then you *know* you didn't do it – unless, of course, you believe that you, too, repressed the memory.

In many cases, there's a sibling domino effect.** One daughter retrieves incest memories and tells her sisters. Some of them not only believe her, but seek therapy to find their own memories. After all, if the father did this to one daughter, isn't it likely he would have done it to the rest? Indeed, if he's such a pedophile, perhaps he also assaulted his son. That's how Frank Schmidt, whose story follows, briefly came to believe that his father had sodomized him. The cases in which multiple

---

* Believe it or not, there is actually a 12-step support group for 'adult children of dysfunctional affluent families' designed to help 'victims of the difficult and debilitating effects of affluence.'

** I know of several families who have lost first one, then several children to recovered-memory therapy. One father I interviewed has lost four of his five daughters, one of whom accuses him of 'incestuous' behavior because, when she was 22, he told her about his job dissatisfaction – a conversation more appropriate with a wife, she asserted. Another couple told me they had lost seven of their eight children. These cases are particularly devastating because so many people assume that if multiple children make the accusations, they must be true. They do not stop to consider the improbability of *several* children completely forgetting abuse for years, let alone one.

siblings cut off all contact are particularly difficult. Not only have the parents lost more, but observers usually conclude that the allegations must be true. Otherwise, why would several children be saying the same thing? (Of course, even if massive repression could occur, what are the odds of *several* siblings failing to recall extensive abuse?)

Most of the parents I interviewed oscillate between anger and compassion for their children. With time, they usually understand that their children are not primarily at fault. They have been 'duped,' as Arlene Schmidt puts it, by their therapists and self-help books. Some, like Julia Hapgood, do not totally forgive their children. 'Everyone is responsible for what they do,' she says, admitting that there are days when she hates her daughter. Another bitter woman wrote to me that her daughter had thrown her mother away, and now she doesn't have a mother to come back to, as far as she is concerned.

Certainly, such bitterness is understandable. Therapists and books encourage accusing children to act as spitefully as possible, as Harold Brightwell's story in this chapter chillingly illustrates. Accusatory letters often arrive on special occasions such as Father's Day, Thanksgiving, or Christmas. One mother told me that her daughter had dumped on her on Mother's Day of 1991; the mother later discovered that one of her best friends had received a similar bomb on exactly the same day.

On the other hand, some accused parents appear almost inhumanly compassionate. In recalling his heart attack following the accusations, for instance, Philip Marsden is *grateful* to his daughter for saving his life. 'If I hadn't had the minor heart attacks, I wouldn't have known I needed surgery.' He holds little bitterness towards his daughter or her therapists, and he is happy to have her back in his life, even though she (a proven virgin) has not retracted her accusations.

I didn't have room for Doug Ellison's full story here, but it is remarkable. The 75-year-old retired clinical psychologist was accused by Flo, one of his four daughters, but he lost *all* of his children, who believed their sister. Then Flo contracted cancer. She finally agreed to see her father, but Flo died at 38 while he was driving across the country to be by her side. At the memorial service, another daughter passed out photocopied letters from Flo accusing her father of incest, so he wouldn't 'get away with it,' as she put it. Despite all of this, Ellison does not blame his children, or even their therapists, whom he sees as victims of dogma themselves. 'I don't think anger serves anybody here,' he told me.

It is difficult not to blame therapists, however, especially when so many hurt, bewildered parents have sought counseling themselves, only to be given advice similar to Gloria Harmon, whose son Robert accused her of incest: 'Acknowledge that Robert is entitled to his feelings, they are valid and he is hurting. Seek to understand what you did and are doing that hurts him.' Either that, or, as with the Schmidts, the therapist gives them John Bradshaw books and encourages them to discover how *they* were abused as children.

Many parents have been sued by their children in either civil or criminal courts. Because of the enormous legal costs, quite a few cases are settled out of court, even though the parents privately admit no wrong-doing. I interviewed Elbert and Josephine Wells, for instance, who are 89 and 83 respectively. Their 53-year-old daughter confronted them at her aunt's 50th wedding anniversary celebration, then sued. They have settled out of court, primarily because of their advanced age. 'We don't want years of court appearances and stress,' Josephine explained. Other accused fathers, such as Jack Collier (his real name) of California, refuse to give in to false allegations. At great expense, Collier won his case, but he has still lost his daughter.[6] Still others lose their cases and find themselves in jail, massive debt, or both.[*7]

Some parents are so devastated that they can barely drag themselves out of bed every morning. In his 1994 book, *What You Can Change and What You Can't*, psychologist Martin Seligman offers the bleakest prospects for those suffering from post-traumatic stress disorder. His prime example is a couple whose 14-year-old son was killed in an automobile accident; the parents cannot shake their grief. The mother is suicidal, and the father can't talk about it.[8] The situation of accused parents is analogous and, in a way, worse. At least with death comes closure, finality. Accused parents live with the constant knowledge of loss that is needless, angry, and on-going. It is hardly surprising that

* I interviewed one retired Tennessee doctor whose two daughters, now in their 40s, recovered hypnotic 'memories' of how he sexually abused them at his summer home, along with 12 prostitutes whom he then allegedly murdered and buried. The police led a hypnotized daughter around the property and dug for the bodies, but they never found them. The daughters have sued their father for $4 million each. At least he is not in jail, as is Rhode Island attorney John Quattrocchi (his real name). In 1994, Quattrocchi was convicted of sexually molesting his former girlfriend's daughter, who is now 19. Her 'recovered memories,' which she discovered after months of psychotherapy, go back to when she was three, just prior to the time she first met Quattrocchi. He has been sentenced to 40 years by Rhode Island Superior Court Judge John P. Bourcier, known locally as 'Maximum John.'

we meet a couple such as the Schmidts in this chapter. Their lives are, as Hank Schmidt puts it, 'in the toilet.'

Quite often, it is the wife of an accused father who takes the most active role in fighting the therapist, seeking reunion with the child, and declaring her husband's innocence. There are several possible explanations. Perhaps the men are so shattered by the experience that they cannot deal with it. Or maybe it's just that males in our society don't generally deal with such emotional issues very well. Finally, it is possible that some wives need to keep asserting their husband's innocence because they inwardly wonder whether he really did molest the children – a possibility most of them entertained at the beginning, at least briefly.

Some wives believe the charges, and marriages blow apart. Thus Bob Sculley, who tells his story in this chapter, lost not only his daughter but his wife. Another father described to me how he first found out about his daughter's allegations one night when his wife confronted him and said, in a shaking voice, 'I know all about you and Lisa.' When he told her he didn't know what she was talking about, she said, 'They always deny it.' Although she left him for a while, she eventually returned to the marriage, which continues under strained circumstances. Although their daughter will not speak with her father, she and her mother talk frequently on the phone. Husband and wife do not discuss the accusations.

If the parents are already divorced when the 'memories' arise, the mother usually believes her daughter immediately, since she is already bitter towards her ex-husband. 'It was the missing piece of the jigsaw puzzle,' one such British mother said. 'I never doubted the veracity of my daughter's words. She has always been honest and serious and never had any illusions about any other aspect of her life, so why should she suddenly start lying about this?'[9]

A surprising number of *mothers* have been accused of incest by their sons or daughters. Gloria Harmon's sad story is, unfortunately, not uncommon, though usually the mothers are brought into the accusations only as the memories expand beyond the father. In reality, evidence from always-remembered abuse indicates that women rarely sexually abuse children.[10]

In several cases I learned about, but had no room for here, it was quite clear that North American influences were at work, leading to devastated parents back in the home country. In 1991, for instance, after recovering 'memories' in Canada, Trysh Ashby-Rolls (of the Rolls

Royce line) published *Triumph: A Journey of Healing from Incest*, in which she described turning her father in to the British police. 'Through discovering her Child Within, she lovingly reparented and got to know herself,' according to the dust jacket, while her grieving father, arrested and released, tried to fathom what had happened.[11]

In another case, I corresponded with an Australian father who sent his daughter to study music at a Christian college in the Midwestern United States and soon found himself accused of incest. Despite several desperate trips to America, he has lost his daughter. A British family sent a daughter to California, where she, too, was diagnosed with repressed memories. And in the case of Harold Brightwell, included here, it was an American homeopath who led his daughter into the search for 'memories.'

Because of the enormous variety of these stories and the number of people who are affected, I interviewed far more people than those represented here. I wanted to include Fred Orr's full interview, because it demonstrates what this process can do to a marriage, but will summarize it here instead. Orr's case is not unusual; I have heard from many other men whose marriages were destroyed after their wives entered recovered-memory therapy.

For three years, Orr believed that his wife Shauna really harbored multiple personalities because of sexual assaults by her father, brother, and grandfather. He read the section for supportive spouses in *The Courage to Heal*, Laura Davis' companion volume, *Allies in Healing*, and tried his best. Orr listened to Shauna's dramatic recounting of therapy sessions, helped her save pickle jars to smash on the garage floor to get out her anger, and even made her a tee-shirt featuring her eight alters (Goodie, Spock, Commando, Ivory, and It, among others). He hated his in-laws, ripping up their Christmas check in self-righteous fury, even though he had heard that Shauna's father was so distraught by the allegations that he often curled up in a fetal position in the corner of a room and wouldn't move. 'I figured he was just feeling guilty.'

Nevertheless, Shauna began to turn against her husband as well. 'She did these boundary exercises,' he told me. 'It started with no sex. Then, it was don't touch, with an invisible line down the middle of the bed. Then it was off to separate bedrooms. Finally, her therapist, a Ph.D. psychologist who ruled her life, told her to get divorced.' In a way, Orr was relieved. 'She'd been chopping up wieners with a butcher knife, fantasizing they were her father's penis. You should see the look on her face when she does that. I was glad to get out of that house.'

I also regret not having room for my interview with John and Thelma Sloan, whose story bears a resemblance to my own. They, too, have lost two daughters, one of whom is a lesbian therapist. 'The fact that Laura has a female partner is not of any concern to us,' John Sloan said. 'In fact, we like her very much.' Neither daughter has come forward with details of the abuse. Both are very bright, college-educated women in their 30s, loved Anne McAffrey fantasy books, and now talk frequently about boundaries. John and Thelma consider themselves feminists, never physically punished their children, and adopted an open parenting style. Ironically, Thelma was a rape crisis counselor in the early '80s and worked with incest survivors who had *always* remembered what happened to them. 'In some ways the progression to an emphasis on repressed memories is understandable,' she told me. 'It was hard at that time to get people to believe that incest was really a widespread problem.'

One of the terrible realities for accused family members is that they cannot seem to do anything right. Even the most innocuous attempts at communication are routinely twisted and re-interpreted for their clients by recovered-memory therapists. 'Dear Sis,' wrote one sibling, 'Mom and I have been thinking about you. Can't wait to see you again . . . In the meantime, take care of yourself. Love, Sis.' While this may appear to be a benign postcard on the surface, therapist David Calof found sinister hidden meaning in every word. 'Take care of yourself,' for instance, he interpreted as a hidden injunction for the client to kill herself.[12] It is this inability to break through on any level that is so heartbreaking and frustrating to accused family members.

HANK AND ARLENE SCHMIDT, ACCUSED PARENTS, AND FRANK SCHMIDT, THEIR SON

On the big-screen television set in their Utah living room, we watch the video of Stephanie, made in 1990 when she was a senior in high school. A radiantly beautiful young woman with long, dark hair, she sings a solo, part of a special program for aspiring professionals. Quietly, Hank and Arlene Schmidt weep, which is rare for them. In public, Hank hides his grief behind a jovial exterior, and Arlene behind a wall of competence. They have not seen their daughter since she accused them of incest early in 1992. Hank, a doctor, and Arlene, an editor, became so depressed that neither could work. They spend most of

their time at home now, living on Hank's retirement funds, trying to under-
stand what happened.

'Stephanie was a dream child,' Arlene tells me. 'We always thought we had
the most wonderful, stable, well-adjusted, in-charge daughter in the world.'
Even as a baby, she was a delight, singing softly to herself in her crib. 'As a
teenager,' Hank adds, 'she never rebelled like her friends. We felt so fortunate.'
Notes she wrote to her parents as a teenager bear them out. 'I love you and
think that you're the strongest man alive,' she wrote to her father when she
was 15. 'You are the best parents in the world and I love you.' Three years
later, she wrote to her mother, 'I love you and I appreciate all the things you
do, even the little things you think nobody notices.'

Their first hint of trouble came in the fall of 1989, her senior year, in a
letter Stephanie left on the kitchen counter. 'I need help,' the letter began.
'I've got this really bad emotional problem.' She described how she periodically
suffered from 'terrible emotional battles with myself.' When she wasn't in this
state, 'I feel fantastic and I'm very happy,' but then 'I get so upset over nothing
I can find, and a billion different thoughts and feelings collide and I get all
confused.' She concluded that something was wrong with her, but 'I'm afraid
of finding out what it is.'

Completely surprised and dismayed, her parents arranged for her to see a
psychologist. After three months, Stephanie said she thought she was all right,
and the matter was dropped. After graduation, Stephanie decided not to go to
college, took a job, and continued to dream of a singing career. Just before her
21st birthday, she moved out of her parents' home to live in an apartment
with two friends, Marianne and Winston, but she continued to see her parents
regularly. Then Stephanie became close friends with Josie, an older woman at
her work, and spent less time with her parents. She began to read self-help
books Josie recommended. Still, Christmas of 1991 passed uneventfully. It was
the last holiday they would celebrate together.

ARLENE: 'On Feb. 20, 1992, we got this letter from Stephanie, completely out of the blue. It began, "Dear Hank and Arlene," something
she'd never done before. "I'm writing to tell you that you won't be
hearing from me for a while, and I don't want you contacting me
either. I am working through some childhood issues, as I'm beginning
to remember my childhood." She said she needed a complete separation
from her family and was "taking responsibility" for her life. She ended
by writing, "This is what I need for myself, and my needs come first
for me now."

HANK: We said, "Huh?" It didn't sound like her at all. It sounded
like some robot was talking. It didn't make any sense. It was just

unbelievable. By this time, she had kicked her very best friend Marianne out of their apartment. They had been like sisters since they were 15. We had worried because Marianne seemed to manipulate Stephanie emotionally. Stephanie became whoever she was with; she'd take on the persona of whoever she was infatuated with. Now she dumped Marianne big-time, and shortly afterward, she dumped Winston, too.

ARLENE: I called Winston, after we got this letter, and he said, "Mrs. Schmidt, she's saying all kinds of crazy things. I don't know what to think." That's when I found out that Josie, her new friend from work, had gotten Stephanie to see this psychic, Ramona. Apparently, Ramona was hypnotizing Stephanie to help her remember all kinds of abuse in her past lives. Soon afterward, Winston showed up on our doorstep and told us she'd kicked him out, too. One night she had come back from seeing Ramona and told him, "I found out my parents did horrific things, so horrible I can't even tell you. They sexually abused me and did all sorts of things to me." He was dumbfounded. And because he didn't get right in there and say how sorry he was in the right way, she booted him out.

He told us that night that Stephanie was having memories that we were in some sort of ritual abuse cult along with our Mormon friends. That was the most preposterous thing yet. Can you imagine anything more ridiculous than a devout Mormon couple inviting a group of other devout Mormon couples into their home for the purpose of sexually abusing their daughter? What a way to get into the Celestial Kingdom!

I'd written Stephanie a letter, of course, saying that "it is quite devastating to have someone you thought you had a great relationship with all your life drop this kind of bomb on you with no explanation at all." I told her we'd agonized over this and couldn't figure out what we might have done to her, but that we should discuss any problems openly under the supervision of a trained counselor. No response.

Finally, I couldn't stand it any more. We'd received some mail addressed to her, so I used that as an excuse to go see her, and I wrote her a little note along with it, telling her how I was crying all the time and couldn't eat because of this, and pleading to talk. When she opened the door, she just stood there with this weird robot smile. "I can't talk to you now," she said without changing her expression. I kept saying, "Why not? When do you think we could get together?" No matter what I said, she just kept repeating, "I can't talk to you now," and I realized she'd been rehearsed to say this. I left the letters and walked away. She was still smiling. That's the last time I've ever seen her.

[Though Arlene didn't know it, her 25-year-old son Frank was asleep in Stephanie's apartment during their little conversation in the doorway. Stephanie had called and told him the new memories she was having, and he believed them. He'd traveled a thousand miles to come see her. I interviewed Frank separately and will allow him to tell part of his story here.]

FRANK: 'Stephanie called me in January of 1992. She'd dropped some hints about sex abuse before this. It's funny. As she told me about these awful memories, she'd say she thought it was our father, but she wasn't quite sure. She'd say, "I think he did this," then a minute later, she'd turn around and say, "He did this." She had a lot of specifics. She said she had been threatened and brutalized and had been raped with a gun in her vagina and her anus. She claimed she had gotten venereal disease from Dad, and that he'd gotten her pregnant and done an abortion on her at home. And that when she was younger, Mom and Dad routinely locked her in a large chest at my grandfather's house. She told me the abuse had lasted from when she was four until 14. I was utterly stunned and shocked. It was unbelievable, but why would she make it up?

Also, you have to understand that I was still very angry at my father. We had a bitter falling out when I was 18 over his refusal to pay full college tuition so I could go to a little-known school near Mary, my girlfriend, who is now my wife. So I could imagine this horrible thing being done by him. I talked to Mary about it at length. She was horrified and angry at my father.

I called Stephanie the next week and offered to visit in March. She seemed genuinely surprised and pleased at my show of support and willingness to come. In the meantime, I was more and more distraught. I became quite depressed and found it difficult to go to work. I took a voluntary leave for six weeks and sought counseling at a local clinic with Lucille Hart, an M.S.W. She was about 36, very attractive, with long blond hair. She seemed very friendly and supportive. During our first session, I told her I was confused and depressed. I said, "My God, if this happened to Stephanie, could it have happened to me?" She said, "Of course. It probably did."

That night, I was lying in bed and couldn't sleep. I sort of relaxed, and then I felt my whole body tense up, and I had a kind of pain in my anus and felt terribly afraid. At my next session, Lucille said, "Oh, that's an abreaction." I said, "What's that?" She said it was a body memory. The natural conclusion was, "Oh, I've been raped anally."

I was uncomfortable with the idea of being hypnotized. She told me, "This isn't really hypnosis, I'm just going to help you relax and think."

She explained that it was similar to the meditation I do before I write short stories. So we did guided imagery, where I would imagine myself flying around through the air, like flying into the past. I flew back to the house where we lived when my father was in his residency, when I was six. I opened the door to my bedroom, and there I was tied down to my bed. My father was cutting on my penis with a scalpel. I got really frightened, so I flew back to the present.

[*When Frank arrived in Arkansas to visit Stephanie that March, he believed that they were both incest victims, but he wanted proof. He convinced her to go to a gynecologist to check for the scars she claimed as a result of the abortion. When the doctor found none, Stephanie became enraged and said he was part of a conspiracy. She took Frank to visit Ramona, the psychic. He concluded that she was a quack and a fraud. Frank was upset when Stephanie told him about her mother's visit and how she had driven her away. 'She laughed a wicked laugh and burned Mom's note.' Instead of the suffering soul-mate he expected, he found his sister to be 'cold and calculating, downright cruel.' By the time he left, it was clear that she had no use for him, because he wasn't the strong ally she wanted. In the meantime, Arlene was trying other avenues.*]

ARLENE: After my failed attempt to talk to Stephanie, I didn't know what to do. I decided that her behavior might stem from her lupus, a rare disease she'd been diagnosed with when she was 16. Lupus affects the autoimmune system, attacking connective cell tissue. It can cause depression, delusions of paranoia, and other symptoms which seemed to match Stephanie's situation. She had really liked Dr. Strunk, the lupus specialist, so I called him and explained the situation. He agreed to contact her and arrange an appointment. But she refused. I was so worried. I thought, "My God, Stephanie will have convulsions and die!" I tried to talk to Josie from her office, but she wouldn't talk to me.

HANK: Then we got another short letter from Stephanie, dated March 20, 1992. It started right out, "My memories are of sexual abuse. And although there were some others, primarily my abusers were the two of you. These are my *memories*. Whether you remember them or not, I know what I know, and I have to deal with it and heal my life. I have plenty of support, many very good friends, and an excellent counselor. I am doing well." What can you do with something like that, knowing that your daughter thinks her parents were black-robed monsters who ate baby flesh? Oh, God. [*laughs*]

ARLENE: Wherever we turned, we hit stone walls. When all this started, before we knew about the sex abuse allegations, I called Betty Carson, one of my best friends, to ask if she might help us find out what was going on. Betty is a psychiatrist. "It's funny you should call today," she said. "Stephanie just called and is coming by for dinner tonight. She said she wanted to play some new songs for us." But when Betty called back, she said Stephanie hadn't told them anything. Later, when I told Betty about the incest allegations, she appeared to be truly shocked and upset. A month or so after that, I discovered that Stephanie was *living* with Betty and Sam Carson. I couldn't believe it! And when I tried to talk to either of them, they told me they couldn't talk to me without Stephanie's permission. These are people we've been friends with for 17 years. We just wanted to explain what we were going through and find out how Stephanie was doing, and they wouldn't even talk to us.

[*Hank and Arlene became clinically depressed. They would stay up until 3 a.m. and sleep until noon. Neither did the dishes until they overran the sink. Arlene, not normally given to emotional scenes, would suddenly burst into gut-wrenching sobs. They were afraid to leave the house, for fear they might miss a possible phone call from Stephanie. They obsessively read books about child abuse, trying to find some explanation for what was happening. They began seeing a therapist who gave them recovery books to read. When their answers to a checklist in John Bradshaw's* Homecoming *matched the abuse profile, they began to search for their own repressed incest memories. Finally, they realized that it was a futile exercise. 'All the talk about codependency and possible abuse took my mind off Stephanie for a while, all right,' Arlene says, 'because I spent all my time thinking about me, me, me.'*

They had not told Frank anything about the situation, hoping it would resolve itself without involving him. Then they accidentally learned that he had been in town to visit Stephanie and had not contacted them. Arlene called Frank.]

FRANK: Around that time, my mother called to fish for information about Stephanie. I was trying to act normal and be noncommunicative, but finally, I dropped my voice to a whisper and told her, "Dad did it to me, too." It was not an easy thing to say. At the time, I felt a real physical fear of my father. I told her not to tell him because I was afraid for her safety.

Eventually, I came to realize that my father had not abused me. I started to have doubts when my wife Mary went to see a different counselor at the same clinic, trying to understand what I was going through. Mary's therapist wanted to know all about her childhood, and when she mentioned that her parents drank too much, the therapist immediately decided that they were dysfunctional alcoholics who had sexually abused her. Mary wouldn't buy it and never had another session. Looking back, we should have figured out that these therapists were sex-abuse happy, but at the time I still believed my sister. And after all, these people were professionals and had degrees.

What really got me thinking was when I visited Dr. Kurtz, the psychiatrist who headed the clinic. He was an old-style type, actually an Austrian. I had to see him before my insurance would pay for my therapy. When I told him my story, I kept seeing shock on his face. He obviously wasn't doing the best job of supervising; he was in it for the bucks. Finally, he said, "Boy, you *are* taking this well, aren't you?" His tone of voice hit me hard. That's when I came to realize that I wasn't feeling as much pain as the abuse would seem to warrant. My doubts spiralled rapidly. Then I went to a urologist because I thought there was a scar on my penis, this line running up the backside. He was a nice old guy and didn't laugh at me, but he told me it was perfectly normal, that everyone had that line.

I sat down on Father's Day and wrote Dad a card, telling him I no longer thought he did anything to me. Then we started talking, and I'm closer to him now than I've ever been. So in a way, this process has given me my father back. By the way, I've since learned from Winston that, at the beginning of the process, Stephanie thought it might have been *me* who abused her. I'm sure I'm on her list of perpetrators by now.

[*In October of 1992, Arlene received another letter from Stephanie, though it was dated in August. 'I have come to assume that you have made yourself unconscious to a lot of things,' the letter began. She told her mother that she could never love her again, that her life was 'full and rich and very happy,' and that she simply wanted to be left alone. 'I love someone else as my mother now,' she ended. 'This is my life now, and you are never going to be a part of it.'*]

ARLENE: When I got that letter, I snapped. I cried all night long. But then I began to get angry. I was tired of fighting, of trying to understand. I whipped out a quick note and mailed it: "Stephanie – You got it – you won't hear from me again unless you initiate the communication." I signed it, "The real victim, your Mother." But I didn't really mean it. In the letter, I told her I was going to throw out all her stuff if she didn't come get it, but I couldn't do it.

In the next few months, I discovered the False Memory Syndrome Foundation and came to understand much more what Stephanie was going through. I also ran into a "retractor" who had met Stephanie in a hospital unit for those diagnosed with multiple personality disorders. Stephanie was supposed to be a satanic ritual abuse survivor, which is why she developed MPD. This retractor told us that Stephanie would stand up in group and say, "I just can't believe this. My parents are the most wonderful people in the world. They wouldn't do this." And then the group would jump on her and convince her again.

I wrote Stephanie again early in 1993, trying to get her to see what was going on. I told her I would never understand why she couldn't face us or even write about the things she supposedly remembered. "Are your memories that insecure?" I asked. I told her how I had gone to visit Ramona anonymously and that she had not come up with anything accurate. Ramona did suggest that I was overweight because of something to do with sex and my father, though. I also mentioned that this same exact process had happened to thousands of other families, and I hoped she would eventually realize she had been duped. "Our love for you will never die, no matter what you say or do," I wrote. "We will ALWAYS be here for you."

HANK: Of course, she didn't answer the letter. We know now that Stephanie is seeing a psychiatrist in Betty Carter's group. She doesn't see Ramona the psychic any more. But educational level doesn't seem to matter, when every therapist sees sex abuse behind every bush. [*He laughs. I comment that it's good that he has retained his sense of humor.*] This is the face everyone sees, the laughing man. But I can't work, I can't do anything. There are days we don't get out of bed. Our lives are in the toilet.

ARLENE: I sit around and daydream that the front doorbell will ring and she'll be there, and she'll throw her arms around me.

HANK: We're going to sell this house. There are too many memories here. Maybe that will help us snap out of this.'

PHILIP MARSDEN, ACCUSED FATHER

Philip Marsden, a bank manager in Devon, England, worries about his daughter, Emma, who at 27 still lives in a community home for the mentally ill and who has yet to retract her allegations of sexual abuse against him. Yet he is hopeful. She is at least back in contact with the family as a 'returnee.'

'The first inkling I had of this whole mess was in the summer of 1989. Emma was 21 and suddenly disappeared. She had been on holiday with our son Simon's girl friend. When she came back, she was very upset because his girlfriend had been going out with other boys, and she felt sorry for Simon. There were a few tears about that. A couple of days later, I was working late and came home to find the house empty. Emma had just vanished. My wife Diane and I were desperate. We phoned the police and reported her missing. We sat up all night hoping she would call.

Until this time, she had been living with us, studying for a degree in sociology. Before all of this, she seemed great. Most people said, "You're so lucky to have the ideal daughter." She was very close to us, especially my wife, Diane. We never had to worry about her.

There were signs that Emma had problems, though. When she was 17, in the sixth form of Grammar School, she started to become very withdrawn. She didn't want to go out, just wanted to spend all her time at home. She's got very strong moral principles and was upset that other girls were sleeping around, and she didn't want to. She did have a couple of boyfriends, but they didn't last long.

To a lesser extent, this pattern continued in university. She studied pretty hard. I would say, "You ought to go to a social club or something." She'd say she just didn't want to. I felt, "Oh, well, she'll get a job and her life will change that way."

Then she told us she had been raped at university. She told us this in 1988, but she said it had happened a year before that. She'd been going to a rape crisis center for it. We believed it at the time and were very upset, but she seemed to be getting help for it, so what else could we do?

The day after she disappeared in 1989, she phoned to say she was all right and was coming home soon. She did come for a visit, but she wouldn't tell us where she was living. This became a regular pattern. We used to take her back to town, but she would very carefully avoid letting us know where she lived.

She would visit once a week or so. This didn't go on for long, because the rape crisis center called Diane and said, "You've got to come over here immediately. Emma has something to show you." Diane thought it might be a tattoo or something. She went over, and there were two counselors, young women in their early thirties. We never learned their names. They said, "Give your mother the letter." Emma did, then ran out of the room. The counselors told Diane that she must read the letter immediately. And that was when the allegations were made against me. The letter was very vague but said Emma had been abused from an early age, right up until the time she left home at 21. Of course, it said the mother must have known what was going on, too.

Diane drove home with this letter and showed it to me. We both went into a state of shock. The next morning, we went down to see our family doctor and personal friend. He was very kind, but he had no idea at that time what was going on.

That weekend, I started to have pains in my chest, and they went on for two or three days. Finally, they took me to hospital and said, "You've been having a series of heart attacks." I was 52 then, and the shock of Emma's accusations probably triggered the attacks. After that, they carried out tests on me, and I had to have a heart bypass. It was apparently a big success, since I'm still alive. I have subsequently told Emma that she actually saved my life. If I hadn't had the minor heart attacks, I wouldn't have known I needed surgery.

While I was in the hospital, Emma wanted to talk to other family members. Diane asked her sister Louise, and her best friend Charlotte, to go and see Emma. So her Aunt Louise and her mother's friend Charlotte went to visit. To our horror, when they came back, they said, "Of course, it's all true. Nobody could make all that up." They made it clear they would support Emma and would not help us. We asked for a family conference because the psychiatrist Diane had gone to see recommended it, but they refused to talk to us.

After I got out of the hospital, it just went into stalemate. Emma didn't want to see us. Diane's family had all been persuaded by her younger sister, so they wouldn't talk to us, either, including her parents and her older sister. And of course the assorted nieces and the rest of the cousins were warned off, told to have nothing to do with us. My side of the family has been quite supportive. My parents are both dead, thankfully. My brother and cousins have been very kind. They think the whole thing is absolutely ridiculous.

Diane's former best friend and her husband started to get to some of our other friends, too. It's amazing how some people react, even when they've known you a long time. They just cut you off without ever talking to you, and that's it. But we kept most of our friends. I live in a smallish town, and because I am something of a public figure, this whole affair has been even more difficult.

Fairly soon, Emma called her mother and said she would be willing to see her, but not me. Diane and I discussed it, and we both agreed it was the only way to move forward, to keep in touch with her on whatever terms she imposed. So Diane would go and meet her in town.

In the summer of 1990, a man and woman walked up the drive to our home and asked if they could talk to me. They identified themselves as police officers from the county. They said, "You know what it's about." I said, "Yes, I can guess, it's Emma. Thank goodness something is happening at last." They were a bit surprised at my reaction. They said they wanted to interview us, and they had two other police with a warrant to search the house. They climbed about in the loft, went into the garden shed, and took away all my video films, most of which were of Turkish archeological sites. I said, "Well, you're in for an interesting evening of viewing."

We went down to the police station the next morning and were interviewed separately. For the first time, I discovered what had been said about us. It was so ridiculous and over the top. I had supposedly been abusing Emma from the age of three, and it went on and on and on. When she was 15 or so, I had somehow got her and a whole group of grammar school boys to perform sex acts on the stage of the school. Don't ask me how I got into the school. Then a year or so after that, I decided she had to become a prostitute, so I took her off and introduced her to men I knew who paid her for her services.

Then, not content with that, I decided to form a satanic ring for ritual abuse. I got together a whole crowd of men, mostly civic leaders from Devon, a fire chief, a lot of the people who worked with me, about twenty men altogether. And don't forget the vicar and a doctor friend. So it was a nice little group we had going. We all dressed up in black robes with yellow sashes. There was apparently one other girl there, the daughter of a friend of mine. We tied her and Emma down on a big oval table in my office. It all happened at my office.

Those were the allegations. The police wanted to come and look at the office. I said, "You'd better look at the boot of my car, too." They laughed at that. The police seemed to know it was crazy. They said, "We believe you, but what can we do to prove your innocence?" I said, "Have Emma medically examined." By this point, I suspected her story of being raped at university was fabricated, too. Emma agreed to the examination, and it showed that she was a virgin. After the police told me the results, they did a remarkable thing. They went to see Diane's family and her former best friend, and they told them about the medical exam results. They told them that they had made the most terrible mistake and had blackened my name and maligned my character and had not in fact helped Emma at all, and they must stop encouraging her.

And do you know what? Diane's two sisters and her former best friend refused to believe them! They ran off to Emma and got her to tell them that all those awful things had actually happened. Charlotte's husband is a doctor, and he thinks all those things happened and she could still be a virgin. He's got himself so involved that he cannot admit that he has made a mistake. What hope is there? Diane's family was boxed into a corner. They can't now bring themselves to say, "My God, we've made a mistake." And Emma is getting so much support from so many silly people, she can't take it back.

Then the police referred Emma to social services, who contacted the Crisis Centre, and she went there. Beginning with the summer of 1991, she lived there, then went to a community center halfway house, and that's where she still is.

But ever since the police involvement, our relationship with Emma has been getting better and better. She now comes to see us once a week. She's been on holiday with us twice. We went together to Crete earlier this year. She sends me presents. If you saw us together, you'd think, "Well, this is ridiculous." She sent me a birthday card recently that read, "To a great Dad on your birthday."

In the early days, I tried to talk to her about how she was a virgin and how impossible her allegations were, but she didn't want to know. She wouldn't talk about it. Now she'll talk to me about false memory syndrome, and she accepts that it's perfectly possible to have false memories, but she won't say it happened to her.

I think her "memories" came from a combination of television programs, nightmares, and the influence of the counselors at the rape center. She also studied sociology, and I don't think that helped. I think Emma did genuinely believe it.

The trouble with being a parent is, you think you know your children, but you probably don't know them as well as you think. She was probably a genuinely troubled child and we didn't realize it. We've tried to figure out what went wrong. We don't know. Our only conclusion is that we were too caring and protective.

We don't blame Emma, but I am getting to the stage where I think she ought to take some responsibility for what's happened. She's a lovely girl, and though it may sound stupid, she's a very caring daughter. As time went on, I think maybe Emma had to keep everyone's attention by making the stories more and more bizarre.

We can't have sensible conversations with the therapists at the Crisis Centre. They aren't interested in what Emma said about her past. They say whether it's true or not doesn't matter. They say she's emotionally disturbed. From where things were, Emma is indeed much better and has more confidence. But they haven't helped her come to terms with reality.

Sometimes I think she really is emotionally disturbed. Because she's over 21, we have no rights at all and can't ask for more information. I suppose I could make a stink about it, but I don't want to make things worse. I don't want to spoil what we have. What we have is not perfect, but it's a damn sight better than no contact at all.'

BOB SCULLEY, ACCUSED FATHER

Bob Sculley, 56, is a short, balding fireplug of a man – slow to speak, hesitant to express emotion. He admits that he was mostly an absent father to his daughter Nicole, 27, but that situation developed in part in response to his wife's devotion as a Jehovah's Witness – he tried to stay out of the way. Because of Nicole's accusations, Sculley's marriage, never on firm footing, has dissolved, and he has moved away from Georgia. He is a confused and bitter man. Nicole's initial hostility stemmed from her stay in an eating disorders unit.*

'I always thought Nicole was a happy, well-adjusted little kid up through eighth grade. She had friends, was outgoing, bubbly. Her two older brothers took care of her pretty much as the youngest in the family, though they excluded her from the typical boy's world. She didn't get to play cowboy, I mean. Yeah, I played with her some, not a lot. We all went fishing some, played some sports, went family camping.

We moved to Georgia when she was in eighth grade, and that was really hard on her, leaving all her friends and having to adjust to a new school. At the same time, my new job in computer repair was very stressful and demanded 60 or 70 hours a week. So I couldn't really pay much attention to her. Finally, I got a less-demanding job three years later.

Nicole had a lot of difficulty in high school, especially around boy–girl relations. She felt very guilty about anything she got into. I don't

---

* I recently sat next to Sculley while listening to a 'retractor' describe the mental agonies she had gone through while in therapy. I looked over and saw tears quietly streaming down his face.

think she had sex, just normal things teens did. I pretty much stayed away from all that – that was her mother's world.

Nicole and her mother are both Jehovah's Witnesses, and I don't share that faith. Debby, my wife, converted 25 years ago. One of their major claims is that they are the only ones who have the truth, and they don't believe in celebrating birthdays or holidays. I believe that was the major source of Nicole's guilt, having to live by extremely strict moral rules. She couldn't go to dances, only to social activities with kids from the church.

At 16, Nicole quit school. Her guidance counselor agreed it was the best thing. She went to hairdressers' school and got a job doing that for a while. But then she quit to witness for the church, going door to door, and she cleaned houses to support herself. When she was 20, she got married to Fred, a church member 15 years older than her. He's never been able to hold jobs, because he dreams too much and has delusions of grandeur.

We saw Nicole fairly frequently until two years ago, when she moved to Texas. Now she's got two little kids and they've had a rough time, because she can't work and Fred can't keep a job. They're always in debt. So I gather things got pretty tense between them. I think Fred hit her, from what I understand. Nicole had a recurrence of bulimia, which she'd had when she was 16. So she entered a three-week in-house program in Texas around April, 1992. We knew about it. Yes, she talked to me about it. She thought it was because of trouble with her husband at the time.

When she got out, she got into some kind of support group. By the time she got out of that damn thing, I think she was into this ACOA [Adult Children of Alcoholics] program. Have you ever read the list of criteria for what makes you an ACOA? Basically, what they say applies to 75 per cent of the people in the world. Communication with me went down to next to nothing. She wasn't openly angry with me, but I started to hear talk about "dysfunctional family" and "emotionally unavailable." I got that through her mother telling me.

Yes, I certainly did drink too much for a few years from the mid-1970s to the early '80s, anywhere from four to seven beers a night, sometimes Scotch.

Well, we got to around Thanksgiving. We were supposed to make a trip down to Texas, and I got uninvited. Through her mother. They talk regular. So Debby went down, and I stayed home. I knew there was some kind of problem, but I didn't know what it was.

At that point, my marriage was reasonably decent. We weren't fighting or anything. The religion thing had been quiescent; we just stopped talking or fighting about it. We traveled together, and Debby liked that. I do business all over the world. I guess our children were the other real common denominator. But it was hard, mostly because of the religion, which covers almost every fiber of your life.

Anyway, Debby calls me from Texas on Monday, and all I got were vague statements about something very serious, but she wasn't at liberty to say what. She was obviously pissed and upset. They were very tense phone calls. So come Thursday, she asked me to go home and check my mailbox. "Nicole wrote you a letter on Friday, and you should have it by now." There the letter was, all right, about two pages, fairly succinctly written, full of hate and anger, accusing me of raping her when she was three years old, forcing her to have oral sex, all kinds of trash about "It's not my shame, it's your shame, and I give you back your shame."

It didn't sound like Nicole at all. For one thing, she would have rambled on for twice as long, and this was just full of all this jargon. You know, my first reaction was, "What a relief. I thought she was accusing me of something I really did. This is ridiculous." You know, there *were* things I wasn't proud of. When she was three, we had a terrible debate about whether she would eat or not, and I whipped her ass. I'd say, "Eat," and she'd say "No," and I'd give her a crack on the butt or the side of her leg. You know, in retrospect, I wish I hadn't. I made it a test of wills. No, this wasn't when I was drinking too much.

Anyway, then I realized that Nicole was serious in this letter. I went into shock. I called my wife. It was some conversation, let me tell you. Talk about crossed communications! I was saying, basically, "Isn't this awful, what can we do to help our daughter who has this perceptual problem?" And she was saying, "You dirty bastard, why did you do this to my daughter? Repent and be saved." Those weren't her exact words, but that was the emotional gist behind it.

I told Debby I didn't do any of those things, and she said she had to believe the evidence she'd seen. She had observed Nicole go through some sort of physical, emotional thing where she curled up in a fetal position and became extremely distraught, just lay there whimpering. Afterward, she explained it was a flashback to when I was supposedly doing these things to her.

My wife went to this therapist's office, where Nicole told Debby all this stuff. All I know is that she's a female therapist; I run into a wall when I ask questions about her. There were a number of therapists through this whole thing, at the hospital, and then for out-patient care.

After that, Debby and I talked every few days, but it was very tense. My wife came back in mid-December and stayed with friends. She has never moved back with me. I talked her into going to see a psychiatrist with me, who tried to explain how false memories can come about, but she wouldn't hear it. She has fundamentally embraced at the heart level some of the tenets of this recovery movement. It's turned into another kind of religion for her.

Trow, my middle son, was in Texas with Debby, and he got the same fetal position show, same meeting with the therapist. He seems to believe it all. I saw him once in person since then, and he isn't as definite as his mother. He'll say, "It's more likely you did than that you didn't."

All I got from Nicole was that damned letter. Everything else has been second-hand. I wrote down everything Debby and Trow said, and it sounded like four different rapists. The stories were contradictory. When it started, she told them, "I specifically remember when I was three, but I think he was doing it regularly until I was twelve." In more recent conversations with her mother, she said, "I'm willing to believe it only happened once or twice when he was drunk, and that he doesn't remember it because of that."

Early in the game, I was willing to say, "Maybe something happened I don't remember." But not 12 years of it. I've gone through the whole process now, and I just don't believe it.'

JULIA HAPGOOD, WIFE OF ACCUSED

Julia Hapgood, a no-nonsense British woman, is married to Arthur, a Maine pharmaceutical salesman. The first hint of serious trouble came when Julia got a call from the local police saying that their daughter Lisa's car had been found abandoned outside her therapist's office. Lisa, 18, had developed an overly close relationship – complete with love letters and daily phone calls – with Janine Woodley, an RN licensed as a social worker. Later that day, Lisa called Julia. 'I have admitted myself to a psychiatric hospital for anxiety attacks,' she told her. That was Feb. 11, 1991. Everything since then has been one long nightmare, culminating in Arthur and Julia finding Lisa's journal, in which she revealed that she thought Arthur had sex with her at the age of eight while he held a knife to her throat. It was this memory, coming out under hypnosis, which had prompted her mental break.

Heavily drugged, Lisa, diagnosed with a dissociative disorder, stayed in the hospital until Good Friday, when her insurance ran out. She was immediately released without any referrals. For a while, Lisa stayed in an apartment attached to the Hapgood home, but she continued to talk to Janine Woodley for hours every day.

Today, Lisa, 21, has made tentative steps toward reconciliation with her family. She visits every Saturday, but she refuses to discuss the sexual-abuse allegations, walking out of the room whenever anyone raises the issue. She continues to see Janine Woodley.

'Nothing can hurt us after this. It would be a joke if it weren't so horrible. You know, in one of her journal entries Lisa wrote that she had a dream about "The Teddy Bears' Picnic." It's true that she used to go to sleep to that song every night. Well, she wrote that the song was playing while Arthur was abusing her, and that he cut off her teddy bear's head with a Swiss Army knife. He's never *owned* a Swiss Army knife. I found the teddy bear packed up in the basement, not a mark on it. But none of that matters to Lisa.

The happiest day of my life was the day Lisa was born. I have racked my brain, and I can't for the life of me figure out what we did wrong in raising her. Arthur keeps saying, "We must have done something wrong," but I refuse to feel guilty. We tried to teach her to be honest and trustworthy. Arthur would give her a whack on the rear end if necessary, or he'd ground her, but only if she broke house rules. Arthur has always traveled a lot, so Lisa is probably closer to me. But even now, if he's not around when she visits, she asks, "Where's Dad?"

Lisa's childhood seemed so good and happy. She was just a pleasure, with dark curly hair, great big brown eyes, lots of friends. When she got to high school, I thought to myself, "I am so fortunate that she's not into alcohol or drugs." She seemed so open with me as a teen. And you've never seen anyone happier in college, right before this happened. She loved it, was on the Dean's List. It was a delight to see her.

That first day at the psychiatric hospital, we saw our daughter, slumped over in a chair, her eyelids droopy. She never once looked at us, just stared at the floor. It was dreadful. She was obviously drugged. We were told we should think of her as a distant relative, because she needed her space, but it was very important for us to continue to financially support her. I thought Arthur would burst a blood vessel. He was turning purple in the face. He asked, "Why haven't we been informed before?" They said it was because she was over 18, so they had no right to tell us. We were told we could not see her or call her. It was such a shock, like someone hit you as hard as they could in the stomach with a two-by-four, to see your child like that. I'd had enough. We got nowhere. No one would tell us anything. I was on the verge of tears and just had to get out of there. We didn't know what to do, where to turn.

She was released when her insurance ran out. I arranged for Lisa to go to a private psychiatric clinic in England, where I'm from, but she didn't like the psychiatrist. He said to her, "Has it ever occurred to you that this incest never happened?" He told me, "We're different over here – we'll talk to the parents." I tried to talk her into seeing a woman therapist, but she wouldn't.

[*Back in the United States, Lisa began to see Janine again, while she lived in an apartment adjoining her parents' house. Arthur and Julia decided in desperation to tap her phone, which led to a lawsuit. They eventually settled out of court by paying Janine Woodley $5,000.*]

Janine would call her constantly, all calls of 90 minutes or more, and we learned how pushy and manipulative she was. She coerced her into saying she loved her. The day Arthur told Lisa he never sexually abused her, Lisa called Janine and told her she was having doubts. Janine answered, "In that case, it would mean that it was all just in your mind, and that would mean that you're crazy, and I know you're not crazy. Maybe your father just forgot. Maybe he dissociated. With all my years of experience, I know that you've been abused, and your family is a textbook dysfunctional family." And this woman has never met us!

During this time, Lisa would be like two different people. She would come into the kitchen, bouncy, happy-go-lucky, just like she always was before all this happened. Then she'd get on the phone with Janine and would be depressed, tell her how we yell at each other and throw things – none of which was true at all.

It's all so unreal. Talk about fairy stories! Janine started giving Lisa these children's books and encouraging her to act like a little kid, get in touch with her inner child.

At least we're seeing Lisa now, and it has made a world of difference, but it's so frustrating not to have an open, honest relationship. I don't feel very warm toward her. She's caused so much hurt. Arthur nearly went to jail over this tape-recording business. We are now broke, both emotionally and financially.

How has this affected our marriage? I don't know how to express that. It's caused us so much pain. We never relax and have a good time any more. There were times I doubted Arthur, when I was feeling low. I'd think, "Could this possibly have happened?" But when I saw his face, his reaction, I knew he didn't do it. And I certainly know that the things she said about me and my mother are ridiculous.

There are days when I hate Lisa, but basically I blame the therapists. Arthur gets very upset with me when I say I hate Lisa. He says, "You can't blame her." At the same time, I believe that everyone is responsible for what they do. She knew about this court business, for instance, and her attitude was, "Well, he broke the law." It made me so angry, but I managed to keep my mouth shut.

No, I haven't gone to therapy for myself. We never did think much of the mental health profession, but now we think even less of it. We don't trust anyone. How could it help? The only thing that would help would be if our daughter came to her senses.

The FMS Foundation meetings have done me a lot of good, just talking to other parents in the same situation. I wasn't surprised when we found out about the organization. I'd said all along, "There have to be other parents like us, but how do we find them?" I was thinking of putting an ad in the paper, when one of Arthur's business associates clipped an article about the foundation for us.

I wouldn't have believed this could happen if you'd told me a few years ago. When I saw someone accused of sex abuse, I always believed it. "Castrate the bastard! Of course he did it." Now, I want to know all the circumstances before I make a judgment."*

DR. AARON GOLDBERG, ACCUSED FATHER

I met Dr. Aaron Goldberg at a 1993 Harvard-sponsored seminar entitled 'Trauma and Memory,' which turned out to be a one-sided event. The main objective appeared to be slamming the False Memory Syndrome Foundation and 'validating' all repressed memories. Goldberg had two reasons for attending the conference: (1) he was a child psychiatrist specializing in child sexual abuse, and (2) his daughter, an Ivy League graduate, has accused him of raping, torturing, and impregnating her, based on memories she recovered during therapy with a trauma specialist. On the third day of the conference, Goldberg announced his displeasure with the slanted proceedings. Someone near me

---

* On Father's Day, 1996, Lisa wrote a note of apology to her father, taking back all her allegations. She added that she did not want to talk about it, and just wanted to get on with her life.

whispered, 'He's got to be dissociated to dare say that here.' Then a woman in the audience identified him as having been accused by his daughter. The room, filled with therapists, social case workers, lawyers and judges, erupted. 'Pig!' someone screamed. 'How dare you!'

I had dinner that night with Dr. Goldberg, a self-contained man who speaks calmly and deliberately. He told me about the day he had contemplated suicide:

'I realized that my life as I had known it had ended. I sat down in front of the fireplace in my living room and listened to Bach's cello suites for eight hours while I seriously considered whether to put a shotgun into my mouth and blow my brains out. Finally, I came up with four reasons not to do it. (1) I couldn't do that to my wife, leaving her to find my brains splattered all over the living room. (2) If I did, people would think it was evidence that my daughter's accusations were true, and I had killed myself out of guilt. (3) I thought about what I told the abused teenagers I work with. "Just learn to survive. You can do it. Your life is not over." I told them stuff like that all the time. So I had to take the same advice. (4) I grew up in Brooklyn, where I learned a maxim: Don't let the bastards get you.'

[Addendum: After the furor at the conference died down, a young woman spoke: 'I'm a Harvard graduate and an incest survivor, and I have yet to hear from the FMS people any convincing explanation of what a survivor has to gain by this. My experience is that all of us have lost a great deal: family members we love, the belief that they were there for us, who we were as children, the image we had of ourselves. I don't know many people who would do that on purpose to themselves, just for a civil suit.' Goldberg joined the applause for her. So did I, because she quite eloquently stated the pain I knew that these young women are going through. Nonetheless, genuine misery does not translate automatically to genuine incest.

Goldberg's daughter has recently initiated contact again, though she has not taken back her allegations.]

HAROLD BRIGHTWELL, ACCUSED FATHER

Retired British naval officer Harold Brightwell has lost all contact with two of his three adult daughters. Although he didn't know it at the time, his troubles began when his middle daughter, Priscilla, sought help for her long-term backaches, kidney infections, candida, and thrush. Having sought traditional medical attention without success, she went to see Rebecca Acceber, an American homeopath practicing in London. (Acceber's name must have been her own creation, since it is a palindrome.) Somehow, during the treatment,

Priscilla came to believe that her physical ailments all stemmed from long-repressed memories of sexual abuse. In September of 1991, she called her father and told him that she needed to see him because of what she had 're-remembered.' Puzzled and apprehensive, he drove several hours to her apartment in London . . .

So on Thursday afternoon, I arrived at Priscilla's London flat, and the door was opened by a young woman whom I didn't know who introduced herself as Lena. She said that she was there to help Priscilla. She ushered me into the front room of the flat, which had a bay window, and in the bay window there was a raised dais where normally Priscilla's boyfriend had his drum kit. But the drums had been replaced by my daughter, who was sitting there in a lotus position like a little Buddha. In the center of the room was a large chair, and she motioned me to sit in the chair. Lena came in behind me, shut the door, and sat by the door in the chair, like a guard.

Priscilla then said something like, "I want you to listen to what I'm going to say and what I'm going to read to you, and when I'm finished, I shall get up, leave this room, go into the garden, and you are to leave the house. I don't want you to say anything. I don't want you to ask any questions. I just want you to listen to me."

My mouth went dry. I felt as if I was about to drop my guts on the floor. I said, "Can't I even have a cup of tea, Priss?" She said, "No, I don't want you to speak."

She then started reading from a handwritten statement. The opening was a sort of preamble describing how she'd had a poisoned life up until now, that she'd managed to strip away the poisoned outer layers of her personality, and she'd been able to discover her true inner self. She then explained the reasons she had these poisoned layers. "When I was a baby of nine months, you started to tickle my clitoris, and you liked it. At two, you started sticking pencils into me. At four, you started buggering me. At eight, you started raping me." There was a whole catalog of things, the most gross sexual abuse that you can imagine. Fingers, pencils, penises. It was all a complete shock to me.

I went numb. I could not believe what I was hearing. I remember thinking, "This is not real, this couldn't be happening." The only sound or gesture I made was when she said, "And when we were in France, you wanted to rape me." This referred to a very recent holiday I'd taken with another couple and Priscilla. She'd come because Gloria, my second wife, had to drop out at the last moment. Gloria had suggested I take Priscilla, who used to think I favoured her sisters. Because it was prearranged, we shared a twin-bedded room. She wasn't ill at ease at the time, because she came back home with me and stayed another night in my house before going back to London. So when she said I wanted to rape her during this trip, I guffawed and said, "Oh, Priss!" Whereupon Lena exclaimed from the back of the room, "You laughed! You must be guilty!"

Priscilla moved into a second part to talk about the compensation she wanted to help her overcome the pain and suffering the supposed abuse had caused her. This was broken down into sections. She needed psychotherapy for two more years. She needed a safe place to live. And at the end of each item, she gave a monetary figure. At the end, she said, "So the total is 70,000 pounds," but quickly added, "I'll settle for 50,000." I hasten to add I never paid her any money, other than to help pay for psychotherapy that I thought would help her.

Then Priscilla read out a letter from Rebecca Acceber, her homeopath. I subsequently got a copy of it, so I will read part of it to you. It is dated August 21, 1991 and addressed, To Whom It May Concern. "As a professional practitioner, I wish to state that all Priscilla Brightwell's symptoms, whether physical, mental or psychological, are consistent with her being a survivor of father/daughter rape, over a continued period of time. I have a great deal of experience in working with people who have been abused as children, and sadly Priscilla is one of them.

"Her recent re-remembering is also very consistent with survivors of childhood sexual abuse. The obscured memories are a very common coping mechanism for children where the reality of the abusive acts are shelved, often for years . . . Amnesia often occurs, where the memories may not surface for years, or may come back in vague flashbacks or nightmares or hallucinations, leading to a great deal of mental anguish. The healing only starts to begin with the re-surfacing of the memories."

Then, in this letter, the homeopath talked about Priscilla's schedule of monetary demands and how important they were. Finally, Priscilla read the end of the letter: "The abusive father, who could face many long years in prison, should seek help for himself and not deny the damage he has done to his daughter, whose safety was in his hands. He must not expect forgiveness from her."

This whole scene lasted about half an hour. It seemed like an eternity, though. The only other thing I said was at the end. I said, "Those things didn't happen, Priss." Any person with an ounce of common sense would know they never happened. And anyone who knew her as a child would know she couldn't have been the Priscilla we knew had these things been happening to her.

I left Priscilla's flat literally in a state of shock. I got in my van and drove round the corner to a phone box and rang up Rachel, my youngest daughter, who lived nearby. (My oldest daughter, Mary, was married and living on the Continent, so she wasn't part of this.) I said, "Rachel, I just had the most disastrous meeting with Priscilla," and she said, "Yes, I know. And I believe her." So that was sort of a double blow. I said, "Well look, can I come round and talk to you about it?" She wasn't at all keen, but I insisted. I went round and she came out of her flat in a semi-hysterical state and started shouting at me. The essence was, "Why would Priscilla say these things to you if they're not true?" It occurred to me that maybe Rachel was catching the bug, too. I said, "Do you think those things happened to you, then?" She said "No," then added the enigmatic phrase, "But if they did, it was only minor." I said, "I assure you, Rachel, I did nothing to you or Priscilla." She said, "Well, why is she saying it then?" And of course back in September of 1991, before the False Memory Syndrome Foundation had even started in America, it was a very difficult question to answer. I said I didn't know.

We walked down the road and sat on a park bench and talked about two complaints she had against me. Neither was about sexual abuse. I said, "Well, how are we going to resolve this?" And she said, "I never want to see you again in my life." We were both crying. I got up from the park bench and walked away, and I haven't seen Rachel or Priscilla since. I have just celebrated the fourth anniversary of the loss of two daughters.

[*When Harold told his wife Gloria about the accusations, she went to see Priscilla. While sitting at the kitchen table, she saw a number of books, including* The Courage to Heal *and* Father-Daughter Rape. *After listening to Priscilla, Gloria told her, 'I feel sorry for you, Priscilla, that you think those things happened, because I know they didn't.' Priscilla became enraged and asked her to leave. Back home, Harold contacted his ex-wife (the girls' mother) Hannah.*]

I went to see Hannah. Of course, she knew all about it. These accusations had been coming out for weeks, apparently. A meeting was set up with Hannah and two other friends of hers. I went to a sort of kangaroo court, where I was grilled by these three women. Why had I gone on holiday with Priscilla without a dressing gown? Why had I shared a room with her? I explained that I didn't have a dressing gown and I hadn't thought tuppence about it. Priscilla and I had never had any problems before. The thought didn't cross my mind that I was transgressing any boundaries or anything. Finally, Hannah and I agreed we would seek proper therapeutic help for her. So we found a well-recommended therapist in London, Stephanie Brent, at the London Institute.

So off went the two girls to have therapy with Stephanie. I soon became very concerned that this woman had not made a proper diagnosis of their problems. She was treating them for the wrong disease. She was treating them as if they were victims of real childhood sexual abuse. She should have treating Priscilla as someone deluded into believing it. There was some pretty acrimonious correspondence between us which got nowhere. When I pleaded with her to help arrange some joint therapy, she wrote, "Both your daughters have to make their own decisions about their beliefs, I cannot change nor implement these. Should they wish to make contact, that too is their decision. You would need the agreement of your ex-family before they would enter therapy with you." I was so outraged that she should call my daughters my "ex-family." In the end, I stopped paying for them to have therapy.

[*Two weeks after the disastrous confrontation in Priscilla's flat, Harold wrote her a long letter. 'My love for you has been assailed on all sides by every emotion a father could possibly have: shock, outrage, anger, humiliation and despair. Now I have an overwhelming feeling of anxiety for your safety and well-being . . . Priscilla, I know, and somewhere inside you, you must know too that those terrible things did not happen to you . . . Anyhow, Priscilla, when the truth does dawn for you, I'll be here and I know that we will enjoy an even better relationship than before. Let that day be soon.' But it was not soon. A year later, an acquaintance in America sent Harold a copy of an early False Memory Syndrome Foundation Newsletter.*]

For me, that newsletter was a revelation. It was the first ray of sunshine through dark clouds. I could clearly see that my daughters had been clobbered by this new seemingly American phenomenon called False Memory Syndrome. Naively and probably stupidly, I thought I had only to show Priscilla and Rachel the evidence of FMS and they would quickly see that they had become victims of it. I had not taken into account that I was not dealing with rational people. I sent them a copy of the newsletter and Melody Gavigan's early *Retractor Newsletter*. Then all hell broke loose.

[*Priscilla called and left a message on Harold's answering machine. Her words tumbled out onto the tape in a bitter torrent: 'Just fuck off, you're a fucking wanker, you're pathetic. Just because you raped me, you want to give me back the responsibility of your pain, your shit. Well, I'm not going to take it back, because it's yours, you fucker, you raper of children. You know what you did to me? You want me to remind you? When I was a baby, you used to get me on the floor and stick pencils in my vagina. When I was two, you used to tie me down and stick your fingers in me, didn't you? You used to put rubber gloves on like a bloody Nazi, you're such a freak. Then when I was having stories told to me you used to come in and you'd get into bed with me and you'd fucking stick your fingers in my vagina, wouldn't you, and it really hurt me so much, you bastard. And then when I was four, you took me to that fucking meeting where they killed a baby and then, and then, you watched, you stood at the back, didn't you, in your bloody fucking uniform while you watched other men bugger me, didn't you? And then when I was eight, you started raping me, oh how exciting, you used to come into my room every night you fucking bastard. I fucking hate you for everything you've done to me, and I'm over it, and I'm not going to ever let you get away with it, and I'm never ever ever ever going to forgive you for anything.'*]

To me, the most important thing that comes across from that tape is that she really believes that those things happened to her and has integrated it into her personality. And she is not mad, I assure you. If you met her, you would see that she is perfectly normal. She simply *believes* all of this. It's really frightening.

After a while, Priscilla wrote, "Now Rachel has remembered too, but it's different." I never discovered what the difference was exactly. But in August of 1994, Gloria and I went down to the Welsh coast, a place where I had gone camping when my children were young. So to remind her of the good times, I sent a postcard to Rachel. That provoked a letter by return in which she wrote, "I have remembered all the abuse you made me suffer. You did sexually abuse me and you did take me to a ritual abuse meeting where I was made to partake in the killing of a baby." And she called me a great many names – "child molester, sicko, monster, buggerer, weirdo, abuser, pervert, freak torturer demon user." So here's another one, apparently believing she was taken to different meetings where different babies were murdered.

So I now have two daughters out there, seemingly believing that I did those terrible things to them, when of course I didn't. The whole thing is so stupid and implausible. I sometimes go back and read old letters, like the postcard Rachel wrote in 1986 after a holiday visit. She wrote, "I feel so lucky to have your caring and understanding – much appreciated. Lots and lots of love, Rachel." But that now seems like another world, another eon ago. And reminding her of that letter wouldn't help, I'm sure. She would find a way to turn her former feelings into evidence of abuse, just as Priscilla told a journalist in 1992. "As a small child," she said, "I idolised my father. To survive, I had to see him as the perfect daddy, separate from the monster who abused me." It makes me shudder to read what else she told that reporter. "I have endless fantasies of what I'd like to do to him, like chopping up his willy and shoving it in his mouth, burning him or putting him in a box and burying him." [*Harold sighs.*] How she must be suffering if she thinks such things!

There doesn't seem to be much I can do about anything. Very little has happened on my personal front for quite a long time now. One wonders whether one is doing the right thing by not chasing them up, and then if one does, one is rebuffed. So I honestly don't know how to help them realize that their nightmare images never actually happened, except to try to let them know that I still love, miss them, and think about them every day. My door is always open for their safe return. I hope it's soon.'

JOE SIMMONS, ACCUSED FATHER

Joe Simmons nearly represented the United States in the Olympics in judo. Now 49, his barrel chest fills out his shirts. Despite his clean-cut good looks and physique, however, he speaks hesitantly. It's little wonder. Joe and his entire family have lived through a nightmare, mostly because of their involvement with Dr. Patsy Linter, their long-time psychologist. At Dr. Linter's urging, they institutionalized Johnny, their teenage son, for most of his high school years, though his 'behavior disorder' never amounted to more than normal developmental issues. Eventually, under the therapist's prodding, Johnny recovered memories of sexual abuse at the hands of both his parents, and Joe Simmons, eager to help his son, came to believe that he had been a high priest in a satanic cult.

'In the fall of 1987, we moved to a new city, and Johnny was very depressed over going to a new school. He was 16. So we ran to Dr. Linter, who told us his depression was serious, suicidal, and he should go back into the hospital. She said she wanted to really get to the core of the problem and didn't want us to see him for a time. She had begun to get into MPD and sex abuse issues, but we didn't know it at the time. We wilted like a leaf and went along with it. She told us not to have contact for 40 days. She put him on the closed unit, which we didn't learn until later, and pressed him hard. That's when he came up with the allegations.

Dr. Linter called Phyllis, my wife, and told her about it, but ordered her not to tell me. I was identified as the perpetrator. Dr. Linter called me and said she knew what was the matter with Johnny, and she wanted me to meet her at another hospital. She met me in the lobby and escorted me to the closed unit, which I thought was a little unusual. She said, "Well, we have some good news and some bad news. We know what's the matter with Johnny. It's a disorder, but it's completely curable. With this particular type of disorder, usually another family member has it. We believe you have it and want you to be tested for it." Not a word about sex abuse or Satanism. I asked what sort of disorder, and she said dissociative disorder. She told me she wanted me to check myself into the hospital for a few tests.

I got kind of nervous, but I had a lot of faith in her. You see, I have a learning disability and didn't do well in school at all. I had a great respect for anyone who appeared intellectual because of my own insecurities. Patsy Linter was married to a psychologist, and she came on in a very caring sort of way, very charismatic and nurturing. She looks sort of like the actress Sally Field.

So I thought, "Gee, I don't want to do this. I'll have to be off work a couple of days. I don't think I have anything. They'll run these tests and they'll be negative." But Dr. Linter convinced me it would help Johnny and I needed to do it. I didn't even have time to call Phyllis and ask if it was a good idea. She made me make a decision on the spot.

From there, it went totally to hell, a complete nightmare. They took me to the locked unit of the psychiatric hospital. A day goes by, nobody even sees me. I found out later that Dr. Linter had told the staff that I was a real dangerous character, had a black belt in judo, kept a gun under the seat of my car, and to be careful of me. Then I started going to group sessions run by Dr. Linter for patients who had been diagnosed as multiple personality disorders. During one of those sessions, she said, "Joe, this is the type of disorder you have." There had been no testing. People came in to see me and talk. Oh, she might have had me fill out a questionnaire, but I didn't know what it was for.

At this point, I didn't know anything about the allegations of abuse. I pushed myself back in my chair. I didn't want this disorder. She said, "Don't fight the therapy, it will just take longer." In the meantime, I found out later, she was seeing Phyllis, who was going frantic, getting information about Satanism, scared to death for Johnny. She was told not to talk to me about it. Phyllis was running from one hospital to another to see Johnny and me, after working all day.

Finally, Dr. Linter came to group and said, "Your son says you did some things to him." She told me that my son cared about me, and no matter what I did, he would forgive me. "Don't worry, the memories will come back to you." I began to think that maybe this was true, that I had this disorder. Dr. Linter assured me, "*You* didn't do anything, it was another part of you, and we have to get these other personalities to come out. Your memories are repressed and will begin to come out."

You have to realize that I was in a captive environment, and there was a lot of craziness going on all around me. Obviously, some of these people really did have major problems. I was afraid of take-downs. If you're not cooperative, they call a Code Green, and half a dozen orderlies jump the patient, take him and strap him down in four-point restraints and medicate him. I was afraid if they took me down, I might hurt somebody, might instinctively try to defend myself. So I went into compliance. That's the word I've learned for it now.

I realized that in order to leave the hospital, I had to get the doctors to release me. Oh, I could have left "AMA" – against medical advice – but they wouldn't have taken me back at my job without a release form. I was active in the union, and my boss didn't like me much anyway.

Once a week, a hospital psychiatrist, Dr. Cohen, came to see me. He didn't believe my diagnosis or what he read in my charts. He asked me if I'd heard of the Salem witch hunts. Dr. Linter told me, "You need to fire Dr. Cohen because he's jeopardizing your treatment. He doesn't understand MPD." So I did.

After two or three weeks, my mental state deteriorated. My son said I did some horrible, terrible thing. Dr. Linter came out with it gradually. She told me that another doctor wanted me to be committed to a hospital for the criminally insane. "But don't worry, I'm not going to let him do that to you." One minute, I was a responsible member of the community, trying to be a good father, and the next I'm like Charles Manson.

Now I was beginning to get paranoid, trying to make sense out of all this. Dr. Linter would have marathon sessions with me and my wife for two or three hours, trying to get me to recall stuff that was never there. Gradually, it came out from her and the other patients that my son said I was a satanic priest in a cult, that I took him to ceremonies where they sacrificed babies. I was supposed to have been involved in murders, eating body parts. I was one of six men who raped my son. At that point, Phyllis wasn't supposed to be part of it.

Dr. Linter tried to hypnotize me, but I just hyperventilated and almost passed out. She had me see a friend of hers, Larry White, a Christian counselor from a local children's services unit. He would explain to me about Satanists and how they worked, and he helped me to develop alters. Plato was the first one. I like intellectual people and was always attracted to those with an ability to write. So I started getting intellectual with Larry. That was Plato; Larry gave me the name. Another alter was the Comedian. When you're under stress, you relieve it in different ways. I would try to be humorous, and they would identify that personality state as the Comedian. That was acceptable to the group. Depending on the mood I was in, they would say, "Who am I talking to now?" And I'd say, "This is Plato."

I began to believe that the way I felt and reacted was actually the alter pushing itself forward, and I began to develop this MPD mentality. They brought in a big-deal psychiatrist who had worked on the Hillside Strangler case. He videotaped me, asked me certain questions, looked at some of the paintings I had made. Yeah, I did basket weaving and painted whatever fit with the therapy. This psychiatrist wrote out a report confirming the diagnosis. It was a done deal. This took all of 15 minutes.

I was saying to myself, "Do I have to become like these other patients before I get better?" It was very frightening. My employer kept calling my doctor, saying, "When's he going to get out? We need him back at work." My wife was getting frantic because we were getting way behind on our bills. I started pressing Dr. Linter about it. Finally, I went to the open unit for two weeks, and then they let me out, but I had to return for sessions twice a week. I got out after 74 days. I was a real mess when I was released. I had bought the MPD agenda completely by that time. Later on, Dr. Linter told me that the Satanists had deprogrammed me with electric shocks, that I had a rare type of MPD. She told me, "They know where you are, your phones will be tapped." She created a very paranoid environment for everyone.

At that point, Johnny was out of the hospital. When I came home, I wasn't allowed to be alone with him; my wife had to be in the room. Then, in one rare session, Dr. Linter had Johnny and I together. Johnny said, "He didn't do it, he's not the one." She flipped out and said to me, "Have you been talking to him?" So all of a sudden, I was asking myself, "If I wasn't this high priest, what's happened?" In the meantime, I'm still seeing Larry, who's convincing me of the reality of satanic cults. I'm really getting crazy with this stuff and still trying to hold down a job.

Then, at a special intervention session, Dr. Linter got Johnny to say that my wife was the one. Phyllis had been under tremendous strain already, and she couldn't handle it. When Johnny accused her, she lost it. I was thinking, "Maybe these things really did happen with her, not with me." I didn't know what to believe. Maybe this was a case of mistaken identity. They put Phyllis in the locked unit right there at the hospital against her will. She was told either to walk over or be carried by three men. To save her dignity, she walked.

When Phyllis left the hospital AMA, Dr. Linter told me I had to get away from her. I sold the house, took the boys, and moved to an apartment. Phyllis moved close to us. Dr. Linter said, "Don't worry, she'll soon be homeless and dysfunctional." Though she was a wreck, Phyllis left us alone and got on with her life, trying to heal herself. I began to see Dr. Linter less and slowly got my critical thinking back. Gradually, I began to realize that none of it was true. It didn't happen. I was frightened at what I had done. Eventually, I got the courage to call my wife. She was cautious at first, she was hurt so bad. I asked to see her over coffee. Together, we began to sort out what had happened to us.

Phyllis and I have been back together for three years now. We found that Dr. Linter's approach was actually like a cult itself, so we talked to a cult exit counselor and began to understand how coercion, compliance, and mind control work. I would try to talk to Johnny from time to time, but he had to make his own break from Dr. Linter. She just burned him out.

I feel extremely fortunate to win back the trust of my son. I had to take a lot and show him I was a decent guy after all. I acknowledge that I *did* do some stupid things. I used to really push my kids to excel at sports. I would pitch baseballs to Johnny, even though he didn't want to do it. I would get really upset. I threw the ball hard at him once, and another time I knocked him down at the net with a tennis shot. You also have to understand that my father was the oldest of 14 children in an Irish Catholic family. My Dad had a strap, and we got it. I had one, too, and I used to spank the kids with it. When Johnny was little, I grabbed him, picked him up by one leg, and spanked him upside down because he was covering his rear with his hands.

I know Johnny loves me now, though. It's strained, but our relationship is healing. Two years ago, knowing I love old cars, he gave me a 1949 Packard to tinker with. I'm concerned about the long-term effects on him, though. He still won't allow me or Phyllis to hug or kiss him. He told us once that he felt his emotions were dead. Looking back on this whole thing, I feel the worst about what my son went through. I was a grown-up, an adult, and it was horrible for me. But when it happens to your kid, you get the hair on the back of your neck standing up. That's what makes me so bitter.

Thinking you're crazy and evil is a frightening, scary place to be. It's like going insane slowly, not knowing you're insane, then trying to find your way back. I get hauntings from this. I went to get a newspaper the other day, and a young woman, obviously a schizophrenic, was in front of the store talking to herself. I thought, "There go I but for the grace of God."

GLORIA HARMON, ACCUSED MOTHER

For Christmas in 1987, Gloria Harmon's oldest son, Robert, then 34, gave her an inscribed copy of the family genealogy which he had helped to write. 'To my one and only mother from your grateful son,' he wrote in the inscription. 'Thank you for life; I wouldn't have wanted to have missed it. May our line always continue. Such fine heredity has to be passed on.' It seemed a typical, thoughtful act from a wonderful son. Charles, Robert's younger brother, had gone through a difficult period in his teens, but Robert had been the golden child – always smiling and happy. Creative and enthusiastic, he married Beth, a soul-mate who shared his values. They lived simply, ecologically, sharing Gloria's liberal politics. Robert taught music for a living and played gigs on weekends. The only dark spot was their failure thus far to have children, whom they desperately wanted.

Finally, a year later, Beth gave birth to Jessica. Just when everything seemed perfect, however, Robert became inexplicably enraged whenever Jessica cried too long. As a consequence, he entered therapy with Jane Foster in the summer of 1989. Five months later, in December, Robert called his mother (divorced in 1975), brother Charles, and younger sister Rachel together for a therapy session. Though Gloria Harmon, now 66, did not know it at the time, this meeting would mark the beginning of a process which would culminate early in 1993 with a letter she cannot forget . . .

'I liked Jane Foster, Robert's counselor. She was very attractive, in her early 40s, and she seemed to really listen to you. I had nothing against therapy. In fact, I thought it was a good idea in general. We had sought out family counseling once before when Charles was having trouble in high school. But I wasn't prepared for what happened that December of 1989. Robert and I sat on opposite ends of a sofa, with him leaning away from me. For an hour and a half, everything I'd ever done to Robert came out. It was a real beat-up Mom session. He complained about things I never dreamed would upset him. He didn't like the way I patted him on the back when I hugged him. He said he hated the articles or tapes I'd send him.

I was so hurt and confused. He was an amateur astronomer, so I'd sent him Carl Sagan articles. We both enjoyed folk music, and I had brought a tape recorder to a music festival and sent him a tape of it. He said, "I don't even listen to those tapes you sent me." There were lots of little complaints that just tore me up. I ended up crying and leaving the room. Jane came out on the balcony and apologized for letting the session get out of hand. That was nice of her, but it didn't take away my misery. Although Robert didn't complain about anything I could really feel bad about, I apologized profusely, as if it were my fault. I thought maybe I *had* overdone it, sending him things.

The whole next year, Robert would send pictures of the baby and short notes, nothing nasty. I stopped sending him anything, afraid it would be the wrong thing to do. In November of 1990, I had open-lung surgery for cancer, a tumor, and was given six months to live. My son Charles sent me *Love, Medicine and Miracles* by Dr. Bernie Siegel, which was right up my alley. Back in the late '60s and early '70s, I had developed an interest in reincarnation, past lives, and visualizations. Both Robert and I took a course in Silva Mind Control. I loved the Bernie Siegel book and was determined to take charge of my own health, to beat this thing with a positive attitude. Also, I was taking an experimental medication.

In January of 1991, Robert and Beth had a son, Richard. I wanted to see my new grandchild in case I died soon, so I went out there to Colorado. I was so excited about how well I was doing. I told Robert and Beth how I visualized my body killing tumors with natural radiation. Robert abruptly got up and left the room. I thought, "Oh, gee, he doesn't want to hear about tumors or think about poor Mom dying." But in March, I got a letter from him. "You may have noticed that I've been avoiding talking to you lately," he began. "I enjoyed your visit up until the afternoon when we discussed your goals and you pushed it too far, disregarding my obvious discomfort and unhappiness. You forced your will on me and I had to leave the room to get free." I couldn't understand this, and the next few lines were even stranger. He said it reminded him of his childhood feelings from the first few years of his life. "I was afraid of you hurting me. My body felt constantly invaded and manipulated against my will. Any feelings of warmth and comforting had sexual overtones attached to them. I felt helpless and trapped."

This was such a strange letter to get from a 38-year-old man! He talked about feeling all alone with no one to help him and how he left his body behind and retreated into his mind. He wrote he was grateful to have "begun the healing process" and to be in therapy, though he still had "huge reservoirs of anger which I'm draining as fast as I can. I feel more and more detached from you and am relieved about that." At least he still said he loved me, though, and he signed the letter with "Love, Robert."

I shared this letter with an old friend who had known Robert a long time, too. I told her, "I'm trying to figure this out. Maybe it's because we took his temperature anally until he was six." My friend said, "But everybody did that then." I asked her, "Did he really feel bad like this all those years? How could I not have noticed? Was he hiding all this?" I didn't think I was an insensitive parent. Even my sister-in-law, who doesn't much like me, always said she envied the way I took care of my children.

But I thought I must have done something. I still think that sometimes. What could I have done to bring this on? Maybe psychological abuse? Maybe I wouldn't let him go to a movie one night or something? It's true that we didn't talk much about negative emotions in our family, but Robert always seemed happy to follow our example, he seemed just naturally to enjoy himself. Was it my drinking, maybe? By 1989, when I quit and joined AA, I was drinking three martinis a day. But that was long after Robert was a boy.

Robert is a very expressive writer, but I had never heard him speak this way, as in this letter. A couple of my friends doubted that he even wrote it. I think he did. It's so bizarre, though. If *he* says this, who would doubt it? He's kind, loving, truthful. Me – I've not always been kind and truthful. I'm a normal, human, imperfect parent.

Then in August, I got a letter which Robert had apparently written back in June, on Mother's Day. He sent it to both my ex-husband and me. "Dear Mom and Dad," it started, "You each caused me more pain and suffering in my childhood than you or I ever could have imagined. You each abused and neglected me so much that as a child I wanted to die myself or to kill you. I know this to be true to the bottom of my heart because my feelings are still there." He went on and on, saying that he forgave us because we were acting out of our own unfulfilled needs, that we were both sick and couldn't help ourselves. He ended the letter, "Goodbye and good luck."

This is so painful. To think he wanted to die? How could he look so happy in the pool with his grandfather? I don't understand it. Where's his common sense? For the first time, when I got this letter, I allowed myself to get angry. "I forgive you, Mom." For what? What did I do? If you had only known this kid! There's a woman Robert grew up with who lives near me. She also happens to be a therapist now. I took both these letters to her and her mother, my friend June, and we all cried for three hours. They couldn't believe it. Two of June's friends, both therapists, had been accused by *their* children because of repressed memories.

In January of 1992, Robert called to tell me he had been diagnosed with temporal lobe epilepsy, which his father also had. I was full of questions, wanting to know if he was taking drugs for it, but I got perfunctory answers. I've done a lot of reading on this since then, and epileptics often have inexplicable anger. I believe that may be what sent Robert to therapy in the first place.

Then, that May, Charles told me on the telephone that Robert had said something about sex abuse. I said, "What?" He didn't know any details. I hung up crying. It had graduated from sexual overtones to sexual abuse. So finally, in October, I wrote Robert my first letter in a long time. I told him that I'd gone to see two professional counselors, and that their advice had been: "Acknowledge that Robert is entitled to his feelings. They are valid and he is hurting. Seek to understand what you did and are doing that hurts him." I continued: "Where and *how* could I have been so insensitive, abusive, callous, unfeeling, indifferent, cruel and oblivious to you, my little child?"

Then I said that I had always felt bad about the difficult divorce, but that I always thought that his early childhood was happy and secure, filled with "playing with John Deere toys, building blocks, relatives for dinner, swimming at the club, fireflies and just normal everyday things." Then I hypothesized that maybe his crib accident when he was two was behind all of this. He had to have three stitches when he fell against the iron bars, and no one discovered him for a long time. "You must have felt so abandoned and frightened and I didn't come to you," I wrote. Then I asked if I could attend another therapy session.

The next month, I went to Colorado for the session. I had a few minutes alone with Jane before we began and I asked, "What's going on? When this first happened, I thought maybe he had regressed to a past life, or a babysitter had molested him, or a therapist led him down a path." When Robert came in, the first thing Jane said was, "Have I been leading you down this path?" He said, "No." Then he accused me of playing with his penis and said that the crib accident was actually a suicide attempt. He was sitting there so serious, so sad. When you see an adult child in such pain and suffering, your heart just bleeds to see it. You almost don't dare to say, "You must be crazy." You're almost scared it will set off a rage or something physical. But I did say, "I never played with your penis. I may have brushed it when changing your diapers." Robert talked about hitting pillows with his fist so hard he got bruises. Jane just sat there. Still, it ended well. Robert and I got into his truck together and we could talk about it, so I felt something had been accomplished. "Maybe your grandfather played with your penis or something," I guessed.

The next major thing that happened was in February of 1993, when Robert went to a hypnotist. At that point, I believed in hypnosis. I would have suggested going to one to get at the truth. Charles called to tell me the results, which were bad, but he wouldn't tell me exactly what came out. "I don't know if I can ever feel the same about you or Dad again," he told me. Shortly after that, I found out about the False Memory Syndrome Foundation from my new therapist. Finally, I got really angry, and I wanted to know what I was supposed to have done. So I wrote a short note to Robert asking for specifics.

In response, he wrote this horrible letter. I cried for a week. It took me eight times before I could read it aloud to anyone without breaking down. For the first time, there was no "Dear" at the beginning, or "Love" at the end. He wrote that he was enraged that I apparently couldn't remember what I had done. "Through hypnosis," he said, "I have established contact with my unconscious. It has been keeping track of everything since I was born." He said it provided the missing pieces to the puzzle, the key to the mystery. "When I was one and two years old, you and Dad had me play with your genitals as part of your foreplay ritual before intercourse." He said we had sex while he was right there, and that I had kissed him sexually on the mouth even when he was a

338

teenager. "But by far the worst sexual abuse you did to me was the ritual you called 'our secret.' As I said, you started playing with my penis when I was just weeks old. You continued this routine almost daily until I was seven years old, by first forcing me to have an erection and then stimulating me until I had a climax."

Finally, he said that he was getting better "after four years of intensive individual therapy, recently with two therapists each week, two years of group, countless thousands of dollars and countless thousands of bad moments for my wife and children." He ended: "It would have been better for me if you had both died when I was born or been locked up for your crimes and I had been raised by someone else, practically anyone else would have been better."

In between my crying jags, I realized that at least now I knew what he thought. I know it's this horrible, bizarre confabulation. I was almost sorry it didn't include satanic ritual abuse. In a way, I was relieved to finally know the worst. A few months earlier, I had asked Charles, "Does he know I was unfaithful to your father once?" You know, that was actually the worst thing I could think of for my children to know about.

Since then, I've had some contact with Robert. I saw him at Charles' wedding, but we barely spoke. Robert called me recently on Richard's third birthday thanking me for his card. He said, "I'm baking a cake in the shape of a baseball, got to go, just wanted to let you know we appreciated it." I hung up and started to cry. I couldn't get to sleep that night. It was a crumb being sent my way, just a crumb of love. It just reminded me of everything that isn't in my life now.

I've been trying to keep contact with my grandchildren. I send postcards for Valentine's, Easter. It's terrible to weigh every phrase to see whether it could be taken wrong somehow or other. I'm lucky, compared to some grandparents in my situation, because the cards don't get sent back. Sometimes I talk to them on the phone now. Jessica is five, old enough to throw me a kiss over the phone.

I'm 66 now, and with the cancer, there's a certain immediacy about everything in my life. I want to do everything today. I don't know if Robert will ever come out of this. I try not to think about a future that includes Robert and his family. If I allow myself to do that, to dwell on what could be, it ruins my entire day, and I become very depressed.

For a while, even my relationship with Charles and Rachel changed for the worst, but now we're back on track again, except that Rachel won't talk about Robert with me. For my granddaughter Jessica, I'm starting to write the story of her Daddy, in photograph and scrapbook form, starting with his birth. I hope it will remind me of who he really was.'

BART STAFFORD, ACCUSED SIBLING

When Bart Stafford's younger sister Cindy told him that she had recovered incest memories about their deceased father, he was horrified and supportive. A few months later, however, she identified him, too. Stafford, 40, is a North Carolina public relations man, the second oldest of five children. His sister Cindy, 33, is the youngest. When Bart chose to go public with his story, he discovered who his real friends – and enemies – were.

'Cindy and I had lunch at a New York coffee shop just before Thanksgiving in 1991. For the first time, she told me she had started to recover memories about my father. She didn't get real specific, just said she'd been sexually abused as a kid. I was completely shocked and didn't think it was something my father would do, but why would I not believe her? She had been in therapy for a long time. I didn't realize it then, but she had recently switched therapists.

She was 30 at the time. I should mention that my mother was also undergoing recovered memory therapy at the same time, at the age of 62. It's a little unclear whose memories came first. I think my mother's did, but then they overlapped. My mother's started when she was six months old, so the memories were buried for over 60 years. Subsequently, Mom discovered abuse by the chauffeur, the maid, her brother and her father. But I didn't know any of this when I was talking to Cindy.

At the coffee shop, I said, "Gee, that's awful. If there's anything I can do to help, let me know." The last thing I said was, "Well, at least you know the root cause of some of your problems now." Cindy was physically obese, never went on dates. She had only a few friends, and she hated her job. In other words, she fit the profile of a miserable young single woman in New York City.

My father had died long ago, when I was 17 and Cindy was 10. Our mother had been ill a lot with manic-depression and was addicted to Valium and alcohol. So Cindy had no parents, in a way. She really did have a lousy childhood.

I saw no indication of tension toward me that November, and Cindy gave me a nice Christmas present. Then on February 4, 1992, I got a Federal Express letter from Cindy covering both sides of a single sheet of legal paper. It essentially said, "You raped me orally, anally, and vaginally, over and over. I don't know when it started or stopped, but it went on for years, and you're a sick and disgusting person." She said she'd sent copies to my mother and brothers, and that I should never contact her again.

I sat reading this in my living room. There was no one else home. I was just flabbergasted. I read it several times, thinking, "What is this about?" It could not have been more out of left field, a total mystery. I was too shocked to be hurt at the time. It just seemed like an act of insanity. She accused me of doing things I've never done with *anybody*. What was so startling was the breadth of the accusations. I would have had no time to do anything else. I was actually away at boarding school and college during much of this period. I would have had to cram in a lot of activity during vacations. I would have had to rape her every spare minute I had.

The next day, I wrote a letter I didn't mail, basically saying, "This is crap. First it was Dad, now me. When are you going to take responsibility for your life?" Then I mailed a much more measured response, saying, "Obviously, something did happen to you and I feel sorry about that, but it has nothing to do with me. I'll be glad to help you in any way, meet with you and your therapist to try to get to the bottom of this, but it wasn't me." I sent copies to my mother and three brothers.

Nobody in my family sided with me. No one called, with one exception. My mother called to tell me she believed Cindy. "I love you, I'll always love you," she said, "but I believe Cindy." I had to initiate all other contact. My older brother began a two year fence-straddling exercise. He says he doesn't believe or disbelieve her or me. Mind you – in this letter, there was *no* evidence, simply pure accusation, pure venom. Only one brother has ever wanted to hear my side of the story.

That's been the focus of this tragedy for me as much as Cindy's accusations – trying to understand why my family wasn't there for me. It was crunch time, and they abdicated. They never tried to find out the truth. Instead, they kept saying *I* would find the answer inside me, that somehow it was my responsibility to – what? Go back in and recover memories. I should go through years of therapy to find what really happened.

I went through a six-month period when I considered whether it could have happened. I went to a therapist who had worked with victims and perpetrators. I asked him, "How can you tell if someone is really a perpetrator? What do they sound like?" He said, "A perpetrator would be saying exactly what you're saying, only he would be lying."*[13]

I only saw him a few times. I stopped going because he was too understanding. I wanted him to be a devil's advocate, to flush me out, see if there was any truth to what Cindy said. Then I went to see a woman therapist, who seemed very reasonable. My wife Cheryl had been seeing her, too. When I stopped, she told Cheryl that I didn't want to learn about myself, that I was in denial.

Cheryl has always felt that I have a dark side that I'm trying to hide all the time, so she wasn't sure about the allegations. She would use them against me when we were arguing. "Cindy was right about you." But I didn't think Cheryl really believed that. Now that she's gone to some FMS Foundation meetings, she understands.

I found out about the FMS Foundation in August of 1992. It was a real life raft, like a life preserver from the deck of the *Titanic*. You just feel total isolation, accused of doing the most hateful things you could do to a person.

I went public in April of 1993, doing an on-the-record interview with a local newspaper columnist. I thought it was important for someone using his real name to say, "This is going on, and it's screwed up." Anyone who knew me would never look at this issue again the same way. Also, I lived in fear of this getting out, even though I hadn't done anything wrong. I didn't want this thing hanging over my head. It gave Cindy power over my life.

My big mistake was in not calling up everyone I knew beforehand and informing them. I also didn't enlist the support, advice, and counsel of my wife. Her bitterness and resentment over how it affected our family were hard to cope with.

The newspaper article was generally accurate, but it left out one tremendously important fact – that my sister had also accused five other people, including my father, a maid, and a few more I didn't even know. I think the reporter thought it would make a better story, just her word against mine.

A lot of people in the community read that article and had a field

---

* The widely-held belief that *real* sex offenders usually deny their guilt may not be true. A 1978 book on family violence, for instance, found that nine out of ten fathers accused of incest admitted it. A 1983 article noted that of all suspected criminals, those accused of sex abuse had the highest confession rate. It appears that only in the past few years has the stereotype of invariable denial been accepted.

day with it. I am now the world's authority on the knowing glance from across the room, field, or road. People in this nice little suburban neighborhood closed up shop. My eight-year-old son Jeffrey got picked on at school. He became a pariah. One day we were walking around the block with Jeffrey and ran into neighbors, out with their son, who was in Jeffrey's class. They refused to let them play together. The mother said, "You are sick. If any of you come to our house, I'm going to kill you."

When the story came out, any relationship that was the least bit strained started to crack. Anyone who had ambivalent feelings about me or a shade of negative opinion turned on me. The good part is that a lot of my friends came up and said, "That's awful." I got a lot of sympathy. One of the hardest things to go through is the silence, when you feel so terrible but can't tell anyone.'

CHAPTER EIGHT

The Retractors

> I did it not out of any anger, malice or ill-will to any person, for I had no such thing against one of them, but what I did was [done] ignorantly ... I desire to lie in the dust, and to be humbled for it, in that I was a cause, with others, of so sad a calamity to them and their families.
>
> ANN PUTNAM, *writing in 1706,*
> *14 years after her accusations helped spark the Salem witch trials[1]*

INTERVIEWS IN THIS CHAPTER:

OLIVIA MCKILLOP, *retractor*
LINDA FURNESS, *retractor*
LAURA PASLEY, *retractor**
MARIA GRANUCCI, *retractor*
FRANCINE BOARDMAN, *retractor from deliverance ministry*
LESLIE HANNEGAN, *Christian retractor*
NELL CHARETTE, *MPD retractor*
STEPHANIE KRAUSS, *retractor from a psychiatric hospital*
ROBERT WILSON, *MPD retractor*

Some of the most compelling voices in this book belong to those who were once convinced that they had recovered memories of incest and have since changed their minds. I call them 'retractors,' for lack of a better term, though that sounds awfully clinical. A longer but more accurate description would be ventured-to-hell-and-back-survivors. They offer startling personal insights into the repressed memory phenomenon.

I hope that, after reading these stories, readers will better understand how and why someone could come to believe in bizarre, unreal allegations. Most entered therapy wanting to get *better*, to find answers to extremely

---

* Laura Pasley is her real name.

unsettling problems. Recovered memory therapy offered those answers, along with initial hope. 'I had been constantly living with frustration and disappointment. I never felt fulfilled,' Linda Furness explains. In therapy, as she first perceived it, 'I was finally getting myself sorted out, finding out what made me tick, and I would become everything I could be.' Similarly, Laura Pasley observes, 'I was desperate. It was like I was drowning and this person reached out a hand to me, and he was my only hope.' As a result, the retractors usually became extremely dependent on their therapists. 'It's like I sold my soul to this man,' Pasley explains.

It is difficult to read these stories without becoming enraged at the therapists who fostered these illusions, even when they appear well-intentioned. Some of these professionals clearly brought their own needs, neuroses, and insecurities to their work. Nell Charette's therapist, for instance, styled himself as a mini-guru and had sex with clients, while ex-Marine Robert Wilson's counselor took a more intellectual approach. 'She was trying to create a monster,' he observes, 'and I happened to be her monster.' Clearly, there is something sick about these therapists' voyeuristic delight at their patients' self-destruction. Olivia McKillop recalls bitterly how her therapist *smiled* in triumph after a particularly harrowing memory retrieval session, then practically ordered her to hurt herself.[*2]

Yet blaming only the therapists is too simplistic. Leslie Hannegan provides an example of a self-made repressed memory survivor who convinced herself, largely *without* a therapist's assistance, that her father had committed incest on her. She read Christian Survivor self-help books and interpreted sleep paralysis and panic-induced choking as evidence of returning memories. Later, Hannegan promptly dumped a therapist who expressed skepticism about whether her father had really committed these acts. Similarly, Francine Boardman clearly needed little coaching to come up with grotesque stories of ritual abuse, which made her feel special. 'All of a sudden, I had this childhood background that nobody else had,' she explains. 'I thought it was exciting in a way, I really did. This couple were giving me all their attention. They were basically pandering to whatever I said.' Yet Boardman takes 'absolutely

---

* McKillop's experience is not uncommon. 'This began a pattern,' one Survivor wrote in 1992. 'I would cut myself, resolve not to do it again, she [the therapist] would say it was going to happen again, and I would cut myself again. It became a vicious cycle. I came to feel like no matter what I did, I would never be able to control what I was doing.' Such women are tacitly *encouraged* to mutilate themselves by a newsletter aptly titled the *Cutting Edge*, filled with poetry such as: 'Slip slash slide enters the blade / and all the pain will fade.'

no responsibility' for what happened. Clearly, all of these retractors 'bought into' the process and, at least at some level, enjoyed the resulting attention, drama, and sympathy.*[3]

I have come to regard the process as a warped kind of tango in which therapist and client dance through a fractured hall of mental mirrors. During most of the dance, the therapist leads, but at other times, the client takes over. Between them, they clasp childhood photos and *The Courage to Heal*, implicated in nearly every case, or other self-help recovery books. My dance analogy breaks down, however, at its height. It is not the therapist who cuts herself, tries to commit suicide, develops multiple personalities, writes hate letters to her parents, becomes a drugged-out zombie, gets divorced, or finds herself bound in psychiatric ward restraints.

I am not sure these early retractors are entirely representative. It takes great courage to admit that you were wrong about something so major and serious. Though these retractors are indeed courageous, I believe that most of them *had* to get out of therapy or die. In general, their therapy was so coercive and horrible, their mental and physical state so shattered, that they had little choice but to flee. There are other 'Survivors' who remain firmly convinced of their recovered memories, because they have not had such atrocious experiences – though they have all gone through the pain of losing their families and redefining their identities.

Nonetheless, the nine stories recounted here provide lessons and hope. They make it clear that to escape from harmful therapy and begin to question memories, people need to *get away from their recovered memory therapists* and *stop taking massive, inappropriate drug doses*.** Once they take these two steps, their minds begin to clear, and they can begin to make more rational life choices. It also helps if trusted acquaintances or authority figures plant seeds of doubt. When Olivia McKillop's friend Fran told her she didn't believe in the incest memories, McKillop was livid – but she began to question her therapy. Similarly, when Leslie Hannegan's pastor confronted her, she refused to believe him at first, but then 'it was like a wall coming down around me.'

---

* Indeed, it is remarkable the lengths some people will go to secure sympathy for fictitious mental or medical ailments. There is even a name for the phenomenon: Munchhausen's Syndrome, in which patients actually fake their illnesses, sometimes going so far as to inject themselves with saliva or urine. Psychiatrists Marc Feldman and Charles Ford explore these extraordinary cases in *Patient or Pretender* (1994).

** I do not mean to imply that retractors should abandon all therapy, just the search for repressed memories. Nor should they necessarily avoid all medication that could ease their suffering. For some, such as those suffering from manic depression (bipolar disorder), proper medication appears to be essential.

As I have already stressed, it is difficult to find a reliable common denominator for those who have recovered memories. Most are women, though macho ex-Marine Robert Wilson offers proof that this delusion can be fostered in either gender. Most are white and come from middle- or upper-class backgrounds, probably because they could afford therapy. Many, such as Nell Charette and Maria Granucci, find memories as housewives in their 30s and 40s, while others, such as Olivia McKillop and Leslie Hannegan, are much younger.

I did not have room here for Faith Sylvester's narrative, one of the saddest stories I heard. When she was only 12, Sylvester's aunt persuaded her to read *The Courage to Heal* and recover 'memories' of being abused by her stepfather. As a consequence, Sylvester spent most of her adolescence living with a man she thought had molested her. When her mother discovered her journal about it, the situation blew up. Even though Sylvester, now 19, has realized that her allegations were wrong, her mother and stepfather have yet to forgive her.

Some of the retractors, including Olivia McKillop, fit the pattern of young women who never rebelled as teenagers and who became incest Survivors partly to individuate from their parents. Like many others, McKillop is highly creative, dramatic, empathetic, and suggestible. Nell Charette told me that she had discovered her artistic and literary creativity in the process of becoming a multiple personality. 'I do have a lot of talents in me that I probably wouldn't have known about, but they're *my* talents, not my alters',' she concludes.

Others who seek memories may suffer from an inherited biological disposition toward depression. Leslie Hannegan and Robert Wilson appear to be examples where such tendencies run in the family. Some retractors, such as Laura Pasley and Stephanie Krauss, really *were* sexually abused as children, though this always-remembered experience wasn't enough for their therapists. Many others weren't victims of incest, but certainly endured difficult childhoods. Robert Wilson, for instance, was harassed by his alcoholic father, while Leslie Hannegan was raised by a chronically ill mother and depressive father. Olivia McKillop, on the other hand, grew up with adoring parents, but she still felt neglected. Maria Granucci wasn't abused, but missed parental hugs and affection. The bottom line? Regardless of their backgrounds, the retractors – like all children – felt some resentment toward their parents. Essentially, I agree with Olivia McKillop and Robert Wilson, both of whom said, '*If this could happen to me, it could happen to anyone.*'

Once they finally realized that their induced incest memories weren't real, all of the retractors experienced profound shame, guilt, and depression – particularly if, like Maria Granucci, their accused father nearly died before they retracted their allegations. Or, like another woman I interviewed, it took her mother's death to snap her out of it. 'Post-retraction is no bed of roses,' Granucci told me. Some people, like Olivia McKillop, Laura Pasley, and Stephanie Krauss, seek qualified counselors to help them sort out issues and reestablish family relations. Others, like Maria Granucci or Robert Wilson, are too distrustful to go anywhere near therapists.

In the aftermath of those who recovered memories in a Christian context, religious faith can be strained. In the case of Francine Boardman, it was broken. She has lost her belief in God and thrown away her Bible. For Leslie Hannegan, however, her experience has renewed her faith and determination to ring alarm bells within the Christian counseling community.

Even when the incest accusations have been dropped, family relations inevitably remain strained. Spouses of retractors, who supported them throughout the ordeal while watching their families disintegrate, often express deep bitterness over what they've had to go through. In rare cases, such as that of Faith Sylvester, the formerly accused parents may be so hurt that they won't take their children back. Even in the majority of the cases, where mothers and fathers gladly forgive and celebrate the prodigal's return, there may be an abundance of love – but trust takes longer to rebuild. Sometimes retractors can't get the well-rehearsed abuse images out of their heads. 'I still have flashbacks in a way,' one retractor told me in an unpublished interview. 'The memories still seem so real. It's frightening.'

Retractors struggle to understand how they could have been so sure of such unlikely events. What does it all mean? How could it have happened? As Melody Gavigan put it in the first issue of her newsletter, the *Retractor*, 'We are frightened, we are embarrassed, we are confused, and we are in shock.' While attempting to understand the process that engulfed them, however, she recognized that they must learn to forgive themselves. She quoted Dante, who also journeyed to hell and back: 'Midway life's journey I was made aware / That I had strayed into a dark forest / And the right path appeared not anywhere.'[4]

Fortunately, the following people have found their ways out of their own dark mental forests.

OLIVIA MCKILLOP, RETRACTOR

She was one of those 'perfect' children who had never given her parents the least cause for concern. 'We used to call Olivia LPWC, for "Little Perfect Wonder Child," her father Harry told me. An avid church-goer, Olivia McKillop seemed thoughtful, compassionate, and well-balanced. A professional child actress, she had appeared in bit parts in Hollywood films. During her senior year in high school, however, she fell apart and began therapy with Tricia Green. Soon, she began to retrieve memories of abuse. Now 20, McKillop has broken with her therapist and is trying to rebuild a good relationship with her family.

'I was the good kid. Everybody liked me. I was very compliant to people's faces. But there were a lot of things sleeping beneath the surface. I got everything in the way of material things, but I missed my Dad. He's a high-power businessman, and he just wasn't there a lot in the last few years. I was jealous of my older brother Jerry. Dad seemed much more interested in Jerry's sports than in my plays. I completely love my Mom, but she lives out a lot of dreams through me. I felt that I couldn't just be a normal kid, I had to be the brilliant actress.

The pressure just kept building on me. One day in October of 1991, in the fall of my senior year, I just went berserk. I threw my school bag down and was banging my head on the floor. I had this horrible feeling of total despair. My Mom came in and said, "Get up off the floor, you're fine, get up, get up." Mom is very reserved and controlled. I screamed, "I don't feel loved, I don't feel loved." Finally, I calmed down. "I'm sick of being the perfect kid," I told her. And I went to bed. I just felt this coldness and started to shake. That was the beginning of my panic attacks.

My parents had some meeting behind closed doors, as always, and they took me shopping. I got lots of new clothes. I just got more and more angry. Then one morning I couldn't wake up. I broke down and checked out. For six weeks, I lay in bed 20 hours a day. I couldn't go to school. My Mom just kept saying, "You're stressed, you're stressed."

[The family doctor diagnosed McKillop as clinically depressed. He put her on antidepressants and strongly suggested she receive counseling. Harry McKillop distrusted the mental health profession, but when his friend told him that local therapist Tricia Green had helped his wife through a bad depression, he relented.]

I was looking for a savior. Tricia lived only ten minutes away. I went in, and she had Georgia O'Keeffe paintings on the wall, and it was so soothing and nice. I thought, "This is great, I'm going to get better." Tricia is divorced, in her 40s, has a master's in counseling, and is also an artist. She's licensed by the American Association of Marriage and Family Counselors. I told her what I was going through, but I got the feeling she didn't quite believe anything I said. She was after something. At the end of the hour, she said, "Well, Olivia, your prognosis is really good, but it's going to take a lot of time."

She gave me *Outgrowing the Pain: For Adult Survivors of Childhood Abuse* by Eliana Gil. It was a short little book. I thought, "This is funny. I don't remember telling her about abuse." But I read it from cover to cover, three times that week. Suddenly, I could not wait to go back to counseling. It wasn't so much the book, but her. The atmosphere was so soothing, and I loved the attention Tricia gave me.

I made sure I looked really nice the next week. I wanted to please her. The second session, she grilled me about my Dad and my older brother Jerry. She asked all these questions, but I never knew what she wanted. She never seemed to believe me, no matter what I answered. "Is he nice to your Mom? How does he treat Jerry? What would you say his typical day is? Olivia, would you say that your Dad is a very angry man?" I'd say, "Yeah," just to agree. Gradually, I began to see my family as really abusive and dysfunctional.

She asked me to bring in pictures of myself as a child. I pored over our family photo albums, and we worked from these pictures. I looked kind of sad in one. I said, "Oh, I hated wearing that sweater." And she said, "Oh, really?" as if she didn't believe that was all there was to it.

Then she made me visualize a safe place. It was like a ring, and I would lie down in the middle of it. She'd talk me through guided imagery, with this really soothing voice. "Now just imagine that you're this little girl in the white sweater. Imagine you're a helpless, vulnerable, defenseless little girl." I had told her how I used to go to a day care and lie under the piano, staring up at it. So she took me back to that scene. I was totally seeing all of this as she said it. "Are you scared?" she asked, and I found that I was. "Do you see somebody?" I saw this piano repair man. "Does he come and sit by you?"

And then suddenly I visualized him lying on top of me. Tricia was really silent at this point, letting me live this scene. I imagined this man taking off my pants and sweater and totally licking me and kissing me from my crotch to my neckline. I didn't say this out loud. "Is he hurting you?" Tricia asked. "Yes, yes," I whispered. Then I opened my eyes and screamed, "Stop! Stop! I want out of this." Tricia was calm, really calm, and she was *smiling*. I grabbed my stuff. I was hyperventilating. She said, "If you need to stay here a minute and settle down, that's fine. But I have another client coming." As I walked out the door, she said, "You're probably going to feel self-destructive, because flashbacks are really hard. So call me any time." I went straight out and bought *The Courage to Heal*, which she'd told me to do.

That night, after everyone was asleep, I got up, went to the kitchen, and took out this knife. I started cutting myself up on my arms. I was very calm. I just cut and cut and cut, lots of little cuts. Then I put the knife away, cleaned everything up, and just stared at my blood. I liked it! It was so weird. I went to my room and stayed up all night.

I gobbled up *The Courage to Heal* – just read it, read it, read it, particularly the stories by Survivors at the back of the book, like "Michelle and Artemis" and "Gizelle." They were so awful. The phrase kept coming back, "If your life shows the symptoms and you don't remember it, you were still abused." I just lived with that phrase. And I bought *Secret Survivors* and *Silently Seduced* and a bunch of other recovery books, too. I read them all.

By the time I went for my next appointment, I was an Incest Survivor, and there was no turning back. I did this drawing exercise with my left hand, showing what I felt like as a little girl. At this point, I wanted Tricia's approval. I wanted her to help me so bad. Sometimes I would exaggerate or even lie. My parents were turning into these monsters of dysfunction. I started to believe my Dad was an alcoholic and Mom was codependent and neurotic. Tricia wanted me to talk to my sister Casey, who's four years older than me, to form a liaison with her, but I resisted that.

I kept worrying that I wasn't like the women in *The Courage to Heal*. It wasn't like I was driving my car and *kazam*, I had this flashback. I was really concerned that I wasn't a true Survivor. If I felt I wasn't acting the right way, I would freak out.

Eventually, I came to believe that six men had abused me, including my grandfather, Dad, and my brother Jerry. Tricia would take a real incident and help me turn it into something awful. "Olivia, remember when you and your brother were fighting downstairs," she said during one guided imagery session. "He throws you up against the wall. What are you doing?" "I'm screaming back at him. Now I'm on the ground." "Is he on the ground, too?" I said, "Oh my God, we're rolling around on the ground together!" And then I saw him raping me. That night I went home and cut all my long, curly hair off, my pride and joy. I think I wanted to punish myself for thinking this about my brother.

I stayed in therapy once or twice a week for six months. I deferred college, gave up a potential music scholarship, and moved out of my parents' house on Tricia's advice. I went to be a live-in Nanny. I began to tell my friends that I had been abused, but I didn't confront my family. "You stay away from people who don't believe you." Tricia told me. "Those people aren't worthy of you!"

[*That fall of 1992, a friend got Olivia to go on a six-month Mission Quest program for young people. After extensive training, she volunteered in Central America with her group, but she continued to conduct weekly phone sessions with Tricia. After a near-rape by a Latino, Olivia told her group leader Fran, 'I'm so afraid I'm going to have nightmares and remember much more abuse now.'*]

Fran just stopped and said, "Olivia, you were not sexually abused." I said, "What?" I was livid. She said, "I'm sorry, but at the risk of you hating me, I have to say this. I've listened to you for the last four months, and I just don't believe it. You're the product of bad counseling. This woman Tricia is a psycho. It kills me to watch it. Every time you call her, you're worse the next day. I can't continue and not tell you the truth. Get out of it."

I didn't believe her, but this seed of doubt was planted. I thought, "Olivia, look at how much better you are. Look at your life. You're so much better than when you were in therapy." I said to myself, "Hey, I was a pretty happy person before." I wished for that peace again. This was a few days before my 19th birthday. I looked back at my past year, and it was just gone, wasted.

At the end of March, 1992, I came back home. I was different, really softened. My depression was gone. I came in the house and saw my family there in the living room by the fire, and I really saw them as this treasure. My God, after a year of being in this daze, I really saw them again. I thought, "I don't want to go back to Tricia. I don't want my family to turn into these horrible people any more." So I called her up that night and told her. She was really okay about it. She said, "Olivia, promise me that you'll continue to work on this, and if you need to come back, come see me. But get into a support group."

By this time, I was accepted to a few colleges. But I realized that my relationship with my parents was still just like ice. So I decided to go back into therapy again. I was having nightmares about the man who assaulted me in Central America. At first, I went to see a male therapist, but when I told him about my repressed memories, he said, "Let me get this straight. You didn't remember anything at all until you went into therapy?" When I told him that was right, he said, "I'm sorry, I can't take you as my client. I can't work from that basis." I was so pissed. He had a woman associate, so I saw her. On her advice, I bought *The Courage to Heal Workbook*, and we started working more on my memories of my grandfather. I started getting nervous again, starving myself again. I started slipping back. I couldn't afford the $85 sessions, though, so I stopped. But I was still doing the workbook and telling people I was a Survivor, even though some of my oldest friends were confronting me about it, saying "That didn't happen to you."

Finally, what really turned me around was an experience that summer, when I was a camp counselor. I was in a boat on the pond with this beautiful, sweet, sad little ten-year-old girl. She was really quiet and shy and never dressed in front of anyone. She said, "Counselor, my Daddy is doing something bad to me, when he sleeps with me in my bed." I turned around and looked at her, and I started to cry. And I thought to myself, "My Dad did not rape me." I was not like this child. She remembered. She always remembered. So we reported what she said to the authorities.

[*Even after the camp experience, however, Olivia continued to waver. 'The hold these therapists can have over you, it's so bizarre,' she observes. She discovered the FMS Foundation, but she still hadn't rid herself of her 'memories.'*]

In the fall of 1993, when I was a freshman in college, I was crying one day about this whole mess. A male friend who knew my story said, "Tricia still has a hold on your life. Can you say out loud, 'I was not sexually abused'?" So I said the words out loud, then again, then screamed them in the middle of my dorm, three or four times. It was a liberating moment. After that, I wrote Tricia a letter and told her the same thing. In a ceremony, I ripped up and burned my copy of *The Courage to Heal*.

When I told my family about this, my father and brother were totally upset and astonished. They had no idea what I'd thought. We're in counseling together now, with a good therapist who understands FMS [false memory syndrome], and I'm so grateful for their forgiveness. My Dad is an amazing man, and he is really trying to rebuild a relationship with me. And I love my brother to death.

But I still have nightmares from these "flashbacks." Sometimes I still

353

say to myself, "Maybe something happened," just to give myself some peace. It's like security, like your savior. It's like coming out of a cult. Something so powerful doesn't just disappear.

Looking back, what makes me the angriest is how Tricia turned me into this pathetic victim. When that man nearly raped me, I froze, and all I could hear was Tricia saying, "You're a helpless, vulnerable, defenseless little girl." She practically *told* me that I would be revictimized because of what had happened to me, and she led me into cutting myself. Also, I think she had kind of a sick relationship with me. She said I reminded her of her daughter. She kept my picture on her desk and my poetry by her bed. She gave me these long hugs.

Before therapy, I was always a strong person who could stick up for myself. I grew up in a good family. I'm bright. I'm the kid next door. If this could happen to me, it could happen to anyone.

It has really helped to contact the FMS Foundation and to speak out about this, but I don't want being a Retractor to become the focus of my life the same way being a Survivor was.

Something that has been really difficult for me is realizing that my relationship with my father will never be the same. I can feel it. I'm not the same person to him, and I know that's hard for him. We're adults now. I don't need him like I did as a little girl. It's different now. He's Harry, not Dad. I mean, he'll always be my dad, but it's not the same. I think the sad thing is that, due to FMS, my Dad lost me prematurely. The whole natural process of breaking away from parents and coming of age was sped up and distorted. I came of age by turning into an incest survivor. Yeah, I had to break away from my parents, but it shouldn't have been out of fear and hate.'

LINDA FURNESS, RETRACTOR

When she was 32, Linda Furness of Bath, England, felt abandoned and rejected by her two previous lovers. She had plenty of money, but she felt empty inside. Desperately, she began to spend money on designer clothes and skiing holidays, and she took up with a fast London crowd, where she was introduced to psychedelic drugs. She had a bad trip, and her boyfriend in the group said she must have some deep-seated psychological problem to react that way. He suggested she go for therapy. At the same time, her mother expressed concern over her fast lifestyle and said she should find someone to talk to. 'So two key people

*in my life said I should get outside help.' She found Mary Beth Snodgrass, a
therapist who specialized in transactional analysis, better known as 'TA.'*

'During our first session, Mary Beth talked about my aspirations and
asked me about my childhood. She said, "What we need to do is to
form a contract to say what are the outcomes you want to achieve in
your life." She explained that therapy was a process of understanding
myself and reaching my potential. This was quite exciting. This was
like a hammock, a safety net. I was finally getting myself sorted
out, finding out what made me tick, and I would become everything I
could be.

I had been constantly living with frustration and disappointment. I
never felt fulfilled, despite my achievements. There was always a gap.
I wonder now if I was being selfish to be so introspective. She invited
me to become extremely self-centered and introspective.

In our sessions, Mary Beth concentrated on negative emotions. I
didn't express anger very much. She concentrated on me being able to
get my anger out. She used lots of different techniques, but mostly Eric
Berne's Transactional Analysis. Very early on, she wanted me to learn
the methodology of TA and buy these books. I was going to become
intimate and break down barriers, have loving relationships. She helped
me understand that I was just playing games most of the time.

Some sessions we would do chair work. She would ask me to imagine
my mother or father in a chair. More often, she asked me to become
the other person, go and be my mother. It was a strange and scary
experience. Sort of like trying to split my mind. But I went along
with it.

In April 1993, I left my job. I had a new tall, dark male boss who
frightened me to death. He was verbally abusive, didn't believe I could
do the job. He was absolutely ruthless. I couldn't respond positively. I
became unable to do the work. I ended up leaving by mutual agreement.
So I wondered what I was doing to myself, why I was self-destructive.
I was full of self-doubt. I thought maybe I could do freelance, design
management and communication. I thought I could speed up the therapeutic process, really get somewhere. I wanted to be right before I could
take on another job.

The dreamwork became quite central to my therapy around this
time. I came in with more and more dreams and nightmares. This one
particular dream led to my sexual abuse accusations. I dreamed I was
in the same house with my parents, in a room that had hundreds of
bolts up and down my bedroom door. I was quite happy with this

355

privacy, with the door shut, with a male I felt comfortable with. Outside in the hallway, on a cold floor, my mother was sitting on a quilt. I was thinking, Why doesn't she go back to bed? There was a voice, my father's voice, shouting for my mother to come back upstairs to bed. And that was it.

The method Mary Beth used for dream work was to split the elements down. The theory was, each was a part of your psyche. So she said, "Linda, you are the bolt, what are you doing in Linda's dream?" I was into it, like a kid's play, but I felt pretty silly. I had gotten accustomed to this process, though. I said the bolts are barriers, keeping people out, achieving my own privacy. I could have said anything. I was trying to please her, give her an answer, say the first thing that came into my mind.

So then we went, Door, what do you want? Quilt, what do you want? Mother, what do you want? The quilt was to keep my Mum warm, away from the cold floor. Then we were going to put the dream together. The male wasn't threatening. He was holding me and it was comforting. He was a married man I was in a relationship with at that time, but he was unattainable.

What really bothered me was that my mother was cold, sitting on this quilt. I wanted to put Mum and Dad together again, put her back there. The quilt was bothering me. I wanted to put the quilt on top of both of them. But when I did, I felt a searing pain, a visualization of this quilt on my father, as if the quilt were me. That's when I got the pain, as if I was being penetrated, almost up to my chest. By this time, I was rocking back and forth. It felt so real, I was clenching my fists, nursing myself. This voice came out of me that sounded very childlike. "It hurts, it hurts, stop it, it hurts." I freaked myself out.

Mary Beth was looking fairly concerned, like there was a breakthrough going on. She then had to take me back up to being an adult so I could walk out without being a gibbering wreck. Often in these sessions, I'd get very tearful. I would cry just about every time.

I didn't actually tell her what was going on; I was in a state of shock. She gently brought me round without talking about it at all. At the next session, I said, "I'm very confused, I don't understand the experience." She explained that I had had a body memory, a memory of being sexually abused by my father.

I was open-minded to the fact that this repressed sexual abuse might be why I had been so pained and upset and introspective and putting up a front that everything was OK. Maybe there was this big trauma.

She explained that I would have blocked it out because it was too painful to remember consciously. I said, "If it was an abuse issue, it could be anybody. Why would it need to be my father?" I tried to come up with other ideas of who might have taken care of me. She would say, "I think you'll find it's your father who is revealed in the end." Every session, I went in and would deny it. I wanted to understand the body memory process, I was intrigued by this. She explained, "Your body is capable of storing the memories in a way that's so traumatic that your brain doesn't remember." I never got more than that; I just had to believe it.

Then I started to have more body memories, when I was agitated, distressed, and dehydrated. I said, "I feel like I can't breathe. I feel hot, like a hot baby in a pram." She asked how old I felt. I said I felt as if I were 18 months old, or maybe up to about four. I thought my father had actually abused me with his penis in my mouth, that's why I was feeling suffocated and phobic, with pain on my chest. It was probably from the weight of him.

I went into a severe depression, almost suicidal. I didn't want to believe it. I was paying my money for absolute hell. I was desperately trying to get her to change her mind, but she wanted me to believe that she was right. It was a struggle of belief systems. And eventually, she won.

I did not really want to believe that anyone had abused me, but because of these body memories, I had no way to dispute it. People I wanted to get answers from were on a track, and they wouldn't get off it.

After the blackest days of my life, on one occasion, I woke up and literally couldn't see, it was total darkness. I thought, "This is the darkness of depression." I told her I just couldn't cope with this. I just lay in bed with my clothes on. I just didn't want this to be the truth. And she would say to me, "These dark days, you have to go through them to become a better person." I had to go through one more dark depression before I got out of it. So she headed me off for another one. It's almost like becoming masochistic, I kept going back for more.

Eventually, I accepted that my father had abused me. I became very withdrawn. I still saw my parents, but very infrequently. I didn't say anything to them, but I started to reveal these terrible awful secrets to others. The more people I told who accepted it, the more I thought it must be true. I told all my friends, even very new friends. I was getting my strokes and my attention from these people. You know, "Oh, you poor thing."

Some people told me later that they never believed it and thought I was being brainwashed. Yet even my closest friends went along with it. My closest childhood friend and I were bathing our children together when I burst into tears. I said, "I think I believe it, but I don't want to." She said, "Well, there's no reason *not* to believe you. What you believe is real to you." I wish somebody had said, "Linda, come out of this."

I finally disclosed it to my brother, and he said, "There's no way this happened. Don't ever accuse my father, or I'll never talk to you again. You really should stop seeing this therapist." To me, that was, "Oh, well, he's in denial." By this time, I believed that my father abused me because *he* was abused, and my mother married him because *she* was abused, going on for generations, a family taboo, and my brother was abused as well and was in denial, and he had married someone with an eating disorder who was abused. And if I didn't get better and accept it, I would be an abuser or marry an abuser.

This all gave me a key to everything. It explained why I lost my job: I had transferred my feelings towards my father to my new boss. He was trying to control me and being abusive, just like my father had been.

I decided not to go home for Christmas in 1993. It would have been a sham. Instead, I spent the holiday miserably walking the moors on my own. I just told them I had things going on and didn't want to upset them during Christmas. They were upset, but they said, "If that's what you want, OK."

Then, around Easter in 1994, I went home. By that time, I was thinking, "OK, he did it, but I forgive him. He was abused and he didn't know what he was doing." So I was trying to figure out how to help my family realize this truth. As soon as I clapped eyes on my Dad, I had trouble. We ate together, but I couldn't hack it after the meal. He said, "What on earth is wrong with you? We don't like you any more. You shouldn't see that woman. We don't know you any more."

We had a buster. My mother asked, "What on earth have we done for you to treat us this way?" I said, "You'll never get me to tell you." He said, "We've racked our brains, and we can't figure out what we did wrong when you were growing up. You'd better go. I've finished with you. I wash my hands of you." And he left the room.

Mum said, "Before you go, will you come upstairs and talk with me? What is it? Have you got AIDS? Are you a lesbian? Are you taking drugs? Has your father ever done anything bad to you?" That sort of triggered me, and I said, "OK, come upstairs and I'll tell you." I told her that I'd been exploring in therapy that he had abused me. I didn't go into any detail. I never actually confronted him directly. Then I left the house. In retrospect, I think that was a cruel thing to do.

She didn't tell him for a week, going through in her own mind, wondering if it was true. She finally confronted him; they went through medical records. He totally denied that it ever took place. She was in a dilemma of who to believe. Finally, she made a decision that this could not have happened. From there, I realized that I didn't have any allies in my family. To me, they were all in denial. I was getting more and more into believing it totally. I was in such deep pain, it was evidence that it was true.

I felt like I understood the pain and why it was there. When I became a whole person, the pain would go away. I had to take on the dark side of my nature and go through it and purge it and accept the terrible truth. Then I could choose to live in a happier frame of mine. I would be one of the few who really understand and can help the rest of the world. I was starting to speak their language, I was taking it all on board.

Once I was saying and doing the "right" thing, my next step began. I went to group induction training for TA. There were aromatherapists, massage people, NHS therapists, psychiatric nurses. I moved from being a victim to being a rescuer. I was on a crusade to save the world by this time.

But I didn't like the former psychiatric nurse who was the trainer. I thought he was playing God. He really got into the sound of his own voice. I asked him about body memories, and he said, "Trust me, all I can say is that the body stores the memories that the brain can't cope with. Your memories are coming out in a safe environment, a lot of inner child work is going on, so you feel safe. The body never forgets." I said, "Yes, but where is the scientific evidence for this?" He said, quite agitatedly, "You must trust me."

I began to doubt it then. One massage guy was hoping to use TA to convert massage clients. He put it to a 60-year-old that she had to have hip replacement because she had been abused. I found that plausible, but where were the facts to back it up? I started to get a bit rebellious.

My Mum, Dad, and brother came to the clinic around this time and met with the head psychiatrist. I was invited to listen. I thought the therapists would get my family to see the truth. Mary Beth told my father that he needed help. As Mum and Dad left, they said, "If she's hurt, we hold you responsible." My Dad was the last one out, and he turned and said, so sorrowfully, "When will this process be finished?

Where's the end to all of this?" It touched me, it really touched me. The therapists said to me afterwards, "Those are very sick people; your family is dysfunctional." I struggled with this. I really wanted to go after my family. I got very distressed because they had left me. I was more vulnerable than ever.

I kept awake all that night, and I suddenly recalled the Peter Pan play I rewrote when I was in the Sixth Form. We wanted the audience to shout, "We believe in fairies," and the crew would hoist Tinkerbell on wires. But they couldn't pull her up, so I kept having to go out and urge the audience to shout louder, stalling for time. I thought, "It's just like that play. This is about belief, and it's up to me to choose what I want to believe. I don't *want* to believe that this is the truth."

I phoned Mum and Dad and told them I felt unwell, that I didn't know what to believe any more. I went home, and at first they were cool towards me. I told them I didn't want to believe it was true. Then my Dad got hold of me and gave me the biggest hug he ever gave me. He looked into my eyes and said, "I thought I had lost you forever." It was at that point that I converted 100 per cent, looking right into his eyes. That was what was missing all my life. I had never had the closeness I wanted from him.

I never went back to the TA people.

Now that I'm thinking for myself, I realize that these negative states are normal to us as human beings sometimes, and they don't necessarily indicate that we were abused. We all know what it feels like when you can't breathe because you're so stressed out. It doesn't mean it's a body memory of oral sex. I'd love to discover what it would be like to concentrate on all the *positive* aspects of your childhood and see how that was in therapy.

For the time being, I'm living here at home, and I'm trying to get myself a permanent job. Even though I am still dependent on my parents and feeling rather vulnerable, it has been good to be home for a while. Dad and I agree this time has been invaluable. We are considerate of each other. I am treated as an adult, with my own ideas and views. I enjoy my parents now.

Every now and again, I remember the therapy process, but I don't allow myself to think of the details. That's why it's hard to talk to you. I wonder if it will trigger me again. I'm talking to you so that others can read my story and understand what has happened to them. If one other person reads this and gets themselves out of this environment, it will be worth it.'

LAURA PASLEY, RETRACTOR

Laura Pasley, 39, is one of the first retractors to sue her former therapist successfully, though he settled out of court, so no precedent was set. A somewhat overweight, no-nonsense Southern American, Laura dropped out of college to work in a police station, where she has made a career.

'I really was a sad kid, you know, with a real distorted view of myself. I felt invisible growing up. When I told my mother this, she said, "No, you didn't." [*laughs*] My counselor, Steve, was the first person who really heard me, my anger and need for acceptance. He would sit and listen no matter what, without boundaries, whether it was 3 a.m. or whatever. I could call him any time.

I went into counseling because I had an eating disorder. I'd been bulimic since I was ten, so I'd been throwing up for 22 years. I was desperate, and I'd read about Steve in a book, how this girl supposedly got healed by him in a four-month period. I went to my pastor, who was like my best friend, and he said, "Well, this man is a Christian counselor, so he must be all right." Steve had a master's of divinity. He was overweight and balding, like the perpetual nerd, someone you'd avoid in high school. My Dad tells me he can't believe all these women fell for this short, fat, balding, wimpy-looking guy. But he became my whole life.

At my first counseling session, in 1985, Steve asked if I'd ever been sexually abused. I told him I had. When I was nine, a boy, a stranger, inserted his finger in my vagina through my swimming suit under the water. The biggest trauma was that I couldn't tell anybody. I didn't feel comfortable. I was ashamed. So I told that to Steve, right up front, but it didn't matter to him, because I always remembered it. He told me I needed to find buried stuff with deeper roots. He told me that since I had an eating disorder, it automatically meant I was seriously abused. So we went to work trying to find buried memories.

From the second visit on, I closed my eyes every time. He'd say weird stuff which I couldn't understand. I would tell him I didn't understand him, and he'd say that was okay, that my subconscious caught it. He used big words like counter-super-autonomous. I tell you, he could use some big words!

You have to understand my mind state. I was desperate. It was like I was drowning and this person reached out a hand to me, and he was my only hope. It's like I sold my soul to this man. I became incredibly dependent on him, wouldn't make a move without him. I went to therapy constantly. It ruled my life. I had just bought a house when I met him. My insurance wouldn't cover him, so every penny I got my hands on went to him. I got into incredible debt, went a year and a half without a car.

I'm convinced that Steve didn't do it for the money. At the time, he really felt that he was anointed by God, he had a mission in life. He said it was his calling. It was a combination of ego and a personal mission to save the world.

He had me get a picture of myself as a little girl, and to imagine her as my inner child. I could close my eyes and just see her sitting on the floor, surrounded by toys, playing. She was a tiny little thing with big, sad eyes. Then, one day when I was vacuuming, I had a visualization of a three-year-old boy trying to smother an infant. I couldn't breathe, broke out into a terrible sweat. Steve kept badgering me the whole hour of our next session to get me to accept that my brother had tried to kill me. After that, I would usually have flashbacks either when I was hypnotized or right after the sessions.

At first, he had me relax while he counted backward to hypnotize me. But it got to a point where I could just go into an immediate trance by closing my eyes, and I was his. He had a very hypnotic voice.

Next I started having flashbacks of being in a bathtub, being abused by either my Mom or my brother. I kept having fingernails molest me, hurting my vagina. I couldn't put a face on it, but Steve said it had to be my mother. And it really did physically hurt, like it was happening right then. The focus came to be on my mother. Steve really hated her; I think he had a thing against mothers.

I never totally cut off from my parents. I'm a single mother, and they helped me with my daughter Jennifer. Steve tried to convince me that my parents were sexually abusing her, but I never bought it. My daughter was different from me, so bubbly and self-assured. And they seemed to be so good with her. Steve called a social worker once to evaluate the situation, and I was so scared I would lose my child. I had to take her to counseling, and the lady said, "I see no indication of sexual trauma, but just to be certain, she should have a gynecological exam." No way, I wouldn't do it, I thought it would be too traumatic for her. It's a good thing I didn't, or I might have lost her.

What I was going through was terrible for Jennifer. She loved my parents, and she loved me. And I just hated my mother through this whole thing – it confused Jennifer and tore her up. Jennifer was basically the mother in the family for a while. I would be in my room chain-smoking for days at a time, and she was pretty much left on her own. Also, when I would be having a flashback and would call Steve, he told me it was healthy to beat on the bed in front of her. He said it was a healthy way to exhibit rage.

Along about April 1986, I started having flashbacks of Mom sexually abusing me with a coat hanger. That went on for quite a few months. I would be like a little child, curled up in a ball screaming. It was still going on when we started the group. There were about ten of us. Steve brought in a co-leader, Dave, who had a Ph.D., but it was really Steve who was the leader. They were like Frick and Frack, Tweedledee and Tweedledum. Dave wore this very obvious, gross toupee, and he had on real tight pants. He'd sit with his legs spread apart. Mostly, he was just a puppet for Steve.

At first, we just interchanged ideas and talked in the group, and it was kind of neat. I felt a camaraderie with these women. But it kept escalating. Late in 1987, I was really bad off, and I'd accidentally over-dosed on Xanax and had nothing in my stomach. I went into the hospital on a Friday night for the first of two stays. They were both 30 days long. Oh, yeah, I was only sick for as long as my insurance lasted, 30 days per calendar year [*laughs*]. It turns out that Steve was the therapist for the psych ward at the hospital, so I saw him three days a week individually, every day in group, and on Monday nights. Plus, on Sun-days he'd lead what he called a "spiritual rap session," and he'd wear this ridiculous motorcycle jacket for that.

Anyway, the following Monday night we had the group. Someone said, "You look tired; are you okay?" I lied and said, "Yeah," and Steve lit into me. For two hours, he screamed. He made me talk about my mother, have more flashbacks. It was a very loud, traumatic few hours. They put a coat hanger up on the clay wall for me to throw clods at. Did you see that TV show where those MPD women were doing that? They couldn't hold a candle to me. I had clay on my eyelashes. I was awful. I tell you, I could throw some clay! There's no doubt that I was angry, all right, but it wasn't "getting out" my anger. It was creating it. It just makes you madder. I was so mad by the time I left that group. I was in a rage for four consecutive years.

After that, the group got more like that all the time. The next week, some other girl would scream and carry on. It was like they all wanted to get into that, getting more loud and hysterical. We'd be sitting there tearing up phone books, beating on chairs with bataaka bats, and Steve or Dave would be screaming in our ears, reading aloud from the terrible things we had written about what we had "remembered."

Then the blood drinking and satanic abuse stuff started. First one girl had an alter, then she started cutting herself. That really got Steve's attention. Then it started with more horrific rapes, the whole nine yards. I had these horrible flashbacks of being given cold enemas and various objects inserted into my vagina. Another time, I remembered my brother and his friends hung me by my feet. It was only recently that I realized where those particular images came from. The enemas and insertion came from the book *Sybil*, and the upside down hanging came from a movie called *Deranged*, which I saw when I was 17. And I had incorporated some of a story I once wrote about identifying a prostitute's body in the morgue. So different pieces of my life that had nothing to do with me being abused became part of the flashbacks. It's amazing to me that my subconscious mind had served them up without my knowing where they came from.

I eventually came up with scenes of group sexual abuse and being raped by animals. After I had a vision of a dead man hanging from a rope, my grandfather, the murderer, got added to the abuser list. But it was mainly my mother who was the target of my anger. Steve convinced me that she had been trying to kill me for years. I interpreted everything she did that way, so when she bought cookies, it was to encourage my binges. Everybody in the group was encouraged to divorce their families and make the group their new family. If anybody expressed any doubts, Steve and Dave would goad them. "You're in denial." The rest of us would join in. "You want to stay sick for your family. You don't want to get well."

I got worse. I vomited more and more, and my life seemed out of control. Even though I landed twice in the hospital with overdoses, my doctor kept prescribing Xanax for me and pills for every other ailment – to sleep, to stop depression, to mellow out. Some of my friends at the police station where I worked saw me going through this. One officer told me, "This guy is a quack. You're turning into a pillhead." I pulled the phone out of the wall and threw it at him. I said, "You don't understand, I've got to get worse before I get better, and this man is going to save my life."

By 1989, my mind was so cluttered with cults and Satanism, I didn't know where I was half the time. In one of my last sessions, I actually started to talk about some of my real-life problems – money, my daughter, my job – and Steve just sat there with this big smirk on his face. I stopped and said, "What the fuck is your problem?" He said, "You're avoiding your real issues; you're not working." If you weren't screaming or having flashbacks, you weren't working. I just lost it. "Let me tell you something, asshole. Every single day of my life is work, just to stay alive." At that point, I would just sit in my room smoking and thinking of ways to kill my Mom.

All this time, Steve kept telling me I had to get worse before I got better. I was sick of hearing how you have to get worse. I was about as worse as you could get. By that time, I was about to lose my house. I had given every penny, every ounce of energy, to this therapy. I had used up all my sick time and vacation time. I was still horribly bulimic, but I had gained a hundred pounds during the four years of therapy. One day late in 1989, I called him, all excited about writing a book about my experiences at the police station. And you know what he said to me when I called? "You're not finished with the flashbacks." And something snapped. I thought, "Oh, yeah, asshole, I am. Four years of getting worse is enough."

So I quit and went to Linda, a woman therapist. She believed I had been an incest victim, all right, but she didn't egg it on. I couldn't deal with anything except grieving over the loss of Steve for a long time. I was so depressed, I didn't really accomplish anything. Then one day in 1991, I read an article in a local magazine about false memory syndrome, with an interview with parents who had lost their daughter. They sounded like nice people. I had been in the group with their daughter, and I'd heard all these horrible stories about them. So I sought them out and met them. They're no more Satanists than I am. One night Steve told us he had to call the police on them, that they had come to their daughter's house threatening her. It turns out they were bringing her Christmas presents.

It was like a light came on in my head. When I realized what had been done to me, I called a good psychologist. I told him, "These flashbacks seemed so real, I mean they were *really* real." He said, "They were real, honey, but not reality." I'll never forget those words. I like, fell off this bed, because I had put my life into a fantasy. After I realized that none of these flashbacks were true, I filed my lawsuit. I also went back to Linda, my good counselor. She accepted that I had made up all the abuse. Now, all of us from the group have called it quits except one girl, who is a tragic case. She accused her mother of satanic ritual abuse, of murdering her twin at birth. It didn't matter that there was a single child registered on the birth certificate. The coven had taken care of that.

I strongly recommend getting a good counselor to people coming out of this mess. They need to set boundaries and appropriate limits, to find a way to feel good about themselves – all the stuff these trauma counselors talk about but don't really do. My Mom and I really do have some problems to work out, but nothing about sexual abuse. It's getting better, not so bad. My bulimia is completely gone now. I don't really know why. In these last few months, I've really taken responsibility for my own life. No more playing the blame game. I realized that if anything was going to change in my life, I'd have to do the changing. I'm more assertive now, don't hold things in as much.'

MARIA GRANUCCI, RETRACTOR

It's an all-too-familiar story. Maria Granucci, now 37, was too smart and competent for her own good, since she had an insecure, incompetent male boss at her accounting firm. By November of 1988, she couldn't take his verbal and physical abuse any more. When she complained to senior management, they 'solved' the problem by taking her and her boss to lunch for a chat. On the verge of a nervous breakdown, Granucci quit. Soon afterward, she thought she was dying of a heart attack but was diagnosed in a local Virginia emergency room as suffering from a panic attack instead. A nurse suggested she see clinical psychologist Karen Meynert.

'Karen seemed very concerned and compassionate but also very assertive from the beginning of our therapy sessions. She's four years older than me. She probably did more talking than I did. She always insisted on me paying and scheduling the next appointment before our session began.

I kept trying to focus the sessions on why I could not handle this boss, so the same thing wouldn't happen again. Karen kept refocusing them back on my childhood. At the very beginning, she asked if I was ever sexually abused. I said, "Absolutely not!" and she backed off. But she harped on the fact that I could not handle this work relationship because I had been emotionally abused by my father. She also intimated that I had married a man somewhat like my father, so I continued to live in this emotionally abusive situation by choice. She said it was good that I had this breakdown so I could now break this pattern and learn to be my own person.

In a way, I really was emotionally neglected by my parents. When I was 10, my parents told me I was too old to kiss them good night any longer, telling me, "You're a grown-up now." I strove to be an adult at age 10 to please them. So there has always been this emotional void in my life due to lack of open affection from my parents. Also, I was the oldest of four girls in a blue-collar family, but I had this 157 IQ, which is two points higher than Einstein's. They really didn't know what to do with me.

Still, I wasn't buying into the dysfunctional family scenario too well until Karen finally realized that she had to take the intellectual route to get to me. She started giving me written assignments. At first, it was writing unmailed letters to my former boss, then to my parents. Then I read *Little Miss Perfect* by Melody Beattie. I did see a lot of myself in that book. It did not talk about incest, but it identified emotional abuse. Then we went on to *The Drama of the Gifted Child* by Alice Miller, and all the rest of the Alice Miller books.*[5] I did writing assignments on all these, analyzing the books.

Finally, in April 1993, Karen asked me if I was willing to discuss possible incest issues. She had groomed me for over four years to get to this point. In desperation to get well, I said I was willing to entertain the thought. Karen gave me a copy of *The Courage to Heal*, and soon after that, I succumbed completely and became a Survivor.

I never developed any specific times and places, but I was sure the abuse had occurred on a continual basis between the ages of 5 and 15, when I met my future husband Tom. Karen wanted to hypnotize me to do age regressions, but I wouldn't do it. Instead, we did relaxation exercises, which I have since learned were really hypnotic sessions. Karen would turn off the lights, tell me to shut my eyes and relax my body, and she would put on relaxation tapes. She always took me to a safe place, which was my bedroom, sitting on my bed with a pile of books. I always have been an avid reader and still read six books a week, on average. The door would always be shut.

---

* Here is how Alice Miller begins her 1991 book, *Breaking Down the Wall of Silence*: 'The truth about childhood, as many of us have had to endure it, is inconceivable, scandalous, painful. Not uncommonly, it is monstrous. To be confronted with this truth all at once and to try to integrate it into our consciousness, however ardently we may wish it, is clearly impossible.' She goes on to recommend recalling and resolving 'every facet of the original experience within a process of careful therapeutic disclosure.'

Then I would remember my father invading my safe spot by entering the room and closing the door behind him. I would picture him demanding that I take off my clothes. At first, I would remember him just looking at me. Then it proceeded to, "My God, he fondled me!" Finally, as I got older in my memories, I realized that he repeatedly penetrated me.

I began to have flashbacks during sexual relations with my husband. Karen interpreted these as flashbacks for me. If Tom touched me in a certain way, I would scream and back off, sometimes picturing my father above me. For about two months, Tom and I stopped having sex, at Karen's suggestion. It was making the flashbacks occur too often.

Karen asked me if my father ever hit me. I said, "No." She asked if I ever hurt myself, and I told her how I had fallen on the ice when I was seven and broken my nose. She convinced me that I was protecting my father, that he had broken my nose while forcing me to have sex. This was my life pattern, she said, to take the blame on myself.

I became completely distraught throughout this summer and fall of 1993. I was put on medical leave from my bank job, but then I couldn't go back. I lost 65 pounds. I became very ill and suicidal. Karen told me I was in no condition to see my family, so I cut off all contact, but I didn't tell them why. Karen referred me to a psychiatrist, who put me on Prozac, the tranquilizer Klonopin, and lithium. I became a walking zombie, I was so heavily medicated.

My husband and children did not know what to do with me. Tom didn't know if he should institutionalize me. I got in car accidents because I was on medication. Luckily, no one ever got hurt. In July, Tom took my license away from me. Karen suggested that I should divorce him because our relationship was dysfunctional, like my childhood. She said I could not get well and remain married to Tom. But even in this state, I clung to him. Still, I was totally dependent on Karen. To pay for my sessions, I spent all our savings and remortgaged the house.

Tom believed all of the incest allegations against my parents. They became the answer to my behavior and explained our marital problems.

Finally, on October 4, 1993, I sat down at my computer and typed out a four-page confrontation/accusation letter to my parents in which I told them my pain was "beyond horrendous." I wrote, "You thought you had got away with it. The 'good' daughter had repressed forever. Not a chance, Dad." I accused my father of repeated rapes, but I also blamed my mother, who must have known what was going on. "Why didn't you save me? I am your child. Was your fear of Dad so great it came before my safety?" Finally, I told them how much all this was costing – over $4600 just in the last two months – and complained that we had lost virtually all our old friends. I wrote, "Our world has shrunk so small."

I mailed the letter before I could have second thoughts and brought a copy with me to my next therapy session. I was so proud that I had the guts to do it on my own. Karen went wild. She stood up, shook her fist, and said, "How dare you do something like this without asking my approval first?" She was livid. I had never seen her like that, and it scared the shit out of me. Our roles were that she was the mother and I was the child. I had done something wrong again. I agonized over disappointing her.

My father, an electrical engineer who had retired a few years earlier after a serious heart attack, responded on October 18 with a 20-page letter accounting for every minute of his life. He denied everything. He said he knew I'd like to hear him say he was sorry, but that would be wrong. He said he and my mother still loved me, but they were very hurt. I showed the letter to Karen, and she said, "There is guilt written all over this letter. This is a very guilty man. You should think about pressing charges."

At that point, I began to question what she wanted from me. I just wanted to get better. I did not want to put my father in jail for something that happened so long ago. I wanted to live my life ahead. I was also internally doubting all this, but I was afraid to tell Karen.

During this period, I sometimes did not sleep for five days straight. Then I would catch a few hours and go without sleep for another few days. I had a lot of medical problems as a result of the stress and weight loss – boils, cysts, a broken hand and foot. After I received the letter from my father, I became even more distraught, if that was possible. Tom became very concerned about the stability of the household, which had been in jeopardy for so long. He took my medication away and said, "You are not taking any more." I became very angry. He said he was only trying to help me, that he didn't know what else to do besides institutionalize me.

So Tom and I agreed to a withdrawal plan. I was off all the medication in four weeks. As I came off it, I started to become myself again, started to feel clear, real, tangible. I also stopped seeing Karen during that time, on my husband's insistence. He is a very smart man, a saint. He saved my life.

In November, I told Tom that I was beginning to question the accusations. He was horrified. "If that's so, how are we going to fix what we have done to your family?" He jointly took responsibility. Over the next two weeks, I reread the letters and parts of *The Courage to Heal.* Finally, I said, "I have got to fix this."

The last week of November, I made an appointment with Karen. I told her I no longer believed the accusations, that I felt nothing but shame for these bogus memories. I asked her for help to fix the mess I'd made. Karen said, "Oh my God, you've re-repressed and you are in denial again. It was too painful for you. Now we have a lot of work ahead of us. We've taken quite a step backwards." I saw what she was up to, because I had been away from her for a while and was not medicated. She said, "Do not apologize to your parents until this is straightened out. Do not call or see them."

The next day, one of my mother's best friends, who knew nothing about any of this, called to ask me how my father was. He had suffered a massive stroke. I called my mother and told her I had to see her, that I was so sorry, that I wanted to see Dad. I thought she understood that I was taking the accusations back, but I've since learned that Mom didn't understand that. Because of the stroke, my father didn't remember anything about the allegations. Mom was afraid that if he saw me, it would trigger his memory of it and would cause him to have another stroke which might be fatal this time. So she had a restraining order put on me to keep me away from his hospital room.

I was in hell with worry and guilt. Finally, I was called to come to the hospital. It turned out that my father kept asking for me, wondering why I wasn't there. My father cried when he saw me and hugged me. It felt so good. He asked, "Where have you been? Why haven't you visited me?" I made up some excuse so as not to upset him. Later, I spent a long time explaining myself to my mother, my three sisters and their husbands. They finally accepted my retraction.

Since then, I have worked very diligently to regain my parents' and family's trust. At first, they thought I would change my mind again. Once they realized it was not temporary and that I had broken off therapy with Karen, it was better.

My father now knows what went on. When he moved to a rehabilitation center from the hospital, I spent 12-hour days by his side. He cries a lot. He is the most wonderful man. He calls *me* now and asks me how I'm doing. He tells me, "Please, don't get too depressed again." He's recovering nicely. He's 59. He's regaining his memory capacity slowly. Since the stroke was on the left side of the brain, he's paralyzed and blind on the right side. Dad is medically disabled and has to count on all of us now for a lot of support. I am just so grateful to be in his life again. Since the stroke, he's much freer with his affection. The void I always felt is finally full of wonderful love, hugs and kisses from my parents. I love them so.

My family had compiled articles and taped talk shows about something called false memory syndrome. I spent nine hours, all alone, reading this material and watching the tapes. I saw myself in them! I cried and cried, and I became very angry at Karen. I realized that my mind had been raped. I now feel that I was the perpetrator rather than the accuser. It is the shame I live with every day.

Now that there are more and more retractors, it's important to talk about it. Post-retraction is no bed of roses. There is a lot of pain and shame. I still have trouble dealing with it, but I will never go to a therapist again. The therapy I need right now is just what I am doing, being an advocate in any way possible for the FMS Foundation and telling my story. I only wish that I could tell my parents how sorry I really am. They will not let me. They don't want to talk about it. And my relations with my sisters are still very strained.

There's one thing I want to clear up. After hearing my story, somebody asked me, "Did you always have sexual fantasies about your father?" I was repulsed by the question. When I would picture my father on top of me instead of Tom, it was a sick delusion fostered by my toxic therapy, not a wish-fulfillment fantasy. I have never thought of my father in those terms. Similarly, I never had any sexual problems with my husband until this therapy.

I entered therapy in 1988 because of a job-related harassment issue, and I left in 1993 a suicidal wreck. It stole five years of my life. I became completely irresponsible and self-involved, but I blame Karen Meynert for what happened. She was the professional therapist who systematically led me down this road.'

FRANCINE BOARDMAN, RETRACTOR FROM DELIVERANCE MINISTRY

Francine Boardman and her daughter, May, have always been very close – too close, according to some members of the Liverpool Baptist church they

371

attended in 1989. The vicar and several elders had attended seminars at Ellel Grange, a Christian healing center in Leicestershire, where they learned about 'deliverance ministry' and how to identify and exorcise demons. Unbeknownst to her mother, 29-year-old May went for church counseling and became convinced that her mother was a witch. Distraught over her daughter's inexplicable distance, Francine sought out her vicar . . .

'I went to Vicar Tom Raseford and told him, "My family is falling apart, I don't know what's happening. Help." But he didn't seem interested in that. All he wanted to know was about my childhood. I told him that I couldn't remember much. My mother died when I was seven. I just didn't remember all that much, that was all there was to it. I said I came from a large family, a father and five children. My childhood was not especially unhappy. My older stepbrother was a bully, that was the only problem I could think of. He was 12 years older than me.

Tom Raseford didn't say much. He prayed a bit, then looked at me in a very strange way, and said, "Who are you?" I had no idea at the time what he was talking about, but it scared me to death. I nearly fainted. It was if he knew that it wasn't Francine speaking. The room went black, I went dizzy, and if I hadn't been sitting down, I would have passed out. Then it clicked with me that he was talking about demons. He got his wife Phyllis with him. She said the name of the demon was Malice, and they proceeded to try to cast out this demon. They held their hands up and said, "In the name of Jesus, come out."

I started coughing. A doctor told me since then that when you're frightened, your throat dries up. But Tom and Phyllis thought it was the demon coming out. The more I coughed, the more demons they thought I had. And the more frightened I got, the more I coughed. I was there for three hours that night, got exhausted, cried a lot, and got terribly upset. I was shocked and didn't quite know what to make of the whole thing.

As soon as I left the vicar and his wife the first time, I started getting pictures in my mind, hallucinations. They had suggested to me that there was witchcraft in my family. They probably knew that May thought I was a witch. I started having hallucinations of witches in the family. I had probably seen a TV program or movies, I'm sure that's where I got my fantasies from.

My imagination just went to work on it; I came up with this terrific story. Week after week, it got more lurid. It's hard to describe why I got into all of this. All of a sudden, I had this childhood background that nobody else had. All these stories of witchcraft were coming out.

I thought it was exciting in a way, I really did. This couple were giving me all their attention. They were basically pandering to whatever I said. They agreed with me, supported me, encouraged me to keep on bringing these things up, because they were convinced they were real memories. They sympathized with me. There were a lot of incest stories, so they prayed for me. I kind of became regressed into being like a child. I didn't think I could function without Tom and Phyllis as parents, and I became totally dependent on them, which they encouraged.

In these stories, my mother was a high priestess; my father wasn't really my father at all. My biological father was a local doctor, a satanist who had an affair with my mother. I was conceived specifically for devil worship. They operated a coven from the crypt of the local village church. I was born during the war and had been brought up specifically for child prostitution. When I reached the age of four, my assignment was to service the American Air Force personnel who were stationed in the Lincolnshire Airfield. I was given male semen to drink as part of the ritual. I was raped by the devil in the shape of Anubis, an Egyptian dog-god.

Where did I come up with these things? Well, I'm fairly well read, but I only read a book on satanism after all of these "memories" came up. Child prostitution was very common in Europe a few thousand years ago, and I probably had read about it.

Over time, the stories became even more elaborate and grotesque. I was laid in a coffin full of snakes with my mother and buried underground for a couple of hours, to prove that I was the devil's child and couldn't be killed by snakes. I really believed these things. It's rubbish, isn't it? They just came into my mind. You have to understand that I was in a terrible mental state, not calm and stable. I didn't sleep much for two years. I'd sleep about an hour a night. Somehow, I managed to hold down my job as a typist.

I wouldn't get visions during the sessions with the vicar and his wife. I'd usually get them in the middle of the night. They would happen just when I was going to sleep or waking up. I would be relaxing, just about to go to bed, when pictures would wake me up. They were quite vivid. On one occasion, I had the picture of this doctor who was supposed to be my father, and I couldn't get it out of my mind. Sometimes I actually saw witches and black cloaks outside the house at night.

I would go see Tom and Phyllis every Friday afternoon at 2 p.m., and I'd be there until 5 p.m. They did more than exorcisms. They would cut "soul ties." They would try to cut you off from your family and pray that God would cut the bond between mother and child, because they thought that would cut off the demons that came from me. This was for May's own good. But May kept seeing me anyway. I kept telling May this story, and she believed it. We found it quite a talking point. She said it actually made sense when she looked at her own deliverance.

The vicar and his wife were terribly interested in my sexual habits, and they asked questions and encouraged me to tell them all about my sexual exploits. For each one, they'd say there was a demon of intercourse or sex. Every person you've been to bed with, you have a soul tie, so they make an enormous meal out of it. I was divorced, which was a sin to start with. They wanted to know about sex before, during, or after my marriage. I wasn't having sex with anyone during the time of my counseling. I wasn't particularly interested in men at the time.

One day when she was sitting in church, Phyllis had a vision that I had a demon of murder. They then proceeded to exorcize this demon in a little room at the side after the service. When they exorcized this demon of murder, I got a picture of having murdered a baby. The satanic rituals were sacrificing babies to Satan, and they came from the female prostitutes having children by the U.S. Air Force men. After being murdered, their bodies were burned.

This went on for one and half years. I finally stopped it. I reached a stage when I was in terrible mental anguish. I would freak out, would try and scream because I felt so bad about everything, but nothing came out. If you've ever experienced real mental pain, you'll know what I'm talking about. This went on day after day after day. I started to turn away from Tom and Phyllis. I hated Phyllis. She was quite cruel. She always spoke to me as a demon. She never treated me like a human being.

I was aware of others who had been through exorcism, but I was their prize pupil. They told me that I would have to see them for about five years, and that was when I decided, no, I would not. I got some strength from somewhere. I rang them up and said, "I'm not coming any more."

They came to see me and just sat there looking at me, watching me. They asked how I was; I said I felt really ill. They said they would pray for me. I told them to get out of the house. They wouldn't go. I went into another room; they followed me. I again told them to leave, and they eventually went after a half hour.

When I told them to go, it was in June of 1991. Gradually, I realized that all of my stories were just stories. None of it was true, but I was still frightened and confused. I went to see a doctor in October. By this time, I had given up work. It became impossible to function. I was terrified everywhere I went. I was terrified of shopping, of speaking to people. I stayed at home all the time, just sat and watched Clint Eastwood movies on TV. The state was pushing me to go back to work, so I went to my doctor. I told him what had been going on, and he was wonderful. He sent me to a psychiatrist. She said I had been so badly hurt that I had become unbalanced, and she gave me drugs to make me sleep and for depression. They really helped, but that's how I lost my faith. The logic in my brain started working overtime. I haven't been to church since then.

The ironic thing is, May left her husband in June, and we bought a house together, and she was with me through all of this, coming out of the church, and she agreed with me. We decided it was all a load of rubbish and threw away our Bibles.

Tom and Phyllis get absolute power out of this. They are incredibly arrogant, and they have power over people. If you tell people they have demons and they are Christians, they will be horrified. The vicar and his wife say God tells them that there are demons inside people. I firmly believe that Tom's intention from the beginning was to split our family up. He felt we were too close together.

I take absolutely no responsibility whatsoever myself for what happened. I lay the blame at the vicar's door. The only part I played was, I was extremely vulnerable and unhappy. Me and May and her daughter live together. I'm 52 now. I am still taking medication. I live on invalidity benefits, long-term sickness benefits. I have difficulty with relationships to a certain extent. I don't want to get too close to anybody. I won't let them get close to my inner thoughts.'

LESLIE HANNEGAN, CHRISTIAN RETRACTOR

As a child, Leslie Hannegan suffered from a severe stutter. Lonely and imaginative, she lived, as she put it, 'in my own world,' even though she had two younger brothers. Her father was often deeply depressed, while her mother was frequently ill. 'I grew up Catholic, and that helped get me through,' she remembers. Whenever the other school children's taunts got to her, she'd listen to the choir sing 'Be Not Afraid,' and she felt the Lord's comforting presence. She suffered from the same depression as her father, however, from the third grade on. 'The only thing that gave me joy were ballet classes.' Still feeling awkward and lonely at 24, Hannegan met a man in 1991 who broke her heart. In the stressful wake of that disappointment, she attended a church function at which a Christian incest survivor spoke. It changed her life.

'I met Ray at a dance performance. He was involved in dance, drama, and singing. He was gorgeous and he was a Christian. We just fell in love with each other. A week later, he was calling, telling me I'd be his wife, wanting to know if I felt the same way. Oh, yes! He swept me off my feet.

[But when Hannegan visited him two months later, he acted completely coldly. The visit was a disaster. She cried the entire flight home.]

A week after I turned 24, he sent me a card saying, "You're not the one for me. I'm not going to marry you." That's when I started to hear this voice inside of me. I believed it was God's voice, telling me that Ray was going to be my husband. This could have been just my desires talking, but it seemed like a real voice to me. So I believed it. I kept hoping and hoping.

Because of this, I was very unhappy with myself. I started searching for what was the matter with me. I attended a large interdenominational Christian meeting here in Texas. The woman speaker was an incest victim from Washington State. She said, "There are women in the audience who don't remember any abuse, but their lives show it." She said, "You're going to start to remember it." It was just like a little light went off inside of me. I thought, "She's talking about me." It's kind of funny, but I finally felt special. It made me feel better, because it wasn't my fault why Ray didn't want me.

My mother went with me to this meeting, and I told her afterwards I felt I had been sexually abused. She asked, "Who could have done this to you?" At first I thought it was a 12-year-old babysitter when I was two. I went to the Christian bookstore and bought *Freeing Your Mind From Memories That Bind*, by Fred and Florence Littauer. They go around the country and give lectures and pass out a quiz asking, "Do you have these kinds of feelings?" They tell you that three out of four people were abused but just don't remember it. They take people through age regression and say that the Holy Spirit is leading them back through time. This is all described in the book.*[6]

---

* Even in comparison to *The Courage to Heal*, the Littauers' book is incredibly suggestive. *Freeing Your Mind From Memories That Bind* offers an extensive list of 'symptoms' of repressed sexual abuse memories, including pre-menstrual syndrome, asthma, migraines, insomnia, vague bodily pains, or even nose-picking. The book is loaded with 'Christian' advice. The Littauers suggest keeping a 'prayer journal,' for instance: 'In it, each day, write out to God your pleading to find the truth of your past, no matter how painful it may be. Write out your prayers, word for word, just as though you were writing a letter to God, asking Him to come and help you.'

Because they wrote that the Lord had told them this truth, I trusted them. I put all my faith in what they told me to do. I also read *The Wounded Heart* by Dr. Dan Allender, which encourages you to write stuff without thinking about it. So I did a lot of that.

Ever since I was little, I've had paralysis in my dream state, where I feel like I'm awake, but I can't move. I would see things, like another realm opened up to me. There would be incredible fear with it. It always seemed that something came into my room and touched me. This got more intense after I converted to evangelical Christianity when I was 19. After I accepted that I was an abuse victim, it got much worse. It was constant, almost every night. Most of the time, I was frozen. I couldn't even scream. Things would be flying into my room, getting on top of me, molesting me. Some were evil-looking inhuman things.

I told my mother about these episodes. When this happened to me, when I could finally get up, I'd run sleep with her, because I didn't want to be alone. Dad had taken early retirement by then and was away at a church retreat for a month. I put two and two together and thought that these dream experiences must have been memories of torments, maybe satanic.

My anger and fear were getting worse and worse, but I didn't know where to direct them. I had this dream two nights in a row, of this dragon. The second night, it had my father's face. And I just knew the dragon's name was Incest. Something inside me screamed, "Daddy, Daddy, why did you hurt me?" I felt so betrayed. The horror and shame came flooding in right then, in the middle of the night. I was in shock.

Prior to this time, I did have a hard time with my father. We were both depressed and living at home. I had a hard time talking to him but couldn't figure out why. Now the pieces started to fit together.

I didn't tell my mother right away. I wanted to deal with it and get healed. I thought the Lord was helping me and would bring the past up and let me be healed. That's what these books were telling me. So I just trusted myself to the Lord. After two weeks, though, I told my mother, because it hurt so bad. I don't know if she believed me at first. I just know I sure needed her. We called Sharon Purcell, a Christian social worker with a private practice. I told her I was an incest victim and needed help. I said I didn't have clear pictures, and she said, "We'll work on those."

Sharon would pray and lead me into age regression. She'd bring me back to the womb and I'd go from there. Anything painful we came across, she'd bring Jesus into it, so the Lord would be there for this painful time. Only nothing ever surfaced during the sessions. It was always on my own. She encouraged me to journal more, so I did. And she wanted me to look at old photographs. Dad has taken so many great pictures of us. There was this one picture of me as a little girl by my parents' bed, with a pocket book on my shoulder, that really triggered me. I'm so uncomfortable about the story that got built around this picture, I'd rather not talk about it.

I got a lot of body memories. One day when I was journaling, my head got thrown back and I was gagging and could not breathe. It was almost like I was choking. That's why I assumed that he forced his penis into my mouth and I was remembering it.

I was so convincing. I would beat myself, scratch my arms, hit my legs, and try to pull out my hair. I hated myself so much. It was hard to believe that nothing had happened to me. The betrayal I felt seemed to indicate it was someone close to me who had done this.

After a month of therapy, Sharon told me I was healed and that the next step was for me to write to my father, so my family would get better and come to counseling. So I wrote him a letter, telling him I forgave him for the incest. I truly believed it would take a load off his shoulders, and we could be a family again. I wasn't trying to get back at him. I saw my father as a hurting person who had been abused himself. I felt compassion for him.

He was crushed. He cried hysterically and told the other people at the retreat about the letter. He told my brothers, and I didn't want them to know about it until he admitted it. My brothers were really angry at me. I became more of a mess. My father came back home. He went to see my counselor and said he was very concerned about me.

Then Sharon met with me and said she wasn't sure he did it. That was the ultimate betrayal. She had committed me to writing something so horrible, something you can't back away from – when she wasn't even sure herself. I was amazed and hurt. I left her.

So I went through agony for another year without counseling. After a year, I went to another Christian counselor, a blind woman in her late 40s, and she was wonderful. She said, "Well, what do you remember about this abuse?" I said, "Not much." She asked, "Are you sure this really happened to you?" I felt angry at first that she didn't believe me, but she was just asking questions. Finally she said, "We're not going to go into your past. We're going to help you get strong again, to be able to get out of bed every day." She didn't say, "I don't believe you." She just said, "Let's help you to cope." She prayed with me. I really started feeling God's love again. For a while I was angry at Him for letting me go through this.

I was sick of trying to look at my past. I just wanted to get on with my life and forget about it. I was still going to the Christian Church of God, an evangelical, charismatic nondenominational church. My pastor does not believe that psychiatry offers any permanent solution. He believes that only the Lord heals. When I told him at the beginning of all this that my father had done this to me, he didn't say anything to me. One weekend, my pastor and his wife saw a newscast on false memory syndrome. They realized that the Holy Spirit was telling them that what I was remembering was false. They prayed on that.

The following Monday night, just before Good Friday, my pastor gave a sermon, saying many of the same things as usual. "We're a new creation. The old one is gone. We're born again, and we don't have to look into our past." Then he said something that was directed straight at me. "There is a deception, an evil spirit from the pit of Hell, crossing the earth, causing false memory syndrome."

I couldn't believe my pastor was saying this. I was shocked and hurt. I made an appointment to see his wife to show her that God was healing me. I brought my journals in, but she didn't want to hear them. She was very strong with me. She said, "Leslie, you are having a nervous breakdown. We care about you so much, and we don't want this to happen to you." A couple of times I almost got up and left, I was so angry. But after an hour, it was like a wall coming down around me. I suddenly realized that it wasn't that terrible if I was wrong. I've always wanted to be perfect, to stay in complete control. But at this point, the fear and pride left, and it wasn't that bad to be wrong. I realized how selfish I had been, how much I had hurt my family. Being a Christian, I needed to release my father. I felt so awful.

I waited three days and wrote him a card on Good Friday of 1993. When he got it, he cried for joy. I was afraid he'd be angry, that he would never speak to me again. But we all embraced – my father, my mother, and me, and started the healing. It was wonderful.

Ever since I came out of this, it's incredible how rapidly I've been healed. I don't listen to that voice any more. I've come to realize it was different from the Lord's voice. It had a selfish intent, focused only on me. To be honest, I do actually believe it was an evil spirit.

Now I am a whole, productive human being. I'm doing well at my job in human resources at a major corporation. I love myself now. I'm coordinator of a Christian dance team, too. Someday, I want to have a good relationship with a man. I'm looking forward to having a husband and kids.

I speak out now about what happened to me. I'm particularly concerned about the misuse of Christianity. These Christian therapists say, "Get the anger out at your parents." But Jesus never said that. He said, "Don't let the sun go down on your anger." When you're angry, you're sinning against someone. I'm concerned that the Christian church is being deceived. These therapists truly believe the Lord is showing them this and that it is a real healing process. If they believe the Lord is telling them, they won't listen to anyone else. There's a stubbornness there.

Maybe if they hear from another Christian, they might listen. I am going to write to the Littauers and to the first speaker who led me into this deception.'

NELL CHARETTE, MPD RETRACTOR

Nell Charette, a 35-year-old Canadian cleaning woman, believed until recently that her alcoholic father had violently sexually abused her during her childhood. Her numerous interior alter personalities told her so during therapy sessions and in her copious journal entries. Yet something inside her resisted confronting her parents, and she eventually rebelled against the diagnosis – and against Milt Kramer, her therapist, a charismatic American expatriate with a master's in counseling who convinced many of the women in this 5,000-person town that they possessed multiple personalities which only he could cure. Nell first visited Kramer after work in an ACOA (Adult Children of Alcoholics) group. She had already read John Bradshaw and watched his videos, and she had heard that this new American therapist did wonderful inner-child work . . .

'I liked Milt from the beginning. He seemed to be one of the nicest men I'd ever met. Very kind, very understanding of anything I said, no matter how off the wall it was. If I did something totally irresponsible at work, he would turn it around so I was the victim in the situation. It felt good. He's about 42, very attractive, with a mustache, a very kind face, sort of like a left-over hippy-type look. Laid back. He made you feel like he very much believed in feminist ideals, that women have been so wronged.

At first, Milt just gathered basic information about my childhood. My Dad is a recovering alcoholic, and we talked about that. There were many times I couldn't remember in detail from my childhood – nothing major, no giant gaps, I just couldn't remember every incident. Milt asked me a lot about abuse. He said I was definitely emotionally abused, and he wondered about physical and sexual abuse. I remembered Dad spanking me, though not very often, but no sexual abuse. So Milt left that alone for a long time. But he encouraged me to read *The Courage to Heal*. I must have read that book about eight times.

Then, after about six months of weekly sessions, we started doing what he referred to as mild relaxation technique, which I've since learned was really hypnosis. We created together a safe spot. At first, I didn't know what that was, but he helped me to find this place in my own head that I could go to. I would close my eyes, and I would walk up some steps, and by the time I reached the ninth step, there would be a door, and when I went through, there was my safe spot. It was a wooded area with water, trees, and what-not. It was weird. I was always amazed that it seemed so real, so very real. You don't usually see your thoughts so clearly.

The first time, I met my inner child, which he referred to as "Little Nellie." She was a pathetic little thing, very real, like looking at a real eight-year-old. This was the wounded me, he told me. I could hardly bear to look at her, and there was so much pain in her voice. I didn't want to be around her. She had memories of my childhood, he told me, and I was to embrace her and tell her that I was there for her and to trust me. We would work together, and whatever memories she had, she would safely release them to me.

I don't remember feeling that bad when I was eight. But I wasn't real happy with my childhood, had some anger toward Dad, because he just was never there. But Mom was wonderful – she picked up the pieces. Dad and I were too much alike – we rubbed each other the wrong way. I was cold toward him, and he has a hard time showing his feelings. He's a laborer for the town he lives in.

I eventually got so I could just close my eyes and be in my safe spot without going up the steps or anything. Milt was always talking in a soothing voice. Around the third time I went to the safe spot, lo and behold, there's two more parts of me, one a boy of fourteen named Pete, and the other a one-and-a-half-year-old baby. Milt was just thrilled that I would come up with these other two. No, he didn't suggest them to me. They were just there. He *would* often say to me about Little Nellie, "Are you sure she's the only one?"

I had no idea of multiple personalities at the time. We had talked about dissociative disorder, but I had no idea what it was. Milt explained that it was parts of me that had taken trauma or pain as a child, so I split off in my own head. I was really upset about that idea, and I said, "What are you talking about, like Sybil?" He laughed and said, "No." I said, "Well, if there's something wrong with me, I want to fix it." Oh, yes, I guess I *did* know about multiple personalities, I'd read about Sybil and Eve. But I never, ever dreamed it would be something I had.

That was a weird session, with Pete and The Baby. I was really upset after it, blown away. One inner child I could handle, but a couple more scared me. So I began to keep a journal. Milt told me to let my inner children write it. I had to go to my safe spot and use my left hand if I was having difficulty.

I began to write the most horrifying things you can imagine. This Little Nellie said my Dad repeatedly sexually abused her, beat her, just horrible things. I was writing it all down. I was thinking I was nuts. I brought it to Milt and said, "This is all garbage, you might as well call Watkinsburg [the local provincial hospital]. I need to be there, there's something wrong with me, none of this is true." That's when he started talking MPD talk. He said, "You're angry, you're in denial. These aren't *your* memories, they're your alters'." That was the first time that word came up. I was really blown away. I thought, "My God, what am I doing, this is nuts." But I kept going back to see him.

I kept writing these notebooks. I couldn't understand why I was writing this crap. I mean it was horrible, it was pornographic. In the next two years, I filled 15 notebooks. And that's nothing, one girl in our MPD group has 75 notebooks filled with poetry, artwork, and stuff. I was really freaked by this alter stuff, so that's when Milt integrated Pete. He just said, "Pete will walk through your back." I didn't really feel much.

But lo and behold, the next session, I go to my safe spot, and there's a whole slew of them, coming out from behind trees. It was terrifying. This started about nine months before I left therapy. All these alters – one named Flo, she was 21 maybe, the tart in me; June, she was the spiritual one; Fred, who wanted to die; Sarah, who was a child about 11; Herbert, who was this paranoid little thing. They told me their names and I told Milt. This was all frighteningly real to me. And each and every one remembered all the horrible things my Dad did to me.

I never confronted Dad, but I started alienating myself from my parents, and I kept asking my mother for information from my childhood, at Milt's suggestion. I asked her about hospital visits I had, certain times in my life, what did we do, where was Dad, was she working then. We were pretty close prior to this. I stopped visiting home. I couldn't talk with her about her memories of the past, because I thought she was in denial. I'd say, "Why talk about the past? You don't remember it in reality anyway." She didn't understand what I was talking about. Milt wanted me to confront my father, say, "I know what you did to me," and see how Dad would handle it. But I didn't really buy into it. I knew a girl who did bring her father in. He was just outraged, told the therapist, "You're off the wall, what are you doing to her?" She was devastated and didn't have a family any more. I mean, these were all alters' memories, not mine. It wasn't a real truth to me yet. But I did start to take on the feelings of a Sexual Survivor.

Meanwhile, I joined this group of MPDs, all being treated by Milt. It seemed kind of weird that all of us had alters, but he said, "You know, you do attract your own kind." This was all very culty, in retrospect. I didn't know these gals other than to say, "Hi, how are you," before this group. Then I became very close to them.

We all became really ill. I went for three months before I left therapy. It was really sick. Milt only attended the first session, then said it was our group. We shared our journals, talked about our work, our feelings, our alters. Now I see that those of us who were in longer, who accepted MPD, were teaching the ones just coming in to be it, to live it. It was like we fed off each other, and the sicker we were, the better. It was sort of like, "Who can top this?" with the journals. Milt said, "If you accept it, and stop denying, we can deal with it." There was a lot of jealousy in that room about him. Somebody would say they spent three hours with him, another went for a walk with him, and we were like cats. I'd think, "Why not me?"

There was a lot of what they call transference going on. You kinda start liking him for more than a therapist, and he fed off it. He'd take me for drives in the country, and we'd talk. He didn't charge for that. I even went to his house a couple of times and cleaned it, I'm embarrassed to say. We'd have coffee. He lived alone, and he told me how lonely he was, how hard it was to meet people in a small town, and how people always expected something from him. I found out later that he was having sex with one of his patients, and another one thought he was going to marry her.

I became really ill through this. At the end, I was hallucinating, seeing myself as other people. I'd look in the mirror and it wouldn't be me, it would be one of my alters. I was just a mess. I wasn't sleeping, running on an hour of sleep a night. I wrote in my journals at all hours. I started eating compulsively, crazy things like bags and bags of popcorn. I always had headaches, and I started mutilating myself, really disgusting. I started pulling my toenails off, and I'll tell you, I didn't feel anything. I would rip the whole nail right off, blood all over the place.

Milt said it was one of my alters in pain, and they were trying to get my attention. If I didn't get into this abreactional work, they would turn on me. I was terrified of abreaction work, where you relived your trauma, and I wouldn't do it. I had seen one woman in my group who was black and blue from head to toe after a three-hour abreaction session. Her nose was bleeding, her breast was bruised, the middle part of her back, and supposedly her alters were doing this to her. I think now Milt did it to her. My God, the shape I saw that woman in!

We all started showing signs of satanic ritual abuse. Upside-down crosses started to show up in pictures, lots of blood. And in my safe spot, I had a black shadowy sort of figure in a robe with a priest's hood and couldn't see his face. A lot of the other girls had grown up here in town, and they started to remember a lot of the same abusers. Milt asked one girl to get a list of the priests around here. Oh, yeah, he was working on it.

I became really worn down and exhausted, and because I do have a lot of good friends, they said, "You're looking like shit, not making any sense, what are you doing?" I finally met with Milt one day outside the office and said, "I can't handle it right now, I'm going to stop for a month, give myself a break." He said, "By all means," because I wasn't planning to leave permanently.

During that month, I started noticing how goddamn sick we all were. I wasn't writing in my journal, and things started to become clear. One girl was suicidal, another's relationship was breaking up. I thought, "Something is really wrong here." The longer I stayed out of therapy, the more I started seeing it for what it was. The voices started disappearing from my head, that was a biggie. Before that, there were constant conversations going on in my head. Even making a cup of coffee was a major ordeal. One alter drank coffee black, one regular. There were eight different people telling you what to do. My headaches started going away. I was sleeping again.

I decided to get a second opinion and met with the director at Milt's health clinic, a psychiatrist. Before that, I was terrified to see a psychiatrist, because Milt had told me that they treated MPD with shock treatment and drugs. Instead, Milt had me see a woman who specialized in MPD, and of course she confirmed the diagnosis, since she's on this kick, too. Anyway, Milt's boss was blown away by what I told him. He gave me a paper on false memory syndrome to read, to take home. He told me he didn't think I had MPD, that it was being created in me.

I finally got the courage to talk to another MPD group member. She got out for a couple of weeks, and we started comparing journals and sessions, how we felt about Milt, our safe spot. It turns out we all had the same safe spot, all had a shadowy hooded figure. It was like waking up from a bad dream and thinking, "What the hell have I done?" That was sort of the end of the beginning for me. I went to see an independent psychiatrist, took a bunch of tests. He said I'm fine, that I did not have MPD, never did.

My marriage was ruined by my therapy. All along, Dick, my husband, thought it was really sick, wanted me to get out of therapy. As a sexual survivor, I had stopped having sex at all with him. I wasn't able to function in that area. Dick didn't understand this dependency I had with Milt. He thought I was probably in love with this man. I was horrified that he would think that. But I *was* really dependent on Milt. I couldn't even go for a ride in my car without his permission. But I felt my husband didn't support me. Milt often told me that Dick was emotionally abusive to me, and that he was sexually abusive if he insisted on having sex. He told me to leave Dick towards the end and suggested a lawyer I should see.

We separated after I left therapy. There was too much already destroyed. I have three children – 12, 8, and 2 years old. They're with me. We've been separated a month and a half. Now I have a real fear of counselors.

My Dad knows now that I thought he sexually abused me. I had to tell him, because I'm involved in a civil suit against Milt. Mom and Dad have both been really understanding. Now they have an explanation for my behavior over the last couple of years. Dad has a really warped sense of humor. He said, "Didn't anybody ever tell you that some shrinks are crazier than we are? They hang around too many nuts; it rubs off on them." Mom got together different eight-millimeter films from my childhood for me to watch and got records of all my hospital visits. None have anything to do with sexual abuse. Everything that the alters wrote in those journals – it was all lies.

I can't really explain those journals. Maybe Milt gave me some kind of post-hypnotic suggestion. A lot of times – in my safe spot, I don't really remember what he said, but I know he was talking. We all just lived and breathed MPD. Oh, I functioned, took care of my children. I had a high-functioning alter, that's how Milt put it.

Yes, in a way being MPD made me feel special and creative. The bottom line is, I do have a lot of talents in me that I probably wouldn't have known about, but they're *my* talents, not my alters'. I'm creative, but it doesn't mean I'm MPD. When you have three children, you don't usually sit down and draw, but I've found I'm pretty good at it.

No, that discovery certainly isn't worth what I've been through and my ruined marriage. The hunt for sex abuse memories is the con of the '90s. If you don't want to take responsibility for your problems, what better way than to blame it on an alter? I've learned now to be responsible. But it was a road through hell and back again. I feel humiliated and stupid to have been so gullible. I hear "inner child" now and I cringe. What's the point of dwelling in the past? I have a hard time with the concept of repressed memories in general. I have a pretty good memory – I can remember my teachers' names. Who cares? It's like you're digging and you're digging, when it's all a lie. And I think this is taking away from dealing with actual sexual abuse. I know gals who really *were* sexually abused, and they have always remembered it, maybe not every detail, but why would they want to? Life does go on, and they don't obsess over it.'

STEPHANIE KRAUSS, RETRACTOR FROM A PSYCHIATRIC HOSPITAL

Stephanie Krauss really was sexually abused by her father, who began fondling her at a very young age. A salesman, he was very religious, as well as abusive and alcoholic. Eventually, other people, including members of her extended New Mexico family, also coerced her into having sex with them. Though she aspired briefly to be a marine biologist and diver, she dove into depression instead, dropping out of school when she was 15. 'I got involved in a number of promiscuous relationships. I went from one man to another to another. I think my lifestyle was a reflection of my upbringing.' As a young adult, Krauss sought counseling, which helped turn her life around. 'I was able to let the hate go.' She married, had two children, and was determined to get on with her life. When she was 34, however, she found herself becoming depressed and having marital problems. In 1991, she entered therapy again, but this time it was not to be a pleasant experience.

'I went to see a clinical social worker for what were really quite normal family problems. When she found out about my sexual abuse, though, she said I had post-traumatic stress disorder and should see Dr. Eugene Deming, a psychiatrist who specialized in that sort of thing. Dr. Deming seemed *wonderful* to me. He was gentle, sincere, intelligent, and articulate. He seemed so warm and trustable, and he listened with his whole heart. I felt that he was going to help me with all my troubles. I didn't worry as much. I had hope that things would get better.

I told him about my current problems, but he was more interested in my childhood. So I told him about my sexual abuse, but I didn't really feel the need to talk about it. I had been to therapy before and dealt with all of that. I don't like thinking about it. I always remembered I was abused. Even when you try to forget, the memories come back to haunt you, like ghosts rising to taunt you again.

Abuse does wound a person. Those wounds can heal, but they leave scars that may stay tender for the rest of your life. You may not dwell on it, but you never really forget that you were abused. After a while, though, that's all Dr. Deming wanted to talk about. He had lots of questions that he said needed to be answered before he could really help me. Some of his questions seemed a bit strange, but I just thought, "Well, he's the psychiatrist, he should know."

The sessions with Dr. Deming rekindled one of the things about my past that did still bother me. Why did I still love my father and yearn for his love in return? I think I saw in him and my other abusers the possibility of a life wasted. I realized that my own life could have been just as wasted as theirs if I did not rise above the bitterness and unforgiveness they harbored for whatever life had brought them. They took it in and it poisoned them.

In the middle of my therapy sessions, my father unexpectedly died of a heart attack. I had to make the funeral arrangements, and a lot of emotions came up for me – fear, guilt, numbness, disbelief, anger, confusion, love and hate. When I came back from the funeral, I was raw-nerved. It was the first time I'd been in the same room with this man that he had not hurt me some way. All of the years I had spent as an adult trying to get his love and attention in a healthy way were over. There would be no more chances.

So I told Dr. Deming about all this emotional turmoil and the flood of memories that had come back. He told me that I had many more memories that needed to come back if I was to get well. That was my real problem, not anything related to pressures of family or job. That confused me, because I didn't know I was sick. But Dr. Deming offered a concrete solution; he had the answers to the perplexing questions of my life. So when he told me that he thought I should enter this special unit at a nearby hospital, I listened.

He said that it was very important that I go in as soon as possible. He made it sound so wonderful. The hospital had programs and facilities especially geared to my needs, all covered by my company insurance. I could have a break from my regular life. That sounded tempting. I felt a bit guilty about taking advantage of the insurance company, but he said that's what it was for.

I felt like I could use a rest for a few days. I talked to my husband about it, and he was all in favor of it. It turns out that Dr. Deming had already called him and convinced him that I was deathly ill, and he should sign me in involuntarily if I wouldn't go on my own. But I didn't know that at the time.

In Dr. Deming's description of the hospital, he had compared it to a fine hotel. When I got there, I was in total shock. It wasn't anything like what he had said. The recreation facilities, the library, the manicured grounds, the jogging trails, those things were there, all right, but I was never allowed to use them. From the very first, I was treated more like a criminal than a patient. I saw people in restraints. Some of them were taken down by nurses and techs if they resisted. I was shocked to find children as patients in this environment. Even now, I cannot stand to hear a child cry, because the sound reminds me of the voice of a young patient in the hospital, begging to see her mother, crying to go home.

Because of my background, I've always felt that I deserved the bad things that happened to me. That was my initial reaction to the hospital. When Dr. Deming finally came to see me, I was so relieved. I didn't want him to leave me there. But he turned so cold. In our sessions, he was hostile. He kept insisting that I close my eyes and picture my abuse. I tried to cooperate, but my efforts were never enough. He told me I had been in a satanic cult, and that I had split off all these alters to cope with it. I knew about satanic cults from watching TV and from things I had read, but I didn't think I had been in one.

Still, if my dear Dr. Deming told me, maybe it was so. I loved him. I felt valued and important when I was with him. But I gradually came to realize that I was only valued if I stayed sick. He couldn't keep me in the hospital if I didn't have grave psychological problems. I had to be suicidal or homicidal. He interpreted all my actions and words that way, even though I told him I wasn't in a cult, and I wasn't suicidal. His response always indicated that I simply did not know the truth about myself.

If I did not behave in a way conducive to what he or the staff believed, I was "in denial," and "regressing," and I would be denied any privileges, like using the telephone or even sleeping in a bed. I finally managed to talk to my husband on the telephone. I told him that this place was not like we were told, that they had lied. I said that bad things were going on, that it was hurting and not helping, that I thought I would go nuts if I had to stay there. He didn't know what to think or what to do. A tech was listening in, it turns out. After that, they told me I couldn't make phone calls for a long time. I wasn't even allowed to see my children. I was put on "constants," where a tech sat with me all the time.

When my family and friends asked why I wasn't allowed to have visitors or phone calls, Dr. Deming would only say that there were "some things" going on. When they asked what he meant, he said he couldn't talk to them about it, because it would break the patient confidentiality law.

There sure was *something* going on I didn't understand, and I was terrified that it was a possibility that I really was a multiple personality and didn't know it. But I could see that most of the alters the patients had were created there in the hospital. Most of us went along with it so we wouldn't be put on restriction. Often they would threaten us, saying that if we didn't act right, we'd be considered untreatable, and they'd have to put us in the state hospital. They pushed people to the breaking point. I was close to mine.

I was drugged and obsessing over all the pain I had inside. I tried to explain what I felt, but they wouldn't listen to me. So to show them my pain, I started scratching myself up. They had told me that people like me would do those things, so I did. I figured they would understand that. All it got me was these mitts on my hands, kind of like boxing gloves. I couldn't even take them off to eat, so I had to kind of wedge a spoon up inside the mitt or I had to have a tech feed me.

It was like a drug store in there. One of the patients had been given over 20 different drugs at one time or the other. All of us were given at least one addictive drug. Many patients suffered various physical problems. We were physically sick a lot, but they ignored it most of the time, saying that everything was a body memory. A lot of the women had extremely long periods because of the drugs, or had two a month, or stopped having them at all. This was interpreted as evidence that different alters were out.

I was exhausted from fighting them – confused, drugged, and hopeless. I could feel myself emotionally slumping into compliance. I began to just go along with it all more and more. No matter how bizarre or unbelievable, I just did what I thought I was supposed to do to "get well." Some of the people there supposedly had animal alters. Nobody I knew actually had them for real. They were all made up to suit the doctors and their insatiable appetite to help us poor patients [*laughs*]. We patients tried to help one another by exchanging information on what worked or didn't work to get more privileges or stay out of trouble with the staff. We even managed to make jokes to keep ourselves going. Since Dr. Deming had told most of us that this would be like a hotel, we renamed the unit "Hell Hotel."

The smallest things became precious to me. I began to realize that the problems I had originally sought counseling for were trivial in comparison to what was happening to me in the hospital. Everything the patients did supposedly had some deep, troubling meaning to the staff. For example, in art therapy, if you put apples on your tree, or used different colors for your stick people – it meant something really significant. Every movement, every expression could help or harm you in the eyes of the staff. I think one of the scariest moments for me was when I realized that my doctor's wild imagination was becoming my reality. I fought to hold on to even a semblance of the truth I had once known. I knew I had to get out of that "twilight zone" of a hospital.

But it was almost impossible to get out. I know a woman who called 911 and told the police that these crazy people were holding her hostage. They came to the address, but when they found out it was the nut house, they just laughed and left. The unfortunate thing is that it was really true.

I finally did get out when a member of the hospital housekeeping staff took pity on me and helped me contact my husband, who contacted my insurance company. They stopped certifying any more treatment, and I was released.

So I got out after five months of pure hell. Dr. Deming told me if I left his care and went home, that the cult would arrange for me and my family to be killed, either by sending a hit-man, or triggering me to do it myself. I am still struggling to overcome the fear implanted by that suggestion. I rarely go outside and constantly worry that Dr. Deming's predictions may come true. It makes me nervous just talking to you about the things that happened in the hospital. I still have nightmares about what I saw and experienced there.

As terrible as the incest in my childhood was, that dissociative disorders unit was worse. I've been raped physically, and I know what a person goes through. What happened to me in that hospital was worse than being raped. And I'm one of the lucky ones. I got out sooner than most people, and my husband was still there for me. So many people lost everything. Their children were taken away from them and their spouses divorced them. They had no home to return to. I did, and I went.

Still, my family has been virtually destroyed. My husband wants his lover, his wife, his friend. My children want their mother back. But I'm not the same person I was. I have lost the joy in things I used to do. I can barely function. I'm afraid to leave the house alone.

I'm seeing a good counselor now. She doesn't believe I was ever in a satanic cult, MPD, or anything else Dr. Deming said about me, and now neither does my family. But I'm still afraid to read the Bible, because Dr. Deming convinced me that there were cult messages there that would trigger my programming. I don't *think* I was in a cult. I don't remember anything about it. Yet I'm afraid to trust my own feelings and memories now, even good ones.

When we went into the hospital, we were your neighbors, your coworkers, your family. Now, we're nuts. Dr. Deming put so much self-doubt and fear into me that I get confused a lot now. If any of Dr. Deming's patients were really in a cult, this man would be dead. He was so paranoid about the cults that he kept bodyguards to protect him. I think now that he was really afraid of the people whose lives were destroyed by him.

They told me in the hospital to beware of this False Memory Syndrome Foundation, that it was a terrible cult full of pedophiles. I've met some parents in that Foundation now, and they're some of the nicest people you'll ever meet. One man at an FMS meeting was angry, though, and vented at me a bit. "How could you let somebody put these lies in your head and believe them?" he demanded. I told him as respectfully as I could, "It's not that I *let* anyone. That carries the connotation of giving them permission to screw up my head. I gave no one permission. I didn't even know they were doing it."

Some people may believe that, because we were stupid enough to trust these doctors in the first place, we deserved the bad things that happened to us in the hospital. I can only say that human beings can be fooled. They can misplace their trust in another person, and few of us are so wise that we never put faith in someone who may end up hurting us.

I know it's important to get to the root of a problem and deal with it, but I don't believe in this repressed memory theory. It is destructive and does not help get to real problems or truth. Most real victims of sexual abuse that I know, going to counseling, do have some memories. They may try to push them out of their minds. Most of them don't want to talk about it. On the other hand, in my experience, those who have "recovered memories" are usually excited to talk about it and get all the attention they can. It seems to be *all* they want to talk about.

One thing I've learned through this is that having a bunch of letters after your name doesn't make you wise. People can become so prideful in their knowledge that it makes them fools. You take someone with a big degree like Dr. Deming has and put them on a panel with a laundromat attendant, and I'll put my money on the laundromat attendant every time to display more sanity. A lot of therapists are screwier and more messed up than the patients they treat. They get hold of this impressive-sounding theory and it goes through some metamorphosis in their minds and is transformed into *fact*. Then they go treat patients with this new information that only causes more havoc in the lives of persons with normal problems. They have this zeal to treat a disorder that doesn't even exist – at least, not until after treatment starts, and that's when the suffering really begins.'

ROBERT WILSON, MPD RETRACTOR

A rugged, 38-year-old former Marine, Robert Wilson cannot find a job in Illinois. 'Who wants to hire a former mental case who hasn't worked in years?' Piecing his life back together after thinking he was an incest survivor with MPD, he is still trying to understand what happened. Wilson really did endure emotional and physical abuse during his childhood. Both of his parents were deaf and possessed limited education. His father, a weekend alcoholic, made life hell for his three children. A Vietnam veteran, Wilson became severely depressed at the age of 29 and entered a VA hospital for four months. Diagnosed with post-traumatic stress disorder, he was put on lithium, had a good counselor, and received support from other veterans. 'I thought I was on top of the world when I came out,' he told me. The hospital counselor suggested that he continue

with follow-up sessions at a local hospital near his home. In 1986, he entered
therapy with Dr. Donna Lovins, a 27-year-old Ph.D. clinical psychologist.

'I thought Donna was pretty young, but she was a doctor, and I
trusted her. She wanted me to talk about my childhood. I told her my
father was an alcoholic who used to come and flip the bedroom light
on, on Friday and Saturday nights, and yell and scream at us. Because
he was a deaf mute, he couldn't hear his own screaming. Then he'd
wait till we were asleep and do it again, all night. He did the same thing
to Mom, shaking her awake. All of us kids became adults real quick.
My older sisters and I had to communicate for our parents.

Depression probably runs in our family. My middle sister Jill went
through it, and so did our father. Everyone on Dad's side of the family
was alcoholic and abusive. His mother punctured his ear drums with
large bobby pins, for instance, and his father went to prison for murder.

Donna Lovins put me on full, permanent disability in 1987, the year
after I started therapy with her. Until then, I was a welder, an auto
mechanic. I can look back now and see how she suggested me into it.
I told her about a real incident from when I was 12. I was working at
a corner store, and my Dad came in one Friday night, screaming and
yelling. I was so embarrassed, I quit the job. So Donna told me that I
would probably have trouble at work. And I did. When I asked her
why, she said, "The machinery and noise remind you of your father,
and you'll have to walk off the job, just like you did when you were
12." So I wound up doing that.

Donna was fascinated by the stories from my childhood, but they
weren't enough for her. She kept saying, "There's more to this than
what you're telling me," and I'd say, "No, there isn't. I remember my
childhood." That's when she said I was repressing it, and there was a
way to get it all out, through hypnosis. At first, I went to see her once
a week for an hour, but then it was two hours, and then two sessions a
week, two hours each. Donna gave me a book, *Outgrowing the Pain* by
Eliana Gil, written for survivors of childhood abuse. Later, when *The
Courage to Heal* came out, she gave that to me, too.

Before we did formal hypnosis, Donna trained me to relax. I'd concentrate on my breathing, then relax my feet, work up to the calves, legs,
chest, relax every part of my body. It's sort of like meditation. It was
no problem for me to relax, because I was on 200 milligrams of Mellaril
and 100 milligrams of thorazine, which is very heavy medication.

After the relaxation sessions, we started doing hypnosis. I never
remembered anything about it afterwards. I felt like I just fell asleep,

and when I woke up she had so much to tell me. She said my father raped me when I was six years old and that my mother sexually abused me by kissing me, like a girlfriend would. At the age of seven or eight, my father and my sister Jill got me into a satanic cult, where I witnessed human sacrifice.

I was devastated by thinking these things had happened to me. I totally believed all of this, though I couldn't remember saying it. And I developed real memories of these things. I could see it all in my head. Donna had a tape recorder in her office, but when I asked her to record a hypnotic session, she said, "I don't advise it," so I dropped it. I totally depended on her. If she'd told me to jump, I'd have asked how high.

I wanted to confront my family, but Donna said, "No, they'll just deny it. They'll say you're crazy." Donna convinced me that Jill had tattooed "666" on my ankle, which is a satanic number. I was really angry at Jill for that. Donna said I was not just abused, but *tortured*. She used that word over and over again. I almost brought charges against them, but instead I would call them up and harass them. People now tell me I looked like a shark, with that cold stare.

I had to talk to Donna daily just in order to get through a day. She gave me relaxation tapes of her voice, and when I started to experience anxiety, I was to listen to her voice, telling me what to do, like hypnosis all over again. She would tell me to relax and go to this safe place in my head – a green pasture, a sunny day, where there were animals but no human beings, a nice, quiet, warm place.

Donna convinced me that everyone in my life had abused me. When my mother died in 1987, she told me to go to her casket and remember all the pain she had caused me, to remember my sexual abuse. So I did. I said, "I hate you for what you did to me." And at the time, I felt no grief, no pain.

Then Donna started telling me I had different personalities. I said, "No, I don't have that. If anybody knows, it's me." She said I was in denial and I had to face it. She named different parts. One was Paul, who was like my protector. When I was a child, Paul would come out and take the pain. Damion was the one who participated in the satanic cult. Bobby was supposed to be the intelligent one who did all the paperwork. I was Robert, the core alter. She also said I had a female personality, and I had a real hard time with that. I thought maybe it meant I was gay or something.

What's so awful and makes me so ashamed is that I started to act out

394

these roles. As Damion, I started acting out satanic rituals, like in a dream state. It's hard to explain. I sacrificed a stray dog. I cut its throat in my back woods. And I stole money from my union, over $50,000, and burned it as a sacrifice. My mind was so twisted and warped, the money was supposed to take care of my mother in hell. Each time I burned the money or did something else awful, I called Donna and told her I was out of control. "I'm committing a felony. I need help." She didn't respond. She'd just say, "We'll talk about this in therapy." Actually, I think my being out of control excited her. At one point, I tried to commit suicide with an overdose of my medication. They found me passed out on the street, and I woke up in the hospital with a tube down my throat.

Then she told me about George, another personality, who was a male prostitute specializing in older women. The next thing you know, I was on a street corner acting out being a male prostitute. I really did have sex with older women for money. To me, it was like a dream. I would find myself in situations I didn't believe. I was making money, wearing fancy jewelry. I honestly didn't consciously know what I was doing until it was over.

In 1989, Donna sent me to this special hospital unit in Chicago for MPDs run by this famous specialist, Dr. Bennett Braun. The first thing they did was inject me. Then before I even went to my room, Dr. Braun showed me the Control Room. It had all glass walls with curtains all around, and a bed with thick straps. I thought, "Oh my God, I'm in trouble here." I was terrified. I called my wife and said, "You've got to get me out of here." Two days later, I was out. Dr. Braun told me I needed to be there. Donna was very upset with me for leaving.

By 1991, I was so afraid of being out of control that I wouldn't leave my house. I confined myself to my bedroom for a year, only coming out to go to the bathroom. It's amazing to me that my wife stuck with me. My three sons were active in sports, but I couldn't go to the baseball games. I would still talk to Donna on the phone during this time. She convinced me that all my friends were against me, that they would try to hurt me. She told me my wife was cheating on me, that my children were my enemies. She was the only one in the world who would help me.

During that year, I stopped taking medication, and I started to feel better. I couldn't understand it. Gradually, I started to come out of my bedroom and reconnect with my family and the rest of the world. I started going to my kids' baseball games. I saw Donna for the last time in person in April of 1992, but I still hated my father and sisters, and I'd talk to Donna on the phone frequently.

On Christmas Eve in 1993, I had been thinking about my sisters a lot, and I decided to call Jill and Barbara. Barbara wouldn't talk to me and still won't. I started to question Jill, and she assured me that the sexual abuse never happened. "Dad would say vulgar, awful things, but he never touched us sexually." It was the first time we had talked in eight years. A few weeks later, Jill called and said, "I saw this program. Would you please call this 800 number for the FMS Foundation?" Two days later, I called, and everything seemed to fall into place. I heard so many stories that were similar to mine. Finally, I could relate to someone else. I had gone through this same thing.

I got a call from Donna six weeks ago, and I told her I was talking to the FMS Foundation. She went ballistic. She threatened to get a court order to put me back in the hospital. I got an attorney, and he told me not to worry. In fact, I'm going to sue my therapist now. She stole eight years of my life. She should be in jail. I didn't get sick until I saw her. She turned a minor problem into a life-threatening mental disorder. She took advantage of me. She took the truth and intertwined it with lies.

Why did Donna do this to me? I've thought a lot about that. I would say she's Dr. Frankenstein. She was trying to create a monster, and I happened to be her monster. Maybe she wanted to write a book about this case for the publicity. She always told me males were more aggressive and would act out more.

What I went through in therapy reminded me of the Marine Corps, the same sort of brainwashing. They would tell you to attack a machine gun nest, and you'd automatically do it. That training was really hard, the hardest thing I've done in my life. They would drill and drill us to kill. Donna would drill and drill me about my past in an almost identical manner.

I still have memories and feelings, even though I intellectually know they're not real. The other day, I got mad at Jill about that tattoo, even though I know an "alter" put it on under Donna's influence.

I'm starting to speak up about this now. I know there's other men out there. People say, "You're a big guy. How could this happen to you?" We're strong on the outside, but weak inside. I'm ashamed. It's embarrassing. I can't really explain it. But I think if it happened to me, it could happen to anybody.

One of my biggest regrets is that my mother died thinking I still hated her. Oh, God, it bothers me. I can't even ask her to forgive me. She was the sweetest, kindest woman on earth.

I cannot go to a therapist now. I know there are good therapists, but I'm scared of them. Talking about what happened to me is my therapy.

I feel fine now. I don't even feel depressed any more. I think everyone on the planet gets depressed sometimes. I did have a very hard childhood, but I went to therapy to be a better person, not to get worse.

This has been really hard on my wife and kids. My wife is still very bitter about it. I think she's only staying with me because of the children. The boys are 15, 13, and 9. We've sat and talked about what I went through. They're very angry – partly at me, partly at the therapist. But they're glad to see I'm a Dad again. It's not too late. Considering everything that's happened, they're doing well.'

CHAPTER NINE

And a Little Child Shall Lead Them (and Be Led)

> Is it not plain that the people had frightened their children with so many tales that they could not sleep without dreaming of the devil, and then made the poor women of the town confess what the children said of them?
>
> FRANCIS HUTCHINSON, *Historical Essay Concerning Witchcraft* (1718), describing the 1669 'seduction' of 300 children in Mora, Sweden, which resulted in the burning of 85 'witches'[1]

While the search for repressed memories began in earnest only after the publication of *The Courage to Heal* in 1988, it was preceded and augmented by another witch hunt in which little children were led to accuse innocent adults of sexual abuse. Although this book focuses primarily on the adult recovery of supposedly repressed memories, the cases involving preschoolers are equally distressing, often resulting in unnecessarily traumatized children and lengthy jail terms for people who had committed no crimes. As we will see, the two phenomena – induced child accusations and adult recovered memories – are not only parallel, but often interact with one another within the same family.

As a result of increased awareness of the true horrors of child abuse, Walter Mondale championed the passage of the U.S. Child Abuse Prevention and Treatment Act in 1974. This landmark legislation offered matching federal funds to states which passed their own laws mandating that doctors, psychologists, police officers, teachers, nurses, and other professionals report any suspected child abuse to the appropriate child protection agency. The act offered anonymity and immunity from prosecution to anyone reporting child abuse. Those who failed to report suspected abuse faced fines or prison sentences.[2]

The legislation has produced a self-sustaining bureaucracy of American social workers, mental health experts, and police officers who specialize in rooting out sex abuse. In the United Kingdom, New

Zealand, and Australia, a similar network of devoted sex abuse hunters arose, along with mandatory reporting of suspected abuse. The more cases they find, the more funds they receive, and the more vital their jobs appear. The result? Beyond question, many cases of actual abuse have been brought to light. But tragically, such legislation and social services policies have also encouraged false accusations that have ruined the lives of innocent people. A network of self-righteous child protective service workers has blanketed English-speaking and other Western countries, eager to find offenses, even in cases where little or no evidence exists. A rumor or malicious allegation is enough to start the wheels rolling. Often, children are taken away from parents without notice, and the accused are arrested without ever being questioned. Those seeking an exhaustive investigative report on the U.S. day care cases should read *Satan's Silence: Ritual Abuse and the Making of a Modern American Witch Hunt* (1995), by Debbie Nathan and Michael Snedeker, describing how, in the authors' words, 'the psychotic delusions of a few individuals were translated into public policy.'[3]

McMARTIN: THE FIRST DAY-CARE SCANDAL

In August of 1983, in Los Angeles, Judy Johnson – diagnosed later as a paranoid schizophrenic – noticed that her two-year-old's bottom was red and decided that he had been sexually abused. She called the police. Although the boy could not speak in complete sentences, uttering only the occasional single word, the police assumed that the mother was correct. They did not question the diagnosis of sexual abuse, but at first, it wasn't clear who had sodomized the boy. Perhaps it had been someone in the park. Soon, however, after repeatedly questioning the child, the mother and police became more certain. It was 25-year-old Ray Buckey, one of his day-care teachers at the McMartin Preschool.*[4]

Without further investigation or observation of the day-care center, on September 9 the local California police sent a letter to 200 McMartin parents, warning of 'possible criminal acts' such as 'oral sex, fondling of genitals, buttocks or chest area, and sodomy, possibly committed

---

* Throughout this chapter, I have used real names for adults, since those involved have become public figures. Thus, Judy Johnson and Ray Buckey are correctly identified. All children's names have been changed, however.

under the pretense of taking the child's temperature.' As a result, concerned parents began questioning their children intensely. They also called one another and compared notes. The young children – most of whom were three or four – at first denied that anything bad had happened to them at the day-care center. Under a barrage of parental pressure, however, some began to tell stories of how they had been touched.

It is almost impossible to reconstruct how these rumors spread, but by the beginning of November, there was a full-scale panic among the parents, many of whom had taken their children to the police, who questioned them aggressively. Parents began to take their supposedly traumatized children to the Children's Institute International (CII), where Kee MacFarlane and other experts in child sexual abuse interviewed them, using leading questions, coercive techniques, and 'anatomically correct' dolls. Eventually, over 350 children submitted to the CII 'therapy.' In *Satan's Silence*, Nathan and Snedeker offer a devastating description of the interview process at CII:

> To put the children at ease, the women [therapists] dressed, clown-like, in mismatched clothes and multicolored stockings, and sat on the floor with the youngsters. They talked in gentle, high-pitched voices, and encouraged discussion about genitals and sexual behavior that young children hardly knew words for. And they used a new diagnostic device: 'anatomically correct' dolls, which came with breasts, vaginas, penises, anuses, and pubic hair. The children were introduced to MacFarlane's collection of hand puppets ... The session became a scene of naked dolls with genitals touching, poking and threatening each other. Cloth penises were being inserted into mouths. 'Did that happen? Ooh, that must have been yucky,' MacFarlane said. 'It didn't happen,' corrected Tanya; 'I'm just playing.' There was talk of being spirited from the school to molesters' homes, though whether they were people's houses or doll houses was unclear. After prompting from MacFarlane, Tanya named Peggy Buckey as a witness to abuse.[5]

About that time, the allegations expanded beyond Ray Buckey to include his sister Peggy Ann, his mother Peggy, his grandmother Virginia McMartin – a septuagenarian in a wheelchair – and three other day-care providers. MacFarlane and her cohorts soon elicited horrifying tales of how the Buckeys and other teachers had forced children to drink blood and urine and had killed animals in front of them, in what sounded like satanic ceremonies.

Meanwhile, Judy Johnson's account of what her inarticulate two-year-old son was supposedly telling her became more graphic and bizarre. Ray Buckey had worn a mask and sodomized her son while sticking his head in a toilet. She also stated that he forced the boy to ride naked on a horse and molested him, while Buckey dressed alternatively as a policeman, fireman, clown, and Santa Claus. Her charges soon escalated to involve other McMartin Preschool teachers. They had purportedly jabbed scissors into the boy's eyes and shot staples into his ears, nipples and tongue; they had also killed a baby and made him drink the blood. (Other abusers Judy Johnson identified included male models she saw in magazines and strangers following her on the highway. Two years later, she was hospitalized for psychosis, and a year after that, she died of an alcohol-related liver disease.)*[6]

Eventually, under intense questioning by therapists, parents, and police, many children came to believe that they had actually been molested, embellishing their stories with wild accusations of having been abused in hot air balloons, on distant farms, in cemeteries, and in tunnels under the school.**[7] Lawrence Pazder, the Canadian psychiatrist who co-authored *Michelle Remembers*, the 1980 book about repressed memories of satanic cults, flew in to tell the police and parents how to spot ritual abuse. Soon, more and more parents and children were convinced that the McMartin Preschool was part of a satanic cult ring of child pornographers and ritual abusers. Testifying before Congress in 1984, social worker Kee MacFarlane stated: 'We're dealing with an organized operation of child predators,' asserting that the preschool served as 'a

---

* In addition to her other mental problems, Judy Johnson probably suffered from Munchhausen's Syndrome by Proxy (MSP), a phenomenon in which parents seek sympathy and attention through their children's fictional illnesses. The lengths to which some parents will go are truly horrifying. Some women have murdered their infants, claiming that they died from Sudden Infant Death Syndrome instead.
** The tunnel issue has recently been resurrected in an attempt to substantiate the McMartin charges. Under the supervision of archaeologist Gary Stickel, parents who have made a career out of their children's supposed abuse dug up the site of the former day-care center. They claim to have found evidence of filled-in tunnels. Roland Summit and Ellen Bass have been quick to publicize this new 'evidence,' although none has been made public. Those who participated in the dig, as critic Debbie Nathan points out, 'not only had an agenda about finding something, but had a history of apparently implanting phony artifacts.' A geologist who gave his opinion in an unpublished report expressed strong skepticism about the supposed tunnels.

ruse for a larger, unthinkable network of crimes against children.'*

The media unquestioningly lapped up the sensational McMartin story. Bumper stickers and placards asserting WE BELIEVE THE CHIL-DREN became popular, and widely quoted misinformation filtered out of California that 'children never lie about such things.' While the preliminary hearing dragged on for a year and a half before a trial even commenced, similar cases popped up all over the United States and Canada at other day-care centers, replicating many of the McMartin charges, with local variations. Within a few years, the example of McMartin had helped to inspire similar overzealous abuse hunts in the United Kingdom, Australia, and New Zealand. Because of unskeptical media coverage and information disseminated by new organizations such as Believe the Children, the necessary ingredients of ritual abuse – including child pornography, sexual 'games,' unlikely travel, chanting, cannibalism, drinking 'magic' liquids, and animal sacrifice – quickly became a part of American and British folk culture.

A widespread witch hunt was on in which social workers, therapists, and non-accused parents (and often police, especially in the U.S.) refused to hear 'No' from children. Convinced that the preschoolers had been terrorized into silence, the interrogators believed that only by encourag-ing, cajoling, and even threatening the children could the 'truth' come out. It is possible that some children, in some of these cases, really had been abused. We will never know, however, because the suggestive questioning clearly contaminated the interviews. Under the barrage of pressure, most three- to five-year-olds eventually succumbed; many undoubtedly actually came to believe that their day-care providers or parents had sexually abused them, even though no abuse had occurred.

RESEARCH ON SUGGESTIBILITY

Recent research by psychologists Stephen Ceci at Cornell and Maggie Bruck at McGill University, as well as others, casts light on how easily young children can come to believe in traumatic events that never occurred. For a comprehensive review of these studies, see Ceci and Bruck's 1995 book, *Jeopardy in the Courtroom: A Scientific Analysis of*

---

* In the McMartin case, as well as its numerous imitators, pornographic films and pictures were supposedly taken. None has ever materialized.

Children's Testimony.[8] With minimal leading, one child in Bruck's study accused a pediatrician of trying to strangle her and of pounding a stick up her vagina with a hammer. Fortunately for the doctor, a video recording of his entire examination showed no such events. Similarly, when Ceci's researchers repeatedly asked a little boy whether his finger had ever been caught in a mousetrap, his initial denials turned into full-blown, convincing accounts of how and where his finger had been caught, how much it hurt, and who had taken him to the hospital. Even after his father told him that the mousetrap memory was a fantasy, the boy insisted to a television interviewer that his finger had really been mangled.[9]

As Ceci has observed, however, the relatively neutral questioning used in his Cornell studies pales in comparison to the browbeating many children receive from sex-abuse investigators. Ceci has watched innumerable videotapes with dialogue such as the following: 'I want to stop, I'm hungry, I want to get out of here,' a child says. 'I'll let you eat, I'll get you a popsicle,' the interviewer responds, 'but only after you tell me what I want to hear. I know you know. Don't tell me you don't know. I know you know.' When the child insists, 'No, I don't know, I never saw her do these things,' the interviewer keeps berating the child. 'Do you want us to tell your friends that you finked out on them, that you won't help them keep her in jail?'[10]*[11]

These are exactly the kinds of coercive approaches used in the McMartin and other day-care cases. In their zeal to unmask perpetrators, the therapists and investigators did not consider that they could be leading the children. They were simply frustrated by the children's stubborn refusal to reveal the horrible things that had been done to them.

Often, the parents were recruited to help their children 'disclose.' In one case, for instance, parents were given a picture book about 'Fuzzy

---

* Some of the actual interview material which has come to light is truly amazing. 'Well, we can get out of here real quick if you just tell me,' one investigator in the Kelly Michaels case said. 'Come on, do you want to help us out?' The child refused, saying he hated the investigator. Finally, the child caved in, asserting that 'I peed in her penis' and that 'we chopped our penises off.' Similarly, in the McMartin case, therapist Kee MacFarlane questioned a child who held a Pac-Man puppet. 'We'll see how smart you are, Pac-Man. Did you ever see anything come from Mr. Ray's wiener?' The child answered, 'He never did that to [me], I don't think.' MacFarlane ignored him and kept insisting that he reveal what the emission tasted like. 'I think it would taste like yucky ants,' he hazarded hopefully. 'Do you think it would be sticky, like sticky, yucky ants?' she suggested. 'A little,' the child conceded.

the Rabbit,' whose teacher started teaching the innocent bunnies 'secret songs, secret touches on their tummies and bottoms,' and warning them not to tell their parents. A fairy rabbit sprinkled 'magic power' on Fuzzy, who then summoned the strength to tell his parents about the evil teacher, who was, in reality, a witch.[12]

At around the same time that the day-care cases were making headlines, mothers in bitter custody or divorce cases began to accuse their husbands of having molested their children. Although some mothers deliberately led and instructed their offspring, more frequently they, too, believed that 'something' must have happened, once the notion occurred to them. And in the overheated, paranoid atmosphere of the 1980s and early 1990s, that notion was not hard to come by. Having conceived the idea that their former husbands might have abused the children, the mothers replicated the same process of intensive questioning, then took their children to therapists and pediatricians to search for 'validation' of abuse.

Similarly, school personnel, instructing children in good touch/bad touch, sometimes suspected abuse because of a child's behavior or comments. Intense questioning led to a call to Child Protective Services, and the wheels were set in motion.

Most of the stories summarized in this chapter involve day-care centers, but there are hundreds of thousands of unpublicized cases in which parents have been jailed or had their children taken from them with no concrete evidence. Often, the parents were never even interviewed. In many ways, the cases involving small children are *worse* than those involving adults with recovered memories. Parents accused on the basis of repressed memories have at least been able to raise their children and can take solace in the reality of those happier times. If they are sued, such older parents generally face civil charges and may lose a great deal of money, but not their freedom. Finally, such parents tend to be well-educated members of the middle or upper class who know how to research their problem and seek appropriate help.

Many of the parents and day-care workers accused by small children, on the other hand, are not terribly well educated or affluent. They are tried in criminal courts and sent to jail. They never get to raise their children, and their children are stripped of their parents at a crucial developmental period. One man, who served as a substitute janitor in a Pennsylvania day-care center when he was 18, is now languishing in jail. 'I'm one of them people that was falsely accused,' he wrote to me recently. He wanted to take a lie detector test but was refused permission. 'I've went up for parole 3 times since 1992 and each time I was turned down because I didn't finish the sex offender program. Well now that I completed the program the psychologist told me that he could not recommend me for parole because I'm in denial of my crime because I won't admit to it.'[13]

His plight is typical of a Catch-22 situation. Those who really *are* sex offenders readily play the prison game and say the right things in their counseling sessions. Innocent people, on the other hand, refuse to confess to a crime they did not commit, and they are routinely denied parole and home leave.

This chapter, as well as most national media attention, focuses mostly on 'high-profile' day-care cases, but I want to emphasize that the same process has put innocent people in prison throughout the United States. One of those men is Kenneth Bruce Perkins of Texas. 'It seems we have convinced the media that the day care witchhunt is exactly that,' he wrote from his cell in 1996. 'Why can they not see that the same people have just moved their tent to the next location with the techniques learned in the big headline cases? How many of us will have to spend the rest of our lives in these hell holes because it is not politically correct to defend an individual who was very obviously falsely accused?'[14] (Perkins was accused of abusing his grandchildren and several other children at a birthday party – regardless of the fact that several of the children were not even in attendance.)

Investigators for social service agencies wield enormous and arbitrary power, and they are usually immune from prosecution for anything they do. In effect, they often operate like a mini-Gestapo. I was horrified by what one pragmatic lawyer wrote to me in 1994: 'Social workers tend to be overworked, underpaid, undertrained, come from offices with insufficient budgets, and have to deal with people who won't cooperate with their investigations. If social workers were liable for any alleged misdeed, they would spend half of their time in court . . . It is conceivable that some states would be unable to continue their child protective services departments without the extension of immunity.'[15]

Once people begin to search for symptoms, they are usually easy to find. Just ask medical students who suspect they are contracting whatever disease they happen to be studying. When parents are told that any trouble their children may be exhibiting is probably due to sexual abuse, or when a pediatrician is told that the anus or vagina probably exhibits signs, the 'symptoms' quickly become convincing. Nightmares, bedwetting, sexual play, or a reluctance to reveal the supposed molestation become evidence. Activities such as mutual masturbation and mock intercourse among children have been labeled deviant, abnormal behavior in our society, although these activities are quite common worldwide and are normally tolerated or ignored.[16*17]

Tiny white lines on an anus or a bump on a hymen are 'consistent with abuse,' even though research reveals precisely the same marks on many nonabused children.[18**19] Highly educated and well-trained child abuse 'experts' are confident that their clinical intuition and experience allow them to differentiate true from false allegations. Yet several controlled experiments have demonstrated their inability to do so. In one such study, the experts performed significantly *worse* than chance, rating the children who gave the most misinformation as the most credible and accurate.[20]

The prior expectations of child interviewers can exert a major influence. In one Ceci study, preschoolers were shown a game-like event and then interviewed about it a month later. Some interviewers were told exactly what had happened, while others were misinformed. They were then asked to elicit the most factually accurate report from each child. Those with the correct information heard no inaccuracies. The others, however, managed to get 34 per cent of the three- and four-year-olds to corroborate false events. Not only that, but the children became more and more sure of themselves as they were encouraged to repeat the stories.[21]

---

* A 1991 study of normal sexual behavior in children revealed that 35.5 per cent of the boys aged two through six, and 19 per cent of the same-aged girls, touched their sex parts in public. In the same population, 22.6 per cent of the boys masturbated with their hands, while 16.3 per cent of the girls did. Finally, 43.5 per cent of the boys and 48.4 per cent of the girls had intentionally felt their mothers' breasts. More aggressive sexual play, such as imitating intercourse or inserting objects in a vagina or anus, were very rare in this study. Given the overt sexual questioning that children are subjected to in these cases, however, such unusual acting out might be expected, even in non-abused children. Related studies have shown that many normal preschoolers bathe with their parents and attempt to touch their parents' genitals. Another study has shown that, contrary to expectations, there is no difference in the level of sexual knowledge between sexually abused and non-abused children.

** In *Satan's Silence*, Debbie Nathan and Michael Snedeker describe how a California general practitioner named Bruce Woodling, a self-proclaimed expert in detecting child sexual abuse, promoted the 'anal wink test' in the early 1980s. He claimed that if a child's anus dilated and closed spontaneously, it indicated repeated sodomy. He also pioneered the use of the 'colposcope,' which could take magnified photos of the hymen, making any irregularities appear horrific. Only in 1988, when Dr. John McCann's studies revealed that normal children also exhibited hymenal irregularities and anal winks, did Woodling's widely accepted theories fall into disrepute.

But if the children's stories are untrue, where do they come from? Are children's imaginations really that morbid and lurid? The answer appears to be 'Yes,' as the Brothers Grimm undoubtedly knew. Most of the details elicited from the children are common motifs in normal children's fantasies. One study, conducted by child psychology researcher Frances Ilg and her colleagues, revealed that preschoolers are typically afraid of clowns, Halloween masks, ambulances, monsters in the dark, animals, policemen, and burglars – all of which appear regularly in the allegations. In addition, the preoccupation with eating feces, blood, or urine probably stem from children's concerns with toilet training or anything they perceive as forbidden.[22]

The parallels with repressed-memory cases are clear. Indeed, in some instances, the cases use identical 'recovered memory' tactics, such as when one therapist in the McMartin case explained to a child: 'And so [for] some of the kids, what we do here is we try to improve their memory and we try to unlock their brain. Sometimes when you're real scared, your brain gets locked up ... You honestly don't remember some stuff. It gets stored right back here in the back of your filing cabinet in your brain under "Z"'[23]

Even without such an approach, however, the day-care cases provide parallels with recovered memory in adults. Prior expectations on the part of therapists play a key role. In both cases, laundry lists of symptoms encourage people to look for signs of sexual abuse. For the adults searching for memories, these include common problems such as poor relationships, low self-esteem, or depression. For the children, they feature common disturbances in normal preschoolers such as fear of school, genital irritation, or incontinence. Once the abuse hunt has begun in earnest, a vicious cycle commences in which real 'symptoms' of trauma are produced by the very process of uncovering the mythical abuse. For hours, children are repeatedly grilled by intimidating adults, asking about sexual matters the children have never even considered. They are then stripped naked while other white-clad adults poke around their vaginas and anuses. Is it any wonder that the children develop symptoms of post-traumatic stress syndrome, or that they begin to engage in sexualized play?

Consider this advice on examining boys suspected of being abused, given in 1990 by American pediatrician Carolyn Levitt: 'To clarify the boy's definition of sexual acts, the physician can perform a rectal examination that includes the penetration of the boy's anus by the physician's gloved and lubricated examining finger ... This allows the boy to compare that sensation with the sensation of abuse.'[24] It is some-what frightening to note that, by her own count, Dr. Levitt has examined over 4,000 children on suspicion of child abuse.[25]

In the same year, a therapist suggested that in interviewing boys, clinicians should 'tell the client that you are going to ask a series of questions that you don't want him to answer . . . because he will probably be dishonest about them.' These questions include: 'What did it feel like the first time you put your finger or crayon or pencil inside your butt? Can you describe how your ("cum") seminal fluid tastes? When did you first become familiar with how your butt smells?'[26]

Ironically, the children are indeed being sexually and emotionally abused by the therapists, officials, and medical personnel who are supposed to be protecting them, and they often develop long-term symptoms as a result, including anxiety, insecurity, insomnia, nightmares, fear of strangers, depression, rages, obsession with death, and suicidal impulses.[27] These, of course, are then taken as proof that the original suspected abuse did, indeed, take place.

ABUSING KIDS IN OUTER SPACE AND
OTHER ALLEGATIONS

Fortunately, public awareness surrounding these cases is building, especially since a fine American public television documentary on the Little Rascals Day Care in Edenton, North Carolina, aired in 1993. No one watching *Innocence Lost* could conclude that the day-care workers were guilty.[28] The children's 'disclosures' included tales of being thrown into shark-infested waters, taking trips to outer space, and worshiping the devil. The program included damning interviews with three jurors who, convinced that day-care provider Robert Kelly was innocent, finally yielded to group pressure and found him guilty anyway to avoid a hung jury. One of the other jurors, it transpired, had been sexually abused as a child and had not revealed that fact during jury selection.

Despite this devastating, widely viewed documentary, however, Kelly remained imprisoned until 1995, when his case was finally overturned and he was released. Before his release, his wife Betsy pled 'no contest' – still maintaining her innocence – rather than risk a trial. So did Willard Scott Privott, who owned a video and shoe-repair store and says he never even went into the day-care center. Dawn Wilson, the day-care cook, was convicted, but her case was overturned along with Robert Kelly's. Meanwhile, three others await possible trials. It is unclear at this writing whether the State will attempt to retry Robert Kelly, but he vows never to accept a plea bargain. 'The state has done me wrong and imprisoned me for over six years. Now they want me to take a plea so they can save face. It will never happen.'[29*30]

Kelly Michaels, once an aspiring young actress and day-care worker, was jailed for five years for alleged sexual abuse. She has finally been released from prison after an appeals court overturned the conviction, questioning the reliability of the children's testimony.[31] There are still eight civil suits pending against Michaels, brought by some parents of the day-care children. Michaels plans to file a $10 million suit against the county, state, and others for malicious prosecution.

As in most other day-care affairs, her preschoolers were subjected to leading, coercive questioning before they finally caved in and made bizarre allegations that Michaels had inserted various objects into their anuses, vaginas, and penises, including Lego blocks, forks, spoons, serrated knives, and a sword. Michaels was also supposed to have forced children to drink her urine, then removed their clothes so that she could lick peanut butter off their privates.[32]

Canadians, too, have fallen for recovered memories and day-care hysteria in a big way. By far the most disturbing instance occurred in Martensville, Saskatchewan, where a two-year-old's 1991 diaper rash sparked the relentless grilling of children at a babysitting service. Eventually, the children asserted that they had been forced to drink blood and urine and to eat feces while locked in cages in 'the devil's church.' One boy said that an axe handle was forced inside his penis, while another said his babysitter had cut off a child's nipple and swallowed it. Two of the nine defendants were found guilty and served prison sentences until their convictions were finally overturned. Many Martensville citizens remain convinced that a satanic cult is operating in the area.[33]

One day-care case has been touted as proof that bizarre, sadistic abuse

* As an indication of shifting public awareness, Dale Akiki was exonerated late in 1993, after being held for two-and-a-half years without bail in a San Diego case. Akiki, who suffers from hydrocephalus, has an enlarged head and bug eyes, which probably led to the 1989 rumors that he had molested children while he provided child care during church services. In typical fashion, the children were taken for 'therapy,' where they revealed that Akiki had sodomized them with curling irons and toy firetruck ladders. They said that he had engaged in animal sacrifice, including the killing of an elephant and giraffe.

does occur. In 1984, 36-year-old Francisco Fuster-Escalona, a Cuban immigrant, and his 17-year-old Honduran wife, Ileana, were accused of molesting children in their home-based babysitting service in Country Walk, Florida, an affluent Miami suburb. The children were subjected to the usual coercive interviews and produced the familiar allegations – oral copulation and sodomy, mind-altering drugs, child pornography, and systematic terrorism. The Country Walk case was distinguished from others by three apparently damning facts: Fuster had been convicted in 1981 for fondling a nine-year-old girl; his six-year-old son tested positive for gonorrhea of the throat; and his wife confessed to the charges and accused him of abusing her as well.[34]

Fuster vehemently denies the 1981 charge,*[35] and the other two pieces of evidence have been seriously questioned by investigative reporter Debbie Nathan. First, she points out that the Center for Disease Control has found that the test used for the son's throat gonorrhea is highly unreliable. More than a third of positive findings sent to the CDC came from children who did *not* have the disease. More disturbing, however, is the manner in which Ileana Fuster came to 'confess.'

Ileana, a frightened teenage immigrant, steadfastly maintained her innocence, as well as that of her husband, for nearly a year, despite being held naked in solitary confinement for much of the time. Her own lawyer, Michael von Zampft, pressured her to 'confess' and turn state's evidence. Finally, Miami psychologist Michael Rappaport and his partner, Merry Sue Haber, who ran a business called Behavior Changers, were brought in to help persuade Ileana Fuster. During August and September of 1985, Rappaport visited Ileana in her cell at least 34 times apparently, accompanied almost every time by Dade County State Attorney Janet Reno.[36]

---

* According to Fuster, he had attended a party along with Lydia Rivera, his sister-in-law's cousin. Lydia was babysitting for her daughter Laura's best friend, nine-year-old Ruth, while her mother went on her honeymoon. After discovering that his van had been towed and retrieving it late at night, Fuster ended up driving with Ruth in his van for ten minutes – she was supposed to keep him awake – as his wife followed them in her car. It turns out that Lydia's daughter Laura had been raped when she was five. Now the tipsy Lydia Rivera asked Ruth whether Fuster had molested her in his van. According to Lydia, the child denied it. 'Well, men do things like that, you know,' Lydia insisted. In the following days, Ruth and Laura discussed rape and molestation, and by the time her mother came to pick her up, Ruth was convinced that Fuster had molested her during their ride together. A year later, Ruth testified that she had complained of molestation that first night. Although Fuster passed two lie detector tests, the jury was never told, and he was found guilty.

Rappaport led Ileana in guided imagery and visualization sessions. Her account of this process is revealing:

[The two psychologists] explained to me that I was having problems and that they were there to help me . . . They diagnosed that I was having a blackout of events . . . they came almost every day. And then I started seeing them at nights . . . I kept saying I was innocent but nobody would listen to me. And they said that I was suffering from a blackout and that those things had happened because the kids said it and the kids don't lie . . . And you know, before I know it, I was having nightmares . . . And they said that that was a way of my system remembering what had actually happened. And then you know, I argue that a little bit, but I got to a point that I was believing that probably those things happened and I just didn't remember because they were so shocking.[37]

The teenager finally confessed, while Reno held her hand and offered encouragement.*[38] Eventually, Ileana came up with suitably outrageous allegations. Her husband had given her drugs and sodomized her with a cross, she said, while he had forced her to give oral sex to a child.

Having confessed, Ileana Fuster was never tried. She did, however, testify against her husband. Before she took the stand, she met with her psychologists to rehearse her testimony. 'They didn't want me to make no mistakes, they said,' she explained later. Ileana served three years in prison and was then released and sent back to Honduras, where she refuses to discuss the case. In her speech in court during sentencing, she told the judge, 'I am pleading guilty not because I feel guilty, but . . . for my own interest . . . I am innocent of all those charges . . . I am pleading guilty to get all of this over.' Francisco Fuster was found guilty and sentenced to six life terms and 165 years in prison. He has now been in prison for a decade, having survived several attempts on his life.[39] A book, *Unspeakable Acts* (1986), which was made into a 1990 movie, presented the abuse as completely factual. The resulting celebrity helped to cinch Reno's reelection, and her reputation as a child advocate

---

* In 1991, Rappaport told journalist Debbie Nathan that Janet Reno had accompanied him on most of these visits. When Reno was nominated for U.S. attorney general and became a national figure, Rappaport retracted his statement. Reno has denied being present during the guided imagery sessions.

later propelled her to the office of U.S. attorney general.*[40] Soon afterward, in her zeal to prevent child sexual abuse inside the Branch Davidian compound in Waco, she sanctioned an attack that resulted in the death of all those inside, including the children.[41]

For a few weeks in 1994, it appeared that Fuster would be granted a new trial. His lawyer flew to Honduras and took a deposition from Ileana in which she retracted her confession and accusations, making it abundantly clear how she was led into making them. Unfortunately, she subsequently became frightened of repercussions and retracted her retraction. Fuster remains in prison.[42]

THE CHILD SEX ABUSE PANIC HITS THE U.K.

While the McMartin case commenced in 1983, it took four more years before a full-blown case exploded in the United Kingdom. By the time it did, however, the atmosphere was ripe. Throughout the early and mid-1980s, British concern with childhood sexual abuse grew dramatically, as Philip Jenkins documented in his 1992 book, *Intimate Enemies: Moral Panics in Contemporary Great Britain*. In the early 1980s, Judianne Densen-Gerber, the American 'expert' who believed that there was a vast international child pornography industry that abducted children for 'snuff' films, flew to England to fan such unfounded fears. Awareness of *real* childhood abuse and neglect also grew, particularly in 1984, when four-year-old Jasmine Beckford was starved, beaten, and ultimately killed by her stepfather in the London Borough of Brent, rekindling memories of the 1973 death of Brighton's seven-year-old Maria Colwell.

Such cases provided emotional ammunition for British feminists such as Emily Driver, who began the Child Sexual Abuse Prevention Education Project in 1984. The same year, an influential conference on childhood sex abuse was held at Teesside Polytechnic, with speeches by American researchers such as Ann Burgess, who explained how to

---

* As the Dade County State Attorney, Janet Reno also spearheaded another sex abuse case in which a 13-year-old boy, Bobby Finjne (pronounced FAIN-ya) was accused of molesting children while he babysat them at a church. In a familiar scenario, it all started with one child's vague nightmares, then rapidly escalated when the children were questioned intensively. Reno insisted on trying the adolescent as an adult, meaning that his name could be released to the media, and that he could be incarcerated. Eventually, after one of the longest criminal trials in Dade County history, Finjne was found innocent.

use children's drawing to diagnose sex abuse and who warned about pedophile sex rings. In the same year, the National Society for the Prevention of Cruelty to Children (NSPCC) celebrated its centennial and revitalized its mission and fund-raising by sounding the alarm about childhood sexual abuse. Also in the early 1980s, consultant child psychiatrist Arnon Bentovim became a vocal spokesman about the dangers of child sexual abuse, and he diagnosed hundreds of such cases at the Great Ormond Street Hospital for Sick Children in London. His interpretation of children's 'disclosures' is illustrated by his response to a child who told him, 'Daddy hit me with a wet fish.' It may sound like a fantasy, the psychiatrist says, but in fact it represents the child's 'coping' with his father hitting him with his penis.[43] Bentovim was a member of the CIBA Foundation working party that published *Child Sexual Abuse Within the Family* in 1984 amidst a barrage of publicity. Slogans such as 'Believe the children' and 'Breaking the silence' became commonplace expressions.[44]

In 1985, Channel Four broadcast three different films about the sexual exploitation of children. The same year, American educational psychologist Michelle Elliott, who was living in Sussex, developed the Child Assault Prevention Program for British schools, and a video (imitating a similar American production) called *Strong Kids, Safe Kids* was distributed by National Children's Homes. The following year, Channel Four aired *A Crime of Violence*, produced by filmmaker Audrey Droisen of the Feminist Coalition Against Child Sexual Abuse. Meanwhile, doctors from the Great Ormond Street Hospital and executives from the NSPCC were planning the Child Sexual Abuse Bexley Experiment, in which police and social workers were taught 'disclosure work' with children. They were sensitized to the sex abuse experience through dramatic role playing and hypnotic regression. In October of 1986, popular television personality Esther Rantzen aired a special on child sex abuse, subsequently sponsoring 'ChildLine,' a telephone hotline for abused children. It received 50,000 calls on opening day, and the media publicity was intense.[45]

Finally, that same year of 1986, two Leeds pediatricians, Chris Hobbs and Jane Wynne, published an influential article in the prestigious British medical journal *Lancet* in which they championed California pediatrician Bruce Woodling's 'anal wink test.' Actually, variations on this purported indicator of sodomy had a long history in England stemming back to the 19th century, so in a sense it was 'coming home,' rechristened the 'reflex anal dilatation (RAD) test' to avoid the somewhat off-color notion of the anal sphincter winking at doctors. 'Buggery in young children,' wrote Hobbs and Wynne, 'including infants and toddlers, is a serious, common and under-reported type of child abuse.'[46]

It was in this highly charged atmosphere that, in 1987, the first major panic commenced in the British county of Cleveland. In January of that year, Australian physician Marietta Higgs arrived as a consultant pediatrician, bringing with her the RAD test, which she taught to fellow physician Geoffrey Wyatt. Within the next five months, the two of them diagnosed 121 local children from 57 families as victims of sexual abuse. They were reinforced by Sue Richardson, the local 'child abuse consultant,' and Deborah Glassbrooke, a veteran of the ChildLine organization, who established a sex abuse therapy center at the Middles-brough General Hospital. Quickly, children were removed from their homes. By the end of June, over 200 children had been referred to social services. Though some actual sexual abuse probably had occurred in Cleveland, the cases became so contaminated by the bogus test and leading interviews that it was impossible to determine the truth.

Eventually, the sex abuse hunt in Cleveland collapsed under its own weight, as numbers grew to crisis proportion. The Cleveland police remained extremely skeptical of the 'evidence' of the RAD test. Manchester police surgeon Raine Roberts criticized Higgs and Wyatt, observing that their test itself constituted 'outrageous sexual abuse' of the children. Dr. Hamish Cameron, a child psychiatrist, offered insightful testimony during the Cleveland inquiry, chaired by Judge Elizabeth Butler-Sloss. 'Whenever a new "illness" or treatment is described, a flurry of excitement develops amongst professionals. This has certainly been the case with child sex abuse. However, in addition to the normal excitement generated by any "new" condition, there is an added voyeuristic component arising from the universality of interest in sexual matters.'

The lengthy Butler-Sloss report, published in 1988, determined that the critics were basically correct, though it tried to apportion blame equally to everyone involved, treating the disaster as a matter of professional disagreement rather than a misguided witch hunt. The report scored Raine Roberts, for instance, for failing to take a 'balanced' approach. Unfortunately, many of the key recommendations of the report were equivocal. It suggested, for instance, that police and social workers should train and work together rather than fight one another. The ironic result was that uncritical belief in pedophile rings spread to the police.[47]

THE BRITISH RITUAL ABUSE FIASCO

With the Cleveland débâcle receiving such coverage in the British media, one would think that the sex abuse panic would have ceased in England. Such was not the case. Feminists, social workers, and evangelical Christians bound together in an odd alliance to declare that the Cleveland children had really been abused after all, that the authorities were covering it up, that if a witch hunt was on, it was directed against the poor social workers and pediatricians. That same year of 1987, Glasgow University sponsored a child abuse conference on the theme, 'Learning from the American Experience,' featuring several American experts on sexual abuse, such as Lucy Berliner of Seattle's Harborview Sexual Assault Center. Arnon Bentovim, of the Great Ormond Street Hospital, defended the use of leading questions under some circumstances. Feminist journalist Beatrix Campbell published *Unofficial Secrets*, a 1988 book defending the Cleveland affair and hailing it as the tip of the iceberg of hidden child sexual abuse.[48]

The harbinger for things to come occurred in Nottingham in 1987, the same year as the Cleveland case. It is unclear how much real sexual abuse took place in Nottingham, but there is no question that the satanic ritual abuse elements – including animal sacrifices, blood being drunk, and adults in ritual robes raping children – were inadvertently planted by overzealous interviewers. In 1988, Ray Wyre helped out. The head of the Gracewell clinic for sex offenders, ex-probation officer Wyre lectured widely about an international ritual abuse network, educating police, social workers, and NSPCC members. He now gave Nottingham social workers Christine Johnson and Judith Dawson a list of 'satanic indicators' he had in turn received from American sources. As it became clear that something was amiss, an inquiry was held. The damning report, suppressed by the Nottinghamshire social services and the Department of Health, concluded that 'witch hunts could develop in this country and grave injustice result.'[49]

The ritual abuse hysteria was coming to a head by the end of the 1980s. In 1989, ritual abuse was a major theme at three conferences at Reading, Dundee, and Harrogate. Sponsors included the Association of Christian Psychiatrists, and speakers included Americans such as cult cop Jerry Simandl and therapist Pamala Klein, as well as Marietta Higgs and Maureen Davies, a ritual abuse believer who was part of a Christian anti-cult organization called Reachout. In December of 1989, Nigel Bartlett published 'Facing the Unbelievable' in the British social work journal *Community Care*, summarizing all of the major ritual abuse dogma. 'One of the most damaging reactions a social worker or any other professional can have is disbelief,' he wrote. 'Trust is eighty per cent of the treatment.' Bartlett asserted that 'children are being used in satanic rituals in towns and areas such as Hull, Surrey, Wolverhampton, Telford, Portsmouth, Manchester and Shrewsbury.' In 1990, Beatrix Campbell produced a *Dispatches* documentary dramatizing the purported perils of ritual abuse, and the NSPCC issued a statement that 'evidence is mounting of child pornography, ritualistic abuse and sex rings involving children.'[50]

The stage was set for a series of ill-advised child-snatches in 1990 and 1991, beginning in Manchester, then Rochdale, Merseyside, Epping Forest, and Ayrshire and the Orkney Islands in Scotland. The Rochdale debacle, typical of these cases, began when a troubled six-year-old boy told frightening stories about ghosts and the living dead. Social workers, convinced that he was the victim of a satanic cult, began the inevitable round of coercive child interviews. Eventually twenty children from six families were taken from their parents. It turns out the boy had been watching horror videos such as *The Evil Dead*.[51*52]

The Orkney Islands crisis proved to be so absurd that it prompted a widespread awareness that social services had run out of control. Without any investigation, social workers and police launched a pre-dawn raid on Feb. 27, 1991, removing nine children from four families. Medical examination of the children revealed no evidence of abuse. The terrified children begged to be returned to their parents. The charges appeared ridiculous – an elderly Church of Scotland minister was supposed to have held large satanic meetings in a local quarry. In a small island community such as South Ronaldsay, the chances of keeping such abuse secret were virtually nil. Fortunately, the children were returned to their homes in April after a quick judgment by sheriff David Kelbie, to be followed by a scathing report by Lord Clyde.[**53] As pediatrician D. H. S.

---

* In most cases, the children in these cases actually came to believe in their accusations. In a few American and British cases, however, they later admitted simply lying under immense pressure.

** Unfortunately, other children from another Orkney family, taken into custody before the dawn raid, remained sequestered from their families, under continued pressure to reveal details of alleged ritual abuse. One of the children was still separated from his family as this book went to press. For the families in the lesser-known case in Ayrshire, it took until 1995, five years after the original allegations, before a legal appeal finally allowed the eight children to be reunited with their parents.

Reid observed in *Suffer the Little Children*, his book on the Orkney case, it repeated a similar witch hunt on the islands four hundred years ago. 'How many times have we been here before?' he wrote plaintively.[54]

It would be comforting to think that unjust accusations and unnecessary child removals are now a thing of the past in Great Britain, but the social workers continue to use the same anatomically correct dolls and the same leading interview techniques, with devastating results. *Poppies on the Rubbish Heap*, a 1991 book by Madge Bray, a British social worker, provides evidence that little has been learned by some professionals. She looked back nostalgically to the 1980s, when 'the beginning of a body of knowledge was emerging and we devoured new treatment methods (mostly American) greedily.' Since Bray and her associates completely believed in these new 'disclosure' methods, and sincerely thought they were only helping children to reveal real abuse, they were bewildered by attacks in the media and courts. 'It's the bits about us interrogating children. It's the language I object to. I mean, Kafka-esque ordeals and all that,' complained a fellow social worker to Bray. 'That's the exact opposite of what we do, what we teach, what we're all about!'[55]

With such blindness and entrenched belief systems, it is not surprising that the Pembroke scandal in West Wales commenced in 1991, resulting in the incarceration of six men in 1994. Ann Done, the social worker for a troubled eight-year-old living with his single mother, decided, with minimal evidence, that the child might have been molested. She commenced 'direct work' with him, an imported American technique involving dream interpretation, drawing, and questions about his past. Later, he underwent 'disclosure work.' In October of 1991, the ubiquitous Ray Wyre organized a three-day workshop at the Gracewell Institute for the Pembroke investigative team.* The same month, guidelines for abuse cases were issued by the Department of Health suggesting that police and social workers work more closely together in these cases.[56]

In December of 1992 – two years after Done began to question the first boy – the arrests began. Eventually, 18 children were taken from nine families, and 11 men and two women were charged. The case came to trial in January of 1994, with the adults accused of 'the most depraved and revolting conduct imaginable,' according to the prosecution. They had purportedly conducted ritual sex orgies in various homes, sheds, tunnels, seaside caves, and boats at sea, and pictures and videotapes were made at these events. Yet no photos or videos ever emerged. There was

---

* Gracewell folded in 1993 due to financial difficulties.

no physical evidence. No child had alleged abuse prior to interviews by social workers. And several accusers recanted on the witness stand, one child revealing that the social workers told him that he could not go home unless he admitted the abuse. Nonetheless, only one man won his appeal; the rest remain in prison.[57]

Just when it would appear that ritual abuse myths had been laid to rest, another case popped up in Bishop Auckland, built on what was apparently a real case of a 14-year-old molester. By this time, the unfortunate effects of the joint training guidelines was evident. It was not simply the social workers, but the police and Crown Prosecution service, who were sucked into the ritual abuse panic. In contrast to many American cases, British law enforcement officers and prosecutors had previously been quite skeptical of the hysteria, demanding firm evidence. In Pembroke and Bishop Auckland, joint training sessions – ironically, one of the suggestions following the Cleveland and Orkney inquiries – apparently infected the police and lawyers as well, binding them together in a closed circle of belief in ritual abuse. Soon, they were hearing and believing tales of voodoo ceremonies featuring devil-worshiping adults and genital mutilation with fish hooks. Fortunately, by January of 1995, the bizarre case collapsed before reaching trial, when the Crown, represented by David Robson QC, determined that it was unwinnable.[58]

It seems unlikely, in the wake of the 1994 La Fontaine report that found no evidence of British ritual abuse cults, that there will be many more such cases in the U.K., although the British believers in ritual abuse continue to hold conferences and assure one another of its reality. Journalist Margaret Jervis is not so sure we have seen the last of the mass abuse cases. 'Satan appears in many guises,' she writes ironically. 'Now they are simply redefining ritual abuse under vague headings such as "organized abuse." I think foster carers and institutional "trusted adults" are next in line.'[59]

At any rate, there is no doubt that social workers will continue to use dangerous 'disclosure techniques' in low-profile, individual cases, particularly in the context of divorce and custody battles, resulting in unjust prosecutions and the traumatizing of otherwise normal children. As British journalist Alasdair Palmer has observed in the *Spectator*, the social services' behemoth allows violation of families' and children's rights that would not be tolerated for any other type of crime. 'Arbitrary and tyrannical uses of state power are tolerated in child-abuse investigations – by local councils, by lawyers, by judges, and ultimately by ministers – which would create uproar if anything similar occurred even in the course of an investigation into the most heinous terrorist bombing.' writes Palmer. 'The councils and their social service departments . . . are protected by the laws of confidentiality and contempt . . . The first step towards a solution is the removal of the secrecy which guarantees that officials who abuse those powers cannot be identified. If that does not happen, families will continue to be poisoned, reputations destroyed, and livelihoods wrecked.' [59a]

SEARCHING FOR ABUSE DOWN UNDER AND ELSEWHERE

The same pattern of sex abuse panic and unjust prosecutions occurred in New Zealand and Australia. In 1987, for instance, a New Zealand mother in a bitter custody dispute accused her ex-husband of molesting their four-year-old twins. Using anatomically correct dolls, the social worker attempted to elicit disclosures. The taped interview is disturbing:

SOCIAL WORKER: Did Daddy ever put his diddle near your vagina?
CHILD: (*laughing*). No.
SOCIAL WORKER: Can you show me how he did that?
CHILD: But my Dad didn't do it.
SOCIAL WORKER: Your Dad didn't? Who did?
CHILD: Nobody . . .
SOCIAL WORKER: Cathy, when you go and see Dad, I wonder if Dad sometimes makes your vagina sore?
CHILD: No, he doesn't.
SOCIAL WORKER: If he did, it would be okay to tell me.
CHILD: He doesn't.
SOCIAL WORKER: But Mummy said you had a sore vagina.
CHILD: Yeah, I used to.
SOCIAL WORKERSW: We want to help so you don't get any more sore vaginas.
CHILD: I used to have one, but now it's gone. I used to have one at home at Mum's.

Despite these repeated denials, the social worker persisted, calling the mother into the room to help out. Eventually, the girl relented and said her father had touched her vagina. The mother and social worker praised her for being a 'good brave girl.'[60]

By that year, a sex abuse therapy center had opened in Christchurch. Its brochure warned parents to expect their children's behavior and mental state to deteriorate as 'disclosure' proceeded. Therapy, they explained, would get 'all the pain, bad memories, worries, fears and feelings out into the open.'[61]

In 1992, Peter Ellis, who worked at the Civic Daycare Centre in Christchurch, was charged with sexual abuse. After the day-care children underwent disclosure interviews, the charges escalated. Ellis had supposedly made them drink his urine and eat his faeces. He had raped one girl, violated others with his finger or a stick, and urinated on their faces for good measure. He allegedly stuck a needle into one child's rear end, making it bleed. When Ellis's four female coworkers denied that these events could have occurred, they, too, were charged with abuse. Many allegations similar to the McMartin case cropped up. The children had supposedly been taken to a private home, had been molested in tunnels under the house, had been forced to stand naked in a circle of adults, and had been used in producing child pornography.

Eventually, all charges against the women were dropped, but Peter Ellis stood trial, despite a complete lack of physical evidence, and was found guilty in 1993 of 16 out of 25 allegations. He lost his 1994 appeal, despite one of the children, then 11, spontaneously coming forward to say she had lied in court. The Appeal Court observed, 'We are by no means satisfied that she did lie at the interviews, although she may now genuinely think she did.'[62]

In Australia, the 'Mr. Bubbles' case broke in Sydney in 1989, followed by the Mornington Childcare case in Victoria in 1991. In both cases, the day-care providers were supposed to have taken children away from the schools and abused them, though there was never any supportive physical evidence. Also, as in many other day-care cases, the abusers were supposed to have dressed up in bizarre costumes to perform their perversions upon the children. All charges were eventually dropped in the Mr. Bubbles case. The owners of the Mornington Childcare and Nursery School were never formally charged, but their business was destroyed anyway. At a closed administrative hearing of the Office of Preschool and Child Care Community Services of Victoria, their license was revoked. A clinical psychologist testified that she felt abuse had indeed occurred – based solely on her second-hand reading of parents' statements. No children ever testified.[63]

Nor have the day-care hysteria cases been limited to English-speaking countries. In the late 1980s and early 1990s, such cases popped up in the Netherlands, Denmark, Sweden, Norway, and Germany as well. In the Bjugn, Norway, case, British influences helped fan the flames. In November of 1992, while visiting Trondheim, near Bjugn, Arnon Bentovim of the Great Ormond Street Hospital first concluded that there was a Norwegian 'paedophile ring' at work. The following year, Eileen Vizard of the Tavistock Clinic and Ray Wyre of the Gracewell Institute attended a conference in Bergen, where they, too, reinforced belief in widespread abuse. Eventually, the repeatedly interviewed Bjugn kindergarten children named numerous abusers, including the local chief of police. Some of the children described adults standing in circles masturbating into buckets, dressing up as ghosts or pirates, and having sex with animals in barns. In the final event, only one teacher was tried, and he was acquitted.[64]

It is alarming that the 'child abuse industry' has apparently spread throughout the Scandinavian countries, as Swedish psychologist Lena Sjögren has observed, with inflated abuse figures and a reversed burden of proof in which the accused must prove their innocence rather than the prosecution having to prove them guilty.[65] It appears that the American and British 'expert' influence is a ticking time-bomb with a delayed fuse. Who knows what the future will bring in the way of unjust prosecutions in other countries?

THE FELLS ACRES NIGHTMARE

But it was in the United States that the majority of the sex abuse hysteria cases occurred, and many innocent people remain in prison there. In a case that was virtually forgotten when the first edition of *Victims of Memory* was published, three innocent people – Gerald 'Tooky' Amirault, now 41, his sister Cheryl LaFave, 37, and his mother, Violet Amirault, 71 – were found guilty of horrendous sexual abuse and sentenced to prison in Massachusetts. Because I have become particularly well acquainted with this situation, and another that relates to it, I hope I can help raise public awareness of these cases.[66*67]

The Amiraults' troubles began one sunny spring day in 1984, when four-and-a-half-year-old Murray Caissie, a newcomer to the long-

---

* See also *The Innocent and the Damned* by Gary Cartwright for comprehensive coverage of another little-known Texas case involving Fran's Day Care, whose owners, Dan and Fran Keller, are in jail for crimes they probably did not commit.

established Fells Acre Day Care Center in Malden, Massachusetts, wet himself during his nap. Deeply embarrassed, he was happy when Tooky changed his pants, cleaned him up, and provided him with alternate clothing kept on hand for such emergencies. Murray carried his wet underwear and pants home in a plastic bag. Nothing more was said of the incident.

Over the summer, Denise Caissie took Murray out of the day care, but she wrote a note of thanks to Violet Amirault, asking her to hold a place for her son in the fall. All was not well in the Caissie household, however. Murray's father, an unemployed custodian with a violent temper, moved out in April of 1984, returned in October, then left again. Murray had always had a bed-wetting problem, but it worsened that spring. He began to imitate the baby-talk of his 16-month-old brother and to act up more often. One night when Murray was crying because he had trouble urinating, his mother told him how one of her brothers had been molested at camp and how Murray should tell her if anyone ever did that to him. The events that followed are unclear, because several conflicting versions were presented in court. What is undisputed is that on Sunday, September 2, the eve of Labor Day, Denise Caissie called a Department of Social Services (DSS) hotline complaining that a man named Tooky had taken her son to a 'secret room' and molested him. It was almost exactly a year after Judy Johnson had sparked the McMartin case.

The following day, two Malden policemen came to the school to request a list of all the children. Violet Amirault sensed that the school, which had been her life for the last 20 years, was in jeopardy, and she protested angrily. 'I'll have you people shut down,' one of the policemen told her. And he did.

On Wednesday, September 5, two days before the birth of his third child, Tooky was arrested on rape charges, without anyone ever questioning him. A week later, the police summoned over a hundred parents to a meeting at the station. There, social workers passed out a laundry list of behavioral symptoms which they said might indicate sexual abuse – bed-wetting, nightmares, poor appetite, crying on the way to school – and asked parents to report any such problems. Very quickly, about 40 cases surfaced.*[68] Of the children questioned, 19 eventually corrobor-

---

* Frantic parents looking for symptoms also had a financial incentive: a $300,000-per-year-per-child insurance policy covered molested children at the day care. Eventually, 18 families would receive about $20 million collectively, over their lifetimes. Money has been a motivating factor in some cases because of Victims Assistance programs, a well-meaning source of funds for crime victims which has, unfortunately, been misused in false accusations of sexual abuse.

ated, after many sessions, that Miss Vi, Miss Cheryl, and Tooky had molested them in grotesque ways. (They also named most of the other teachers, as well as a mythical Mr. Gatt, but they were never arraigned.) Only nine of the most believable children testified in the trial.

The investigators had help. Prosecuting attorney Lawrence Hardoon traveled to California to talk to the McMartin trial team and came back full of information and ideas. Not so coincidentally, the children's allegations took on many of the same ritualistic, bizarre aspects. Like Ray Buckey, Tooky Amirault had supposedly dressed as a clown. Whereas the McMartin molesters had taken the children to tunnels underneath the school, Tooky had performed his sodomy, forced fellatio, and assorted other disgusting acts in a 'magic room' hidden somewhere in the day-care center. Pediatric nurse Susan Kelley, who has published widely about the horrors of ritual abuse, conducted leading interviews with many of the children.

Like Kee MacFarlane in the McMartin case, Susan Kelley refused to take no for an answer. Here is a slightly edited excerpt from one interview, in which she used Bert and Ernie puppets:

SUSAN KELLEY: Would you tell Ernie?
CHILD: No.
KELLEY: Ah, come on [*pleading tone*]. Please tell Ernie. Please tell me. Please tell me. So we could help you. Please . . . You whisper it to Ernie . . . Did anybody ever touch you right there? [*pointing to the vagina of a girl doll*]
CHILD: No.
KELLEY: [*pointing to the doll's posterior*] Did anybody touch your bum?
CHILD: No . . .
KELLEY: Would you tell Bert?
CHILD: They didn't touch me!
KELLEY: Who didn't touch you?
CHILD: Not my teacher. Nobody.
KELLEY: Did any big people, any adult, touch your bum there?
CHILD: No.[69]

Another exchange with a four-year-old shows how Susan Kelley jumped on any comment that might lead to a stereotyped accusation – in this case, the notion that day-care abusers took pornographic photos of naked children:

KELLEY: How about when you went to school at Fells Acres, did anybody look at your vagina?

CHILD: No.

KELLEY: Ohh. Did anybody at Fells Acres ever touch your vagina?

CHILD: No. They took down our pictures.

KELLEY: What pictures?

CHILD: The pictures hanging on the walls.

KELLEY: Ohh. Who took your picture?

CHILD: Not pictures of us – the pictures we drew!

KELLEY: Ohh. Did anybody take pictures of girls with their clothes off?

CHILD: No.[70][*][71]

In testimony before a grand jury, Denise Caissie asserted that Tooky had taken her son out of his classroom to the magic room every day. The evil Amirault also supposedly forced the boy to drink his own urine in front of his teachers, though none of the teachers witnessed such a thing; nor had they ever heard of a magic room, or remembered Tooky taking the child out of the classroom.

Judge Elizabeth Dolan presided over the 1986 trial, pioneering in an attempt to spare the children – who were two to five at the time of the alleged abuse and now a year and a half older – from normal confrontive courtroom procedures. The public was barred from the courtroom. Children were seated in little plastic chairs at a miniature table. To make herself less threatening, Dolan removed her black robes and perched on a small chair next to them. The children were positioned so that they did not have to see the accused, and their parents were allowed to sit just behind them to lend moral support. Rules against leading the witness went out the window for the children. When Hardoon asked the children if they had been abused, they often answered that they had not. With sufficiently pointed questions, however, they usually came around. Defense attorneys had to whisper objections. Judge Dolan routinely disallowed them.

The clear presumption was that the day-care providers were guilty, that these children had been so terrorized and abused that the leading

---

* Susan Kelley's persistence and obvious belief that abuse had occurred isn't surprising, given her published remarks on the reality of satanic ritual abuse. In 1989, she wrote that ritualistic abuse was 'often characterized by forced ingestion of human excrement, semen or blood; ceremonial killing of animals; threats of harm from supernatural powers; ingestion of drugs or "magic potions"; and use of satanic songs, chants or symbols.'

questions were justified, and that to subject them to normal courtroom procedures would be to 'retraumatize' them. It did not seem to occur to anyone that the children were being psychologically traumatized by the Department of Social Services, the police, and the court, and that they might sustain life-long psychic scars as a result.

Logic, in fact, had little to do with the trial. Children said that they had told their teachers they were going to a magic room, even though no teacher had heard of such a room. They told stories of attacks by a robot, being forced to eat a frog Miss Vi had killed, and being molested by clowns and lobsters. One boy told how he had been tied naked to a tree in the school yard in front of all the teachers and children. Though the teachers denied the incident, and no other child verified it, Amirault was found guilty of other offenses this child recounted – how Tooky had raped him with a thick pointed stick which looked like a gun, for instance.* Even the accused man's nickname, which derived from the sound his mother made when she chucked him under the chin as an infant, came to sound sinister and revolting in Hardoon's mouth. 'Yes, and what else did *Tooky* do to you?'

After a 13-day deliberation, the jury returned a guilty verdict. The following year, in a separate trial, his mother and sister were also convicted. For more than seven years, they all languished in prison, losing subsequent appeals and repeatedly being denied parole.

Two days after Tooky Amirault's conviction, his lawyers discovered that Shirley Crawford, a 54-year-old juror, had not told the entire truth about her own background. When she was 14, she had been raped and testified at a trial which sent the rapist to prison for ten years. When confronted with this information, Crawford denied having any memory of the rape. She must have repressed it, she said. Judge Dolan believed her and refused to order a mistrial.

Amirault tries not to hold a grudge. 'I don't blame the kids and parents. They were as much victims as we were,' he told me from his jail cell. He is still bitter that the media coverage and the judge were so one-sided. 'When the kids said "No," it meant "Yes." It was unbelievable. Talk about the deck being stacked against you! You're almost better off killing somebody, really committing a crime. This sex abuse stuff is like fighting ghosts. I just want people to know what really

---

* During Tooky's trial, the boy asserted that he had been hung upside down from the tree and forced to eat white pills; at Vi and Cheryl's trial, however, he claimed to be right-side up and did not recall eating pills.

happened, not what was reported in the scandal sheets or the Boston *Herald American*. I'd sit in the courtroom all day long, and we'd have a real good day in court. Then the paper would come out the next day, and I'd say, "Wow, I can't believe this is the same trial I sat through." Now when I read the newspaper, I only believe the sports pages; the scores and standings are probably accurate. I take everything else with a pound of salt.'

For years, Violet Amirault and her daughter Cheryl LaFave were denied parole because they insisted on their innocence. The parole report for 71-year-old Violet read: 'Parole denied. Vigorously denies the offense(s). Until such time as she is able to take responsibility for her crimes and engages in long term therapy to address the causative factors, she will remain a risk to the community if released.'[72]

Fortunately, in 1995, in the wake of a public outcry fomented primarily by articles on Fells Acres by *Wall Street Journal* reporter Dorothy Rabinowitz, the mother and daughter were released from prison. They won an appeal based on their inability to face the accusing children in court. Unfortunately, unlike his mother and sister, Gerald 'Tooky' Amirault's appeal on the same issue went before Judge Elizabeth Dolan, who had presided over the original trial. Not surprisingly, she denied his appeal, stating in her decision: 'The courtroom seating arrangement at issue reduced the risk of trauma to the child witnesses.'[73] In other words, Dolan continues to assume that abuse took place and that Amirault was guilty. He remains in prison.

THE RAPE OF THE SOUZA FAMILY

Seven years after she ruled on the Amirault case, Judge Elizabeth Dolan also decided the fate of Ray and Shirley Souza, accused of molesting their two grandchildren. As this book goes to press, the Souzas have been found guilty and remain under house arrest in their Lowell, Massachusetts, home, awaiting the verdict of the appeals court. If they lose their case, they will eventually be separated and jailed for 9 to 15 years. Because they are in their early 60s, that possibly amounts to a life sentence.[74]

The Souza case is especially interesting because it combines the two types of sexual abuse allegations – repressed memories recovered by adults, and the repeated questioning of little children. Their story is tragic, but not unique. Throughout the United States, adult daughters have gone to therapy, been encouraged to find repressed incest memories, and then frantically questioned their own small children about what Grammy and Grampa might have done to them. Usually, these family mini-dramas go unpublicized, but because of the criminal trial, the Souzas have lost not only their entire family, but their liberty.

Lifelong residents of Lowell, a classic melting-pot New England mill town, Ray and Shirley Souza raised five children. Products of the Depression, the Souzas were determined to give their children many of the advantages and privileges their parents had lacked. Thus, Ray made sure his kids owned bicycles, because he never had one as a boy. Ray worked as an electrical lineman and Shirley as a part-time nurse. In a way, like many other parents in the 1950s, they reared their children permissively. At the same time, they appeared a bit overprotective and overinvolved. Their children came to rely on them perhaps too much.

Sharon, the oldest daughter, lived only two doors away and ate dinner with her parents frequently. Son Scott lived at home for quite a while, while Tommy also spent a great deal of time there as an adult, playing his drums in the basement. David kept more distance, because his wife Heather didn't get along very well with her mother-in-law. The youngest child, Shirley Ann, had a particularly difficult time breaking away from home when she went to college. After a near date rape and the subsequent trial, Shirley Ann sought counseling with a therapist, who apparently encouraged her to search for repressed incest memories and gave her *The Courage to Heal*.

In a dream she had on Father's Day, 1990, Shirley Ann visualized a horrifying scene in which she was raped by her father, her oldest brother, and her mother. Despite the fact that certain elements in the dream appeared unrealistic – Shirley Ann had no arms or legs, her mother had a penis, while her father inserted a crucifix into her vagina – Shirley Ann immediately called her sister-in-law Heather to inform her that her parents were molesters. 'Please, please,' she said, 'keep your children away from Mom and Dad.'

As a result, Heather took her five-year-old, Cindy, to a child psychologist. At two, Josh seemed too young. The counselor failed to find any evidence of sex abuse, concluding that the mother was pressuring the child unduly. Undaunted, Heather sought another counselor, an 'expert' in spotting abused children. On the very first visit, she proclaimed that Cindy suffered from post-traumatic stress disorder (PTSD) resulting from likely abuse. (Meanwhile, Heather herself, having read *The Courage to Heal*, sought therapy and recovered 'memories' that her grandfather had sexually abused her.)

Eventually, all of the Souzas' children except Scott came to believe the charges, which escalated once the Massachusetts Department of Social Services (DSS) became involved. Although initially skeptical, Shirley Ann's older sister Sharon finally concluded early in 1991 that her four-year-old child Nancy had also been molested by their grandparents, after Sharon herself entered therapy and recovered what she considered previously repressed memories of incest and ritual abuse. In the meantime, as Heather and David's marriage deteriorated, Heather began to suspect that David, too, had abused their children. Under her intense interrogation, Cindy complied, telling her mother how David had molested her. Suffering from a nervous breakdown, he promptly checked himself into a psychiatric hospital. Heather has subsequently divorced David and is now remarried.

Repeatedly questioned by their mothers, therapists, social workers, and police, Cindy and Nancy eventually 'disclosed' how their grandparents sexually abused them.

Because of snowballing allegations and various bureaucratic tangles, the case did not come to trial until January of 1993. Robert George, the Souzas' attorney, advised them to waive their right to a jury trial and rely solely on the decision of Judge Elizabeth Dolan, who had presided over the Fells Acres case.* By the time Ray and Shirley appeared before Dolan in late January, 1993, Cindy and Nancy had not seen their grandparents for nearly two years.

There was no hard evidence against the Souzas other than the word of the children and symptoms reported by their parents. When the children testified, they sat in little chairs at a miniature table, with their backs to their grandparents. Judge Dolan descended from her bench to sit next to them. During her testimony, seven-year-old Cindy revealed that her grandparents routinely locked her and her first cousin Nancy in a basement cage.

Six-year-old Nancy then told Judge Dolan how her grandparents had stuck their entire hands and heads into her vagina, where they would wiggle them around. They also abused her, she said, with a huge multi-

---

* Robert George advised waiving their right to a jury trial because he knew that juries are often swayed by emotional testimony by innocent little children. It is inexplicable why he would have wanted Judge Dolan to be the sole arbiter, however, since George had worked in the office of the Fells Acres defense team, and he knew that she tended to accept children's testimony and the reality of repressed memories.

colored machine, as big as a room, which was kept in the cellar. She did not remember any cage, just as Cindy did not mention any machine.*

Throughout the trial, Judge Dolan indicated that she considered herself an expert on the subject of child abuse. 'You know, I've heard all of this material time after time after time,' she lamented, adding, 'I'm not trying to be a smart mouth or anything ... I'm not saying I know everything but, you know, I have heard a lot in this field over the years. And I've done a moderate amount of reading in this general subject area.' She was overtly hostile to Richard Gardner, the expert witness for the defense. Gardner reviewed videotapes of interviews with five-year-old Cindy during which the little girl commented to investigator Lea Savely, 'Mommy told me that Papa [*her term for her grandfather*] tied me up.' Instead of picking up on this hint of Cindy's confusion, Savely zeroed in on the allegation itself, ignoring the reference to parental pressure: 'Did Papa do that?' Cindy muttered, 'Uh huh,' and Savely followed up with 'And what part of your body?' Cindy mumbled: 'I forget.'

Gardner also objected to the use of anatomically correct dolls because they 'sexualize the interview, they draw the child's fantasies into sexual realms. These dolls have very explicit sexual organs with pubic hair, large breasts, often prominent nipples ... Some of them have open mouths, open anuses, open vaginas, larger than average penises.' He said that, in other contexts, the use of such dolls would be considered inappropriate: 'If this doll were to be used in a school situation, parents would justifiably complain about the competence of a teacher. If a neighbor were to subject the child to such a doll, there would be complaints and indignation.'**[75]

Dr. Leslie Campis, staff psychologist and associate director of the Sexual Abuse Team at Boston's Children's Hospital, was the prosecution's expert witness to counter Gardner. 'Disclosure is understood

---

* During videotaped interview sessions, Nancy had also alleged that her grandparents forced her to drink a green potion. By the time she testified in court, however, she apparently didn't remember it.
** Several studies have shown that the use of anatomically correct dolls can contaminate interviews. Using the dolls in one recent study, Maggie Bruck found that 75 per cent of preschool girls who did not receive a genital examination during a pediatric checkup incorrectly indicated that the doctor had touched their privates. 'A child may insert a finger into a doll's genitalia,' she notes, 'simply because of its novelty.' She and other researchers suggest that children point to their own bodies to indicate what may have occurred. Social workers resist such an idea, assuming that it would somehow traumatize the children.

to be not a single event, but a process,' she told the judge. 'Initially when asked, children might say no, that nothing has happened to them, because they may not be ready to tell their experience.' The second level, she said, is 'tentative disclosure,' followed by 'active disclosure . . . sometimes to the point where they talk about it excessively.' Campis asserted that it is normal for some children to recant, because 'it's their way of trying to make the anxiety go away,' even though the abuse really occurred. She said that it is very rare for children to falsely disclose.

'What might a therapist do in situations where a child is not disclosing?' the prosecutor asked. 'One would want to ask more direct questions,' Campis answered. 'And sometimes, one has to recommend that the child be in an extended therapeutic relationship for them to be able to disclose.' Yet Campis insisted that 'no one who is doing good practice in this area approaches any case with an agenda.'

Dr. Andrea Vandeven, a staff pediatrician at Children's Hospital, took the stand to discuss her examination of the children, during which she spread their labia and examined their hymens carefully, taking photographs of their private areas. She found no irregularities. She then turned them onto their stomachs, rear ends presented to her invading finger, covered by a surgical glove. Vandeven told Judge Dolan that Nancy's exam was 'consistent with anal penetration,' particularly because she felt that her anus 'spontaneously dilated' more than most she had seen. Under cross-examination, the doctor admitted that there was no evidence of penetration. She noted, however, that 'normal rectal exams are consistent with penetration, with or without dilatation.' In other words, *any* exam of a child would be considered 'consistent with penetration.'

Ray and Shirley Souza testified that they never abused their grand-children. It was obvious that their attorneys had not prepared them for cross-examination, and they came across as extremely defensive. Various old friends and fellow workers briefly took the stand, recalling the loving, unfearful relationship the grandchildren seemed to have with their grandparents. These character witnesses were dismissed by Dolan as 'window dressing.'

The trial was also notable for those who did *not* testify. Shirley Ann Souza, whose dream sparked the entire affair, did not appear, nor did her therapist. Carmela Eyal, the therapist who finally concluded that Heather Souza was applying undue pressure on Cindy, did not testify. Jeanine Hemstead, the therapist responsible for getting both Cindy and

Nancy to disclose, never took the stand. Aside from Dr. Gardner, the defense called no expert witnesses – no scientists who had conducted studies on the suggestibility of children, no pediatricians who had studied normal children who present with the same 'fissures' and 'tears' that supposedly indicate abuse.

After a week and a half of testimony, Judge Dolan took another 14 days before she pronounced the Souzas guilty as charged. In her opinion, Dolan acknowledged that 'children are quite capable of *intentional* false-hoods,' but she obviously did not feel that they can easily incorporate false memories into their belief systems. She dismissed any inconsistencies or unbelievable stories because of the children's ages: 'Age impacts upon perception, memory and verbal capacity.' She was particularly impressed by the children's knowledge of wet vaginas. 'As a general premise,' she wrote, 'most young children do not have knowledge of adult sexual activity to support a convincing, detailed lie about sexual abuse.'

On the other hand, Dolan also interpreted *unconvincing* details as proof that abuse occurred. Commenting on Nancy's rather odd testimony about feet and elbows being stuck into her vagina, the judge said: 'A child who has been coached, programmed or rehearsed in a fabrication is unlikely to include elbows and feet.' In other words, if the story appeared plausible, it proved abuse. If the story was implausible, it also proved abuse. Incredibly, Dolan asserted, 'There was no evidence of [Sharon's] malice or bias against her parents' – ignoring her therapy-induced beliefs that her parents had ritually abused her as a child. (The judge had not allowed this evidence to be presented.)

At the end of the trial, Sharon and Heather read emotional statements calling for lengthy jail terms and quoting from letters purportedly written by Cindy and Nancy. Sharon asked Judge Dolan not to be influenced by her parents' age. 'People may say they're so old, why send them to jail? I say, they've not always been 61 years old, and they've been doing this for years.'

Before the sentencing, however, a public outcry erupted, largely due to the efforts of Richard Gardner, the outspoken Columbia University psychiatrist who had testified for the Souzas in the trial. After the media picked up the story, Dolan repeatedly delayed sentencing. Eventually, she handed down a judgment of 9 to 15 years, but rather than sending the couple to jail, she confined them to house arrest pending their appeal.

Unhappy with their first lawyer, the Souzas have secured Dan

Williams, who successfully represented Kelly Michaels in her fight to clear her name. The Souzas have lost an initial round of appeals, but they remain hopeful that they will be freed eventually, especially in light of the decision to free Cheryl LaFave and Violet Amirault in the Fells Acres case.

While awaiting the outcome of their appeal, they continue to live in the home they purchased 25 years ago, wearing awkward electronic ankle monitors and sending their picture by fax telephone ten times a day to the Department of Corrections. Their children speak out frequently on the perils of sex abuse and are trying to sell their story to Hollywood.

'When those kiddos grow up,' Ray Souza says of his grandchildren, 'they're going to realize that these things never happened. They're bright children and they have a mind of their own, and when nobody's prompting them, when they grow up, they're going to remember, and we'll embrace.'*

BELIEVING THE CHILDREN

Richard Gardner has written several books, including *Sex Abuse Hysteria* and *True and False Accusations of Child Sex Abuse*, about the problems that can arise when people question children *too* intently about possible sex abuse. No one – certainly not Gardner, who has worked extensively with traumatized children – denies the reality or horror of child sexual abuse. Adults can and do sometimes take advantage of the innocence and helplessness of small children, and the resulting confusion, shame, and long-lasting psychic damage can be devastating. We must be extremely careful, however, not to jump to conclusions or engage in coercive, leading interviews once a suspicion is aroused.

There is one point that has not been made strongly enough concerning these day-care and custody cases, as well as recovered memories of abuse at a very early age. The majority of child molesters prefer older children, usually beginning with grooming activities around the age of nine or ten. Not only that, but the grotesque, violent abuse of

---

* I hope that Souza's prediction is correct, but the McMartin case offers a less optimistic scenario. Now teenagers, many of the accusing children still maintain that they were abused when they were in day care. It has become an essential part of their belief systems.

preschoolers, commonly alleged in these cases, would cause obvious, permanent damage, if not death.[76] Why, then, did the children in these cases display no ill effects and disclose no abuse until coerced into doing so?

We must beware of therapists such as California psychiatrist Roland Summit, author of 'The Child Sexual Abuse Accommodation Syndrome,' a 1983 paper that has served as a touchstone for overzealous investigators.[77] In that article, Summit noted that 'child sexual abuse has exploded into public awareness during a span of less than five years.' His paper blasted 'any adult who chooses to remain aloof from the helplessness and pain of the child's dilemma.' Few could dispute Summit's sentiments regarding the plight of abused children, or his wrath at adults who refuse to listen to them.

Yet his description of children's reluctance to disclose sexual abuse spawned today's coercive measures and belief in implausible allegations. Summit encouraged investigators to question children repeatedly and to believe their eventual allegations, regardless of their implausible nature. 'The more illogical and incredible the initiation scene might seem to adults,' Summit wrote, 'the more likely it is that the child's plaintive description is valid.' He added, 'It has become a maxim among child sexual abuse intervention counselors and investigators that children never fabricate the kinds of explicit sexual manipulations they divulge in complaints or interrogations.'

As the final stage of his hypothetical syndrome, Summit asserted, '*Whatever a child says about sexual abuse, she is likely to reverse it.*' In other words, even once a child has disclosed, she is likely to take back the allegations, even though they are true. While Summit was correct that sexually abused children often 'accommodate' themselves to powerful adults, it did not occur to him that they might similarly accommodate themselves to powerful adult interrogators intent on hearing abuse allegations.[78]

Summit's original paper was mild and reasonable, however, compared to his more recent statements. 'When there is some level of suspicion,' Summit told a television journalist in 1994, 'the investigation has to go way beyond the ability of children to tell us about it.' The first interview, he explained, rarely results in disclosure. 'There has to be more than one interview, and there are times children will say quite sincerely that nothing happened, only later to begin disclosing their experience.' Not only that, but 'it's not unusual for children in criminal cases to come back and say, "It never happened. I only said those things because the prosecutor badgered me."' These children, he believes, are simply 'in denial' of their very real abuse. Summit also defends Kee MacFarlane's coercive interview techniques in the McMartin case, even though he admits he has never reviewed the tapes.[79]

The parallel mindsets of the repressed memory therapists and child sex abuse specialists are striking. 'Children never fabricate the explicit detail,' Summit insists, just as those who believe in massive repressed memories cite detailed accounts as evidence for their validity. Child investigators are determined to get children to reveal abuse that never occurred – just as therapists root out repressed memories of events that never happened. In both cases, it doesn't seem to disturb them that some of the allegations are, to say the least, improbable. A sword stuck into children's privates, for instance, would certainly leave prominent scars, if it didn't kill them. Both the child and adult therapists brush aside concerns about improbable or downright impossible stories. These exact events may not have occurred, they argue, but they *symbolically* represent some other actual abuse.

I recently interviewed Steven Normandin, one of the 1986 jurors from the Fells Acres case. 'There's still absolutely no doubt in my mind that Tooky Amirault was guilty,' he told me. I asked him how he and the other jurors had reacted to some of the more bizarre allegations, such as the little boy who claimed to have been hung naked upside down from a tree while the entire school watched. 'Well,' he told me, 'some of those things were probably exaggerated. But we knew the kids were telling the truth. Besides, Amirault just didn't seem credible when he testified.'[80]

It is ironic that the battle-cry of those leading the charge in these cases is, 'Believe the children!' In fact, the trouble always begins in these cases when adults *do not* believe children who truthfully report that no one abused them. The mantra would be more accurate if it went, 'Believe the children, but only when or if they say they were abused, no matter how incredible, bizarre, or unrealistic their stories may be.'

PEGGY BUCKEY'S POST-TRAUMATIC STRESS

Even those who have been found innocent in these cases, though, are still coping with how their lives have been altered. They have lost their livelihoods, their reputations, their homes, and millions of dollars. I recently interviewed Peggy Buckey, who is now 68 years old.*[81] A decade ago, she was jailed for two years while awaiting her McMartin trial. 'I survived four attempts on my life,' she told me, 'because other inmates hate anyone accused of child molestation.' Once she and her son Ray were finally vindicated in 1990, she fell apart. 'I was afraid of everything, of everyone. I couldn't leave the house or drive a car. I was heavily sedated. They diagnosed me with post-traumatic stress disorder.' It took three years for her to recover.

Today, Peggy Buckey volunteers at a soup kitchen for the homeless and keeps up an active correspondence with those who have been jailed in similar molestation cases – Bill and Kathy Swan in Kirkland, Washington;**[82] Bob and Betsy Kelly and Dawn Wilson in Raleigh, North Carolina; Kelly Michaels in New Jersey; Brenda Kniffen in Frontera, California; Frank Fuster in Bushnell, Florida; Debbie Runyan and Lynn Malcom in Gig Harbor, Washington. I told her about the Amiraults and Souzas, who can now expect to get a letter from Peggy Buckey.

---

* Peggy Buckey's mother, wheelchair-bound Virginia McMartin, died in 1995 at the age of 88. 'She was the single strongest, most committed, most energetic player in the entire saga,' her lawyer, Danny Davis, commented. Before she died, McMartin got to see herself portrayed as a heroine in the 1995 television movie, *Indictment*.
** The case of Bill and Kathy Swan is one of the worst I have heard. On her first day on the job in 1985, day-care worker Lisa Conradi interpreted remarks made by three-year-old Betty Swan as evidence of child abuse. Conradi had already been fired from several other day cares because she saw child abuse everywhere. She later told a reporter that she herself had been sexually abused by 'damn near everybody that came near ... used regularly, daily, by three or four hundred guys.' At the 1986 trial, Betty was found incompetent to testify, but Conradi's hearsay evidence was admitted. The Swans were found guilty. Now finally out of jail, they still do not have custody of Betty. In fact, they have not even seen her since leaving prison, because the child's therapist deems that she is 'not ready yet.' The Swans saw their four-year-old daughter Hillary, born just before Kathy went to jail, for the first time in 1993.

CHAPTER TEN

A Brief History: The Witch Craze, Reflex Arcs, and Freud's Legacy

Woman! A she hell-cat, a witch! To prove her one, we no sooner set fire on the thatch of her house, but in she came running, as if the devil had sent her in a barrel of gunpowder.

JOHN FORD, *The Witch of Edmonton* (1658)[1]

What history teaches us is that man has never learned anything from it.

GEORG WILHELM HEGEL[2]

'Today, more women are seeking psychiatric help and being hospitalized than at any other time in history,' feminist Phyllis Chesler wrote in her seminal 1972 book, *Women and Madness*. She attributed this intensification of an old trend to the 'help-seeking' nature of the learned female role, the oppression of women, and role confusion in the modern age. 'While women live longer than ever before,' Chesler observed, 'there is less and less use, and literally no place, for them in the only place they "belong" – within the family. Many newly useless women are emerging more publicly into insanity.'[3]

The female 'career' as a psychiatric patient identified by Chesler has a long history, with women often displaying the symptoms expected of them: depression, frigidity, paranoia, vague aches and pains, suicide attempts, and anxiety. Of course, when women have rebelled against their passive state, becoming aggressive and sexually active, they have *also* been labeled mentally ill. Chesler tacitly acknowledged this history with a wry observation: 'No longer are women sacrificed as voluntary or involuntary witches. They are, instead, taught to sacrifice themselves for newly named heresies.'[4]

In Western cultures, both men and women have suffered from bizarre psychosomatic ailments for centuries, always aided and abetted by the 'experts' of the era, whose expectations determined which symptoms

436

they would display. Because of societal bias, females, considered the 'weaker vessel,' have traditionally been expected to act out the role of the 'hysteric' more often than males. Women – frequently repressed and abused, and sometimes powerless to do much about it – have often conformed to the role expectation, which at least allows them sympathetic attention and an emotional outlet for their suppressed and usually justifiable rage.*[5] The only thing that is relatively new about the Incest Survivor movement is its particularly awful slant – the virulent accusations against parents and other early caregivers. We will briefly examine several historical periods, looking for insights into our current crisis.

THE WITCH CRAZE

If its duration is any indication, the Witch Craze is frightening evidence that human beings are capable of maintaining sustained societal persecution based upon fantasies for a long, long time. For two centuries, the 16th and 17th, most of Europe engaged in a frantic search for evil witches, a process which bore an alarming resemblance to the modern hunt for pedophiles – except, of course, that there really *are* pedophiles, which makes the epidemic search for repressed memories more confusing and unlikely to disappear anytime soon. To the clerics, philosophers and lawyers of the 1500s, however, there was also no doubt that witches existed and exerted a malevolent force everywhere. Mostly, witches were older women with extraordinary powers who had formed an underground international organization and practiced hideous rituals involving bestiality, murder, rape, and other atrocities. As Hugh Trevor-Roper, a historian who has written about the period, noted, 'some of the most powerful minds of the time' applied themselves to studying the witch phenomenon. 'And the details which they discover, and which are continually being confirmed by teams of parallel researchers – field

---

* Men are equally susceptible to psychosomatic ailments, but in Western culture, as in many other patriarchal cultures, they are socially molded to act them out differently, usually with more overt aggression. During the Middle Ages, for instance, the various 'dancing attacks,' in which masses of people saw visions and jumped about for prolonged periods, afflicted more men than women. In Malaya, women are subject to 'Latah,' which usually follows a sudden fright, such as stepping on a snake. During Latah, they act in a compliant manner, often wailing. Malayan men, on the other hand, sometimes suffer from 'Amok,' in which they suddenly seize a weapon and kill anyone within reach until subdued or killed. Those who survive claim amnesia regarding the entire episode.

437

researchers in torture-chamber or confessional, academic researchers in library or cloister – leave the facts more certainly established and the prospect more alarming than ever.'[6]

What such experts discovered was that elderly and not-so-elderly women were making pacts with the Devil, at whose command they ate boiled children, engaged in sexual orgies, and generally enjoyed themselves in revolting fashion. In between these witch's sabbats, they rendered bridegrooms impotent, killed off neighbors' pigs, and had sex nightly with the Devil, who aroused them as an invisible *incubus*. Thus, any sexual dreams or nightmares could be easily explained, though it was an unwise woman who was caught having such dreams or who reported them.

The zealous clerics and judges who ferreted out these evil witches had help from numerous manuals which described the symptoms of witchcraft in great detail. The first and most famous, the *Malleus Maleficarum*, or 'Hammer of Witches,' written by Heinrich Kramer and James Sprenger, was published in 1486. It is a remarkable document which, like *The Courage to Heal*, offers an internally logical and quite convincing way to identify the root cause of the problem. In this case, however, it was witchcraft rather than repressed memories of sexual abuse that wreaked havoc in people's lives. 'The *Malleus* lay on the bench of every judge, on the desk of every magistrate,' noted Montague Summers in his introduction to the 1948 reprint. 'It was the ultimate, irrefutable, unarguable authority.'[7]

The *Malleus* included compelling case studies. In the town of Ratisbon, for instance, 'a certain young man who had an intrigue with a girl, wishing to leave her, lost his member.' He was not merely impotent. 'Some glamour was cast over it so that he could see or touch nothing but his smooth body.'*[8] In need of a stiff drink, he entered a tavern, where he described his problem to a woman at the bar, 'demonstrating in his body that it was so.' She immediately adduced that he had been bewitched and asked if he suspected anyone. He did. That night, he accosted an elderly woman in the neighborhood, who maintained her innocence and said she knew nothing of his missing penis. Thereupon he grabbed her, choking her with a towel wrapped around her neck. 'Unless you give me back my health,' he exclaimed, 'you shall die at my

---

* Masculine paranoid delusions such as this story reveals are not unique to Western culture. Chinese men sometimes suffer from *koro*, a state in which they are convinced that their penises are shriveling up, soon to disappear completely.

hands.' Not surprisingly, she submitted. 'The witch touched him with her hand between the thighs, saying, "Now you have what you desire."' And he was cured.[9]

Compared to *The Courage to Heal*, however, the *Malleus* was in some ways a moderate, well-reasoned document. Take, for instance, the section entitled 'Of One Taken and Convicted, But Denying Everything.' True, the accused should be kept 'in strong durance fettered and chained,' and should regularly be visited by officers to 'induce him to discover the truth.' But the authors cautioned the authorities not to 'be in any haste to pronounce a definitive sentence.' Indeed, they should urge witnesses to 'examine their consciences well.' Perhaps their memories were faulty, or 'actuated by malice.' If the alleged witch maintained his or her denial for over a year, however, and the witnesses didn't recant, the witch should be reluctantly turned over to the secular judges for sentencing and burning.[10]

As Montague Summers wrote in his heavily ironic 1948 introduction, 'What is most surprising is the modernity of the book. There is hardly a problem, a complex, a difficulty, which they have not foreseen, and discussed, and resolved. Here are cases which occur in the law-courts today, set out with the greatest clarity, argued with unflinching logic, and judged with scrupulous impartiality.'[11] Summers did not know how germane his observations would be in another forty years, when *The Courage to Heal* would be published. In a rather bizarre case, Lorena Bobbitt has recently acted out the scenario depicted above, but she used a knife, rather than any 'glamour,' to remove the offending penis.

Speaking of the hunt for witches, Trevor-Roper observed: 'Since a system was presupposed, a system was found. The confessions – those disconnected fragments of truth hardly won from the enemy – were seen as the few visible projections of a vast and complex organization, and so every new confession supplied fresh evidence for deductive minds.' He pointed out that this insanity did not take place during the Dark Ages or even the Middle Ages. No, it was during the flowering of intellect of the Renaissance period, during the time of Erasmus, Luther, and Shakespeare,*[12] whose works, not so coincidentally, roil

---

* In 1598, all of England was riveted by the prosecution of the 'witches of Warbois.' Young Joan Throgmorton claimed that Mother Samuel, an elderly neighborhood woman, had afflicted her with spirits with imaginative names such as 'First Smack,' 'Blue,' 'Catch,' 'Hardname' and 'Pluck.' The same year, Shakespeare's *A Midsummer Night's Dream* featured a less harmful cousin spirit named 'Puck.'

with witches. This fact should serve as a 'standing warning to those who would simplify the stages of human progress,' Trevor-Roper dryly observed. 'Even intellectual history, we now admit, is relative and cannot be dissociated from the wider, social context with which it is in constant interaction.'

Arguably, what made the almost universal hunt for witches possible was the same new technology that sparked the Renaissance and allowed the Bard's work to live forever: the invention of the printing press by Johannes Gutenberg in the mid–1400s. The *Malleus* followed only 30 years later. We suffer from the same irony today during the era of CNN and instantaneous information retrieval. Without the talk shows and their voracious appetite for sensation, without our printing presses and the nightly news, it is unlikely that the dogma surrounding repressed memories would have spread so quickly and effectively, spawning the current epidemic of incest charges, nor would the modern rumors of satanic cults have gained such easy credence.

At first, it was mainly the clerics who pressed the charges against witches. Quite soon, however, the lawyers took over. By 1600, noted Trevor-Roper, they were 'more savage and pedantic than the clergy,' having recognized a good source of income when they saw it. The witch trials also lent an enthralling, appalling moral force to their otherwise mundane practices. As one prosecutor bemoaned: 'Was ever age so afflicted as ours? The seats destined for criminals in our courts of justice are blackened with persons accused of this guilt. There are not judges enough to try them.' Every day, he and his colleagues 'return to our homes discountenanced and terrified at the horrible confessions which we have heard.'[13] Similarly, whole law firms now specialize in representing young women who are suing their 'perpetrators' for sexual abuse, based on recovered memories.

Not all of the confessions during the Witch Craze were extracted by torture. Even in England, which abjured such tactics, many 'witches' confessed to the most ridiculous charges. As Charles Mackay wrote in 1841, 'When religion and law alike recognized the crime, it is no wonder that ... the strong in imagination ... fancied themselves endued with the terrible powers of which all the world were speaking.'[14] Trevor-Roper estimated that, for every victim whose story popped out under duress, there were two or three who genuinely believed they were witches. They had developed very coherent, detailed memories of the orgies in which they had taken part, the babies they had roasted and eaten. Young girls would describe in gory detail how they had been deflowered by the Devil, though examination proved them to be virgins.[15]*

It seems strange, of course, that women would admit to being witches, knowing that they would be burned. Yet as one historian noted, there were advantages to the role: 'Think of the power wielded by Satan's Chosen Bride! She can heal, prophesy, predict, conjure up the spirits of the dead, can spell-bind you . . ., cast a love charm over you; there is no escaping!'[16] For a woman without any real authority in society, a belief in such powers could prove quite attractive, despite its hazards. 'Again and again,' Trevor-Roper wrote, 'when we read the case histories, we find witches freely confessing to esoteric details without any evidence of torture, and it was this spontaneity, rather than the confessions themselves, which convinced rational men that the details were true.'

This observation is analogous to what I have heard therapists say over and over: 'You wouldn't doubt these memories if you had seen what I have seen. These women are in terrible pain, reliving the abuse. It is absolutely real, there's no question.' The most famous modern case of a self-confessed 'witch' is Paul Ingram, the Washington State policeman who obligingly told his interrogators that he had raped his daughters as a priest in a satanic cult. Ingram is the subject of Lawrence Wright's book, *Remembering Satan*. Only when Ingram confessed an imaginary event planted by social psychologist Richard Ofshe was it clear that he was not a sex abuser after all. A similar case is presented in Chapter 7 of this book. And as I can attest, anyone accused of a heinous crime that he did not commit goes through self-doubts and guilt that could easily, under the right circumstances, be turned into a belief in the charges.

Exactly why social movements such as the Witch Craze occur is a difficult question, but it appears that periods of general social unrest provide a standard backdrop.[17] When life is too confusing, a scapegoat helps, whether it be a witch, a Jew, a Communist, or alleged pedophile. The Witch Craze seems to have flourished particularly in poverty-stricken rural areas. As Trevor-Roper wrote, 'If the Dominicans, by their constant propaganda, created a hatred of witches, they created it in a favorable social context.' During the two centuries that Europe hunted witches, there were periods of relative prosperity when the tribunals and tortures

---

* The Survivor movement has yielded similar cases in which young women 'discover' through recovered memories that their fathers raped them throughout their childhoods; yet their hymens are found to be intact.

almost ceased. But when times got rough, so did the handling of witches. To apply the lesson to our times: Ellen Bass and Laura Davis may have written a deadly book, but they can hardly be blamed for the current witch hunt for sex abusers. Our society, for a variety of reasons (*see Chapter 11, 'Why Now?'*), was ready and eager for her message.

Eventually, the excesses of the Witch Craze drew criticism. Compassionate souls realized that many of the confessions were merely the result of torture and that many of the supposed 'witches' were the victims of political feuds or long-standing family rivalries.*[18] Still, none of the critics questioned the underlying assumption that there *were* witches who did evil deeds. It wasn't until Descartes came along and changed the entire way we thought, giving us a mechanistic universe – with its own problems and prejudices – that witches receded into mythology. Similarly, few now question the validity of 'repressed memories,' our Freudian legacy, though such repression may not exist at all (*see Chapter 2, 'The Memory Maze'*). As Trevor-Roper wrote, 'the absurdity of inquisitorial demonology should be a salutary warning to us never to trust the accounts which a persecuting society has drawn up of any esoteric heresy ... Once the mythology had been established, it acquired, as it were, a reality of its own ... It had become part of the structure of thought, and time had so entwined it with other beliefs, and indeed with social interests, that it seemed impossible to destroy it.'

By the end of the 17th century, the furious hunt for witches was sputtering out in Europe, but it briefly flourished in one last bright flash in America, where the Puritans lagged behind the times. In 1692, in Salem, Massachusetts, nine-year-old Betty Parris, the local minister's daughter, began to act very strangely.[19] She entered a kind of trance. Her body contorted. She uttered horrible gargling noises and growls. Soon, her cousin Abigail was crawling around the house barking like a dog. 'Their arms, necks and backs were turned this way and that way,' a contemporary observer wrote, 'so that it was impossible for them to do of themselves, and beyond the power of any epileptic fits or natural disease to effect.' Choking, they asserted that the devil himself had stuck invisible balls in their windpipes. They felt thorns piercing their flesh.

* When Boguet wrote his treatise on witches in 1602, he warned that 'torture is both useless and unnecessary,' since extracted confessions were compromised. Instead, he simply said to burn them – but humanity compelled him to suggest they be strangled first. 'Never was judge more conscientious, more thorough, more bent on extermination,' wrote Jules Michelet in his classic history of witchcraft.

The girls' behavior stemmed largely from what they already knew about bewitchment and demonic possession, but it was augmented by Reverend Parris' West Indian slave, Tituba, who could tell a fortune by floating an egg white in a glass. When it revealed the milky shape of a coffin, and the girls' fits amplified, ministers from miles around gathered and asked, 'Who torments you?' When the girls failed to name anyone, the ministers suggested likely older women of the town. Just as modern therapists inadvertently cue their patients into visualizing sexual abuse, these ministers dragged accusations out of the young girls, and the first three witches were charged.

In the courtroom, the girls put on a remarkable show. Of course, they were not pretending. They *believed* that they were under the influence of witchcraft, and their tortures seemed quite real to everyone. When Martha Corey, one accused woman, protested, 'We must not believe these distracted children,' no one heeded her. When Dame Corey clenched her fists, the girls screamed as if they had been pinched. When she bit her lip, their faces twisted in agony and their mouths bled, showing tooth marks. In the mad search for witches, almost any evidence would do. A birthmark, mole, or genital irregularity could be interpreted as a 'witch's teat,' a flap of flesh to suckle the Devil.*[20]

The girls fell into fits from almost anyone who looked at them. Neighbors corroborated the accusations – yes, they had seen shapes at night, yes, they had been choked and tormented by this witch, by that witch. Friend turned against friend, brother against sister. No one was safe. One four-year-old girl, whose specter supposedly bit Betty Parris, was kept in chains for nine months. A pet dog was executed for practicing witchcraft. In the end, when the accusations had spread to some of the most prominent families in Salem, the judges put a stop to the prosecutions.

Why did the Witch Craze afflict Salem? Were the Puritans living in a particularly stressful time? Yes. They scraped out their existence in a strange new land, terrified of the Indians, whom they considered savages and demons.**[21] At the heart of the conflict lay an old feud between the

* In the fourth edition of his *Country Justice*, published in 1630, British jurist Michael Dalton wrote about the scientific search for signs such as 'some big or little Teat upon their body, and in some secret place, where he (the Devil) sucketh them. And besides their sucking, the Devil leaveth other marks upon their body, sometimes like a blew spot or red spot, like a flea-biting.' Because such teats were 'often in their secretest parts,' they required 'diligent and careful search.'
** The Indians themselves were quite puzzled by the bizarre behavior and beliefs of the Puritans.

Porter and Putnam families. Added to that, there was really no town government, and the only established values were those provided by the church, which believed in Satan. It was in this climate of fear that the young girls' antics and accusations were taken seriously, and 20 people died as a result. Fourteen of them were women, the common scapegoats of a patriarchal era. Any women who did not fit the desired cultural stereotypes were suspect – childless women, spinsters, adulteresses, or outspoken 'troublemakers.'

Today, of course, the accused tend to be the exact opposite – men, particularly those in some position of authority, are the preferred targets. If their public behavior appears beyond reproach, so much the better. They must be hiding their abusive behavior, but they can't fool the questing therapist or the regressed daughter. Truth will out!

DEMONS

Demonology, a parallel phenomenon, pre-dated the two centuries of the Witch Craze and lasted well beyond it – to this day, in fact.*[22] The belief in demons is widespread and boasts an ancient lineage. The Jews apparently picked up demonology from the Babylonians and Assyrians during the second and first centuries B.C. The concept was adopted by early Christians; the New Testament records numerous examples of possession and exorcism.[23]

As with witches, most people who were possessed by demons were female. There was a symbiotic relation between the two, because witches were assumed to have the power to inject demons into people. Conversely, demoniacs could then unmask witches who had inflicted this misery upon them. Thus, Betty Parris and her cohorts in Salem were considered to be possessed and able to name the perpetrators. As psy-

---

* There is no room here for an extended cross-cultural foray into demonology. Anthropologist Felicitas Goodman offers a sympathetic look at world-wide beliefs in *How About Demons: Possession and Exorcism in the Modern World* (1988). It is unclear whether Goodman actually believes in possession or not, but she clearly recognizes the efficacy of exorcism for those with the proper belief systems. She notes that 'the respective spirit is "culture-specific." Normally, *hekura* spirits can enter only during a Yanomamo ritual. The Holy Spirit comes to worshipers during a ritual in a Pentecostal church.' It is obvious that cultural expectations account for the possessions. As one informant told Goodman, 'You see it happening to others and you wonder, will it ever happen to me too? And then it does happen.'

chologist Nicholas Spanos has pointed out, those who thought they were possessed by demons were acting out a carefully prescribed social role. They were expected to be insensitive to pain, be amnesic for what occurred during attacks, experience various sensory or motor deficits, exhibit heightened intelligence or clairvoyance, and be under involuntary control by their demons. Quotations from primary sources are revealing:

> [During the possession state,] her Apprehension, Understanding, and Memory, was riper than ever in her life; and yet, when she was herself, she . . . forgot almost everything that passed in these Ludicrous Intervals. (1693)

> Sometimes also she can hear only, and not everybody, but someone whom she liketh and chooseth out from the rest; sometimes she seeth only . . . sometimes both hearing and seeing very well, and yet not able to speak. (1593)

> I cannot help myself at all, for he [the demon] uses my limbs and organs, my neck, my tongue, and my lungs . . . I am altogether unable to restrain them. (1489)

> An even more certain sign [of possession] is when a sick man speaks in foreign tongues unknown to him . . . or when, being but ignorant, the patients argue about high and difficult questions; or when they discover hidden and long-forgotten matters, or future events, or the secrets of the inner conscience, such as the sins and imaginings of bystanders. (1608)[24]

As Spanos points out, 'the components of the demoniac role were generally well-known to the average person in medieval and late medieval Europe, and the potential demoniac's exposure to "experts" (usually clerics) served to define the subtleties of the role in great detail.' The greatest source of educational information came from the exorcism procedure itself. 'As a preliminary to the Catholic exorcism rite,' Spanos writes, 'the priest was required to obtain information from the demoniac concerning the number and names of the possessing demons.' In other words, the priests provided a 'detailed recipe of expected role enactments.' In addition, would-be demoniacs could pick up tips by watching the behavior of those who were possessed, both before and during an exorcism.

Because she shared the same cultural frame of reference as the priest,

445

the demoniac usually truly believed that she was possessed and would involuntarily exhibit all of the expected characteristics. In addition, there were benefits that went along with the role, particularly for women who normally had little societal power. They received a great deal of sympathetic attention, the power to identify witches or predict the future, a lightened work load, a dramatic self-importance. Even so, some women resisted the label. 'Periodic denials of being possessed were expected by authorities,' Spanos notes, 'and were routinely construed as obvious indications of a wily demon attempting to escape divine punishment. Continued refusal to enact the role properly frequently led to punishment administered in the guise of benevolently motivated attempts to free a helpless victim from demonic control.'

THE NERVE DOCTORS AND THE 'HYSTERICS'

Psychosomatic illness didn't originate with the Witch Craze or widespread belief in demonic possession, nor did it perish with the Enlightenment. Indeed, the duality promoted by Descartes – subject separate from object, mind independent of body – prompted a world-view in which all phenomena could be explained rationally and scientifically. Unfortunately, this approach merely transferred the cloak of 'expert' from the cleric to the physician and, eventually, the therapist. The symptoms and treatment didn't change much.

Part of what makes human beings unique is the power of our imagination, and while that quality allows us to create great art, it also means that we are capable of inflicting very real psychological and even physical injury upon ourselves, all through the power of the mind. By the late 18th century, the paradigm and the expected social roles had shifted, however. Demons were gradually replaced by more 'scientific' explanations, and witches were being relabeled 'hysterics,' a pejorative term deriving from the Greek word for uterus.

Numerous cases of what might be psychosomatic illnesses were reported in antiquity. The Bible records sudden loss of the power of speech, the inability to open the eyelids, terrible contractions of the elbows, wrists and fingers, and fits in which the subjects' limbs twitched spasmodically and they screamed, cursed, and tried to bite those nearby.[25] One of the classic symptoms, *globus hystericus*, has already been described in Chapter 3. Shakespeare's King Lear referred to this choking sensation as he struggled to master his anger: 'O how this mother swells up toward my heart! / Hysterica passio, down, thou climbing sorrow.'[26]

After the Witch Craze died down, ailments originating through suggestion took on other forms, always those sanctioned by the particular disease model of the era. In his meticulously researched book, *From Paralysis to Fatigue: A History of Psychosomatic Illness in the Modern Era*, Edward Shorter describes over two centuries of quackery, observing that 'patients' notions of disease tend to follow doctors' ideas.' His conclusion, based on an extensive survey of psychosomatic sickness over the years, is that 'the relationship between doctors and patients is reciprocal: As the ideas of either party about what constitutes legitimate organic disease change, the other member of the duo will respond. Thus the history of psychosomatic illness is one of ever-changing steps in a *pas de deux* between doctor and patient.'

That unconscious dance has now led to the incest accusation craze, which follows a long tradition in which women have been victimized by their doctors and therapists. As we review cases from the past, bear in mind that many of the 'symptoms' that doctors once diagnosed as 'irritable spine' or 'hysterical insanity' are now interpreted as proof of repressed memories of sexual abuse. Thus, *globus hystericus* is taken as evidence that your father forced fellatio on you when you were in your crib, and other psychologically induced bodily pains are labeled 'body memories' of abuse.

Shorter demonstrates that patients in search of an easy answer – or sympathy and attention – conform to the 'symptom pool' of the era. 'The surrounding culture,' he writes, 'provides our unconscious minds with templates, or models, of illness.' When it was considered normal to be paralyzed, lo! they were paralyzed. It is the same with supposed incest survivors, who convince themselves that their anxiety attacks are flashbacks to memories of abuse.

My only criticism of Shorter is that he tends to assume that *all* diagnosed cases of 'irritable spine' and the like were purely psychosomatic. A substantial number may have been misdiagnosed organic ailments such as epilepsy, as Richard Webster documents in his 1995 book, *Why Freud Was Wrong*. Similarly, some women convinced that they harbor 'repressed memories' really do have treatable mental or physical illnesses. Regardless of whether the ailments are real or psychosomatic, however, the root cause is neither 'hysteria' nor buried incest memories.

In 1702, a London physician named John Purcell described 'vapours, otherwise called hysterick fits.' Sufferers exhibited the following symptoms:

> First they feel a heaviness upon their breast, a grumbling in their belly, they belch up, and sometimes vomit . . . They have a difficulty in breathing and think they feel something that comes up into their throat which is ready to choke them; they struggle, cry out, make odd and inarticulate sounds or mutterings; they perceive a swimming in their heads, a dimness comes over their eyes; they turn pale, are scarce able to stand; their pulse is weak, they shut their eyes, fall down and remain senseless for some time.[27]

For centuries, physicians had blamed a 'floating womb' or uterus for 'hysterical' fits. Somehow, they believed that this was linked to perverted sexual desires, including masturbation. In the 1750s, however, Edinburgh physiologist Robert Whytt demonstrated in animal experiments that the spinal cord formed the center of the body's nervous system. A new pseudoscientific era dawned which we unconsciously echo whenever we call someone neurotic or nervous. It was these mysterious 'nerves' rather than the uterus or humors that caused 'hysterical' maladies. Whytt wrote that such disorders were caused by 'a too great delicacy and sensibility of the whole nervous system.' As a cynical commentator wrote in 1786: 'Before the publication of [Whytt's] book, people of fashion had not the least idea that they had nerves. But a fashionable apothecary [general practitioner] of my acquaintance, having cast his eye over the book . . . [began telling them], "Madam, you are nervous." '[28]

The emphasis on nerves led to a new diagnosis by the 1840s: spinal irritation, a disease that mostly afflicted young women. The symptoms were a combination of sensitive spots along the spine as well as peripheral bodily problems – such as pain beneath the breast or near the sternum – which were assumed to be caused by central nervous disorders. It was simple to plant the idea of spinal irritation in a patient, as Dr. Walter Johnson, an 1849 observer, related:

> The examiner stands behind the patient, and, commencing just below the neck, makes firm pressure with his knuckles successively on each projecting ridge, or spinous process as it is called, that stands out from the spinal column. Less usually, he tries the effect of scalding the patient by a sponge dipped in hot water. In the course of his investigations, it frequently happens that as soon as

448

he presses or scalds one particular ridge or vertebra, he perceives his patient [to] wince or give some evidence of pain. 'Aha!' says the physician, 'there it is!'[29]

Because of the doctor's air of authority and certitude, the young women had no doubt that they suffered from an irritated spine and must lie flat on their backs for months at a time. In similar fashion, today's 'network chiropractor' (*see the story of Angela Bergeron in Chapter 6*) has convinced his patients (mostly women) that his mere touch at the proper place on their spines will release repressed memories of abuse. 'Aha! There it is!'

As Dr. Johnson commented back in 1849, 'Attracting the patient's chief attention and filling her head with the fear that some disease exists in that situation [the spine], greatly misleads the practitioner.' A few years later, London surgeon Frederick Skey lamented the spinal irritation rage which had reduced hundreds of healthy young women to a 'horizontal or semirecumbent posture for years' and which 'excluded [them] from society, debarred their education, restricted their natural food . . . simply because a hot sponge created a sensation of uneasiness.'[30]

But why would these women have submitted to such absurd beliefs and treatments? Certainly, the authority of the doctor provided a strong inducement, but another contemporary critic astutely noted in 1851 that the diagnosis 'appeases their relentless desire to be able to explain everything. Therewith the entire domain [of life's troubles] is reduced to a region that may be palpated with the tips of one's fingers.'[31] In remarkably similar fashion, women today seek their 'repressed memories' as a simple explanation of any problems they have experienced in life.

Men, too, conformed to the expectations of the era, but they were firmly separated from their female counterparts, as explained by an 1846 treatise on hysteria by Landouzy, who offered parallel columns for the genders. Hysteria, he asserted, was 'the sole prerogative of women . . . between puberty and the menopause.' Hypochondriasis, however, he proclaimed 'exclusive to Man, affecting both sexes, but especially males, usually between 30th and 50th years of life.' These hypersensitive men displayed depression, obsession with hygiene, and the 'need to consult medical books or to talk to doctors.'[32] Men were not, however, expected to faint or fly into convulsive fits, nor were their spines generally problematic.

When spinal irritation passed out of favor, it was replaced by 'reflex theory.' According to the new dogma, nervous connections running along the spine regulated *all* bodily organs, including the brain, independent of human will. One organ could therefore affect a far-distant organ. Suddenly, the long-suffering uterus came back to the fore. 'As the uterus regained its centrality,' Edward Shorter writes, 'many women in turn became riveted by internal sensations from the abdomen and attributed various symptoms to supposed pelvic disease.'[33] The organs of generation were implicated in numerous troubles, ranging from paralysis to fits. Doctors often diagnosed women by pressing on their ovaries and inducing convulsions. The awful solution? Remove the offending parts, excise the ovaries!

In the latter half of the 1800s, the 'reflex arc' came into full flower. Faced with 'paralysis of the tongue,' doctors deduced its cause: a constipated colon. Similarly, an entire school of German ophthalmologists diagnosed diseases of the eye as stemming from uterine troubles. In a final flourishing of the theory, both European and American doctors concluded that the mucous lining of the nose was neurologically connected to the genitals. Consequently, a nosebleed might supplant menstruation, while chronic masturbation could be cured by nasal operations. In the 1890s, Sigmund Freud, who believed in nasal reflex arcs, allowed his friend Wilhelm Fliess to operate on one of his patients, as we shall shortly see.

Most of the patients who were diagnosed with these ailments were women, and most of the physicians were men.*[34] Nonetheless, there were women such as Dr. Mary Jacobi, a New York physician describing herself as a 'staunch feminist,' who fervently believed in reflex theory. In the late 1880s, she treated a woman with 'transient amblyopia,' or dimness of vision, concluding that her troubles were uterine. She recommended the 'removal of the ovaries for intractable hysteria.' Clitorectomies were frequent 'cures.' There were also a few male patients, diagnosed with irritated mucosal membranes because of excessive masturbation or coitus interruptus. Some underwent nose operations or castration as a solution. But women by far outnumbered men.

Jeffrey Masson has assembled some appalling stories in *A Dark Science: Women, Sexuality and Psychiatry in the Nineteenth Century*, documenting abusive practices. In 1865, Gustav Braun, a German physician, published

---

* At the turn of the century, the typical male attitude toward women was appalling. In 1901, for instance, the German psychiatrist Paul Julius Moebius wrote *On the Physiological Imbecility of Woman*, placing women physically and mentally somewhere between children and men. 'If woman were not bodily and mentally weak,' he stated, 'she would be extremely dangerous.' See also Cynthia Eagle Russett, *Sexual Science: The Victorian Construction of Womanhood*.

a paper entitled 'The Amputation of the Clitoris and Labia Minora: A Contribution to the Treatment of Vaginismus.' He stated that 'under the influence of a salacious imagination, which is stimulated by obscene conversations or by reading poorly selected novels, the uterus develops a hyperexcitability which leads to masturbation and its dire consequences.' Braun then described the case of a single 25-year-old woman who was 'cured' of such troubles by his operation.[35]

Nearly 20 years later, in 1884, Paul Flechsig, a respected Leipzig psychiatrist, dispassionately described the case of a 32-year-old woman with a long history of psychosomatic troubles and suicidal tendencies. He considered her 'hereditarily tainted.' A gynecological examination revealed that 'the left ovary seemed displaced downward, and the uterus seemed situated too far toward the left.' Otherwise, he could discern no abnormalities. Nonetheless, Flechsig concluded that 'the pathology of her sexual organs had caused her nervous anomalies . . . On the basis of these considerations, castration was resorted to on July 10.'[36]

HYPNOSIS

In the meantime, a parallel psychological phenomenon was taking place. It, too, later intersected with the early theories of Sigmund Freud. In the late 1700s, Franz Anton Mesmer invented the 'science' of animal magnetism, posited on the belief that humans have a 'subtle fluid' whose unequal distribution can be realigned by a magnetizer who makes 'passes' over patients. Mesmer practiced his theory in Vienna until he attempted to cure 18-year-old Maria-Therese Paradis of blindness by taking her into his household. Although he declared her cured, she still apparently could not see. Eventually, the girl's alarmed parents tried to extricate her. Mesmer refused to yield her up, causing a scandal.[37]

Fleeing sexual allegations, Mesmer moved to Paris in 1778, where he became increasingly convinced that the power of animal magnetism resided within himself. He emphasized the need to establish 'rapport' with his patients, eliciting an almost mystical bond between the powerful male magnetizer and his weak female patient. He termed this relationship 'magnetic reciprocity.' Mesmer's flashy therapy – he wore purple robes and held court in a dimly lit room full of mirrors, stained glass, gentle music, and the scent of orange blossoms, while he waved his magnetizing rod and stared deeply into his patients' eyes – attracted young women who had vague abdominal complaints and other troubles. Mesmer believed that only when his patients reached a 'crisis,' characterized by convulsive contortions, would their fluids properly realign themselves.

Not surprisingly, his young women obliged by performing as expected, after which, emotionally and physically spent, they experienced at least temporary symptom remission. All of this took place in a group setting. The women sat in a circle around the *baquet*, a barrel filled with magnetized water and iron filings, studded with moveable iron rods to be applied to the afflicted body parts. The patients held hands to facilitate the passage of the magnetic fluid. Because Mesmer could not personally attend to all needs, he hired assistant magnetizers, handsome young men who rubbed patients' spines and breasts while staring intently into their eyes, until they fell into convulsive fits.

'It is impossible,' wrote one contemporary, 'to conceive the sensation which Mesmer's experiments created in Paris.' Eventually, a distinguished scientific commission, whose members included Benjamin Franklin, Antoine Lavoisier, the chemist, and Jean-Sylvain Bailly, the astronomer, was appointed to study the phenomenon. Bailly's report, which completely debunked the proceedings, is revealing:

> The magnetizer acts by fixing his eyes on them. But above all, they are magnetized by the application of his hands and the pressure of his fingers ... an application often continued for a long time – sometimes for several hours. Meanwhile the patients in their different conditions present a very varied picture. Some are calm, tranquil, and experience no effect. Others cough, spit, feel slight pains, local or general heat, and have sweatings. Others again are agitated and tormented with convulsions ...
>
> As soon as one begins to convulse, several others are affected ... These convulsions are characterized by the precipitous, involuntary motion of all the limbs, and of the whole body – by the contraction of the throat – by the dimness and wandering of the eyes – by piercing shrieks, tears, sobbing, and immoderate laughter. They are preceded or followed by a state of languor or reverie, a kind of depression, and sometimes drowsiness ...
>
> Nothing is more astonishing than the spectacle of these convulsions. One who has not seen them can form no idea of them. The spectator is as much astonished at the profound repose of one portion of the patients as at the agitation of the rest ... Some of

the patients may be seen devoting their attention exclusively to one another, rushing toward each other with open arms, smiling, soothing, and manifesting every symptom of attachment and affection.[38]

This scene is startlingly reminiscent of group therapy for incest survivors experiencing 'flashbacks' and 'abreactions.' As one cries out in response to a terrifying 'memory,' others respond in kind. Similarly, the groups provide a social support system to reinforce the process. Their emotional catharses bind them together in a common experience which is extremely powerful, similar to the solidarity felt at an evangelical gathering.

After the commission's report, Mesmer fled Paris and died years later in anonymous poverty, but his influence continued. His successors abandoned most of the mumbo-jumbo, with the exception of the Marquis de Puységur, who renamed the phenomenon 'artificial somnambulism' and described the relationship to his clients as 'intimate rapport.' He encouraged his patients to develop an infantile dependence upon him, a kind of early 'reparenting' approach in which he played the loving mother or father. Puységur also believed that he could magnetize elm trees, which the afflicted could then touch to be healed. 'To me,' noted a fellow magnetizer, 'it is obvious that the effect of the tree was nonexistent, and that which occurred in its shade was entirely the result of the confidence that was placed in its magnetic virtue.'[39]

As early as 1819, Portuguese priest Abadé José di Faria realized that the trance state had nothing to do with magnets. He described the social 'demand characteristics' of the subjects, who performed as expected: 'They immediately lend themselves to fulfilling these [implied] demands, and sometimes even in spite of themselves, by the power of conviction.' The magnets fell into disrepute in America after surgeon Benjamin Perkins began using metallic 'tractors' in 1798 to induce a trance state in his patients prior to operations. Others soon discovered that wooden tractors painted silver worked just as well.[40]

But the trance-like state into which Mesmer's patients fell intrigued his followers. James Braid abandoned the mesmeric passes and magnets and popularized the name 'hypnotism' in 1843. Braid eventually came to believe that hypnosis worked through the suggestibility of the client. He thought that by concentrating on one idea – such as 'my arm cannot bend' – to the exclusion of all else, it would become true. Other magnetizing physicians believed they could cure a new disease called 'catalepsy,' in which women froze into weird positions and couldn't move. In fact, these physicians both *created* and *cured* catalepsy by hypnotic suggestion.*[41]

Nicholas Spanos has pointed out the remarkable similarities between Mesmerism and demonic possession, which it largely replaced. 'In both cases,' he wrote, 'patients convulsed on cue, appeared to be more intelligent and sometimes clairvoyant, reported spontaneous amnesia, engaged in behaviors that were thought to transcend normal capacities . . . , and experienced their role enactment as an involuntary occurrence.'[42] During both exorcism and magnetism, symptoms tended to become more pronounced until there was some sort of peak crisis with dramatic convulsions, followed by a cure or alleviation of the symptoms.

John Joseph Gassner, a German Catholic priest of the 18th century, provides a direct link between demonology and hypnosis. Gassner believed that he had cured himself through exorcism, and he successfully threw demons out of the afflicted throughout Europe. Anton Mesmer observed some of Gassner's demonstrations and concluded that he really obtained his results from animal magnetism. Gassner regarded faith 'an essential condition' for a cure. He almost always touched the affected part. He could reputedly make the pulse of his patients vary by sheer will power. He could paralyze their limbs, make them weep or laugh, soothe or agitate them.[43] It never occurred to either Gassner or Mesmer that such behavior stemmed from the power of suggestion rather than their own overweening egos.

Like the current crop of 'multiple personality disorders,' the cataleptics proved to be intriguing patients who often displayed supernatural powers of vision or touch. The condition purportedly heightened these senses. One woman could hear only through her stomach, while many cataleptics claimed that they could see their own insides. French magnetizer Charles Despine created and treated numerous cataleptic patients in the early 1800s through hypnosis. In 1822, one of his 20-year-old patients reported that she could read with her fingers. She saw the walls of her room as 'diaphanous as glass,' and revealed having 'double vision of the Hebrides.'[44] But Despine's prize pupil was a 21-year-old

---

* Mesmer did not invent the notion of healing by means of some form of suggestion. Similar modes were practiced by the ancient Chinese, Egyptians, Hebrews, Indians, Persians, Greeks, Romans and others. 'More than 4,000 years ago,' writes one historian, 'Wang Tai, the founder of Chinese medicine, taught a therapeutic technique that utilized incantations and manual passes over the body of the patient.'

seamstress named Micheline Viollet who came under his care in 1823. At first, she did not reveal other expected symptoms such as 'ecstasy' (a sort of rapturous trance) and somnambulism. When Despine told her that 'they surely will one day appear,' Micheline obligingly developed the required symptoms. If anyone she disliked so much as looked at her, she would instantly become immobile.[45]

Like many such patients, Micheline went on to become a 'healer' with Despine in her own right. The literature of the age is full of women who converted easily from patient to practitioner, having found a vocation in life. Similarly, many Survivors who have recovered their repressed memories have gone on to become therapists who help others unearth *their* memories.

Over time, cataleptics obliged in such histrionic ways that no one believed them any more. They would pass from conversing perfectly normally to suddenly throwing their heads back and laughing soundlessly, following by rolling around and jumping in the air while whistling. Responding to a few magnetic passes from a doctor, they would be rendered instantly immobile, then switch to sobs, laughter, and an exhausted, convulsive cough. After a half-hour performance, they might strike a pose reminiscent of a praying saint. 'We see cataleptics by the dozen,' wrote a Viennese doctor visiting Paris in 1857. 'The magnetizers put the limbs of the magnetized in positions and directions that defy all laws of gravity and mechanics.'[46] Sometimes the cataleptics' seizures even led to self-induced death.

One early young male hypnotic subject came for treatment in 1803 after a year of having fits. He evinced a repugnance for anything made of metal, but particularly copper. During his hypnotic sessions, he felt a kind of peaceful fog envelop him, which protected him from unwelcome intruders, particularly women and children. Whenever they came within ten paces of him, he went into terrible convulsions and protested this 'violation of my fog.'[47] If he were around today, he would probably be complaining about his violated 'boundaries' and would interpret his aversion to metal as evidence that his mother stuck copper forks up his anus when he was a child.

By the late 1800s, a second wave of hypnotists, following James Braid, came to believe that they could *suggest* whatever they wanted to their patients rather than elicit an underlying problem such as catalepsy. Stage hypnotists such as Carl Hansen got their subjects to become as rigid as boards and lie between two chairs. Amused audiences watched subjects munch on raw potatoes which, they were told, were apples. In 1880,

Sigmund Freud watched one of Hansen's performances and 'became firmly convinced of the genuineness of hypnotic phenomena.'[48]

By the late 19th century, according to one chronicler, 'so much was hypnosis in the air that becoming hypnotized required little more than a bit of experience: One learned what was expected and then unconsciously did it.' This led to many people asserting that they *lived* in a constant state of hypnosis or somnambulism. An 1892 interview with a 26-year-old woman could as easily be a transcript of an early therapeutic session with a future Survivor with repressed memories. 'I tell myself that if I died I wouldn't feel any different than right now. That wouldn't bother me. That's the reason you should just let me die.' During a hypnosis session, she said she didn't really know what she was doing. 'She doesn't feel any of her internal functions . . . Everything around her seems unfamiliar, she has no sense of time, nor things, nor persons . . . She has no sense of the reality of things and "lives as though in a dream." '[49] Such patients were easily convinced a few years later that they were actually multiple personality disorders, a vogue which accelerated soon after the turn of the century.

In the progression from witches and demons to animal magnetism and diagnoses of hysteria, nothing had materially changed other than the role that the patients were expected to play. Many of the symptoms remained the same, although blaspheming against God, speaking in a demonic voice, or defining oneself as possessed became less popular. In many ways, however, as Spanos pointed out, those labeled as 'hysterics' shared many characteristics with demoniacs: 'They tended to be unhappy women who were socialized into viewing themselves as weak and passive, dissatisfied with their lives, socially and economically powerless, and without access to means of voicing their dissatisfactions or improving their lot outside of adopting the role of a sick person.'[50]

The term *hysteria* has been used to cover so many different symptoms that it is virtually meaningless. At various points, it has referred to spontaneous amnesia, convulsions, sensory or motor disturbances, high suggestibility, hallucinations, or anorexia. It has also been applied to a particular type of personality – one prone to violent mood swings, self-absorbed, suggestible, manipulative, frigid, flirtatious – which is, as Harriet Lerner pointed out in a 1974 article, simply a male caricature of femininity, adding that 'a girl's immediate social environment puts enormous pressure on her to develop a style of cognition and personality that will lend itself to this diagnosis.'[51] Spanos noted that the diagnosis 'did not identify a unitary disorder, pinpoint a valid etiology, or lead to successful treatment.'[52] It did, however, provide a legitimation for the new discipline of psychiatry, which yearned for scientific medical trappings characterized by 'diseases of the mind.'*[53]

CHARCOT'S CIRCUS

No history of psychosomatic ailments would be complete without examining the psychiatric circus created by Jean-Martin Charcot at his Salpêtrière, a combination poorhouse, home for the aged, and asylum for insane women.[54] Charcot was a great neurological systematizer who, in the 1870s and 1880s, became fascinated by what he termed 'hysteria.' It happened that women with mental disorders were housed alongside epileptics, and some who had no apparent organic problems began to imitate the epileptic fits, so Charcot initially labeled them 'hystero-epileptics.'

Freud critic Richard Webster has argued that many of Charcot's (and, later, Freud's) purportedly psychosomatic patients may have actually suffered from real, undiagnosed neurological disorders such as temporal lobe epilepsy, organic brain damage, tuberculous meningitis, encephalitis, Tourette's syndrome, multiple sclerosis, or syphilis.[55]** By ignoring their real ailments and focusing on 'hysteria,' Charcot effectively blamed the patients for the disorder. On the other hand, it is probable that many of his cases were indeed psychosomatic. Unfortunately, he himself *induced* and *encouraged* their problematic behavior rather than helping to alleviate it. In other words, many of his 'hysterics' were iatrogenically influenced to believe in a mythical disease and to act out its appropriate symptoms.

Eventually, the Parisian neurologist charted an inflexible set of rules which he thought characterized such a disorder. Given their cue, the inmates obligingly performed as he thought they would. By pressing

---

* The term *hysteria* could be satisfactorily applied to women who conformed to the social expectations of the era by succumbing to weakness, paralysis, or convulsions. Those who were too independent, who demanded equality or sexual freedom, were considered to be 'morally insane,' another pseudomedical diagnosis, and were locked away in institutions.

** It is also possible that some of Charcot's patients were faking in order to secure insurance payments. 'Railway brain' and 'railway spine' were recently-named ailments in claims against train companies.

on their ovaries, Charcot could switch various bizarre behaviors on or off. His hysterics went through four phases: (1) an epileptic kind of fit; (2) a 'period of contortions and *grands mouvements*' otherwise known as 'clownism,' during which patients flung themselves about, emitted piercing screams, and often took the position of *arc-de-cercle*, arching backwards so that only the head and heels rested on the ground; (3) a period of impassioned poses in which patients assumed exaggerated postures of prayer, crucifixion, accusation, or the like; and (4) a 'terminal period' in which anything could occur, often characterized by hallucinations such as seeing snakes.

Charcot was convinced that hysteria was an organic, hereditary disease, and he would delve vigorously into a patient's family background until he found 'evidence' for his theories. In what Edward Shorter calls a 'crucible of suggestion,' the women at the Salpêtrière received further instruction in bizarre behavior when Charcot invited an old-style magnetizer named Victor-Jean-Marie Burq to demonstrate 'metallotherapy' on his wards. Soon, Burq was dragging symptoms from one side of a woman to the other with his metallic rods. Fascinated by hypnosis, Charcot began to induce hysteria. When professional colleagues expressed doubts, he threw his demonstrations open to the public.

It became clear to several of Charcot's young associates that he was deluding himself, creating the conditions he was supposedly discovering. 'These stage performances,' assistant Alex Munthe later wrote, 'were nothing but an absurd farce, a hopeless muddle of truth and cheating.' While some patients actually thought they were hypnotized, others were simply play-acting. It was also clear that a certain amount of 'contagion' was present. One woman would begin screaming and rhythmically beating her fists, and another nearby would take up the same behavior.

In 1885, Charcot began to admit that psychological mechanisms rather than heredity might have something to do with hysteria. He became interested in hysterical symptoms following psychic shocks or accidents, labelling them 'traumatic neurosis,' or 'hystero-neurosis.' During that same year, a young Viennese doctor named Sigmund Freud came to study under Charcot for a few months. The experience catalyzed Freud, diverting him from neuropathology to psychopathology. In a letter to his fiancée, Freud wrote that Charcot was a genius who was 'uprooting my aims and opinions,' giving him a 'new idea of perfection.' While some critics complained of Charcot's showmanship, the young Austrian physician clearly loved it. 'My brain is sated, as if I had spent an evening at the theatre.'[56]

Charcot's circus quickly collapsed after his death in 1893, and his carefully constructed phases of hysteria fell into disrepute. Without the master to induce them, the symptoms simply vanished, and no more unfortunate young women balanced on their heads and heels.*[57] But by that time, Freud and Josef Breuer had taken his lead and were sowing the seeds of modern psychology and the theory of repression.

FREUD'S MENTAL EXTRACTIONS

Until recently, Freud's pronouncements have been treated almost as holy psychological writ. Now critics are realizing that Freud was just another human being, very much a man of his time. His contributions to the understanding of psychology have been immense. He popularized many ideas which seem self-evident to us now: People often act irrationally, for reasons they don't admit to themselves. Our childhood experiences shape our self-concepts and methods of dealing with the world. Our dreams reveal many personal concerns, fears, and desires, sometimes in symbolic ways reminiscent of myth. Much goes on in our minds below the conscious level. If we become infuriated at one person, we often deflect that anger illogically onto someone else. We can also be grateful to subsequent Freudians for helping to fight the eugenics movement (and Nazism); for promoting a healthier attitude toward human sexuality; for more humane treatment of children, mental patients, and prisoners; and for many other beneficial modern attitudes.

But Freud has bequeathed us a mixed heritage. Much that we have simply accepted as revealed truth has never been proved. Essentially, Freud has provided a convincing mythology for our times, one which has permeated every aspect of our culture. Some of our most fundamental modern assumptions are based on Freud's pronouncements, and those assumptions may not necessarily be correct. Too often, as psychologist Garth Wood has written, Freud 'dreamed up what was for him a plausible entity [i.e., the id, ego, superego, death wish, Oedipus complex], and then set about finding mental phenomena which for him, but not for others, tended to support it.'[58]

* It should be noted, however, that in 1988 neurologist Colin Binnie described a classic *arc-de-cercle* case in a woman diagnosed as epileptic. Thus, there may be some neurological reality to the posture. It may be that Charcot's patients included true epileptics from whom they learned this behavior.

Freud followed in the grand tradition of physicians who identified the precise symptoms they expected to find, then proceeded to induce them. Freud believed in much of the quackery that had preceded him, including the notion that excessive masturbation caused neurosis, that there was such a thing as neurasthenia,*[59] that there was a nasal reflex arc, and that hysteria could be provoked by pressing on the ovaries, which he termed 'stimulation of the hysterogenic zone.' Freud believed in a variety of hands-on therapies, one of which played a significant role in early recovered memory cases, as we will shortly see.[60]

Writing to his friend Wilhelm Fliess in 1895, Freud said, 'I have invented a strange therapy of my own: I search for sensitive areas, press on them, and thus provoke fits of shaking which free her [the patient].'[61] That same year, Freud treated a 27-year-old named Emma Eckstein, who came from a prominent socialist family and was active in the Viennese women's movement.[62] Like many 'hysterical' or 'neurasthenic' patients of the era, she came to Freud with vague complaints, including stomach aches and menstrual problems. He deduced that she suffered from excessive masturbation that could be cured by operating on her nose. He prevailed on his best friend, Wilhelm Fliess, to perform the operation.

Fliess was a well-respected Berlin ear-nose-and-throat specialist who complained of the 'immense multitude' of women who rushed from spa to spa without success, 'falling into the hands of quacks.' He, on the other hand, knew the scientific truth that their troubles often stemmed from the nasal reflex. At first, he used cocaine on his patients' noses, which provided temporary relief (and a pleasant buzz, no doubt).**[63] Then he cauterized the noses, but that too didn't do the trick. Finally, he decided that removal of a portion of the left middle turbinate bone would permanently cure female sexual afflictions. Freud concurred, and the unfortunate Emma Eckstein believed them.

---

* 'Neurasthenia,' a catch-all diagnosis coined by American psychologist George Beard in 1881, is discussed in some detail in Chapter 11.

** It is quite possible that Freud suggested the cocaine treatment to Fliess. Ten years before, Freud had proclaimed cocaine a miracle drug, took it himself, and saw it as his road to fame. He introduced his friend Fleischl to the drug as an alternative to his morphine habit. Unfortunately, his friend died a few years later in a cocaine agony, crying that ants were crawling under his skin. In *Freudian Fallacy* (1984), E. M. Thornton argued that *all* of Freud's theories stemmed from his paranoia and hallucinations as a cocaine addict, though her conclusion seems doubtful. Nonetheless, Freud's letters to Fliess are filled with obsessive concern over his nose and its secretions, and Freud frequently applied cocaine as a curative.

Fliess bungled the operation, sewing a large piece of gauze into Eckstein's nose. Before anyone realized that, Freud described her worsening condition in a letter to Fliess: 'Eckstein's condition is still unsatisfactory; persistent swelling, going up and down "like an avalanche"; pain, so that morphine cannot be dispensed with; bad nights.' She emitted an awful odor. Then another doctor opened her nose and, as Freud wrote, 'suddenly he pulled at something like a thread, kept on pulling and before either one of us had time to think, at least half a meter of gauze had been removed from the cavity. The next moment came a flood of blood. The patient turned white, her eyes bulged, and she had no pulse.'[64]

Eckstein survived, though she continued to hemorrhage for some time. Freud managed to rationalize the entire affair, assuring Fliess that it was 'one of those accidents that happen to the most fortunate and circumspect of surgeons.' In the end, Freud even managed to blame Emma Eckstein. Her bleeding was all caused by hysteria! Incredibly, Eckstein remained true to Freud, even becoming a therapist herself. In 1904, using books from Freud's library as her sources, she wrote a short monograph on the dangers of childhood masturbation, recommending special bandages and restrictive clothing to prevent such mishaps. Soon afterward, she took permanently to her couch, convinced that her legs were paralyzed. She died in 1924.[65*66]

Emma Eckstein was one of the first patients upon whom Freud practiced another form of questionable therapy that became the cornerstone for his psychological theories. He concluded that her problems stemmed not only from masturbation (known as 'self-abuse' in those days) but from a repressed memory of sexual abuse when she was eight. He prompted her to recall a visit to a confectioner's during which the shopkeeper had grabbed her genitals through her clothing. This memory was mild, however, compared to those he eventually elicited from Eckstein in 1897: 'I obtained a scene [i.e., a "memory"] about the circumcision of a girl. The cutting of a piece of the labia minora (which is still shorter today), sucking up the blood, following which the child

---

* In fact, Freud's vanity probably condemned Eckstein to her fate, through his authority and her suggestibility. Dr. Dora Teleky, a well-known Viennese physician, 'discovered' an ulcer in Eckstein's abdomen and either operated on it or pretended to do so. Immediately, the invalid miraculously recovered. Freud, indignant at this interference, broke off his analysis, declaring, 'Well, that's the end of Emma. That dooms her from now on. Nobody can cure her neurosis.' Taking her cue from Freud, Eckstein relapsed, never again to leave her couch.

was given a piece of the skin to eat.'[67] Like many modern physicians who are 'experts' in child sexual abuse, Freud had found physical 'evidence' to corroborate this memory.

Taking his lead from Charcot and Bernheim, Freud had begun hypnotizing patients late in 1887, primarily using direct suggestion in an attempt to ameliorate their symptoms. Until then, he had relied primarily on various forms of ablutions ('hydrotherapy'), mild electrical stimulation, massage, and the 'rest cure' popularized by American physician Weir Mitchell (*see Chapter 11*).[68]

Soon, Freud also started to use hypnosis to access what he suspected were repressed memories. In 1895, in uneasy collaboration with Joseph Breuer, Freud published *Studies in Hysteria*, in which he elaborated his theory that unconscious repressed memories caused hysteria, obsession, and other neurotic symptoms. 'The patient only gets free from the hysterical symptom by reproducing the pathogenic impressions that caused it and by giving utterance to them with an expression of affect, and thus the therapeutic task *consists solely in inducing him to do so*,' Freud wrote.[69] The following year, he elaborated on this theory in three essays, making it clear that he considered *repressed memories of childhood sexual abuse* to be the root cause of all hysterical symptoms. Because Freud's theories and methods provided the template for the modern hunt for repressed memories, and because many modern scholars have argued recently over this crucial aspect of his early work, I will examine his practice during this period in some detail.[70]

Freud based his theory on a small number of cases. He referred to 12 in *Studies in Hysteria*, admitting that most of them were unsuccessful. 'But it is my opinion that the obstacles have lain in the personal circumstances of the patients and have not been due to any question on theory,' he asserted. 'I am justified in leaving these unsuccessful cases out of account.' By February 5, 1896, when Freud sent off his first two papers openly proclaiming sex abuse as hysteria's long-sought 'source of the Nile,' he had added only one new case, bringing the total to 13. Surprisingly, by April 21, less than three months later, when he gave a lecture on the subject (published as his third paper, *The Aetiology of Hysteria*), Freud claimed to have treated 18 hysterical patients with his revolutionary method. This is particularly confusing, because Freud wrote to his friend Fliess on May 4, 1896, complaining that 'my consulting room is empty' and that 'for weeks on end I see no new faces.'[71]

Until the end of 1895, Freud relied at least partially on hypnosis to delve into his patients' unconscious. Frustrated by his inability to hypnotize some subjects – and by the outright unwillingness of others – Freud had already invented a new 'pressure procedure' in which his patients lay down, closed their eyes, and allowed Freud to press on their foreheads or squeeze their heads between his hands. They were then to report whatever images or words popped into their heads.[72] In his 1892 treatment of Elisabeth von R., he first 'made use of the technique of bringing out pictures and ideas by means of pressing on the patient's head.' Sometimes this pressure prompted detailed scenarios, 'as though she were reading a lengthy book of pictures,' but when Elisabeth was in a cheerful mood, she often failed to recall anything while Freud pressed on her cranium. Undeterred, the psychologist 'resolved, therefore, to adopt the hypothesis that the procedure never failed; that on every occasion under the pressure of my hand some idea occurred to Elisabeth or some picture came before her eyes,' but she was simply unwilling to report it. When he insisted that she report these thoughts, she finally obliged him, though it often took two or three head squeezes. 'I derived from this analysis a literally unqualified reliance on my technique,' Freud wrote with satisfaction.[73]

To his credit, Freud realized that he was not *literally* pressing memories out of his patients' unconscious. It simply seemed to be an appropriate metaphor, 'the most convenient way of applying suggestion.' Without apparent irony, he asserted that he could as easily have made his patients stare into a crystal ball. 'As a rule,' Freud wrote, 'the pressure procedure fails on the first or second occasion.' Then, however, the flood gates opened, and the patient cooperated, engaged in a fascinating intellectual pursuit. 'By explaining things to him,' Freud said, 'by giving him information about the marvelous world of psychical processes . . ., we make him himself into a collaborator, induce him to regard himself with the objective interest of an investigator.'[74]

Freud emphasized that this method worked only if the physician assumed an extraordinary importance to the patient akin to a 'father confessor who gives absolution.' He described one female patient's 'quite special relation to the figure of the physician,' and another who wanted to kiss him.*[75] Because this personal relationship was so important, Freud observed that he had to work with attractive, intelligent patients. 'I cannot imagine bringing myself to delve into the psychical mechanism

---

* Thirty-five years later, Freud still vividly recalled this incident involving 'one of my most acquiescent patients' who, upon awakening from hypnosis, 'threw her arms around my neck.' Freud was saved from any temptation to respond when a servant unexpectedly entered the room.

of a hysteria in anyone who struck me as low-minded and repellent.' It also helped if they manifested complete confidence and dependence upon him, the physician, because 'a good number of the patients who would be suitable for this form of treatment abandon the doctor as soon as the suspicion begins to dawn on them of the direction in which the investigation is leading.'[76]

Before arriving at the crucial traumatic scene, Freud believed that he had to go slowly, establishing rapport and gaining patients' confidence. Then, through 'repeated, indeed continuous, use of this procedure of pressure on the forehead,' he delved for memories like an archeologist digging ever deeper. 'We force our way into the internal strata, overcoming resistances all the time; we get to know the themes accumulated in one of these strata and the threads running through it.' Finally, after pursuing numerous side paths, he could 'penetrate by a main path straight to the nucleus of the pathogenic organization ... Now the patient helps us energetically. His resistance is for the most part broken.'[77]

In 1895, though he had been using this method for some time, Freud had not yet concluded that all hysteria stemmed from sexual abuse. Perhaps, however, he was merely remaining circumspect, as he later asserted Breuer wished him to be. Even in 1895, he described two sisters who 'shared a secret; they slept in one room and on a particular night they had both been subjected to sexual assaults by a certain man.' By February of 1896, Freud explicitly blamed hysteria on *precocious experience of sexual relations with actual excitement of the genitals, resulting from sexual abuse.* These 13 cases were 'without exception of a severe kind' that could be classed as 'grave sexual injuries; some of them were positively revolting.' Seven of the perpetrators were other children, usually older brothers, while the others were nursemaids, governesses, domestic servants, or teachers. In late April, Freud provided a similar list, then added that the abuser was 'all too often, a close relative.' He asserted that disgust at food or habitual choking was caused by repressed memories of oral sex, just as indigestion and intestinal disturbances could be explained by forgotten sodomy. In one case, he believed, a child had been forced to masturbate an adult woman with his foot.[78]

During the rest of 1896, Freud appears to have zeroed in on fathers as the culprits. 'It seems to me more and more that the essential point of hysteria is that it results from *perversion* on the part of the seducer,' Freud wrote to Fliess on December 6, 1896, 'and *more and more* that heredity is seduction by the father.' In the same letter, he discussed a patient with a 'highly perverse father.' On January 4, 1897, he wrote in detail about a patient who balked at his seduction theory. 'When I thrust the explanation at her [that her father had sexually abused her], she was at first won over; then she committed the folly of questioning the old man himself.' When her father indignantly declared himself innocent, Freud's patient believed him, much to her therapist's disgust. 'In order to facilitate the work,' he concluded, 'I am hoping she will feel miserable again.'[79]

Soon afterward, Freud was finding more and more disgusting memories (presumably in other clients), going back to earliest childhood. 'The early period before the age of one-and-a-half years is becoming ever more significant,' he wrote to Fliess on January 24, 1897. 'Thus I was able to trace back, with certainty, a hysteria that developed ... for the first time at eleven months and [I could] hear again the words that were exchanged between two adults at that time! It is as though it comes from a phonograph.'[80] By September 21, 1897, in a famous letter expressing doubts about his theory, Freud asserted that 'in all cases, the *father*, not excluding my own, had to be accused of being perverse.'[81]

DID FREUD LEAD HIS PATIENTS?

What are we to make of Freud's briefly held 'seduction theory?' Did he indeed uncover horrifying repressed memories of paternal incest, or did he merely provide a misguided template for the modern brand of memory seekers? We can get a clue from Freud's arrogance. 'We must not believe what they say [when they deny having memories], we must always assume, and tell them, too, that they have kept something back ... We must insist on this, we must repeat the pressure and represent ourselves as infallible, till at last we are really told something.' Or again: 'It is of course of great importance for the progress of the analysis that one should always turn out to be in the right *vis-à-vis* the patient, otherwise one would always be dependent on what he chose to tell one.' Freud refused to accept no for an answer. 'We must not be led astray by initial denials,' he wrote during this period, sounding just like the *Malleus Maleficarum* or *The Courage to Heal*. 'If we keep firmly to what we have inferred, we shall in the end conquer every resistance by emphasizing the unshakable nature of our convictions.' No wonder he could write that 'the pressure technique in fact never fails.'[82]

It is instructive to read Freud's 1896 description of how he unearthed repressed memories:

> The fact is that these patients never repeat these stories spontaneously, nor do they ever in the course of a treatment suddenly present the physician with the complete recollection of a scene of this kind. One only succeeds in awakening the psychical trace of a precocious sexual event under the most energetic pressure of the analytic procedure, and against an enormous resistance. Moreover, the memory must be extracted from them piece by piece, and while it is being awakened in their consciousness they become the prey to an emotion which it would be hard to counterfeit. Conviction will follow in the end, if one is not influenced by the patients' behavior.[83]

It is clear that Freud's expectations contributed heavily to what he found in his patients' unconscious. 'If the memory which we have uncovered does not answer our expectations,' he wrote, 'it may be that we ought to pursue the same path a little further; perhaps behind the first traumatic scene there may be concealed the memory of a second, which satisfies our requirements better.' It required the 'most energetic pressure' to 'extract' such memories; they never surfaced spontaneously or as whole, coherent events. 'Before they come for analysis the patients know nothing about these scenes,' Freud proudly noted. 'They are indignant as a rule if we warn them that such scenes are going to emerge. Only the strongest compulsion of the treatment can induce them to embark on a reproduction of them.'[84]*[85] Once they finally produced a suitable memory, they often tried to deny it. 'Something has occurred to me now, but you obviously put it into my head,' they would say, or 'I know what you expect me to answer,' or 'Something has occurred to me now, it's true, but it seems to me as if I'd put it up deliberately.'

---

* Freud critics Jean Schimek, Malcolm Macmillan, and Allen Esterson believe that Freud's patients never actually produced any memories at all, but that Freud only *inferred* incest. It seems quite clear from several quoted passages, however, that many of his patients did indeed 'relive' highly emotional traumas in which they eventually came to believe. 'The behavior of patients while they are reproducing these infantile experiences is in every respect incompatible with the assumption that the scenes are anything else than a reality which is being felt with distress,' Freud wrote. There is no question, though, that Freud cajoled and bullied them unmercifully, exhorting them to remember. In 1896, he wrote to Fliess that he was 'almost hoarse' from pressuring patients ten to eleven hours a day.

To these protestations, Freud turned a deaf ear. 'In all such cases, I remain unshakably firm.' Often, the doctor was even more blunt. 'The principal point is that I should guess the secret and tell it to the patient straight out.'[86]

Even 35 years later, when Freud supposedly realized that he had been mistaken, he wrote, 'It was necessary to make efforts on one's own part so as to urge and compel him [the patient] to remember. The amount of effort required . . . increased in direct proportion to the difficulty of what had to be remembered.'[87] These passages, as revealing as they are, hardly convey the extent to which Freud encouraged his patients' 'memories' and enthusiastically validated them. His disciple Sandor Ferenczi later described how the early Freud 'involved himself passionately and selflessly in the therapy of neurotics, lying on the floor for hours, if necessary, next to a patient in the throes of a hysterical crisis.'[88]

When the patients finally brought forth the fantasies their therapist sought, they displayed profound emotions which Freud (and many therapists after him) took to be proof that the memories were real. 'While they are recalling these infantile experiences to consciousness, they suffer under the most violent sensations, of which they are ashamed and which they try to conceal.' Sounding precisely like Ellen Bass or Renee Fredrickson, Freud dismissed their subsequent denials: 'Even after they have gone through them . . . in such a convincing manner, they still attempt to withhold belief from them, by emphasizing the fact that, unlike what happens in the case of other forgotten material, they have no feeling of remembering the scenes.'[89] Compare this statement to therapist Renee Fredrickson's observation that 'repressed memories rarely seem real when they first emerge.'[90]

Incredibly, Freud dismissed the notion that he might have planted any of the memories. '*We are not in a position to force anything on the patient about the things of which he is ostensibly ignorant or to influence the products of the analysis by arousing an expectation.*' How did Freud know this? 'I have never once succeeded, by foretelling something, in altering or falsifying the reproduction of memories . . . for if I had, it would inevitably have been betrayed in the end by some contradiction in the material.'[91]*[92] Because the stories appeared self-consistent, he believed them. Later, when the memories floated up from as early as one-and-a-

---

* Later, Freud reiterated that 'I have never yet succeeded in forcing on a patient a scene I was expecting to find, in such a way that he seemed to be living through it with all the appropriate feelings.'

half years old, Freud explained why he believed them. 'I should not lend credence to these extraordinary findings myself if their complete reliability were not proved by the development of the subsequent neurosis.'[93] In other words, Freud, like Lenore Terr today, insisted that the *symptoms* of the adult *proved* the validity of the memories.

Freud also believed that the remarkable similarity of the stories proved that they were true, just as those who hear about ritual abuse nowadays are positive that similar tales constitute validation. Freud wrote about the 'uniformity that they exhibit in certain details, which is a necessary consequence if the preconditions of these experiences are always of the same kind, but which would otherwise lead us to believe that there were secret understandings between the various patients.'[94] Of course, it was not necessary for the patients to confer with one another for them to confabulate similar stories. Freud probably *cued* them without realizing it.

Finally, Freud asserted that he had found external corroboration for two cases. Like Judith Herman, however, he appears to have been eager to accept circumstantial evidence as 'proof.' One patient's older brother admitted having sexual contacts with her in late childhood, so Freud assumed that he had also done so when she was an infant. In another instance, two patients recalled having been abused by the same man.[95] This fact could indicate nothing more than Freud's success at suggesting abuse to his patients, who probably conferred with one another as well. Similarly, many sisters nowadays recover similar abuse memories at the hands of their father and take that to be corroboration.

Freud himself saw a parallel to the confessions of 'witches,' but he apparently concluded that the unfortunate witches had *really* all been victims of incest: 'Why did the devil who took possession of the poor things invariably abuse them sexually and in a loathsome manner? Why are their confessions under torture so like the communications made by my patients in psychological treatment?'[96] It did not occur to Freud, at the time, that the reason for the similarity was probably quite simple. In both cases, determined interrogators induced the confession/memory of horrors, whether they ever really happened or not. Freud went even further, foreshadowing the current rage to find memories of satanic cults. 'I dream,' he wrote, 'of a primeval devil religion whose rites are carried on secretly, and I understand the harsh therapy of the witches' judges.'[97]

In 1896, Freud summarized his real reason for believing the 'scenes' of abuse which his patients revealed. They explained everything. They were necessary for his theory. 'It is exactly like putting together a child's picture-puzzle: after many attempts, we become absolutely certain in the end which piece belongs in the empty gap; for only that one piece fills out the picture.'[98] As we have seen, this same analogy – finding the missing piece which explains the puzzle of one's life – has cropped up repeatedly nearly 100 years later, during the great repressed-memory hunt of the late 20th century.

By 1897, Freud had become less certain of the validity of such memories. He realized that he may have applied too much pressure. Still, in December, he was encouraged by a report from Emma Eckstein, now acting as a therapist, as he wrote to Fliess: 'My confidence in the father-etiology has risen greatly. Eckstein treated her patient deliberately in such a manner as not to give her the slightest hint of what will emerge from the unconscious, and in the process obtained ... the identical scenes with the father.'[99]

This passage is somewhat confusing, as it appears that Freud may have already treated the same patient and elicited the identical memory, which surfaced again. Even assuming that Eckstein was dealing with a new patient, however, we have only Freud's second-hand assurance that the therapist didn't give the 'slightest hint' of the sort of incest memories she sought. In my own interviews with therapists, I repeatedly heard this same assertion: 'I never ask leading questions or make suggestions.' Yet in virtually every case, the therapist had informed the patient that memories of abuse are often repressed and may resurface during therapy. They did not consider this to be a strong cue. I suspect that Emma Eckstein – obviously a rather troubled and emotional woman who had just recovered her own 'memories' – was not quite so circumspect as she thought.

Later that month, Freud again wrote to Fliess, describing another dreadful repressed memory session in which the patient supposedly recalled a scene from when she was six months old, during which her mother nearly bled to death as a result of an injury inflicted by her father. When she was two, she continued to remember, her father 'brutally deflowered her and infected her with gonorrhea, so that her life was in danger as a result of the loss of blood and vaginitis.' Finally, she vividly described a scene (complete with dialogue) between her father and mother which Freud interpreted as anal intercourse. Clearly, Freud was both repelled and intrigued by these 'filthy stories,' as he called them, and he apparently believed them, as implausible as such early recollections might have been.

Hypothesizing that the patient's mind had blotted out many details,

Freud drew an analogy to 'Russian censorship' in which 'words, entire phrases and sentences [are] obliterated in black, so that the rest becomes unintelligible.' Then, quoting Goethe, Freud suggested a new motto, which the 'incest survivor' advocates have now inscribed on their hearts: 'What have they done to you, poor child?'[100]

Eventually, Freud changed his mind, concluding that most of these incestuous events never occurred, that the 'memories' were actually a form of fantasy, even wish-fulfillment. He couldn't admit, however, that he had actually *planted* these memories.*[101] Instead, he concluded that they were innate fantasies. As a result, he concocted the Oedipus and Electra complexes, asserting that young children yearned to displace the parent of the same gender and have sex with the other. Freud's entire elaborate edifice was based on his obsession with childhood sexuality. Indeed, children are sensual beings, but whether an 'Oedipus complex' accounts for our psychological problems or whether the way we were toilet trained determines our personality is subject to dispute. Controlled scientific studies have repeatedly failed to corroborate such notions.[102]

Much to his credit, Freud emphasized the reality of incest in a 1916 lecture. 'Phantasies of being seduced are of particular interest,' he said, 'because so often they are not phantasies but real memories,' reiterating that 'you must not suppose . . . that sexual abuse of a child by its nearest male relatives belongs entirely to the realm of phantasy.' On the other hand, he confused the issue by asserting that 'in the case of girls [for whom] their father figures fairly regularly as the seducer, there can be no doubt . . . of the imaginary nature of the accusation.' Finally, Freud muddied the waters by saying that it didn't really matter whether the incest was real or imagined. 'The outcome [i.e., neurotic symptoms] is the same, and up to the present, we have not succeeded in pointing to any difference in the consequences, whether fantasy or reality has had the greater share in these childhood events.'[103] Such relativistic sophism has become a standard line for modern therapists, particularly those hunting for repressed memories. 'It doesn't matter whether your memories are literally true or not,' they tell their patients. 'The emotional

* In 1925, Freud wrote that 'these scenes of seduction had never taken place,' adding that 'they were only phantasies which my patients had made up or which I myself had perhaps forced on them.' He still couldn't really bring himself to admit his own role, though. Later in the same paragraph, he asserted: 'I do not believe even now that I forced the seduction-phantasies on my patients, that I "suggested" them. I had in fact stumbled for the first time upon the *Oedipus complex*.'

truth is valid.' Of course, it *does* matter very much to parents as well as to accusing children whether these events actually took place or not.

Despite his retraction of the 'seduction theory,' Freud continued to promulgate the notion that patients could banish certain traumatic events from their consciousness, and that only by recalling and reliving these crucial moments could they be whole and healed. In fact, Freud never really repudiated his early work. He did not publicly distance himself from the seduction theory until 1906, and in his 1925 autobiography, he still maintained that sexual experience lay behind all neuroses. Writing of his work on repressed sexual abuse memories, he asserted: 'I was not prepared for this conclusion and my expectations played no part in it.' He still believed that uncompleted sex acts, sexual abstinence, or excessive masturbation caused anxiety and neurasthenia. And he most certainly still believed in repression, which, in 1914, he called 'the foundation stone on which the structure of psychoanalysis rests.' In 1925, he repeated that 'the theory of repression became the corner-stone of our understanding of the neuroses . . . It is possible to take repression as a centre and to bring all the elements of psychoanalytic theory into relation with it.'[104]*[105]

By enshrining the concept of repression, Freud planted the seeds for the current epidemic of incest accusations. At the same time, as Jeffrey Masson** has pointed out, Freud's flip-flop also had a disastrous effect

---

* The 'procedure method' also provided the prototype for classical psychoanalysis. Although Freud later concluded that he should never touch his patients, he continued to have them lie down and use 'free association,' as he described in a 1913 essay, 'On Beginning the Treatment.' He remained out of sight, since 'I cannot put up with being stared at by other people for eight hours a day (or more).' Freud still preferred well-educated, wealthy clients with mild neuroses. He insisted on hour-long sessions six days a week (along with prompt payment of a substantial fee). He continued to break through his patients' 'resistance' to inform them of their true problems. 'It remains the first aim of the treatment to attach [the patient] to it and to the person of the doctor.' Freud believed that 'the patient's first symptoms or chance actions' often betrayed their problems. Thus, he concluded that a young philosopher who straightened the creases of his trousers must have been 'a former coprophilic of the highest refinement,' or that a young girl who pulled the hem of her skirt over exposed ankles revealed 'her narcissistic pride in her physical beauty and her inclinations to exhibitionism.'

** In his 1984 book, *The Assault on Truth: Freud's Suppression of the Seduction Theory*, Jeffrey Masson complained about the effect of Freud's flip-flop, as well as documenting other Freudian flaws, including the horrendous nose operation on Emma Eckstein in 1895. But Masson miraculously swallowed the 1896 repressed memory scenario without a qualm, asserting that the incest horrors Freud extracted from his patients were all true. Masson's book, with its illogical conclusion, has unfortunately served as one of the cornerstones of the incest survivor movement.

on *real* incest victims. Even though Freud himself never denied the reality of some incest memories, until recently many psychoanalysts routinely dismissed their patients' all-too-well-remembered stories of sexual abuse. 'Ah, yes,' they would nod knowingly. 'Those are just fantasies. Your father didn't *really* do that to you! Your unconscious only *wishes* that he had.'

MULTIPLE PERSONALITIES

As the turn of the century approached, another fascinating concept emerged – that people could harbor several distinct personalities within the same body and brain. Robert Louis Stevenson prepared the way with *The Strange Case of Dr. Jekyll and Mr. Hyde* (1886), while Oscar Wilde contributed *The Picture of Dorian Gray* (1891).*[106] The fictional stories reflected the underlying Victorian tension between science and irrationality, between puritanical sexual codes and pornographic imaginations. Freud expressed these feelings in his concept of the submerged and violent id, a turbulent repressed unconscious held down by the beleaguered forces of the conscious ego and the prudish superego.

Ian Hacking, a philosopher specializing in 19th-century statistics, describes that period's obsession with 'the statistics of deviance.' He dates the emergence of intense interest in multiple personalities to 1875, the year in which one Felida X was diagnosed by a French surgeon who had an interest in hypnotism. The surgeon was largely motivated by a philosophical argument in support of 'psychological positivism,' trying to prove to conservatives and the Church that there was no inherently unitary 'soul.' Felida's dual personality was held to refute the 'dogmatic transcendental unity of apperception that made the self prior to all knowledge.' In their struggle to sound lofty and scientific, the experts of the age delighted in pedantic jargon. As Hacking puts it, the Victorian age introduced 'a particular medico-forensic-political language . . . The sheer proliferation of labels in that domain during the 19th century may have engendered vastly more kinds of people [i.e., diagnoses] than the

* Stevenson wrote his Jekyll/Hyde story after reading a 'French scientific journal on subconsciousness.' There were a few cases of 'double' personality documented earlier in the 19th century, but they weren't full-blown multiples. For a skeptical summary, see Michael G. Kenny, *The Passion of Ansel Bourne.* For a more credulous overview, see Henri Ellenberger, *The Discovery of the Unconscious*, pages 126–170.

world had ever known before.'[107] After Felida, a multitude of multiples ensued, particularly in France, where Pierre Janet applied himself to its proper identification.

Like Freud, Pierre Janet had studied with Charcot and was fascinated with the mechanisms of the mind.*[108] Janet coined the term *dissociation* to describe a mechanism that he assumed to exist, just as Freud presumed the reality of repression. Janet theorized that the mind was capable of splitting off from itself in some form, usually to protect itself from distress. The more sensitive, neurasthenic, or hysterical the patient, and the more pronounced the trauma, the more likely that severe dissociation, or even multiple personality, would occur. Janet emphasized the importance of naming each psychic part: 'Once baptized, the unconscious personality is more clear and definite; it shows its psychological traits more clearly.'[109]** In 1887, he hypnotized Lucie, a young woman with a history of 'hysterical' symptoms. The following exchange took place while Lucie was hypnotized and practiced automatic writing:

How are you?
I don't know.
There must be someone there who hears me.
Yes.
Who is it?
Someone other than Lucie.
Ah. Another person. Would you like us to give her a name?
No.
Yes. It would be more convenient.
All right. Adrienne.

* Also like Freud, Janet had his mystical side. He believed, for instance, that time travel would be possible. 'Everything that has existed,' he proclaimed, 'still exists and endures in a place which we do not understand.' While Janet sometimes seemed aware of the dangers of suggestibility ('Most frequently, psychotics are acting'), he fell into the familiar trap of validating anything his patients said. One visitor was startled to find 'housed together many persecutionist patients who fired one another emotionally with fantastic tales.' Janet dismissed his criticism, asserting, 'I believe those people, until it is proven to me that what they say is untrue.' By 1925, however, Janet had become much more cynical, particularly about Freudians, writing: 'The psychoanalysts invariably set to work in order to discover a traumatic memory, with the *a priori* conviction that it is there to be discovered ... Owing to the nature of their methods, they can invariably find what they seek.'
** Anthropologist Sherrill Mulhern, who has written extensively in French about MPD, insists that Janet has been mistranslated and misrepresented, and that he realized that naming 'parts' was not a good idea. I have not read Janet in the original.

Very well, Adrienne. Do you hear me?
Yes.[110]

It is fairly obvious from this dialogue that Janet was creating the multiplicity he expected to find. Lucie, already compliant in her hypnotic inductee role, went along with it. This process replicated the exorcist's methodology. He, too, insisted on speaking directly to internal demons, each of whom needed a name. The similarity of the process was not lost on early proponents of multiple personality. They proclaimed that demoniacs had actually been multiple personalities, misdiagnosed by the ignorant, superstitious clerics. In fact, both exorcist and psychologist practiced the same stratagem, and their clients simply complied by acting out the expected role.

The real blossoming of multiple personality diagnoses took place in America, however, after the publication of *The Dissociation of a Personality* by Morton Prince in 1905. Prince, who founded and edited the *Journal of Abnormal Psychology*, saw the exploration of multiple personalities as his ticket to fame. 'Abnormal psychology is fast forging to the front as an important field of research,' he wrote in the book's preface. He asserted that the field had 'long awaited investigation by modern methods.' In his introduction, he explained that Janet had revealed simpler forms of dissociation through hypnosis and automatic writing. Trance mediums displayed a more fully developed form. But he, Morton Prince, had identified a full-blown case of multiplicity for the first time. 'Such cases are generally overlooked,' he assured the reader, because 'such persons often pass before the world as mentally healthy persons.' Finally, he revealed that he found these cases to be 'fascinating objects of study.'[111]

In 1898, Miss Christine Beauchamp (an alias for Clara Fowler), arrived on Prince's doorstep at the age of 23. He described her as 'a neurasthenic of an extreme type, [suffering from] headaches, insomnia, bodily pains, persistent fatigue, and poor nutrition.' In other words, she displayed all the psychosomatic symptoms expected at the time. Even as a child, she was 'impressionable . . . given to day dreaming and living in her imagination.' She clearly attracted the psychologist, who identified in her 'that natural refinement of thought and feeling which is inborn, and which is largely made up of delicacy of sentiment and appreciation of everything that is fine in thought and perceptions . . . She is well educated and has marked literary tastes and faculties. She is essentially a bibliophile, and is never so happy as when allowed to delve amongst books.' Finally, he noted that she was 'very suggestible.'

Over the next seven years, Prince encouraged an extremely close and dependent relationship with Beauchamp. 'During most of this time,' he wrote, 'she has been under constant, and often for long periods, daily observation.' Even when she went away for summer vacation, 'a considerable correspondence with each personality has been kept up.' In other words, Prince would write to each of the three personalities, and they would respond, using different handwriting, samples of which were reprinted in the book. Prince noted that the multiple parts engaged in 'a comedy of errors, which has been sometimes farcical and sometimes tragic.' That is quite a good description of the entire book, in which Prince painstakingly and unwittingly conned both the young lady and himself.

Yet Prince was utterly convinced that he had not cued his patient. During an early hypnotic session, he was surprised when she denied remembering something she had previously told him. Then he understood her to refer to herself in the third person as 'She.' Although he sincerely believed that he had discovered a new personality 'against my protests and in spite of my skepticism,' it is obvious that he eagerly jumped on what he considered a significant clue. 'I hastened to follow up the lead offered and asked, as if in ignorance of her meaning, who "She" was.' Not satisfied, he 'pursued her relentlessly in my numerous examinations.'

> Why are you not 'She'?
> *Because 'She' does not know the same things that I do.*
> But you both have the same arms and legs, haven't you?
> *Yes, but arms and legs do not make us the same.*
> Well, if you are different persons, what are your names?

Maddeningly, Beauchamp refused to take the bait, remaining 'evasive, unable to answer; [she] made every effort not to commit herself.' Finally, after quite some time, this newly 'discovered' personality was labeled first B II, then Chris, and finally Sally.

It seems obvious that Prince unwittingly cued his patient into multiplicity, as his friend William James suspected: 'Where you see occasion for singling out definite phases, there is nothing in Nature but a flux of incoherent memories, emotions, impulses, and delusions.'[112] James wasn't terribly concerned, however, assuring Prince that to 'define any continuum,' arbitrary labels had to be applied. That wasn't all there was to it, however. As social anthropologist Michael Kenny observes, 'Morton Prince was scarcely a detached scientific observer; he and Miss Beauchamp mutually, though unconsciously, colluded in the composition of a medical drama based on stereotypic nineteenth-century roles.'[113]

In many ways, Christine Beauchamp was the ideal candidate for multiplicity. She had a highly developed imagination, read widely,* and craved the attention Prince gave her. Once she entered into the spirit of the roles she was to play, she obviously relished them. She probably came to believe in them herself, until Prince triumphantly discovered 'the Real Miss Beauchamp' (a fourth personality) and reintegrated all of them.**[114] At the end of the book, he wrote, without intended irony, that 'these states [now] seem to her very largely differences of moods. She regrets them, but does not attempt to excuse them, because, as she says, "After all, it is always myself." '[115]

EMIL KRAEPELIN AND HIS PATIENT

I will conclude this chapter with a case that serves as a parable and warning to both therapist and patient.

Munich, 1904. Emil Kraepelin, author of an influential psychiatric textbook and creator of the term *manic-depression*,[116] introduces a patient to his lecture hall colleagues in the most humiliating, demeaning way: 'Gentlemen – the young lady, aged 30, carefully dressed in black, who comes into the hall with short, shuffling steps, leaning on the nurse, and sinks into a chair as if exhausted, gives you the impression that she is ill.'[117] Clearly, the doctor thinks otherwise. When he asks her where she is and what the date, she answers correctly in a low, tired voice, without looking up.

A few minutes later, she apparently falls into a deep sleep. 'Her arms

---

* It is entirely possible that the whole business about who 'She' was stemmed from a misunderstanding, since Beauchamp had apparently read Rider Haggard's book entitled *She*.

** Not to be outdone, Morton Prince's namesake and competitor W. F. Prince, a firm believer in psychic phenomena, soon hypnotized Doris Fischer, a medium, and announced that she, too, contained multiple personalities. Not surprisingly, her case developed along precisely parallel lines to that of Miss Beauchamp. W. F. Prince eventually adopted Miss Fischer as his daughter.

have grown quite limp,' Kraepelin observes. 'If you raise her eyelids, her eyes suddenly rotate upwards. Needle-pricks only produce a slight shudder.' He sprinkles her with cold water, and she starts up, opening her eyes. She apologizes for having another one of her sleeping attacks.

The doctor then proceeds to describe her history and treatment while she listens. He never names her, but we will call her Sonia. Both of Sonia's parents died when she was 14. Educated thereafter in convent schools, she suffered from headaches that were 'relieved by the removal of growths from the nose.' (The treatment was presumably designed to cure masturbatory tendencies as well.) 'She very readily became delirious in feverish illnesses.' At the age of 17, she took a job as a governess, but she soon became ill, and for the last seven years, she has been 'wandering out of the hands of one doctor into those of another.'

Sonia had violent abdominal pains and menstrual difficulties. These were ascribed to 'stenosis of the cervical canal and retroflection of the uterus.' Consequently, five years ago, 'recourse was had ... to the excision of the wedge [in the uterus] supposed to cause the obstruction, and the introduction of a pessary.' Later, Sonia lost her voice. Her right forearm contracted, as did her left thigh. Doctors treated her with massage, administered electrical shocks, restricted her movement with bandages, and stretched her limbs under an anaesthetic.

Next, Sonia complained of 'heart oppression and spasmodic breathing, [followed by] disturbances of urination, diarrhoea, and unpleasant sensations, now in one, and now in another part of the body, but particularly headaches.' She was also subject to violent mood swings. Seeking a cure, she underwent a series of ablutions in 'brine baths, Russian baths, pine-needle baths,' followed by more electric shocks. Blessedly, the next treatment involved breathing country air, living at summer resorts, and a stint on the Riviera.

Two years earlier, Sonia's 'sleep attacks' grew worse. They would come on even when she was standing up and could last as long as an hour. Hypnotic suggestion didn't help, but cold water and the Faradic current were 'fairly effective.'

During her current residence, Sonia has begun to have 'great attacks,' in addition to her other troubles. 'We will try to produce such an attack,' Kraepelin says hopefully, 'by pressure on the very sensitive left ovarian region.' After one or two minutes of increasingly strong prods, Sonia has had enough. She throws herself to and fro with her eyes still shut, screaming, 'You must not do anything to me, you hound. Pig! Pig!' She cries for help, pushes him away, and twists 'as if she were trying to escape from a sexual assault,' the doctor explicates, out of breath, but still master of the situation. 'Whenever she is touched, the excitement increases. Her whole body is strongly bent backwards.'

Suddenly, she collapses and sobs, begging not to be cursed. Kraepelin sprinkles more cold water. Sonia shudders, appears to come to herself with a deep sigh, and looks around as if she doesn't know what has happened. The doctor explains that 'we have to deal here with the disease known as *hysteria*.' He notes that in her 'great attacks,' she often repeats a 'dream-like recollection' about a horrible gynecological examination she once endured at the hands of a rough Dutch doctor. She also remembers a traumatic curse pronounced on her by an aunt.

Kraepelin believes that all of Sonia's symptoms are psychosomatic, giving as an example how he cured her spasmodically clenched hand by applying a gold coin to her wrist. Her sleep was improved by giving her sugar water. 'All the various troubles gave way to measures of the same kind, working on the imagination alone.'

Finally, near the end of his lecture, the doctor reveals his hostility toward Sonia. 'Her illness gives her a certain satisfaction,' he observes, 'and she resists involuntarily when steps are taken to cure it . . . Invalidism has essentially become a *necessity of life to her*.' He complains that 'with her growing expertness in illness, the emotional sympathies of the patient are more and more confined to the selfish furthering of her own wishes. She tries ruthlessly to extort the most careful attention from those around her, obliges the doctor to occupy himself with her by day or by night on the slightest occasion.'

Despite such attentions, 'she calls herself the abandoned, the outcast, and in mysterious hints makes confession of horrible, delightful experiences and failings, which she will only confide to the discreet bosom of her very best friend, the doctor.' Kraepelin ends by dismissing the possibility of recovery. 'Hysterical insanity is the expression of a *peculiar, morbid tendency* . . . In our patient, the beginning of the illness goes back to an early age. We cannot therefore expect that treatment will be successful in altering her personality.'

The lecture is over, Sonia dismissed. Kraepelin's associates congratulate him on a fine presentation and commiserate with his lot, having to deal with such difficult patients. A few months later, Sonia dies of tuberculosis. The fatal symptoms were undoubtedly misdiagnosed as more hysteria.

What morals can we draw from this dreadful story? The all-powerful Dr. Kraepelin appears to be a monster who treats his patients as objects. The treatments are often inhumane and abusive. He sprinkles water on her, sticks needles into her, pokes and prods her. He apparently gets some kind of sexual, voyeuristic, sadistic thrill from her reactions. Then he interprets her rage as mental illness. He ignores her traumatic stories about a rough pelvic exam (a rape?) and her hostility toward her aunt. He condemns her to eternal pain, telling her that she is incurable. Then he allows her to die. In many ways, she truly *is* 'the abandoned, the outcast,' as she agonizingly asserts.

Yet Kraepelin also has a point. Her invalidism has become a way of life. Her symptoms are her only way to obtain attention in the context of the institution and, by extension, her society. She has learned to perform the psychological *pas de deux* with her doctors, to comply with their expectations. In the unreal world of the hospital, she has become completely self-absorbed.

Fortunately, society has changed dramatically since this 1904 scene. But were Sonia alive today, her expert therapist, her modern-day Kraepelin, would immediately interpret her behavior and her symptoms as evidence of sexual abuse – and not just by a Dutch gynecologist. Her cries of 'Pig! Pig!' would automatically be perceived as the reliving of a repressed memory of sexual assault, even if no such assault had taken place. This expert, like Kraepelin, would be a voyeur, titillated by his patient's troubles. He, too, would tell her that her problems stem from childhood, that unearthing all the memories may take years, that she may never truly recover.

Perhaps the therapist would hypnotize Sonia and ask, 'Can you see your aunt's face? What is she touching you with? How old are you now, Sonia?' From there, the memories might expand to include her mother and father, conveniently deceased and unable to deny anything. And the 30-year-old, in search of sympathy and attention, would be only too eager to confide her 'horrible, delightful experiences,' regardless of whether they occurred in reality or were produced by dreams, trance states, or massages to unleash 'body memories.'

I began this chapter by quoting Phyllis Chesler's 1972 book, *Women and Madness*, so let me end with her prophetic warning. 'In what ways can therapy "help" women?' she asked. 'Can female therapists "help" female patients more differently than male therapists? Can feminist or "radical" therapists "help" female patients in some special or rapid way?' Her answer was that 'people and social structures change slowly if at all,' and that 'most people simply obey new myths, as inevitably as they did old myths.' Consequently, she was both excited and disturbed by the possibilities she saw in feminist psychotherapy. It could, she feared, simply turn into 'authoritarianism with a new party line.'[118]

CHAPTER ELEVEN

Why Now?

I don't know a soul who's not been battered,
I don't have a friend who feels at ease.
I don't know a dream that's not been shattered
Or driven to its knees.
But it's all right, it's all right,
For we've lived so well, so long.
Still, when I think of the road we're traveling on,
I wonder what's gone wrong.
I can't help it, I wonder what's gone wrong.

PAUL SIMON, *American Tune*

The current repressed-memory craze represents the continuation of a long-standing historical trend in which authorities have encouraged troubled women to act out the 'symptom pool' of the era and accept an inappropriate diagnosis. But that does not explain why this particularly virulent form of delusion has become so popular at this time in our particular culture. The inevitable questions arise: Why now? Why in the English-speaking world, particularly America?

Revelations about *real* incest initially led to the search for repressed memories, as I documented in Chapter 1. But how could an idea with such shallow scientific grounding receive such ready and widespread acceptance? Although it is tempting to try to construct elaborate, convincing hypotheses, I believe that there are no simple answers. Rather, several historical and cultural threads seem to have woven together to produce a social fabric that is receptive to the current sex abuse witch hunt. These threads include, among many others, victimology, the codependency movement, and a general tendency to seek specific causes for a multitude of problems. Permeating all of these factors is a high level of societal stress.

In this chapter, I will focus on American history, sociology, and psychology, since it is in the United States that the recovered memory boom commenced. Nonetheless, many of these observations apply to Britain and other industrialized countries – particularly the sections on feminism, political correctness, Christianity, the New Age movement, victimology, and fragmented families. While Americans have had to cope with their diminishing economic power and prestige since the Vietnam War, for instance, the British have had similar problems ever since their political sovereignty was reduced in 1973, with entry into the European Community. By the 1980s, Great Britain was coping with inner-city poverty, drug use, and high crime rates. In short, many of the ills attributed to Americans in this chapter have also contributed to a witchhunt mentality in other countries, as Philip Jenkins points out in his book, *Intimate Enemies*.[1]

As we saw in the last chapter, a frantic search for scapegoats often surfaces during times of cultural upheaval. As Frederic Bartlett observed in 1932, 'times of social stress, threat from outside, insurrection from within, any state of high social tension' tend to exacerbate such 'persistent tendencies' within a society.[2]

By almost any standard, Americans feel disjointed, pressured, and confused as they approach the turn of the century. They face an insurmountable national debt, a shortage of decent jobs, the spread of AIDS, gratuitous random violence, the breakup of families, newly discovered dangers to their health and environment, an unwieldy health-care system ... the list goes on. Is it any wonder that they want to lay the blame somewhere? Who allowed things to get this way, anyway? It wasn't them, that's for sure! It was the previous generation. They messed everything up, including their children.

But there have been other times of generalized, free-floating anxiety. Why, this time, has the malaise taken the bizarre form of unwarranted accusations of incest? Why aren't Americans searching for witches or branding political subversives instead? Perhaps clues can be found in historical trends involving the American national character and attitudes toward psychology, religion, women, and sex.

A NATION IN SEARCH OF A DISEASE

In 1881, Dr. George Beard published *American Nervousness: Its Causes and Consequences*, in which he asserted that the stress of modern life, with its telegraph, steam engine, and frantic pace, was causing more and more people to come down with 'neurasthenia,' a disease that Beard both invented and treated. Its symptoms, which he himself described as 'slippery, fleeting, and vague,' included sick headache, exhaustion, ringing in the ears, nightmares, insomnia, flushing and fidgetiness, palpitations, dyspepsia, vague pains and flying neuralgia, spinal irritation, uterine troubles, hopelessness, claustrophobia, lack of sexual interest, and several more pages filled with other options. Beard hypothesized that people inherited a certain finite amount of 'nervous force,' and that when it was over-strained, neurasthenia resulted.[3]

Beard proclaimed that neurasthenia was primarily a disease of the upper class, whose refined, sensitive nervous systems were overwhelmed by the pace of modern life. While delicate women came down with the ailment most frequently, hard-pressed businessmen could also be afflicted. Overwork, the volatility of economic booms and busts, repression of turbulent emotions, and too much *thinking* – particularly by women, unaccustomed to such brain strain – supposedly contributed to this high state of nerves. 'The rapidity with which new truths are discovered, accepted and popularized in modern times,' Beard wrote, 'is a proof and result of the extravagance of our civilization.'[4]

While we may laugh at Beard's naïveté, his diagnosis clearly struck a chord with the public in his time, a period remarkably similar to our own.

In the '60s (1860s, that is), the United States was torn apart by a controversial war that sometimes pitted family members against one another. In the post-war period, physicians developed an interest in war-induced stress and soon identified similar syndromes in the normal population. The pace of scientific and technological change seemed overwhelming. Religious faith lost ground to materialism and greed in the nation's value system. A flood of immigrants entered the country. Reformers attempted to stem the tides of alcoholism, child abuse, and sexual deviance. Homelessness in the midst of affluence became common. Interest in alternative healing methods using herbs and traditional native American remedies blossomed, along with belief in psychic phenomena. Psychological self-help books proliferated. Some women rebelled against their traditional subservient roles, and many men reacted defensively. In this turbulent society, which stressed individualism over community, the psychologist replaced the priest, as people sought respite from their confusion and unhappiness.

Sound familiar? The above commentary could apply equally to the late 20th century.*

* People appear to undergo psychological stress near the end of *every* century, perhaps because of awareness of a major transition point. As the year 1000 approached, Western Europeans went into a frenzy, believing the world would come to an end at the 'millennium.' The Witch Craze commenced at the end of the 15th century, but it became most intense a hundred years later during the 1590s. One century later, the Salem witch trials occurred in 1692. Mesmerism surfaced along with the French Revolution in the late 18th century.

'Americans are the most nervous people in the world,' Dr. John Pemberton wrote in 1885, the year before he invented Coca-Cola as a 'nerve tonic' for neurasthenics.[5] For Pemberton and Beard, this observation was a point of curious pride. Because Americans were so inventive, energetic, and sensitive, they suffered more magnificently than others. 'Beard's was an ambivalence characteristically American,' observed medical historian Charles Rosenberg, noting that Beard was torn between an 'arrogant nationalism and a chronic national insecurity.' Nor was Beard alone. Since the late 1700s, Rosenberg continued, physicians such as Benjamin Rush had concluded that 'the unique pace of American life, its competitiveness, its lack of stability in religion and government, was somehow related to an incidence of mental illness higher than that of other Western countries.'[6]

Alexis de Tocqueville, who mused over the American character in the early 19th century, commented on the national obsession with self. The citizens were 'apt to imagine that their whole destiny is in their hands.' For the Frenchman, who was accustomed to philosophical acceptance of adversity, it was 'strange to see with what feverish ardor the Americans pursue their own welfare, and to watch the vague dread that constantly torments them lest they should not have chosen the shortest path which may lead to it.'[7] As an ironic consequence, the impatient individualistic American, straining after an instant cure, has traditionally placed a dependent faith in the latest theories and self-help books produced by self-proclaimed experts.

George Beard exemplified both the sufferer's search for certainty and the expert's assertion of authority. His father and two brothers were ministers, but Beard could not bring himself to accept that vocation, largely because of his belief in Darwin's theories of evolution. Until the age of 23, when he graduated from Yale, Beard experienced his own brand of neurasthenia, with ringing in the ears, acute dyspepsia, pains in the side, nervousness, morbid fears, and chronic exhaustion. As medical historian Barbara Sicherman observed, intellectuals such as Beard 'suffered acutely from the loss of faith that accompanied Darwinism ... and the growing authority of Science. In a society of changing and often conflicting values, the decline of spiritual certitude intensified feelings of isolation.'[8]

Beard and his fellow nerve doctors, the forerunners of therapists, made a religion out of their supposedly scientific approach to emotional and spiritual problems. Beard declared that the physician must not only heal, but enlighten the public and become 'a *power in society*.'[9] Although

Beard died in 1883, his colleague S. Weir Mitchell did indeed become a powerful figure, pulling down $70,000 a year while treating neurasthenics with his 'rest cure,' which he first tried out on Civil War soldiers. Most of his subsequent patients, however, were upper-class women. According to an 1899 survey of neurasthenic patients, two-thirds were between the ages of 20 and 40, with an average age of 33.3.

In a typical rest cure, Mitchell ordered an afflicted woman to take to her bed, where she was fed and washed by attendants and forbidden to read, use her hands, or even speak. 'Mitchell subsequently systematized the treatment to include total isolation of the patient from the family,' Barbara Sicherman writes. Such isolation enhanced the doctor's control over the patient, which Mitchell considered all-important, writing: 'The man who can insure belief in his opinions and obedience to his decrees secures very often most brilliant and sometimes easy success.' He sought a 'trustful belief' and was at first surprised 'that we ever get from any human being such childlike obedience. Yet we do get it, even from men.' Mitchell implicitly recognized that he was usurping the role formerly occupied by a minister. 'The priest hears the crime or folly of the hour,' he wrote, 'but to the physician are oftener told the long, sad tales of a whole life.'[10]*[11]

In *The Autobiography of a Neurasthene* (1910), Margaret Cleaves provided, as Sicherman puts it, 'a classic study of unresolved dependency needs that were at least partly met by her long-term relationship with her physician,' who visited her daily during her worst attacks. Cleaves blamed her rearing for all of her troubles, noting that the arrival of a younger sister deprived her of milk. Also, her father died when she was 14, and she had a recurrent dream of being a child cradled in his arms. Her doctor provided a fine substitute, however. 'It seemed worthwhile,' she wrote, 'to have suffered for the sake of all this comfort.'[12]

I have taken us back a century in some detail for obvious reasons. As noted, the similarities between the two eras are striking.**[13] The late 19th century spawned the psychoanalytical enterprise, the shift from

* In 1873, feminist writer Abba Goold Woolson protested 'Invalidism as a Pursuit' in her book, *Woman in American Society*. 'Society,' she wrote, was 'ever doing its best to crush out of them every trace of healthy instincts and vigorous life, and to reduce them to the condition of the enfeebled young ladies that meet us on every side, who are all modelled after one wretched pattern, and as much alike as so many peas.'

** In 1900, H. G. Wells made an accurate observation and prediction: 'Life is already most wonderfully arbitrary and experimental, and for the coming century this must be its essential social history, a great drifting and unrest of people, a shifting and regrouping and breaking up again of groups, great multitudes seeking to find themselves.'

priest to therapist, and the abnegation of personal responsibility in the face of social turmoil. By medicalizing neurosis, the early psychologists and physicians initiated a disturbing trend that has now reached crisis proportions. As Barbara Sicherman notes, 'They were interpreting behavioral symptoms that some found morally reprehensible (an inability to work for no apparent cause, compulsive or phobic behavior, bizarre thoughts) as signs of illness rather than wilfulness. They thus legitimized the right of individuals with such difficulties to be considered, and to consider themselves, victims of disease.' Beard, she writes, urged that 'kleptomania, inebriety, and pyromania – all safely medical – replace the traditional moralistic designations of stealing, drunkenness, and arson.'[14]

VICTIMS ALL

In the late 20th century, we have taken such excuses to new and extraordinary heights. As numerous commentators have lamented, virtually everyone now claims to be a victim of *something*. In his 1992 book, *A Nation of Victims*, Charles Sykes provides numerous examples. 'An FBI agent embezzles two thousand dollars from the government and then loses all of it in an afternoon of gambling in Atlantic City,' Sykes writes. 'He is fired but wins reinstatement after a court rules that his affinity for gambling with other people's money is a "handicap" and thus protected under federal law.' Similarly, overweight people sue McDonald's because the chairs are too small, and those who are chronically late protest being fired, because they suffer from a psychological affliction. With such precedents, it is little wonder that sex abuse allegations – far more serious than habitual tardiness – provide a ready excuse for murdering or maiming a parent, spouse, or other accused molester.[15] One Kentucky woman even managed to avoid responsibility for her admitted adultery by claiming that it was not she, but her *alter*, who had illicit sex. The courts bought her MPD excuse.[16]

Since its third edition appeared in 1980 (the fourth was published in 1994), the *Diagnostic and Statistical Manual of Mental Disorders*, the psychiatric Bible, has encouraged this trend by codifying almost any human behavior as a potential mental illness.*[17] Some of the diagnostic

---

* Among the various 'personality disorders' enumerated by the *DSM-IV* are Narcissistic Personality Disorder (selfishness, grandiosity, and a sense of entitlement), Avoidant Personality Disorder (socially inhibited, feeling inadequate, hypersensitive), Dependent

categories are truly ludicrous. In a 1994 review of the fourth edition of the *DSM*, *Scientific American* asked, 'Do you use grammar and punctuation poorly? Is your spelling horrendous, and penmanship bad, too? You may be mentally ill.' Why? You may suffer from the 'Disorder of Written Expression.'[18] The *DSM-IV* further describes someone with an 'Identity Problem' as suffering from 'uncertainty about multiple issues ... such as long-term goals, career choice, friendship patterns, sexual orientation and behavior, moral values, and group loyalties.'[19] Certainly, these are difficult issues, but hardly unique. As Sykes puts it, 'Is this a psychological disorder or a description of existential angst? Is this illness or man faced with the disorder of modern life?'[20]

In his book, *The Diseasing of America*, social psychologist Stanton Peele objects to the creation of ever more specialized grievance categories, each of which can blame its difficulties upon some kind of 'addiction,' each with its own 12-step recovery group. Sex addicts cannot help being promiscuous. Gamblers, shoppers, gluttons, thieves, procrastinators, and television viewers can all now qualify for medical treatment. 'We see,' Peele writes, 'the ultimate definition of the ordinary discomforts and challenges in life as diseased events.'[21]

The modern prototype for this flood of maladies is alcoholism, a very real, devastating problem to millions of people. Alcoholics Anonymous published its 'Big Book' in 1939, and since that time, AA has helped many people to achieve and maintain sobriety. As a result, it has saved lives and reunited families that had become dysfunctional because of alcohol.

Unfortunately, in the early 1980s, other less helpful movements attempted to emulate the success of AA, using the same 12-step methodology, allocating disease and victimhood to other people.* The alcoholic's wife, who remained with him despite his habits, was labeled

---

Personality Disorder (inability to make decisions, needs reassurance from others), or Oppositional Defiant Disorder (angry, resentful, deliberately annoys people). If you find someone obnoxious but can't quite find the proper category, there's always 'Disruptive Behavior Disorder Not Otherwise Specified.' In other words, we appear to have turned character traits into certifiable ailments. As sociologist Carol Tavris points out in a scathing 1994 article on the *DSM*, the majority of these 'diseases' are aimed at women: 'When men have problems, it's because of their upbringing, personality or environment; when women have problems, it's because of something in their very psyche.'
* It is important to note that many traditional AA members disapprove of the newer forms of 12-step groups. 'I hate all this talk about codependence and dysfunctional families,' one veteran AA member told me. 'We were drunks, period. That's the problem, not all this psychobabble.'

'codependent,' locked into a sick relationship. His children, raised in a dysfunctional household, were irrevocably damaged, according to the book *Adult Children of Alcoholics* (1983). ACOA groups sprang up throughout the country, probably providing a therapeutic outlet for adults who had suffered childhood abuse from alcoholic parents, but also providing a new scapegoat for those wishing to escape responsibility for their own problems. Now it became a badge of honor to have an alcoholic parent. If Dad had a beer after work or a glass of wine with dinner, that meant he was an alcoholic, thus allowing his adult offspring to blame everything on him.

Charles Whitfield, an internist-turned-psychotherapist, masterfully tapped into this new market with *Healing the Child Within* (1987), written not only for alcoholics' offspring, but *any* adult who grew up in a dysfunctional family, which he estimated to be between 80 per cent and 95 per cent of the population. Whitfield stressed that such adults should go to therapy and contact a suppressed inner child, the 'True Self.' To do so, they must abandon false beliefs such as 'Oh, my childhood was fine,' and get suitably angry at their parents. 'When working in recovery,' Whitefield wrote, 'most adult children *are* able to work through the denial and to gradually uncover their ungrieved losses or traumas.'[22]

In *Codependent No More*, published the same year, Melody Beattie declared that codependency was rampant in American relationships, independent of alcohol. Everyone was stuck in debilitating marriages, coercive friendships, maladjusted work situations. CODA groups (Codependents Anonymous) sprang up to take their place next to the ACOA meetings. Soon, drug counselors jumped on the bandwagon as well, explaining that substance abuse often stemmed from traumatic childhoods.

The following year, in *Bradshaw On: The Family*, John Bradshaw reiterated what he had already said in his popular television series: 96 per cent of American families are dysfunctional, even without the presence of Budweiser or Jack Daniels, and everyone must search out their impoverished inner children. By the 1990s, parents had become pariahs, the monsters who had nearly destroyed their now-adult children, all of whom rushed to buy the latest self-help books, entered therapy, and declared themselves 'in recovery' from numerous abuses.

The point here is not to downplay the horrible damage that can be caused by truly dysfunctional families, whether the dysfunctions involve drunkenness, spousal abuse, sexual or other physical abuse of children, or any combination thereof. But if 96 per cent of families are really that sick, then just about everybody needs self-help 'recovery' books and years of therapy.*

The phrase 'adult children' is particularly disturbing. It goes well beyond describing now-grown offspring. Instead, the term apparently means that these are *literally* children stumbling around in adult bodies. Some Americans have turned themselves into irresponsible spoiled brats, constantly pointing the finger at someone else – usually parents, but a mate will do. 'The National Anthem has become The Whine,' as Charles Sykes puts it.[23] Or, as commentator Joseph Epstein says, 'We have become connoisseurs of grievance – one nation problematical, with anxiety and aggravation for all.'[24]

Similarly, is it necessarily *bad* to be 'codependent,' to depend on one another? Isn't that in part what mates are for? Of course, there is a grain of truth in all of this psychobabble. But by naming a disease, we often create it. Sure, all families have problems and could easily be called dysfunctional. Yes, all relationships have their strains, and those in them could be called codependent. Unfortunately, these easy labels prevent us from seeing ourselves as unique people with the power to make our own decisions.**[25]

By constantly defending ourselves against imperfect relationships, refusing to be sucked into the codependent role of caregiver, and severing ties with newly perceived abusive families, we run the risk of narrowing our world to only ourselves – a process which, as de Tocqueville warned long ago, 'throws [every man] back forever upon himself alone and threatens to confine him entirely within the solitude of his own heart.'[26]

By the end of the 1970s, Americans were clearly fulfilling de Tocque-

* *The Codependency Conspiracy* (1991), by Dr. Stan J. Katz and Aimee E. Liu, is a realistic appraisal of the dangers inherent in becoming overly dependent on therapists, written in the inimitable tradition of recovery books, complete with charts and questions. Even the subtitle is delicious: 'How to Break the Recovery Habit and Take Charge of Your Life.'
** One indication of how our personal worlds are rapidly shrinking is the trendy emphasis on *boundaries*. 'Picture a bubble surrounding you, separating you from all that is not you,' read the directions for 'Boundary Formation Exercises' handed out in a psychiatric ward. 'The bubble is your boundary. Make it a color that is pleasing to you.' The Bubble Boy, tragically born without an immune system, must live in a protective sheath all of his life. Yet we have adopted a kind of psychic Bubble Boy as an emblem of our age. He is safe, insulated by well-defined, healthy boundaries. He will not suffer from the indefinable plagues of our era, which physicians have actually named *twentieth-century disease*. According to a 1992 article in the *Journal of the American Medical Association*, patients suffering from this illness complain of 'difficulty in breathing, depression, headache, fatigue, irritability, insomnia, palpitations, and other cardiovascular symptoms' – in other words, all of the classic psychosomatic symptoms.

ville's prophecy, as Christopher Lasch pointed out in his 1978 book, *the Culture of Narcissism*. Lasch noted that Americans had 'carried the logic of individualism to the extreme,' constituting 'the pursuit of happiness to the dead end of a narcissistic preoccupation with the self. Strategies of narcissistic survival now present themselves as emancipation from the repressive conditions of the past.'[27]

Today, that trend has become yet more extreme. 'The self is now the sacred cow of American culture,' Australian essayist Robert Hughes observes in *Culture of Complaint* (1993), adding that we have enshrined the victim-as-hero. 'Hence the rise of cult therapies which teach that we are all the victims of our parents: that whatever our folly, venality, or outright thuggishness, we are not to be blamed for it.' Rather, our rearing caused all our current problems. 'We have been given imperfect role models, or starved of affection, or beaten, or perhaps subjected to the goatish lusts of Papa; and if we don't think we have, it is only because we have repressed the memory and are therefore in even more urgent need of the quack's latest book.'[28]

While intellectuals such as Hughes may sneer derisively at the recovery movement, it is not a joke. As we have seen, the *I've-been-abused* mindset ultimately leads to splintered families and shattered lives, suicide attempts and psychiatric wards. Even when it does not reach such drastic proportions, the self-absorption now in vogue has produced people such as this young woman who recently wrote to a *Psychology Today* advice columnist:

> I've had a lot of therapy and read a lot of self-help books. I've learned to really love myself. I always pamper my inner child. I have overcome any tendency to feel guilt for anything I do. I'm real good at asserting myself and expressing my anger, and I don't let anyone abuse me in any way. I've worked particularly hard on my codependency. I've cut off all my dysfunctional relationships. I'm now ready for a perfect relationship but no one I meet matches my level of mental health. What can I do to get the love I deserve?

Fortunately, she received some old-fashioned common-sense advice from psychiatrist Frank Pittman:

> You are suffering from a deficiency of appropriate guilt. Forget about your mental health, forget about your own feelings, spend some time studying other people's feelings and practicing your

manners in dealing with them. See if you can go a whole day talking about everything except your complicated state of mind and the manifold ways in which other people have failed to pamper you sufficiently.[29]

POP THERAPY

We have seen that another incandescent thread leading to the current incest hunt is the American reliance on experts, self-help books, and therapists. Americans have always jumped into the latest craze faster than any other nationality. In the 1830s, de Tocqueville observed that Americans 'frequently allow themselves to be borne away, far beyond the bounds of reason, by a sudden passion or a hasty opinion, and sometimes gravely commit strange absurdities.' Speaking of religion, the Frenchman noted that 'from time to time strange sects arise which endeavor to strike out extraordinary paths to eternal happiness.'[30] In our time, that 'fanatical and almost wild spiritualism' has largely turned from organized religion to psychology. The therapist has replaced the evangelist.

As veteran psychologist Henry Gleitman recently put it, 'the only time American psychology could be said to have been moderate is when the pendulum happened to be swinging through that mid-point.'[31] In the early 19th century, Americans embraced phrenology, spiritualism, and magnetism. A few decades later, neurasthenics with irritated spines tried out rest cures or reflexology.

During the late 19th century, many experts espoused 'New Thought' or 'mind cure,' asserting that people could profitably tap into their subconscious. 'In just the degree in which you realize your oneness with the Infinite Spirit,' wrote one enthusiast, 'you will exchange disease for ease.' Another urged readers to 'substitute self-realization for self-sacrifice, and development for self-effacement.' A third stated that the key to happiness was to 'affirm and persistently maintain as *true now* that which you desire.'[32] Those who could not solve their problems with such mental gymnastics could purchase patent medicines containing cocaine, morphine, alcohol or cannabis, or buy electric belts to rejuvenate their sex lives.

When Sigmund Freud delivered his 1909 Clark University lectures, Americans avidly took his dogma to their bosoms, and psychoanalysis became popular in the urban United States.[33] Members of the upper crust sought the true meaning of their dreams, ferreted out repressed 'primal scenes,' and increasingly relied on their therapists to tell them how to live, sometimes with disastrous results. In 1921, for instance, American psychiatrist Horace Frink journeyed to Vienna for a personal analysis with Freud himself. Freud advised Frink and his mistress/patient to divorce their respective spouses. As a consequence, the guilt-ridden Frink became profoundly depressed and suicidal.[34]

Until World War II, only psychiatrists (trained as physicians) served as licensed therapists, and most Depression-era Americans were too absorbed in the daily survival struggle to worry about their psyches. After the war, however, returning soldiers with psychological problems overburdened Veterans Administration hospital psychiatrists. As a 'temporary' solution, psychologists were recruited to treat them, and the field of clinical psychology was born.[35]

The 1950s could easily be termed the Freudian decade. Because of the Nazi menace, many prominent European analysts had fled to the United States. German émigré Ernest Dichter told advertisers how to manipulate consumers through subtle use of phallic symbols and 'motivational research,' while Dr. Benjamin Spock advised mothers on the best ways to avoid traumatizing their children. In 1950, Theodor Adorno and fellow researchers published *The Authoritarian Personality*, which essentially equated the stern *pater familias* with Hitler. The family and, by extension, society, were sick, according to Adorno. As Charles Sykes has pointed out, 'everyday life – especially family life – was demonized, while attacks on the social structure were redefined as therapeutic.'[36] As early as 1953, one social commentator could write about 'the staggering number of clinics, conferences, lectures, pamphlets and books on the subject of relations between parents and child, between husband and wife.'[37] During the '50s, almost every psychological problem – from schizophrenia to anorexia – was blamed on 'iceberg' mothers who hadn't provided proper childhood nurturing.

During the '60s, psychology went pop, with encounter groups and the like, and by the '70s, we were poised for an onslaught of diverse therapies. Social workers joined clinical psychologists as licensed therapists.*[38] As their governmental agency jobs disappeared along with the '60s' War on Poverty, social workers increasingly turned to private practice, especially after California led the way in 1977 by mandating insurance benefits for therapy provided by social workers and other licensed therapists. 'Psy-

---

* California was the first state to license social workers in 1945, but the vast majority of the licensing took place in the 1970s and 1980s.

chiatrists became the experts on medication,' recalls one veteran social worker. 'It left the "walking wounded" to social workers.'[39] In most states, anyone could call themselves psychotherapists, regardless of training. As investigative journalists Debbie Nathan and Michael Snedeker have observed, 'The mental health field during this period was undergoing profound changes, producing increasing numbers of therapists who were less trained than their predecessors and more apt to accept at face value patients' accounts of their pasts.'[40]

During the '70s, which critic Tom Wolfe declared the 'Me' decade, people sought all manner of therapy, including Synanon, est, Silva Mind Control, transcendental meditation, primal scream, co-counseling, rebirthing, direct analysis, gestalt, and transactional analysis. As Wolfe wrote in 1976, 'The new alchemical dream is: changing one's personality – remaking it, remodeling it, elevating, and polishing one's very self . . . and observing, studying, and doting on it.'[41] The following year, journalist R. D. Rosen published *Psychobabble*, exploring the 'bewildering proliferation of self-improvement manuals and popular psychotherapies.' As a result, he wrote, 'a manic, self-regarding, relentlessly psychological atmosphere had developed.'[42] What all of these approaches had in common was the notion that technologically repressed people had to get in touch with their *feelings* in order to feel better.

As I discuss elsewhere (*see Chapters 6 and 13*), the relationship between client and therapist can be fraught with danger. Far too many therapists have abused their powerful positions; in an effort to 'heal' clients, they have actually harmed them. In *Against Therapy* (1988), an impassioned tirade of a book, Jeffrey Masson documents case after case of malpractice, including John Rosen's 'direct analysis,' which Rosen practiced from the late 1940s until finally forced to give up his license in 1983. Rosen believed that his patients did not receive adequate love as children. 'The therapist, like a good parent, must identify with the unhappy child,' he wrote. 'He must make up for the tremendous deficit of love experienced in the patient's life.'[43]

However, Rosen's notions of love and concern often took the form of emotional and physical torture.* Several patients died under his 'care,'

* Like many current therapists, Rosen seemed to go out of his way to alienate patients from their parents. 'As I continued my pressure toward reality,' he wrote about one case, 'I called Mary's attention to the fact that in the three weeks that she was in the hospital her mother had not come to see her once. The patient fainted dead away. I should say, in all fairness, that the mother had been acting on my orders . . . My purpose was to focus the patient's attention on the pathogenic lack of love rather than to allow her to be confused by the mother's loving attitudes.'

and he forced fellatio, intercourse, and group sex on other clients. For our purposes, his treatment of Sally Zinman is most informative, because it resembles the current hunt for repressed memories in many respects. In 1970, the 33-year-old Zinman, an English professor, woke up one day and felt that she was not herself. She remembered her past, but felt it was not *hers*. At Rosen's private inpatient facilities, no one asked her about her real problems. Rather, Rosen informed her that her mother's milk had been sour and that she had incestuous fantasies about her father. After a month-long stay, she asked to leave. Rosen and an ex-Marine aide stripped and beat her. As Masson wrote, 'John Rosen is one of many, many therapists who harm their patients under the guise of their greater wisdom. He merely had the misfortune of being caught.'

Rosen's therapy was similar to 're-parenting,' an approach developed in the late 1960s by Jacqui Lee Schiff, a psychiatric social worker, as an off-shoot of transactional analysis. Like Rosen, Schiff got away with it for a while because she specialized in chronic schizophrenics whom other professionals had given up on. She would regress patients *literally* to an infantile status, diapering and spanking them, allowing them to suck on her thumb. To discipline her charges, she would stand them in corners or strap them into heavy wooden 'restraining chairs,' all methods detailed in her 1970 book, *All My Children*. Eventually chased out of the United States, she restarted her practice in India and landed in England in the mid '80s. In 1992, she received a thunderous ovation when she addressed the European Transactional Analysis Association.[44]

There are only a few hundred therapists in America who still admit to 're-parenting,' but the practice of regression in which the therapist acts as a surrogate parent is widespread. The most widely publicized recent case is that of Paul Lozano, a medical student who sought therapy with Margaret Bean-Bayog, a Harvard psychiatrist who encouraged Lozano to regress to a three-year-old state and to call her 'Mom,' while she composed sado-masochistic fantasies about him. Bean-Bayog also convinced Lozano that he was recovering repressed memories of incest. When she terminated his therapy, he committed suicide.[45] (*See Chapter 13 for a more detailed account of this case.*)

But it was psychologist Arthur Janov who provided the prototype for the current trauma therapist with his wildly popular 1970 book, *The Primal Scream*. Janov's patients were told that they must recall repressed memories of trauma at the hands of their parents, and that only in reliving them – and screaming bloody murder – would they be healed. 'It is possible that a major Primal Scene can occur in the earliest months of life,' he wrote, an event 'so intrinsically shattering that the young child cannot defend himself and must split away from the experience.' The therapist didn't have to worry about a particular symptom list because '*all* neuroses stem from the same specific cause.' Once cured by the Primal Scream(s), a patient would lead 'a tensionless, defense-free life in which one is completely his own self and experiences deep feeling and internal unity.'[46]

The process by which Janov elicited his screams would be familiar to any brainwashing expert. For three weeks, patients must not work or attend school. During the first week, they must stay in a hotel room without TV, radio, or any other distraction. The night before their first session, they should not sleep. 'The isolation and sleeplessness are important techniques which often bring patients close to a Primal,' Janov noted. 'Lack of sleep helps crumble defenses.' Noting with satisfaction that patients arrive already suffering, the therapist instructs them to lie spread-eagle on a couch 'in as defenseless a physical position as possible.' Patients are then encouraged to 'sink into the feeling' of childhood. After a 'chipping away process' of several hours – during which Janov urges 'Feel that! Stay with it!' – they finally arrive at their Primal Scene and scream something like, 'Daddy, be nice!', 'Mommy, help!' or 'I hate you, I hate you!'[47]

Janov stressed repeatedly that this was an anti-intellectual therapy. 'In no case are ideas discussed,' he noted firmly. Of course, the *therapist's* ideas are quite clearly conveyed. 'Letting down and being that little child who needs a "mommy" helps release all the stored-up feeling.' At the end of the day, the patient returns to his hotel room. 'He still may not watch television or go to the movies. He really does not want to because he is consumed with himself.'

Virtually any trauma, no matter how trivial, could provoke a Primal Scream from the Primal Pain Pool. Nonetheless, the parents were always to blame, as with a father who forced his child to ride a horse. After the patient finished venting his rage at his father, he switched to the 'enabling' mother: 'Why didn't she stop him? She was so weak. She never protected me from him.' Of course, Janov savored any incest he managed to uncover, even if it wasn't altogether necessary. He recounted one man's memory of a mother's kiss: 'She stuck her tongue in my mouth. Can you imagine? My own mother. My God! She always wanted me instead of Father. Mother! Leave me alone! Leave me alone!'

Joe Hart and Richard 'Riggs' Corriere soon founded the Center for Feelings Therapy in Los Angeles, an off-shoot of primal screaming.

During the '70s, their Center turned into a psychotherapeutic cult, as documented by Carol Lynn Mithers in her disturbing 1994 book, *Therapy Gone Mad*. The indoctrination/therapy process she describes involved rewriting the patients' past and fostering a complete dependence on therapists. 'Men and women with different histories and personalities all emerged similarly furious at their parents, denouncing their past lives and speaking the same loud phrases ... And when patients started feeling confused or lost, they didn't turn to old friends or ways of coping. They turned to the only people who really knew how to feel ... They turned to their therapists.'

The Center eventually self-destructed in 1980, spasmodically dying off in numerous lawsuits. Mithers' tragic conclusion sounds eerily similar to the aftermath of recovered memory therapy: 'There was no way to undo years of family estrangement, no way to bring back missed Thanksgivings and Christmases or to reconcile with parents who'd died before the Center's end. There was no way to bring back marriages destroyed a decade before.'[48]

I have only scratched the surface of this subject here, but it should be clear that the repressed memory craze is part of a continuum of therapeutic approaches that blame parents for all problems. Now, however, it is not so much the iceberg mother as the deviant father who is to blame.

THE FRANTIC PURSUIT OF HAPPINESS AND
THE BOOMERS

The American Declaration of Independence proclaims every citizen's right to 'life, liberty, and the pursuit of happiness.' Ever since, Americans have specialized in the sprint after fulfillment as a national pastime, though they sometimes drive themselves crazy in the process.*[49]

That national tendency reached an extreme in the materialistic era

---

* In the 1830s, Alexis de Tocqueville noted the American 'fear of missing the shortest cut to happiness' that ironically rendered the citizenry 'more stricken and perturbed.' All of his life, the typical American chased 'that complete felicity which forever escapes him.' A century later, F. Scott Fitzgerald created Jay Gatsby, whose relentless pursuit of the ever-receding 'orgastic future' cost him his life. 'It eluded us then,' Fitzgerald wrote, 'but that's no matter – tomorrow we will run faster, stretch out our arms farther ...'

following World War II, known as the Baby Boom. Coming out of the Great Depression and war rationing, Americans renewed their pursuit of individual happiness with a vengeance. Mothers, carrying the hope of the future in their wombs, were determined that *their* children should be raised correctly. This new generation would be reared with all the benefits of modernity, including Cheerios, television, Barbie dolls, and G.I. Joes. To help the anxious mother, Dr. Benjamin Spock provided avuncular advice in his record-setting best seller, *Baby and Child Care*.

The Boomers were the first generation to be raised permissively. Their parents worried about whether they would become anally fixated or whether they would feel deprived of affection. The underlying message was: 'Life is good. You are important, the center of the Universe, and you have every right to expect that when you grow up, you will be happy and fulfilled.'* The family, which had in the past been viewed largely as a necessary economic unit, became a life-long source of true and perfect love. They grew up expecting to find a perfect love-mate who would work with them, in absolute harmony, to raise their own perfect children. Not surprisingly, few of them have actually achieved this ideal. That probably accounts for the extremely high divorce rate among Boomers, and the popular view that almost all families are dysfunctional.

The Baby Boomers came of age during a decade when future prosperity seemed assured. Yet at the same time, it was also the 'Age of Anxiety,' with the constant threat of the mushroom cloud. They were born in the dark shadows of Hiroshima and the Holocaust. 'Since 1945,' psychologist Bernie Zilbergeld observes, 'we have suffered one setback after another, and even our successes were somehow never good enough. The result was the replacement of optimism and faith with cynicism and pessimism.'[50] The Korean War proved that Americans were not invincible, while Sputnik patrolled the very air over their heads, spying on them.

As a result, some curious cultural phenomena emerged. The late 1940s saw the birth of UFO sightings, with the first 'abductions' in 1961. The fifties produced *The Search for Bridey Murphy* and *The Three Faces of Eve*. Invisible, threatening psychic forces boiled within, while Joe McCarthy's communists lurked under beds. Horror movies featuring

---

* Obviously, this is a generalization. There were plenty of '50s children who were not spoiled, but deprived or abused. Despite these exceptions, however, the overall *feeling* of the age was one of entitlement.

threatening 'blobs' and aliens became popular. Evil creatures skulked in black lagoons.

In 1959, Robert Heilbroner wrote of 'our contemporary feeling of unease and confusion. We feel ourselves beleaguered by happenings which seem not only malign and intransigent, but unpredictable.'[51] Despite this underlying *angst*, however, Americans pretended as a society that they were blessed, that they represented true democracy and freedom for all. They added the phrase 'under God' to the pledge of allegiance.[52] Meanwhile, all of the unsolved problems – racism, sexism, poverty, child abuse, environmental pollution – continued to fester. As the Boomers' parents took them to Disneyland, they were, as de Tocqueville had put it so many years before, 'serious and almost sad, even in their pleasures.'[53]

The Vietnam War shattered any illusions about living in the best of all possible societies. It pitted the Boomer generation against that of their parents and irrevocably changed the nation. As a college student at Harvard in the late '60s – I graduated with Vice President Al Gore in 1969 – I protested against the war, and I felt some kinship with those who spoke of the inevitable Revolution that would forever change our repressive society. In retrospect, of course, some of the 'revolutionaries' were not particularly altruistic. Although I am proud that my generation helped to force the United States out of an immoral war and to face many societal injustices, I am not proud that some of my preppie classmates talked about all policemen as pigs, and that some even threw bricks at Cambridge firefighters as they responded to a call.

Perhaps the 'us-versus-them' mentality is inevitable within major social movements that involve life and death or basic human dignity. Those on 'our' side are beyond reproach, even if their statements sometimes become extreme and hurtful. 'We' have to stick together. Those on 'their' side are the enemy, and don't deserve to be heard. In the post-Vietnam era, this pattern seems to have infected, to some extent, most important social struggles, including factions of the feminist and other 'politically correct' movements.

At any rate, Boomers have found it difficult to grow up and take responsibility for their lives. They keep thinking that life is going to be fair, that they will find the perfect relationship, that they will find the happiness that was promised to them. In 1980, journalist Landon Jones, in his book *Great Expectations*, wrote: 'Unlike previous generations, which found happiness only as a by-product of doing something well, the Baby Boomers [have] pursued it as an end in itself.' Consequently, as they entered their 30s, they felt 'alienated, fragmented, shattered and disenchanted,' according to Jones.[54] They still feel cheated. The promise of the '60s never arrived. There was no Revolution. They are left with their own problems and mortality, just like every other generation.

Horror writer Stephen King, born in 1947, observes of the Boomers: 'We went on playing for a long time, almost feverishly. I write for that buried child in us.' King cleverly taps into a generational discomfort. 'He knows that we have been set down in a frightening universe,' one critic has noted, 'full of real demons like death and disease, and perhaps the most frightening thing in it is the human mind.' King says that he presses 'phobic pressure points' in order to exorcize fears. Trauma therapists also know how to find those points, and how to *fan* the paranoid mental flames. As a consequence, many people accept the notion that they were irretrievably wounded as children.[55]

Many feel they must become infants again, nurturing their damaged inner children, clutching their teddy bears along with John Bradshaw, finding a way not to grow up. It is the Boomers who began to discover to their horror that they were victims of secret incest. Ironically, the pampered generation has turned on its parents, blaming them for the very love they tried so hard to give, twisting it into memories of sexual abuse. The example has filtered downward to those in their 30s and 20s, and now even teenagers are recalling repressed memories.

In other words, the Baby Boom legacy has been passed along to the 'twenty-something' generation. Born too late to experience the legend-ary '60s, they were raised in the troubled '70s, often with single parents who were too busy trying to 'find themselves' to pay enough attention to their children. As William Straus and Neil Howe point out in their 1991 book, *Generations*, these children grew up in a 'nightmare of self-immersed parents, disintegrating homes, schools with conflicting mis-sions, confused leaders.'[56] Consequently, they, too, can find plenty of symptoms that could be interpreted as evidence of buried incest. Not only that, but because of their upbringing, they can choose from a number of possible perpetrators – not only their mothers and fathers, but multiple parental lovers, step-parents, step-siblings, several sets of grandparents, or housemates. Often raised in homes where nudity and discussions of sex were relatively open, they can now blame their parents for creating or allowing a sexualized environment.

PSYCHICS AND EXORCISTS

Another thread contributing to the hunt for recovered memories stems from the apparent failure of traditional religion to provide answers to life's problems. As a result, at least since the 1960s, interest in the 'New Age' and in evangelical, charismatic churches has burgeoned.

In part, the growing popularity of psychic phenomena, channeling, angels, near-death experiences, UFO abductions, past lives, demon possession, and trance states reflects disenchantment with science and logic. Clearly, humans need transcendence. We want meaning in life, and we will sometimes seek it in irrational or destructive ways.

America is a nation in search of spirituality and meaning. Ever since the Vietnam War, the United States has suffered a massive loss of confidence, with sporadic attempts to recapture a mythic past in which father knew best, God could be trusted to watch over us, and life was good. Instead, Americans find themselves heading toward the third millennium in a state of unprecedented upheaval. As they near the turn of the century, more and more Americans are turning toward miraculous, sometimes fringe belief systems and radical solutions. Human beings have always hungered for spirituality, for transcendence beyond the dimensions of their daily lives. In times of stress, when traditional values and belief systems lie in ruins, they tend to search (desperately) for alternative ways to fill this spiritual void.

It is no surprise, then, that so many people are looking for a miracle, for a benevolent, all-wise guardian angel to see them through, or for a secret message of divine guidance.[57] That's why books such as *The Celestine Prophecy*, by James Redfield, have such appeal. Redfield assures us that, in mysterious ways, we are moving toward a break through into a wonderful new transcendental awareness. 'Perhaps more than any other people in any other time, we intuit higher meaning in mysterious happenings,' he writes. We can tell that this magical transformation awaits us precisely because of the overwhelming *angst* of our age. 'This insight always surfaces unconsciously at first, as a profound sense of restlessness.'[58]

The degree to which modern American society has embraced the New Age is quite remarkable. For most of the 1970s and 1980s, for instance, the CIA and the Pentagon spent millions of dollars on psychic consultations.[59] We may shake our heads over trusting military intelligence operations to crystal gazers, but what's so bad about looking for answers in this fashion? Going to see a psychic would at first glance appear to be relatively harmless. Why not? Perhaps there is something to it after all, and if what the psychic says resonates, maybe it will help with major decisions about jobs, moves, or relationships.

Unfortunately, when we begin to rely on other people to make our decisions, we are usually in trouble. Even more unfortunately, all too many psychics inform clients that they were sexually abused as children and have repressed the memories. The same is true for past-life hypnotists, UFO specialists, channelers, automatic writers, or those who simply read auras. Nurses who espouse 'therapeutic touch' (which involves no touch, just hovering hands) sometimes think they can identify hidden sex abuse victims, just as massage therapists diagnose 'body memories.'

In the meantime, traditional churches – Catholic, Protestant, or Jewish – have failed to address the raging spiritual hunger of many Americans. Pentecostal and Charismatic non-denominational churches have sprung up to fill that need. Here, there is no dry ritual. A lively soft-rock band backs up a choir that sings almost constantly. Everyone in the congregation hugs and praises the Lord throughout the service. Everyone seems happy, transported. Hands are raised on high in a semi-trance. The sermons are brief and punchy. In many churches, the Devil is a major topic of conversation. Troubled parishioners may be exorcized of their various demons.

Those demons are all too often associated with a belief in repressed memories of sexual abuse, mythical satanic ritual abuse cults, and presumed multiple personality disorder. In a disastrous melding of New Age influence, secular psychology, and fundamentalism, many pastoral counselors are destroying families in the name of Christ, uncovering illusory incest memories and holding down terrified parishioners to cast out non-existent demons. Not only that, but the traditional churches have, in turn, been heavily influenced by the charismatic movement and psychology, so that the same recovered memories and exorcisms are taking place there as well.

THE WOMEN'S MOVEMENT

In the late '60s and early '70s, the protest movements diversified, splintering from concern primarily with civil rights and Vietnam.[60] Americans had always prided themselves on their compassionate respect for individual rights, but in many ways this attitude had not applied to women, children, homosexuals, or the handicapped. Most conspicuously, an angry women's movement came into being.

The movement's core demands – equal pay and opportunities, relief from sexual harassment, and general recognition of the degradation caused by male sexism – were basic and overdue.* And it isn't surprising that the Women's Liberation Movement split off from the anti-war and civil rights protests of the '60s, as many female activists realized that the men who most loudly proclaimed the Revolution still expected them to wash all the dishes, raise the kids, be subservient at meetings, and put up with their sexual promiscuity.

Taking their cue from 'black power,' books such as *Sisterhood Is Powerful* (1970), featuring a raised fist on the cover, announced a new, militant feminism. 'This book is an action,' wrote editor Robin Morgan. 'It was conceived, written, edited, copy-edited, proofread, designed, and illustrated by women.'

Morgan tapped into a well-spring of seemingly infinite rage. 'I couldn't believe – still can't – how angry I could become, from deep down and way back, something like a five-thousand-year-buried anger.' Once she realized how endemic sexism was, *everything* triggered her – her unequal pay, her husband's jokes, television commercials, rock-song lyrics, pink blankets for girl babies. 'It makes you very sensitive – raw, even,' she wrote. She became angry at men as a class with their 'linear, tight, dry, boring, male super-consistency.' Moreover, she announced, 'the nuclear family unit is oppressive to women,' forcing them into a 'totally dependent position.'

But what were the alternatives? 'No one,' she admitted, 'has any answers yet, although a host of possibilities present themselves to confuse us all even further. Living alone? Living in mixed communes with men and women? Living in all-women communes? Having children? Not having children? Raising them collectively, or in the old family structure?' Perhaps men were entirely superfluous. 'Test-tube births? Masturbation? Womb transplants?' Or, finally, 'Parthenogenesis [reproduction from an unfertilized egg]? Why? Why not?'[61]

---

* Even by 1969, sexism was thriving enough so that Frank Gray could publish *Scoremanship*, in which he explained how '*you too will be able to score with any woman you choose*' by applying the 'basic principles of salesmanship.' Before he realized that 'women like to be mastered,' Gray said he had 'attempted to *force* a sale too fast' or had not 'applied the *right pressure* when it was time to close.'

Later in the book, Martha Shelly's 'Notes of a Radical Lesbian' announced, 'Lesbianism is one road to freedom – freedom from oppression by men.' By choosing this alternative sexual lifestyle, women could free themselves from dependence upon males for love, sex, money, orthe 'drudgery of child raising.' Clearly, most men were included in her sweeping indictment, since 'hostility toward your oppressor is healthy.' After all, 'isn't love between equals healthier than sucking up to an oppressor?' Besides, women could be far more patient, nuanced lovers, freeing women from 'hasty and inept [hetero-]sexual encounters.'[62]

Since then, of course, the basic beliefs of the feminist cause – equal rights, equal pay, equal opportunity, freedom from harassment – have been adopted in principle by mainstream America. Turning principle into reality has been painfully slow, but people throughout the political spectrum have joined the struggle. The shrill condemnations of the entire male gender by some of the early activists might well be compared to the self-righteous and sometimes silly rages expressed by those of us in the anti-war movement. And yes, sexism did permeate almost every aspect of American culture, so it is not surprising that some of the early expressions of long-festering rage may have lacked focus.

Yet as many feminist authors have noted, even today there are factions of the feminist movement – including the Incest Survivor faction – whose extreme positions seem to be hindering, rather than furthering, social progress. It is this kind of misguided 'feminist' approach that led Bonnie Burstow to write *Radical Feminist Therapy* in 1992. 'Faced with any female client,' she wrote, 'we can assume some degree of childhood abuse ... Whenever we encounter a woman who has such large gaps in her memory of childhood, we can usually conclude that she experienced ongoing and severe trauma as a child.'

It is little wonder, then, that one commentator wrote in 1991 that 'a sort of reverse sexism seems to be creeping into the training of therapists ... I've heard [case consultants] make numerous sexist, sarcastic, and derogatory comments about male clients that would have been vehemently challenged if they had been made about women. Gender prejudices in psychology can lead to a man's disadvantage, even to his harm.'[63]

Feminist historian Alice Echols complained in 1984 that what she terms 'cultural feminism' has embraced the old negative stereotypes, simply trying to turn them into positive stereotypes. According to cultural feminists, women are by nature gentle pacifists, nurturers, intuitive, poetic.*[64] Men, on the other hand, are aggressive, brutish, compulsively logical. 'Cultural feminists are so convinced that male sexuality is, at its core, lethal, that they reduce it to its most alienated and violent expressions,' Echols wrote. 'Sexual intercourse becomes a mere euphemism for rape.' She urged fellow feminists to fight anyone who wanted to 'make our sexuality conform to our political ideology . . . We must abandon the belief so deeply entrenched in the feminist community that particular sexual expressions are intrinsically liberated or intrinsically degraded.'[65]

More recently, other feminists have challenged the politically correct stance of woman-as-victim. 'Let's not chase the same stereotypes our mothers have spent so much energy running away from,' Katie Roiphe writes. 'Let's not reinforce the images that oppress us, that label us victims, and deny our own agency and intelligence, as strong and sensual, as autonomous, pleasure-seeking, sexual beings.'[66] Harvard feminist Wendy Kaminer has also dared to question the dogma of what she terms 'feminist victimology,' which underscores women's helplessness.**[67] 'Today discussions about date rape and sexual harassment also reflect some belief in women's emotional as well as physical fragility,' she writes in *I'm Dysfunctional, You're Dysfunctional*. She laments 'the growth of the memory-retrieval industry during a period of hysteria about child abuse, ritual abuse, Satanism, and pornography.' Because of her criticism, Kaminer has been labeled 'in deep denial,' or 'part of the backlash.'[68] Similarly, social psychologist Carol Tavris has been bitterly disparaged for her perceptive 1993 article, 'Beware the Incest-Survivor Machine.' 'To want to throw a small wrench into the abuse-survivor machine,' Tavris wrote, 'is like opposing censorship of pornography: nowadays, you feel you have to apologize for any support you might be providing to molesters, rapists, pedophiles and other misogynists.'[69]

---

* Compare this attitude with that of gynecology professor William H. Walling, who described the generic woman in his 1904 book, *Sexology*: 'She is in more intimate relation with Nature. Her instincts are stronger, while her personal intelligence is less. She readily achieves many things by instinct at which man arrives less surely by reflection. Man is guided by calculation and personal interest, woman by passion and feeling. Man *sees* truth, woman *feels* it.' In 1976, feminist Betty Friedan warned against adopting 'the assumption that women have any moral or spiritual superiority *as a class*, or that men share some brute insensitivity *as a class*. This is male chauvinism in reverse; it is female sexism.'

** 'A Martian would be forgiven for thinking,' writes columnist Barbara Amiel, 'that the primary problem of North Americans is a population of females totally absorbed in their personal misery – addictions, abuse experiences and pain.'

Debbie Nathan begs critics to note that 'feminist theory and practice are not monolithic, and that many women's advocates abhor that part of the movement that demonizes masculinity, forges alliances with the antifeminist right, and communicates such a profound fear and loathing of sexuality that – as the ritual-abuse cases demonstrate – it is even willing to cast women as demons.'[70] In return for her pleas for reason, Nathan herself has been demonized by some who call themselves feminists.

If women such as Echols, Roiphe, Kaminer, Tavris and Nathan cannot safely question the ideologies of some feminist factions, what reception can I expect? I am painfully aware of my masculinity as I write this book.*[71] How *dare* I criticize any aspect of the feminist movement? How can I claim to be a feminist myself? For many people – including some men – that's enough to brand me a manipulative perpetrator, part of the patriarchal denial of women's abuse. In response, I can only agree heartily with Wendy Kaminer, who observed plaintively, 'I wish we were less threatened by debate. It is possible to criticize the recovery movement without condoning child abuse.'**[72]

Please hear my personal credo: *I believe that all human beings, male or female, should be free to pursue their lives, including sexual inclinations, without interference, as long as they do not harm anyone else in the process.**** Women have been and continue to be subjected to ill treatment at the hands of too many men, ranging from rape to subtle sexism. This does not mean that all women are automatically victims or that all men are

* On a 1994 cover, *Time* portrayed a pig dressed in coat and tie, along with the caption, 'Are Men Really That Bad?' In the article, commentator Lance Morrow observes that 'the overt man bashing of recent years has now refined itself into a certain atmospheric snideness – has settled down to a vague male aversion, as if masculinity were a bad smell in a room ... We have reached the point where the best a man can say for himself is that he is harmless.' Morrow has a point, but only a few months earlier, the same magazine ran a story about a group of Los Angeles teenage boys who competed with one another to see who could have sex with the most girls. They remained unrepentant about their sexual exploits, which included rape. 'Nothing my boy did was anything any red-blooded American boy wouldn't do at his age,' one father says. With such attitudes still prevalent, it is understandable that men should be vilified.

** Garrison Keillor can get away with complaining about man's lot because he is so funny. In *The Book of Guys* (1993), he writes: 'Years ago, manhood was an opportunity for achievement, and now it is a problem to be overcome.' Or, as he has one of his characters say, 'Nuts to sensitivity. Go ahead and fart.'

*** Of course, defining 'harm' becomes difficult. Some pedophiles, for instance, assert that it is perfectly fine to have sexual relations with children. I do not agree. On the other hand, if women or men choose a homosexual lifestyle, I don't see that anyone has any business judging them.

automatically aggressors, however. Nor does it mean that any 'recovered memories' of abuse are necessarily true. All humans deserve a fair hearing. *Whenever a cause classifies an entire group as the Enemy, it is dangerous, regardless of how just the cause may appear.* It is dangerous for all concerned. The Incest Survivor Movement has victimized, in horrendous fashion, not only fathers, but women – in the name of feminism.

POLITICALLY CORRECT EXCESSES

In this 'Revolution of Rising Sensitivities,' as Charles Sykes puts it, politically correct (PC) college students and their equally PC professors have led the charge.

For perspective, it's important to note that the PC movement has taken on some very important causes. Certainly, America needs better understanding and communication among racial and ethnic groups and among people of different genders and sexual orientations.

But tragically, some who are in conspicuous positions in the movement have taken their rhetoric to destructive extremes. And many otherwise sensible people who identify with the movement have been reluctant to distance themselves from those excesses.

In the current climate in some quarters, 'lookism' (looking at a woman with a facial expression that might be interpreted as lustful) is called as sexual harassment. We are witnessing a new puritanism in which justice for all doesn't seem to matter. 'If a woman did falsely accuse a man of rape,' one female student opined recently, 'she may have had reasons to. Maybe she wasn't raped, but he clearly violated her in some way.' Similarly, an assistant Vassar dean thinks a false accusation could actually be *good* for a male: 'I think it ideally initiates a process of self-exploration. "How do I see women? If I didn't violate her, could I have?"'[73]

In women's studies classrooms around the United States, male students are often treated as pariahs, hardly daring to open their mouths. 'For women, participation [in class] means making verbal contributions,' one first-day handout advises. 'For men, participation means seriously listening more than contributing to discussions.' In one remarkable 1990 *Harvard Educational Review* article, Professor Magda Lewis triumphantly reveals how she routinely squelches any male attempts to question her classroom dogma. Even if they remain mute, the men are not safe, since 'the subtleties of body language' give away their inherently abusive attitudes.

Lewis approvingly quotes a letter from one of her female students, praising the course for creating feminist 'anger and a pervading sense of injustice' that is 'self-perpetuating.' The student is, however, 'frustrated and impatient with people who can't see the problems.' Consequently, she has cut off most social contact and spends most of her time writing furiously – in both senses of the word – in her journal.[74]

Liberal parents sending a daughter to college are likely to nod approvingly when told that she plans to take a course in women's studies. After all, the historical treatment of women has been lamentable, and female accomplishments have traditionally been minimized. There is, however, a difference between academic exploration and anti-male rhetoric. Naïve parents have no idea that the women's studies curriculum in many colleges has been hijacked by those whom Christina Hoff Sommers describes as 'gender feminists' in her extraordinary and disturbing 1994 book, *Who Stole Feminism? How Women Have Betrayed Women.* Teachers in these classes are not interested in encouraging open debate, but in indoctrinating students into a particular belief system with its own jargon. 'If the classroom situation is very heteropatriarchal,' one St. Louis professor wrote in 1988, 'I am likely to define my task as largely one of recruitment . . . of persuading students that women are oppressed.' Sommers not-so-facetiously suggests that these new 'feminist' bastions print the following announcement on the first page of their bulletins to parents:

> We will help your daughter discover the extent to which she has been in complicity with the patriarchy. We will encourage her to reconstruct herself through dialogue with us. She may become enraged and chronically offended. She will very likely reject the religious and moral codes you raised her with. She may well distance herself from family and friends. She may change her appearance, and even her sexual orientation. She may end up hating you (her father) and pitying you (her mother). After she has completed her reeducation with us, you will certainly be out tens of thousands of dollars and very possibly be out one daughter as well.[75]

Indeed, accused father Ralph Vance wrote recently in the *Chicago Tribune* about how his 20-year-old daughter turned away from him during her college years, eventually accusing him of ritual sexual abuse. He describes his family's 1990 holiday season:

> Kristin announces during Christmas break that she has changed her college major from English to 'gender studies.' She is toting around a book titled *Intercourse* by Andrea Dworkin. I've always considered myself a card-carrying feminist, but I know that Dworkin is a radical-fringe lesbian feminist and that the relentless message of *Intercourse* is that any heterosexual intimacy is innately violative of the woman, essentially a euphemism for rape. I sense trouble.[76]

Three months later, Kristin was hospitalized for suicidal tendencies as a result of recovered memories that first involved her Uncle Jack, then her father, and finally her mother as well. Her younger brother, a college freshman, soon entered therapy and discovered similar memories. Now both children refuse to have anything to do with their parents.

One of the major efforts of the PC movement has been to alter the English language. Giving credit where it's due, I believe that effort has had some beneficial results. We're much more conscious than in the past that some commonly-used words and expressions may, unintentionally, imply bigoted, sexist, hurtful sentiments. But the effort sometimes crosses the line between raising of consciousness and stifling of free speech. Such appears to have been the case for University of New Hampshire German professor Roger Brown, who had to sue to clear his record after a student complained that he had used 'offensive and intimidating language' in class. His sin? He had quoted a German saying which translates: 'A pretty back can be charming.'[77] The University of Missouri School of Journalism's handbook of forbidden phrases and words, for example, says that the word *glamorous* is sexist; the exclamation *Ugh!* will offend native Americans; *Mafia* obviously bothers Italians; and the word *community* 'implies a monolithic culture in which people act, think, and vote in the same way.'[78]

THE FRAGMENTATION OF THE FAMILY

With this last item, the journalistic print patrol has a point. Whatever sense of community Americans once had appears to have been shattered.

Up until World War II, the extended family of grandparents, aunts, uncles, and cousins at least provided some sense of grounding, especially in small-town communities.*[79] 'Time was,' writes historian Peter Laslett, 'when the whole of life went forward in the family, in a circle of loved, familiar faces, known and fondled objects, all to human size. That time is gone forever.'[80]

I do not want to idealize the family of the past, which was often a constrained, unhappy institution, as several recent books have pointed out. In *The Way We Never Were* (1992), historian Stephanie Coontz observes that 'families have always been in flux and often in crisis.'[81] Similarly, in *Embattled Paradise* (1991), family studies professor Arlene Skolnick notes that 'the image of a warm, secure, stable family life in past times' is an illusion.[82] I recently discussed this issue with my father, now in his late 70s. 'My father,' he said, 'thought that his role was to provide for his family, but raising the children wasn't really part of the job description. He didn't spend much time with me. When my generation became fathers, we tried to be more involved, but we felt inept at it, like Ozzie Nelson.' I think he's right, even though he went a long way toward overcoming the modeling *he* received. A gentle, kind, thoughtful father to his seven children, Dad did tell us stories, romp with us on the living room floor, and show us that he loved us, but there was always an unspoken awkwardness.

Like many other Boomers, I was determined to be a new kind of father – involved, open, nurturing, playful. My generation may have put too much faith in the possibilities for social revolution. We felt that we understood the mistakes of the generation that preceded us, and we were determined not to repeat them. On one level, we brought about some remarkable progress in family life. For example, physical punishment of children is no longer considered acceptable, even if it still occurs in some families.

Yet compared to past generations, there are fewer support systems in place, and far fewer parents stay together to raise their children. 'Even if things were not always right in families of the past,' Stephanie Coontz admits, 'it seems clear that some things have newly gone wrong.'

---

* Americans have always been mobile, restless people, and American families have always been more unstable than their European counterparts, as de Tocqueville lamented in the 1830s: 'New families are constantly springing up, others are constantly falling away, and all that remain change their condition; the woof of time is every instant broken and the track of generations effaced.' Under such conditions, people 'acquire the habit of always considering themselves as standing alone.'

She points out that the American divorce rate tripled between 1960 and 1982, then leveled off with 50 per cent of first marriages and 60 per cent of second ones failing. Between 1960 and 1986, the number of children growing up in single-parent homes doubled.[83]

Some observers have speculated that Americans' unease over having to send their children to day-care centers or leave them with babysitters was an underlying cause for the day-care sex-abuse-hysteria cases. 'It seems it had something to do with this fear that we'd turned our kids over to total strangers,' sociologist Catherine Beckett says. 'It's as if there was guilt that people we didn't know were raising them for us.'[84]

In her 1994 book, *Reviving Ophelia: Saving the Selves of Adolescent Girls*, psychologist Mary Pipher suggests that overburdened families are having a difficult time coping with the increasing pressures daughters experience in the 1990s. These teenagers 'know that something is very wrong, but they tend to look for the source within themselves or their families rather than in broader cultural problems.' Pipher observes that girls are 'coming of age in a more dangerous, sexualized and media-saturated culture.' It is little wonder, then, that so many young women are searching for answers to their generalized *angst*. Pipher's next book is called *The Shelter of Each Other: Rebuilding Our Families*. Let us hope that it will be a best-seller.[85]

In a sense, the search for incest may be a logical extension of the fragmentation of the family.*[86] We find ourselves more and more alone, afraid. We fear being overly dependent on anyone, yet we yearn for love. We want to be innocent children again, but we cannot be. We feel betrayed somehow, brought into the world and abandoned without much explanation. Recovered incest memories provide a rationale – however misdirected – for some of these feelings.

---

* The demise of the extended family may also partially account for an increase in *real* incest. Some anthropologists believe that the incest taboo is a universal human trait, the evolutionary result of kinship exogamy. In *The Red Lamp of Incest*, anthropologist Robin Fox argues that the taboo is *'built into the cortical processes.'* In other words, Fox believes that the incest taboo is wired into our evolutionary circuitry, based on dominant male primates in well-defined family groups. But 'it looks as though less and less control by the older males is going to be the order of the day in many societies,' he notes. As a consequence, in developed nations such as the United States, where we are rootless, mobile, and abandoning kinship patterns, the incest taboo may be weakening.

RIGHTING WRONGS

One of the most positive aspects of the women's rights and PC movements is a receptive environment for confronting hurtful and abusive sexual behavior. Ugly family secrets have been brought out of the closet. The United States has now passed laws *requiring* doctors, teachers, and anyone else who has knowledge – or even suspicions – of child abuse to report to social service agencies.

As more people came forward to report the terrible indignities they had suffered in silence for so many years, Americans became appalled at what a poor job they had done, as a society, in protecting their children. They learned horrible things to which they had turned a blind eye because they didn't *want* to believe they could happen. Children in schools for the blind were being molested by older students and adult supervisors. Altar boys were being sodomized by priests. Teenage girls were forced into sex with their own fathers. For generations, Americans had wanted to believe that in their great country such things couldn't happen.

When they learned that such things did happen, and with some frequency, their instinct was to 'get the bastards.' They moved from an assumption that anybody accused of such atrocities was innocent to an assumption that anybody who is accused is guilty. They wanted to right the past wrongs, and felt that if some people were unfairly accused, perhaps that would be a small price to pay – unless, of course, they found themselves among those who were unfairly accused.

MEDIA MADNESS AND SEXUAL SCHIZOPHRENIA

Whatever the trends, they have only been exacerbated by sensation-hungry media. In the world of infotainment, sex abuse sells. So do satanic ritual stories, murder, high-profile trials, multiple personalities, and female victims of all kinds. It seems that every other American movie-of-the-week features a wronged woman of one sort or another. It would be nice to believe that all TV executives really care about women's issues, but that isn't the case. Victimized women are the 'in' topic, and whatever will grab ratings is what viewers will get.

In their 1995 book, *Tuning in Trouble: Talk TV's Destructive Impact on Mental Health*, psychologists Jeanne Heaton and Nona Wilson make an observation about multiple-personality disorder coverage, but it could apply to a vast array of talk-show topics. Such shows, they write, 'work to create interest in a disorder, present it as an exciting eccentricity, and then tell viewers that anyone could have it ... Perhaps if MPD is indeed the "syndrome of the '90s" we can all thank Talk TV for helping to make it so.'*[87]

Even in cases where *real* sex abuse survivors are presented on talk shows, the implicit message is negative and misleading. 'Watching Talk TV can lead [incest] survivors to believe that they will go on to abuse their own children,' Heaton and Wilson write, 'that good relationships are out of the question, and that at best they can hope for years of therapy with little hope of adequate coping.'[88]

It's tempting to raise a chicken-or-egg-type question here. Are Americans paranoid about incest because they see it constantly in their movies, soap operas, talk shows, news broadcasts, read about it in books, newspapers and magazines, and hear about it on the radio? Or is it simply that the media reflect the reality of their concerns? I suspect that it is a mutually reinforcing vicious cycle.

Roseanne Barr Arnold is an unfortunate symbol of how the media work, creating and then destroying their own. The more bizarre her statements, the more attention she gets. Now she is not only an Incest Survivor, but also a battered wife with multiple personalities. At the time I'm writing this, her public statements about her private life seem to be remarkably changeable, depending on her mood (or perhaps depending on which 'alter' is speaking).

As a nation, the United States appears to need a collective Enemy, or so it seems many nights on the evening news. With the end of the Cold War, the communists no longer serve, and Saddam Hussein was only temporary. The 'international conspiracy' of satanic cults came along at the right time to serve that function, and the secretly incestuous family seems to be close behind.

---

* Even public radio has helped spread the word. In 1994, Daniel Zwerdling introduced a credulous segment on Beth Hafling, a woman who 'discovered' her MPD status with a therapist who 'wanted to be another Cornelia Wilbur.' Zwerdling solemnly announced: 'She has dozens of personalities, an unusually severe case of a mental illness nicknamed MPD. Researchers believe the disease can be triggered in childhood by repeated physical and sexual abuse.' Indeed, Hafling recovered memories of torture and rape by family members and others.

The other day, I saw an American public service spot in which a man tells a female office mate that he dreads a forthcoming family reunion because his father will be there. 'Yeah, but why so blue?' she asks. 'I've never told anyone,' he answers, 'but I think my Dad molested me.' He explains that 'whenever I'm around him, I feel so anxious and uncomfortable. Sounds crazy?' She reassures him that it does not, since *she* has remembered being molested by her brother and a female babysitter. She tells him to call Survivors of Incest Anonymous, as the phone number and address flash onto the screen.[89]

Fortunately, the media are also capable of providing forums for legitimate public discussion. In the recent case of Cardinal Joseph Bernardin, in which Steven Cook retracted his hypnosis-based allegations, some newspapers had the grace to apologize for their earlier knee-jerk condemnations of the cardinal.

It's worth noting that the schizophrenic attitude toward sex predates the modern media. In colonial times, when adultery was often a capital crime, it was considered a civic duty to spy on miscreants. In 1643 Maryland, for instance, one couple, hearing suspicious snores, stood on a hogshead of tobacco to peer over a wall, where 'Richard Jones Laye snoring in her plackett [a slit in a skirt] and Mary West put her hand in his Codpis.' Prying a loose board away, the spies then witnessed Mary West 'with her Coates upp above her middle and Richard Jones with his Breeches down Lying upon her.'[90] This puritanical disapproval, along with a prurient interest in the proceedings, represent two sides of the same coin – an obsession over an act that is, at once, both disgusting and titillating.

In their 1988 book, *Intimate Matters: A History of Sexuality in America*, John D'Emilio and Estelle Freedman observe that 'sexuality has been associated with a range of human activities and values: the procreation of children, the attainment of physical pleasure (eroticism), recreation or sport, personal intimacy, spiritual transcendence, or power over others.' They add that 'certain associations prevail at different times, depending on the larger social forces that shape an era.'

In 1990s society, those forces are pulling in opposite directions. On the one hand, the media are saturated with images of overt, erotic sexuality, celebrating women as sexual objects and men as hunk-studs. The same media tell viewers that men are evil, often incestuous rapists, and that women are perpetual victims. Again, this is the flip side of the same ambivalent coin. Americans are giving their children extremely confusing, mixed messages. 'Sex is easily attached to other social concerns,' D'Emilio and Freedman observe, 'and it often evokes highly irrational responses.'[91]

A CONCLUDING NOTE

As I stated at the beginning of this chapter, the question, 'Why now?' has no simple answer. To summarize briefly, a great many social, historical, and attitudinal factors seem to have conflated into a receptive climate for today's flurry of bizarre incest accusations. In the tension-filled '90s, Americans have been eager for a new scapegoat for their personal and societal problems. Meanwhile, the horrors and extent of *real* incest have emerged from the national closet, so after imagination had run its course about iceberg mothers and communists under our beds, the snake oil of repressed memories may have come along at just the right time.

CHAPTER TWELVE

Survivorship as Religion

No one can understand mankind without understanding the faiths of humanity. Sometimes naïve, sometimes penetratingly noble, sometimes crude, sometimes subtle, sometimes cruel, sometimes suffused by an overpowering gentleness and love, sometimes world-affirming, sometimes negating the world, sometimes inward-looking, sometimes universalistic and missionary-minded, sometimes shallow, and often profound – religion has permeated human life since obscure and early times.

NINIAN SMART, *The Religious Experience of Mankind* (1969)[1]

We see the bloodshed, terror and destruction born of such generous enthusiasms as the love of God, love of Christ, love of a nation, compassion for the oppressed and so on.

ERIC HOFFER, *The True Believer* (1951)[2]

Human beings are religious animals. We cannot exist, it seems, without finding a higher meaning for our lives. We sense that there is more to life than our five senses convey. Perhaps other species worship their unseen gods as well, but I suspect that we are unique in this respect. Every society or tribe ever discovered has its own brand of religion, complete with creation myth, ethical imperatives, rituals, and shamans. Many of our most sublime insights have come from inspired religious leaders, and their messages have often echoed one another. *We are all one. All life is holy.* Every major religion has taught its own version of the Golden Rule, urging us to *treat others as we wish to be treated.* Similarly, devotees have described the utmost bliss during ecstatic mystical moments in which they have been consumed by the Holy Spirit.

Yet religions also have their dark side. More people have been slaughtered in the name of ideological holiness than any other cause. As Blaise Pascal observed in 1670, 'Men never do evil so completely and cheerfully as when they do it from religious conviction.'[3] This continues to be the case around the world. All too often, our faiths make us intolerant rather than compassionate, holier-than-thou rather than humble, filled with righteous anger instead of understanding, forgiveness, and love. If you're not saved, you're damned. The Manichean division of the world between God and Satan, pitting the forces of light and goodness against those of darkness and evil, has led far too many people to demonize one another, to search out the witch or the warlock.*[4]

It is this darker aspect of the religious impulse that I will explore in this chapter in regard to the Incest Survivor Movement. Survivorship, I believe, has become a pseudo-religion that provides intensity and meaning to people's lives in a destructive manner. In making that statement, I do not wish to disparage any religious faith. In fact, belief in God has sustained many of the accused parents as well as the retractors who are trying to put their lives back together.

THE SUBSTITUTE FAITH

'In a period of religious crisis,' historian of religion Mircea Eliade wrote in 1969, 'one cannot anticipate the *creative*, and, as such, probably unrecognizable, answers given to such a crisis.'[5] Indeed, no one could have predicted the particularly bizarre answer that would arise some 20 years after Eliade made that observation. As I pointed out in Chapter 11 ('*Why Now?*'), one of the primary appeals of the Incest Survivor Movement is that it serves as a substitute religion in an era of shifting values, uncertainty, and confusion. Being a Survivor provides many of the advantages of a born-again sect, including self-righteous indignation or pity for those who have not been saved, a warm feeling of communion with those who share similar beliefs, a strong spiritual/mystical component, and the opportunity to become a martyr for the cause. For therapists, the movement is a crusade against the forces of evil. They are valued priests who can unlock the secrets of the mind.

To identify the Incest Survivor Movement as a religion, you have only to listen for the telltale words and phrases. It is astonishing how

---

* The Manichean movement was founded by a Persian named Mani, who lived from 216 to 277 A.D. and taught that the forces of light (good) were continually imprisoned by those of darkness (evil). The evil forces dominated this material world. Consequently, the best way to release the light was to practice severe asceticism and refrain from all sexual intercourse. The Manichean mindset – with its dualistic approach and horror of sex – has had an enormous influence on our culture.

often the words 'belief' and 'faith' come up. 'Letting go takes faith,' Bass and Davis write in *The Courage to Heal*. 'You have to trust your capacity to heal yourself.'[6] Therapists must *believe* their patients, or they will retraumatize them. Social workers and judges must *believe* the day-care children. It requires a *leap of faith* to *believe the unbelievable*. To doubt any of these stories or to ask for some sort of evidence is tantamount to heresy.

There is also a mystical, non-rational component to this religion. On a computer bulletin board for Survivors, for instance, Randy Emon, a California policeman who once appeared in videos warning about satanic cults, began to question his beliefs. He asked for some sort of proof and cited an FBI study that failed to find any evidence of such cults or the murders supposedly perpetrated in them. In response, another bulletin board subscriber took the skeptic to task for attempting to apply logic to ritual-abuse stories. 'When you wish to speak of feelings instead of data and studies, I and many others will welcome your comments,' he wrote. 'LIFE IS FEELINGS. STRUCTURE IS DEATH OF THE CHILD WITHIN.'[7]

Over and over again, I have heard Survivors speak passionately of their spiritual journeys. The search for memories, for the precious child within, clearly resembles religious meditation in some respects. 'I sense that you are quite spiritual,' one woman wrote in 1992 to another on the same computer network, 'just in the way you talked about sitting in the meditation (hypnosis) mode and burning your incense while trying to reach your inner child. I have done that many times, and the memories do get clearer and clearer as you continue.' She urged her correspondent to find a wise, understanding therapist, then continued: 'I guess when one goes in search of their true self and faces the demons that appear along the way, then nothing can get much more spiritual than that, huh? It involves so very much TRUST that we will survive and make it through. I want to share with you that my spiritual growth through this journey has made everything I have experienced – TERROR, nightmares, panic, depression, phobias – the WHOLE 9 yards, well worth it. I would do it all again just to be able to discover my true spirituality.'

It is clear, then, that we are dealing with a religious phenomenon, which begins to explain why so many Christian therapists and pastoral counselors are among the most zealous memory retrieval advocates. In an era when the ministerial role has become more secularized and less influential, the Survivor ideology provides a renewed sense of mission and urgency. As in the past, good Christians can do battle against demons, exposing evil satanic cults while delving into the mysteries of the mind.

DEFINING RELIGION

Perhaps because the religious impulse is so universal, defining it is no simple matter. Philosopher Ninian Smart has written that religion is 'a six-dimensional organism, typically containing doctrines, myths, ethical teachings, rituals, and social institutions, and animated by religious experiences of various kinds.' Let us examine each of those six dimensions in turn.[8]

By now, we are well acquainted with the Survivor *doctrine*, which holds that all life's difficulties are explained by forgotten sexual abuse. Recalling the suffering is necessary and redemptive, though only after a 'dark night of the soul.'

By *myths*, Smart doesn't mean to imply truth or falsehood, but oft-repeated stories that demonstrate the essential truth of the doctrine. For the Survivor, these stories are retold and dramatized endlessly in therapy and group sessions – how the perpetrator entered the room, seduced the child, and terrorized her into silence; how the victim repressed or dissociated, watching from a disembodied vantage point on the ceiling; how the perpetrator always denies; how memories surface but seem doubtful at first.

Ellen Bass and her co-disciples offer plenty of *ethical teachings*. Getting in touch with anger is good. Forgiveness is unnecessary, or even, as some Survivors assert, a sin. Sharing abuse stories is a necessary part of healing. Separating from the dysfunctional family of origin and bonding with fellow Survivors is part of the process.

Rituals? 'It is worth remarking,' Smart wrote, 'that even the simplest form of religious service involves ritual, in the sense of some form of outer behavior (such as closing one's eyes in prayer) coordinated to an inner intention to make contact with, or to participate in, the invisible world.'*[9] What better description could there be of a guided imagery session? In most traditional religions, this 'invisible world' was sought

---

* 'In some ways therapy is similar to prayer,' clinical psychologist Bernie Zilbergeld has noted. 'Both can be comforting and useful even when one does not get what one asks for. Both can keep hope alive; combat boredom and demoralization; decrease loneliness and alienation; help us get things off our chests and clear our minds.'

somewhere outside the body. In our psychological inner-directed era, Survivors seek it in their own mindscapes. In *The Courage to Heal*, Bass and Davis recommend what they term 'anger rituals,' such as burning a perpetrator's photo or writing a divorce decree from one's parents.[10]

As for *social institutions*, Survivors of Incest Anonymous as well as innumerable other associations, 12-step groups, and publications provide as recognizable and widespread a network as any organized religion. A Survivor can move anywhere in the English-speaking world and quickly hook up with fellow believers.

That leaves only the sixth dimension of the organism – *religious experiences of various kinds*. What gives a religion its exceptional power is its *personal* significance, its ability to transform the individual it touches. In its most elemental form, religion involves a dramatic conversion experience, defined by a recent sociologist as *'a radical transformation of identity or orientation.'*[11]*

CONVERSION

In 1902, philosopher and psychologist William James delivered a series of lectures entitled *The Varieties of Religious Experience* in which he explored, among many other topics, the commonalities of sudden religious conversion. 'Were we writing the story of the mind from the purely natural-history point of view,' he said, 'with no religious interest whatever, we should still have to write down man's liability to sudden and complete conversion as one of his most curious peculiarities.'[12] James offered several first-hand accounts, including one man's wrenching experience:

> I fell on my face by a bench, and tried to pray, and every time I would call on God, something like a man's hand would strangle me by choking ... I thought I should surely die if I did not get help, but just as often as I would pray, that unseen hand was felt on my throat and my breath squeezed off. Finally something said,

---

* Many genuinely religious people, of course, have never gone through a dramatic conversion experience. I explore this aspect of sudden belief change because it is clearly relevant to the recovered memory phenomenon.

'Venture on the atonement, for you will die anyway if you don't.' So I made one final struggle ... The last I remember that time was falling back on the ground with the same unseen hand on my throat ... When I came to myself, there were a crowd around me praising God.[13]

James hypothesized that those who were most susceptible to conversion were easily hypnotized and highly suggestible. 'On the whole,' he said, 'unconsciousness, convulsions, visions, involuntary vocal utterances, and suffocation, must be simply ascribed to the subject's ... nervous instability.' Nonetheless, he was careful to admit that this condition might actually predispose special people to receive 'higher spiritual agencies,' adding a significant caveat: 'The mere fact of [these forces'] transcendency would of itself establish no presumption that they were more divine than diabolical.'[14]

The philosopher/psychologist actually mentioned a possible connection between repressed memories – a new concept that fascinated him – and the conversion experience. In the 'wonderful explorations' of Sigmund Freud, Pierre Janet, Morton Prince, and others, James believed that 'we have revealed to us whole systems of underground life, in the shape of memories of a painful sort which lead a parasitic existence, buried outside of the primary fields of consciousness, and making irruptions thereinto with hallucinations, pains, convulsions ...' He admitted that 'these clinical records sound like fairy-tales when one first reads them, yet it is impossible to doubt their accuracy.' He wondered whether all 'unaccountable invasive alterations of consciousness' – such as dramatic religious conversion – might not stem from 'subliminal memories reaching the bursting-point.'[15]

Fifty-five years later, British psychiatrist William Sargant also noted the similarity between religious conversion experiences and the psychotherapeutic process, though he attributed both to a physiological process of heightened arousal that promotes changes in belief systems. In fact, in *Battle for the Mind* (1957), he dared to equate coercive communist brainwashing – very much on people's minds after the Korean War – with religious conversion and experiences in psychotherapy. Sargant disagreed with James' hypothesis that those prone to conversion were somehow abnormal and exhibited 'nervous instability.' On the contrary, Sargant asserted, 'The ordinary person, in general, is much more easily indoctrinated than the abnormal,' because the everyday member of society is more susceptible to social influence.[16]

Sargant pointed out that while the dramatic moment of conversion seems an instantaneous watershed, it is usually preceded by a period of intense anxiety and self-doubt, often generated by the 'priest' or therapist. Sargant quoted a personal patient of Sigmund Freud: 'For the first few months I was able to feel nothing but increasing anxiety, humiliation and guilt. Nothing about my past life seemed satisfactory any more, and all my old ideas about myself seemed to be contradicted.' Only after this patient's former identity was stripped away could Freud 'piece everything together in a new setting.'[17]

Sargant also referred specifically to the dramatic moment of 'abreaction,' the emotional catharsis of supposedly recovered trauma memories, as a crucial component in the conversion process. 'Many patients who have been subjected to repeated abreactions, during a period of months and even years, on the psychotherapist's couch, are known to become increasingly sensitive to the therapist's suggestions ... They respond more willingly when he attempts to implant new ideas in them ... which they would have rejected without hesitation before.'[18]

The psychiatrist hypothesized that some kind of literal biological alteration occurs somewhere in the brain cells to precipitate this shift in belief systems. 'Before being able to change behaviour patterns of thought and action in the human brain with speed and efficiency,' Sargant wrote, 'it is apparently in many cases necessary to induce some form of physiological brain disturbance. The subject may have to be frightened, angered, frustrated, or emotionally disturbed in some way or another.'[19]

The dramatic, emotional moment of conversion helps to convince skeptics. Clearly, *something* extraordinary is going on. Thus, in 1739, evangelist John Wesley reported with satisfaction how a local doctor had become a believer:

> We understand that many were offended at the cries of those on whom the power of God came; among whom was a physician, who was much afraid there might be fraud or imposture in the case. Today one whom he had known many years was the first who broke out 'into strong cries and tears.' He could hardly believe his own eyes and ears. He went and stood close to her, and observed every symptom, till great drops of sweat ran down her face and all her bones shook. He then knew not what to think ... But when both her soul and body were healed in a moment, he acknowledged the finger of God.[20]

Perhaps this woman really was touched by 'the finger of God.' On the other hand, her experience sounds disconcertingly similar to that of the modern Survivor, whose 'strong cries and tears' convince her therapist that the recovered memories are real and that the patient is re-experiencing the true horror of the past.

In 1964, seven years after Sargant wrote his book, Abraham Maslow published *Religions, Values, and Peak-Experiences*. Maslow stated that all true religious experiences were ased on magical 'peak experiences,' which all humans could naturally experience. In other words, he stripped religion down to only one of the components identified by Ninian Smart: the intense personal experience. In fact, a 'non-peaker' is some-one 'who suppresses them, who denies them, who turns away from them, or who "forgets" them' – a statement that sounds alarmingly similar to attitudes toward 'repressed memories.'[21] Maslow's book helped promote the intense search for individualistic, ecstatic fulfillment during the hippie era of the late '60s, including experiments with LSD.

In the introduction to his second edition in 1970, Maslow sounded a note of caution to those intent on finding peak moments. 'Instead of being temporarily self-absorbed and inwardly searching, he may become simply a selfish person ... This trend can sometimes wind up in mean-ness, nastiness, loss of compassion, or even in the extreme of sadism.' He warned that the hunt for peaks could move into 'the occult, the dramatic and effortful, the dangerous, the cultish. Healthy openness to the mysterious, the realistically humble recognition that we don't know much ... all these can shade over into the anti-rational, the anti-empirical, the anti-scientific.' Finally, he noted 'the possibility that the inner voices, the "revelations," may be mistaken, a lesson from history that should come through loud and clear.'[22]

As William James observed back in 1902, 'emotional occasions, especially violent ones, are extremely potent in precipitating mental rearrangements.'[23] More recently, psychiatrist Jerome Frank has observed that 'a sense of isolation and estrangement from others charac-terizes the pre-conversion state. The dominant affects include despair, hatred, resentment, and helpless fury, often directed toward a parent or parent-substitute.' Those previously admired or emulated are either shunned or become targets for conversion to the new faith. Like James, Frank noted that adolescents are particularly susceptible to sudden con-version, perhaps in an effort to establish an independent identity.[24]

Frank referred to the moment of *kairos*, which the Greeks identified as an auspicious moment of intense emotional involvement – either positive or negative – precipitating profound personality change. 'A great variety of psychological states in combination with certain external circumstances may be followed by abrupt, large, enduring changes in a person's outlook, values, and behavior.' Or, as one Survivor put it in *The Courage to Heal:* 'It's a quantum shift in my perception of the universe.'[25] Frank concluded that 'psychotherapy is always an emotionally charged experience, and the emotions are more often unpleasant than pleasant. To be sure, there are interludes of hope, optimism, even elation; but episodes of unpleasant feelings such as fear, anger, despair, and guilt are apt to be more frequent and more prolonged.' Why would anyone continue such treatment, then? For the same reason that a parishioner endures the hell-fire sermon: 'expectation of benefit.'[26]

ECSTATIC RELIGION AND THE POSSESSED SHAMAN

In his 1971 book, *Ecstatic Religion*, anthropologist I. M. Lewis studied tribes in which spirit possession and shamanism were common.* His comments on this type of dramatic 'conversion' reinforce what James, Sargant, and Frank observed. 'The initial experience of possession,' Lewis wrote, 'is often a disturbing, even traumatic experience, and not uncommonly a response to personal affliction and adversity.' Even so, many 'victims' actually desire to become possessed, because it confers a special status and otherwise unattainable insights.**[27] Those seeking visions during a possession experience attempt to induce them through some form of trance. Lewis reviewed 'time-honoured techniques' such as hypnotic suggestion, hyperventilation, ingestion of mind-altering drugs, self-inflicted wounds, meditation, or fasting – all of which, of course, are characteristic of many modern Survivors as they search for their memories.[28]

Lewis noted that *women* in many different cultures appeared to be particularly susceptible to dramatic possessions, but he did not attribute this fact to any inherent biological gender difference. Rather, 'such

* A tribal shaman acts as a medium to communicate with the invisible spirit world and practices magic or sorcery.
** Also like Survivors, most shamans do not *consciously* seek their vocation. As one anthropologist observed of a typical Vietnamese shaman: 'The more he ostensibly refuses this destiny, the more he resists, the more striking will be the signs, the more gripping and dramatic his vocation.'

women's possession cults are,' he observed, 'thinly disguised protest movements directed against the dominant sex ... in cultures where women lack more obvious and direct means for forwarding their aims.'* In other words, the extent to which women act out these roles is evidence of the near-universal oppression of their gender. Though the anthropologist did not accuse the possessed women of consciously enacting a role to gain their ends, he believed that their form of 'illness' did, in fact, offer benefits. 'Women who succumb to these afflictions cannot help themselves and at the same time bear no responsibility for all the annoyance and cost which their subsequent treatment involves. They are thus totally blameless.'[29]

For many women, Lewis noted, possession becomes a chronic condition. 'The patient learns, in effect, to live with her spirit,' which is considered 'tamed' for the moment, but only at the cost of numerous ceremonies in a group with other women, under the direction of a female shaman. These activities are essentially cures, Lewis wrote, 'and in psychiatric terms, the cult meetings assume much of the character of group therapy sessions.' As with Survivors, those initially afflicted often go on to become therapists in their own right: 'In the course of time, she may then graduate to the position of female shaman, diagnosing the same condition in other women.'[30]

Lewis also observed that these 'peripheral possession cults'**[31] appeared to thrive during times of social upheaval. 'New faiths may announce their advent with a flourish of ecstatic revelations,' he wrote, 'but once they become securely established they have little time or tolerance for enthusiasm.' So what factors keep radical possession experiences 'on the boil'? Lewis asserted that 'the answer lies in acute and constantly recurring social and environmental pressures which militate against the formation of large, secure social groups.'[32]

Finally, Lewis acknowledged the similarity between psychotherapy and possession experiences in primitive tribes. 'The psychoanalyst's mythology both evokes and moulds the putative experiences of his

---

* Lewis also pointed out that men sometimes belonged to peripheral possession cults as well – usually when they, too, found themselves in a subordinate, oppressed condition.
** Often, peripheral possession cults involve some form of what could be called sexual abuse or deviance. In Italian 'tarantism,' for instance, the onset of the possession was incorrectly believed to stem from the bite of the tarantula spider. Those seeking a cure summoned the appropriate saint by calling out, 'My St. Paul of the Tarantists who pricks the girls in their vaginas: My St. Paul of the Serpents who pricks the boys in their testicles.'

patient,' he observed. Similarly, in a peripheral possession cult, 'everything takes on the tone and character of modern psychodrama or group therapy. Abreaction is the order of the day. Repressed urges and desires, the idiosyncratic as well as the socially conditioned, are given full public rein.'[33]*[34]

MINIRTH-MEIER AND THE CHRISTIAN HUNT FOR MEMORIES

Unfortunately, many of the 'peripheral possession cult' characteristics described by I. M. Lewis have appeared in mainstream Christian counseling, particularly in the American chain of Minirth-Meier New Life Clinics (formerly Minirth-Meier Clinics) founded by psychiatrists Frank Minirth and Paul Meier in 1976. Until the '70s, 'Christian counseling' generally meant going to confession or talking with a pastor about marital difficulties. But in the late 1970s and 1980s, pop psychology invaded the field, and Christian psychologists such as Larry Crabb, James Dobson, Frank Minirth, and Paul Meier began their lucrative psychological ministries through counseling centers, radio programs, newsletters, and organizations. The Minirth-Meier Hour, nationally syndicated in the U.S. on many Christian radio stations, offers advice on everything from tobacco addiction to bipolar disorder and repressed memories.

In 1982, Dr. Richard Flournoy joined the Minirth-Meier Clinic in Richardson, Texas. He co-authored several books with Frank Minirth and other therapists. In 1985, Gloria Grady, the 27-year-old daughter of a Baptist minister, sought counseling with Flournoy. She was overweight, depressed, and overly dependent on her parents, with whom she still lived. Flournoy asked Gloria to write down everything bad that had ever happened to her. She had a hard time with the assignment, finally coming up with the fact that her parents wouldn't let her square dance in the first grade. Concerned about Gloria's new attitude toward

* No cross-cultural anthropological study of 'recovered memory' has ever been conducted, but there is at least one case in which early traumatic events are presumed to cause distress in later life. Members of some Latin American tribes sometimes suffer from *susto*, stemming from a long-ago 'fright,' which may have occurred as far back as the womb. Diagnosed by divination, *susto* results in 'soul loss,' as evidenced by lethargy, vague physical complaints, and depression. The cure involves inducing the soul to return by means of complex rituals.

them, her parents asked for a meeting with Flournoy, but it went poorly. 'He wouldn't address us at all,' Gloria's mother recalls. 'He would say, "Gloria, how does that make you feel?" She would look to him for answers.'[35]

By 1986, Gloria was seeing Flournoy four times a week – twice for individual therapy and twice with a group. With his encouragement, she bought a teddy bear and carried it with her everywhere. She transferred her dependency from her parents to her therapist. In 1987, she cut off contact with her parents. Eventually, with Flournoy's help, Gloria Grady came to believe that from the age of ten until she entered college, her father had repeatedly raped her and inserted a rifle barrel, pistol, and a knife into her vagina. Her parents had been in a satanic cult along with her brother, grandfather, and other family members; they had forced her to undergo five ritual abortions and eat parts of the fetuses.

To be fair to Minirth-Meier, it should be noted that Richard Flournoy left the clinic late in 1986, and Frank Minirth did make a belated effort to get Gloria out of his therapy.*[36] But Minirth and Meier have continued to espouse recovered-memory therapy, and their clinic has recently been involved in another disturbing example of therapeutic abuse. On March 15, 1994, a young Georgia father named John Scott Rogers was listening to a Minirth-Meier radio program while driving his car. The program stated that people who were abused as children are likely to abuse their own children in turn.

Rogers, whose father beat him severely as a child, was concerned enough to stop the car and call the 0800 number from a pay phone, looking for information and prayer. He spoke with Melody, who quickly secured his name, address, and insurance carrier. Emotionally overwrought by the radio broadcast, Rogers explained that although he had not yet abused his children, he was afraid that he might at some point, if the radio show was correct. Melody told Rogers, 'If you feel you may become an abuser, maybe you're actually doing it now and subconsciously you're shielding it from yourself.' He told her that anything was possible, but he didn't think so. By the end of the conversation, Melody told him that he needed to be hospitalized at the Minirth-Meier

---

* In 1986, Richard Flournoy went into private practice with Michael Moore, who had worked at Minirth-Meier for six years. Between the two of them, they counseled numerous patients who came to believe that they had been sexually abused in satanic cults but had repressed the memories. Moore was recently sued by a former client. It should also be noted that Frank Minirth left Minirth-Meier New Life late in 1995 to found his own Texas clinic.

clinic in Atlanta for a minimum stay of 14 days. He must go home, pack, and leave immediately, or she would turn him in to the Georgia Department of Family and Children's Services (DFCS). Rogers begged her to let him see his wife first; she was driving up from Florida with their son and daughter, ages three and two. Finally, Melody agreed.

Terrified and distraught, Rogers went home and packed. Then he called his pastor, who rushed over. When the pastor heard the full story, he told Rogers not to go to the hospital, that he had done nothing wrong and had nothing to worry about. Relieved, Rogers called Minirth-Meier and told Melody he wasn't coming in. She told him she had no choice but to turn him in to DFCS.

The next day, Rogers' wife pulled into the driveway with two exhausted children. Right behind her, a county sheriff pulled in, along with a local DFCS worker, who informed Rogers that he was accused of molesting his son, even though there had been no talk of sexual abuse in his conversation with Melody. In the ensuing two months, Scott Rogers' marriage was nearly destroyed. He was not allowed to be with his children alone. His children were stripped naked, their private parts examined. In addition, the children were subjected to sexualized interviews using anatomically correct dolls. Finally, the case was dropped.[37]

What is particularly disturbing about this fiasco is that no one at Minirth-Meier has ever apologized or acknowledged any wrong. Frank Minirth was sent a videotape, 'A Family Betrayed,' in which Scott Rogers poignantly tells his story. Minirth did not to respond.[38]*

Given Minirth's published beliefs about repressed memories in his 1995 book, *The Power of Memories*, his lack of response to Scott Rogers is ominous. In the book, he tells the story of Hannah, who entered therapy at the Minirth-Meier New Life Clinic suffering from postpartum depression and was soon having nightmares of satanic ritual abuse. 'A lot of horrible memories came pouring in like a flood,' she recalls. Minirth recounts her memories without a hint of skepticism. 'The unspeakable acts she witnessed during the few years of her involvement culminated in the murder-sacrifice of an infant,' he concludes. 'Traumatized, she recalled none of this until her own son was born.'

Minirth also recounts the story of Martha, who couldn't remember fourth grade. 'The blank spot at ages ten and eleven was significant,' he asserts. 'A dark spot in otherwise retrievable memories is a warning flag. Here is something the memory has deliberately blocked out.'

* Melody is no longer employed by Minirth-Meier. Neither Frank Minirth nor Paul Meier responded to my requests for an interview.

Eventually, of course, Minirth helped her recall being sexually abused in a shed. 'And the torrents came, floods of tears and floods of memories.'

Not only does Minirth espouse a belief in repressed memories, he implicates Jesus and God in the process of their retrieval. 'Memories are so powerful you must lead them forth from the depths carefully, or they will crush you. As you do it with Christ's spiritual help, He will protect you from receiving too much too fast.' Minirth suggests asking God directly for help in a prayer journal. 'Tell God you are now ready and willing to go to work on bad memories. Ask Him to accompany you down the pathway to those memories, opening up what He wants to show you. Remind Him that you realize the two of you can face it together.'[39]

Equally disturbing were the comments of Dr. Paul Meier on a nationally aired 'Focus on the Family' show in February of 1995. True, Meier recognizes that some false allegations may arise from hypnotic age regression, which he does not recommend. But he also revealed that the 300 therapists in Minirth-Meier clinics routinely search for repressed memories through 'conscious' processes. Meier himself has helped 'literally hundreds' of clients to unrepress 'memories' of abuse. Not only that, Paul Meier, like his colleague Frank Minirth, believes in the myth of widespread satanic ritual abuse cults. 'I saw a real case of it just this past week,' he said, explaining that his client 'didn't even remember how she got pregnant, but she does remember when she delivered the baby, and the baby was sacrificed at a satanic cult.'

Meier told listeners that Minirth-Meier has a 'Chicago clinic that specializes in satanic ritual abuse' and that 'there are Satan-worshiping cults all around the country.' Of all the people who recover SRA memories in the Minirth-Meier clinics, he said that he believed two-thirds of them. Considering that between 15,000 and 20,000 people seek Christian counseling at Minirth-Meier clinics *every week*, we have every reason for concern.[40]

Minirth-Meier New Life's current literature boasts that the clinic chain is the 'nation's largest and most trusted provider of Christian mental health services,' offering a 'sound integration of medical and psychological principles with Christian beliefs of love, hope, and restoration.' Yet this 'trusted provider' of services has almost certainly helped to destroy families. Among their listed specialties are sexual abuse and multiple personality disorders. Espousing a belief in MPD is, as we have seen, a telltale sign of trouble.[41]

James Dobson, the enormously popular director of Focus on the

Family, based in Colorado, is clearly concerned about false allegations of sexual abuse. 'The memory is an imperfect function of the brain,' he said on the first day of his February 1995 broadcast on this issue. 'Imagine how much more imperfect it is when you're going all the way back and trying to resurrect what happened when you were two or three or four. I simply don't believe it in most cases.'

Yet by the time he introduced the second day's broadcast, he had apparently changed his mind. 'There are circumstances where a child is sexually abused either by a parent or an uncle or a brother or a sister,' he intoned, 'and they repress that because it's so painful they can't deal with it emotionally.' Later on in life, he explained, 'they suddenly remember those experiences that were so horrible during childhood. It does happen, it does happen.'[42]

The Christian hunt for repressed memories has been encouraged by Fred and Florence Littauer in their 1988 book, *Freeing the Mind From Memories That Bind*, by Dan Allender in his 1990 book, *The Wounded Heart*, and by James Friesen in 1991's *Uncovering the Mystery of MPD*. Allender's book is the more subtle and less obviously leading, but for that very reason, its message may be more persuasive. He does not recommend strong measures such as sodium Amytal interviews. The memories will come back 'slowly, progressively,' he writes. 'Choosing to open oneself to memories will, over time, draw them to the surface, where they can begin to be dealt with constructively.' This process will be painful, he warns. 'Marriages will need to be reshaped; sexual relations may be postponed while the partners devote themselves to prayer and fasting. The fabric of life will need to be unraveled piece by piece as the Master reweaves the cloth to His design.'

Throughout *The Wounded Heart*, Allender simply *assumes* that his readers harbor repressed memories. 'At times, I wonder if every person in the world ... has been sexually abused,' he muses. If all the world's population were to read his book, everyone might indeed *think* so. 'The denial [of repressed memories] is an affront to God. It assumes that God is neither good nor strong enough to help during the recall process. Ultimately, the choice to face past memories is the choice not to live a lie.'[43]

All too many American and British Christian counselors have taken such books to heart, and it is usually good Christian families that are being blown apart as a result. In 1995, I met Tom Rutherford, an Assemblies of God minister in Springfield, Missouri. His three daughters all believed at one point that one of them was abused. They were counseled by the wife of a fellow Assembly of God minister. One daughter accused her father of multiple rapes and came to believe that she had been impregnated twice. No one bothered to ascertain that Rutherford had a vasectomy when his daughter was four, making it impossible for him to have impregnated anyone. A subsequent medical exam revealed the daughter to be a virgin. Fortunately, all of his daughters have realized that the 'memories' were illusory, and they are back with their family. The Rutherford family is represented by veteran lawyer Sidney L. Willens, who has successfully prosecuted lawsuits against therapists for over a decade.[44]

Fortunately, concerned Christian counselors such as Colorado pastor Ed Bulkley have begun to warn against the hazards of recovered-memory therapy. Bulkley's 1995 book, *Only God Can Heal the Wounded Heart*, is an explicit rebuttal to Dan Allender. Bulkley also reviews Frank Minirth's book, worrying that Minirth's readers 'will be convinced that they can find peace of mind by reworking their memories. What a disaster! Instead of finding the peace that God offers through His divine power, Christians are being offered counterfeit solutions that lead them back into pain, sin, bitterness, and defeat.' And while many psychologists are questioning the recovered-memory dogma, all too many Christian counselors continue to unearth illusory memories. 'Just when secular authorities are dismissing the reliability of recovered memories,' Bulkley writes, 'Christian therapists are buying into it like it's a revelation from God!'[45]

Paul Simpson is another Christian therapist sounding the alarm, even though he himself once helped clients unearth 'memories.' Now Simpson counsels those whose lives have been upended by this form of misguided therapy. In 1995, he recounted a disturbing story one Christian retractor told him. 'The Holy Spirit took her back in time. She could see her father molesting her as an infant. Then the Holy Spirit took her back to her mother's womb, and she could hear hateful things being said at that time. Finally, the Holy Spirit took her right back in time to the presence of God, where she was talking with God before she was born.' With such belief systems being advanced in the name of religion, it is little wonder that so much damage has been inflicted.

It would be interesting if every minister in English-speaking countries were to act on Paul Simpson's suggestion. 'Pastors,' he advises, 'I encourage you next Sunday to ask that any families that have been impacted through these kinds of false accusations, whether in the immediate or extended family, come to you privately and share that with you. I think that you will be shocked to see how prevalent this phenomenon is within your own congregations.'[46]

THE BRITISH EVANGELICAL SEARCH FOR MEMORIES

British ministers who take Simpson's advice might be particularly surprised – though others might not, since they themselves have helped
unearth recovered memories. 'The satanism panic originated in the
United States,' observes Philip Jenkins in his book, *Intimate Enemies*,
'but such stories could not have attained the power they did unless there
was already in existence a domestic audience willing and eager to hear
them; and this was found among the swelling ranks of fundamentalist
and Charismatic Christians within Britain itself.' As far back as 1934,
popular British author Dennis Wheatley had published *The Devil Rides
Out*, in which the Devil himself leads an orgy involving every imaginable
perversion. 'A little cannibalism, my friend,' one character in the book
observed. 'It may be a still-born baby or perhaps some unfortunate child
they have stolen and murdered.' The book was re-issued in 1966 and
made into a film two years later.[47]

Concepts such as spiritual warfare and exorcism had been popular
among British evangelicals for many years, along with speaking in
tongues. Between 1979 and 1989, membership in independent fundamentalist churches swelled from 44,000 to 128,000 in England and
Wales – and that ignores evangelical branches sprouting within the
Anglican ranks.[48]

An interdenominational Christian Exorcism Study Circle was formed
in 1972, and by 1985, it was counseling some two hundred people who
claimed to be fleeing from satanic or occult groups. The group's secretary warned that 'Satanists can be found at the highest levels in our
society, in political life and on the boards of multinational companies.'
Several prominent British clergymen wrote books warning against
Satan's influence. The Reverend Russ Parker, who had worked with the
Manchester Deliverance Advisory Group, went on to minister to two
Leicestershire parishes within the established church and to write
Battling the Occult in 1990. Anglican vicar Kevin Logan wrote *Paganism
and the Occult* in 1988, describing in it a London occult group composed
of 'high ranking civil servants, top industrialists and prominent City
figures.' It was in Logan's Lancashire home that 'Hannah,' the famed
British ritual abuse survivor, committed suicide (*see Chapter 4*).[49]

In 1988, the Evangelical Alliance, which claims to represent a million adherents, formed a committee to look into ritual abuse claims,

particularly those of adult survivors. Among the prime movers were Maureen Davies, who claimed to have identified the first British ritual abuse case in 1985, and Diane Core, the organizer of Childwatch on Humberside. Core told a reporter, 'About four thousand babies a year are born into covens to be used for sacrifices and cannibalism. This is only the tip of the iceberg.' Davies described the job of 'brood mares,' teenage girls or older women who are intentionally impregnated. 'When they are five and a half months pregnant the birth is induced. At this stage, the foetus is alive and can be sacrificed. The blood of the infant is then drunk, then the body is eaten.'[50]

In 1990, in his popular book *The Hot Line*, Anglican cleric Peter Lawrence described an exorcism that had apparently become a common-place event for him: 'When I asked the Spirit to come, horrific demons manifested, growling and snarling and throwing her to the floor. Like so many Christians we find with resident demons, she had been an incest victim.'[51]

'Deliverance ministries' have become quite popular in Great Britain, as we saw in retractor Francine Boardman's story in Chapter 8. Some cases are bizarre almost beyond belief, however. In 1995, British readers were shocked to discover that a former Anglican vicar, 70-year-old Andy Arbuthnot, had induced illusory memories of satanic ritual abuse in Mary Llewellyn, 50, one of his parishioners at his London Healing Mission. That explained many of her problems, he said, including her bad back. 'When I started talking about my childhood, so much was blank,' Llewellyn recalls. 'He said God wanted me to find out.' Arbuth-not treated Llewellyn as a seven-year-old, giving her teddy bears and writing her pornographic love letters. Eventually, he sought to exorcize her demons through 'internal ministry,' which involved inserting his fingers, soaked with consecrated wine, into her anus and vagina. Finally, Llewellyn, who had become completely dependent on Arbuthnot, rebelled and went public with her story. 'I do have real memories of being abused as a child,' she says. 'They are very few, and those are the ones that I am keeping.'[52]

RAGE AND THE WORSHIP OF SELF

Anthropologist Clifford Geertz defines religion as a system of thought and belief 'which acts to establish powerful, pervasive, and long-lasting moods and motivations ... by formulating conceptions of a general order of existence and clothing these conceptions with such an aura of factuality that the moods and motivations seem uniquely realistic.'[53] Note that an *aura* of factuality is sufficient to establish a religion, which requires no objective evidence. That certainly describes the belief in repressed memories.

It is striking that Geertz should single out *moods* as such an important component. The heart of an evangelical religious movement isn't the particular philosophy, then, but the emotional content that it promulgates. There's no question that the Survivor movement fosters one mood above all others: *rage.* Love, tenderness, turning the other cheek, and the Golden Rule may have worked well enough for Jesus, but not for Survivors. The movement's bible, *The Courage to Heal,* calls anger 'the backbone of healing' and encourages, sanctions, and foments blinding, furious rage. 'You may dream of murder or castration,' write Bass and Davis. 'It can be pleasurable to fantasize such scenes in vivid detail. Wanting revenge is a natural impulse, a sane response.' With approval, the authors quote a woman named Vicki who convinced her mother, on the basis of recovered memories, that Vicki's father had violently abused her. 'She got fiercely angry at my father. She wanted to go over to his house and shoot his brains out. She wanted to kill him. I loved it.'[54]

Anger is a powerful motivator, which most religions understand. If you can demonize your enemies, making them Evil incarnate, denizens of Satan's empire, it is much easier to maintain community. As Eric Hoffer noted in his 1951 classic, *The True Believer,* 'Hatred is the most accessible and comprehensive of all unifying agents,' allowing its members to become selfless workers for a righteous cause. 'Mass movements can rise and spread without belief in a God,' Hoffer observed, 'but never without belief in a devil.'[55]

That is why so many religions, in their formative years, remain remarkably cohesive. Like the early Christian martyrs, they are combating a common enemy, ready to die for the cause. With time, if the religion thrives and puts down roots, it inevitably loses that early fire. It develops an organization, a fixed creed, a hierarchy. It becomes part of the status quo, and in doing so, it begins to miss its early enemies. Without satanic forces to fight against, without an underdog status, the adherents revert to normal human bickering and in-fighting. Some seek to rekindle the old-time religion through breaking off a new sect or identifying a new Enemy.

Survivorship is still in its infancy as a new religion, so the original fire in the belly still burns brightly. As we have seen, the allegations have been expanded into a *literal* fight against Satan, who supposedly sponsors ritual abuse cults throughout the land. These monstrous perpetrators specialize in murdering and consuming babies and skewering every available orifice not only with tumescent penises, but with red-hot pokers, knives, and other implements of destruction. They are Evil, pure and simple.

The 'moral crusader' was described by sociologist Howard Becker in 1963 as identifying 'some evil which profoundly disturbs.' Such a zealot 'operates with an absolute ethic; what he sees is truly and totally evil with no qualification. Any means is justified to do away with it. The crusader is fervent and righteous, often self-righteous.' Becker pointed out that such reformers tend to up the ante, searching for ever-greater evils to correct, or they would be out of business. 'First, they say that by reason of their efforts the problem they deal with is approaching solution. But, in the same breath, they say the problem is perhaps worse than ever (though through no fault of their own) and requires renewed and increased effort to keep it under control.'[56] Becker's observations certainly seem to be borne out by the Survivor Movement.

One of the advantages of a religion based on accusing innocent parents of horrible crimes is that they are bound to fight back eventually. Hence, the creation of the False Memory Syndrome Foundation, or some such organization, was inevitable. It was equally inevitable that the Survivors would fiercely attack the Foundation as part of the 'backlash' effort to deny the reality of sexual abuse. It doesn't matter how often members of the Foundation wearily explain that they are well aware that incest exists, and they deplore it. No Survivor wants to hear that. Instead, they have found a new enemy, and they spread the word that the Foundation is a group of perpetrators in denial, well funded and dangerous.

But a religion cannot function solely on rage. Survivorship does promote love, tenderness and devotion for those within its bosom. Survivors support one another in 12-step groups, seminars, computer bulletin boards, and numerous organizations such as Survivors of Incest Anonymous. Mostly, however, the natural need for love is turned inward in self-absorption.

In 1976, journalist and social critic Tom Wolfe identified what he called the Third Great Awakening of American religious evangelism.*

* The Great Awakening came about in the 1740s with Jonathan Edwards and other evangelical preachers. The Second Great Awakening occurred from 1825 to 1860, out of which many modern-day religions, such as Mormonism, arose.

534

Its mantra, he said, was 'the holiest roll of all, the beat that goes . . . *Me* . . . *Me* . . . *Me* . . . *Me*.' Wolfe wrote that this new psychological religious wave – epitomized by *est* and primal screaming – was on an 'upward roll,' predicting that the wave would crest some time in the future.[57]

He was right. That wave is now cresting, with the cult of the wounded inner child. Its message: Be kind to yourself, for you have been so terribly wounded in life. Surround yourself with stuffed animals. Allow yourself to feel enormous self-pity. One of the Survivors I interviewed told me, with awe and tenderness, how she had literally fallen in love with herself in a mirror. Her story is worth quoting at length:

> I was real upset one day because of a love affair that wasn't working out, and I was so tired of having this happen to me. I was 46 years old and just utterly tired of having it not work out, you know, and I was crying really hard, and finally I started thinking, 'It's just not worth it, I don't ever want to go through this again. I'll do without love affairs, or I'll find a way to be in love by myself. That's it! I'll find a way to be in love *all by myself*.' And I was pounding the bed, angry.
>
> Then the crying stopped, and all of a sudden, I looked at myself in the mirror, like trying to check out my reality. And for the first time in my life, the eyes were real. Always before it was like looking at a photograph in a magazine when I looked in the mirror, or just looking *at* my eyes, never *into* my eyes. This I knew was me, because that was what I was demanding, a way to be in love all by myself. And here was this real person looking back at me from the mirror, and I really did *love*. I know this sounds really ridiculous, but I acted like a little tiny kid, like a two-year-old with a baby, touching the face and the mouth, coming closer and going farther away, just *love*, an exploration with myself in the mirror. And I was giggly and it was wonderful, just wonderful! So for about 48 hours I was constantly running to the mirror to be sure I was still there. Constantly. And for weeks, this was the most exciting thing that ever happened to me. It was like your average person falling in love.

By quoting this passage, I do not intend to mock the very real grief Frieda obviously felt. Like many of us, she has suffered isolation, loneliness, depression, unrequited love, disappointment, feelings of abandonment and loss. She has wondered if she will ever feel happy or whole. And it is probably true that you must accept and love yourself before you can love others. Yet there is something very sad about her solution. A year after this experience of falling in love with her image in the mirror, Frieda began to seek out her repressed memories of abuse, ultimately graduating to visualizations of satanic cults. Now, she has found her niche in life, her new religion. She is a Survivor.

Like many such women, Frieda's home has numerous New Age accoutrements: hanging crystals, stuffed unicorns, books on meditation. She talks earnestly about spiritual growth, and she believes in guardian angels. There is nothing wrong with such New Age beliefs, many of which intrigue me, but it is disturbing that the belief in parapsychology and spiritualism – in invisible powers – seems so closely allied to the Survivor Movement and *its* invisible memories.*[58] There is a chapter entitled 'Spirituality' in *The Courage to Heal*, a book whose title itself sounds soothing and positive, even though the book is full of bile. Bass and Davis wax quite lyrical: 'There's a part of everything that wants to become itself – the tadpole into the frog, the chrysalis into the butterfly, a damaged human being into a whole one. And that's spirituality: staying in touch with the part of you that is choosing to heal, that wants to be healthy, integrated, fully alive.'[59]

It sounds so peaceful, so seductive. Yet the mental state that the Survivor Movement really produces is the precise opposite. Rather than becoming healthy, integrated, and fully alive, its members routinely become ill, fragmented, and suicidal. They don't eat or sleep. They experience repeated panic attacks. They become convinced that they are not even themselves, but a conglomeration of other wounded beings, multiple personalities. They are led to wound themselves not only psychically but literally, cutting or burning their own flesh.

But why would anyone willingly undergo such horrors, winding up in a locked ward in a psychiatric unit? The creed of the Movement explains it all, of course, as part of the slow healing process. 'You have to get worse before you get better.' The panic attacks, the sleepless

---

* A 1993 *Time* poll indicated that 69 per cent of Americans believe in angels, and 46 per cent believe they have their own guardian angel. This widespread faith may be harmless and comforting, but its flip side is not. A 1990 survey indicated that 60 per cent of Americans believe in the existence of the Devil, up from 37 per cent in 1964. Also, the surge of interest in angels may not be quite so harmless as it appears. A California minister, for instance, calls on angel power to help his clients work out 'unresolved traumas.' This sounds alarmingly familiar.

nights, the self-hurt – all stem from the terrible sexual abuse experiences of your stolen childhood. Everything can be blamed on the evil Perpetrator. It isn't a surprise that you are feeling so awful, that you want to hurt yourself. You were systematically taught to blame yourself for the incest. The wonder is that you have remained alive at all!

BRADSHAW: THE EVANGELIST OF DYSFUNCTION

If Ellen Bass has written the scriptural text that fomented the Survivor Movement, John Bradshaw has served as her John the Baptist, a voice crying in the wilderness, preparing the way, telling us that we are all abused children from dysfunctional families, whether we were literally victims of incest or not – but if we can come up with incest memories, all the better. Bradshaw informed *Lear's* readers in 1992 that 60 per cent of all incest memories are repressed. 'Victims have often cited the smell of chlorine bleach and the sight of toothpaste as provoking memories of childhood exposure to ejaculate,' he explained. 'Accept the *theory* that you were sexually abused,' he advised, 'live consciously with that idea for six months . . . and see whether any memories come to you.'[60]

Although his books have been enormously influential, you have to attend a Bradshaw lecture to appreciate the power of this Recovery Movement guru. As journalist Emily Mitchell writes, 'Bradshaw has a high-octane style that is too big for the TV screen. On stage, he is commanding and works a room like a pro. Cordless mike in hand, he is a stand-up psychologist, slinging one-liners or deepening his voice to repeat self-pitying monologues.'[61]

She hardly does him justice. Bradshaw, now in his early 60s, lived in a monastery for years, quitting the day before his ordination. Even after that, he went back to school for degrees in psychology and religion. Despite evident bitterness at organized religion, Bradshaw, a reformed alcoholic, still calls himself a theologian. He also collects wizard figurines with which he may well identify.[62]

You don't need to know any of this background, however, to identify his approach as psychological evangelism. You simply need to listen, swept up by his earnest Houston twang. He speaks in staccato cadences, with the urgent intensity of Billy Graham in his glory years. The words spill forth, the italics and exclamation points practically visible in the air. He repeats the same key buzzwords, the same phrases – *shame*, *dysfunctional family, abandonment, abuse* – hammering them hypnotically home. Nearly every sentence ends with an upward keen, bringing audiences to the edges of their seats with tense anticipation. Everything Bradshaw says seems to be *terribly* important. He is conveying a message of salvation. He has discovered the Truth. Every now and then, he throws in some self-deprecatory humor, but mostly, he whips up emotions – notably grief and rage.

Bradshaw, apparently, doesn't want you to think. Indeed, there is a decidedly anti-intellectual slant to the Survivor Movement. Feelings are superior to rationality. 'Staying in your head's a way to cut off your heart,' he intones. 'We've gotta feel as bad as we really feel. Because feelings *move* you. I am *moved* to *tears* by my sadness. I am moved to do something about it by my anger. My anger is my *power*. The Incredible Hulk phenomenon. When I'm angry, I have my power. When I'm sad, I cry and I ventilate and I heal. Grieving is a healing feeling. When I'm afraid, I'm wise and discerning. If I don't ever feel as bad as I feel, I won't change. I'll go to my death never having known who I was. So you've gotta feel as bad as you feel.'[63]

No one in the audience stops to analyze the words. Like any effective evangelist, Bradshaw knows how to build emotion. Now, like the old-time tent preacher, he practically invites people to come down the aisle and be saved. 'Hey! A night like this can do it. You can be confronted enough tonight in your delusion and denial. You see, as children are abused and abandoned, they do something really strange. They idealize their parents.' Consequently, people can begin to heal when they recognize the Truth and give up the 'mirage in the desert of their family,' the myth that Mom and Dad really loved them. Unless they can do this, they will continue with their 'spiritual bankruptcy,' he asserts. 'There's no kingdom within. Codependency is a conflict of gods.'

If you're not sure you have enough dysfunction to warrant attention and salvation, don't worry. 'It's so widespread, this cultural dysfunctionality,' Bradshaw assures his audience, 'that *everybody* is able to identify and say, hey, we're *all* – kind of like the old church – we're *all* sinners. We're *all* sinners and we *all* need help. We *all* need salvation. See, and then we can come together as a family. And it does my heart good to look around and to know I'm not alone.' In a moment of utter honesty, Bradshaw revels in the powerful religious ecstasy. 'It's *wonderful* to get this kind of energy. It's almost like I feel the energy of a movement in this room. It's exhilarating to be here. So you see some of my self-worth is coming from your faces.'

538

'The first step in recovery,' Bradshaw continues, 'is to break down these denials and go find what I call a family of choice. Find a new family of choice, some place where you can go and you won't feel shamed.' Here it comes, the appeal to community, as the real parents and siblings are jettisoned. 'So the process of healing will probably mean *leaving* that family of origin, that closed system, that relationship that's destructive to you, going into a group where you can be accepted just for the very one you are. You know, where you share your crud and they *love* on you! I mean, in these groups, you go and tell them all this *crud* and they tell you they love you! And they accept you and listen to you.'

Bradshaw's message is seductive. In the unnatural world of the support group, you can whine about your troubles and everyone will not only listen, they'll *encourage* you. The more feeling, the more anger, the more tears, the better. 'You see, it's like a new family, with new rules. Everybody's equal here, everybody's a sinner here, there's nobody better than anybody else. We're all equally screwed up. We all have a common problem. And there's something that's so *healing* in that.' Exactly what is so healing about feeling so screwed up he does not bother to explain, but rushes onward. 'You know, we need some Adult Children of Dysfunctional Families groups,' Bradshaw says. 'Start one, start a movement!'

In the hierarchy of abuse, Bradshaw makes it quite clear that sexual abuse qualifies the victim for the most pity, the most love, the most rage. He doesn't spend much time on it, just enough to point listeners in the right direction. 'An incest victim will depersonalize. She'll dissociate, she'll be up on the ceiling somewhere, or she'll see monsters in the hall instead of Daddy coming in the room. That's the way that nature allows us to survive this. But what happens 35 years later? You see, we've got to know what happened to us. You can't change what's real. So you have to make the abandonment real.'

At the end of his lecture, Bradshaw becomes more overtly religious as he rhapsodizes about the child within. 'You've got to embrace yourself and love yourself. You're the only one that you'll never lose or leave.' Does this sound familiar? Shades of Frieda, who probably got the idea from Bradshaw. 'So it's crucial work. You know, as the Bible says, unless you become as children, you cannot enter the Kingdom.' He goes on to suggest that 'you accept your powerlessness, you embrace your shame, and you turn to something greater than yourself. And you pray and you meditate and do what all those spiritual masters said.' Then he wanders off into a pseudoscientific New Age sideline, expressing his belief in 'morphic resonance' and 'remote viewing ESP experiences' in which 'people can know what they're gonna see two hours later.' Finally, he ascends to his platitudinous peak: 'So at some level of higher consciousness, we are all one. When we get out of limited socioculturally conditioned ego, narrowed consciousness, the flashlight self as opposed to the spotlight self.'

Before sending people – agitated, angry, and uplifted – into the night, Bradshaw brings it all back to his main theme. 'We're on a journey, a beautiful journey, an exciting journey. And thank God there's some brothers and sisters on the journey, because I wouldn't want to be on the journey alone. So go ahead and love that little kid in you. 'Cause they've been hiding in that closet for years. And they really want to come out. And if you stay in your idealization and your delusion and your denial and your-family-was-really-okay-and-nothing-really-happened-to-you, then nothing's really going to happen to you. Go read the Psalms or the Scriptures or any of the religious literature. The call is always that I love you, I think about you every day. I will always be faithful to you no matter what. May God bless you all.'*64

SAVING THE WORLD

As disturbing as Bradshaw may be, he is merely a popular synthesizer for the Recovery Movement. 'Bradshaw is a Geiger counter, a loudspeaker for what a million people are doing and saying,' Andrew Meacham told me. Meacham, a former editor of *Changes Magazine*, a Health Communications publication, is intimately acquainted with the self-help movement and knows Bradshaw personally. 'He's not even the primary messenger, just the person who has honed the presentation to a fine art.'65 Nonetheless, it is disconcerting that Bradshaw has become the

---

* Bradshaw's latest book, *Family Secrets*, continues to promote his dogma that most families hide evil abusers, though he at least acknowledges the possibility of illusory memories. His message is being received a bit more skeptically now, though. For example, an interviewer for *New Age Journal* couldn't swallow Bradshaw's self-pitying assertion that 'I was having the shit abused out of me' because he was a straight-A student and president of his class merely to please his mother. 'Do you mean to say that every good thing you did as a kid was the result of dysfunction?' she asked incredulously. 'That your childhood was a total washout?'

darling of Hollywood liberals. His specials have been aired prominently on American educational television as part of fund-raising efforts. What other televangelist could have attained such mainstream acceptance?

Bradshaw's brand of evangelism has helped to promote the more virulent religion of the Incest Survivor Movement. It is no accident that the 'Christian counselors' tend to be the worst kind of suggestive therapists, encouraging memories of satanic ritual abuse. There is a crusading aspect of the trauma therapists who unearth these memories. They call themselves 'witnesses' and repeatedly talk about the need to 'believe.' Many who choose the helping professions do so because they genuinely want to save the world. Given the complexity of real mental troubles, which are often intractable, it must be very frustrating for a minister or therapist to listen to problems without being able to offer a simple solution. The uncovering of previously unknown memories provides an exciting way to really help. In addition, it has a mysterious spiritual component, delving within the psyche to heal the ravaged soul.

Similarly, there is a religious aspect for the Survivors as well. The therapists may be the priests, but the Survivors are the movement's acolytes, its martyrs, its devotees, and often its prophets. For many of the women I interviewed, the hunt for memories has become an exciting spiritual adventure. Those who haven't 'gotten their memories yet' feel left out. They haven't passed through the required initiation rite. True, they may have a vague feeling that they were abused, but they haven't experienced the Pentecostal moment, the flashback, the abreaction, the screaming, the delicious horror. When they achieve this *kairos* moment, they are finally true inductees into Survivorship. Not only that, but if they manage to graduate to the status of multiple personalities, they can commune with their godlike 'inner self-helpers' and develop extraordinary clairvoyant powers.

SURVIVORSHIP AS SECT

Some have called the Survivor Movement not only a religion, but a cult. I am uncomfortable with that word and all that it implies. It is all too easy to label any fervent group a 'cult,' with all of its negative connotations. I prefer the word 'sect' for most cases. There is no question, however, that some self-contained psychotherapy groups qualify for the term 'cult.' Take, for instance, the counseling center run by Doranda Blevins in Chesterfield, Missouri. Blevins isolates her young female wards from their families and friends, controls what they read and hear, helps them recover repressed memories of incest, and screams at them for hours in confrontation sessions. Her center is guarded by a pit bull.[66]

Similarly, Genesis Associates, a Philadelphia therapy center run by Pat Mansmann and Pat Neuhausel, espouses 'detachment' from family as its primary therapeutic modality. Most clients are diagnosed as 'people addicts' who also must uncover hidden memories of sexual abuse. Husbands and wives are told to 'detach' from one another as well. Control rests completely with the therapists.[67]

Doranda Blevins and Genesis Associates are extreme examples, but even run-of-the-mill recovered memory therapy, conducted one-on-one in a private therapy setting, shares certain characteristics with a cult. I found a great deal of insight in *Combatting Cult Mind Control*, by Steven Hassan, an ex-Moonie, licensed therapist, and exit counselor who helps people to leave what he terms destructive cults. As I read Hassan's book, I was struck by the remarkable similarities between Survivors and many of the general characteristics he ticked off.*[68]

This form of cult-like thinking is 'a *system* of influences that disrupts an individual's identity (beliefs, behavior, thinking, and emotions) and replaces it with a new identity,' writes Hassan.[69] Certainly, that is what has happened to many who have recovered 'memories.' They are no longer someone's daughters; they are Survivors. Hassan points out that in many such religions, new inductees are literally renamed and given new identities. Patty Hearst, for instance, became Tania the Revolutionary. Similarly, books such as *The Courage to Heal* and *Secret Survivors* encourage those who have recovered memories of abuse to change their names, assuming a new label completely separate from the perpetrating father.[70]

Hassan believes that hypnotism can be used to rewrite the past, creating a 'fantasy world that can be used to enslave us.' He notes that many sects tell their members to 'become like little children' – just as the Incest

---

* Hassan's observations are not original. He has synthesized and popularized the theories of many sociologists such as Robert Jay Lifton, Margaret Singer, J. Gordon Melton, and Thomas Robbins. Hassan's use of the phrase 'mind control,' which implies some Zvengali-like power over people, is unfortunate. I prefer Lifton's concept of 'thought reform,' Lowell Streiker's nomenclature of 'mind bending' in his book of the same name, or Robbins' description of 'ideological totalism.'

Survivor Movement encourages its members to become psychological infants, identifying with their 'inner child.'[71]

Self-enclosed sects encourage a complete dependence on a figure of authority. For the Survivor Movement, that figure is usually the therapist, or a book. As we have seen, many Survivors are totally dependent on their therapists, unable to make the smallest decision without consulting them. Most of the therapists appear to be convinced that they are on an important, nigh-holy mission. Recovered memory guru E. Sue Blume, for instance, writes earnestly of those who are 'driven by conscience and courage to relinquish the safety of their silence,' and likens herself to the lone protestor facing the tanks in Tiananmen Square.[72] That fits Hassan's general observations: 'They believe that what they are doing is truly beneficial for you. However, they want something more valuable than your money. They want your mind! Of course, they'll take your money, too, eventually.'[73] Similarly, trauma therapy guarantees a protracted period of recovery and, hence, a steady income.

People are most often recruited into such belief systems at a *vulnerable time of stress in their lives*,' Hassan emphasizes. 'The stress is often due to some kind of major transition: moving to a new town, starting a new job, breaking off a relationship, experiencing financial instability, or losing a loved one.'[74] For quite a few of my interview subjects, that generalization appears to have been true. For some, the triggering stress involves the transition from adolescence to adulthood – moving far away, going to college, finding an independent adult persona. For others, it may be marital stress, job difficulties, postpartum depression, the death of a parent, or even the onset of menopause.

The process of induction into a sect involves learning as much as possible about the potential recruit – 'his hopes, dreams, fears, relationships, job, interests. The more information the recruiter can elicit, the greater his chance of manipulating the person. The recruiter strategically plans how to bring him step by step into the group,' Hassan writes. The 'recruiter,' in our case, is the therapist – and what better person to elicit all of this information! That's the whole point of therapy. Then the therapist brings the client 'step by step' into the sect by telling the potential recruit that these memories come slowly, that this is a gradual process. Whenever she expresses doubts, the therapist assures her that this is a normal process of denial, and it will pass as she becomes more convinced of her memories.

Another universal characteristic of such groups is black-and-white thinking. Everyone is either good or bad, a victim or a perpetrator.

You either believe, or you're in denial. All communication outside the religion's belief system is cut off. Members are programmed automatically to plug any breaches in that fortress, the self-contained world view.

Typically, a specialized vocabulary, usually with religious overtones, helps solidify member participation. Thus, many therapists call themselves 'witnesses' and repeatedly speak of the need to 'believe your memories.' They 'validate' the feelings. All family members are either 'perpetrators,' 'enablers,' or 'victims.' Like most jargon, these words and phrases become an ingrained way of looking at the world. By labeling something, you often make it reality. Insidiously, the Survivor Movement's pet buzzwords have entered the vocabulary of accused parents. They often find themselves talking about denial or validation, perpetrators and victims. (*The therapists are in denial about what they are doing. The parents are victims of a witchhunt. It is so validating to hear other parents' stories.*') They sometimes become mirror images of their accusing children.

Many groups, according to Hassan, resort to pseudoscientific claims. The entire psychoanalytic movement was founded, as we have seen in Chapter 10, on pseudoscience. Freud and his followers established a mythology of the mind that strove to imitate the medical advances of the time. The concepts of repression and dissociation have never been scientifically demonstrated, however, and tossing around words such as 'abreaction' or 'endogenous opiates' does not make manufactured memories any more factual.

Most groups create a mechanism to keep members from straying. 'Fear is used to bind the group members,' Hassan writes. For one thing, there is usually an outside 'enemy' who is persecuting you. In addition, however, the group keeps members off balance, 'foster[ing] a feeling of dependency and helplessness . . . People are made to have a panic reaction at the thought of leaving [the sect]. They are told that if they leave they will be lost and defenseless in the face of dark horrors: they'll go insane, be killed, become drug addicts, or commit suicide.'[75] Does this sound familiar? Incest Survivors are convinced that if they don't remain in therapy and deal with these memories, their lives will be ruined, they'll go insane. The ritual abuse therapists assure their clients that they have been 'programmed' by the satanic cult to return to it. Only by staying in therapy will they be safe.

Most destructive sects bombard their inductees, Hassan asserts, with the notion that 'they are badly flawed – incompetent, mentally ill, or spiritually fallen. Any problems that are important to the person, such as doing poorly in school or on the job, being overweight, or having trouble in a relationship, are blown out of proportion to prove how completely messed up the person is.'[76] How much more 'badly flawed' can you get than to be the victim of repeated sexual abuse in your childhood? The Survivor Movement zeroes in on incest as *the* central issue in people's lives that 'explains' why they are unhappy, have troubled relationships, or eat too much.

Finally, Hassan comes to the crux of the matter. When I read this passage, I was astonished by its applicability to those who have recovered 'memories':

> An individual's memory becomes distorted, minimizing the good things in the past and maximizing the sins, the failings, the hurts, the guilt. Special talents, interests, hobbies, friends, and family must be abandoned . . . The group now forms the member's 'true' family; any other is just his outmoded 'physical family.' Some cults insist on a very literal transfer of family loyalty . . . The member's past is rewritten. He tends to look back at his previous life with a distorted memory that colors everything dark. Even very positive memories are skewed toward the bad.[77]

First, they strip you of your real family, your real past. Then, in the midst of the confusion, hurt, and pain, they give you a new family – your 12-step group, your fellow Survivors, those who share your anguish. 'One of the most attractive qualities of cult life is the sense of community that it fosters,' Hassan observes.[78] Indeed, the sisterhood of victimhood is powerful, and there is a real sense of bonding and community.

So close can this bond become, and so paranoid the threat of contact by grieving parents, that some 'incest survivors' have been deliberately spirited away and hidden by cult-like support groups. In a state of total panic, others with recovered memories have literally abandoned their normal lives – complete with house, possessions, and automobiles – and fled, who knows where.

SEEING CULTS EVERYWHERE

As insightful and compelling as Hassan's book is, however, I have come to have doubts about cult exit counseling, particularly since it is a descendant of 'deprogramming,' which sometimes refers to an illegal

545

use of force. Hassan disavows the kidnapping and deprogramming that once freed him from the Moonies, however, and says that he has not participated in such activities since 1977. His *modus operandi*, as described in his book, is simply to get the group member to listen to an alternative point of view, usually for several days. To gain entree, he uses a neutral friend or acquaintance, and he also brings an ex-member of the particular group, someone who knows all the feelings and the jargon.

Hassan claims a very high success rate with cult members who agree to listen to him for several days, though that does not count cases in which they run at the first sign of an 'intervention.' Families must be fairly desperate and well-heeled before hiring Hassan, who makes no guarantees and charges $150 an hour. 'That's a lot less than some psychiatrists charge,' he points out, 'and they don't travel.'

More troubling, however, is Hassan's unquestioning belief in 'massive repression.' I discovered his attitude the hard way, when I arranged for him to give a one-day seminar to a group of accused parents. It became clear over the course of the day that he has severely conflicting feelings about this issue. Yes, he thinks that some therapists overstep their bounds and lead their clients into false memories. His consciousness was raised when his own sister went to a therapist and was told at her first session that she probably harbored repressed memories. On the other hand, he informed the group that people often repressed memories of years of abuse. He presented this not as an opinion, but as scientific fact.

Later, I asked Hassan for any specific cases that would prove the reality of massive repression. He referred me to Colin Ross, the notorious 'expert' on multiple personality and ritual abuse who believes the CIA is programming Manchurian candidate MPDs (*see Chapter 4*).*

Thus cued, I asked Hassan if he believed in satanic ritual abuse cults. He did, though he now disavows a belief in an international satanic conspiracy. Still, when Survivors come up to him after a speech to tell him about their recovered memories, in which their parents killed their little siblings and roasted them in satanic rituals, he doesn't dispute them. He just shrugs.**[79] Consequently, when one of the ritual abuse

---

* I did call Colin Ross, but I never got through to him. His secretary called back and referred me to the Linda Williams study described in Chapter 4.

** Hassan recently wrote to me: 'I also often ask them if they have cut off from their families, and if they have, I tell them that I believe in using professionals to build bridges to family members and not cut them off in a wholesale fashion. I tell them that unless they are making noticeable improvement in the course of therapy to get another opinion. What is most important is the present and the future, not the past. And if they are open to it, I tell them about false memory syndrome.'

Survivors I interviewed began telling me all about 'mind control' and the strobe lights that were used to 'program' her as an infant, I was disturbed. The pseudonymous Elizabeth Rose quoted from Hassan's book in her 1993 *Ms.* magazine article in which she claimed to be a ritual abuse survivor. Hassan's *Combatting Cult Mind Control* is, in fact, listed as a recommended resource in the second edition of *The Courage to Heal*, under the heading 'Ritual and Cult Abuse.' On the other hand, Hassan's book has also been praised in retractor newsletters – surely one of the few works to appeal to those on both sides of this debate.

My reservations about Hassan's belief in repression are symptomatic of a problem that threatens to discredit the entire anti-cult movement. The 'academic arm' of this movement is the American Family Foundation (AFF), which publishes *Cultic Studies Journal*. On its editorial advisory board sits Susan Kelley, the pediatric nurse (now a professor at Georgia State University) who coercively interviewed the Fells Acres Day Care children and who has maintained a firm belief in ritual abuse cults (*See chapter 9*).[80] In 1993, Michael Langone, the editor of *Cultic Studies Journal*, edited a book entitled *Recovery From Cults*.[81] In it – you guessed it – is an article by Susan Kelley called 'Ritualistic Abuse of Children in Day-Care Centers.'*[82]

In late 1995, I wrote to Michael Langone, begging him to disavow a belief in mythical ritual abuse cults and to remove Susan Kelley from his board. 'Save your organization further embarrassment,' I wrote, 'by coming out *strongly and clearly* with a statement about so-called satanic ritual abuse cults.' He wrote back, declining to 'denounce colleagues simply because some people think they have made grievous errors.'[83] Apparently Langone, too, buys much of the ritual abuse scenario. In a 1992 article, he stated, 'ritualistic abuse clearly exists.'[84] He co-authored a 1990 book with Linda Blood entitled *Satanism and Occult-Related Violence*. Blood, the former lover of flamboyant 'Temple of Set' leader Michael Aquino, went on to write *The New Satanists* in 1994, explicitly avowing belief in violent multi-generational satanic cults (*See chapter 13*).

* Social psychologist and recovered-memory critic Richard Ofshe served on the AFF board briefly. He quit in 1993, upset by the Kelley article in *Recovery From Cults* as well as what he terms a 'classic lawyer blackmail letter' sent by a prominent AFF member to a parent accused on the basis of recovered memories.

CONSTANT RAGE CAN'T LAST

Despite my reservations about the anti-cult groups, however, I am grateful to Hassan and other experts for their insights into closed-minded
religious sects. Whether you call the Incest Survivor Movement a cult
or not, it most certainly does foster complete dependence on a figure of
authority, rewrites the past, demonizes the family of origin, encourages
black-and-white thinking, and creates a new identity. Ultimately, I am
consoled by another Hassan observation:

> It is extremely important to always keep in mind that he [the sect
> member] has *two* identities . . . One moment the person is speaking
> cultic jargon with a hostile or elitist know-it-all attitude. Then,
> without warning, he seems to become his old self, with his old
> attitudes and mannerisms. Just as suddenly, he flips back to being
> a stranger . . . When John-cultist is talking, his speech is 'robot-
> like' or like a tape recording of a cult lecture. He will speak with
> inappropriate intensity and volume. His posture will typically be
> more rigid, his facial muscles tighter . . . On the other hand, when
> John-John is talking, he will speak with a greater range of emotion.
> He will be more expressive and will share his feelings more will-
> ingly. He will be more spontaneous and may even show a sense
> of humor. His posture and musculature will appear to be looser
> and warmer. Eye contact will be more natural . . . Good experi-
> ences and positive memories rarely disappear entirely . . . Over
> time, the old self exerts itself and seeks out ways to regain its
> freedom. This process is speeded up by positive exposure to non-
> members and the accumulation of bad experiences he has while
> in the group . . . The 'real' self holds the keys to what it will take
> to undo the mind control process.[85]

Perhaps this insight about the difference between the normal and cultic
personality accounts for the startling disparity between pre-therapy and
post-therapy letters from many children. In May of 1987, one father
received this note:

Dear Dad,
Just a note to thank you for taking such good care of me and my
friend during our much-too-short stay. My friend is impressed

548

and a bit envious of the loving relationship and open lines of communication which you and I share . . . I love you and I'm glad you're my dad!

Love, 'D'

A little over two years later, the same daughter sent a letter without salutation:

I am writing this letter for two reasons: (1) to attain closure for myself regarding my relationship with you and (2) in the hope that you will seek help before you hurt anyone else the way you hurt me.

I have spent 37 years of my life denying and minimizing the torture that was my childhood and adolescence . . . I genuinely hope this letter causes you to seek help – you are a very sick man. I do not wish to hear from you unless you are willing to admit the things you did to me and to seek help for your sickness.

'D'[86]

Many parents have commented that their children's accusatory letters don't sound like them at all, but appear impersonal and robotic. The parents wonder whether the therapists actually wrote them. I don't think that is necessarily the case. As Survivors, the children are writing out of their new personae. In one such letter, the accusing daughter *typed* the Survivor part, sounding just like a prosecuting attorney barely controlling her rage. Then, in a handwritten postscript, she reverted to her real self, almost a still, small inner voice trying to come out, saying that she loved her father and to have patience, that this was a necessary process. Accused parents simply have to hold on to the conviction that somewhere deep inside, buried underneath all of the rage and hurt of Survivors, their real children remember the good times, the love, the laughter and the joy.

Ultimately, I don't think that keeping people in a constant state of upheaval and anger works. Geertz, the anthropologist of religion, talks about *long-lasting* moods and motivations. I agree with Hassan that love is stronger than hatred, truth is more durable than fiction, tenderness can eventually replace rage. Staying angry all the time is self-destructive. It isn't the natural human state, thank God. Some day, I believe that this particularly virulent form of pseudoreligion will pass away.

CHAPTER THIRTEEN

Conclusions and Recommendations

All hatred driven hence
The soul recovers radical innocence
And learns at last that it is self-delighting,
Self-appeasing, self-affrighting.

WILLIAM BUTLER YEATS,
A Prayer for My Daughter

I would like to think that the repressed-memory craze has already crested and will quickly disappear. There has certainly been a great deal of publicity about the issue, much of it fomented by the False Memory Syndrome Foundation and its Commonwealth counterparts, but more by the sheer scope of the problem, which is only beginning to become apparent. *Time* and *U.S. News & World Report* ran simultaneous cover stories on the debate late in November of 1993. Skeptical British stories on recovered memory have appeared in the *Observer*, the *Sunday Times*, the *Daily Telegraph*, the *Independent*, and the *Mail on Sunday*. BBC television and radio programs have highlighted the issue. Various retractors, flanked by professional critics Elizabeth Loftus, Michael Yapko, or Richard Ofshe, have appeared on American talk-show programs. Only two years ago, few people in the media or the public questioned the horrifying stories that self-proclaimed incest survivors told, nor did they differentiate memories that had *always* been there from those that were newly 'discovered.' Today, most people realize that the validity of repressed memory is a hotly debated topic.

Several high-profile cases have contributed to public awareness. In November of 1993, Steven Cook accused Cardinal Joseph Bernardin of having sexually abused him when he was a teenager. He recalled the abuse through hypnosis. Months later, Cook dropped his lawsuit, explaining that he now realized how questionable hypnotically induced memories could be.[1] (His unlicensed hypnotist, Michele Moul, had earned her master's in psychology from an unaccredited weekend insti-

tution and had previously been employed in a print shop and delica-
tessen.)[2]

Also emblematic of the changing public attitude is the 1994 California
decision in the Holly Ramona case, in which 12 jurors found two therapists guilty of misleading a young woman through the use of sodium
Amytal and other suggestive techniques and assumptions.[3] In other lawsuits, angry retractors are suing their former therapists for encouraging
them to believe in repressed memories, multiple personalities, and/
or satanic cult involvement. These court proceedings, in which some
therapists face as many as six separate suits from as many clients, are
bringing into public scrutiny the outrageous paranoid delusions that
passed for therapy until recently. Among those being sued are Houston's
Judith Peterson, Chicago's Bennett Braun, and Minneapolis' Diane
Humenansky. In the first of these suits to go to trial in 1995, in which
Vynnette Hamanne sued Humenansky, the therapist was found guilty
of inducing memories of satanic ritual abuse and fined $2.6 million.[4]
In England, a father committed for trial in 1993 on the basis of his
adult daughter's recovered memories of sexual abuse was finally
cleared in 1995. In its decision, the Teesside Crown Court criticized
the Crown Prosecution Service for proceeding with the case in the first
place.[5]

Meanwhile, several appeals courts have gotten the message from
researchers such as Stephen Ceci and Maggie Bruck that little children
can be led into stating and believing the most outrageous falsehoods.
Robert Kelly has been freed from jail in the North Carolina Little
Rascals Day Care case, Violet Amirault and Cheryl LeFave are out of
jail in the Massachusetts Fells Acres case, while in Canada most
of the Martensville defendants have been exonerated. In my own state
of Vermont, the conviction of Robert Lawton, accused of sodomizing
his three young sons, has been overturned, and a new trial ordered.

Perhaps the most important ruling came in 1995 from Judge William
J. Groff in New Hampshire. Groff insisted on a pretrial hearing before
allowing cases based solely on recovered memories to go forward. One
case involved a woman who believed her father had raped her throughout her childhood, right up until two days before her wedding at the
age of 23. The other featured a woman who believed her eighth grade
teacher had impregnated her when she was 12 – even though she did not
begin menstruating until she was 14. After hearing scientific testimony,
Groff ruled: 'The phenomenon of memory repression, and the process of
therapy used in these cases to recover the memories, have not gained

general acceptance in the field of psychology and are not scientifically reliable.' The judge was even more outspoken later in his opinion:

> The very concept of a 'repressed' memory, that is, that a person can experience a traumatic event, and have no memory of it whatsoever for several years, transcends human experience. There is nothing in our development as human beings which enables us to empirically accept the phenomenon ... It is inappropriately suggestive for a therapist to communicate to a client his or her belief that a dream or a flashback is a representation of a real life event, that a physical pain is a 'body memory' of sexual abuse, or even that a particular memory recovered by a client is in fact a real event ... [Such therapy] thoroughly and schematically violates the guidelines and standards of the practice of psychotherapy.[6]

Despite such unequivocal legal judgments, however, it is unlikely that the sex abuse hysteria phenomenon will disappear quite so quickly. In 1992, Johns Hopkins psychiatrist Paul McHugh published an interesting article called 'Psychiatric Misadventures' in *The American Scholar*. 'During the thirty years of my professional experience,' he wrote, 'I have witnessed the power of cultural fashion to lead psychiatric thought and practice off in false, even disastrous, directions.' He noted that these fads – the notion that schizophrenia was culturally induced, the popularity of sex-change operations, and the proliferation of multiple personalities – seemed to last about ten years.[7] If he is correct, the hunt for repressed memories will probably extend until near the turn of the century, since it began in earnest in 1988 with the publication of *The Courage to Heal*.

Even then, I doubt it will die out completely. Once an idea enters the cultural mainstream, it has a way of resurfacing like a bloated corpse every few years. Ever since Freud applied his 'pressure procedure' to extract repressed memories of incest, psychologists have periodically imitated the Viennese master. Soon after the turn of the century, Morton Prince hypnotized Christine Beauchamp to 'uncover' her multiple personalities, while Boris Sidis and J. E. Donley also used hypnotism to promote 'abreactions.'[8] In the wake of World War I, there was another spate of traumatic reliving in trance. In the 1920s, 'hypnoidalization' was proposed to unearth memories, while Otto Rank convinced his followers that only by reliving the birth trauma could they be healed.[9] Sandor Ferenczi unearthed hidden memories of abuse in the 1930s, while American and British therapists were simultaneously inventing 'narco-analysis,' using barbiturates to facilitate the recovery of supposedly repressed memories.[10]

During the 1940s, psychiatrists encouraged World War II veterans to 'abreact' traumatic memories while under sodium Pentothal or hypnosis. As a result, one soldier acted out the entire battle of Iwo Jima, even though he had never left the United States. In 1944, prison psychologist Robert Lindner published *Rebel Without a Cause** (made into a film in 1955), his account of how he regressed a 'criminal psychopath' to six months old, when he 'remembered' being traumatized by watching his parents engage in sexual intercourse.[11] And we have seen in Chapter 11 how Arthur Janov and others kept the idea alive in the United States throughout the 1960s and 1970s. Consequently, I would be surprised if the search for repressed memories completely disappeared.

Indeed, if recent developments are any indication, accusations based on rediscovered memories continue to sell books and fill the courts. Even though stories of satanic ritual abuse have been thoroughly discredited, a mass market paperback called *The New Satanists* came out in 1994. Author Linda Blood solemnly writes: 'There are thousands of women who report having been childhood victims of mind-numbingly vicious and brutal forms of physical and mental torture at the hands of members of their families. They tell of having been subjected to every conceivable abuse as well as some that would be inconceivable to any normal human being.'[12]

The same year, *Treating Survivors of Satanist Abuse*, edited by Tavistock Clinic consultant child psychotherapist Valerie Sinason, was published. British taxpayers continue to fund Sinason's 'research' into mythical ritual abuse. In 1995, Lavinia Gomez, a therapist heading the Minster Centre for Integrative Psychotherapy and Counselling in London, published an article in the journal *Counselling* in which she repeated all the stereotypical horror stories. 'Children may be forced from infancy to drink blood or urine and eat shit,' Gomez wrote. 'In rituals they may be buried, sewn inside animal corpses to be "reborn to Satan," and raped by groups of adults. They may be physically tortured and forced to participate in the abuse, torture and possibly killing of animals, children and adults, perhaps with cannibalism.'[13] A 1996 conference of the British chapter of the International Society for the

---

* In their introduction to *Rebel Without a Cause*, psychologists Sheldon and Eleanor Glueck dismissed 'such outworn notions as "guilt," "criminal intent," [or] "knowledge of right and wrong,"' thereby paving the way for the current wave of victimology and abnegation of responsibility.

Study of Dissociation featured speakers who espouse belief in recovered memories such as Madge Bray, Maureen Davies, and Sue Richardson, along with high-powered American imports such as Bessel van der Kolk and Joy Silberg from Sheppard-Pratt. Consequently, it is quite clear that this type of misguided therapy will not disappear from either side of the Atlantic any time soon.

In fact, it appears to be spreading. 'Until recently,' wrote an Australian psychiatrist late in 1995, 'it was held that FMS was largely an American phenomenon and that our sensible, empirical approach would prevent any such problem. Well, think again.' He observed that in his home town of Wollongong, 'a self-proclaimed therapist ... lives in a house with something like five women, whom she claims need her there to protect them from their various personalities.' Recovered memory therapy has made inroads in Ireland, France, Germany, Switzerland, Belgium, the Scandinavian countries, Israel, and South Africa.[14]

As late as the fall of 1995, a publication issued by the Institute of Pennsylvania Hospital included this familiar, dangerous misinformation:

There are all sorts of therapeutic techniques to aid in recon-structing the trauma story. These include hypnosis, group therapy and psychodrama, as well as biological methods, such as sodium Amytal ... However, traumatic memories may not be accessible by language since they are sometimes recorded in the form of vivid sensations and images.'[15]

Also in 1995, Sage Publications came out with *A Survivor's Guide*, by Washington State counselor Sharice Lee, on both sides of the Atlantic. Intended for teenage girls, it is a kind of *Courage to Heal* for adolescents. 'Just because you can't remember some of the things that happened to you doesn't mean that these things are gone from your brain forever,' Lee writes. Appealing to computer-hip teens, she explains that retrieving the memories is similar to playing a PC keyboard: 'It's kind of like a computer program that you have to have an access code to get into.' At first, the returning sex abuse memories will come as 'bits and pieces or small flashes.' They may be 'fuzzy at the beginning.' In time, however, they will begin to 'fit together like a jigsaw puzzle.' In the afterword for therapists, Lee explains that the book should be used as an 'edu-cational tool' in group work, with teenagers reading chapters aloud to see if any memories come up.[16]

The same year, a Texas conference for therapists was held by the

Society for the Investigation, Treatment and Prevention of Ritual and Cult Abuse (SITPRCA). It offered an extremely disturbing mix of ritual abuse stories, CIA conspiracy theories, and militia-group warnings about the New World Order to be imposed by Jews and liberals. One of the speakers, Cathy O'Brian, claimed that the CIA had programmed her to be a multiple personality. She had recovered memories of having sex with assorted American political figures, including George Bush, Ronald Reagan, Jimmy Carter, Gerald Ford, and Hillary Clinton. Another speaker, former FBI agent Ted Gunderson, informed everyone that there were 500 satanic cults in New York City alone, sacrificing 4,000 humans each year. Gunderson, famous for his involvement in the McMartin Day Care case, also has close ties with right-wing militia groups. In fact, he believes that the U.S. government itself bombed the Oklahoma City federal building in order to promote passage of anti-terrorism bills.

What is so frightening about this conference is that most of the audience members appeared to *believe* what they were told, according to Evan Harrington, a skeptical psychologist in attendance. Indeed, when he raised the slightest doubts, he was treated as a pariah. 'I frequently observed a categorical rejection of the possibility that there could be false memories of traumatic events,' he writes. 'Strong beliefs are highly resistant to discrepant input and they do have a certain persuasive power.' Harrington quotes an attending physicist: 'I came away with the opinion that cults are far more prevalent, well connected, sophisticated and dangerous than I had ever dreamed.'[17] A second annual conference of the SITPRCA was planned for the following year.

As 1996 commenced, a caller on the psychological American public radio program, 'Voices in the Family,' informed listeners that in 1990, she had suddenly recalled being molested by her grandfather when she was three. The host and guests were not the least bit skeptical of her 'memories.'[18]

Psychiatrist Gary Almy and his physician wife Carol have written a scathing indictment of current psychological trends – including recovered-memory therapy – in their book, *Addicted to Recovery*. As Christians, they are particularly concerned about the extensive involvement of so-called Christian therapists. The Almys conclude their book with this shrewd appraisal:

Do not expect this psycho-fad to go quietly into the night. This searching of the 'subconscious' and probing the past is ... at the heart of the false memory phenomenon and the multiple personality fad . . . This is the heart and soul of the psychotherapy industry, its major theoretical underpinning and resultant practice pattern. This has come to be economically vital. Entire livelihoods, reputations, and businesses depend on the survival of the recovery industry, and sadly, all too many of these are within the Christian community.[19]

The Almys continued by quoting 2 Timothy 4:3–4: 'For the time will come when men will not put up with sound doctrine. Instead, to suit their own desires, they will gather around them a great number of teachers to say what their itching ears want to hear. They will turn their ears away from the truth and turn aside to myths.' Similarly, the prophet Jeremiah long ago warned against false prophets who 'speak visions from their own minds, not from the mouth of the Lord.' (Jeremiah 23:16)

THE SCOPE OF THE PROBLEM

Just how widespread is the recovered-memory business, though? How many therapists are actively searching for repressed memories, and how many people have 'recovered' them, cut off contact with their families, and become Survivors? So far, more than 17,000 families have contacted the American False Memory Syndrome Foundation, and over 700 British families are in touch with the British False Memory Society, but that number is almost certainly a tiny fraction of the actual cases out there. Most accused parents are probably too frightened and embarrassed to tell anyone about their situations. To obtain a realistic estimate, it is necessary to approach the problem via the therapists.

It should be clear to readers by now that a substantial subset of American and British therapists specialize in helping clients to recall what they believe are repressed memories of sexual abuse. It isn't difficult to spot them, even through ads in the yellow pages. Many specifically solicit 'sexual abuse survivors.' Other tell-tale phrases include *inner child work, dream work, adult child of dysfunctional families, hypnosis,* or *guided imagery.* One of the more notorious therapists, involved in several cases that have come to my attention, has placed an aggressive Yellow Pages ad, featuring a black telephone receiver and a red headline: *'Immediate*

Help.' The highlighted problems and solutions offered include: 'Anxiety and Stress, Sexual Issues, Drugs and Alcohol, Isolation, Survivors of Incest and Abuse, Relaxation Training, Depression, Troubled Relationships, Adult Struggles.' Of course, people *do* sometimes need therapy for depression or 'adult struggles,' but this therapist is likely to explain all such difficulties by uncovering repressed memories.

How many such therapists are there, and how many clients have they infected? Several recent surveys offer disturbing figures. Michael Yapko, a clinical psychologist whose 1994 book, *Suggestions of Abuse*, questions the hunt for repressed memories, gathered data in 1992 from more than 860 American psychotherapists, most of whom were attending national conventions. The average respondent was 44 years old, with education beyond the master's degree level, and had been in clinical practice for more than 11 years. Of these, 40 per cent agreed with the statement: 'I believe that early memories, even from the first years of life, are accurately stored and retrievable,' and about the same percentage thought that if people don't remember much about their childhoods, it is because of traumatic events. Almost 60 per cent thought that any events someone couldn't remember must have been repressed. And 36 per cent agreed that 'if a client believes a memory is true, I must also believe it to be true if I am to help him or her.'

An overwhelming majority (84 per cent) of Yapko's respondents thought that hypnotic age regression was a useful technique. Three-quarters believed that hypnosis enables people to accurately remember forgotten events. Nearly half (47 per cent) believed that 'psychotherapists can have greater faith in details of a traumatic event when obtained hypnotically than otherwise,' while 31 per cent agreed that 'when someone has a memory of a trauma while in hypnosis, it objectively must actually have occurred.' Incredibly, 28 per cent of Yapko's respondents believed that hypnosis could be used to recover accurate memories of *past lives!* Finally, 16 per cent thought that it was *impossible* to implant false memories in a client.[20]

Social psychologist Richard Ofshe has called the belief in satanic ritual abuse the 'Achilles' heel' of the recovered memory movement, since the grotesque memories of murder, cannibalism, and aborted fetuses are so unbelievable and never present any confirming evidence.[21] His point is well-taken. Yet in a huge survey published in 1994, conducted by Gail Goodman and her colleagues, 13 per cent of the nearly 7,000 therapists surveyed had elicited recovered memories of ritual abuse, and these respondents 'overwhelmingly believed' the memories.[22]

A 1993 survey yielded equally disturbing results. Debra A. Poole and D. Stephen Lindsay conducted a random national survey of Ph.D.-level American psychologists with a substantial female client base.[23] Of their 86 respondents, 76 per cent reported that they sometimes used one or more memory recovery techniques, including hypnosis, age regression, dream interpretation, guided imagery, use of family photographs as memory cues, or interpretation of physical symptoms as body memories; 60 per cent reported using two or more of these techniques. Most of those surveyed (85 per cent) said that at least some clients who initially denied any memory of sexual abuse subsequently recalled it during therapy. Some therapists reported that *all* of their clients recovered memories. Over half (52 per cent) claimed that they were sometimes 'fairly certain' after the first session that they were dealing with a repressed-memory case.*[24] A disturbing 43 per cent of their respondents sometimes recommended *The Courage to Heal* to their clients. Only 8 per cent never made quick judgments about sex abuse, used no suggestive techniques, and did not regard memory recovery as an important therapeutic goal.

This survey makes it abundantly clear that the *majority* of American therapists sometimes hunt for repressed memories of sexual abuse, using suggestive techniques to do so. (Indeed, results from another national American survey, published in 1995, indicate that 73 per cent of 378 psychologists surveyed had at least one recovered memory patient.)[25] On the other hand, only a minority appear to *specialize* in recovered-memory work. As an extreme example of such 'memory focused' therapists, Poole and Lindsay describe a clinician who routinely tells her clients that they were probably abused, then leads them in an initial two-hour hypnotic age regression. *All* of her female clients eventually come to recall abuse while in her care. Yet she wrote on her survey sheet that 'it is very important not to lead the hypnotized subject.'

Poole and Lindsay found that 25 per cent of their sample are 'memory focused.'** All of these therapists use two or more memory recovery

---

* Some therapists pride themselves on being able to identify repressed memory cases quickly. 'I can tell within ten minutes, I can spot it as a person walks in the door,' one therapist told a TV talk show host in 1992. Others believe they can pick abuse survivors out of a crowd just by the way they walk or talk.

** One Florida retractor told me recently that she had attempted to locate a good counselor for a friend in Daytona Beach. She called over 100 therapists before finding one who did not recommend *The Courage to Heal* or espouse a belief in recovered memories. Thus, Poole and Lindsay's estimate that only 25 per cent are 'memory-focused' may be conservative.

techniques, think that they can often spot hidden abuse victims after an initial session, and believe it is important for clients to recall the abuse if therapy is to be effective. On average, these therapists saw approximately 50 adult female clients per year and reported that 60 per cent of those who they suspected had repressed memories eventually came to remember abuse.

From this first survey, it was not clear what percentage of *all* female clients recalled memories, so Poole and Lindsay conducted a second survey of 59 therapists early in 1994, rephrasing the question. The results confirmed that 25 per cent of the therapists were memory focused, and that 34 per cent of their clients initially denied any memory of abuse but eventually recalled it while in therapy.*[26] Although Poole and Lindsay emphasize that their limited survey cannot be considered definitive, it provides at least a rough approximation of the extent of recovered memory work in the therapeutic community.

In their second survey, Poole and Lindsay were joined by British colleagues Amima Memon and Ray Bull, who gave the questionnaire to 57 psychologists in the United Kingdom, with similar results – about 25 per cent appeared to be memory focused.

Even more alarming are the results of a British Psychological Society survey of 810 member therapists, published in 1995. The overwhelming majority, 97 per cent, believed in the essential accuracy not only of run-of-the-mill recovered memories, but of satanic ritual abuse reports (over half believed such memories 'sometimes,' over a third 'usually,' and 5 or 6 per cent 'always'). Twenty-three per cent of the respondents had clients who had recalled memories from total amnesia while in therapy with them during the previous year. Thirteen per cent had worked with clients with satanic ritual abuse memories and had believed them. Ten per cent used hypnotic age regression. Unfortunately, the BPS chose to interpret these disturbing results as evidence that most recovered memories were probably accurate: 'Memory recovery is reported by highly experienced and well qualified therapists who are well aware of the dangers of inappropriate suggestion

* In her compelling 1993 series in the *San Francisco Examiner*, reporter Stephanie Salter interviewed Laguna Beach therapist Douglas Sawin, who provides a template for therapists who seek memories. Of his 50 weekly clients – virtually all of whom recovered memories of sexual abuse – Sawin said, 'Not one walked in my office and said, "I'm an incest survivor."' This did not stop him from convincing a young client that her parents had ritually abused her, applying carrots, chicken parts, hoses, and broomsticks to her vagina and anus.

and interpretation.' This assertion was made despite the fact that 33 per cent of the respondents did not believe it was even *possible* to create false memories.[27]

It is surprisingly difficult to arrive at a firm figure for the total number of practicing American psychotherapists, because they encompass psychiatrists, clinical psychologists, social workers, psychiatric nurses, master's-level counselors, and pastoral counselors. Nonetheless, in a recent article in *Common Boundary*, journalist Beth Baker arrived at an estimate of 254,600 practicing licensed U.S. therapists. Her figure is unquestionably low, for a variety of reasons. For example, Baker got her figure of 80,000 practicing social workers from membership figures of the National Association of Social Workers (NASW). But, as an NASW official told me, there is probably an equal number of practicing social workers who have not joined the organization.[28] The same holds true for figures from the American Psychological Association and others. Because of high dues, many therapists simply don't belong.

There are other reasons to suspect that Baker's figure is an underestimate. The country's 13,000 school counselors are not included, for instance, although a number of them have been involved in repressed-memory cases. Moreover, in most states, *anyone* can legally hang up a shingle declaring him- or herself to be a psychotherapist – like Lucy in the *Peanuts* cartoon strip – and unlicensed therapists do not show up in these figures.[29] Nor do the body worker/massage therapists, channelers, or other non-traditional memory-retrieval practitioners.

Nonetheless, let us take Baker's figure and round it *down* to 250,000 therapists. Poole and Lindsay's survey indicated that 25 per cent of doctoral-level therapists are 'memory-focused.' That percentage is likely to be *higher* for social workers or master's-level counselors, who tend to accept the repressed-memory dogma more eagerly than do their Ph.D. colleagues *(see Chapter 5)*. Taking that 25 per cent figure as accurate, however – and ignoring the substantial number of 'recovered memories' that arise outside that core group – *we arrive at 62,500 memory-focused therapists*. Poole and Lindsay found that each therapist saw approximately 50 female clients per year, of whom 34 per cent recovered memories.

Using simple math (62,500 memory-focused therapists × 50 clients × 34 per cent who recover memories), we arrive at *over 1 million cases of 'recovered memories' each year*. Even assuming overlap – some clients return to the same therapist year after year, while others change therapists frequently – it is reasonable to assume that, since the hunt for repressed memories came to full flower in 1988, several million have come to believe they are 'Survivors.'

And that is only an estimate of women who have recovered memories at the hands of hard-core, memory-focused, licensed therapists. It doesn't account for *men* who have recovered memories, or for those who worked with clergy or unlicensed therapists, or those who were influenced outside of therapy by books such as *The Courage to Heal*.

It is even more difficult to arrive at a reasonable estimate of British recovered memory cases, since ascertaining the number of therapists is almost impossible. Glenys Parry, director of Psychological Services at Sheffield Consulting and Clinical Psychologists, has been commissioned to write a report on the effectiveness of various types of psychotherapy for the Department of Health. I wrote to her, asking for help. 'The number of psychotherapists in the U.K. is a difficult figure to arrive at,' she responded. 'The definition of "psychotherapists" is problematic.' She further noted that 'the figure would also differ according to whether the psychotherapist was employed in the public service or in private practice, for there is no legal requirement to register.'[30]

Those calling themselves therapists might join several different British organizations, among which are the British Psychological Society (3,000 members), the U.K. Council for Psychotherapy (3,500), the British Association for Counselling (12,000), and the British Confederation of Psychotherapists (1,600). There are also numerous fringe organizations such as the Association for Psychoanalytic Psychotherapy, the Society for Primary Cause Analysis, the International Association of Hypno-Analysts, the Association of Primal Therapists, or the Association of Curative Hypnotherapists. What these smaller associations lack in numbers they often make up in pseudoscientific pursuit of recovered memories. Since many therapists do not join *any* organization, it is quite clear that there are well over 20,000 British psychotherapists, perhaps twice that number.

Applying the Poole/Lindsay/Memon/Bull figure of 25 per cent, we find that *at least* 5,000 British therapists are likely to specialize in extracting abuse memories. It appears that full-time British counsellors see fewer clients than their American counterparts. I will use a quite conservative estimate of 25 clients per year. Thus, using essentially the same math as before (5,000 memory-focused therapists x 25 clients x 34 per cent who recover memories), we arrive at 42,500 British cases of 'recovered memories' each year. Since this form of therapy became popular in 1990 (when *The Courage to Heal* was published in England), it is reasonable to assume, then, that well over 100,000 cases have been fomented in the United Kingdom since that time.

I realize that such an estimate seems startlingly high, and I certainly hope that it is an overestimate. Because this therapy tends to be long-term, there may be an overlap between years. Some recovered memory therapists undoubtedly only work part-time. Nonetheless, considering the fact that the base figure of a total of 20,000 British therapists is extremely conservative, I think that my estimate, while alarming, is probably accurate.

Why, then, have only 700 families come forward to contact the British False Memory Society? There are several explanations. For one thing, it is likely that most British parents accused of incest by their adult children on the basis of recovered memory therapy are too embarrassed, frightened, and depressed to come forward. They are suffering in silence all over the United Kingdom. It is my hope that this book will help them to understand this phenomenon. Many other families may be unaware of their children's new 'memories' because the accused is dead, the therapist advises against confrontation, the client is unsure of the memories, or the client wants to avoid unpleasant scenes. In fact, these cases may represent the majority. In other cases, the 'memories' involve abuse by non-family members.

In summary, by any conservative analysis of the information available, there are millions of cases of 'recovered memories' around the world, each of which represents shattered lives and destroyed families. That astonishing conclusion is also confirmed by anecdotal evidence. I challenge readers to consider how many people they personally know who have been affected, either by retrieving memories themselves, being accused on their basis, or belonging to a family system that has been shaken by such allegations. If you don't know of any, ask your friends and neighbors about this phenomenon. You might be surprised.

THE BACKLASH: WHOSE BACK? WHOSE LASH?

There have been many disturbing responses to the repressed-memory debate. Instead of taking a hard look at what *The Courage to Heal* has done and trying to make amends, Ellen Bass and Laura Davis published a third edition in 1994, adding a chapter called 'Honoring the Truth.' In it, they give grudging, minimal acknowledgment to the problem of induced memories, but they stress that therapists *rarely* push clients into making false allegations. Further, they assert that 'there is no such thing as false memory syndrome' and that 'moving into and out of denial is a natural part of the healing process.' If material about false memories is disturbing, Bass and Davis advise: 'Give yourself a break and avoid it.' They reaffirm their belief in ritual abuse, dredge up the McMartin tunnel story again, recycle the Country Walk case, and urge Survivors to 'honor your own truth' – as long, of course, as they continue to believe they were abused.[31]

Instead of moderating their tone, Bass and Davis have retained all the vitriolic quotations from Survivors, encouraging rage and violent fantasies: 'I have such venomous hatred. I pray to God that [my father] comes down with some terrible disease. I'd like him to get AIDS. That or Alzheimer's. I can't wait for his funeral.' Or this: 'I imagine walking into my parents' house with a shotgun aimed right at my father's balls. "Okay, Dad. Don't move an inch. Not one step, you sucker. I'm gonna take 'em off one at a time. And I'm gonna take my sweet time about it, too!"'[32]

Despite the mounting criticism aimed at *The Courage to Heal*, many counselors are still assigning it as mandatory reading. In the 1994 book, *The Authoritative Guide to Self-Help Books*, 500 prominent therapists across the United States were polled for their recommendations of 350 books. The number one choice? *The Courage to Heal*.[33]

In his 1949 novel, *1984*, George Orwell introduced the concept of 'doublethink,' in which authorities use a positive word to mean its opposite. In Newspeak, they said 'peace' when they meant 'war,' and 'truth' when they meant 'lies.' Those who elicit recovered memories and coercively interview young children are masters of doublethink. They speak of 'healing' when the result is harming. They talk about 'safety' just when they create the gravest mental dangers. They speak of children 'disclosing,' but the children are actually caving in to adult pressures. They complain of the 'backlash' against true revelations of sex abuse, but they refer to the anguish of the falsely accused. A foster mother practiced 'therapeutic holding' on a child by bruising his ribs with her knuckles until he confessed that he had been ritually abused.[34]

George Orwell's description of the rationale for doublethink is eerily prophetic of the recovered-memory movement: 'It means the ability to *believe* that black is white . . . This demands a continuous alteration of the past. [The Party member] must be cut off from the past . . . It will be seen that the control of the past depends above all on the training of memory . . . It is necessary to *remember* that events happened in the desired manner. And if it is necessary to rearrange one's memories or to tamper with written records, then it is necessary to *forget* that one has done so. The trick of doing this can be learned like any other mental technique.'[35]

Recovered-memory therapists such as Judith Herman proclaim that the False Memory Syndrome Foundation is spearheading a despicable 'backlash' against those who heroically expose the extent of sexual abuse. 'For the past twenty years,' Herman writes, 'women have been speaking out about sexual violence, and men have been coming up with denials, evasions, and excuses. We have been told that women lie, exaggerate, and fantasize.' Then she reviews 'the basic facts,' asserting that sexual abuse of children is common and still underreported. 'Most victims do not disclose their abuse until long after the fact, if ever.'[36]

Much of what Herman says thus far is true, but it is irrelevant to the repressed memory debate. By getting up on her ideological soap box, she diverts the debate away from whether massive repression and recovery actually occur – and the highly suggestive methods that therapists use – to a diatribe against societal ills. 'Violence against women and children is deeply imbedded in our society. It is a privilege that men do not relinquish easily. So it's not surprising that we would see serious resistance to change. Historically, every time a subordinate group begins to make serious progress, a backlash occurs.'

Having stacked the deck against anything a *man* might say, Herman then reviews all of the familiar dogma about recovered memories – how the memories come back as sensations or memory fragments, how Survivors don't want to believe these memories themselves and frequently cling to doubts, how support groups are important in the healing process. Finally, Herman admits that 'occasionally' overzealous therapists 'try to play detective, leaping to conclusions about their patients' histories without waiting for the memories to emerge.' Even in these cases, however, she asserts that 'it is most unusual for patients to accept every suggestion their therapists make. Psychotherapy is a collaborative effort, not a form of totalitarian indoctrination.'*[37]

Critics such as Herman, who believe that only the most coercive

---

* In 1995, Judith Herman found other things to worry about besides the 'backlash.' She was fined $30,000 in a U.S. District Court for illegally dispensing psychoactive drugs to non-patients. In addition, an audit revealed that over 4,000 pills, including Halcion, Valium, and Fiorinal with codeine, were missing from her clinic. She was subsequently fined another $5,000 by the Massachusetts Board of Registration and ordered to undergo 50 hours of training in prescribing practices.

methods of memory extraction are dangerous, ignore the well-documented history of *inadvertent cuing* that can occur in therapy sessions. There is a classic study, for instance, in which research assistants showed subjects the same ten photographs of people's faces, asking them to rate the degree of 'success' or 'failure' that the faces showed. The assistants were informed that the purpose of the experiment was to corroborate previous findings. Half of the research assistants were told that the photos depicted successful people, while the other half believed that previous viewers had rated them as failures. As a result, the experimenters given the 'success' expectation obtained uniformly higher ratings than the other group – *yet the experimenters had no idea that they were signalling the subjects* through slight voice inflections or body language.[38] This experiment is also evidence of what researchers call *confirmatory bias*, in which clinicians are likely to find confirmation for their own presuppositions.[39]

In such experiments, as psychiatrist Jerome Frank pointed out in 1973, 'the greater the power, prestige, or status of the experimenter, the greater his biasing effect,' a finding that clearly applies to the 'expert' therapist. Not only that, but as the experiments progressed, it became apparent that the subjects and experimenters reinforced one another, so that the experimenter produced increasingly blatant but unconscious cues. 'These findings would support the assumption that the longer a person receives treatment, the more he may be influenced by his therapist,' Frank commented. 'This would be analogous to the *folie à deux* between hypnotist and subject.'[40]

Nowadays, the term *folie à deux*, which literally means 'folly involving two,' has been replaced in the *Diagnostic and Statistical Manual of Mental Disorders* by the more formal diagnosis of 'Shared Psychotic Disorder,' defined as:

> . . . a delusion that develops in an individual who is involved in a close relationship with another person (sometimes termed the 'inducer' or 'the primary case') who already has a Psychotic Disorder with prominent delusions. The individual comes to share the delusional beliefs of the primary case in whole or in part . . . Usually the primary case in Shared Psychotic Disorder is dominant in the relationship and gradually imposes the delusional system on the more passive and initially healthy second person . . . If the relationship with the primary case is interrupted, the delusional

beliefs of the other individual usually diminish or disappear.[41][*42]

As Judith Herman observed, therapy sessions *are* a 'collaborative effort.' It is ironic, to say the least, that a substantial number of well-educated American psychotherapists appear to suffer from a mental illness that is defined in their own diagnostic manual. Indeed, *they are the transmitters of the disease, and the cure is to get patients away from such therapists.***

WHO'S IN DENIAL NOW?

Now that the extent of damage done in recovered-memory therapy is coming to light, it is remarkable to witness the variety of rationalizations and reactions from the psychology establishment. Instead of welcoming open debate, therapists such as Charles Whitfield, author of *Healing the Child Within*, flatly deny that there is any such thing as false memory syndrome or even recovered-memory therapy.*** Although Whitfield admits that delusive memories can sometimes occur, he has asserted – without recourse to any study – that only 2 *per cent* of parents accused on the basis of recovered memories are innocent. Most of them don't *know* that they are guilty, however, because 90 per cent of them were 'unconscious' as they abused their children.

Whitfield also joins therapist E. Sue Blume in dismissing the horrifying, compelling testimony of retractors. They really *were* abused. Their incest memories *were* accurate. It's just that they have slipped back into denial. 'Why are we so . . . willing to accept the validity of the reported withdrawal of an incest memory – *by persons seen as so suggestible that they*

---

* In the *DSM-IV Casebook*, there is a fascinating case study of Shared Psychotic Disorder relevant to the repressed-memory controversy. In it, a 43-year-old housewife entered the hospital in 1968, asking to be hypnotized to recall her many infidelities and be cured of them. It turned out that she was not, in fact, having numerous affairs. Her dominant, jealous husband was convinced that she was massively unfaithful, and his wife accepted his version of reality, explaining to the doctors that she 'blocked' the memories out.

** While Judith Herman expresses such concern for trauma victims, she and others like her have helped to promote *ageism*, which seems to be getting worse in America. Unlike most societies that defer to the wisdom and experience of the elderly, we appear to have reversed the Fifth Commandment to honor our fathers and mothers. Instead, we heap blame on them in their old age.

*** In denying the reality of false memory syndrome, Whitfield is apparently making a semantic distinction, since he does admit that a few illusory memories may have been created in therapy.

allegedly have been persuaded to accept a "false" experience in the first place?' asks Blume in an aptly-titled 1995 article, 'The Ownership of Truth.' Who, one wonders, is actually in denial here?[43]

At a 1994 Seattle workshop ironically titled 'The False Memory Debate,' Whitfield made participants sign a 'Statement of Safety' which read, in part: 'This is to certify that I am not a False Memory Syndrome Foundation member. I also do not side with them or seriously advocate their point of view that most delayed memories of trauma are false.'[44] By the following year, Whitfield had abandoned such loyalty oaths, but, following MPD guru Richard Kluft, he began to refer to critics of recovered memory as 'falsies' or 'psycho-terrorists.'

Whitfield, who comes across in person as a rather gentle, older man, has become one of the most strident supporters of the recovered-memory dogma. In 1995, he published *Memory and Abuse*, a book filled with all the old misconceptions about memory, intent on 'piecing together signs, symptoms and clues,' which include chronic headaches, neck and back pain, tight jaws, stuttering, eczema, and accident prone-ness. And if you don't have any of the signs? No problem: 'One of these symptoms is not being aware of having any of these manifestations.' Whitfield denies the reality of infantile amnesia. He espouses the value of what he calls 'internal corroboration,' a kind of circular logic in which abuse memories and 'symptoms' provide their own proof. Despite all the publicity about the dangers of leading questions, Whitfield blithely encourages therapists to ask, 'Have you ever wondered if you might have been abused?'[45]

Colin Ross, the former president of the International Society for the Study of Multiple Personality and Dissociation, presents an interesting case of how a self-promoting, charismatic MPD guru can twist in the wind of changing public opinion. Ross is attempting to distance himself from the sins of his past – without, of course, admitting that he ever did anything wrong. In 1994, he began his remarkable metamorphosis. He admitted that 'it is a fact that suggestible individuals can have memories elaborated within their minds because of poor therapeutic technique.'[46] He also stated that 'normal human memory is highly error-prone.' His conclusion? *'False memories are biologically normal and, therefore, not necessarily the therapist's fault* [italics added].' Clients must be responsible for their own memories, because therapists are merely 'consultants.'

Ross then engaged in tortuous psychological logic in which he reversed himself, asserting that the incest memories are really accurate. 'The therapist has been identified with the incest perpetrator, who

567

implanted semen in his daughter.' By a process of 'projective identification,' the therapist is now accused of 'implanting' false memories. 'Logically,' Ross concluded illogically, 'the therapist should be able to sue the parents for false memories of therapy, as much as the parents should be able to sue the therapist, because both parties are pawns of projective identification.' But that's not all. Because the clients with recovered memories are 'suggestible, vulnerable, easily persuaded,' they must have been manipulated by media coverage, the FMS Foundation, and their parents into retracting their allegations. 'Therefore, therapists should be able to launch false memory suits against the parents, lawyers, and background organizations suing them. I am considering doing so.'

After this flight into absurdity, Ross concluded with a reasonable statement. 'Juries need to be instructed in the difficulty of differentiating true from false memories.' True. But if juries should be so instructed, does Dr. Ross not see that the poor *patients* should have been told the same thing? Was it not the therapist's professional obligation to inform clients that hypnosis has been demonstrated to enhance confabulations, that human memory is malleable and error-prone, that expectation effects can severely distort perception? Instead, Ross, along with many other therapists, actively encouraged clients to believe in questionable memories, lending the weight of his considerable authority to the process.

At the end of 1994, Ross attended a Baltimore conference co-sponsored by Johns Hopkins University and the False Memory Syndrome Foundation, where he engaged in a fruitless debate with MPD critic Richard Ofshe and me. At the same time, he gave a clear signal that he wanted a way out of the MPD orthodoxy. By 1995, he was serving as an expert witness on both sides of the fence (charging $5,000 a day plus expenses), sometimes turning on his fellow recovered memory therapists. Soon thereafter, he appeared on the same platform with Elizabeth Loftus to call for 'therapeutic neutrality.'

It is commendable that Ross appears to be 'coming around,' but let us not forget that this is the same man who elicited demonic alters, who encouraged his patients to compete with one another in 'remembering' the most gruesome stories, who told a reporter that undiagnosed MPD was rampant among the general population. This is the same man who espoused a belief that the CIA was clandestinely creating multiple personalities, and who allegedly prescribed massive amounts of inappropriate medication to Roma Hart, a former patient who is currently suing him. Hart claims that Ross saw his female patients as 'nothing more than white rats for use in experiments,' and that he displayed a 'weird pseudoscientific interest in manipulating women's minds for profit,' though other former female clients may feel differently.[47]

Ross continues to promote the idea of massive dissociation and multiple personality disorder, making his living from this supposed malady. In 1994, he published *The Osiris Complex: Case Studies in Multiple Personality Disorder*. Here, he included the case of Charlene, who recovered hideous memories of sexual abuse which he clearly believed, though he doubted her MPD status. This is the 'only case' he has ever doubted, however, and he still believes her recovered memories of torture, rape by a minister, and childhood prostitution. Elsewhere in the book, Ross recounts the story of Margaret, who 'had a clear memory of aliens coming into her apartment, impregnating her, coming back later to remove the foetus, then returning years later to show her the half-human, half-alien child they were raising among the stars.' When he raised the possibility that the aliens might not be literally real, Margaret cried and accused him of ruining the therapy. He quickly backed down. 'Expressing doubt damages the treatment alliance,' he concluded, adding that Margaret taught him that 'there is a connection of some kind between UFO abductions and the use of women as breeders for Satanic cults.' Ross also observed, 'I have met many demons, devils, evil characters, representatives of Satan, and Satan himself in the course of my MPD work.' Not to worry, however. 'All of these entities turned out to be alter personalities, and none was actually a discarnate spirit.'[48]

In 1995, Ross published *Satanic Ritual Abuse*, in which he concedes that many of the SRA 'memories' were probably bogus. Yet he clearly believes in such cults and spends considerable space trying to convince his readers of their reality. He believes that SRA cults could be 'operating in secrecy through a combination of bribery, financial power, political connections, and intelligence expertise.'[49] The fact that he allowed Elizabeth Loftus to write an 'Afterword' to the book in which she rebuts him in no way alters his culpability in encouraging such myths. Ross has given over 120 workshops to fellow therapists, in which he continues to promote his belief in MPD.

AVOIDING THE TRUTH TRAP

Of course, we might expect that someone such as Colin Ross would evade admitting culpability. But there are many other clinicians who continue to blame everyone except the responsible professional. A case study presented in the *Family Therapy Networker* early in 1994 makes this point, even with its headline: 'Avoiding the Truth Trap.' I thought that this title must surely be ironically intended. No. It means just what it says. The truth doesn't matter. 'Clinicians are *not* judges, police officers or legal experts,' explains therapist Bill O'Hanlon, one of the respondents to the case. 'We cannot make informed judgments about the reliability of our clients' reports.'[50] This equivocation comes from a man whose ad for a 'Solution-Oriented Hypnosis' workshop was featured in the same magazine a few months earlier, promoting a methodology intended for 'survivors of trauma and sexual abuse.'[51]

But let us review the case, introduced by Connecticut therapist Henry Schissler, whose presentation is then critiqued by O'Hanlon and two other therapists. 'I have seen enough clients who were sexually abused to understand the reality of incest,' Schissler begins, but he believes this is a case in which 'another therapist jumped to the conclusion that there had been childhood sexual abuse, isolated the client from her family, and provided some very bad therapy.' Schissler describes a familiar situation in which Jane, the accusing daughter, sought therapy following the birth of her first child, became a Survivor, and accused her father of incest. Jane's therapist refused to talk to Schissler or the parents. Jane also attended a support group at the local YWCA, where the group leader told her that if she felt that she had been abused, then she had been, and encouraged her to sever all ties with her biological family.

Schissler's description of his efforts to help this family reminds us that there *are* decent therapists in practice. He interviewed both the mother and father alone, determining that the father had spent little time with his children, drinking to kill the pain of chronic colitis. The father claimed that because of his physical condition, he could not have carried Jane upstairs to molest her, as she asserted. Schissler also discovered that both of Jane's grandmothers had undergone psychiatric hospitalization with severe post-partum depression. He even reviewed the grandmothers' hospital records and 'was struck by the similarities between their behavior and Jane's.'

The first respondents to the case, Mary Jo Barrett and Wayne Scott, immediately proclaim that whether the alleged abuse took place or not is irrelevant. 'Mired in a preoccupation with The Truth, family members avoid directly confronting the toxicity that has permeated all their relationships.' They assert that 'both actual sexual abuse and false allegations grow out of the same psychological environment – one in which children grow up feeling disempowered, violated and angry.' Finally, they conclude that 'the goal of family therapy in cases of alleged abuse is not to magically reconcile the survivor and her family. It is to validate the perspective of the adult child by having other family members hear what her experience has been without anyone needing to deny or redefine it.'[52]

I find this case and the responses to it absolutely appalling. It was published in 1994, *after* the magazine in which it appeared ran a long cover story about the repressed-memory debate. Still, everything is blamed on the parents, nothing on the recovered-memory therapist. Even if this *is* a case of false memory, the respondents maintain, it is *still* somehow the parents' fault. 'If parents insist that their child has been brainwashed by irresponsible therapists,' Barrett and Scott write, 'they should consider what in that child's family experience has made her vulnerable to being brainwashed.'

We have here an Orwellian world where truth doesn't matter, where the therapist can redefine reality and hide behind the sanctity of his 'concern' for the patient. This kind of thinking is, unfortunately, widespread among recovered-memory therapists. 'I don't care if it's true,' one such therapist told a journalist in 1995. 'What's important to me is that I hear the child's truth, the patient's truth. That's what's important. What actually happened is irrelevant to me. It doesn't matter.'[53]

The same kind of wagon-circling rationalizations are documented by journalist Eileen McNamara in *Breakdown* (1994), the story of how Harvard psychiatrist Margaret Bean-Bayog convinced medical student Paul Lozano that he had repressed memories of sexual abuse by his mother. As is the norm with such cases, the psychiatrist refused to meet with her patient's family. The situation was worse than most, however. Bean-Bayog not only encouraged Lozano to contact his inner child, but to *become* a regressed three-year-old. She gave him children's books and wrote him love notes calling him 'the boy,' signing them 'Mom.' At the same time, she penned sadomasochistic pornography about him. 'You kneel between my legs and begin to lick and nibble my inner thighs,' one of the milder fantasies commenced. 'You begin to lick my clitoris. I am ecstatic with the pleasure of it, and adore you. You keep licking and sucking me, taking pleasure and aroused, but watching me.'[54]

Even before Lozano committed suicide in 1991, all of this material had come to light. Not only did Bean-Bayog deny any inappropriate behavior, she claimed that *she* had been a victim of this manipulative patient. Her sexual fantasies (it is unclear whether they were ever acted out) were explained away as 'countertransference.' During a deposition, a lawyer asked Bean-Bayog if she ever had sexual fantasies about Paul Lozano? 'Not as me, myself, no,' she answered. 'It was in a countertransference sense.'[55]

Perhaps this kind of incredible sophistry could be expected from a psychiatrist caught in such flagrant malpractice, but her peers, well-respected Boston-area psychiatrists and psychoanalysts, sprang to Bean-Bayog's defense, as did feminists, other recovered-memory therapists, the Survivor community, and the *Boston Globe*. Clinical psychologist Kathryn Kogan called her colleague Margaret Bean-Bayog 'kind, moral, responsible . . . a shining light.' She defended the reams of pornographic fantasies as a necessary catharsis so that Bean-Bayog could keep her feelings 'in a scientific framework.' Psychoanalyst John Maltsberger lamented that Bean-Bayog had been 'brutalized' by the press. 'She had already taken an emotional beating from Paul Lozano and suffered the expectable pain of losing a patient to suicide.'[56]

Talking about the case on a national television show, psychiatrist Thomas Gutheil repeated the familiar truth-trap dogma. 'If a patient brings up alleged memories or even false memories . . . , you have to take them as true; otherwise you can't treat a patient. If a patient says, "I was butchered and beaten with chains and branded with hot irons," you don't say, "That doesn't sound plausible." You say, "That must have been terrible."' Gutheil did not mention situations in which therapists actively promote the notion that sexual abuse occurred and was repressed. Anyway, it didn't really matter to him whether Lozano's incest 'memories' were true or false. 'Either [Lozano] really had this experience, in which case she [Bean-Bayog] is right and everything is cool, or he is a liar, in which case she is right and everything is cool.'[57]

'MODERATES' AND OTHER THERAPISTS

Even therapists who recognize the widespread havoc that the hunt for repressed memories has caused are often reluctant to address the central problem. For example, psychologist Michael Yapko, the author of *Suggestions of Abuse*, bends over backward to take a 'moderate' position. When Yapko appeared with Lenore Terr on *Geraldo*, he hardly mounted an argument against Terr's pet theories.[58] And on the Maury Povich program, while warning that hypnosis could promote illusory memories, Yapko also stated: 'I can tell you, as an expert in hypnosis, and working with these kinds of memory recovery techniques, you can use [them] to recover accurate memories that have been repressed.' He offered no evidence for this major caveat, but interviewer Povich, calling himself 'not knowledgeable,' accepted his assertion.[59*60]

Psychology professor Kevin Byrd acknowledged in a 1994 article in *American Psychologist* that recall can be 'shaped by the implicit expectations of the therapist [through] subtle means.' Nonetheless, Byrd went on to say that 'when hidden trauma is strongly suspected on the basis of objective criteria and the patient's suffering is severe, methods aimed at "de-repression" are justifiable.' He recommended asking patients to study old family photographs. 'Memory reconstruction should be a gradual process in which the degree of certainty is based on a continuing record of data collected without therapist bias.'[61] Yet Byrd offers no insights on how to distinguish between 'objective criteria' and 'therapist bias.'

Similarly, in their otherwise-excellent 1994 review assessing the problems with recovered-memory therapy, psychologists Stephen Lindsay and Don Read *assume* the reality of repression. 'It is very likely,' they state, 'that some adult victims of childhood abuse have no available memories of the abuse.' Unlike other statements in this meticulously documented paper, Lindsay and Read simply offer this opinion as an unverified assertion. Bending over backward to be fair, they write that unearthing repressed memories may be 'psychologically beneficial,' so that 'it makes sense that memory recovery techniques would be used by competent practitioners.' In their conclusion, Lindsay and Read suggest that 'when childhood sexual abuse . . . is explored in a non-suggestive, open-minded way, without the use of special memory recovery techniques, there is little ground for concern about the creation of illusory memories.'[62**63]

Yet therapists, as we have seen, *never* think their methods are suggestive. They *all* consider themselves open-minded. Those therapists who do not use hypnosis or other intrusive methods are the most likely to convince themselves and their clients that the repressed memories have arisen 'spontaneously.' In fact, if therapists believe in the possibility of

* I asked Michael Yapko about this statement, and he said he had seen 'some cases' in which he was convinced that repressed memories of sexual abuse had returned in therapy. None involved massive repression. Some had been 'corroborated' by friends, siblings, or their diary entries at the time, he said. Yapko could not refer me to specific clients. He said that he thought massive repression is 'statistically unlikely but theoretically possible.'
** Stephen Lindsay has subsequently made much stronger statements: 'The vast majority of victims of traumatic child sexual abuse that occurred after the age of 3 or 4 years are aware of their histories . . . There is not a single controlled study demonstrating any beneficial effect of therapeutic efforts to recovered hidden memories of child sexual abuse in clients who report no abuse history.'

massive repression, they will probably convey this belief to clients, even without being aware of it. Elsewhere in this same paper, Lindsay and Read acknowledge that 'there are sometimes substantial discrepancies between what therapists apparently believe they do in therapy . . . and what they actually do.'[64]

For perspective, it should be understood that recovered-memory therapists regard Yapko, Lindsay, and Read as extremists on the other side of the debate. These scholars undoubtedly face intense professional pressure to moderate their positions, to avoid giving the appearance of extremism.

But if the 'moderate' position prevails in this debate, the recovered-memory movement will probably survive nearly intact. Recovered-memory therapists will simply moderate their approach, telling patients, 'You have all the symptoms of someone who was sexually abused as a child, so it wouldn't surprise me if you recovered memories as you are feeling safer in therapy. But we won't dig for them. If the memories arise, they will do so on their own, in their own good time.' Then, the suggestive seed having been planted, it will indeed sprout into a hideous mental vine.

Another newly popular argument in favor of repressed memories runs like this: 'I recovered my memories outside of therapy. I didn't read any of those suggestive books. I just spontaneously started having these flashbacks, and that's why I went to therapy.' I have heard the same argument regarding UFO abduction memories. 'I knew nothing about UFO literature.' While there is no doubt that these testimonies are sincere, it is quite likely that the *idea* of repressed sexual abuse memories (or UFO abductions) had indeed been implanted, whether consciously or subconsciously, resulting in the 'spontaneous' flashbacks. Then, once entered into therapy that accepted the reality of repression, the seeker would find plentiful validation and amplification.

Because illusory incest allegations seem so strange, there is a natural tendency for commentators to search for underlying disturbances to explain them. Common explanations are: (1) Those who have recovered these memories are pathologically disturbed. (2) The memories reflect unconscious sexual desire for the accused parent. (3) The accusations do not reflect actual events, but they are evidence of severe dysfunction within the family system. Overt sexual boundaries may not have been breached, but the accuser must have been emotionally violated throughout childhood, or the child was raised in an overly sexualized atmosphere.

There may be a grain of truth in some of these explanations for a few specific cases, but as we have seen, such memories can be encouraged in almost *anyone* entering therapy in a vulnerable state, seeking answers to life's problems. When the therapist – the figure of authority – systematically leads the client into believing that buried incest memories provide those answers, and when an entire culture validates the memory-retrieval process, the client develops a new belief system, a new identity as an Incest Survivor. This process has occurred over and over again. It does not take a Ph.D. in psychology to figure it out. *Yet within the psychological community, there is extreme resistance to admitting any responsibility on the part of members of that community. Instead, families continue to bear the brunt of the blame for false accusations.*

Psychoanalyst Lawrence Hedges provides a final chilling example of how therapists can simultaneously realize that delusive memories have arisen in therapy and, like Freud, ignore their own responsibility in having encouraged their creation. Hedges explains in his 1994 book, *Remembering, Repeating, and Working Through Childhood Trauma*, that 'no seasoned psychoanalyst ever assumes any memory, no matter how vivid or seemingly true it appears, [is] an indisputable historical fact.' But then he goes on to search for the 'narrative' or 'emotional' truth which the memory must, he believes, reveal. After a good deal of Freudian jargon about 'counter cathexis' and 'selfobject needs,' Hedges gets to his own pet theory: recovered memories of abuse are *really* screen memories of trauma suffered 'in utero and in the earliest months of life.'* In other words, the fetus or infant who didn't feel loved or safe maintains an unconscious traumatic memory, which will then surface as a false incest accusation.[65]

Hedges then details how one of his female colleagues found herself in a dreadful situation. During six months of therapy with a client, the therapist told Hedges, 'all of these abusive memories began coming out during sessions.'[66] Her client 'became quite fragmented and was having

---

* Like many psychologists, Hedges hides behind a wall of abstract verbiage so thick that it is often impossible to figure out what he means. Here, for instance, he explains (I think) how spurious repressed incest memories arise from other early trauma: 'Since the interaction to be *represented* [remembered] is preverbal, presymbolic, and affectively interactive, it is only when the analyst begins to verbalize countertransference responsiveness to being held in such a tight emotional spot with such rigid expectations that the split-off infant role [memory] will at last be given verbal and emotional *representation*. That is, speaking the countertransference, when done carefully and thoughtfully, brings the split-off "unthought known" into the realm of replicated representation in the scenarios which serve as memories of the earliest symbiotic interactions.'

a hard time functioning,' so she put her on Prozac and sent her to a Survivor support group, where even more terrible memories emerged. Now, at the urging of her group, the client was about to confront her family. 'I don't question whether she has been somehow badly abused,' the therapist explained. 'I know some horrible things must have happened to her.' The therapist was afraid, however, that when the parents denied the abuse, her client would suffer a psychotic break. 'What's got me scared is that I have somehow colluded in all of this without really meaning to,' the therapist concluded. 'I don't know how I got into this jam.' She was worried about the parents being upset and wanting information, but she couldn't reveal it because of confidentiality issues. 'The bottom line is, I'm fucked!'

In response, did Hedges tell her that she had gotten herself into this mess by believing in repressed memories, by helping her client to 'remember' them, by referring her to a Survivor support group, by validating her memories at every step of the process? Did he tell her to stop worrying about herself and start being concerned for a client she had made nearly psychotic rather than better? No! 'Your client has succeeded in molesting you,' Hedges informed this therapist, 'violating your personal and professional boundaries in much the same intrusive or forceful way she may once have experienced herself as a very young child.' He explained that the memories might not be completely accurate (because they presumably stemmed from the womb or the first few months of life), but 'all this time you have been held emotional hostage in a similar helpless and vulnerable position to the one she felt in as a child – without having the slightest idea of how to protect yourself from this violence.'

'Oh, God!' answered the therapist, 'I'm sick in the pit of my stomach just realizing how true what you are saying is. I'm feeling all of the abuse in the symbiotic role reversal of the countertransference.' Readers may be excused if, at this point, they, too, feel sick in the pits of their stomachs as a result of Hedges' arrogance in not only exonerating his colleague, but bragging about it in print.

BRITISH BELIEVERS

It is somewhat surprising that many British therapists still espouse a firm belief in recovered memories, despite the complete lack of scientific evidence for them. There has been an explosive growth in the therapy industry within the U.K. in the last few years, as membership figures for the British Association for Counselling attest. In 1977, the BAC had 1,300 members. By 1988, it nearly tripled to 3,612. But the largest growth has come since then, with current membership cresting 12,000.[67]

Unfortunately, it appears that many BAC therapists are *quite likely* to believe in repressed memories. According to a 1993 survey, 60 per cent pursue a 'psychodynamic model' that believes in dredging the past for clues to current problems, while only 19 per cent were cognitive or cognitive-behavioral.[68] In 1995, the BAC published *Counselling Adults Who Were Abused as Children*, by psychiatric social worker Peter Dale, who sought training in sexual abuse in America in 1987. Dale, who was associated with the NSPCC for several years, now has a private practice in Hastings, East Sussex, where he performs 'Gestalt psychotherapy.'

The bulk of Dale's book does not concern abused adults who have always remembered what happened to them. Rather, it is chock full of advice on how to help people recover 'memories' previously unavailable to them. 'Some clients may have no conscious memory of abuse and may refute any suggestion of this being a possibility,' he writes. 'Yet their specific problems may leave the counsellor wondering whether significant abuse-related material is being repressed.' These 'specific problems' that may be indicative of repressed memories constitute an alarming laundry list: 'sleep disturbances, chronic muscle tensions, regular headaches, genital-urinary problems, frequent infections, menstrual irregularities, vaginismus, skin complaints, seizures, palpitations, dizziness, gastro-intestinal problems, eating disorders, anxiety attacks, depression, mood swings, a wide variety of compulsive and obsessive behaviors, substance abuse, and self-injury.'

Those who deny that they were abused are, of course, usually wrong. 'Such people may maintain an illusion that their childhoods were happy and satisfying.' By contacting their wounded 'inner child,' however, they may get in touch with their memories, according to Dale. Such memories may also return through 'flashbacks' or nightmares, especially after the establishment of a 'working alliance' between therapist and client. The author warns that '*things tend to get worse before they get better*,' and that 'as work progresses new memories tend to return and feelings can be experienced and expressed in more intense and volatile ways' that can imperil marital relationships.

Dale recommends 'planned regressive work' which is a form of hypnosis, though he does not use that term. 'The client begins to relax, breathes more deeply and allows their attention to gradually shift away from external preoccupations and onto sensations and images.' For some clients, such sessions can be 'extremely powerful,' facilitating 'the return to conscious awareness of important repressed memories.' Once such memories return, any family confrontations must be thoroughly planned. 'This can be done by helping the client visualise or enact possible family reactions to the visit and preparing and rehearsing their approach and response in advance for each one.' Clients must accept the fact that parents 'are never going to be able to provide sufficient love' for them.

Without using the term 'multiple personality disorder,' Dale clearly prepares the way for a full-blown MPD diagnosis. Therapists should be alert for 'subtle changes in facial movements, posture or mood.' At such moments, the clinician should ask, *'What is going on inside at the moment?'* and 'specifically enquire as to which voice is currently speaking.'

Clearly, Peter Dale encourages the hunt for repressed memories, and his message is sanctioned by the British Association for Counselling. It is little consolation that he adds an addendum acknowledging that a few false memories may occur.[69]

Another 1995 British publication is equally disturbing. The Social and Community Planning Research branch of the Department of Health decided, quite admirably, to conduct a national survey on sexual abuse. Based on four 'pre-pilot' surveys, Deborah Ghate and Liz Spencer make recommendations for such a study in *The Prevalence of Child Sexual Abuse in Britain: A Feasibility Study for a Large-Scale Survey of the General Population.* Unfortunately, the authors write of 'the tendency for painful, traumatic or deeply confusing events in childhood to be suppressed or "blocked," as a form of psychological coping mechanism . . . . The clinical literature indicates that some people who have been the victims of child sexual abuse may have no memory at all of the abuse.' To back up this assertion, they cite *The Courage to Heal* and *Secret Survivors.*

With this orientation, it is hardly surprising that Ghate and Spencer caution that 'the survey interview itself may act as an "unblocking" or triggering mechanism.' In other words, the interview itself may cause a memory to return. 'The fact that memories of sexual experiences may be retrieved *after* the survey interview suggests that it might be very important . . . to provide for a second round of data collection after the initial interview.' Later in the report, they call this follow-up interview 'indispensable.' The authors give the example of one woman they interviewed who, during subsequent discussions about the survey with her family, recalled her uncle molesting her when she was four.[70]

Such recall is hardly surprising, especially if the interviewers told the woman in question, 'This interview may trigger recall of a repressed memory of sexual abuse.' She would then obsess over it and come up with something. It is quite likely that this national survey, far from providing objective evidence of the extent of real sexual abuse, will encourage confabulations that will then be taken as firm evidence of wide-spread abuse. While Ghate and Spencer give a passing nod to 'false memory syndrome,' they clearly believe in recovered memories – citing Roland Summit, Ellen Bass, Sue Blume, Judith Herman, and Ray Wyre – and encourage their interviewers to look for them.

In much of the British professional clinical literature, the notion of induced memories has been angrily dismissed, as in a 1995 article by Janet Rimmer on 'The Falsehoods in the False Memory Syndrome Debate.' Rimmer, a BAC-accredited counsellor and 'psychosynthesis therapist' based in Harrow, also trains other clinicians. She believes that 'much of childhood trauma is locked away and banished from consciousness' and only re-emerges in 'a supportive trusting environment' such as therapy. She is not surprised that parents accused on the basis of recovered memory deny their guilt. 'They have probably successfully convinced themselves it never happened.' Rimmer reveals that many of her clients say, 'I don't believe this happened. It could not have happened to me. My mum loved me!' She dismisses such outbursts. 'Retractions are part of the process.'[71]

But the leading public advocate of recovered memory therapy emerged in 1994. Marjorie Orr, a well-known British astrologer who doubles as a Jungian psychotherapist, founded Accuracy About Abuse to combat the British False Memory Society. Her newsletter is required reading for anyone interested in this debate, and it includes a good deal of interesting information, along with a protracted smear campaign against anyone associated with FMS organizations. She also believes in ritual abuse and cites research articles purporting to 'prove' that memory for trauma can go back to 3 months of age, or even to birth. She laments the effect that recovered memory critics have had on Survivors. Their faith in themselves and their often fragile memories, so painfully acquired, are undermined. Worse, their faith in their therapists, often their main support, can be damaged.'[72]

On a radio phone-in programme in 1995, Orr asserted that sexual abusers were 'Academy Award winning liars,' implying that parents accused on the basis of recovered memory were lying. Then she qualified her criticism. 'Quite a few abusers probably don't know they have done it because they have to maintain this delusion of a happy contented family.' She didn't understand why the media made 'such a fuss' about false allegations when 'false denials are extremely common.' Finally, she admitted that some illusory memories might have been produced, 'but there is something very unhealthy in the family that a child would come to believe' such a thing.[73]

Although Orr did not mention it on this show, elsewhere she has let it be known that she can spot a perpetrator through the science of astrology. 'A personal birth chart will certainly show up clearly and in some detail the psychological dysfunctions which would indicate that someone was likely to abuse or had been abused.' But she quickly points out that 'astrology will not solve the problem. Only long, painstaking and acutely painful facing up in therapy will do that.'[74]

With such firmly held beliefs, all expressed in 1995 – well after the hazards of recovered memory therapy were widely publicized – it is obvious that there is a major, on-going problem with pseudoscientific therapeutic approaches in Great Britain. Fay Weldon's 1994 novel, *Affliction*, certainly made that clear enough. Therapy is 'very fashionable, all of a sudden,' one of her characters observes. Annette, the main character, goes for counselling when her husband succumbs to a New Age astrologer/homeopath/psychiatrist, whom he is seeing four times a week. Annette's therapist (who turns out to be the homeopath's husband) assures her that her problems stem from repressed incest memories. 'These memories are often buried,' he explains. 'It does not mean they are not there, simply that you have overlaid them.' Annette, a level-headed skeptic, does not buy it. 'I simply cannot believe any such thing about my father,' she tells her friend. 'But perhaps an uncle. Who's to say?'[75]

Herein lies the insidious nature of human suggestibility. When we are told something disturbing, impossible to disprove, by an authority figure, we are likely to obsess over it and come up with something. I can only agree with one common-sense woman who wrote a letter to *The Times* in 1995. 'At one time we laughed at Americans for regarding as a problem what the rest of us considered normal life,' she observed, 'and having car pools to take their children to psychiatrists as we took ours to dancing lessons. However, with the burgeoning consultancy industry catching up, I go to seek, if not counselling, then at least a long, brisk walk.'[76]

THE AMERICAN PROFESSIONAL ASSOCIATIONS
RESPOND

Don't get me wrong. I don't think that therapists intentionally promote illusory memories. And, yes, some people have managed to 'find' their own repressed memories completely outside of therapy, either in support groups, through books ('bibliotherapy'), or triggered by TV talk shows. Nonetheless, *it is the repressed-memory dogma, promulgated primarily by therapists, that has created the disastrous situation described in this book.* These therapists have ignored the most fundamental injunction of the Hippocratic Oath, which exhorts healers: *Primum non nocere – First, do no harm.* As Pamela Freyd, the director of the False Memory Syndrome Foundation, has repeatedly written, 'If any other medical product had more than 13,000 [now 17,000] complaints and had never been shown to be safe or effective, it would be taken off the market.'[77]*[78] A 1995 British editorial in *The Mail on Sunday* made a similar point. 'It seems that there are more safeguards on cold remedies sold over the counter of Britain's High Street shops than there are on some controversial mind-tinkering therapies.'[79]

But with few exceptions, the appropriate professional associations have failed to respond in any meaningful way to this very obvious problem. The American Medical Association is to be commended for issuing a 1993 statement about memory retrieval techniques, recognizing that they are 'fraught with problems of potential misapplication.'[80] The American Psychiatric Association followed late in 1993 with a less satisfactory response to the crisis. It did note that 'human memory is a

---

* Readers should be skeptical when Survivors with recovered memories claim that their 'memories' arose completely spontaneously. Retrospective accounts can be extraordinarily slanted. 'No therapist can be accused of misleading me,' Sylvia Fraser wrote in a 1994 article, 'since none was involved in the initial recovery. I had read no books on incest . . .and had no conscious interest in this subject.' Fraser's 1988 book, *My Father's House*, offers evidence to the contrary. 'Through Freudian and Jungian analysis, I learned how to interpret dreams as messages from my unconscious,' she wrote in her book. 'Through primal and massage therapy, rolfing, bioenergetics, yoga, meditation, I grew more in touch with my body and my emotions . . .Why had I been such an angry child? Why did I hate my father? . . . I was approaching a time when I would remember. The obsession of a lifetime was drawing to a close.' Then Fraser described how her repressed abuse memories came back under hypnosis. Similarly, a Survivor named Vanessa stated in December of 1993 that she had never claimed ritual abuse memories, while she had actually done so on television in January of the same year.

complex process' and that it was impossible to distinguish accurately between true and false memories. Unfortunately, aside from such pro-forma acknowledgments, the rest of the statement embraces Survivor dogma. 'Expression of disbelief is likely to cause the patient further pain ... The issues of breaking off relationships with important attachment figures [parents], of pursuing legal actions, and of making public disclosures may need to be addressed.'[81]

Most distressing, the American Psychiatric Association statement asserted: 'Many individuals who recover memories of abuse have been able to find corroborating information about their memories.' I wrote to the association, explaining that I was writing a book on repressed memories and asking for specific cases that had been confirmed. In response, I received a bibliography including citations from Judith Herman, John Briere, and Lenore Terr, among others.

There is hope, however. Late in 1995, Paul Fink, a Philadelphia psychiatrist and former president of the American Psychiatric Association, wrote to the current president of the APA expressing concern about 'therapists, among whom are some psychiatrists, who are promulgating memory return therapy as well as several fringe therapies including space alien abduction therapy, satanic cult therapy, and past life therapy.' Fink suggested that the American Psychiatric Association co-sponsor a conference with the False Memory Syndrome Foundation to explore these issues. Since Fink had previously taken a strong anti-FMSF position and had appeared on a 1991 television talk show espousing belief in repressed memories, this turn-around is particularly significant. Let us hope that all the professional associations heed the words in Fink's letter: 'As long as we act as if we are two Balkanized camps with little communication between these various organizations, things will smolder or get worse rather than better.'[82]

In the meantime, the American Psychological Association has created a six-person committee to study the repressed-memory issue. Three of the members are experimental researchers who are skeptical of massive repression, including Elizabeth Loftus. The other three are recovered-memory clinicians, including Christine Courtois. The committee has existed on paper for nearly two years and has been unable to agree on a final joint statement. Instead, each side will present separate conclusions and rebuttals.

The February 1994 edition of *Practitioner Focus*, an American Psychological Association newsletter, contained an article about the repressed-memory controversy, concluding that 'nothing less than the integrity of the mental health professions and the trust inherent in the client-therapist relationship is at stake.' I could not agree more. Yet the entire concern of the article is how to respond to 'biased media attention' to therapy-induced memories. Also, 'the directorate's legal and regulatory affairs department would like to know about any instances where psychologists are denied reimbursement in cases involving . . . recovered memories.'[83] In other words, many professional psychologists appear to be worried primarily about their images and their pocketbooks – not about creating illusory incest memories. Rather than cleaning house, the APA has created a $1.5 million war chest to boost the image of therapists.

One hopeful sign is a brief position paper issued by the American Psychological Association in the fall of 1995, admitting that '*most* people who were sexually abused as children remember all or part of what happened to them although they may not fully understand or disclose it,' adding that 'it is impossible, without other corroborative evidence, to distinguish a true memory from a false one.'[84]

On the other hand, two months *after* that position paper was issued, in his presidential address to the American Psychological Association, Ron Fox castigated scientists and therapists who 'harm the profession' by publicly criticizing repressed-memory clinicians. He even called for 'revising the ethical code' of the APA to censure psychologists 'who undermine the public's trust in the discipline' by criticizing their peers.[85] It seems that the wagon-circling at the American Psychological Association has become yet more frantic, drawing in ever tighter spirals to deny any wrong-doing.

In the meantime, the International Society for the Study of Multiple Personality & Dissociation has quietly renamed itself the International Society for the Study of Dissociation – dropping the now-tarnished MPD moniker. In the 'President's Message,' psychiatrist Nancy Hornstein admitted, 'We are "in it," so to speak, deep. If you don't believe me, check recent adjudications, not to mention multi-million dollar settlements, against therapists.'[86] The MPD gurus are running scared, but they have not admitted to their gigantic errors.

The National Association of Social Workers is also studying the false memory issue, but it, too, is unlikely to challenge its members to change their ways. In fact, at the annual NASW conference held in October of 1995, one therapist detailed her clinical experiences with satanic ritual abuse and multiple personalities, and another speaker apparently claimed to have 10,000 personalities![87]

THE BRITISH AND AUSTRALIAN SOCIETIES' STRUGGLES

The American associations are not alone in waffling on the issue of recovered memories. In 1994, the British Psychological Society initiated a survey of some 800 members. The results, reviewed earlier in this chapter, were extremely disturbing. *Not only did 97 per cent of those surveyed believe in the essential accuracy of recovered memories – the same overwhelming majority validated reports of satanic ritual abuse.* Yet far from sounding the alarm that something was amiss, the BPS Working Party on Recovered Memories reached far different conclusions. They published an 'executive summary' in January of 1995, amidst a great deal of media hype. 'Complete or partial memory loss is a frequently reported consequence of experiencing certain kinds of psychological traumas including childhood sexual abuse,' the report stated. 'These memories are sometimes fully or partially recovered after a gap of many years.' The report offered no scientific evidence or corroborated cases to support this conclusion. Rather, it stated: 'Memory recovery is reported by highly experienced and well qualified therapists who are well aware of the dangers of inappropriate suggestion and interpretation.'[88]

There is a curious bit of circular logic going on here, smacking more of an *ex cathedra* Papal pronouncement than the findings of a group of scientists. The argument appears to be that only 'highly experienced and well qualified' therapists belong to the British Psychological Society. Therefore, anything they believe must be true, particularly because they are 'aware of the dangers of inappropriate suggestion and interpretation.' In addition, the authors added, 'the non-doctrinaire nature of these beliefs [in accurate recovered memories] is indicated by the high level of acceptance of false memories.' In the January report, no one could verify that statement, since, inexplicably, it did not include a detailed analysis of the survey results, or even precise information on the questions asked. The survey results were finally published in May of 1995 in *The Psychologist*, the BPS academic journal, without fanfare. Indeed, not a single journalist reported on it, as Working Party chair John Morton told me with evident relief.

The January summary had neglected to mention the startling beliefs about satanic ritual abuse, which now came to light. It also became clear what was meant by the 'high level of acceptance of false memories.'

One of the questions asked: 'Do you think it is possible that a person could come falsely to "remember" that they had been repeatedly sexually abused as a child if no abuse had actually taken place?' Sixty-seven per cent agreed, while 33 per cent thought that inducing such false memories would be impossible. The bland conclusion of the survey authors was that 'the majority of our respondents believed that false memories were possible,' apparently providing justification for the conclusion that these therapists were 'aware of the dangers of inappropriate suggestion and interpretation.' *In fact, however, it is extremely alarming that one-third of the BPS members thought that it was impossible ever to instill false memories.* Even those who believe it is *possible*, of course, do not necessarily worry that *they* might lead someone inadvertently to believe in illusory abuse.[89]

To give the BPS report credit, it did conclude that 'it is important for the therapist to be alert to the dangers of suggestion' and that hypnotic regression should be avoided. It would be nice to believe that the Society took its own conclusion more seriously. Only once – in a footnote – did the report even *mention* highly suggestive memory recovery techniques such as guided imagery, dream analysis, journaling, or sodium Amytal interviews. The overall impression was that a few false memories might occur, but they were really a minor problem in comparison to the great number of accurate abuse memories that had been repressed and then unearthed by the 'highly trained professional members' of the BPS.

When I came to England to conduct research for this book in August of 1995, I interviewed John Morton, the chair of the BPS Working Party. A cognitive experimental psychologist, Morton clearly understands the problems inherent in misguided therapy. He admitted that 'there is no scientific evidence for repression,' that induced memories can occur, and that 'we haven't found a single case of corroborated massive repression yet.' He thinks that it is not necessary to *believe* everything a therapy client says, and he knows that there is absolutely no evidence for the existence of satanic ritual abuse cults. He thinks it is dreadful for parents to be excluded from therapy and their children's lives. 'I can't think of anything more awful than my 22-year-old daughter reinterpreting the warm, physical, loving relationship that I have with her and thinking that I somehow did something sexually abusive to her,'[90] he told me.

Nonetheless, he attempted to justify the BPS executive summary as 'balanced.' He defended the therapists by noting that 31 per cent of their clients' recovered memories had purportedly arisen prior to therapy. I observed that in the late 1980s and early 1990s, our culture was permeated with the idea of repressed memories of sexual abuse, so it wasn't surprising that some memories would 'spontaneously' arise outside therapy. But why weren't such memories surfacing in the 1970s or before?

Morton called the 97 per cent belief in ritual abuse 'bewildering' and 'very disturbing,' but he also justified not mentioning it initially because 'it was really a tiny little issue in the scheme of things.' I disagreed, saying that it was indicative of a very credulous belief system. I wondered aloud what the therapists would have said about past lives or alien abduction memories. 'Oh, thank God we didn't ask them about that!' he exclaimed.

I got the impression that Professor Morton was a well-meaning academic who has found himself caught in an awkward position. 'You've got to understand this socio-political climate,' he told me. 'Some of us wish we hadn't got involved in this issue because the material is so painful.' At one point, he blurted out, 'You have to understand that we have to remain friends with these people!' He was referring to the clinicians, since most of the Working Party included experimental psychologists, with the exception of Phil Mollon, whose disturbing therapeutic treatment of supposed ritual abuse survivors was reviewed in Chapter 4. Even Mollon, however, has apparently come around to a somewhat skeptical position regarding recovered memory.

Because of the furor and criticism that came in the wake of the report, the BPS is conducting a second in-depth telephone interview with 100 of those originally surveyed. Among other things, the survey will ask what percentage of their clients retrieve memories, what kinds of techniques were employed, and what form of corroboration has been found. I cautioned Morton against accepting hearsay corroboration, stressing the need for clear confirming evidence.

Since my meeting with John Morton, the British Psychological Society has lobbied Parliament to pass a law that would make it illegal for anyone to call themselves a psychologist without belonging to the BPS. Given the disturbing beliefs demonstrated by the majority of the BPS members surveyed in 1994, the passage of such a law would seem ill-advised. Rather, I hope that the British Parliament will pass laws requiring anyone calling themselves a psychotherapist or hypnotist to register as such with the government and to receive appropriate education in the hazards of hypnosis, the nature of human memory, and the like.

Following the lead of the BPS, other British societies will address the volatile issue of recovered memory therapy. The U.K. Council for Psychotherapy has sponsored a Working Party on False Memory. One of its members, John Rowan, recently stated that he believes amnesia is frequently caused by repression or dissociation. 'You get delayed memories cropping up suddenly,' he asserted.[91] Given Rowan's beliefs, it is frightening to consider what this committee may conclude. The Royal College of Psychiatrists, the governing body for British psychiatrists, has also assigned a five-member Working Party to report on the issue. The British Association for Counselling has assigned its Research and Evaluation Committee to draft a statement outlining the 'official position' of the BAC.[92]

The Evangelical Alliance, which claims a million members, has sidestepped the debate, even though many of its members unearth abuse 'memories' through deliverance ministry, exorcism, or prayer. In a 1995 set of guidelines, the Alliance urged contact with police and social services as soon as an abuse allegation arises, but it dealt only cursorily with 'word of knowledge,' a process in which a charismatic Christian supposedly receives a message from the Holy Spirit that someone else has been abused.[93]

In the meantime, the Australian Psychological Society issued the most comprehensive and reasonable set of guidelines currently available on recovered memories. Other professional associations around the world should adopt similar guidelines. Here are excerpts:

> Memories can be altered, deleted, and created by events that occur during and after the time of encoding, and during the period of storage, and during any attempts at retrieval.

> Although some clinical observations support the notion of repressed memories, empirical research on memory generally does not. Moreover, scientific evidence does not allow global statements to be made about a definite relationship between trauma and memory.

> The presence or absence of detail in a memory report does not necessarily mean that it is accurate or inaccurate. [Nor does] the level of belief in memory or the emotion associated with the memory.

> The available scientific and clinical evidence does not allow accurate, inaccurate, and fabricated memories to be distinguished in the absence of independent corroboration.

Psychologists should be alert to the ways that they can shape the reported memories of clients through the expectations they convey, the comments they make, the questions they ask, and the responses they give. Psychologists should be alert that clients are susceptible to subtle suggestions and reinforcements, whether those communications are intended or unintended.

Psychologists should obtain informed consent at the beginning of therapy in relation to the therapeutic procedures and process.[94]

Unlike the reasonable guidelines adopted by the Australian Psychological Society, many professional associations are unlikely to take any firm moral stand on this issue which, according to British psychiatrist Janet Boakes, 'threatens to undermine the credibility of the entire profession.'[95] Why won't societies take action? One obvious answer is that they would look bad. Another is that the concept of repression has been accepted for such a long time that it will not be seriously questioned. There is, however, a more compelling reason . . .

WHERE THE MONEY IS

Recovered-memory therapy, in all its variations, is a *lucrative pursuit*. The repressed-memory craze has proved to be a bonanza, not only for private therapists and inpatient psychiatric units, but for retreat centers, continuing-education instructors, and lawyers. As long as insurance companies continue to pay for questionable diagnoses of 'post-traumatic stress disorder' or 'dissociative identity disorder,' therapists will continue to milk the system for all it's worth. One father reported to a psychiatrist recently that his daughter's therapy had cost $300,000 over the last five years. That was nothing compared to the three-quarters of a million dollars another woman spent on MPD therapy and hospitalization in just four years. Others have spent well over a million dollars for 'treatment' that rendered them depressed, suicidal, and utterly dependent.[96]

As psychoanalysts Janice Haaken and Astrid Schlaps noted in 1991, 'Successful clinicians, like salespeople, must believe in what they sell . . . The more competitive the therapeutic marketplace, the more difficult it becomes to question ideas which are the basis of one's economic survival.'[97]

Some advertisements follow in the grand American tradition of huckin the grand American tradition of huckster-sterism. 'Are You Ready to Remember Your Childhood?' one such 1994 ad asks in its headline. 'If you have "blank spots" in your childhood memories,' it continues, 'if you're puzzled by your "strange" responses to certain situations, if you're continually frustrated in achieving certain goals, if you remember some abuse but suspect there's more, you may hold buried memories that need to surface and be healed.'[98] If so, come see the hypnotherapist and lay down your money – and your mind.

A psychiatric hospital placed an even more outrageous ad in *Changes* magazine in December of 1993. 'Remembering incest and childhood abuse is the first step to healing,' the ad began. 'We can help you remember and heal.' There followed a laundry list of symptoms indicative of abuse: 'Mood swings, panic disorder, substance abuse, rage, flashbacks, depression, hopelessness, anxiety, paranoia, low self-esteem, relationship problems,' – on and on, right down to pre-menstrual syndrome and irritable bowels. 'What we do best is help bring up forgotten memories through our powerful combination of massage, body work, hypnosis, psychodrama, and sodium brevitol interviewing.'[99]

It is not just cynical journalists who believe that repressed-memory diagnoses can sometimes be motivated largely by financial factors. In a recent article, psychiatric nurse Sally McDonald complained about the abusive treatment patients in a Houston dissociative disorders unit received. Despite repeated protests from the nursing staff, the hospital administrators refused to censure the doctor who ran the unit. The reason? 'The dissociative disorders unit housed 10 patients billed at an intensive care unit rate of $1,200 per day – plus billable rates of $80 to $100 each for art therapy, expressive therapy, journal therapy, and abreactive sessions,' the nurse wrote. 'One patient's average fee per day was $1,560; multiply this by 10 patients, and the hospital received $15,600 per day from this unit alone.'[100]

One would think that such whopping bills would alert parsimonious insurance companies, who would then send their investigators, but that has not been the case. Some insurance companies actually *own stock* in private psychiatric hospitals, a clear conflict of interest. In addition, according to one angry psychiatrist, insurance companies *like* large bills. 'Big bills mean big premiums and bonuses,' a doctor working for a major insurer told him. Finally, insurance officials are often afraid to crack down on mental health fraud. 'Insurance companies are petrified [of mental illness],' one expert testified before Pat Schroeder's congressional select committee in 1992. 'They don't want to touch it. They don't understand it. All you have to do is threaten to sue them or push them and they back down.'[101] Besides, why should they worry about it when they can pass on the bill to corporations and taxpayers?

Those providing services to therapists are also cashing in on recovered memories. Continuing-education credits are routinely dispensed to those who wish to learn the latest therapeutic techniques to unleash repressed memories. One course at a 1993 conference offered American Psychological Association credits for learning about 'body memories.' The course description: 'Neuroscientists have recently surmised that the mind is no longer in the head but is in every cell. To understand the concept of cellular memory we will look to genograms, eidetic imagery, past lives, holograms, recent research, the triune brain and unified field theory. We will also discuss various healing techniques.' At the same conference, a course taught people how to spot forgotten early childhood trauma through handwriting analysis.[102]

Crash courses in 'hypnotherapy' are advertised as a quick way to make money – for everyone concerned. I recently received a flier for a 'Hypnotherapy Certification Weekend' in Boston or Philadelphia, offered by the Hypnodyne Foundation in Clearwater, Florida. '*In Two Powerful Days You Will Develop Techniques and Skills That Will Enable You to Become a Hypnotherapist Certified by the International Association of Counselors and Therapists*,' it promised, adding that I would discover 'how you can make $3,000 to $10,000 in one evening by conducting group sessions' and 'how to use speed hypnosis and disguised hypnosis.' All of this cost a mere $395 for the weekend. It was touted for psychotherapists, chiropractors, massage therapists, clergymen, and police officers.

Another recent ad in the *Family Therapy Networker* promises a course in hypnotherapy that takes three times as long – '*Certification in 6 days!*' It features a photo of trainer Diane Zimberoff of the Wellness Institute. Like many other Recovery gurus, Zimberoff glows with movie-star quality. Her smile is beatific, radiant, warm. Her course, which offers continuing education credits, promises help with 'unlocking the inner child, codependency, incest issues.'[103]

Then there are the psychological tests that purport to offer scientific methods of determining personality. They, too, naturally cost money, both to purchase and administer. I recently received a flier from Western Psychological Services of Los Angeles promoting 'The Parent-Child Relationship Inventory,' a 15-minute quiz designed for use on parents. 'The PCRI is highly useful in child custody evaluation, family therapy, parent training, and child abuse assessment.' All for just $95.*[104]

There is also a lucrative market for material aimed directly at children, ranging from children's books (*I Can't Talk About It*) and card games (*Let's Talk about Touching in the Family*) to computer disks such as *Psych-Pix*, a new collection of psychological clip art. For a mere $19.95, psychologists can purchase a computer disk in this series called 'No Secrets Anymore,' with more than 50 images 'selected specifically for children who may have been sexually abused,' the ad specifies, including 'partially clothed adults and children; children looking concerned, worried, and angry; a dark closet; beds, etc.'[105]

Money has also flowed freely into the coffers of recovered-memory therapists directly from the government spigot. In a biographical sketch, MPD specialist Colin Ross recently bragged that he had received 'several hundred thousand dollars in research funding.'[106] Despite the clear evidence that facilitated communication does not work, the state of Georgia has awarded a second annual grant of $100,000 for study of this 'promising' technique.[107]

I recently witnessed a disturbing example of how greed, media influence, and pseudoscience often combine. While waiting to appear on a Midwestern talk show, I watched while another guest, a self-professed psychic, touted her skills. 'My findings are 96 per cent accurate,' she boasted, encouraging people to pony up for a dinner at which she would offer psychic counseling. When she came off the set, I asked her whether she could tell if someone had been sexually abused, even if they had repressed the memories. 'Oh, yes,' she said, 'I can read their auras.' Later, I complained to the station manager, who informed me that this psychic *paid* for her periodic spot on the show. In other words, her appearance was a well-disguised infomercial.

Law firms specializing in repressed memories are not content to sit back and wait for clients. In a new version of ambulance chasing, one lawyer began distributing a packet of information to women's centers, including a boilerplate letter intended for accused parents. 'Dear Mr. and Mrs. Blank,' the letter begins. 'Your child has retained me to represent her for the sexual and physical assaults perpetrated on her by Mr. Blank when she was a minor.' It goes on to threaten legal action,

---

* Although it is beyond the scope of this book to cover psychological tests, they have often been criticized for making unwarranted assumptions and validating false conclusions – particularly such subjective tests as the Rorschach Ink Blot or the more recent Dissociative Experience Scale, which is supposed to diagnose multiple personality candidates.

but states that 'we are prepared to settle the case to $250,000.'[108] Another lawyer sent letters to mental health professionals explaining that the statute of limitations for recovered memories had been extended. 'Restitution would provide empowerment and closure' – as well as hefty legal fees, of course.[109] Because parents would have to spend substantial amounts to defend themselves, with the attendant negative publicity and risk of losing, many have chosen to settle out of court when faced with such threats, even while maintaining their innocence.

The situation in Britain is not yet as bad. Still, a 1995 notice appeared in Marjorie Orr's *Accuracy About Abuse Newsletter* advertising the services of The Smith Partnership, a firm of solicitors specializing in sexual abuse cases. 'They offer help to advise on rights for claiming compensation from abusers or carers, from the Criminal Injuries Compensation Board or justice through the Criminal Courts.' When I called the Smith Partnership, solicitor Simon Richardson, who has handled hundreds of cases in the last four years, stated that he would always accept his client's stories at face value even if they claimed to have been abducted by aliens! In order to work within statutes of limitation, he refers his clients to psychiatrists, who can assess them and, where appropriate, certify that they have been mentally ill since the age of 18. Negligence cases, in which employers of alleged abusers are sued, are easier to pursue, since a judge has the discretion to override legal time limits, and there is no need to prove medical or mental illness.[110]

While I do not think that all who claim to have recovered memories of sexual abuse are motivated primarily by money, it certainly lends an added incentive. To receive compensation, the 'crime' must be reported to the police and there must be evidence of harm. In many recovered memory cases, however, it has not been necessary to go to trial to receive money as a purported sex abuse victim, and the 'evidence' of harm can be provided by the therapist who helped unearth the memories in the first place. 'There seems to be little or no awareness among the police and social workers of the possible detrimental aspects of criminal compensation awards,' observes British journalist Margaret Jervis. 'They may lead to both true and false allegations being exaggerated and lengthened, since the nature and longevity of abuse affects the amount of the award.'[111]

Victim compensation has been even more generous in New Zealand and Australia. Until 1993, sex abuse victims in New Zealand could claim lump sum payments up to $27,000. No substantiation is required to make such a claim. All that is necessary is for the alleged victim and her therapist to *believe* that she was abused. The lump-sum payments were finally stopped, but during a three-year transition period, more than $830 million was paid out in over 100,000 claims, mostly for 'loss of enjoyment of life.' In addition, in New Zealand sex abuse counseling is mostly paid by the government. In 1992, that therapy was costing an extraordinary $10 million annually – and the entire country holds fewer than four million people.[112]

THERAPISTS FACING THE FUTURE:
'FLOCKS OF EDGY BIRDS'

As acknowledged by all sides of the debate over health care reform, there are very real limits to how much we, as a society, can afford to spend on health care – including therapy. This obvious fact has therapists running scared, taking courses on brief therapy techniques, and wondering aloud over their future. In 'Endangered Species,' a long and remarkably frank cover article in the March/April 1994 issue of *Family Therapy Networker*, senior editor Mary Wylie describes therapists 'who now fly from one meeting to another like flocks of edgy birds [and] feel they have about as much job security right now as the engineers on the Super Collider project that the U.S. Congress recently abolished.'[113]

Wylie acknowledges that 'the therapeutic community has brought its current woes upon itself by its amazing failure ... to provide decent explanations, let alone measures of cost and outcome accountability, for its treatment methods.' Therapists are 'held to almost no objectively measurable, external standards for deciding what is wrong with the client, what to do about it, how long it should take to do it, when it can be considered done and how anybody knows if it is done.' Wylie reports that managed-care case reviewers she interviewed told her about a rich array of questionable therapies they had been asked to approve – including horseback riding lessons ('equestrian therapy'), exorcisms, past-life regressions, and a request for 500 sessions in advance. 'In another case, a therapist, who had been seeing a client four days a week for eight years at $200 a pop, wanted more.'

The time when 'vastly rich corporate patrons' unquestioningly paid for long-term therapy is coming to an end, however, according to Wylie. 'The Golden Age of private practice, when the term "rich therapist" was not an oxymoron,' is nearly over. Unfortunately, inventive therapists in search of lucrative repressed memories are already finding ways around the system. Some offer 'boutique therapy,' long-term counseling for wealthy clients who can afford it without insurance. It isn't difficult to predict that therapists will diagnose such golden-goose clients with massive amounts of repressed memories that will require years of expensive therapy to root out. Another recovered-memory therapist saw her practice cut in half by managed care. Undaunted, she offered a special after-work program, featuring a catered dinner and evening sessions. Managed care companies tumbled for this program, which supposedly kept people out of the hospital.[114]

Most therapists, however, will band together to offer major employers an 'integrated package' of mental health services, including assessment, outpatient therapy, referrals to self-help groups, crisis intervention, and psychiatric hospitalization.[115] In this context, a diagnosis of recovered memory will still provide much-needed business across the board. More than ever, less-qualified therapists who demand less money will find ready employment, hidden inside such organizations. Psychiatrists, relegated largely to writing drug prescriptions, are a disappearing breed, as noted by a recent *Newsweek* article, 'Psychiatry: Anxiety Over a Shrinking Future.'[116] In short, although health care reforms are likely to produce rhetoric about eliminating coverage for unnecessary or harmful procedures, they are not likely to end the search for repressed memories.

In England, where the National Health Service pays only for limited services by approved therapists, most psychotherapy is *already* privately funded by clients. Therefore, the issue of health reform is not as urgent as in the United States, and the hunt for repressed memories is less likely to be closely regulated in order to save taxpayers' money.

There is hope, however. While those who are deeply invested in the repressed-memory ideology are likely to become even more entrenched as they feel backed into a corner, many other therapists who always felt somewhat uneasy about recovered memories will probably begin to express concern. 'All my life I have experienced that people will seldom stand up on an unpopular or scary issue,' one therapist wrote to me recently. 'Just as dogs turn on an injured member of the pack, we humans want to be on the side that wins more than anything else. The tide is beginning to turn on this issue, and soon many, many people will feel free to talk about how they never really bought this satanic ritual abuse and repressed memory stuff.'[117]

PAT SCHROEDER, LIZ SAYCE, AND THE
POLITICS OF RECOVERY

Nor are most politicians aware of the hazards of recovered-memory therapy, even when the evidence appears overwhelming.

In 1992, U.S. Representative Patricia Schroeder of Colorado chaired a select committee investigation into the flagrant abuses perpetrated by private psychiatric hospitals. The hearing report was appropriately titled *The Profits of Misery: How Inpatient Psychiatric Treatment Bilks the System and Betrays Our Trust*. In her opening remarks, Schroeder deplored 'one of the most disgraceful and scandalous episodes in health care in America that I've seen in a long time.' She lamented the facts that 'patients sometimes were kept against their will until the benefits ran out' and that school counselors were given kickbacks for referring students with good mental health insurance coverage. 'Clearly,' she stated, 'this business of treating minds . . . has not policed itself, and has no incentive to put a stop to the kinds of fraudulent and unethical practices that are going on.' She lambasted a mental health system that could 'bilk patients of their hard earned dollars, strip them of their dignity, and leave them worse off than they were before they went for help.'[118]

In her remarks, Schroeder clearly described the mental health abuses I have documented in this book. Yet she has failed to make the connection between abuses in private psychiatric hospitals (including the MPD units described in Chapter 4) and the mind-warping that goes on during out-patient counseling sessions. A feminist who champions the rights of women, Schroeder has been taken in by the supposedly 'feminist' Survivor movement. She has recently sponsored a resolution urging *all* states to extend statute of limitations to allow prosecution based on recovered memories. 'The trauma of childhood sexual abuse typically causes effects such as denial, repression, and dissociation, which prevent the victim from remembering the abuse or recognizing its injurious effects until many years after the abuse has occurred,' Schroeder's resolution states, echoing familiar dogma – hardly surprising, because the bill was largely written and promoted by the American Coalition for Abuse Awareness, a Washington Survivor lobbying organization.[119]

Congresswoman Schroeder has also introduced a bill to allow the garnishing of federal pensions for those found guilty of sexual abuse.[120] The legislation is specifically aimed at Edward Rodgers, a Colorado man whose three daughters won a $2.2 million award in a lawsuit claiming that he sexually abused them.*[121] A movie-of-the-week version called *Ultimate Betrayal* appeared on television in 1994. While it appears that Rodgers was probably physically abusive to his children, it is not evident that he sexually abused his daughters, who apparently retrieved such 'memories' in therapy.

Until feminist officials such as Pat Schroeder realize that recovered-memory therapy is just another aspect of the abuse of women, it is unlikely that *any* politician will dare confront the tragic consequences of such therapy. Schroeder was appalled when a witness before her 1992 committee revealed that one chain of psychiatric hospitals distributed a pamphlet called 'Books as Hooks,' which touted self-help books as powerful recruiting tools.[122] And yet she does not see that *The Courage to Heal* and its ilk serve as just such 'hooks' for many unwary and unfortunate women searching for answers to their problems. I can only hope that Schroeder will come to understand that her own words apply to this disastrous form of 'healing' that does indeed 'bilk patients of their hard earned dollars, strip them of their dignity, and leave them worse off than they were before they went for help.'

Patricia Schroeder announced late in 1995 that she would not seek re-election in 1996, a blow for those who valued her feisty opposition to right-wing Republicans. In making her announcement, she said she wanted to 'tackle new challenges.'[123] I can only hope that among them will be the challenge to put an end to this misguided form of therapy.

In Britain, several politicians have championed the cause of recovered memory. David Hitchliffe, an ex-social worker and Labour MP, put forward a private members' bill to repeal the statute of limitations in civil suits. Other MPs, such as Lin Golding and David Alton, have supported legislation relating to ritual abuse. But the nearest U.K. equivalent to Pat Schroeder is Liz Sayce, policy director of MIND, a British advocacy group for mental health clients. Like Schroeder, Sayce is a committed feminist well aware of the abuses that women often suffer at the hands of mental health professionals. Yet she, too, has been seduced by the recovered memory dogma. In a 1994 letter to the *Guardian*, she inferred that there was no such thing as 'false memory

* Certainly, the Rodgers case, like that of George Franklin, is disturbing, though it does not prove the reality of repressed memories. I interviewed his son Steve and his ex-wife Dorothy, both of whom allege that Ed Rodgers was physically abusive. Neither believes that he sexually abused his preadolescent children. According to his ex-wife, however, he did make a sexual overture to his 19-year-old daughter one night when he was drunk.

syndrome' or illusory memories resulting from misguided therapy.[124] Hopefully, as more retractors contact her organization for help, she will realize that women mental health clients are being harmed by a pseudoscientific form of therapy.

THE HAZARDS AND USES OF THERAPY

As psychiatrist Jerome Frank pointed out over two decades ago in *Persuasion and Healing*, the therapist/client relationship – whether it involves repressed memories or not – is fraught with inherent danger. 'The patient enters into emotionally charged interactions with someone on whom he feels dependent.' Anyone who seeks counseling automatically does so in a distressed, vulnerable frame of mind, searching for answers to life's dilemmas. The therapist has an opportunity to exert enormous influence – particularly when *appearing* to be neutral. 'The very subtlety and unobtrusiveness of the therapist's influencing maneuvers,' Frank noted, 'coupled with his explicit disclaimer that he is exerting an influence, may increase his influencing power. For how can a person fight influences that he does not know exist?' Furthermore, 'the patient's tendency to scrutinize the therapist for clues of what is expected of him may be heightened by his belief that relief from his suffering depends on his doing or saying the right thing.'[125]

Mental health writer Mary Wylie recognizes how powerful and seductive the therapeutic relationship can be. 'Who does not yearn atavistically, when in pain of body and mind, to enter into a mysterious and deeply personal healing communion with a compassionate and skillful magician?' she writes.[126*127] True, and what therapist can resist playing the magic guru? As *Family Therapy Networker* editor Richard Simon has written, 'Nothing fills the seats in a hotel ballroom like a workshop

---

* The latest fad is 'Eye Movement Desensitization and Reprocessing,' or EMDR, in which guru therapists wave their fingers back and forth in front of patients' eyes, hearkening back to Anton Mesmer and described by one journalist as looking 'like something from a Monty Python skit.' By means of EMDR, clients supposedly relive and resolve past traumas. 'I'm rolling my eyeballs at the bullshit,' one psychiatrist recently commented to a journalist when asked his opinion of EMDR. 'Never underestimate the stupidity of people.' As *Psychology Today* writer Hara Marano notes, this new, quick method is attractive to recovered-memory advocates frightened by the demand for brief therapy. Therapists, Marano notes, are 'dazed from predictions that only one out of three of them would survive professionally.'

that promises therapists a new clinical method, some secret knowledge that can produce sudden, dramatic changes in troubled lives.'[128] This search for a 'quick fix' has led to one dangerous fad therapy after another, usually searching for some secret key in the recesses of childhood.

'Exploration of the patient's past is much more than a fact-finding expedition,' Jerome Frank observed. Rather, it is a reinterpretation in which patients actively participate. 'Evaluation apprehension, as experienced by most patients, makes them highly sensitive to the therapist's influence, which can be transmitted through cues so subtle that the therapist may not notice them.' In conclusion, Frank urged 'caution in evaluating patients' productions. If the therapist has an hypothesis in mind . . . he may unwittingly convey it to the patient, who may oblige by producing supportive material.'[129]

The history of therapist/client interactions is rife with examples that support Jerome Frank's cautions – and more. Because they are placed in such a powerful position, therapists have ample opportunity to abuse their power. In the privacy of their offices, with no supervision, they can – if they choose – play God with their clients' psyches. Ever since Freud's era, when many prominent psychoanalysts, including Carl Jung, had sexual intercourse with their clients, therapists have shown an alarming tendency to sexualize this intensely personal relationship. In several recent surveys, from 6 per cent to 17 per cent of the respondents admitted having sex with clients, and I suspect the percentage of actual instances is considerably higher. In one study, 65 per cent of those surveyed had treated patients who had been sexually involved with *previous* therapists.

Almost all of the therapists who had sex with their clients rationalized their action, asserting that it caused no harm.*[130] Yet 11 per cent of their clients were hospitalized as a result, and a substantial minority attempted suicide.[131] Therapists who encourage clients to visualize fantasies of incest are, in an analogous manner, abusing their clients in a 'therapeutic' context. As a result, their traumatized clients also often require hospitalization and sometimes take their own lives.

---

* In his provocative book, *House of Cards: Psychology and Psychotherapy Based on Myth*, psychologist Robyn Dawes discusses therapist-patient sexual contact, citing its prohibition (even years after therapy) as a 'paternalistic' attitude 'based on the premise that clients are totally under the control of their therapists.' In other words, Dawes thinks that the client should be treated as an autonomous adult capable of making independent decisions. I do not agree. In a relationship with a therapist, the client clearly *is* in a vulnerable, unequal position.

A number of critics have argued, fairly convincingly, that the only real benefit of most therapy is a placebo effect. Although many clients report that they feel better as a result, some studies indicate that simple *attention* and *support* combined with the *passage of time* account for the improvement. In addition, the client who has invested substantial effort and money is motivated to believe that therapy was successful. 'Despite decades of effort,' Jerome Frank wrote in 1973, 'it has been impossible to show convincingly that one therapeutic method is more effective than any other,' with the possible exception of behavior modification for problems such as obsessive-compulsive disorder.[132]

Ten years later, clinical psychologist Bernie Zilbergeld came to precisely the same conclusion in *The Shrinking of America*. 'You can expect about the same results regardless of which therapy you choose,' he explained, citing controlled experiments. Referring to the steady proliferation of therapeutic fads, he added that 'every new approach claims unprecedented success . . . Anyone still breathing at the end of treatment is considered to be cured or greatly improved.' Zilbergeld stated that 'there is no evidence that counselors do better, feel better, or overcome more problems than anyone else.'[133] Consequently, it should come as no surprise that, in one study, professional therapists provided no better results than well-intended, empathetic college professors (with no training in psychology). In 1994, after another decade of research, psychology professor Robyn Dawes, in *House of Cards*, echoes Frank and Zilbergeld: 'The effectiveness of therapy is unrelated to the training or credentials of the therapist.'[134]*

Moreover, *therapy can actually cause considerable harm* because of the biases that therapists convey. Since the 1960s, studies have consistently confirmed that some 10 per cent of clients *get worse* in therapy.[135] 'Mental health researchers and clinicians see problems and not strengths,' Zilbergeld has noted, 'because that is what they are trained to see and because it is in their interest to do so. The more pathology, the greater the need for more studies, more therapists, and more therapy.' In schools and textbooks, psychologists learn to concentrate on dysfunctional families, 'the ways they harm, oppress, and limit. They do not learn what a

---

* The conclusion that well-intentioned, compassionate lay therapists can be just as helpful as those with advanced training seems to contradict another concern I have repeatedly expressed – that poorly trained therapists are enthusiastically misapplying recovered-memory therapy on the basis of faulty notions. There is, however, no real contradiction. It is the hunt for repressed memories that is the problem, not the particular training.

healthy or typical family looks like, the ways in which a family provides security, comfort, love, and direction.'[136]

A retractor wrote to me recently, providing great insight into many counselors' predisposition to find dysfunctional families:

> When I was in graduate school for a master's in counseling psychology, I did a two semester practicum at the college counseling center. I had one case of an eighteen-year-old with major body image issues, which isn't particularly unusual. In the intake, she told me that she had a good relationship with her parents. My supervisor insisted that *no one* likes their parents that much. There had to be something else there. Later, my own therapist said the same things, that I had to be hiding something about my parents. And since I had already been trained in that school of thought, it was easy for me to go the next step and apply it to my own life.

In his 1994 book, *Beware the Talking Cure*, psychologist Terence Campbell includes a list of questions, some of which are reproduced below, to help identify ineffective, dangerous therapeutic approaches.

> Do you feel more worried and discouraged since you began therapy?
>
> Is your therapist intensely interested in the minutiae of your fantasies, feelings, and/or thoughts?
>
> Does your therapist focus primarily on the events of your childhood and overlook the present-day issues of your life?
>
> Does your therapist overemphasize your deficits and shortcomings while ignoring your strengths and resources?
>
> Does your therapist frequently tell you things about yourself which seem wildly speculative?
>
> Does your therapist seem to regard himself [or herself] as intellectually superior?
>
> Does your therapist appear to distrust you; is he quick to assume that you are merely victimizing yourself and sabotaging your therapy?
>
> Does your therapist frequently talk about other people in your life, but refuse to include them in your therapy despite their availability?

Does your therapist attribute malevolent motivations to other people in your life and indict them as a result?

Does your therapist act as if he or she provides you with a uniquely important relationship that is unavailable to you in other sectors of your life?

Does your therapist seek to determine where some feeling or emotion is located in your body?

Does your therapist rely on sympathetic platitudes advising you to 'trust yourself' and/or 'be kind to yourself'?[137]

If you answer 'yes' to many of these questions, it is probably time to switch therapists. I would add another important caveat. It is inappropriate for your therapist to encourage overdependence. The goal should be for you to become independent. Therefore, if you find yourself unable to make any decisions without approval from your therapist, or if your therapist becomes the most important person in your life, something is wrong.

Even if all of the recovered memories were true – which they are not – it is painfully obvious that the obsessive search for them does not usually make clients better. They almost invariably get worse, except for the few who appear to get a positive placebo effect from their new belief system. It is not healthy to live in a tortured past, nor is it healthy to encourage a client to sever all contact with family members.

Several British feminists have, fortunately, strongly protested the potentially detrimental effects of therapy – particularly the kind that elicits 'memories.' Journalist Margaret Jervis observes: 'Encouraging voyeuristic fantasies under the pretext of counselling is not therapy but emotional pornography.'[138] Suzanne Stevens of the Cardiff Woman's Support Group writes:

> The client must subordinate their autonomy to the control of the practitioner . . . . The peculiar and abnormal setting of the therapy furthermore is designed to create a tension and an expectation that something significant will happen. A client becomes vulnerable in this kind of situation and, as they have invested a great deal in the therapy, whether financial[ly] or emotional[ly], will quickly start colluding with the assumption that the therapist and his/her special abilities will be a central focus of the client's life . . . . The meeting between two hitherto equal people can become quite bizarre . . . . There are often covert messages that the therapist is the only

one who could deal with such material and the feelings attached
... All in all, the relationship, far from being therapeutic, can
become skewed, unbalanced and potentially unhealthy.[139]

Should people *ever* seek therapy, then? Of course, the answer is 'Yes.'
There are times when it makes sense to pay for a professional listener.
Sometimes friends and family members offer too much unwanted advice
because they are too close to a situation. Or maybe they don't have the
time to sit down and pay sufficient attention. Psychologist Peter Gray
describes the virtues of a good therapist:

> By devoting time to the client, listening warmly and respectfully,
> and not being shocked at the client's statements or actions, any
> good psychotherapist communicates the attitude that the client is
> a worthwhile human being ... In addition, most therapists make
> at least some common-sense suggestions that have little to do with
> their theories, of the sort that anyone's wise friend or relative
> might make, but carrying more weight because they come from a
> recognized authority.[140]

Also, a professional counselor can sometimes help open clogged communication channels, facilitating understanding and dialogue. Research
has shown that true family therapy – involving biological family
members, friends, or others concerned with the client – to be quite
effective, especially when therapy helps families identify their resources
and strengths to support a troubled family member.[141]

While therapy is, indeed, an art form of sorts, it should be based on
logic and common sense. Truth does matter. Proven effectiveness matters. As veteran therapist Paul Meehl advised his colleagues in 1992,
clinicians should continually ask, 'What do you mean? How do you
know?' If therapists ignore such questions, they are 'little more than
be-doctored, well-paid soothsayers.' Meehl continued: 'I see disturbing
signs that this is happening and I predict that if we do not clean up
our clinical act and provide our students with role models of scientific
thinking, outsiders will do it for us.'[142]

At last count, there were more than 400 supposedly different forms
of psychotherapy, with the practitioners of each sure that *their* approach
offers the key to mental health.[143] Consequently, it can be confusing
when you're shopping around. The particular therapist and his/her personality may make more difference than any orientation, but controlled

research has clearly demonstrated that *cognitive and behavioral therapies* are more effective than other approaches. Psychodynamically oriented therapies (including psychoanalysis) have proven less useful, though usually slightly better than a placebo. The most effective therapeutic approaches are short-term (under 20 sessions).[144]

Cognitive therapy – as exemplified by Albert Ellis' 'rational-emotive' approach, Aaron Beck's treatment for anxiety and depression, or George Pransky's 'psychology of mind' – concentrates on current problems. Rather than rehashing and reinterpreting the past, cognitive therapists stress how people's belief systems – the ways they think about themselves and others – interfere with their lives. By reframing and modifying self-defeating attitudes, people can better cope with their lives, without years of lying on an analyst's couch.[145]

Behavior modification methods can be a component of the cognitive approach, particularly for anxiety disorders. Such methods as systematic desensitization or counter-conditioning can sometimes help people cope with panic attacks or obsessive-compulsive behavior. I should note, however, that some behavioral approaches, such as 'flooding,' have been used by recovered-memory therapists in destructive ways. Any method that deliberately manipulates strong human emotions has great potential for harm.

Appropriate use of medication can also provide much-needed relief in some cases. I am personally concerned about an over-reliance on drugs, but there appears to be no question that Prozac and other medications have made an enormous difference to many suffering from depression or other difficulties, when no form of therapy did much good.[146]

For those suffering from panic attacks, the CHAANGE program – the acronym stands for Center for Help for Agoraphobia/Anxiety through New Growth Experiences – has helped over 13,000 people to overcome this severe psychological problem. *Free from Fears*, an inexpensive paperback by Ann Seagrave and Faison Covington, provides a simple introduction, or readers can write to CHAANGE National Headquarters, 128 Country Club Dr., Chula Vista, CA 91911 U.S.A..

For further information on any of these promising therapeutic approaches, readers should check this book's bibliography.

If you decide to seek therapy, you should ask what orientation your therapist has and how long the process will probably take. Never forget that *you* are paying for a service and you deserve straight answers. There should be no mystery involved in this interaction between two people.

By and large, overly stressed people in Western cultures tend to place entirely too much faith in therapists. Life isn't fair, and every person's time on earth includes challenges, disappointments, and even tragedies. But most people are basically resilient and resourceful, quite capable of surviving and thriving with a little help from their friends, as the Beatles once sang. 'It's not clear that long discussions of childhood are necessary or useful,' psychologist Bernie Zilbergeld has observed. Nor do we need constant monitoring or psychic repair by experts. 'We may take pride in living more honest lives,' he wrote, 'bearing the limits, contradictions, vulnerabilities, and burdens of our humanity as best we can, taking our place in the long stream of men and women who have done the same since the beginning of time.'[147]

THE VERDICT ON REPRESSED MEMORIES

Since writing Chapter 2, 'The Memory Maze,' I have kept an open mind about the possible validity of 'massive repression,' in which years of abuse may have been forgotten. Actively seeking *just one case* in which such a mechanism clearly occurred, I wrote to over 50 professional psychological associations, including the American Psychological Association, the American Psychiatric Association, the American Association for Marriage and Family Therapy, and others. I asked for any official statements they might have on repressed memories, sexual abuse, hypnosis, or dream analysis. I wrote:

> Although I have conducted numerous interviews with those who have recovered memories of abuse, I have thus far been unable to find a case with firm corroboration – that is, where the accused perpetrator admits to the abuse, contemporary diary entries verify it, or where pediatric records confirm the complaints. If you know of any such cases, I would really appreciate it if you would help me out. I make all interviews completely confidential and anonymous, changing names and locations. You are welcome to copy this letter and give it to colleagues or clients, who could contact me directly.

So far, I have received no useful responses.*

---

* I received my original letter back from the American Psychosomatic Society with a short note attached: 'Sorry, we have no information that will be helpful to you.' Since the repressed-memory phenomenon involves considerable psychosomatic displays such as 'body memories,' I found this response surprising.

As documented earlier in the book, in the cases of Ross Cheit, some Father James Porter victims, and survivor Melinda Couture, I believe that some cases of sexual abuse can be forgotten, only to be recalled later in life. But in such cases, the abuse covered (1) only a single incident or a very limited period of time and (2) was not perceived as particularly traumatic at the time. In other words, I believe that we are dealing here with simple forgetting, not repression.

Other cases of actual forgetting (and possibly remembering) involve children on the cusp of the infantile amnesia period. In the television documentary, 'Divided Memories,' Ofra Bikel interviewed a mother whose five-year-old daughter told her that her husband had put his penis in the child's mouth. When confronted, he confessed and swore he would stop. The matter was never mentioned again, and the child forgot it. When the daughter was in her late teens, she was experiencing difficulties. Her mother thought perhaps they stemmed from the sexual abuse, so she told the daughter. Soon afterward, the daughter was sure she remembered the incident from when she was five.[148]

Frankly, I question whether she really recalled the sexual abuse. It is not terribly surprising that she would have forgotten something that happened when she was five, but it is likely that it really was just forgotten. Told that she had been abused, and desperate for an answer to her current problems, the daughter would naturally strive mightily to remember. What she then pictured in her mind could well have been fantasized, however.

I have been unable to find any corroborated cases of 'massive repression,' however, in which *years* of terrible abuse were completely forgotten, only to be recalled later.

I asked Ellen Bass for cases of massive repression that had firm corroboration, and she referred me to three women I will call Nancy, Pat, and Laura. None of them, in fact, could provide firm corroboration. Laura subsequently changed her mind about having her story told, so I will not include it here. Since the other two were referred directly by Ellen Bass, whose book has played such a central role in encouraging 'memory' recovery, I will briefly summarize them.

Nancy is 60 years old and did, indeed, experience severe abuse and neglect as a child, by anyone's standards. She spent her early years with her disturbed mother, who was diagnosed as a paranoid schizophrenic her alcoholic father, and her mother's various boyfriends. When she was nine, she was taken from her mother and placed in an institution. Nancy always remembered her mother leaving her on a window ledge to die when she was four years old. She recalled the starvation, living in sleazy hotels, the constant parade of strange men, her father's abusive rages at her mother. She always remembered the 'nameless men' who fondled her. She vividly recalls a female social worker trying to seduce her when she was 13.

It was only in the late 1980s, however, that Nancy retrieved memories of sexual abuse by her father and mother. Her corroboration came second-hand, when her sister-in-law told her that her husband, Nancy's twin brother, was also abused and confirmed that Nancy had been, too. Her brother won't talk about it, though. Similarly, Nancy's aunt, now deceased, supposedly confirmed that she had known about the abuse perpetrated by her sister, 13 years her junior. Since the aunt is dead, there is no way to ask her about this, but it is quite possible she was only referring to the truly awful childhood she knew Nancy had endured. That is one reason I never accept second-hand, hearsay testimony in these cases. It is very easy for those who have recovered 'memories' to grab onto a relative's halting reaction as clear corroboration. A relative may say, 'I always knew your mother was abusive to you,' but that does not constitute corroboration.

Pat, 28, has recalled being sexually abused by her cousin Tom, seven years her senior. The memories began to come back in 1994, when she was reading *The Courage to Heal* and writing in her journal. Then she had a dream in which Tom abused her and told her threateningly, 'I had fun this weekend. I lit a cat with gasoline.' Eventually, she recalled him molesting her for years, then raping her when she was in the sixth grade. As with Nancy, there is at least some truth to these allegations. When she was five or six, Pat told her mother that Tom had touched her in places he wasn't supposed to. 'We figured it was maybe just curiosity with him,' Pat's mother told me when I interviewed her. They spoke to Tom's parents and thought nothing more about it.

Ironically, Pat now says she does not remember this initial incident, but she does recall the others. She is sure they are true, because from her dreams and journals she can identify the different rooms – the bathroom, the basement, the bedroom – where the abuse occurred. Also, Tom's mother wrote to her recently, 'No, he is not denying it. He said every time the family got together for a gathering he would wonder about things.' She appears to be writing only about the initial, acknowledged incident, however. 'Tom at that time was only 13 or 14,' she wrote in the letter. Therefore, it is not clear what he is not denying or what he meant by wondering about 'things.' I called Tom, but he would not discuss the allegations with me. It would appear that Tom may not remember these incidents either, but he feels that perhaps he repressed them, too. This is a confusing case, in which some sexual abuse apparently took place, but again, the new 'memories' are not firmly corroborated.

When I contacted Judith Herman to ask for confirmed cases of recovered memories, she referred me to Roger Pitman at the VA hospital in Manchester, NH. In his turn, Pitman referred me to his associate, Danya Vardi, who told me that completely repressed memories were extremely rare in her experience. Finally, however, she referred me to Lisa, a 43-year-old Massachusetts woman who supposedly had corroboration for her returned memories.

My extended interview with Lisa only confirmed everything I had already heard. After a year in Adult Children of Alcoholics, 'trying to figure out why my life was screwed up,' Lisa joined Overeaters Anonymous, then sought therapy. She eventually 'remembered' being abused by eight different people, including her mother and older sister, a grandfather and grandmother, an uncle, two neighbors, and a priest. As her 'proof,' she cited her younger sisters who were two and three at the time of the abuse. 'As I would be telling my sisters about a memory, they would remember a piece of it.'

It should be clear by now that many people claim that their memories were 'corroborated,' when in fact they were not. There is a kind of self-confirmatory bias that kicks into gear once a belief system is in place. I spoke to one woman who retrieved memories of abuse by her junior high swimming coach. As clear 'proof' that the memories must be true, she says, 'When I heard his wife was pregnant, I got really upset. Why would I have reacted that way otherwise?' Of course, there could be any number of reasons, but once the recovered memory hypothesis is in place, every intuition or reaction is taken as confirming it.

Similarly, many women told me that their memories must be true because they retrieved them outside of therapy, or because their therapists never led them in any way. I am quite skeptical of such claims, especially if the 'memories' came back after the mid–1980s, and particularly after *The Courage to Heal* was published in 1988. By that time, for women, the idea that repressed memories of sexual abuse might account for any life problems had become all-pervasive. By 1990, most women must have at least briefly considered the idea that they harbored repressed memories. They might not recall precisely where they heard about this phenomenon – a friend, a talk show, a short story, a book – but the odds are very good that the idea was indeed planted.

· And I most assuredly do not believe those cases in which the therapist was supposedly neutral and did not lead the client at all. In all such cases, I suspect the therapist conveyed the idea that massive repression was a *possible* explanation. 'It could be anything, including repression, but let's not jump to conclusions,' the therapist warns. 'I don't want to lead you into anything. These memories will come on their own if they're there.' And by that very statement, the therapist is indeed leading the client down repressed memory lane.

These supposedly corroborated, unforced stories have led many otherwise responsible journalists to write that cases of massive repression have been confirmed, even though they never explore any specific cases in detail. In her excellent 1995 piece in the *New York Times Magazine* on Kelly Michaels, for instance, Nancy Hass wrote: 'While some of the thousands of people who, aided by therapists, have recalled long-ago instances of sexual abuse have had their claims substantiated, many others are thought to have been grossly manipulated by suggestions.'[149] I wrote to Hass, questioning this statement. 'If you have any cases in which massively repressed memories have been firmly corroborated, *please* let me know about them, since I am preparing a second edition,' I wrote. She never answered me.

One final case deserves attention. I was initially excited when one of the therapists I interviewed put me in touch with Betsy, a 43-year-old Texan whose father had confessed to her incest allegations. Not only that, but Betsy had retrieved her memories on her own, outside therapy, using Christian recovery books as her guide. She told me that she had always remembered an incident when she was learning to drive at 16. Her father had touched her breast, and she had become very upset and told him never to do that again. Now, she has recalled how he fondled and raped her from the age of four until that last attempt at molestation when she was 16 – and he has confessed to it.

Then I interviewed George, her 70-year-old father. 'Praise the Lord, hello,' his wife Rose answered the phone. It turns out that George, Rose, and Betsy all attend a charismatic born-again church. George told me that he, too, had always remembered the incident when Betsy was 16. He did not, however, actually recall any other abuse. A blue-collar factory employee, he had routinely worked from 5 a.m. until the evening, often arriving home as late as 11 p.m. He would then drink straight shots of whiskey to put himself to sleep, and start the routine again the next morning. 'I don't remember anything about what Betsy says I did,' he told me. 'I used to be an alcoholic, so I probably had black-outs. I told her that if she says that I did something, I did. Because I brought my children up to be truthful. So she wouldn't lie. I've tried many a time to get a picture of it. How could I do such a thing? It isn't easy to believe, but when an innocent child tells you what you've done, you've got to know it's true.'

In other words, George – like Paul Ingram in Lawrence Wright's *Remembering Satan* – is a devout father who thinks he may have a 'dark side' and loves his daughter enough to confess to anything she accuses him of doing. Unlike Ingram, George has not been able to visualize virtuoso ritual abuse performances, but he seems equally willing to accept blame for incest, whether or not it ever occurred.

Perhaps people can forget a single traumatic incident and then recall it years later, but I find it difficult to believe that years of abuse could be repressed or dissociated, only to pop back to consciousness with the proper trigger. If such massive repression routinely occurred, why is it only in the past decade that recalling years of abuse has become a wholesale American pastime? Some might answer that uncovering such memories requires a skilled therapist to elicit the proper abreaction. Yet consider Arthur Janov's primal screamers of the early 1970s, all of whom were encouraged to relive buried trauma memories. Of all of Janov's cases related in his first book, only *one* involved incest memories. Why? Clearly, Janov didn't *expect* or *need* sexual abuse as an etiology. Any old trauma would do, so that's what his patients produced. If indeed there were truly so many repressed incest memories, they most certainly would have swamped primal scream sessions.[150]

My views remain unaltered. Although the human mind is clearly capable of many things, 'massive repression' is probably not one of them.

HOW TO TELL TRUE FROM ILLUSORY MEMORIES

One of the few things that adversaries on both sides of the repressed memory debate agree on is that, without firm external corroborative evidence, it is impossible to distinguish definitively between true and false memories. Given what we now know, however, I think it is possible to hazard a reasonable guess in many cases. First, if a sex abuse memory stems from massive repression – memories of long-term abuse retrieved after lengthy amnesia – I believe the memory is untrue. There may be always-remembered elements that are correct, but the superstructure built upon those elements is probably confabulated. Beyond that simple criterion built around the concept of massive repression, there are other indicators. In general, I distrust 'checklists,' since people tend to regard them as iron-clad criteria in an ambiguous world. Nonetheless, I think a positive answer to several of the following questions may legitimate appropriate skepticism for the 'memories' involved.

Did the memories come back during memory-focused psychotherapy, incest group work, or after reading a book such as *The Courage to Heal*?

Does the claimed abuse go back to the crib, during the period of infantile amnesia?

Do the recovered memories extend into the teenage years or beyond?

Do the recovered memories involve actual rape or bizarre ritual abuse elements?

Do the memories have a 'horror movie' stereotypical quality to them, standing alone, outside a normal life narrative?

Has the accuser been diagnosed with multiple personalities?

Did the accusations begin with one person, then spread to multiple perpetrators?

In order to retrieve the memories, were hypnosis, guided imagery, massage, dream analysis, or other such techniques employed?

Does the accuser feel that the memories explain most life problems, such as physical illness, depression, troubled relationships, or work-related issues?

Does the accuser cut off all contact with anyone who expresses even the mildest doubts?

Does the accuser seem motivated by monetary compensation?

Does the accuser appear to be enraged much of the time?

Has the accuser made being a 'Survivor' the main source of identity?

Did the memories come back during the height of media attention and societal belief in recovered memories, in the late 1980s
to early 1990s?

Positive answers to several of these questions *could* provide an indication
that the accusations *may be* based on illusory memories. I want to caution
readers, however, that they are not fool-proof, nor have they been
scientifically tested in any kind of controlled situation. Furthermore,
negative answers to these questions do not necessarily indicate that the
memories are accurate. Indeed, it is quite likely, as time goes on, that
many of those who have recovered memories will hide or distort that
fact. We already see that beginning to happen. Memories retrieved
during therapy have now become questionable to many knowledgeable
people. Therefore, some accusers convince themselves that the memories arose outside of therapy. Similarly, some who previously stated
that their memories sprang back full-blown after a long period of
amnesia have now revised their stories. 'I always sort of remembered.
I just pushed the memories to the back of my mind.'*

This kind of vagueness makes for a gray area in trying to distinguish
true from false memories. It need not be a matter of conscious duplicity.
One of the lessons we have learned from recovered-memory therapy is
how readily human beings can manipulate their pasts. It is quite possible
for those who have recovered illusory 'memories' to convince themselves
that they had *always* remembered. This possibility makes it very difficult
indeed to jump to conclusions. According to several studies, a sizeable
minority (up to a third) of 'UFO alien abductees' claim continuous
memory for their experiences, which usually includes sexual abuse
aboard a spaceship.[151]. This statistic should, at least, make us somewhat
cautious about accepting all always-remembered claims in the current
social climate. Each case must be examined carefully. Above all, I do
not want us to go back to an automatic denial of sex abuse accusations. In general, all things being equal, I believe always-remembered

* Cases involving older children or teenagers are particularly difficult. It is quite possible
for an adolescent daughter to feel trapped by a personal dilemma and want to 'get back'
at her parents. She knows that accusing her father of sexual abuse will give her automatic
power and attention. Once the allegations are made, they take on a life of their own,
with social workers and the police involved. Often, the teen wants to take back the
accusations once she sees their effect, but is deterred by fear of prosecution. These cases
are particularly disturbing because they often arise outside of therapy and do not involve
recovered memories. And, of course, in some cases the daughters really *are* being sexually
abused by their fathers.

accusations of sexual abuse, and I do not believe in those involving massive repression.

WHEN A FRIEND REMEMBERS

Because there has been much publicity about the recovered-memory debate, and because many people now recognize that the intrusive methods of many therapists can lead to false accusations based on bogus memories, most of my acquaintances agree that the hunt for repressed memories can be dangerous. Many have a close friend, however, who has recovered such memories. *Those* cases are accurate, they assure me, and if I express doubts, they sometimes become outraged.

It's an understandable attitude. When you watch a friend going through the process of memory recovery, it is extremely convincing. After all, this is someone you know very well. She (or he) is not stupid, not faking, not crazy or hallucinatory. This is Suzy, your best friend since high school. So when she tells you that she's going to therapy for her relationship problems, and the therapist thinks it might stem from sexual abuse, you just listen. When she expresses her anxieties and her doubts, you're there for her. And when she tells you with genuine horror that she really *has* remembered something awful that her father did, you believe her. How dare someone like me doubt her memories, when I've never even met her?

I respond that if I told them a good friend of mine were convinced through hypnosis that she had been abducted by a UFO, or that she was possessed by demons, what would they think? Well, they would be very skeptical. That, I explain, is an analogous situation. I don't *need* to meet their friend. If she follows the classic pattern – she's in a stressful life situation, searching for answers, goes to therapy, reads *The Courage to Heal*, has dreams of abuse, has mysterious bodily pains – then it is very unlikely that she was actually sexually abused. She has suggested herself into it. I explain that there is no scientific evidence that people can completely forget such long-term trauma. It just doesn't make any sense.

Generally, however, such arguments make no difference. *We're not talking about UFOs! We're not talking about demons! This is sexual abuse. This is incest and this is my friend! How dare you make such comparisons?* I explain that I'm not saying that incest doesn't exist. I'm saying that *massive repression* of incest memories probably doesn't exist. The pattern of memory 'recovery' matches everything we know about how people create stories of UFO abductions, past lives, or multiple personalities. I go on about suggestibility, panic attacks, and the like. My acquaintance remains unmoved.

Look, I say, has your friend confronted her father about these memories? *Yes.* And does he deny them? *Of course he denies them, but that doesn't mean anything.* What about pediatric records? Do they show anything? *I don't know. I wouldn't think of questioning her that closely on this delicate subject.* Has she cut off all contact with her parents because of this? *Well, yes.* Don't you think it would be important to really get the other side of the story, to search for some validation for 'memories' which come back in fuzzy fragments, in dreams, in odd bodily manifestations?

No. Absolutely not. I would never suggest such a thing to my friend, not after all the pain she has been through. How could I even think of expressing doubts to her?

Not surprisingly, I feel rather strongly about this issue. It is tragic to watch people develop their 'memories,' tear themselves apart emotionally, and cut off all contact with their parents. If you, the reader, have a best friend who has recovered memories, I urge you to suggest, in as gentle a manner as possible, that there is a possibility that such memories do not represent real past events. Don't push it, or you'll be cut off, too. Remain there for your friend, but you might consider loaning her this book at an appropriate moment.

A HUG IS NOT SEX ABUSE

One of the unfortunate consequences of the current paranoia in this country over sexual abuse is that we're afraid to express physical affection for our children any more. One of my friends, a teacher, told me that she has been instructed only to use a 'tent hug' to console a student. She demonstrated it, leaning stiffly forward from the waist so that only her head touched mine as she patted me on the back. Day-care providers do not dare hold children on their laps during story hour. My father, well into his seventies, told me that when he gives his four-year-old granddaughter a bath, he refuses to help her wash her private parts. As a consequence, she doesn't rinse the soap off very well and, according to my sister, sometimes complains of an itchy crotch. (Thank goodness my sister hasn't taken her to a social worker in fear that this is a symptom of sex abuse!)

In 1971, when my children were one and three years old, Ashley Montagu wrote *Touching: The Human Significance of the Skin*. At the time, I read the book and thought it made sense. 'Fondling of the infant can scarcely be overdone,' he concluded. 'Any abrupt cessation of fondling should be avoided, and it is recommended that in cultures of the Western world, and in the United States in particular, parents express their affection for each other and for their children more demonstratively than they have in the past. It is not words so much as acts communicating affection that children, and, indeed, adults, require.'[152] No one would dare say such a thing now. The word *fondling* has been demonized and now refers only to invasive sexual acts.

That's too bad, because Montagu was right. Many Americans have always been uncomfortable about expressing physical affection. We are somehow afraid of one another, and the new puritanism, with its emphasis on 'boundaries,' is likely to deprive an entire generation of natural, affectionate touch. In a recent poll of Virginia mental health and legal professionals, *20 per cent of the respondents felt that frequent hugging of a 10-year-old child justified intervention by state authorities. Over half thought that a parent giving a child a brief good-night kiss on the lips was sexually abusive. And 75 per cent thought that intervention would be required in families where parents appeared nude in front of their five-year-olds.*[153]

Ugandan native Joshua Rubongoya, now a Virginia political science professor, recently wrote an article complaining about how difficult it is to be a good father in the United States. He muses about 'why raising children is so burdensome in America and not so much so in Africa.' Part of the answer is that in Uganda, 'children were brought up by the community, the neighborhood, the extended family, the school and church.' He also recognizes that in America 'if a dad frequently changes diapers and gives evening baths to the kids, this could become grounds for child molestation charges.' He wonders whether fathers will all be 'stripped of the joys of parenting, or can fatherhood be retrieved from the heap of social history?'[154]*[155]

---

* A 1994 newspaper article provides chilling evidence that Rubongoya's concerns are realistic. In the article, Tennessee Circuit Judge Muriel Robinson said that she has heard so many false allegations of child sexual abuse in her divorce court that she advises divorced fathers to limit physical contact with their children. 'It's very dangerous nowadays for a loving father to be around his children, especially little girls,' the judge stated.

It is a good question. Yale child psychiatrist Kyle Pruett wrote *The Nurturing Father*[*][156] in 1987, the year before *The Courage to Heal* appeared. Pruett called for fathers to be much more involved in the daily care of their children. His ideal father 'would be loving and nurturing without embarrassment or fear, open and vulnerable without being a victim. He could foster in his children the freedom to be strongly feminine or tenderly masculine but, above all, abidingly human.'[157] These are wonderful sentiments, but increasingly difficult to fulfil in these troubled times.

HUMANS ARE RESILIENT

Another unfortunate result of the current atmosphere is the assumption that people who really *were* sexually abused are irretrievably damaged by it, and that all unwanted sexual incidents – ranging from comments on breast size to rape – have an equally harmful effect. Certainly, violent sexual abuse of children is very traumatic and its effects should not be minimized. Nonetheless, humans are far more resilient than the Survivor Movement would have us believe.

Psychologist Terence Campbell draws an analogy between victims of automobile accidents and sexual abuse. Some people involved in a car wreck suffer severe injury or whiplash. Others walk away with minor injuries, and some appear completely unscathed. Similarly, some victims of sexual abuse appear to suffer severe sequelae, while others do not. The diagnosis on medical charts does not say 'victim of auto accident,' but 'neck injury.' Similarly, Campbell says, it is absurd to diagnose someone for treatment as a 'sex abuse victim.' Instead, specific problems such as panic attacks or low self-esteem should be treated.[158]

Maya Angelou's terrible childhood experience with sexual abuse is instructive. At the age of seven, she was raped by Mr. Freeman, her mother's boyfriend. 'He called me into the living room. Then he was

---

* Reading Kyle Pruett's book was a bittersweet experience for me because it brought me back to the time my children were infants. The book opens with Pruett's meeting with a 19-year-old father who could have been me. Later, he describes the immense pain caring fathers go through after a divorce. 'It hit me so hard I started crying,' one such father says. 'I just couldn't help it. And I kept on crying. I'd never done that before in front of her [his daughter].' Pruett saw his tears as 'a gift to his daughter.' Ironically, therapists such as Patricia Love would interpret such tears as 'emotional incest.'

holding me too tight to move and his pants were open and his "thing" was standing out and he grabbed down my bloomers. And then there was the pain and I passed out.' She was not going to say anything about it, but her mother discovered her bloodied underwear, and the story came out. After the trial, Mr. Freeman was murdered by Angelou's uncles. Irrationally, the little girl felt terrible guilt, and she simply stopped speaking for four years.

Clearly, if anyone could complain of life-long problems resulting from childhood sexual abuse, it is Maya Angelou. Yet she went on to become an inspirational example to us all through her poetry and speeches. 'I tell you there's not one thing I would undo, not one,' she told an interviewer. 'Because look at who I am. I am so grateful to be who I am ... I laugh a lot. I am greatly loved and love greatly, and I cry and I'm pleased with human beings. So I wouldn't undo it, not one thing, not even the rape.'[159]

In his classic 1959 book, *Man's Search for Meaning*, Holocaust survivor and psychotherapist Viktor Frankl concluded that 'man [or woman] is *not* fully conditioned and determined; he determines himself whether to give in to conditions or stand up to them. In other words, man is ultimately self-determining.' As an example of how psychological theory can promote the very symptoms it supposedly cures, Frankl discussed a client who had been sexually abused by her father and sought therapy for her unsatisfactory sex life. 'Through reading popular psychoanalytic literature,' he observed, 'the patient had lived all the time in the fearful expectation of the toll that her traumatic experience would some day take. This anticipatory anxiety resulted in ... excessive attention centered upon herself.'[160]

I edited a moving Holocaust* memoir, published in 1994.[161] It tells the story of a husband and wife who were separated when their ghetto was liquidated, then survived years of starvation, torture, and abuse in many different concentration camps. They watched their friends slowly die. They saw children arbitrarily shot. Nothing could compare to the

---

* It disturbs me that repressed-memory advocates such as Judith Herman and Ellen Bass equate the unequivocal horror of the Holocaust with supposedly recovered abuse memories. In 1994, for instance, Holocaust survivor and historian Elie Wiesel addressed a national convention of therapists, who clearly wished to co-opt his real suffering in the name of repressed memory Survivors. (Fortunately, Wiesel specifically warned his audience of the potential hazards of recovered-memory therapy.) As a falsely accused parent, I also deeply resent being lumped with modern neo-Nazis who deny that the Holocaust ever occurred.

horror they experienced. Yet they picked up the pieces of their lives after the war. They moved to America and started anew. They had children, raised them in a loving manner, and contributed to their community. Like other Holocaust survivors, they experienced (and continue to experience) profound grief over the loss of their families. The wounds of the Holocaust will never fully heal for them or other survivors. But the experience has not ruined their lives. Nor did they ever forget what happened to them.

Wendy Kaminer draws the same conclusion in her book, *I'm Dysfunctional, You're Dysfunctional*. Having listened to the stereotypical stories of self-identified Survivors in 12-step groups, Kaminer attended several meetings of Cambodian refugees, *true* survivors of Khmer Rouge atrocities. 'These Cambodian survivors don't glibly proffer their stories to strangers,' she found. Instead, she heard about their agony secondhand from social workers and doctors. One woman, for instance, had watched soldiers split her husband's head with an axe and was then unaccountably spared after being forced to dig her own grave. 'There is more laughter and lightness in these meetings of vulnerable, impoverished survivors of genocide than in any twelve-step group I've attended,' Kaminer observes, 'where people pursue recovery with deadening earnestness.'[162]

Similarly, true incest victims don't often speak of their experiences, which are too private, too painful. When Melody Gavigan (who has since retracted her allegations) formed the first Survivors of Incest Anonymous group in Reno, Nevada, she attracted those who had always remembered their abuse along with those who had recovered 'memories' in therapy. Soon, the group split in two. The real incest victims couldn't stand to listen to the gory details of retrieved-memory Incest Survivors. It wasn't that the real survivors necessarily doubted the recovered memories. They just felt no need to rehearse and relive the pain continually. They wanted to get on with their lives.[163]

Somehow, we have come to regard sexual abuse as a *special* category of trauma that inherently causes more damage than anything else. In a way, this is similar to the Victorian view that saw 'fallen' women as irretrievably soiled. By concentrating almost exclusively on sexual abuse, we have minimized and neglected the far more prevalent *physical* abuse of children, which was the focus of concern in the 1960s. As feminist therapist Janice Haaken bluntly asks, 'Is fondling a child worse than beating her with a belt?'[164] Simple *neglect* is, by far, the most prevalent form of child abuse. 'Many more children die from neglect than from physical abuse or sexual abuse,' sex researcher Allie Kilpatrick points out, but neglect is 'less dramatic than physical abuse and certainly less titillating than sexual abuse.'[165]

Consequently, 'child abuse' is automatically taken to mean child *sexual* abuse nowadays. We have also concluded that the only way to 'save' sexually abused children is to destroy their families, even if the children are already adults. Some studies have suggested that helping families work through their problems and stop abusive behavior is preferable to splitting them.

Ever since Freud, we have tended to accept a kind of grim psychological predestination. Experts assume that the traumas of the past not only *affect* our current lives, but *determine* them. Thus, a 1994 *Time* review of Mikal Gilmore's book, *Shot in the Heart*, about his murderous brother Gary, contains the following statement: 'Both Gilmore parents, haunted by their past, took their frustrations out on their children, dooming them to lives of anger and abuse as well.' It is true that screwed-up parents usually produced screwed-up children, but the absolute assertion that 'his mother's shattered Mormon faith [and] his father's secret criminal past' *doomed* Gary Gilmore to murder people is absurd.[166]

Several recent studies indicate how resilient humans can be. In a 1993 review of numerous surveys on the impact of child sexual abuse, Linda Williams and David Finkelhor – two sociologists who lean toward belief in repressed memories – noted that one-third of the victims displayed no apparent symptoms, while two-thirds seemed to have recovered within a year and a half. 'The findings suggest the absence of any specific syndrome in children who have been sexually abused and no single traumatizing process,' they stated. Not only that, but a comparison between sex abuse victims and other children in therapy revealed that the former were actually *less* symptomatic.[167]

In a 1996 review of the literature on sexual abuse sequelae, Bruce Rind and Evan Harrington concluded that brutal sexual abuse was indeed likely to cause negative repercussions later in life. They warn, however, that 'focusing on early sexual experiences when they have little or no influence on later adjustment, while ignoring other factors that have greater influence, represents misplaced attention and is also likely to be counterproductive.' Rind and Harrington concluded, from the college samples and general population surveys they reviewed, 'that permanent harm [from non-penetrative molestation] is rare and that effects are small on average.'[168]

Similarly, a 1992 follow-up study of people who were severely battered as children more than 20 years before revealed surprising adult adjustment. As a group, they *did* display relatively high levels of resentment and suspiciousness, which is certainly understandable. Still, 'many subjects maintained ties with their troubled parents ... Several had developed long-term stable marriages, and social supports appeared adequate for most subjects in the group. Overall, study findings indicate that early abusive trauma and adult functioning have no simple relationship.'[169]

Elizabeth Loftus published a 1990 study of college students in which she asked them to 'think of the most traumatic event you have experienced in your life.' Of the reports, only 6 per cent listed 'shootings, sexual assault, dead bodies, and so forth.' Over 60 per cent reported that their worst memories went back no further than the previous three years.[170]

Two other long-term studies, following children born in the 1930s, indicate that people have an astonishing capacity for regeneration and change throughout their lives. Harvard psychiatrist George Vaillant, who now heads the studies, describes the key factors that allowed his subjects to overcome trauma and adversity: *a sense of humor, empathy for others (including parents), creative resourcefulness, and a supportive mate.* Those less likely to rebound from childhood or adult trauma tended to remain bitter, blaming their problems on others.[171]

In his 1994 book, *What You Can Change and What You Can't*, psychologist Martin Seligman, having reviewed all the studies on childhood trauma's effects, came to similar conclusions. 'The major traumas of childhood,' he writes, 'may have some influence on adult personality, but the influence is barely detectable ... There is no justification, according to these studies, for blaming your adult depression, anxiety, bad marriage, drug use, sexual problems, unemployment, beating up your children, alcoholism, or anger on what happened to you as a child.'

Seligman is particularly concerned about our culture's obsession with sexual abuse as the supposed root of all adult problems. He relates his own experience as a nine-year-old with Myron, an unkempt retarded man who sold newspapers on a street corner by which young Martin walked every day on the way to school. 'He and I had a special friendship. He kissed me and we hugged for a few minutes.' Then, one day, Myron disappeared. Seligman later surmised that his parents discovered the sexual abuse and had the police quietly scare Myron off. As a result, Seligman was never bothered by the abuse. In fact, he retains warm memories of Myron.

'[My parents] did not interrogate me about the intimate details,' he writes. 'No emergency-room doctor probed my anal sphincter. I did not go to court. I was not sent to therapy to undo my "denial." I was not, years later, encouraged to rediscover what I had "repressed" and then to relive the trauma to cure my current troubles.' Like me, Seligman is concerned that 'well-meaning parents, therapists, and courts of law can slow healing. Sometimes they even repeatedly rip the protective scar tissue off the wound.'[172]

It seems clear, then, that the Survivor dogma promotes unhealthy attitudes, even if the repressed memories *were* accurate. Therapists are not helping their clients by encouraging them to obsess over the wounds of the past, assuring them that they are badly flawed for life because of them, and urging them to rage at those who abused them.

CRYING WOLF

Another ironic result of the repressed memory craze may very well be the 'backlash' that Judith Herman and others are worried about. When *everyone* claims to be an incest survivor, the attention and healing that *real* victims should receive may be diluted or denied. It is now becoming clear that many allegations of sexual abuse based on recovered memory are false. I am very much afraid that some people, including therapists, may make the mistake of confounding always-remembered abuse with newly-recalled illusory 'memories.' Then we would return to the terrible old days in which paternalistic therapists assured real incest victims that they were simply fantasizing and *wanted* to have sex with their fathers.

In addition, incest has been so broadly defined now that you don't *need* to retrieve memories of overt genital fondling or intercourse to claim Survivor status. Incest can be an inappropriate glance, an overlong hug, discussion of sexual topics, or parental nudity. Add to that the claims that Dad raped his daughter for years and she forgot all about it until recently, and you have the potential for a 'cry wolf' syndrome. With our compassion and credulity drained, we face a danger that *real* incest may be discounted, and again, as in the past, the wolf will be allowed to roam at will.

And if family members and therapists start to doubt all incest claims, will they know when to listen? How will over-worked social workers decide which clients to see first?

Those who have succumbed to therapeutically induced memories tend to become chronic patients, draining health care insurance that may become less and less available in the future, or only at a much higher price. Who will pay the costs then?

Finally, if claims of incest based on recovered memories are perceived as false, how *do* we help these people who are genuinely suffering, though not necessarily from past abuse? It is all too likely that many will impatiently dismiss the self-proclaimed 'victims,' ignoring their cries for help.

UNWANTED BEDFELLOWS

Because I do not want my book to be misperceived as supporting viewpoints I find reprehensible, I feel compelled to address several issues before closing.

I believe that any sexual relations between adults and children are wrong. Even if the children appear to suffer no harm, or sometimes report favorable feelings from the experience, they are too young to make such choices, because of the inherent power inequality and the potential for physical or psychological harm.*[173]

I was extremely disturbed by an interview, published in 1993, with Ralph Underwager, one of the founding members of the False Memory Syndrome Foundation. Underwager, a Minnesota psychologist and Lutheran minister, has written in a scholarly, intelligent manner about the sex abuse hysteria engulfing English-speaking countries, and I respect him for that. Long before many other critics (including this author) began to express concern over innocent lives being shattered by induced memories, Ralph Underwager was a lone voice crying in the wilderness. He and his wife have recently published *Return of the Furies*, a thoughtful book about the recovered memory disaster. But the views he expressed in an interview that appeared in a 1993 issue of

---

* Unlike the child-sex-abuse industry, I define a 'child' as being prepubescent. I also disapprove of sexual contact between adults and adolescents, but such behavior, if consensual, *sometimes* falls into more of a gray area. As sex historian Vern Bullough has noted, 'adult/adolescent sexual behavior has not simply been tolerated throughout much of history but, in some time periods, has been the norm.' Bullough illustrates his point with anecdotes about St. Augustine, Mohammed, Gandhi, and historian Will Durant. Durant, for instance, met his wife Ariel as his student when she was 14. They were married just over a year later.

Paidika, a Dutch journal for pedophiles, were disturbing. 'Paedophiles can boldly and courageously affirm what they choose,' he said. 'They can say that what they want is to find the best way to love. I am also a theologian and . . . I believe it is God's will that there be closeness and intimacy, unity of the flesh, between people. A paedophile can say, "This closeness is possible for me within the choices that I've made." '[174]

As a result, Underwager was asked to resign from the FMS Foundation Scientific Advisory Board, although his wife, Hollida Wakefield, who did not make such inflammatory statements, remains on the board. Underwager and Wakefield have issued defensive statements regarding the interview, asserting that 'we do not believe sexual contact between an adult and a child is ever acceptable,' saying that Underwager had only meant to emphasize the 'individual responsibility' of the pedophile. He said his remarks were taken 'out of context,' that the *Paidika* interview was merely intended to 'begin and create an ongoing discussion with pedophiles aimed at producing a primary prevention program.'[175] I have read the entire interview, and I do not see how they can make such claims. Underwager's views were quite unequivocal and were not just taken out of context.

In fact, Underwager dug himself a deeper hole in his response, stating that 'people may have ethical systems that are different. There is no way to select which one is best other than arbitrarily.' To do so is to be a 'cultural imperialist and . . . to force your own values on other people.' Such blanket moral relativism is scary, if it is used to defend the 'right' of one person to victimize another.*

I also want to make it clear that I do not automatically accept claims of innocence by those accused of sexual abuse. I am extremely skeptical of charges based on recovered memories, but, except in my own situation, I cannot state positively that no abuse occurred in any particular case, because I just don't know. I have great admiration for the False Memory Syndrome Foundation and the work it has done. Many of the world's most widely respected psychologists and memory researchers

---

* Because of his outspoken position, Ralph Underwager has been subjected to a smear campaign by the National Center for Prosecution of Child Abuse, a federally funded Virginia organization (a branch of the National District Attorneys Association) that keeps extensive files on Underwager and other experts who testify in sex abuse court cases, including Lee Coleman, Richard Gardner, David Raskin, and others. When I called the NCPCA, they faxed me an 11-page bibliography covering every court appearance and publication involving Underwager – even including a mortgage foreclosure notice! Underwager told me that the NCPCA has spread defamatory rumors about him, asserting, among other things, that he is a 'known pedophile.'

sit on its board. But this book is neither sponsored nor supported by the FMS Foundation, and I certainly cannot vouch for every member's innocence.

I interviewed one father who had contacted the FMS Foundation who told me a disturbing story. Call him Larry. Larry's daughter, who was hospitalized in a dissociative disorders unit, has accused him of being in a satanic cult and killing babies, as well as raping her throughout her childhood. He convincingly denies ever touching his daughter sexually. Toward the end of our interview, however, he told me that he had been 'indiscreet' with his stepdaughter. When I asked what he meant, he told me in a round-about way that he had fondled her breasts as soon as they started developing, and had stopped when she was 15. He said he felt terrible about it and had apologized long ago. I do not think Larry is representative of those who have joined the Foundation, but I certainly do not want to be perceived as proclaiming people like him completely innocent.

Similarly, I was quite disturbed when I got a call from a mother who told me she suspected her daughter suffered from 'false memory syndrome.' I asked her how old her daughter was. Fourteen. Had she gone to therapy to recall these memories? No. When did she claim her father had abused her? When she was fourteen. Did she say she had forgotten it and then remembered? No, she had always remembered. Did the father deny it? He denied it at first, but then admitted it after failing a lie-detector test. I had to tell this mother that it sounded as if her husband had indeed sexually abused her daughter, and that she should not deny that fact and hide behind the words 'false memory syndrome.'

I am also concerned that my book may be misconstrued as support for anti-lesbian or right-wing views. In a 1993 editorial, the lesbian magazine *Off Our Backs* labeled anyone questioning repressed memories as 'obviously right wing, heteropatriarchal, misogynist and anti-feminist.'[176] On the contrary, I have nothing against women in general or lesbians in particular. I think lesbians should be able to march in St. Patrick's Day parades, express affection in public, and be treated just as any other human beings – with respect.

LEGAL AND PROFESSIONAL RECOMMENDATIONS

Finally, I have a few recommendations that, if implemented, may help to resolve the problems I have described in this book.

I don't think the problems can be magically solved by 'passing a law' or adopting new professional standards. But I do think constructive action in some areas could dramatically reduce the scope of this unfortunate phenomenon. For example, some of the provisions of the U.S. Child Abuse Prevention and Treatment Act should be reviewed and carefully revised, so that it will continue to protect children without inadvertently encouraging persecution of innocent people. No one calling in an accusation should be granted anonymity or immunity, nor should social workers or other investigators be granted absolute immunity.*[177] Once the accused are cleared of official charges, their names should be removed from all lists kept by officials.

All too often, the employees hired by child protective services organizations are undertrained, overworked, or incompetent, resulting in a sometimes disturbing track record. Sometimes, as one family-violence expert put it, they are '26-year-old art-history majors with 20 hours of training who do risk-assessment based on how the toys are lined up.' On the one hand, unabused children are ripped from their parents without warning and no physical evidence. The parents are frequently never even interviewed. On the other hand, truly abused children with all the evidence of broken bones and awful bruises are frequently returned to their abusers, whether parents or foster homes. Some children die as a result, as a 1995 *Time* cover story, 'Abandoned to Her Fate,' documented all too clearly. The situation is so bad that in nearly half the American states, the courts have ruled that the child-protection systems are inadequate.[178] The situation is not much better in the United Kingdom.

In Massachusetts, where innocent people such as the Souzas and Amiraults have been indicted as a result of overzealous child protection workers for the Department of Social Services (DSS), a 1995 scandal emerged. A DSS case worker hosted a sex party during which a nine-year-old girl was raped as her father watched approvingly.[179] Clearly,

---

* In 1995, California passed a law limiting the immunity of child protective workers. It is to be hoped that other states and countries will follow suit.

screening and training of child protective workers need to be drastically improved, and the workload must be reasonable.

In particular, all interviews with children should be taped, and the children should not be subjected to repeated, coercive interviews. The questioning of children should be open-ended. For instance, if it is suspected that a four-year-old has been molested by his grandfather, the interviewer should ask questions such as, 'What do you do with your grandfather? Do you like spending time with him?' The interviewer should *not* ask, 'Does your grandfather ever touch you in your private parts? Show us on this doll where he touched you.'

In courtrooms, the qualifications for 'expert psychological witnesses' should be strengthened so that testimony is allowed only on the basis of scientifically controlled, replicated studies.* That would automatically disallow any 'expert' testimony espousing the concept of repressed memories. For years, American courts relied solely on the 'Frye test,' a 1923 ruling that allowed scientific evidence if it had 'gained general acceptance in the particular field in which it belongs.' But just because a notion has gained general acceptance is no guarantee that it is scientifically valid. In 1692, for instance, the search for 'witches' teats' would have passed the Frye test with flying colors. In 1993, the Supreme Court replaced Frye with the 'Daubert' ruling, at least for federal trials. The Daubert precedent was intended to take a 'general approach of relaxing the traditional barriers to "opinion" testimony.' Ironically, however, it is being used by many judges to keep 'experts' off the stand if they cannot demonstrate a scientific basis for their theories. 'The court in *Daubert* is telling judges not to be so deferential to the scientists,' according to law professor David Faigman. 'I would say that as a theory it's going to be very difficult to introduce repressed memory as scientific evidence.'[180]

Hearsay evidence should be disallowed, with no exceptions made for cases involving preschoolers. Interviews that elicit 'memories' of sexual abuse, whether conducted by therapists, social workers, lawyers, parents, or police, should be taped, so that juries and judges can witness the circumstances under which the allegations were first made.

In court, if young children are to testify, they should certainly be

---

* In his book *Reign of Error: Psychiatry, Authority, and Law*, psychiatrist Lee Coleman argues that *all* expert psychological witnesses should be banned from the courtroom, allowing juries to form their own conclusions, since psychologists cannot judge criminal intent, predict dangerousness, or read anyone's mind. I do not, however, feel that such drastic measures are needed.

treated gently, but they should testify in court just like any other witness. They should not be allowed to testify by remote video. When the court allows children to be kept away from defendants, or the defendants are situated so that the children cannot see them, the clear, prejudicial message to the jury is that the defendants are guilty perpetrators who are a threat to the children by their very presence.

Laws that extend the statute of limitations for 'decades-delayed discovery' of sexual abuse should be repealed. (If the abuse was always remembered, but not reported because of fear, coercion, or other factors, the perpetrator should not be protected by the statute of limitations, as long as the abuse can be corroborated by external evidence. But that's different from bringing charges against an elderly parent based on dreams or hypnosis.)

All cases in which adults have been jailed or heavily fined because of children's allegations of abuse or adult children's recovered memories should be systematically reviewed by a specially appointed judicial panel, national commission, or some other official body. In light of current scientific knowledge, the cases should be re-evaluated and new trials allowed – based on this new evidence – for those where a miscarriage of justice may well have occurred. (Our legal system generally provides excellent protection to those accused of offenses until all appeals have been exhausted. Once found guilty, however, the convicted rarely receive new trials. Appeals are usually won only on technicalities, not on fundamental issues of injustice. If the original defense lawyer did not object sufficiently, there may be few grounds for appeal, even if it is clear that the case was based on inappropriate, repeated, coercive questioning of small children.)

British law differs from American regarding statutes of limitation. In England, civil suits must be brought by the age of 24 or within three years of the alleged injury. This law has been challenged, however, by four women who claim recovered memories of sexual abuse. They won a 1995 favorable judgment from the European Commission of Human Rights in Strasbourg. The matter has been referred to the Law Commission, the official law reform body for England and Wales.[181] Let us hope that this body will not sanction civil suits based on a mythical 'block-out syndrome.' Hypnotically refreshed memories are already subject to strictures by Home Office guidelines, but many suggested memories do not involve formal 'hypnosis' – merely relaxation, meditation, or guided imagery sessions, which amount to the same thing. British juries may convict on the basis of completely uncorroborated evidence, which is unfortunate. Until recently, judges were supposed to caution juries that such allegations were easy to make and difficult to defend, but this duty was abolished by the Criminal Justice and Public Order Act of 1994, on the grounds that the warning was degrading to sex abuse victims. Such a ruling assumes guilt and should be reversed.[182]

There is no statute of limitations on British criminal charges. Nonetheless, long-delayed criminal charges must be understandable and justifiable for the evidence to be admissible. It is to be hoped that British courts will have the sense to prevent cases involving recovered memories from jailing innocent people.

Two British cases are problematical. In 1993, three adult daughters were awarded £57,000 damages for sexual and physical abuse suffered at the hands of their father, Endre Kelemen. This has been cited as a ground-breaking case. The eldest daughter had undergone therapy at Peter Dale's NSPCC group in East Sussex, and with Mary Rees, who told the court: 'When you have children, especially girl children, it can be a trigger back for you, and you can start to remember your own abuse, especially if you have made every effort to suppress and bury that, and certainly Helen had done this for a considerable length of time.' An appeal was lodged by Kelemen with an application to present new evidence, but it was refused on technical grounds.[183]

In March of 1995, a father was sentenced to eight years in prison by a Winchester Crown Court, based on the uncorroborated oral evidence of his daughter, who had apparently recovered incest memories while in psychiatric care for post-partum depression. He remains in prison while his appeal is pending. On a more favorable note, five law lords in the House of Lords ruled in 1995 that someone bringing false accusations resulting in lawsuits could be sued for malicious prosecution.[184]

The legal climate in Australia appears to be improving as well. Three men jailed on the basis of recovered memories were freed in 1995, their convictions reversed because the juries were not confronted with the possibility that the 'memories' might have been fabricated. While the Appeal Court has ordered re-trials, however, the scientific validity of recovered memories was not addressed. Late in 1995, Melbourne barrister Ian Freckelton, president of the Australian and New Zealand Association of Psychiatry, Psychology and Law, called for a ban on repressed memories from Australian courtrooms. Despite such reasonable appeals, however, several Australian men remain incarcerated as a result of recovered 'memories' of abuse. National health minister Peter Beattie recently skirted the issue in State Parliament, saying only that 'the efficacy or desirability of a particular treatment or therapy is one for experts within the relevant profession to determine.'[185]

Whether through legislation or through actions by the professional associations, the standards should be strengthened for those who call themselves psychotherapists or hypnotists. On the national or regional level, a single law should be enacted to cover all therapists. Currently, each U.S. state hosts a hodgepodge of regulatory peer review boards for psychiatrists, psychologists, social workers, marriage and family counselors, and the like. Usually, the fringe therapists using past life regression or channeling are completely unregulated.

Standards for therapists should be similar to those for teachers – a specified level of education from accredited institutions, periodic continuing education in approved subjects, and some form of ongoing observation and review. Most therapists are never observed as they conduct sessions. Instead, they periodically report their own versions of what happened to a supervisor. Supervisors should implement the use of one-way mirrors so that they can observe sessions directly and randomly (always maintaining strict confidentiality, of course).

The issue of confidentiality is a delicate one. Clearly, clients should feel secure that, under normal circumstances, their unguarded, frank comments during a therapy session will not go beyond the session. On the other hand, in cases of incest accusations based on recovered memory, there should be some kind of obligation to include parents in the therapy. Frankly, I do not know a simple way to resolve this issue, but it needs to be studied by ethics committees of professional associations.

Continuing education programs should be subjected to systematic review. Therapists should no longer receive credit for learning how to dig for memories, spot UFO abductees, or hunt for past lives.

As part of their training, all therapists should receive education in current memory research, the hazards of hypnotic confabulations, inadvertent cuing, sleep paralysis, panic attacks, and related topics. Therapists should inform clients that the concept of repression is a hotly contested issue within their own field and, despite anecdotal clinical reports, that it has not been proven to exist at all. As psychiatrist Harrison Pope has suggested, clients who have already recovered 'memories' should not be told abruptly that they have created imaginary events but, once the therapist suspects that such is the case, clients should be 'gently confronted' with that idea.[186]

Professional associations should adopt statements acknowledging the lack of evidence for massive repression. Associations should provide balanced brochures on the topic, which may be given to clients or left in therapists' waiting rooms.

And regional and national licensing boards should become true watchdog agencies rather than peer groups that are more interested in protecting the reputation of their profession than enforcing sound therapeutic practice.

Perhaps most significantly, using the Ramona case as a precedent, third-party suits should be allowed against therapists for malpractice and family disruption.*[187] I personally don't like the idea of solving social problems through lawsuits, but the simple truth is that therapists will be less likely to destroy families if they are legally liable for their actions.

In the wake of the Ramona suit, one California insurance firm has tripled the cost of malpractice insurance for therapists, sending a clear message to the profession. Hit in their pocketbooks, most therapists will respond with alacrity. It is encouraging that the British Psychological Society has advised its members to take out additional insurance to protect themselves against negligence claims, including allegations of having planted false memories of sexual abuse. Over 35 per cent of the BPS membership has signed up.[188]

It would appear that U.S. insurance companies could put a stop to American recovered-memory therapy much more quickly than any legislation.**[189] They should begin to look more closely at claims for 'post-traumatic stress disorder' or 'dissociative disorders' – the two most likely diagnoses based on repressed memories. Major corporations and the military, both of which pay whopping insurance premiums for mental health care, should demand investigation of claims based on memory-focused therapy.[190]

A number of organizations already exist that should be addressing

* The Ramona suit relied on California law, so that it cannot serve as a legal precedent elsewhere. Nonetheless, now that the judicial climate is changing, other states could follow suit, using their own laws. In 1995, a Pennsylvania federal district court judge allowed such a third-party suit to go forward. It was filed by accused parents Kenneth and Joan Tuman against their daughter's therapists at Genesis Associates. Also in 1995, a Washington State monitoring agency became the first to take disciplinary action against therapist Linda MacDonald, based on accused parents' complaints. MacDonald was fined and her license temporarily suspended.

** In 1995, Aetna Life Insurance Company sued Paracelsus Healthcare Corporation for allegedly luring patients into treatment, lying to insurers, and giving kickbacks. Other such suits are likely to follow.

this issue. The American Protection and Advocacy for Individuals with Mental Illness Act (PAIMI) has set up an advisory council in every state that must include those diagnosed with mental illness and/or their family members. PAIMI needs to hear from retractors and involved family members about the mental health abuses caused by recovered-memory therapy.

Finally, the United States has a 'Mental Health Bill of Rights,' but it applies only to patients in hospitals. If legislation were passed to apply it to all who seek therapy, it would go a long way toward providing protection for unwary clients. Here, in part, are the rights covered by the current statute:

> The right to an individualized, written treatment plan, providing for periodic reassessment and revision.
>
> The right to know the objectives of a treatment, the possible adverse effects of treatment, and any available alternative treatments, services and providers.
>
> The right not to receive a mode or course of treatment in the absence of informed, voluntary and written consent.
>
> The right to appropriate protection in connection with one's participation in an experimental treatment.
>
> The right and opportunity to revoke one's consent to an experimental treatment.[191]

Many of the above recommendations and points will be included in the 'Mental Health Consumer Protection Act,' a draft of which has been written by Christopher Barden, a Minnesota lawyer and clinical psychologist. His bill, which he plans to publish initially in a prestigious academic journal such as the *Harvard Journal of Legislation*, will mandate (a) informed consent for clients entering therapy, (b) a ban on harmful treatments, (c) banning pseudoscience from court, (d) criminalization of fraudulent practice, and (e) a model licensing act, to be enacted by individual state legislatures.[192]

Advice to Parents, Children, and Therapists

In the aftermath of the repressed-memory disaster, accused parents, their adult children, and therapists who realize what has happened will have to come to grips with it. All of them will have to deal with feelings of guilt, distrust, anger, and depression. In short, they really *will* suffer from a form of post-traumatic stress. Because I have spent the better part of three years studying this phenomenon and interviewing many of those involved, I have some general ideas which may help. (I am, of course, addressing this section to families torn asunder by false incest allegations, not situations in which real sexual abuse took place.)

PARENTS: There is no magic wand anyone can wave to bring your children back. Usually, they come out of their belief systems *only* when they get away from their recovered-memory therapists and incest support groups. Generally, sending them books such as *Victims of Memory* is counterproductive, as long as they come from you. Your best bet is to find someone who can legitimately maintain contact with your accusing child – a sibling, a friend, a former teacher, minister, lawyer, or a fellow worker. If you can gently educate these potential intermediaries about repressed-memory issues, they may eventually be able to introduce *Victims of Memory* or other such material in a non-threatening way. (See advice to siblings, below.)

You should seek a support group while you prepare yourself for the hoped-for reunion with your children. To understand what has happened to them, you should read extensively on the subject, if you can stomach it. Let other relatives know what is happening so that they, too, will understand. That is one of the reasons I wrote this book.

If your children accept letters or phone calls, try to be as positive and brief as possible. Don't try to argue with them: you will lose. Simply repeat the truth, that you love them, that you miss them, that you'd be happy to see them. Tell them that you have no memory of having abused them, if such is the case, but that you'd be glad to talk about it all. Those of you who are allowed no contact whatsoever (which includes me at the moment) cannot do much except wait and try sending a brief letter or postcard every now and then, hoping it will not be returned. You might leave a brief, loving message on their answering machines on their birthdays or other holidays.

In the meantime, you should get on with your lives as best you can. Don't allow anyone to guilt-trip you for being depressed sometimes.

631

That's a natural consequence of your situation. But try to overcome the depression by staying active, enjoying friends and your remaining family.

If possible, try to get beyond your inevitable anger at recovered memory therapists, accusing children, or the general unfairness of it all. Such anger is normal and understandable, but rage is not a healthy emotion, and it will eat at you. It only hurts you, and, unfortunately, it prevents many people from hearing you. Do not demonize the 'other side' as they have demonized you. Try to rise above the situation and look at it somewhat philosophically. You can still try to change the situation without living with constant anger. Let peace of mind and compassion be your best revenge – otherwise, those who hate you win, and you become their bitter mirror image.

Some parents have found that volunteering for worthy causes helps. That could include working in schools, with businesses, the homeless, or any organization that interests you. Instead of spending all of your time obsessing over your own troubles, you will be helping others.

If your marriage has been shaken by the allegations, which is likely, try to provide much-needed support for one another during this difficult period. One accused parent, who also happens to be a therapist, offers the following sound advice:

> Don't let the horror of this subject take you away from the precious moments of loving your partner, or you will be eaten alive yourself. Family is first. It's so easy to become haunted by the compelling nature of this material, so much so that one can become as cynical and feverish and negative as the True Believers. I was a True Believer at one time myself. I had no idea the damage I could potentially be doing until it was done to me. But on the other side of things, I see that there is an equal potential for blindness, fervor, and self-righteousness by FMS advocates.

It helps to talk about your situation. If you've been too ashamed to talk to your friends and acquaintances, I urge you to do so now. If you have done nothing wrong, you have nothing to be ashamed of. You've been caught being a parent at the wrong time, in the wrong place, and your children have been swept up in a malignant social movement. Contact the appropriate national support association and ask about local meetings. Here are the addresses and phone numbers:

The British False Memory Society
Bradford on Avon
Wiltshire BA15 1NA
U.K.
01225-868682

Australian False Memory Society
P.O. Box 363
Unley
South Australia
5061
61-3-9740-6930

Casualties of Sexual Allegations
P.O. Box 35
Albany
New Zealand
00-64-9-415-8095

False Memory Syndrome Foundation
3401 Market Street
Suite 130
Philadelphia
PA 19104
U.S.A.
00-1-215-387-1865

If you feel the need, seek counseling for yourself, but walk out the door if your therapist suggests you read self-help books by people like John Bradshaw, or tells you to hold a symbolic funeral for your children – that's the sort of 'ritual' that recovery therapists love.

When your children return, they may do so in gradual stages. Many such 'returnees' are simply re-entering their parents' lives, pretending that nothing happened and refusing to discuss it. Your initial reaction may be to force the issue, but it is probably wise to let the matter be for quite some time. By promoting contact, you are at least reminding your children of old times, that you are not demons or ogres, and that you love them. In time, they may be able to process and discuss what happened to them. As one parent writes, 'I think it's important to think positively and not demand apologies, explanations and a pound of flesh as the price of family unity.'[193]

On the other hand, some parents are uncomfortable just ignoring the hurtful allegations. 'We are troubled by the idea that by making it too easy for her to just come back, we are doing precisely what we did that contributed heavily to her susceptibility to this awful syndrome: protecting her from reality, bailing her out, not insisting she take responsibility for her own life,' one accused father writes. 'She is 32 years old, college educated and a mother. But she needs to grow up.'

One accused mother's son returned and said, 'It's OK, Mom. I love you and want a relationship ... but I still think you did something to me.' She asks plaintively, 'Do my feelings count in all this? For what it's worth, I still feel violated. I know I did not sexually abuse any of my children. So what am I to do with my feelings?'[194] I would advise this mother to renew contact, on the condition that she say at the beginning of each meeting, 'I know you think I did those awful things to you, but I also know I didn't. Now let's drop the subject and get on with our visit.' In other words, for the time being, agree to disagree. As strange as it may sound, treating the debate over repressed memories as a philosophical dispute – nothing personal – can help reduce blame and allow a more relaxed, friendly atmosphere to develop.

It is natural, of course, that parents would want a full retraction. Some parents insist on a retraction before allowing contact, assuming that by ignoring the matter, they would only be allowing their children to continue to impose absurd rules. There really is no right or wrong answer. I cannot tell you what you *must* do. Nonetheless, I hope that you now understand the tremendous pain that this process has put your children through, and that you can sympathize with them, as difficult as that may be for you.

In some cases, your children might apologize and tell you they know you never sexually abused them, only to go back to their therapists and renew the accusations. Be prepared for a difficult period of readjustment. They have been well indoctrinated into hating you, and their 'memories' of abuse have been so well-rehearsed that they may be difficult to forget. On the other hand, if they have made a clean break with their therapists, they may rush back to you totally convinced that you are innocent and that they have missed you terribly.

If possible, discuss what happened with your children. If you can find a decent counselor who is not imbued with recovery movement attitudes and jargon, and who understands the consequences of illusory memories, you should consider going with your children, because talking about this confusing, emotion-laden topic can be too difficult to handle on your own. Paul Simpson, an Arizona psychologist and family mediator who has rejected his former involvement in regression therapy, now offers a program called *Project Middle Ground*. In an effort to initiate contact between estranged children and parents, Simpson sets up mediation sessions which allow for safe communication between both parties. The accusing children don't demand confessions and parents don't demand retractions. Instead, the idea is to find some middle ground, a way for both parties to communicate and reach reasonable points of understanding and agreement. This can be the first step toward reconciliation. Simpson also offers 'exit-counseling' for full retractors, helping them to better understand how they were abused by the process of recovered-memory therapy and assisting them in healing the broken relationships in their families. You can contact Project Middle Ground at 5240 E. Knight Dr., 120, Tucson, AZ 85712; phone 520–751–0101. It is to be hoped that family mediators in Commonwealth countries will also develop a subspecialty in helping families to reunite.

Of course, rather than spending money on a counselor, you and your children may all sit down to talk with a mutually trusted family friend. Regardless of whether you seek professional counseling, remember that healing the breach will take time. Love has never departed, but rebuilding trust will take patience – not just for you, but for your children.

ADULT CHILDREN: Once you realize that your parents did not sexually abuse you, you will feel enormous confusion and guilt, along with relief. For many of you, your therapist and support group have become your new family, and breaking ties with them will be difficult and painful. Still, you must get away from their destructive influence in order to see your situation more clearly. If you are on massive doses of medication, try to find a reputable psychiatrist – *not* an MPD specialist – who will supervise your withdrawal, or who will help you adjust to a proper dosage.

Do not be afraid to call your parents *now* and ask for reconciliation. With very few exceptions, your parents will welcome you back with joy, love, tears, and celebrations similar to the Biblical story of the Prodigal Son. Don't wait. One good thing that can come out of this mess is a renewed awareness of how much family really means, and of how limited our time on earth really is.

Another positive outcome can be a new openness. Once you've renewed contact comfortably, take advantage of this time to talk about *real* problems that concern you. All families have their problems, and some are quite severe. Without relying on abstract jargon – please don't talk about boundary violations – discuss specific issues. Don't expect your parents to change all that much, though. They've lived a long time, and they're probably not going to alter in any fundamental way. Enjoy them for who they are.

You will need to rebuild relationships not only with your parents, but with your long-suffering spouse (if you have one) and your friends and relatives. Many mates of self-identified Survivors watched their marriages deteriorate and their children suffer, but they tried to be supportive, thinking that the repressed memories of abuse were all true, and that the process was necessary. Once it is clear that it was all a terrible delusion, many spouses will release pent-up frustration and fury, misdirected at you. You will have to weather this understandable reaction. Similarly, your children will probably need a great deal of attention and may feel bitterness over your former self-obsession. While you may feel guilty about what you did to your spouse and children – and it is important to apologize sincerely and repeatedly – you must not grovel or accept an inferior status. Re-establish yourself as a viable, independent member of the family who deserves respect and love.

If your therapist will not admit what he or she has done and continues to practice recovered-memory therapy with others, you face the difficult decision of whether to lodge formal complaints with state licensing boards or to sue the therapist. Many retractors simply want to walk away and never see their therapists again. Others cannot live with themselves unless they try to prevent the same thing from happening to others. This is a decision each of you must make for yourselves.

You may feel the need to seek a counselor, too, to cope with all your residual feelings of confusion and guilt. If so, use the same criteria I described above for your parents.

SIBLINGS: If you are still coping with a sister or brother who is accusing your parents of incest, you have been placed in a very uncomfortable position. Many of you believe in the reality of the abuse, go to therapy and find your own 'memories,' and cut off from your parents. If so, the advice to returning children applies to you as well. Often, siblings side with their parents, which means they are cut off, too. In this case, they tend to become extremely angry at their accusing siblings and want nothing to do with them or the issue. Still others try to maintain a 'neutral' stance, neither affirming nor denying their parents' guilt.

I don't think there really *can* be a truly neutral stance, but for those of you who do not believe the allegations or don't know what to think, it is imperative that you understand this issue. Educate yourselves about what has happened. Stop being so angry at your accusing siblings and begin to worry about them. They are in deep trouble, sucked into a cult-like mindset. You are one of the few people who might be able to help them.

Therefore, if you care enough, it is a good idea for you to maintain a relationship with your accusing sibling, even as you educate yourself about what has happened to her (or him) by reading books such as this. Don't ever agree that your parents were molesters, but remain sympathetic toward your accusing sibling. Say things like, 'I hate to see you suffering like this. Is there anything I can do to help you? Would you like to come over for dinner? I care for you so much. I'm always here for you. I'm going to call you once a week just to check in with you.' At least that way, you will maintain contact, and you can also tell your poor parents how their lost child is doing.

If you can maintain rapport with your accusing siblings, you might ask them for reading material to help you understand what they are going through and how they got back their 'memories.' It is likely that they will give you *The Courage to Heal* or other similar material to read, and in reading it, you will, indeed, gain insight into what they have been through. Then, at an appropriate time, you might say, 'Gee, I've been reading this other book, and it's got me really confused, because it criticizes some of what *The Courage to Heal* says. I don't quite know what to make of it. Would you mind reading it and telling me what you think?' (Or read this article or watch this video.) If the approach is gentle enough, accusing siblings may actually read the material with an open mind. It will *not* help to shove *Victims of Memory* at them and say, 'This is what's the matter with you. You've been duped by bad therapy.'

When your accusing sibling finally takes back the accusations, you may feel like the always-faithful child at the feast for the Prodigal Son – resentful that the one who caused all the problems is now getting all the attention. Try to understand that your parents' relief and joy are natural. They also love you, the one who was always there for them.

THERAPISTS: It will take enormous courage for you to admit what you have done to dozens, perhaps hundreds, of clients, validating their belief in horrible events that never took place.

I first realized how difficult it would be when I interviewed Heather, a speech therapist who formerly used 'facilitated communication' and was responsible for one child typing sexual abuse allegations against her parents. After a controlled test with her and the child unequivocally showed that the messages were coming from the facilitator and not the child, she denied the truth for a month. 'When I found out the test results, I was crushed,' she told me. 'I thought, "No way!" I thought that the person validating FC had a stake in making it fail. I felt I was the only one who cared about this kid at all. I had no reason to believe it was coming from me. I did not intentionally type those allegations.'

What finally got to Heather was a journalist who asked her point-blank, 'How long do you have to use FC, how many people have to get hurt, before you stop it?' And he sent her a great deal of documentation showing how FC failed to work in test after test. That shook her confidence, but within an hour, she was rationalizing it again. Finally, that weekend, she suddenly came to the realization that she had indeed been responsible for the allegations. She halted all use of FC in her school and publicly declared her position.

As a result, Heather spent over a year in mental agony. She lost all of her old friends in the FC network, who said she was simply a bad facilitator. People in the community were disgusted with her for having created false allegations. Her therapist insinuated that Heather herself must have been sexually abused as a child to have unconsciously typed such things. People at her school didn't want to talk about it for fear of a lawsuit. It has taken her a long time to come to grips with her guilt and to figure out how this could have happened.

'The trainers tell you that if you don't believe in FC enough, if you don't believe in the integrity of your client enough, it won't work for you,' she explained to me. 'So they set you up. To be the one that this works for is a real thrill. At this time in my life, I wanted a cause, something to strive for. I would say that FC was like a religion for me.' Heather still isn't sure where the allegations came from, but she did tell me she'd read 'a ton of self-help books,' and she was aware that many FC clients had allegedly been sexually abused.

After hearing Heather's story, I realize what a personal challenge it will be for therapists to examine what they have done. Unlike for facilitated communication, there is no iron-clad test for repressed memories, and you have a much larger professional community to lend you support in your continued rationalizations and denials. When you can admit the truth to yourselves, however, I hope that you have the integrity that Heather displayed and try to reverse the harm. Heather's healing really began, she told me, when she went to apologize to the parents she had accused through facilitated communication. 'They were more compassionate than I could have hoped for. I had hoped for the moment when I could just apologize. The father said, "We want you to know that we have no hard feelings for you. You got caught up in this, just like we did." The mother later said she thought we could be friends. It blew me away.'

Similarly, I hope that you – like retractor therapists Robin Newsome (see Chapter 8) and Paul Simpson – will go beyond merely admitting the mistakes you have made and will become an active force for good. Rather than losing your practice or career, you can redirect it to a much-needed specialization in helping families to reunite and process what happened to them. After all, who better understands the Survivor syndrome than you? You can facilitate the healing process, reversing the terrible delusion that you helped to foster.

As former recovered-memory therapists, you have a moral obligation to contact every former client and attempt, as gently as possible, to tell them that you were wrong, that you no longer believe in the concept of massive repression, and that they should consider reuniting with their families. It will be difficult for you to do this, but consider the following analogies. If you were an automobile manufacturer and discovered that one model had a fatally flawed part, would you simply stop manufacturing the car, or would you recall the faulty vehicles? If you were a doctor and prescribed medicine that you now discovered was a slow poison, would you just stop dispensing it, or would you warn patients who might still be taking it?

Please, clear your conscience. You have a precedent from 300 years ago. On Jan. 14, 1697, Massachusetts declared a 'Day of Repentances' for the Salem Witch Trials, which had taken place only five years earlier. In a public statement, the jurors wrote: 'We do therefore hereby signify to all in general (and to the surviving sufferers in especial) our deep sense of and sorrow for our errors in acting on such evidence to the condemning of any person, and do hereby declare that we justly fear we were sadly deluded and mistaken.'[193]

In the wake of this national tragedy, many critics from all sides of the political and ideological spectrum will inevitably search for the ultimate villains who were responsible for fomenting it, and you therapists will become targets. Yet few human beings set out to do evil. It is, ironically, almost always accomplished with the goal of doing good. With very few exceptions, I believe that therapists urged clients to unearth what they thought were real incest memories, convinced that they were performing a real mental health service.

FINAL WORDS

It will do little good to demonize recovered-memory therapists in the same way many of them have encouraged the demonization of parents. There can be no doubt that the therapeutic community must be held *primarily responsible* for promoting this disastrous and misguided form of 'therapy.' Ultimately, however, no one *intended* harm – not the therapists, not the children, and certainly not the parents.* You were all caught up in a very unfortunate, destructive phenomenon, and you need to acknowledge it, talk about it, and then get on with your lives, leaving judgmental hatred behind.

---

* Some therapists cannot be let off so easily, however. A small minority appear to be paranoid sociopaths who enjoy wielding power over their patients' lives and who refuse to acknowledge the harm they have done, even when directly confronted with it.

Myths and Realities*

MYTH	REALITY
1. You must identify the root cause of your unhappiness (from your past) in order to heal and be happy in the present.	1. *It is unfortunately the normal human lot to be frustrated and unhappy at various points in your life. There is no magic pill to make you happy, and your attitude in the present is much more the issue than anything that happened to you in the past.*
2. Trauma in your past, particularly sexual abuse, is so harmful that you will never fully recover from it.	2. *Humans are resilient. There are thousands of examples of people who succeed in spite of their handicaps. Although severe trauma is terrible and does indeed leave life-long scars, it need not be the sole focus of your life.*
3. All good therapy takes a long time and involves delving into the past.	3. *The forms of therapy that have proven to be the most effective are cognitive and behavioral therapy that do not dwell on the past, but help clients cope with current life stressors, often by reframing the way they perceive their problems. Such therapy can often be short-term.*
4. Memories are always accurate.	4. *All memories are reconstructions of likely scenarios in which you fill in the gaps. Thus, all memories are somewhat inaccurate, though they serve us well enough under normal conditions. Under severe social influence, however, memories can be distorted or even entirely rewritten. Memory is largely a matter of rehearsal. The more often a scene is rehearsed, the more real it becomes to you. Experiments have shown that people can be induced to remember events that did not occur*
5. Repeated trauma is so distressing that it must be	5. *There is no scientific evidence that human beings are capable of 'massive repression.' On*

* Thanks to Bob Koscielny for the original idea and help for this list.

repressed or dissociated. You could have been raped for years and not remember anything about it.

the contrary, there is much evidence that repeated traumatic events are more likely to be remembered than others. There is no way to prove that massive repression does not exist, however, just as one cannot prove that ghosts or witches do not exist; one cannot prove a negative

6. You must remember and relive all traumatic events from your past in order to heal.

6. *Although talking through recent painful events is often helpful, dwelling on long-past traumas tends to make people worse rather than better. The idea that you must 'relive' or abreact the trauma to get better is simply not true. On the contrary, therapists who tell clients, 'You must get worse before you get better,' are misleading them. The endless downward spiral into retrieving more and more 'memories' is harmful rather than helpful.*

7. If you were a victim of incest, you must completely detach from your family in order to heal. You must detach from anyone who does not completely support you or who questions your memories

7. *Even in cases of real, always-remembered incest, it is doubtful that complete detachment from the biological family is ultimately helpful. If the incest is on-going, temporary separation is clearly indicated. However, therapy should involve the entire family, including the perpetrator, in order to promote change and healing. True family therapy has proved to be helpful in many cases. Unfortunately, some therapists encourage separation and isolation from the family without ever meeting other family members. There is an inherent danger in isolating already disturbed and vulnerable people from their family and friends.*

8. You have a huge storehouse of unresolved anger. You must 'get your anger out' in order to heal.

8. *It is natural to want to express justifiable anger, but it is seldom healing in and of itself. When rage is encouraged as a healthy outlet, it tends to feed on itself and create more rage rather than less. People need to learn to express their differences in an appropriate and helpful manner. Often, it is best to avoid confrontations until anger has subsided and a more rational discussion can ensue.*

9. Confrontation is necessary for healing.

9. *Confrontation should only be undertaken with the idea of achieving a better understanding and relationship. In other words, mediation in*

which all parties participate is preferable to judgmental confrontation. Confronting someone as a 'hit-and-run' tactic, without allowing any dialogue, is cowardly and unfair – certainly not 'courageous.'

10. Group therapy is always a good way to treat survivors of sexual abuse.

10. *Group therapy can indeed be helpful in some cases, but it can be extremely damaging in others, particularly when there is peer pressure to conform to group expectations. In an 'incest survivor' group, for instance, retelling and embellishing horror stories can create an emotional hothouse atmosphere in which those who do not have 'memories' feel inadequate or left out, and they feel pressured to 'remember' similar horrors. Similarly, they are often told that if they react strongly to a story, it is proof that they were abused.*

11. Your therapist should become an extremely important person in your life, a surrogate parent.

11. *Good therapists never encourage a client to become overly dependent. The goal of therapy should be to make you a fully functioning person capable of independent judgment. Any therapist who relishes the role of authority figure or guru should be avoided. Any therapist who tells you that he or she alone cares about you and understands you is a bad therapist. Good therapists constantly guard against 'countertransference' in which they bring their own egos, needs, and biases into the therapy session.*

12. Self-help books are always helpful and authoritative.

12. *Self-help books can indeed be very useful, but readers should never forget that many publishers are interested primarily in profits, not accuracy. In other words, just because something is written in an authoritative style and is published in a best-selling book doesn't mean that it is true. Books such as* The Courage to Heal *are full of misinformation and have caused untold damage. Intelligent readers of such books should employ their own critical thinking skills and should also read books expressing contrary views.*

13. You can trust any therapist who seems compassionate, warm, wise, and caring. You do

13. *Just because a therapist is warm and caring does not mean that he or she is competent or can help you. Training, philosophy, and treatment*

not need to ask about credentials, experience, training, philosophy, treatment approach, or techniques.

modalities are extremely important. Therapists who dwell unceasingly on your past are unlikely to help you cope with your present-day problems. Therapy should challenge you to change your way of thinking about and dealing with the present-day conflicts that sent you to therapy in the first place.

14. Therapy is an art, not a science. Therefore, it is inappropriate to ask for a treatment plan.

14. *Therapists who hide behind statements about how therapy is an art-form should take up painting and stop practicing their 'art' on unsuspecting minds. Patients should not be used as guinea pigs for experimental techniques. Like brain surgeons, those who treat mental problems should base their treatment on scientifically proven, safe and effective methods. Patients should seek alternate opinions from therapists with different clinical orientations.*

15. Your therapist is an intuitive genius who does not need to consult with other therapists or refer you to a physician for any physical problems. Therapists have an uncanny ability to discern the truth or falsity of your statements.

15. *Therapists are no better than anyone else at determining truth or falsity. Enormous confidence in one's intuition turns out to be a drawback in terms of predictive outcome. 'Clinical intuition' is notoriously inaccurate. In one study, clinical psychologists were correct less than 50 per cent of the time in assessing sexual abuse. That being the case, therapists should remain suitably humble and seek outside consultation frequently, especially if clients present physical problems. Such clients should be referred to competent psychiatrists and physicians for a full mental and physical evaluation.*

16. Your panic attacks are probably flashbacks to repressed memories.

16. *About 35 per cent of the American public have panic attacks at some time in their lives. Panic attacks are extremely frightening. If you have one, you may fear that you are having a heart attack. You may feel dizzy, experience a choking sensation, and feel disconnected from reality. Cognitive and behavioral therapy approaches can quickly help you with panic attacks, which stem from current life stress, not from past trauma. Panic attacks are neither life-threatening nor dangerous. They are treatable.*

17. Therapists must treat your 'narrative truth' without

17. *It is indeed important for therapists to listen to clients and to distinguish narrative from*

consideration or investigation of historical truth. Therapists are not detectives.

historical truth – but that does not mean that what actually happened is unimportant. Indeed, if clients believe that they have recalled previously 'repressed' memories of sexual abuse, it is very important to the client whether these events actually took place. By validating these memories, the therapist is already acting as a 'detective.' It is the therapist's obligation to explain that such memories are questionable at best and must be corroborated by firm external evidence before they are taken seriously.

18. Your eating disorder most probably stems from repressed memories of sexual abuse.

18. *Careful studies have shown that there is no significant correlation between eating disorders and a history of sexual abuse. The percentage of those with eating disorders who were sexually abused is about the same as in the normal population.*

19. Therapists are experts at interpreting (a) dreams, (b) writings, (c) artwork, (d) bodily pains.

19. *No one knows what dreams really mean, but true experts on dreams know that they reflect daily concerns. Therefore, it is not surprising that someone obsessed with an issue might dream about it. Dreams should never be taken literally. Similarly, just because someone concerned with an issue writes a story about it or draws a picture does not mean that the story or artwork reflects reality. Intense self-examination often leads to vague bodily pains. Therapists who believe that such pains are 'evidence' of so-called 'body memories' are practicing pseudoscience.*

20. Multiple personality disorder is a common response to childhood trauma and is often only diagnosed during adult psychotherapy.

20. *Multiple personality disorder (MPD, now renamed Dissociative Identity Disorder, DID) is a fad diagnosis of the last decade. If MPD exists naturally at all (which is doubtful), it is exceedingly rare. It appears that people only come to believe they harbor internal 'alters' after entering therapy or reading a book or seeing a movie.*

21. Therapists do not need to inform patients of the potential hazards of a particular form of treatment or technique.

21. *All clients seeking help from a medical or mental health professional should give informed consent before accepting treatments. Any therapist who does not inform clients of potential hazards is committing malpractice.*

22. Hypnosis is a good and accurate method of

22. *Hypnosis is defined as being a state of 'enhanced suggestibility.' Hypnosis may be*

recovering memories from your subconscious.

useful for suggesting someone into a desired frame of mine; i.e., some people have used it to stop smoking. But hypnosis should never be used to retrieve memories. Research indicates that memories retrieved under hypnosis (or guided imagery or sodium Amytal) are likely to be confabulations – a mixture of truth and fantasy – based on the expectations of the hypnotist and subject.

23. Checklists of 'symptoms' are reliable tools to identify disorders.

23. *Beware of symptom checklists, particularly if they apply to nearly everyone in the general population. At one time or another, most people experience depression, troubled relationships, ambivalence towards family members, and low self-esteem. These are not necessarily 'symptoms' of anything other than the human condition.*

24. If you cannot remember chunks of your childhood, you were probably so traumatized that you forgot them.

24. *No one remembers every event from his or her childhood. Most people recall the high and low points, but not much in between. This is normal and does not necessarily indicate any trauma in childhood.*

25. One-half of all women are likely to be sexually abused before the age of eighteen.

25. *Statistics about sexual abuse vary, depending on the study methods and the definition of sexual abuse. Most women experience some form of unwanted sexual approach in their teenage years, which is unfortunate, but should not necessarily be considered sexual abuse. The incidence of sexual intercourse between fathers and daughters appears to be less than 1 per cent in the general population, according to several studies. Incest is indeed a terrible problem, but it is far from the inflated figures often bandied about.*

26. There is a network of satanic ritual abuse cults around the world involving many 'upstanding' citizens. These cults are usually intergenerational.

26. *There is absolutely no evidence that satanic ritual abuse cults exist at all, at least as defined in popular culture. In other words, there are no cults in which babies are bred, sacrificed, and eaten. Isolated psychopaths, such as Charles Manson or the drug cult in Matamaros, Mexico, may commit hideous atrocities, but they are not organized ritual abuse cults. Rebellious teenagers may draw pentagrams and murder stray cats, but they too are simply imitating popular cultural myths.*

27. All 'Christian therapists' and pastoral counselors can be trusted because they are sincere and in touch with the Lord.

27. *Unfortunately, more atrocities have been committed in the name of God than any other cause. True Christians believe in love, family unity, and forgiveness. Too many so-called Christian counselors and ministers are promoting hatred, family destruction, and no forgiveness. In the name of the Lord, they inadvertently conduct the Devil's work. Jesus warned that false prophets would arise in His name; He was correct.*

28. If you have a tiny intuition or a feeling that you may have been sexually abused, you probably were.

28. *If you have a 'tiny intuition or a feeling' that you may have been sexually abused and that you have repressed the memories, you have probably been influenced by* The Courage to Heal, *similar books, or the general culture that has made such notions so popular. If you were truly sexually abused, the odds are very good that you would remember it all too well.*

29. If you first remember one perpetrator, you probably were abused by multiple perpetrators and will remember them in time.

29. *Illusory memories of sexual abuse frequently progress from one perpetrator to multiple perpetrators, from limited incidents to rapes throughout childhood, from vague intuitions to detailed, horrifying scenarios. True memories of long-term sexual abuse have always been remembered, even if the memories have been 'parked' away from day-to-day attention.*

30. If you recalled traumatic events on your own, outside therapy, they are reliable because you could not have been led into them.

30. *Beginning in the mid-1980s, and extending into the 1990s, the idea that personal problems may stem from long-forgotten sexual abuse became so prevalent that almost all women have considered whether they might have been incest victims without knowing it. Many seeking answers to their problems have desperately sought 'memories' both in and out of therapy. Many have recovered such 'memories' after reading self-help books, being 'triggered' by a talk show, or talking to a friend. They are led into this false belief system just as surely as in formal therapy.*

Endnotes

INTRODUCTION TO THE BRITISH
EDITION

1. Hellman, *Pentimento*, p. 112.
2. Hart, *MPD/FMS Retractor's Story*.
3. Tavris, *Mismeasure*; Epstein, *Deceptive Distinctions*.
4. Castro, 'New Age Therapy.'
5. MacLean, 'Some Therapists.'
6. Orr, *Accuracy About Abuse*, June 1995, p. 14–15.

CHAPTER ONE

1. Bass, *Courage to Heal*, p. 42.
2. Bass, *Courage*, p. 22; Dyer, 'Victory.'
3. Russell, *Secret Trauma*, p. 59.
4. Bullough, 'History of Human Sexual Behavior' in *Pedophilia*, p. 72–76.
5. Bullough in *Pedophilia*, p. 77–82.
6. Kilpatrick, *Long-Range Effects*, p. 47, 67.
7. Kinsey report and Pomeroy quoted in Russell, *Secret Trauma*, p. 6–8.
8. Brownmiller, *Against Our Will*, p. 281.
9. Bass & Davis, *Courage to Heal*, p. 13.
10. Bass, *I Never Told*, p. 51; Bass, *Courage*, p. 327.
11. Monroe in Bass, *I Never Told Anyone*, p. 90.

12. Armstrong, *Kiss Daddy*, p. 19, 23, 224–225.
13. Butler, *Conspiracy*, p. 48–49.
14. Bass, *I Never Told Anyone*, p. 86–87, 103–105.
15. Monroe in Bass, *I Never Told*, p. 92.
16. Yarrow in Bass, *I Never Told*, p. 87.
17. Finkelhor, *Sourcebook*, p. 64, 126.
18. Herman, *Father-Daughter Incest*, p. 8.
19. Herman, *Father-Daughter Incest*, p. 69.
20. Nathan, *Satan's Silence*, p. 43–44, 156.
21. Gelinas, 'Persisting Negative Effects of Incest.'
22. Herman, 'Time-Limited.'
23. Freud, *Complete Letters*, p. 31.
24. Ward, *Father-Daughter Rape*, p. 6, 50, 91, 120, 211.
25. Nathan, *Satan's Silence*, p. 107.
26. *Incest Survivor Campaign Newsletter*, 1981, Sept. 1983.
27. Smith & Pazder, *Michelle Remembers*, p. 18.
28. Grescoe, 'Things That Go Bump'; Nathan, *Satan's Silence*, p. 45.
29. Russell, *Secret Trauma*, p. 60–62.
30. Russell, p. 68–70.
31. Paul Okami, 'Sociopolitical Biases,' in *Pedophilia*, p. 99–102.
32. Finkelhor, *Sourcebook*; Finkelhor, 'Sexual Abuse in a National Survey,' p. 20–22; Russell, *Secret*

Trauma, p. 72–74; Laumann,
Social Organization, p. 340–343;
Wassil-Grimm, *Diagnosis*,
p. 15–16; Lopez, 'Prevalencia';
Kelly, 'Exploratory Study.'

33. Russell, *Secret Trauma*, p. 34.
34. Matthews, *Breaking Through*,
p. 19–21.
35. Mary Ann Donaldson & Russell
Gardner, Jr., 'Diagnosis and
Treatment of Traumatic Stress
Among Women After Childhood
Incest,' in *Trauma and Its Wake*,
v. 1, p. 370–373.
36. Jervis, 'Paradox.'
37. Fogarty, 'Journey.'
38. Bass, *Courage*, p. 22.
39. Bass, *Courage*, p. 23.
40. Bass, *Courage*, p. 35–39.
41. Bass, *Courage*, p. 40–54.
42. Peele, Stanton. *The Diseasing of
America*, p. 117; Bikel, 'Divided
Memories,' Part II, p. 1.
43. Bass, *Courage*, p. 218.
44. Bass, *Courage*, p. 62, 65–66.
45. Bass, *Courage*, p. 62–63.
46. Bass, *Courage*, p. 66–67.
47. Bass, *Courage*, p. 67.
48. Bass, *Courage*, p. 75–77.
49. Bass, *Courage*, p. 78–80.
50. Bass, *Courage*, p. 72.
51. Bass, *Courage*, p. 80.
52. Bass, *Courage*, p. 81–82.
53. Bass, *Courage*, p. 82–83.
54. Bass, *Courage*, p. 86–88.
55. Bass, *Courage*, p. 90–91.
56. Bass, *Courage*, p. 100–101.
57. Bass, *Courage*, p. 113.
58. Bass, *Courage*, p. 125–127.
59. Bass, *Courage*, p. 128–129.
60. Bass, *Courage*, p. 125.
61. Tavris, *Anger*, p. 45, 148.
62. Bass, *Courage*, p. 133–135.
63. Bass, *Courage*, p. 137–139.
64. Bass, *Courage*, p. 137.
65. Bass, *Courage*, p. 143–148.
66. Bass, *Courage*, p. 149–151.

67. Bass, *Courage*, p. 345–349.
68. Bass, *Courage*, p. 103, 265.
69. Bass, *Courage*, p. 262.
70. Bass, *Courage*, p. 256, 269.
71. Adrienne Rich, 'Compulsory
Heterosexuality and Lesbian
Existence,' in *Powers of Desire*,
p. 177–205.
72. Hollibaugh and Moraga in *Powers
of Desire*, p. 395.
73. Blume, *Secret Survivors*, p. xxvii-
xxx.
74. Blume, *Secret Survivors*, p. xxi-
xxiii.
75. Blume, *Secret Survivors*, p. 5.
76. Hall, *Surviving*, p. 54–55, 88–99.
77. Love, *Emotional Incest*, p. 1.
78. See *The Evil Eye*, edited by
Maloney; Siebers, *The Mirror of
Medusa*.
79. Love, *Emotional Incest*, p. 8.
80. Bass, *Courage*, p. 82.
81. Fredrickson, *Repressed Memories*,
p. 70.
82. Love, *Emotional Incest*, p. 163.
83. Adams, *Silently Seduced*, p. 40, 45,
64.
84. Adams, *Silently Seduced*,
p. 101–103.
85. Bass, *I Never Told*, p. 30–31.
86. Konker, 'Rethinking Child Sexual
Abuse,' p. 148; Maisch, *Incest*,
p. 21–41; Twitchell, *Forbidden
Partners*.
87. Lew, *Victims No Longer*, p. 69,
98–99.
88. Lew, *Victims*, p. 101, 104.
89. Lew, *Victims*, p. 234–235.
90. Lew, *Victims*, p. 247–248.
91. Hunter, *Abused Boys*, p. 149–151.
92. Hunter, *Abused Boys*, p. 165–196.
93. Hunter, *Abused Boys*, p. 206–241.
94. Fredrickson, *Repressed Memories*,
p. 17.
95. Fredrickson, *Repressed*, p. 27–28.
96. Fredrickson, *Repressed*, p. 104.
97. Fredrickson, *Repressed*, p. 32, 53.

98. Fredrickson, *Repressed*, p. 73, 84–86.
99. Fredrickson, *Repressed*, p. 59–60, 66, 85.
100. Fredrickson, *Repressed*, p. 43.
101. Fredrickson, *Repressed*, p. 109–112.
102. Fredrickson, *Repressed*, p. 113–114.
103. Fredrickson, *Repressed*, p. 115–116.
104. Fredrickson, *Repressed*, p. 161–162, 203–204.
105. Fredrickson, *Repressed*, p. 206.
106. Bobrow quoted in *FMSF Newsletter*, July 3, 1993, p. 6.
107. Maltz, *Sexual Healing*, p. 50–51.
108. Herman, *Trauma and Recovery*, p. 2–3.
109. Herman, *Trauma*, p. 175–178.
110. Herman, *Trauma*, p. 177, 182.
111. Herman, *Trauma*, p. 177–179.
112. Herman, *Trauma*, p. 179–180.
113. Herman, *Trauma*, p. 180.
114. Herman, *Trauma*, p. 229.
115. 'Multiple Personality,' *APA Psychiatric News*, Nov. 20, 1992.
116. 'The Experience of Ritual Abuse,' Survivors of Incest Anonymous flier, undated.
117. Hill, 'The Many Hearts,' p. 3.
118. Rose, 'Surviving the Unbelievable,' *Ms*, p. 42.
119. Bennetts, 'Nightmares on Main Street,' *Vanity Fair*, p. 42, 52.
120. Victor, *Satanic Panic*, p. 119, 244; Margaret Jervis email, Jan. 14, 1996.
121. Brunvand, *Vanishing Hitchhiker*.
122. Steinem, *Revolution From Within*, p. 157–166.
123. 'A Star Cries Incest,' *People*; Arnold, *My Lives*, p. 243.
124. Vanderbilt, 'Incest.'
125. Nathan, 'Cry Incest.'
126. *Ultimate Betrayal*, March 21, 1994, CBS.
127. Smiley, *Thousand*, p. 228, 280.
128. Britton, 'Terrible Truth.'

CHAPTER TWO

1. St. Augustine, *Confessions* X.viii.15, p. 220.
2. Baker, *Hidden Memories*, p. 50–54; Rose, *Making of Memory*, p. 2.
3. Hilts, *Memory's Ghost*, p. 163.
4. Roediger, 'Memory Metaphors.'
5. Leman, *Unlocking the Secrets*, p. 14.
6. Tetens quoted in Loftus, 'On the Permanence,' p. 109.
7. Tulving, personal communication, Nov. 21, 1995.
8. Bartlett, *Remembering*, p. vi, 204, 213.
9. Schacter, 'Cognitive Neuroscience.'
10. Miller, *Family Pictures*, p. 4.
11. Schacter, 'Memory Distortion,' p. 2.
12. See *Human Suggestibility* (1991).
13. Frank, *Persuasion*, p. 220–221.
14. Jaspers, *General Psychopathology*, p. 75–76.
15. Bartlett, *Remembering*, p. 212, 227.
16. Bartlett, *Remembering*, p. 205.
17. Stephen Crites, 'Storytime,' in *Narrative Psychology*, p. 160.
18. Bartlett, *Remembering*, p. 209.
19. Bower, 'Brain Scans.'
20. Bass & Davis, *Courage*, p. 1.
21. Bikel, 'Divided Memories,' Part I, p. 11.
22. Freud, *Standard Edition*, vol 2, p. 160.
23. Petersen, *Dancing*, p. 62–65.
24. Petersen, *Dancing*, p. 70.
25. Petersen, *Dancing*, p. 73–75.
26. Bartlett, *Remembering*, p. 217–220.
27. Gray, *Psychology*, p. 454–455.
28. Neisser, 'Memory: What Are the

Important Questions?' *Memory Observed*, p. 4.

29. Tulving, personal communication, Nov. 21, 1995.

30. Haberman, 'A Criticism of Psychoanalysis,' p. 266.

31. Haberman, p. 277.

32. P. D. Medawar in Crews, *Skeptical Engagement*, p. 25.

33. Holmes, 'The Evidence for Repression,' in *Repression and Dissociation*, p. 85–99; see also Holmes, 'Is There Evidence for Repression?'; Gruenbaum, *Foundations*, p. 95–266; Crews, *Skeptical*, p. 18–111.

34. Wilson quoted in Merskey, *Analysis*, p. 242.

35. Herman and Schatzow, 'Recovery and Verification,' 1987.

36. Wright, *Remembering Satan*, p. 184–185.

37. Briere and Conte, Self-reported.

38. Williams, 'Recall of Childhood Trauma'; Linda Meyer Williams interview, Oct. 27, 1993.

39. Van der Kolk, 'Dissociation and the Fragmentary Nature.'

40. Williams, 'Recovered Memories.'

41. Loftus et al, 'Memories of Childhood Sexual Abuse,' p. 73.

42. Femina, 'Child Abuse,' p. 227–231.

43. Loftus et al, 'Memories of Childhood Sexual Abuse.'

44. Elizabeth Loftus personal correspondence, June 5, 4.

45. Terr, *Unchained Memories*, p. xiv, 10–11.

46. Terr, 'What Happens,' p. 96–104.

47. Larry Squire interview, March 21, 1994.

48. Terr, *Unchained*, p. 96–119.

49. Terr, *Unchained*, p. 120–151.

50. Horn, 'Memories Lost and Found.'

51. Frank Fitzpatrick speech, 'Trauma & Memory' Conference, Colonnade Hotel, Boston, MA., April 2, 1993.

52. Gwen Mitchell interview, Oct. 23, 1995.

53. Atler, *Story of Hope*; Tape of speech to Family Services Agency of San Mateo, CA, May, 1994.

54. Ross Cheit interview, July 1994.

55. Stuart Grassian interviews, May 26, 1994, Dec. 13, 1995.

56. Atler, *Story of Hope*.

57. Fitzpatrick, *Survivor Activist*.

58. Elizabeth Feigon, personal correspondence, May 1994.

59. Erickson, 'Negation or Reversal.'

60. Neisser, 'Phantom Flashbulbs,' in *Affect and Accuracy*; Neisser, 'Snapshots or Benchmarks?' in *Memory Observed*.

61. Baddeley, *Handbook of Memory Distortion*; Baddeley, *Psychology of Memory*; Baddeley, *Working Memory*; Broadbent, *Biology of Memory*; Broadbent, *In Defense of Empirical Psychology*; Tulving, *Elements of Episodic Memory*; Tulving, *Organization of Memory*; Warrington, 'Amnesia'; Weiskrantz, 'Conditioning in Amnesic Patients'; Weiskrantz, 'Problems of Learning and Memory.'

62. Loftus, *Witness*, p. 20.

63. Loftus, *Witness*, p. 84.

64. Loftus & Loftus, 'On the Permanence,' p. 116.

65. Robinson, 'Memories of Abuse,' p. 20.

66. Loftus, 'When a Lie,' p. 120.

67. Loftus & Hoffman, 'Misinformation and Memory,' p. 103.

68. MacLean, *Once Upon a Time*, p. 398–401.
69. MacLean, *Once Upon a Time*, p. 345–357.
70. Terr, *Unchained Memories*, p. 22.
71. MacLean, *Once Upon a Time*, p. 80–81, 106–108, 155–193.
72. Terr, *Unchained Memories*, p. 60.
73. MacLean, *Once Upon a Time*, p. 80–81. Also, thanks to Harry MacLean for portions of the preliminary hearing and trial transcripts upon which this information is based.
74. MacLean, *Once Upon a Time*, p. 372–373.
75. *FMSF Newsletter*, Sept. 1995, p. 17.
76. Loftus, 'Repressed Memories,' p. 5; Loftus, 'Reality of Repressed Memories,' p. 532; Loftus, *Myth of Repressed Memory*; Loftus, 'Formation of False Memories.' Loftus' findings were replicated and expanded in Hyman, 'False Memories of Childhood Experiences.'
77. Herman and Harvey, 'The False Memory Debate,' p. 4.
78. Olio, 'Truth in Memory,' p. 442.
79. Robinson, 'Memories of Abuse,' p. 18–19.
80. Loftus, *Witness*, p. 149.
81. Robinson, 'Memories of Abuse,' p. 21.
82. Loftus quoted in Jaroff, 'Lies of the Mind,' p. 56.
83. Penfield in Loftus, 'On the Permanence,' p. 111.
84. Loftus, 'On the Permanence,' p. 114; Penfield, *Mystery of the Mind*, p. 22; Rosenfield, *Invention of Memory*, p. 163–166; 201–209; Squire, *Memory and Brain*, p. 75–84.
85. Penfield, *Mystery*, p. 21–27.
86. Penfield, *Mystery*, p. 62.

87. Lashley quoted in Squire, *Memory and Brain*, p. 59–62; Johnson, *In the Palaces*, p. 14–16; Lashley, 'In Search,' p. 479.
88. Squire, *Memory and Brain*, p. 63–64, 77, 236.
89. Campbell, *Improbable*, p. 157; Gardner, *Mind's New Science*, p. 275–278; Taylor, *Natural History of the Mind*, p. 123–126; Squire, *Memory and Brain*, p. 179–218.
90. Campbell, *Improbable Machine*, p. 163.
91. Rose, *Making of Memory*, p. 125–128; Squire, *Memory and Brain*, p. 179–218; Hilts, *Memory's Ghost*.
92. Tobias, Kihlstrom and Schacter, 'Emotion and Implicit Memory,' p. 71; Roediger, 'Implicit Memory.'
93. Schacter, 'Implicit Knowledge'; Schacter et al, 'Implicit Memory'; Tobias, Kihlstrom & Schacter, 'Emotion and Implicit Memory.'
94. Tobias, Kihlstrom, Schacter, p. 84; Schacter, 'Implicit Knowledge,' p. 1116.
95. See *Memory in Context*.
96. Schacter, 'Functional Amnesia,' p. 214.
97. Terr, *Unchained*, p. 137.
98. Daniel Schacter, personal correspondence, June 2, June 13, 1994.
99. Schacter in Goleman, 'Miscoding.'
100. Kihlstrom, 'The Recovery of Memory,' p. 7–14.
101. D. M. Thomson in *Memory in Context*, p. 298.
102. James, *Principles*, p. 438–439.
103. McGaugh, 'Affect, Neuromodulatory Systems, and Memory Storage,' in *Handbook of Emotion and Memory*; Cahill &

McGaugh, 'Neurobiology of Memory for Emotional Events,' in *Trauma and Memory*; McGaugh, 'Emotional Activation, Neuromodulatory Systems and Memory,' in *Memory Distortion*; Ledoux, 'Emotion, Memory.'

104. Blakeslee, *Beyond Diagnostic*, p. 424; Terence Keane et al in *Trauma and Its Wake*, v. 1, p. 265; Charles Figley in *Trauma and Its Wake*, v. 2, p. ix; Langer, *Holocaust Testimonies*.

105. 'Child Sex Abuse Leaves Mark'; Schacter, *Searching for Memory*, Chapter 8.

106. Weiskrantz, personal correspondence, Oct. 12, 1995.

107. McGaugh, personal correspondence, Nov. 11, 1995.

108. Loftus, 'Remembering Dangerously,' p. 26–27.

109. Kandel, 'Flights of Memory, p. 36–38.

110. Rose, *Making of Memory*, p. 215–240.

111. Van der Kolk, 'Body Keeps the Score.'

112. Smith, *Survivor Psychology*.

113. Pert, 'Wisdom of the Receptors.'

114. James McGaugh, personal correspondence, Dec. 17, 1995.

115. Gould, *Mismeasure*, p. 22.

116. Huber, *Galileo's Revenge*, p. 27.

117. Dawes, *House of Cards*, p. 48–49, 193–194.

118. Rose, *Making of Memory*, p. 189–199.

119. Smith, *Survivor Psychology*; Van der Kolk, 'Body Keeps the Score,' p. 255; Mark Twain and Lewis Carroll, quoted in Huber, *Galileo's Revenge*, p. 24–5.

120. Webster, *Why Freud Was Wrong*, p. 88.

121. Richet quoted in James, *Principles*, p. 422.

122. Johnson, *In the Palaces*, p. 182–183; Allman, *Apprentices*, p. 1–3, 177–189.

123. Campbell, *The Improbable Machine*, p. 12–35.

124. Campbell, *Improbable*, p. 49; 140–141.

125. Loftus, *Witness*, p. 137; Loftus, *Eyewitness Testimony*, p. 77–79.

126. Campbell, *Improbable*, p. 143.

127. Campbell, *Improbable*, p. 164; 238.

128. Yates, *Art of Memory*, p. 1–3; Rose, *The Making of Memory*, p. 62–72.

129. Spence, *Memory Palace of Matteo Ricci*, p. 1–13; Johnson, *In the Palaces*, p. xiii–xiv.

130. Albertus Magnus in Yates, *Art of Memory*, p. 68.

131. Piaget quoted in Loftus, *Witness*, p. 17–19.

132. Usher and Neisser, 'Childhood Amnesia'; Loftus, 'Desperately Seeking Memories.'

133. Freud, 'Screen Memories,' *Standard Edition*, v. 3, p. 303–306.

134. Usher & Neisser, 'Childhood Amnesia,' p. 155–156; Howe & Courage, 'On Resolving,' p. 305–326.

135. Rymer, *Genie*, p. 35–38, 84–94, 125, 163–164, 175.

136. Bikel, 'Divided Memories,' Part I.

137. Freud, *Standard Edition*, v. 3, p. 322.

138. McHugh, 'Psychotherapy Awry,' p. 25.

139. Merskey, *Analysis*, p. 75–79; 98–113.

140. Schacter, 'Functional Retrograde Amnesia,' *Neuropsychologia*, p. 529; Schacter & Kihlstrom, 'Functional Amnesia,' in

Handbook of Neuropsychology,
p. 210.

141. Schacter, 'Functional Retrograde
Amnesia,' p. 529; Estabrooks,
Hypnotism, p. 109.

142. Symonds in Merskey, *Analysis of
Hysteria*, p. 264–265.

143. Malmquist, 'Children Who
Witness'; Pynoos and Eth, 'The
Child as Witness'; Lindsay,
'Memory Work.'

144. Martha Churchill cartoon.

CHAPTER THREE

1. Carroll, *Alice's Adventures*, p. 230.
2. *Comprehensive Textbook of
Psychiatry*, Part IV, v. 2, p. 1516.
3. Smith, 'Hypnotic Memory
Enhancement,' p. 399.
4. Baker, *They Call It Hypnosis*,
p. 193–195; see also Smith,
'Hypnotic Enhancement;' Parkin,
Memory and Amnesia, p. 44–45.
5. Baker, *They Call It Hypnosis*,
p. 18.
6. Orne and Loftus quoted in Baker,
They Call It Hypnosis, p. 110, 195.
7. Laurence and Perry, *Hypnosis,
Will, and Memory*, p. xiv–xv.
8. Merskey, *Analysis*, p. 165–166.
9. Laurence & Perry, *Hypnosis*,
p. xiii.
10. Baker, *They Call It*, p. 17, 174.
11. Spanos, 'Hypnotic Amnesia;'
Spanos, 'Multiple Identity
Enactments.'
12. Baker, *Hidden Memories*, p. 148.
13. Baker, *They Call It*, p. 109.
14. Spiegel in Woodward, 'Was It
Real or Memories?' p. 55.
15. Bernheim in Ellenberger,
Discovery, p. 172.
16. Estabrooks, *Hypnotism*, p. 43.
17. Lynn & Rhue in *Theories of
Hypnosis*, p. 13; Kirsch, 'Altered
State.'

18. Bernheim in Laurence & Perry,
Hypnotism, p. 237–238.
19. Laurence & Perry, 'Hypnotically
Created,' p. 524.
20. Spanos, 'Hypnotically Created,'
p. 155–159.
21. Orne in *Hypnosis and Memory*,
p. 46; Sheehan in *Hypnosis and
Memory*, p. 95–125.
22. Orne, 'Use and Misuse,' p. 323,
334.
23. Udolf, *Handbook*, p. 131–133.
24. Baker, *They Call It*, p. 130; Baker,
Hidden Memories, p. 152.
25. Nash, 'What, If Anything,'
p. 49–50; see also Perry in *Hypnosis
and Memory*, p. 128–150.
26. Rubenstein, 'Living Out,'
p. 473.
27. Verny, *Secret Life*, p. 190; Loftus,
'Therapeutic Recollection,' p. 6;
Bikel, 'Divided Memories,' Part I,
p. 9.
28. Woolger, *Other Lives*,
p. 137–138.
29. Baker, *Hidden Memories*, p. 154;
Wilson, *All in the Mind*, 101–106.
30. Wills, *Reagan's America*,
p. 162–170.
31. Wilson, *All in the Mind*; Baker,
Hidden Memories, p. 78–92;
153–164; Spanos, 'Secondary
Identity Enactments'; Loftus,
Witness, p. 84; Goleman,
'Miscoding Is Seen.'
32. Baker, *Hidden*, p. 153.
33. Jacobs, *Secret Life*, p. 25.
34. Mack, *Abduction*, p. 3–27.
34a. Bryan, *Close Encounters*, p. 419
35. Neimark, 'The Harvard
Professor,' p. 46–48; Orlans,
'Potpourri.'
36. Trace, Robert, 'Research
Findings;' Green, 'Quality of the
Evidence' in *Facilitated
Communication*; Howard Shane
interview; Gina Green interview;

Green, 'Facilitated Communication,' *Skeptic*.

37. For background on Ouija boards, see Jastrow, *Wish and Wisdom*, p. 129–143.
38. Biklen, *Communication Unbound*, p. 132.
39. Haskew & Donnellan, *Emotional Maturity*, p. 31.
40. 'Prisoners of Silence,' *Frontline*; Chideya, 'Language of Suspicion.'
41. Gray, *Psychology*, p. 25–27; Jastrow, *Wish and Wisdom*, p. 203–213.
42. Allan Hobson, personal correspondence, Oct. 12, 1995; Hobson, *Dreaming Brain*; Hobson, *Chemistry of Conscious States*, p. 114–115; Dolnick, 'What Dreams.'
43. Borbely, *Secrets of Sleep*, p. 63–64.
44. Shapiro, 'Rush to Judgment.'
45. Hall, *Meaning of Dreams*, p. 14, 17.
46. Jastrow, *Wish and Wisdom*, p. viii.
47. Loftus, *Witness*, p. 22.
48. Kirsch in *Theories of Hypnosis*, p. 439. See also Reed, *Psychology of Anomalous*, p. 41, 58–59.
49. Frank, *Persuasion*, p. 52–54; Goodman, *How About Demons?*, p. 89–94.
50. Frank, *Persuasion*, p. 212; see also Ellenberger, *Discovery*, p. 306.
51. Sargant, *Battle*, p. 59.
52. Fredrickson, *Repressed Memories*, p. 134–137.
53. Baker, *They Call It*, p. 179–182; Hufford, *Terror*, p. 115–170; Reed, *Psychology of Anomalous*, p. 37–40.
54. J. Bond, *An Essay on the Incubus or Nightmare*, in Robbins, *Encyclopedia of Witchcraft*, p. 356.
55. Hufford, *Terror*, p. 40–41; see also Barlow, *Anxiety*, p. 73, 85–87.
56. Bass, *Courage*, p. 65.
57. Borbely, *Secrets of Sleep*, p. 156–157; see also 'Sleep Disorders'; Hobson, *Sleep: Principles and Practices of Sleep Medicine*.
58. MacCurdy, *War Neuroses*, p. 4–7.
59. Sargant, *Battle*, p. 51.
60. Kolb in *Hypnosis and Memory*, p. 268–269.
61. Yapko, 'Seductions of Memory,' p. 31–32.
62. 'The Grade Five Syndrome,' *Cornerstone*, p. 16.
63. Fredrickson, *Repressed Memories*, p. 146–147.
64. Baker, *Hidden*, p. 150–151.
65. Wilson, *All in the Mind*, p. 142–145; 'Stigmatics' interview with Ted Harrison; Harrison, *Stigmata*.
66. Wilson, *All in the Mind*, p. 143–149.
67. Estabrooks, *Hypnotism*, p. 44.
68. Smith, *Michelle Remembers*, illustrations.
69. Beck, *Anxiety*, p. 8.
70. Barlow, *Anxiety*, p 22, 28, 102–103.
71. Foxman, *Dancing with Fear*, p. 3.
72. *Diagnostic*, p. 395.
73. Beck, *Anxiety*, p. 4–6, 90.
74. Barlow, *Anxiety*, p. 226–229, 252–259.
75. Seagrave, *Free from Fears*, p. 26.
76. Barlow, *Anxiety*, p. 78–80, 148–151.
77. *FMSF Newsletter*, March 1995, p. 7; *FMSF Newsletter*, Jan. 1996, p. 11.
78. Whitfield, *Healing . . . Continued*, Tape 1.
79. Lenore Terr on *Maury Povich Show*, May 25, 1994; Pope, 'Recovered Memories,' p. 5.
80. Rader, 'Incest and Eating Disorders.'

81. Toni Luppino interview, Rader Institute, June 14, 1994.
82. March, 1993 conversation with anonymous psychiatric nurse at Hollywood, FL, Rader Institute.
83. June Treacy interview, June 15, 1994, National Association of Anorexia Nervosa and Associated Disorders.
84. Ads for Shades of Hope and The Meadows in the 1994 Gurze Eating Disorders Bookshelf catalog, Carlsbad, CA.
85. Hall, *Surviving*, p. 55.
86. Eating Disorders Association literature, 1995.
87. Grant, 'Are Women Mad?
88. Barton, 'Therapy of Danger.'
89. Pope, 'Is Childhood Sexual Abuse a Risk Factor?'; Pope, 'Childhood Sexual Abuse.'
90. Nelson, 'Symbolic Rejection'; Sue Hutchinson in *Treating Survivors*, p. 304.
91. McElroy, 'Misattribution.'
92. Otani, 'Memory in Hypnosis.'
93. Pamela Freyd interview, May 1994.
94. Pope, 'Recovered Memories,' p. 10–11.
95. Kihlstrom, 'Recovery of Memory,' p. 5–6.
96. Piper, 'Truth Serum'; Loftus, 'Therapeutic Recollection,' p. 9.
97. Frank, *Persuasion*, p. xi.
98. Bass, *Courage*, p. 66, 90, 146–147.
99. Festinger, *Theory*, p. 3, 83, 180.
100. Cialdini, *Influence*, p. 66.
101. *FMSF Newsletter*, Nov./ Dec. 1995, p. 15.
102. Bass, *Courage*, p. 108.
103. Festinger, *Theory*, p. 177, 192, 200.
104. McGrath, *Motel Nirvana*, p. 52.
105. Gray, *Psychology*, p. 545–546.
106. Festinger, *Theory*, p. 252–259; Festinger, *When Prophecy Fails*.
107. Bartlett, *Remembering*, p. 241, 256, 300.
108. Cialdini, *Influence*, p. 82–83.
109. Roesler, 'Network Therapy.'
110. Ceci, *Jeopardy*, p. 208.
111. Rosenhan, 'On Being Sane.'
112. *CNN Special Assignment*, May 3, 1993.
113. Loftus, 'Remembering Dangerously,' p. 24.

CHAPTER FOUR

1. Thigpen, *Three Faces of Eve*, p. 1–22.
2. Thigpen & Cleckley, 'A Case.'
3. Schreiber, *Sybil*.
4. Spiegel in Bain, *Control*, p. xi.
5. Schreiber, *Sybil*, p. 18.
6. Herbert Spiegel interview, March 23, 1994.
7. Ludwig, 'Altered States,' p. 229.
8. Ludwig, 'Objective Study.'
9. Allison, *Minds*, p. 31–34.
10. Allison, *Minds*, p. 25–65.
11. Allison, 'Effects on the Therapist,' p. 15; Ralph Allison interview, July 1, 1994.
12. Allison, *Minds*, p. 66–100.
13. Allison, *Minds*, p. 4–5.
14. Personal correspondence with Ralph Allison, June 1994; Allison, 'A Debate: Satanic Ritual Abuse.'
15. Thigpen, *Three Faces*, p. 7.
16. Alpher, 'Introject and Identity.'
17. Peck, *People of the Lie*, p. 150–196.
18. *FMSF Newsletter*, Oct. 1995, p. 9; Patrick Clancy email, Dec. 9, 1995.
19. Friesen, *Uncovering*, p. 42, 64–65, 82–83, 98, 108, 136, 151–153, 166, 170, 175–177, 200–201, 263–264.
20. Spanos, 'Demonic Possession'; Kenny, 'Multiple Personality.'
21. Peck, *People of the Lie*, p. 185.
22. Allison, personal correspondence, June 1994.

23. Sherrill Mulhern interview, July 1994; Ralph Allison interview, July 1994.
24. Ross, *Multiple Personality Disorder*, p. 44–53.
25. North, *Multiple Personalities*, p. 127.
26. Putnam, *Diagnosis*, p. vii. The following quotations come from pages 71–102.
27. Kluft in Taylor, John, 'The Lost Daughter,' p. 85; Peck, *People*, p. 186.
28. Bliss, *Multiple*, p. 124.
29. Putnam, *Diagnosis*, p. 223–249.
30. Mulhern interview; *FMFS Newsletter*, June 1994, p. 6; Kluft, 'Clinical Presentations,' p. 607; Frank Putnam, personal correspondence, Aug. 19, 1994.
31. Putnam, *Diagnosis*, p. 103–130, 227; Simpson, 'Gullible's Travels,' p. 95.
32. Hacking, 'Two Souls,' p. 857.
33. Simpson, 'Gullible's Travels, Or The Importance of Being Multiple,' in *Dissociative Identity Disorder*, p. 121.
34. Ganaway, 'Historical vs. Narrative,' p. 209.
35. Ganaway, 'Hypnosis,' p. 6.
36. McHugh, 'History and Pitfalls,' p. 13
37. Putnam, *Diagnosis*, p. 98.
38. Schreiber, *Sybil*, p. 374.
39. Schwarz, *Hillside*; Coleman, *Reign*, p. 13–16.
40. Ralph Allison post, Witchhunt computer bulletin board, June 13, 1994.
41. Schwarz, *Hillside*, p. 138–139.
42. Spanos, 'Multiple Personality.'
43. Spanos, 'Hypnotic Interview.'
44. Aldridge-Morris, *Multiple Personality*, p. 107–108.
45. Spencer, *Suffer the Child*.
46. Karle, *Filthy Lie*, 6, 11–12, 21, 35, 47–48, 76, 147, 167, 210, 253, 271, 284, 291–294, 305.
47. Jervis, 'Book Review.'
47a. Ray Aldridge-Morris, email, Feb. 7, 1996.
48. *Treating Survivors* p. 98–99, 140–147, 178, 243, 250, 254–260, 268, 288; Cornwell, 'True Lies,' p. 26.
49. Jervis, 'Recall Totalled,' p. 44; Jervis email, Jan. 14, 1996.
50. Merskey, 'Manufacture,' p. 337.
51. Kenny, *Passion*, p. 14.
52. Simpson, 'Gullible's Travels, Or The Importance of Being Multiple,' in *Dissociative Identity Disorder*, p. 88, 101, 104.
53. Piper, 'A Skeptical Look at Multiple Personality Disorder,' in *Dissociative Identity Disorder*, p. 137.
54. World Health Organization, *ICD–10*, quoted in Simpson, 'Gullible's Travels.,' p. 91
55. McHugh, 'Multiple,' *Harvard Mental Health*. See also Piper, 'Multiple'; Piper, 'Treatment.'
56. Putnam, 'Recent Research'; North, *Multiple Personalities*, p. 59–64.
57. Merskey, 'Manufacture,' p. 335.
58. Sizemore, *Mind*, p. 118, 166, 174; Sizemore, *I'm Eve*.
59. Loewenstein, 'An Office Mental Status Examination,' p. 568, 570.
60. Ross, 'Discussion,' p. 127.
61. Freud, *Standard Edition*, v. 20, p. 17.
62. Taylor, 'Lost Daughter'; *20/20* documentary, July 22, 1994.
63. Anonymous interview, June 13, 1994.
64. Goffman, *Asylums*, p. 4, 14.
65. Ofshe, *Making Monsters*, p. 225–251; Bikel, 'Search for Satan.'

66. Ofshe, *Making Monsters*, p. 236–237, 248.
67. Keenan, 'The Devil and Dr. Braun,' p. 10.
68. McDonald, 'An Ethical Dilemma'; Smith, 'Haunted Dreams'; Bikel, 'Search for Satan'; Gangelhoff, 'Devilish Diagnosis.' The material that follows comes from these sources, as well as August 1994 interviews with Sally McDonald and an anonymous former dissociative disorders unit nurse at Spring Shadows Glen.
69. 'Sabbats/Festivals,' VOICES in Action, no date.
70. Smith, 'Haunted Dreams.'
71. Anonymous interview with former Spring Shadows Glen dissociative disorders nurse.
72. Smith, 'Haunted Dreams.'
73. Anonymous interview with Judith Peterson's former patient, June 27, 28, 1994.
74. Mary Shanley interview, Sept. 12, 1994.
75. Bikel, 'Search for Satan.'
76. Sharkey, *Bedlam*, p. 55, 77–79.
77. Smith, 'Haunted Dreams.'
78. McDonald, 'An Ethical Dilemma.'
79. Christy Steck interview, Aug. 9, 1994.
80. Judith Peterson interview, Aug. 3, 1994.
81. Peterson, 'When the Therapists.'
82. Ibid.
83. Gangelhoff, 'Devilish Diagnosis.'
84. Janet quoted in Frankel, 'Hypnotizability and Dissociation,' p. 824.
85. Frankel, 'Hypnotizability and Dissociation,' p. 825.
86. West quoted in Putnam, *Diagnosis*, p. 6.
87. Tillman, 'Does Trauma Cause Dissociative Pathology?'
88. Gray, *Psychology*, p. 504.
89. Kenny, *Passion*, p. 9.
90. Epstein, 'Self-Concept,' p. 407.
91. Spanos, 'Hypnotic Interview,' p. 310.
92. Kluft, 'Hospital Treatment,' p. 695–696.
93. *Multiple Personality Disorder from the Inside Out*, p. 124.
94. Robbins, *Encyclopedia*, p. 395.
95. Troops, *When Rabbit*, p. xiv–xvi, 412.
96. Hart, *MPD/FMS Retractor's Story*
97. Spiegel, *Trance and Treatment*, p. 55; Herbert Spiegel interview, Aug. 5, 1994; Webster, *Why Freud Was Wrong*, p. 62, 87.
98. Spiegel, Herbert, 'The Grade 5 Syndrome: The Highly Hypnotizable Person,' *The International Journal of Clinical and Experimental Hypnosis*, 1974, v. 22 (4), pp. 303–319.
99. 'Reticular Formation,' in *McGraw-Hill Encyclopedia*, v. 15, p. 434–435.
100. Spiegel interview.
101. Makarec & Persinger, 'Electroencephalographic,' p. 323–329.
102. *Psychiatric Aspects of Epilepsy*, p. viii.
103. Persinger, *Neuropsychological*; Rogo, 'Is Religion in the Brain?'
104. Persinger, 'Elicitation of 'Childhood Memories."
105. Putnam, *Diagnosis*, p. 258.
106. *Psychiatric Aspects of Epilepsy*, p. 49, 279, 286.
107. Devinsky in *Epilepsy and Behavior*, p. 1.
108. Bear et al in *Psychiatric Aspects*, p. 197–224; Orrin Devinsky in *Epilepsy and Behavior*, p. 1–21.
109. Devinsky in *Epilepsy*, p. 12–14.
110. Mark R. Elin, 'A Developmental Model for Trauma,' in *Dissociative Identity Disorder*, p. 230–231.

111. Bass, *Courage*, p. 417–419.
112. Ellis, 'Satanic Ritual Abuse'; Nathan, *Satan's Silence*, p. 36–37; Wright, *Saints and Sinners*, p. 121–156.
113. Ganaway, 'Historical vs. Narrative,' p. 210.
114. Lanning, 'Investigator's Guide,' p. 40.
115. Goodman, 'Characteristics,' p. 5, 11; Nathan, *Satan's Silence*, p. 1.
116. La Fontaine, *Extent and Nature*, p. 24–25.
117. Robbins, *Encyclopedia*, p. 105–106.
118. Giandalone, 'Guidelines for Therapists and Support Service Providers,' August 1990.
119. Cohen, *Folk Devils*, p. 9
120. 'The Adult Survivor of Ritual Abuse,' VOICES in Action.
121. Passantino, 'Satan's Sideshow.'
122. Michaelson in Stratford, *Satan's Underground*, unpaged foreword.
123. Stratford, *Satan's Underground*, p. 18–162.
124. Jenkins, *Intimate Enemies*, p. 167; Hebditch, 'Ritual Fabrication.'
125. Cohn, *Europe's Inner Demons*, p. xi.
126. Wright, *Remembering Satan*, p. 197; Hsia, *The Myth of Ritual Murder*; Moore, *Formation of a Persecuting Society*.
127. Cohn, *Europe's Inner Demons*, p. xi–xiii.
128. Braun quote in Mulhern, 'Satanism and Psychotherapy,' *The Satanism Scare*, p. 166; Braun in 'Ritual Child Abuse' Cavalcade video, 1989.
129. Harold Crasilneck in Hammond, *Handbook*, p. ix.
130. Hammond videotape at Parkwood Hospital, Atlanta, GA, March 2, 1991, quoted in *FMSF Newsletter*, March 1994, p. 6–7; Hammond in 'Ritual Child Abuse' Cavalcade video, 1989; Hammond audiotape, no date, from Debbie Nathan.
131. Marks, *Search*, p. 3–22, and following; Condon, *Manchurian Candidate*; Thomas, *Journey Into Madness*.
132. Ross, 'CIA Mind Control.'
133. Ross on *Fifth Estate*, Nov. 8, 1993, quoted in *FMSF Newsletter*, April 1994, p. 3.
134. Pendergrast, *For God, Country & Coca-Cola*, p. 267–268.
135. Blume, 'Ownership of Truth,' p. 134.
136. Rockwell, 'One Psychiatrist's View,' p. 448.
137. *Treating Survivors*, p. 175–178, 243.
138. Coleman in *Treating Survivors*, p. 250.
139. Phil Mollon, 'The Impact of Evil,' in *Treating Survivors*, p. 136–147.
140. Mollon, 'Clinical Psychologists.'
141. Curtiss, 'Some on Ritual Abuse'; Johnson, 'The "Phantom Anesthetist".'
142. Keyes, *Minds*, p. xi–xvii, 143, 148.
143. Thigpen & Cleckley, 'On the Incidence.'

CHAPTER FIVE

1. Campbell, *Improbable Machine*, p. 254.
2. Poole and Lindsay, 'Psychotherapy and the Recovery.'
3. Cornwell, 'True Lies.'
4. Feldman-Summers, 'Experience of Forgetting,' p. 637; Allison, 'Effect on the Therapist,' p. 14.
5. Philipson, *On the Shoulders*, p. 1, 144.

CHAPTER SIX

1. Blake, *Complete Writings*, p. 663.
2. Bass, *Courage*, p. 45, 166.
3. Davidson, *The Agony*, p. 4.
4. Bass, *Courage*, p. 52.
5. *FMSF Newsletter*, Jan. 1996, p. 6.
6. Bass, *Courage*, p. 47.
7. Ganaway, 'Dissociative Disorders,' p. 11–12.
8. Beck, *Anxiety Disorders*, p. 133–135, 142–143.
9. Bass, *Courage*, p. 48.
10. Lipinksi and Pope, reported in Loftus, 'The Repressed Memory Controversy,' p. 445.
11. Bass, *Courage*, p. 163.

CHAPTER SEVEN

1. Kafka, *The Trial*.
2. Wright, *Remembering Satan*, p. 8; Ofshe, 'Inadvertent Hypnosis.'
3. Gudjonsson, *Psychology of Interrogations*, p. 228; Ofshe, 'Coerced Confessions.'
4. *Book of Job* 4:7; 6:21.
5. *FMSF Newsletter*, May 3, 1993, p. 13.
6. 'Repressed Memories: Can They Be Trusted?' *Santa Cruz Sentinel*, March 21, 1993.
7. J. Alexander Bodkin, July 2, 1994 unpublished letter to the *New York Times*; John Quattrocchi interview, Sept. 6, 1994; Smith, Martha. 'The Bulldogs,' *Rhode Islander Magazine*, July 31, 1994, p. 11.
8. Seligman, *What You Can Change*, p. 133–144.
9. Orr, 'Accuracy About Abuse,' p. 26.
10. Finkelhor, 'Victimization of Children.'
11. Ashby-Rolls, *Triumph*.
12. FMSF Newsletter, June 1995, p. 3.

13. Manchester, 'Incest and the Law,' in *Family Violence*; Mitchell, 'Confessions.'

CHAPTER EIGHT

1. Putnam, quoted in Robbins, *Encyclopedia of Witchcraft*, p. 402–403.
2. *The Cutting Edge*, Fall 1992, p. 4, 7.
3. Feldman, *Patient or Pretender*; Franzini, *Eccentric & Bizarre Behaviors*, p. 21–38.
4. Gavigan, *The Retractor*, Dec. 1992/Jan. 1993, p. 1–2.
5. Miller, *Breaking Down the Wall*, p. 1.
6. Littauer, *Freeing Your Mind*, p. 87–217, 226.

CHAPTER NINE

1. Hutchinson in Robbins, *Encyclopedia of Witchcraft*, p. 348–350.
2. Gardner, 'Modern Witch Hunt,' *Wall Street Journal*; Coleman, 'False Allegations of Sexual Abuse,' p. 15–16.
3. Benedek, 'Problems in Validating.' For general books on the child abuse industry, see Wexler, *Wounded Innocents*; Pride, *Child Abuse Industry*; Tong, *Don't Blame ME*; Costin, *Politics of Child Abuse*; Nathan, *Satan's Silence*, p. 53.
4. Material about the McMartin case comes from Nathan, *Satan's Silence*; Nathan, *Women and Other Aliens*, p. 116–167; Eberle, *Abuse of Innocence*; 'From the Mouths of Children,' *Fifth Estate*; Ceci & Bruck, 'Child Witnesses,' p. 1–2; 'The McMartin Pre-School,' *60 Minutes*, CBS TV, Nov. 2, 1986; Debbie Nathan, 'Satanism and Child Molestation' in *Satanic*

Panic, p. 75–94; interviews with Peggy Buckey, Virginia McMartin; and correspondence with Sherrill Mulhern and Debbie Nathan.

5. Nathan, *Satan's Silence*, p. 78–80.
6. Franzini, *Eccentric & Bizarre*, p. 21–38; Feldman, *Patient or Pretender*.
7. Summit, 'Dark Tunnels'; Bass, *Courage to Heal*, 3rd ed., p. 520–521; Nathan, June 13, 1994 personal communication; Nathan, *Satan's Silence*, p. 242.
8. 'From the Mouths of Babes,' *ABC News 20/20*; Ceci, 'Cognitive and Social Factors'; Ceci & Bruck, 'Child Witnesses'; *Suggestibility of Children's Recollections*; Ceci, *Jeopardy*, p. 218–220.
9. Ceci, *Jeopardy*, p. 218–220.
10. Ceci in 'From the Mouths of Children.'
11. Ceci, 'Cognitive and Social Factors,' p. 11–13; Taylor, 'Salem Revisited, p. 10; Coleman & Clancy, 'False Allegations.'
12. Ceci, *Jeopardy*, p. 223–224.
13. July 7, 1995 letter from prisoner.
14. Bruce Perkins to Mark Pendergrast, Jan 12, 1996.
15. Aaron Larson, May 7, 1994, message on 'Witchhunt' computer bulletin board.
16. Nathan, *Satan's Silence*, p. 110–111, 130.
17. Friedrich, 'Normative Sexual Behavior'; Rosenfeld, 'Determining Incestuous Contact'; Rosenfeld, 'Familial Bathing Patterns'; Gordon, 'Children's Knowledge of Sexuality.'
18. McCann, 'Perianal Findings'; McCann, 'Genital Findings'; Coleman, 'Medical Examination.'
19. Nathan, *Satan's Silence*, p. 178–179.
20. O'Neel & Dalenberg, 'True and False Allegations'; Horner et al, 'The Biases of Child Sexual Abuse Experts'; Ceci, 'Cognitive and Social Factors'; Ceci & Bruck, 'Child Witnesses,' p. 11; Campbell, 'Challenging Psychologists.'
21. Ceci & Bruck, 'Child Witnesses,' p. 9.
22. Nathan, *Satan's Silence*, p. 114.
23. *Satan's Silence*, p. 82.
24. C. Levitt quoted in Howitt, *Child Abuse Errors*, p. 51.
25. *Family Sexual Abuse*, p. 244.
26. Gerber quoted in Howitt, *Child Abuse Errors*, p. 52.
27. Nathan, *Satan's Silence*, p. 123, 188.
28. Bikel, 'Innocence Lost: The Verdict.'
29. Robert Kelly interview, Jan. 15, 1996.
30. Fine, 'Seeking Evil.'
31. Taylor, 'Salem Revisited'; Hass, 'Margaret Kelly Michaels.'
32. 'From the Mouths of Babes,' *ABC News 20/20*.
33. Roberts, 'Martensville Horror'; 'From the Mouths of Children,' *Fifth Estate*.
34. All material regarding Country Walk comes from Nathan, 'Reno Reconsidered' and Nathan, *Satan's Silence*, p. 169–177.
35. Frank Fuster interview, July 27, Aug. 20, 1994; Fuster form-letter summary of his case, Sept. 26, 1988; State of Florida vs. Francisco Fuster Escalona, Case No. 81–21904, Sept. 21–22, 1982.
36. Nathan, *Satan's Silence*, p. 169–177.
37. Ceci, *Jeopardy*, p. 229.
38. Cockburn, 'Beat the Devil.'

39. Fuster interview.
40. Armbrister, 'Justice Gone Crazy.'
41. Boyer, 'Children of Waco.'
42. Ceci, *Jeopardy*, p. 228–230.
43. Jenkins, *Intimate Enemies*, p. 73, 104–113; Nathan, *Satan's Silence*, p. 43–44, 244; Orr, 'Accuracy About Abuse,' p. 25.
44. CIBA, *Child Sexual Abuse*; Jervis email, Jan. 21, 1996.
45. Jenkins, *Intimate Enemies*, p. 116–119; Jervis, 'Spectral Evidence.'
46. Hobbs, 'Buggery in Childhood'; Nathan, *Satan's Silence*, p. 196; Debbie Nathan, email, Jan. 6, 1996; Jenkins, *Intimate Enemies*, p. 134.
47. Jenkins, *Intimate Enemies*, p. 136–144; Butler-Sloss, *Report of the Inquiry*, p. 11; Department of Health, *Working Together*; Jervis email, Jan. 28, 1996.
48. Jervis, 'Objectivity Compromised'; Campbell, *Unofficial Secrets*; Jenkins, *Intimate Enemies*, p. 111.
49. Jenkins, *Intimate Enemies*, p. 85, 160–161, 185; Woffinden, 'Out of the Mouths'; Waterhouse articles; Jervis email, Jan. 11, 1996.
50. Jenkins, *Intimate Enemies*, p. 117, 152, 168–171; Victor, *Satanic Panic*, p. 244; Bartlett, 'Facing the Unbelievable.'
51. Jenkins, *Intimate Enemies*, p. 177–185; Victor, *Satanic Panic*, p. 117–119; McKain, 'Ayr "Abuse" Case Closed.'
52. Victor, *Satanic Panic*, p. 115.
53. Jervis email, Jan. 28, 1996.
54. Jenkins, *Intimate Enemies*, p. 185–187; Reid, *Suffer the Little Children*.
55. Bray, *Poppies*.
56. Department of Health, *Working Together*.
57. Woffinden, 'Out of the Mouths'; Booker, 'Men Who Say.'
58. Jervis, 'Panic Over Satanic'; Jervis, 'Spectral Evidence,' p. 14.
59. Jervis email, Jan 20, 1996.
59a. Palmer, 'Get the Baby'
60. Goodyear-Smith, *First Do No Harm*, p. 98–99.
61. Goodyear-Smith, *First*, p. 101.
62. Goodyear-Smith, *First*, p. 82; Goodyear-Smith email, Jan. 10, 1996.
63. Norman Shulver interview, Jan. 22, 1996.
64. Scotford, 'The Bjugn Case.'
65. Jervis, 'Rise.'
66. Information on the Fells Acres case came from interviews with Gerald and Patty Amirault and Susan Leighton; extensive local newspaper coverage; trial transcript, Commonwealth v. Amirault, Massachusetts Superior Court, Cambridge, Mass.
67. Cartwright, 'The Innocent and the Damned.'
68. Weiss, 'Citizens Group'; Moya, 'Sparks Man.'
69. Transcription of videotaped Susan Kelley interviews, property of Jonathan Harris, Cambridge, Mass.
70. Mashberg, 'Defense: Tapes Tell It All.'
71. Kelley, 'Stress Responses,' p. 503.
72. Rabinowitz, 'A Darkness.'
73. Mashberg, 'Judge Nixes.'
74. Material on the Souza case comes from interviews with Ray and Shirley Souza; the trial transcript [Commonwealth of Mass v. Shirley Souza, Raymond Souza, Middlesex Superior Court]; Shapiro, 'Rush to Judgment,' *Newsweek*; 'Grandparents Being Sent to Jail,' *Donahue*; 'From the

Mouths of Babes,' *20/20*; and coverage of the case by the *Boston Globe* and *Lowell Sun*.

75. Ceci & Bruck, 'Child Witnesses,' p. 13–14.
76. Nathan, *Satan's Silence*, p. 70, 75; Muram, 'Child Sexual Abuse.'
77. Summit, 'The Child Sexual Abuse Accommodation Syndrome.'
78. Coleman, 'False Accusations,' p. 549.
79. Summit in 'From the Mouths of Children,' *Fifth Estate*; Coleman & Clancy, 'False Allegations,' p. 44.
80. Steven Normandin interview, May 22, 1994.
81. Woodhull, 'McMartin Held.'
82. Armbrister, 'When Parents Become Victims'; Kathy Swan interview, Aug. 3, 1994; Peggy Buckey interview, July 1994.

CHAPTER TEN

1. Ford in Mackay, *Extraordinary Popular Delusions*, p. 462.
2. Hegel quoted in Ganaway, 'Dissociative Disorders,' p. 5.
3. Chesler, *Women and Madness*, p. 34.
4. Chesler, *Women and Madness*, p. 34–35, 40, 118.
5. J. F. C. Hecker, 'Epidemics of the Middle Ages,' in Merskey, *Analysis of Hysteria*, p. 266–276; for a cross-cultural survey of Amok and other psychosomatic complaints, see Merskey, *Analysis of Hysteria*, p. 211–219; Kenny, 'Paradox Lost.'
6. Trevor-Roper, *The European Witch-Craze*, p. 93. For an earlier treatment, see Mackay, *Extraordinary Popular Delusions*, p. 462–564.
7. Montague Summers, introduction to Kramer, *Malleus Maleficarum*.

8. Reed, *Psychology of Anomalous*, p. 129.
9. Kramer, *Malleus*, p. 119.
10. Kramer, *Malleus*, p. 259–261.
11. Summers, in Kramer, *Malleus*, p. x.
12. Mackay, *Extraordinary Popular Delusions*, p. 489–490. Anne Barton in Shakespeare, *The Riverside Shakespeare*, p. 218.
13. Mackay, *Extraordinary Popular Delusions*, p. 479.
14. Mackay, *Extraordinary Popular Delusions*, p. 477; see also Robbins, *Encyclopedia of Witchcraft*, p. 104.
15. Trevor-Roper, *European Witch-Craze*, p. 123; Michelet, *Satanism and Witchcraft*, p. 145.
16. Michelet, *Satanism and Witchcraft*, p. 89.
17. Schoeneman, 'Witch Hunt as a Culture Change Phenomenon.'
18. Michelet, *Satanism and Witchcraft*, p. 148.
19. Watson, 'Salem's Dark Hour,' p. 117–131; Mackay, *Extraordinary Popular Delusions*, p. 552–555; Demos, 'Entertaining Satan'; Hansen, *Witchcraft at Salem*; Hill, *Delusion of Satan*.
20. Fox, *Science and Justice*, p. 77–90.
21. Mackay, *Extraordinary Popular Delusions*, p. 554–555.
22. Goodman, *How About Demons?* p. 3–4. See also Bouguignon, *Possession*, and *Altered States of Consciousness and Mental Health*.
23. Spanos, 'Demonic Possession, Mesmerism, and Hysteria,' p. 531–532.
24. All material quoted from Spanos, 'Demonic Possession . . . ,' unless otherwise noted.
25. Shorter, *From Paralysis to Fatigue*.
26. Shakespeare, *King Lear*, II: iv: 55, p. 1270.

27. John Purcell in Shorter, *From Paralysis*, p. 6

28. James Makittrick Adair, quoted in Shorter, *From Paralysis*, p. 24.

29. Walter Johnson in Shorter, *From Paralysis*, p. 30.

30. Frederic Skey in Shorter, *From Paralysis*, p. 32.

31. Moritz Romberg in Shorter, *From Paralysis*, p. 38.

32. H. Landouzy, 'Traité Complet de L'Hystérie,' 1846, in Merskey, *The Analysis of Hysteria*, p. 250.

33. Shorter, *From Paralysis*, p. 40.

34. Moebius in Ellenberger, *Discovery*, p. 292.

35. Gustav Braun, in Masson, *A Dark Science*, p. 128–138.

36. Paul Flechsig, quoted in Masson, *A Dark Science*, p. 45–54.

37. The history of Anton Mesmer and early hypnosis is related by Shorter, *From Paralysis to Fatigue*, as well as numerous other sources, including Baker, *They Call It Hypnosis*; Melvin A. Gravitz, 'Early Theories of Hypnosis,' in *Theories of Hypnosis*, p. 19–42; Mackay, *Extraordinary Popular Delusions*, p. 304–345.

38. Bailly in Mackay, *Extraordinary Popular Delusions*, p. 327–328.

39. Gravitz, in *Theories of Hypnosis*, p. 28.

40. Baker, *They Call It Hypnosis*, p. 61.

41. Gravitz, in *Theories of Hypnosis*, p. 19–20.

42. Spanos, 'Demonic Possession,' p. 533–534.

43. Spanos, 'Demonic Possession,' p. 538.

44. Shorter, *From Paralysis*, p. 139.

45. Shorter, *From Paralysis*, p. 140–142.

46. Shorter, *From Paralysis*, p. 144.

47. Shorter, *From Paralysis*, p. 146.

48. Shorter, *From Paralysis*, p. 153.

49. Shorter, *From Paralysis*, p. 158.

50. Spanos, 'Demonic Possession,' p. 542.

51. Lerner, 'Hysterical Personality,' p. 157.

52. Spanos, Nicholas and John F. Chaves, 'History and Historiography of Hypnosis,' in *Theories of Hypnosis*, p. 60.

53. Masson, *Against Therapy*, p. 26–44.

54. Shorter, *From Paralysis*, p. 166–200.

55. Webster, *Why Freud Was Wrong*, p. 71–167.

56. Freud, *Standard Edition*, v. 3, p. 9–10.

57. Webster, *Why Freud Was Wrong*, p. 86–87.

58. Wood, *Myth of Neurosis*, p. 77.

59. Beard, *American Nervousness*, p. 9; Lutz, *American Nervousness, 1903*.

60. For other critiques of Freud, see Crews, *Memory Wars*; Crews, *Skeptical Engagements*; Crews, 'The Unknown Freud'; Esterson, *Seductive Mirage*; Gray, 'The Assault on Freud'; Grünbaum, *Foundations of Psychoanalysis*; Israels, 'The Seduction Theory'; Lakoff & Coyne, *Father Knows Best*; Macmillan, *Freud Evaluated*; Masson, *The Assault on Truth*; Schatzman, 'Freud: Who Seduced Whom?'; Schimek, 'Fact and Fantasy in the Seduction Theory'; Schultz, *Intimate Friends, Dangerous Rivals*; Shorter, *From Paralysis to Fatigue*; Sulloway, *Freud, Biologist of the Mind*; Thornton, *The Freudian Fallacy*; Torrey, *Freudian Fraud*; Webster, *Why Freud Was Wrong*; Woods, *The Myth of Neurosis*.

61. Freud, *Complete Letters, Freud to Fliess*, p. 120; Shorter, *From Paralysis*, p. 191.

62. Masson, *The Assault on Truth*, p. 55–106.

63. Baker, *Hidden Memories*, p. 66–67; Freud, *Cocaine Papers*; Thornton, *Freudian Fallacy*.

64. Freud, *Complete Letters, Freud to Fliess*, p. 113, 117.

65. Masson, *Assault*, p. 241–258.

66. Masson, *Assault*, p. 257.

67. Freud, *Complete Letters, Freud to Fliess*, p. 227.

68. Freud, *Standard Edition*, v. 2, p. xi–xiii, 110–111.

69. Freud, *Standard Edition*, v. 2, p. 283.

70. See also Powell & Boer, 'Did Freud Mislead Patients?'

71. Freud, *Standard Edition*, v. 2, p. 260–262; v. 3, p. 152, 164, 203, 207; *Freud to Fliess*, p. 185.

72. Macmillan, *Freud Evaluated*, p. 91; Freud, *Standard Edition*, v. 2, p. xi–xiii, p. 267–271.

73. Freud, *Standard Edition*, v. 2, p. 153–154.

74. Freud, *Standard Edition*, v. 2, p. 271, 282.

75. Freud, *Standard Edition*, v. 20, p. 27.

76. Freud, *Standard Edition*, v. 2, p. 265, 284, 303.

77. Freud, *Standard Edition*, v. 2, p. 272, 294–295.

78. Freud, *Standard Edition*, v. 2, p. 276; v. 3, p. 152, 164, 180, 208–215.

79. Freud, *Freud to Fliess*, p. 220–221.

80. Freud, *Complete Letters, Freud to Fliess*, p. 226.

81. *Freud to Fliess*, p. 212–213, 264.

82. Freud, *Standard Edition*, v. 2, p. 279, 281; v. 3, p. 269.

83. Freud, *Standard Edition*, v. 3, p. 153.

84. Freud, *Standard Edition*, v. 3, p. 195, 204.

85. Esterson, *Seductive Mirage*, p. 19; Macmillan, *Freud Evaluated*, p. 223–224; Schimek, 'Fact and Fantasy'; Freud, *Standard Edition*, v. 3, p. 204.

86. Freud, *Standard Edition*, v. 2, p. 280–281.

87. Freud, *Standard Edition*, v. 20, p. 29.

88. Ferenczi in Masson, *Against Therapy*, p. 89.

89. Freud, *Standard Edition*, v. 3, p. 204.

90. Fredrickson, *Repressed*, p. 116.

91. Freud, *Standard Edition*, v. 2, p. 295.

92. Freud, *Standard Edition*, v. 3, p. 205.

93. Freud, *Standard Edition*, v. 3, p. 165.

94. Freud, *Standard Edition*, v. 3, p. 205.

95. Freud, *Standard Edition*, v. 3, p. 206.

96. Freud, *Complete Letters, Freud to Fliess*, p. 224.

97. Freud, *Complete Letters, Freud to Fliess*, p. 227.

98. Freud, *Standard Edition*, v. 3, p. 205. For a compelling analysis of how Freud forced the repressed memory puzzle pieces into place, see Robert S. Steele, 'Deconstructing Histories,' in *Narrative Psychology*, p. 265–268. For a somewhat different interpretation, see Allen Esterson, *Seductive Mirage*, p. 11–31.

99. Freud, *Complete Letters, Freud to Fliess*, p. 286.

100. Freud, *Complete Letters, Freud to Fliess*, p. 288–289.

101. Freud, *Standard Edition*, v. 20, p. 34.

102. Torrey, *Freudian Fraud*, p. 214–239; Wood, *Myth of*

Neurosis, p. 69–97; Baker, *Hidden Memories*, p. 61–77.

103. Freud, *Standard Edition*, v. 16, p. 370.

104. Freud, *Standard Edition*, v. 14; v. 20, p. 24–30.

105. Freud, *Standard Edition*, v. 12, p. 126–139.

106. Kenny, *Passion*; Bell, *Dreams of Exile*, p. 173.

107. Ian Hacking, 'Making Up People,' in *Reconstructing Individualism*, p. 222–226.

108. Janet quoted in Ellenberger, *Discovery*, p. 351–353; Janet quoted in Powell, 'Did Freud Mislead?', p. 1290–1291.

109. Janet in Ellenberger, *Discovery*, p. 139.

110. Merskey, 'The Manufacture of Personalities,' p. 331–332.

111. Prince, *Dissociation*, vii–28; for detailed coverage of this case, see Kenny, *Passion of Ansel Bourne*, p. 129–156.

112. James quoted in Kenny, *Passion of Ansel Bourne*, p. 141.

113. Kenny, *Passion*, p. 146.

114. Estabrooks, *Hypnotism*, p. 105–108.

115. Prince, *Dissociation*, p. 525.

116. 'Kraepelin, Emil (1856–1926),' in *International Encyclopedia of Psychiatry*, v. 6, p. 314–315

117. Emil Kraepelin, 'Hysterical Insanity,' in Merskey, *Analysis of Hysteria*, p. 252–257.

118. Chesler, *Women and Madness*, p. 111–113.

CHAPTER ELEVEN

1. Jenkins, *Intimate Enemies*, p. 29–56.

2. Bartlett, *Remembering*, p. 261.

3. Beard, *American Nervousness*, p. 1–12.

4. Beard, *American Nervousness*, p. 96–133; Sicherman, 'Doctors, Patients.'

5. Pendergrast, *For God, Country and Coca-Cola*, p. 26.

6. Rosenberg, 'The Place of George Beard,' p. 254, 256.

7. de Tocqueville, *Democracy*, v. 2, 105–106, 144.

8. Sicherman, 'The Uses,' p. 45.

9. Rosenberg, 'Place,' p. 257.

10. Sicherman, 'The Uses,' p. 40, 50, 54.

11. Abba Goold Woolson, quoted in Dijkstra, *Idols*, p. 27–29.

12. Sicherman, 'The Uses,' p. 48–49.

13. H. G. Wells in *The Nineties*, p. 143.

14. Sicherman, 'The Uses,' p. 53.

15. Sykes, *Nation*, p. 3–10, 131.

16. *FMSF Newsletter*, March 1995, p. 5.

17. Tavris, 'Illusion of Science,' p. 80; *Diagnostic*, p. 91–94, 658–669.

18. Leutwyler, 'Sick.'

19. *Diagnostic*, p. 685.

20. Sykes, *Nation*, p. 152–153; Kirk, *Selling of DSM*; Szasz, 'Diagnoses Are Not Diseases'; Dershowitz, *Abuse Excuse*.

21. Peele, *Diseasing*, p. 117, 141.

22. Whitfield, *Healing the Child Within*, p. 2, 95–105.

23. Sykes, *Nation*, p. 15.

24. Joseph Epstein in Zilbergeld, *Shrinking*, p. 193.

25. Council on Scientific Affairs, AMA, p. 3465.

26. de Tocqueville, *Democracy*, v. 2, p. 106.

27. Lasch, *Culture of Narcissism*, p. xv.

28. Hughes, *Culture*, p. 7.

29. Pittman, 'Ask Dr. Frank,' p. 95.

30. de Tocqueville, *Democracy*, v. 2, p. 142, 234.

31. Henry Gleitman, introductory remarks at 'Memory & Reality'

conference, April 16, 1993, Valley Forge, PA.

32. Zilbergeld, *Shrinking*, p. 44.
33. Hale, *Freud and the Americans*; Torrey, *Freudian Fraud*.
34. Esterson, *Seductive Illusion*, p. 121–123.
35. Dawes, *House*, p. 14.
36. Sykes, *Nation*, p. 51–60.
37. Robert Nisbet in Sykes, *Nation*, p. 45.
38. *State Comparison*.
39. Belleruth Naparstek quoted in Baker, 'Changing Face,' p. 34.
40. Nathan, *Satan's Silence*, p. 47.
41. Wolfe, 'The "Me" Decade,' p. 32.
42. Rosen, *Psychobabble*, p. x.
43. All information and quotes on John Rosen are from Masson, *Against Therapy*, p. 124–147.
44. Meacham, 'Call Me Mom.'
45. McNamara, *Breakdown*.
46. Janov, *Primal*, p. 20–30.
47. Janov, *Primal*, p. 79–85. These pages also cover the following quotes.
48. Mithers, *Therapy Gone Mad*, p. 99, 357.
49. de Tocqueville, *Democracy*, v. 2, p. 136, 144–147; Fitzgerald, *The Great Gatsby*, p. 189.
50. Zilbergeld, *Shrinking*, p. 62.
51. Heilbroner in Zilbergeld, *Shrinking*, p. 63.
52. Oakley, *God's Country*, p. 321.
53. de Tocqueville, *Democracy*, v. 2, p. 144.
54. Jones, *Great Expectations*, p. 252.
55. 'King, Stephen Edwin,' *Contemporary Authors*, p. 220–222.
56. Strauss, *Generations*, p. 321–324.
57. Nickell, *Looking for a Miracle*.
58. Redfield, *Celestine Prophecy*, p. i, 5.
59. Waller, 'The Vision Thing.'
60. See Chafe, *Unfinished Journey*, p. 406–445.
61. Morgan in *Sisterhood*, p. xiii-xxxiv.
62. Martha Shelly in *Sisterhood*, p. 306–309. See also Adam, *The Rise of a Gay and Lesbian Movement*.
63. Kipnis, *Knights Without Armor*, p. 270–272; Burstow, *Radical Feminist Therapy*, p. 114.
64. Walling, *Sexology*, p. 131; Friedan, *It Changed My Life*, p. 244.
65. Alice Echols, 'The Taming of the Id: Feminist Sexual Politics, 1968–1983,' in *Pleasure and Danger*, p. 59, 66.
66. Roiphe, 'Date Rape Hysteria.' See also Roiphe, *The Morning After*.
67. B. Amiel in Sykes, *Nation*, p. 12.
68. Kaminer, *I'm Dysfunctional*, p. xx–xxvi.
69. Tavris, 'Beware,' p. 16.
70. Nathan, *Satan's Silence*, p. 247.
71. Morrow, 'Men: Are They Really That Bad?' p. 54; Smolowe, 'Sex With a Scorecard.'
72. Keillor, *Book of Guys*.
73. Sykes, *Nation*, p. 166, 184–185.
74. Sykes, *Nation*, p. 191–196.
75. Sommers, *Who Stole Feminism?* p. 91–92. See also Patai, *Professing Feminism*.
76. Vance, 'After the Fall,' p. 14.
77. Trott, 'Campuses.'
78. Sykes, *Nation*, p. 6, 11.
79. de Tocqueville, *Democracy*, v. 2, p. 105–106.
80. P. Laslett in Sykes, *Nation*, p. 48.
81. Coontz, *The Way*, p. 2.
82. Skolnick, *Embattled*, p. xvii.
83. Coontz, *The Way*, p. 2–3.
84. Catherine Beckett in Hayward, 'Upheaval in '80s.'
85. Pipher, *Reviving*, p. 12–13; Pipher, *Shelter*. See also Netzer, *Cutoffs*.
86. Fox, *Red Lamp*, p. 180, 216.
87. 'I Am What We Are.'
88. Heaton, *Tuning in Trouble*, p. 135, 138.

89. Public Service Spot, Baltimore, MD, Survivors of Incest Anonymous.
90. D'Emilio, *Intimate Matters*, p. 29.
91. D'Emilio, *Intimate Matters*, p. xv-xix.

CHAPTER TWELVE

1. Smart, *Religious Experience*, p. 23.
2. Hoffer, *True Believer*, p. 94.
3. Pascal, quoted in Hartug, 'Love Thy Neighbor,' p. 86.
4. Smart, *Religious Experience*, p. 355–359.
5. Eliade, *Quest*, unpaginated preface.
6. Bass, *Courage*, p. 157.
7. This and the following quotes from Prodigy computer interactive personal service, Nov.-Dec. 1992.
8. Smart, *Religious Experience*, p. 6–16, for this and following material.
9. Zilbergeld, *Shrinking*, p. 157–158.
10. Bass, *Courage*, p. 120, 129, 144.
11. Robbins, *Cults, Converts*, p. 64. For a thorough review of different varieties of conversion, see Robbins, p. 61–99; Lofland and Skonovd, 'Patterns of Conversion,' p. 1–24, in *Of Gods and Men*.
12. James, *Varieties*, p. 189.
13. James, *Varieties*, p. 204.
14. James, *Varieties*, p. 198–199, 205.
15. James, *Varieties*, p. 193–194.
16. Sargant, *Battle*, p. 60–61.
17. Sargant, *Battle*, p. 58.
18. Sargant, *Battle*, p. 52.
19. Sargant, *Battle*, p. 62.
20. Wesley in Sargant, *Battle*, p. 75–76.
21. Maslow, *Religions*, p. 22.
22. Maslow, *Religions*, p. viii–ix.

23. James, *Varieties*, p. 166.
24. Frank, *Persuasion*, p. 80–81.
25. Bass, *Courage*, p. 163.
26. Frank, *Persuasion*, p. 80, 205, 337.
27. Guy Morechand quoted in Lewis, *Ecstatic Religion*, p. 187.
28. Lewis, *Ecstatic Religion*, p. 39, 66.
29. Lewis, *Ecstatic Religion*, p. 30–31.
30. Lewis, *Ecstatic Religion*, p. 88–89, 93.
31. Lewis, *Ecstatic Religion*, p. 89–90.
32. Lewis, *Ecstatic Religion*, p. 34–35.
33. Lewis, *Ecstatic Religion*, p. 194–195.
34. Rubel, *Susto*.
35. Whitley, 'Seduction.'
36. Whitley, 'Abuse of Trust.'
37. 'A Family Betrayed.'
38. 'Minirth-Meier New Life Clinic Betrays.'
39. Minirth, *Power of Memories*, p. 98–112.
40. Meier in 'Repressed Memories: True or False?'
41. 1995 Brochure for Minirth-Meier New Life Clinics.
42. Dobson in 'Repressed Memories: True or False?'
43. Allender, *Wounded Heart*, p. 25–26, 185–187.
44. Tom Rutherford interview, Dec. 14, 1995; Sid Willens interview, Dec. 16, 1995.
45. Bulkley, *Only God Can Heal*, p. 66, 71.
46. Paul Simpson in 'Repressed Memories: True or False?'
47. Jenkins, *Intimate Enemies*, p. 154–156; Wheatley, *Devil Rides Out*, p. 93.
48. Jenkins, *Intimate Enemies*, p. 45, 161; Walker, *Restoring the Kingdom*.
49. Jenkins, *Intimate Enemies*, p. 162–169.
50. Jenkins, *Intimate Enemies*, p. 166–169.

51. Lawrence, *Hot Line*; Jenkins, *Intimate Enemies*, p. 164.
52. Beaumont, 'Fear and Loathing.'
53. Clifford Geertz, 'Religion as a Cultural System,' in *Anthropological Approaches to the Study of Religion*, p. 4.
54. Bass, *Courage to Heal*, p. 128, 136.
55. Hoffer, *True Believer*, p. 85–86.
56. Becker, *Outsiders*, p. 147–148, 157.
57. Wolfe, 'The "Me" Decade,' p. 39–40.
58. Gibbs, 'Angels Among Us'; Lotto, 'On Witches,' p. 388; Woodward, 'Angels.'
59. Bass, *Courage to Heal*, p. 156.
60. Bradshaw, 'Incest,' *Lear's*, p. 43–44.
61. Mitchell, 'Father of the Child Within,' *Time*, p. 83.
62. Mitchell, 'Father,' p. 82–83.
63. Bradshaw, *Adult Children of Dysfunctional Families*. The rest of the quotes in this section are taken from this tape.
64. Bradshaw, *Family Secrets*; Taylor, 'Family Man,' p. 68.
65. Andrew Meacham interview, April 1994.
66. 'Doranda Blevins.'
67. Bikel, 'Divided Memories,' Part II.
68. Streiker, *Mind Bending*; Singer, *Cults in Our Midst*; Singer, 'Coming Out of the Cults'; Melton, *The Cult Experience*; Lifton, *Thought Reform*; Robbins, *Cults, Converts*, p. 70.
69. Hassan, *Combatting Cult Mind Control*, p. 7.
70. Blume, *Secret Survivors*, p. 57, *Courage to Heal*, p. 188.
71. Hassan, *Combatting*, p. 47.
72. Blume, 'Owning the Truth,' p. 140.
73. Hassan, *Combatting*, p. 49.
74. Hassan, *Combatting*, p. 49.

75. Hassan, *Combatting*, p. 63–65.
76. Hassan, *Combatting*, p. 68–69.
77. Hassan, *Combatting*, p. 71–72; 83.
78. Hassan, *Combatting*, p. 81.
79. Hassan e-mail, Sept. 26, 1995.
80. Hayward, 'Experts Split.'
81. *Recovery From Cults*.
82. Richard Ofshe interview, Dec. 5, 1995.
83. Michael Langone to Mark Pendergrast, Dec. 4, 1995.
84. Langone, 'Treatment of Satanism,' p. 190.
85. Hassan, *Combatting*, p. 73–74.
86. FMSF Newsletter, June 1995, p. 3.

CHAPTER THIRTEEN

1. Woodward, 'Was It Real?'
2. Andrew Greeley, quoted in *FMSF Newsletter*, Feb. 1994, p. 12.
3. Smolowe, 'Dubious Memories.'
4. Bauerlein, 'Mirror Cracked'; Gustafson, 'Jury Awards.'
5. Wilkinson, 'Father Freed.'
6. Groff, *Decree*. See also a similar 1995 California case reported in *FMSF Newsletter*, Oct. 1995, p. 7.
7. McHugh, 'Psychiatric Misadventures.'
8. Brenman, *Hypnotherapy*, p. 66–75.
9. Rosen, *Psychobabble*, p. 149.
10. Masson, *Assault*, p. 145–188.
11. Rosen, *Psychobabble*, p. 199; Kihlstrom, 'Recovery of Memory'; Watkins, *Hypnotherapy of War Neuroses*; Lindner, *Rebel Without*, p. xi, 205–282.
12. Blood, *The New Satanists*, p. 140.
13. Gomez, 'Satanist Abuse.'
14. Robert Kaplan in *FMSF Newsletter*, Oct. 1995, p. 14; Waterhouse, 'Families Haunted'; Pamela Freyd email, Jan. 26, 1996; Sherrill Mulhern email, Feb 8, 1996.

15. *Notebook*, vol 4(3), Fall 1995, quoted in *FMSF Newsletter*, Oct. 1995, p. 2.
16. Lee, *Survivor's Guide*, p. 23, 139.
17. Harrington, 'Conspiracy Theories.'
18. 'Voices in the Family,' WHYY-FM, Philadelphia, NPR, Jan. 2, 1996.
19. Almy, *Addicted to Recovery*, p. 196.
20. Yapko, *Suggestions*, p. 42–61; 229–236.
21. Ofshe, *Making Monsters*, p. 194.
22. Goodman, *Characteristics and Sources*, p. 4–6.
23. Poole & Lindsay, 'Psychotherapy and the Recovery of Memories,' (versions 1 and 2).
24. Yapko, *Suggestions*, p. 43, 127.
25. Pope and Tabachnick, 'Recovered Memories.'
26. Salter, 'Buried Memories,' April 4, 1993, p. A-14.
27. Andrews, 'Recovery of Memories'; British Psychological Society, *Recovered Memories*.
28. James Brennan, director of mental health services, National Association of Social Work, phone interview, May 11, 1994.
29. McNamara, *Breakdown*, p. 265–266; Sharkey, *Bedlam*, p. 77–79.
30. Glenys Parry to Mark Pendergrast, Jan. 3, 1996.
31. Bass, *Courage to Heal*, 3rd ed., p. 475–534.
32. Bass, *Courage*, 3rd edition, p. 371, 470.
33. Santrock, *Authoritative Guide*.
34. Loe, 'Judge Dismisses.'
35. Orwell, *1984*, p. 175–178.
36. Herman, 'Abuses of Memory.' Subsequent quotes by Herman from this article.
37. 'U.S. Attorney Settles'; Langner, 'Two Doctors'; 'Boards of Registration.'
38. Frank, *Persuasion*, p. 118–119.
39. Lindsay and Read, 'Psychotherapy and Memories', p. 18.
40. Frank, *Persuasion*, p. 120–121.
41. *Diagnostic*, p. 305.
42. *DSM-IV Casebook*, p. 279–281.
43. Whitfield, *Healing*; Whitfield in Waterloo, 'Healing ... continued,' tapes 3–4; Blume, 'Ownership of Truth,' p. 139.
44. Whitfield, 'False Memory Debate' conference, Jan. 15, 1994, Seattle, WA.
45. Whitfield, *Memory and Abuse*, p. xiii, 9, 24–26, 149, 184–187, 244.
46. Ross, 'President's Message.' All subsequent Ross quotes from this source.
47. Roma Hart letter to Mark Pendergrast, Oct. 24, 1995.
48. Ross, *Osiris Complex*, p. 32–45, 124, 148–149.
49. Ross, *Satanic*, p. 53.
50. O'Hanlon in Schissler, 'Avoiding the Truth Trap,' p. 76.
51. O'Hanlon ad in *Family Therapy Networker*, Sept./Oct. 1993, p. 101.
52. Barrett and Scott in Schissler, 'Avoiding the Truth Trap,' p. 73–75.
53. Douglas Sawin in Bikel, 'Divided Memories,' Part I, p. 14.
54. McNamara, *Breakdown*, p. 136–137.
55. McNamara, *Breakdown*, p. 240.
56. Kogan in McNamara, *Breakdown*, p. 225, 269.
57. Gutheil in McNamara, *Breakdown*, p. 237–238.
58. *Geraldo* Show, May 25, 1994.
59. Yapko on *Maury Povich Show*, May 25, 1994.

60. Michael Yapko interview, June 10, 1994.
61. Byrd, 'Narrative Reconstruction,' p. 439.
62. Lindsay and Read, 'Psychotherapy and Memories,' p. 14, 25, 32.
63. Lindsay, 'Beyond Backlash.'
64. Lindsay and Read, 'Psychotherapy and Memories,' p. 18.
65. Hedges, 'Taking Recovered Memories Seriously,' p. 4, 14–15.
66. Hedges, 'Taking Recovered,' p. 20–21. The rest of the Hedges quotes from these pages.
67. Jervis email, Dec. 7, 1995.
68. British Association for Counselling, 'Survey.'
69. Dale, Counselling Adults, p. 1, 3, 8–14, 22, 24, 28–29, 40–51.
70. Ghate, Prevalence, p. 68–69, 87–88.
71. Rimmer, 'Emperor's New Law Suit.'
72. Orr, Accuracy About Abuse, July 1994, p. 2, March 1995, p. 6, June 1995, p. 10; Orr, '"False Memory" Syndrome,' p. 27.
73. Orr, 'First Sight Forum,' BBC Radio, Feb. 16, 1995.
74. Marjorie Orr email to 'Witchhunt' bb, Feb. 15, 1995.
75. Weldon, Trouble, p. 41, 57, 76, 94.
76. Hudson, 'All Psyched Out.'
77. Freyd, FMSF Newsletter, June 3, 1994, p. 1.
78. Fraser, 'Freud's Final Seduction,' p. 57; Fraser, My Father's House, p. 211–212, 225; FMSF Newsletter, Feb. 1994, p. 7.
79. 'Mind-bending Treatments.'
80. 'AMA Wary of Using "Memory Enhancement"'; AMA, 'Report of the Council.'

81. American Psychiatric Association, 'Statement on Memories of Sexual Abuse,' Dec. 12, 1993.
82. Jane Wallace Live, Philadelphia TV Talk Show, Oct. 30, 1991; Paul Fink to Mary Jane England, Oct. 26, 1995.
83. Herndon, 'False and Repressed Memories.'
84. American Psychological Association, 'Questions and Answers.'
85. Fox, APA Monitor, Oct. 1995, p. 6.
86. Hornstein, ISSD News, Aug/Sept. 1995.
87. Allen Feld in FMSF Newsletter, Nov./Dec. 1995, p. 4.
88. British Psychological Society, Recovered Memories.
89. Andrews, 'Recovery of Memories.'
90. John Morton interview, Aug. 23, 1995.
91. Orr, 'Accuracy About Abuse,' p. 25.
92. Barton, 'Danger Therapy'; Alec McGuire to Roger Scotford, May 22, 1995.
93. Bunting, 'Evangelical Guide.'
94. Australian Psychological Society, 'Guidelines.'
95. Boakes, 'False Memory Syndrome.'
96. August Piper, FMS Foundation Newsletter April 1994, p. 8.
97. Haaken, 'Incest Resolution Therapy,' p. 45.
98. Advertisement in Open Exchange, March/April 1994, p. 68, quoted in FMSF Newsletter, April 1994, p. 4.
99. ACTA ad, Changes, Dec. 1993.
100. McDonald, 'An Ethical Dilemma,' p. 20.
101. Sharkey, Bedlam, p. 279–281; Walter Afield in Profits of Misery, p. 148; Robert F. Stuckey letter in

Profits of Misery, p. 279; Hendricks, 'Insurance Invested Billions in Hospitals.'

102. Flier for conference of the Association for Humanistic Psychology, March 26–28, 1993, quoted in *FMSF Newsletter*, March 5, 1993, p. 2.

103. Wellness Institute ad, *Family Therapy Networker*, May/June 1994, p. 80.

104. Dawes, *House of Cards*, p. 146–154; Frankel, 'Hypnotizability and Dissociation, p. 827.

105. Childswork/Childsplay 1994 catalog, The Center for Applied Psychology, PO Box 61586, King of Prussia, PA 19406.

106. Ross, 'CIA Mind Control' proposal.

107. Wisniewski, 'Technique for Teaching.'

108. *FMSF Newsletter*, April 1994, p. 9.

109. *FMSF Newsletter*, Feb. 1994, p. 9–10.

110. Simon D. Richardson interview, June 17, 1996.

111. Orr, *Accuracy About Abuse*, June 1995, p. 12; Jervis email, Jan. 21, 1996.

112. Goodyear-Smith, *First Do No Harm*, p. 105–106; Goodyear-Smith email, Jan. 10, 1996.

113. Wylie, 'Endangered Species.' All quotes from Wylie from this source.

114. Butler, 'Surviving the Revolution.'

115. Butler, 'Surviving the Revolution.'

116. Rogers, 'Farewell to the Couch?'

117. Sharma Oliver, personal communication, Nov. 21, 1995.

118. Schroeder in *Profits of Misery*, p. 1–3.

119. H. Con. Res. 200, Feb. 1, 1994; Elaine Foster, 'Legislative Update.'

120. H.R. 3694, Nov. 22, 1993.

121. Steve Rodgers, Dorothy Rodgers interviews, July 1994.

122. Mike Moncrief in *Profits of Misery*, p. 7.

123. Yoachum, 'Democrat Schroeder.'

124. Sayce, 'Looking Back'; Jervis email, Jan. 29, 1996.

125. Frank, *Persuasion and Healing*, p. 213, 216–217.

126. Wylie, 'Endangered Species,' p. 22.

127. Butler, 'Too Good To Be True?' p. 3, 20; Marano, 'Wave of the Future.'

128. Simon, 'From the Editor,' p. 2.

129. Frank, *Persuasion*, p. 219, 335.

130. Dawes, *House of Cards*, p. 256–258.

131. Herman, 'Psychiatrist–Patient Sexual Contact,' p. 166–167; McNamara, *Breakdown*, p. 198–201, 220–222; Markowitz, 'Crossing the Line,' p. 26; Kenneth Pope, 'Sexual Involvement.'

132. Frank, *Persuasion*, p. 2, 19.

133. Zilbergeld, *Shrinking*, p. 103, 142, 163, 179.

134. Dawes, *House of Cards*, p. 5, 56.

135. Butler, 'Shadow Side of Therapy.'

136. Zilbergeld, *Shrinking*, p. 18, 22.

137. Campbell, *Beware*, p. 248–251.

138. Jervis, 'Book Review,' p. 12.

139. Stevens, 'Post Therapy.'

140. Gray, *Psychology*, p. 674–675.

141. Campbell, *Beware*, p. 218–228.

142. Meehl, 'Philosophy of Science,' p. 728–729.

143. Gray, *Psychology*, p. 652.

144. Kingsbury, 'Where Does Research.'

145. Gray, *Psychology*, p. 662–670; Ellis, *Reason and Emotion*; Pransky,

The *Relationship Handbook*; Beck, *Anxiety Disorders.*

146. Kramer, *Listening to Prozac*; Bodkin, 'What Antidepressants Do.'

147. Zilbergeld, *Shrinking*, p. 8, 270, 279.

148. Bikel, 'Divided Memories.'

149. Hass, 'Margaret Kelly Michaels.'

150. Allen Esterson correspondence; 'Primal Scream Therapy,' *BFMS Newsletter*, May 1995, p. 11.

151. Bryan, *Close Encounters*, p. 50, 128, 144; Constance Dalenberg email, Jan. 31, 1996.

152. Montagu, *Touching*, p. 334–335.

153. Okami, 'Child Perpetrators,' p. 126.

154. Rubongoya, 'Raising Our Children.'

155. Loggins, 'Divorced Fathers.'

156. Pruett, *Nurturing Father*, p. 1, 273.

157. Pruett, *Nurturing Father*, p. 300.

158. Terence Campbell, interview, Nov. 4, 1995.

159. Angelou in Fleming, *First Time*, p. 20–31; for a remarkable book about human resilience, see Reynolds Price, *A Whole New Life.*

160. Frankl, *Man's Search*, p. 194–195; 206.

161. Lilienheim, *Aftermath.*

162. Kaminer, *I'm Dysfunctional*, p. 80–83.

163. Melody Gavigan interview, September 1993.

164. Haaken, 'Debate over Recovered Memory,' p. 15.

165. Kilpatrick, *Long-Range Effects*, p. xvii.

166. Farley, 'Growing Up With a Killer.'

167. Kendall-Tackett, 'Impact of Sexual Abuse,' p. 164–165.

168. Rind and Harrington, 'A Critical Examination of the Role of Child Sexual Abuse in Causing Psychological Maladjustment,' in *False Memory Syndrome.*

169. Martin, 'Battered Children Grown Up,' p. 75.

170. Christianson, 'Some Characteristics,' p. 196–197.

171. Bass, Alison, 'Putting the Pieces'; Vaillant, *Wisdom of the Ego*, p. 284–325.

172. Seligman, *What You Can Change*, p. 231–235.

173. Bullough, 'History in Adult Human,' p. 69–72.

174. Underwager, 'Interview,' p. 4.

175. Underwager, 'Statement'; Underwager, 'Misinterpretation,' p. 100.

176. 'FMS: The Latest.'

177. *FMSF Newsletter*, Nov./Dec. 1995, p. 12.

178. Van Biema, 'Abandoned'; Smolowe, 'Making the Tough Calls.'

179. Barnicle, 'Absent.'

180. Frye vs. U.S.; Daubert vs. Merrell Dow; David Faigman in MacNamara, 'Fade Away,' p. 86.

181. Dyer, 'Euro Appeal'; Dyer, 'Victory for Victims.'

182. Jervis, 'Sex Trial Storm'; Jervis email, Jan. 11, 1996.

183. Jervis email, Jan. 29, 1996; Mary Rees in Kelemen High Court transcript, Re P, Queen's Bench Division, Nov. 8, 1993.

184. Cornwell, 'True Lies,' p. 28; Lewis, 'Week in Britain.'

185. Arndt, 'Dark Memories'; Fife-Yeomans, 'Call to Ban'; Madigan, '"Memory" Sex Cases Attacked.'

186. Pope, 'Recovered Memories,' p. 12.

187. *FMSF Newsletter*, March 1995, p. 1, Sept. 1995, p. 2, 8.

188. Dobson, 'Increase.'
189. *FMSF Newsletter*, Jan. 1996, p. 13.
190. Hochman, 'Recovered Memory Therapy,' p. 61.
191. *FMSF Newsletter*, March 1995, p. 7.

192. Barden, 'A Proposal to Finance.'
193. *FMSF Newsletter*, April 1995, p. 13.
194. *FMSF Newsletter*, Oct. 1995, p. 16.
195. Hansen, *Witchcraft at Salem*, p. 267.

Bibliography

Adam, Barry D. *The Rise of a Gay and Lesbian Movement*. Boston, MA: Twayne, 1987.

Adams, Kenneth. *Silently Seduced: When Parents Make Their Children Partners: Understanding Covert Incest*. Deerfield Beach, FL: Health Communications, 1991.

'The Adult Survivor of Ritual Abuse: A Personal Perspective,' VOICES in Action, PO Box 148308, Chicago, IL, no date.

Affect and Accuracy in Recall: Studies of 'Flashbulb' Memories. Ed. by Eugene Winograd and Ulric Neisser. Cambridge MA: Cambridge U. Pr., 1992.

Aldridge-Morris, Ray. *Multiple Personality: An Exercise in Deception*. London: Lawrence Erlbaum, 1989.

Allender, Dan B. *The Wounded Heart*. Colorado Springs, CO: Navpress, 1990.

Allison, Ralph, 'A Debate: Satanic Ritual Abuse and Multiple Personality, The Negative Side of the Argument,' March 22, 1991 speech, Society for the Anthropology of Consciousness annual meeting.

Allison, Ralph, 'Effects on the Therapist Who Treats Patients With MPD,' presented at conference on 'Trauma, Dissociation & Multiple Personality,' April 22–24, 1993, 'Version 1: What I Planned to Say,' from Ralph Allison.

Allison, Ralph, with Ted Schwarz. *Minds in Many Pieces: The Making of a Very Special Doctor*. NY: Rawson, Wade, 1980.

Allman, William F. *Apprentices of Wonder: Inside the Neural Network Revolution*. NY: Bantam, 1989.

Almy, Gary and Carol Tharp Almy, with Jerry Jenkins. *Addicted to Recovery: Exposing the False Gospel of Psychotherapy, Escaping the Trap of Victim Mentality*. Eugene, OR: Harvest House, 1994.

Alpher, Victor S., 'Introject and Identity: Structural-Interpersonal Analysis and Psychological Assessment of Multiple Personality Disorder,' *Journal of Personality Assessment*, April 1992, v. 58(2), p. 347–367.

Altered States of Consciousness and Mental Health: A Cross-Cultural Perspective.
Ed. by Colleen A. Ward. Newbury Park: Sage, 1989.

'AMA Wary of Using "Memory Enhancement" to Elicit Accounts of
Childhood Sexual Abuse,' *Clinical Psychiatry News*, Aug. 1, 1993.

American Medical Association, 'Report of the Council on Scientific
Affairs,' CSA 5-A–94.

American Psychiatric Association, 'Statement on Memories of Sexual
Abuse,' Dec. 12, 1993.

American Psychological Association, 'Questions and Answers about
Memories of Childhood Abuse,' Washington, DC: APA, Aug. 10,
1995.

Amiel, Barbara, '"Memories" That Surface to Destroy Us,' *Sunday Times*,
May 15, 1994.

Andrews, Bernice, et al, 'The Recovery of Memories in Clinical Practice:
Experiences and Beliefs of British Psychological Society Practitioners,'
The Psychologist, May 1995, p. 209–214.

Anthropological Approaches to the Study of Religion, ed. by Michael Banton.
NY: Praeger, 1966.

Armbrister, Trevor, 'Justice Gone Crazy,' *Reader's Digest*, Jan. 1994,
p. 33–40.

Armbrister, Trevor, 'When Parents Become Victims,' *Reader's Digest*,
April 1993, p. 101–106.

Armstrong, Louise. *Kiss Daddy Goodnight: A Speak-Out on Incest.* NY:
Hawthorn Books, 1978.

Arndt, Betina, 'Dark Memories,' *Weekend Australian*, July 1–2, 1995, p. 28.

Arnold, Roseanne. *My Lives.* NY: Ballantine, 1994.

Ash, Angie. *Father-Daughter Sexual Abuse: The Abuse of Paternal Authority.*
Bangor, Wales: Dept. of Social Theory and Institutions, University of
North Wales, 1984.

Ashby-Rolls, Trysh. *Triumph: A Journey of Healing from Incest.* Montreal:
McGraw-Hill Ryerson, 1991.

Atler, Marilyn Van Derbur. *A Story of Hope.* P.O. Box 61099, Denver,
CO 80206. Videotape of speech given May 23, 1991.

Augustine, Saint. *The Confessions of St. Augustine.* Trans. by F. J. Sheed.
NY: Sheed & Ward, 1943.

Australian Psychological Society Limited, 'Guidelines Relating to the
Reporting of Recovered Memories,' *The Bulletin of the Australian
Psychological Society*, 1995, vol. 17, no. 1, p. 20–21.

Baddeley, Alan D., ed. *The Handbook of Memory Disorders.* NY: John Wiley,
1995.

Baddeley, Alan D. *The Psychology of Memory*. NY: Basic Books, 1976.

Baddeley, Alan D. *Working Memory*. NY: Oxford U. Pr., 1986.

Bain, Donald. *The Control of Candy Jones*. Chicago: Playboy Press, 1976.

Baker, Beth, 'The Changing Face of Social Work,' *Common Boundary*, Jan./Feb. 1994, p. 32–38.

Baker, Robert A. *Hidden Memories: Voices and Visions From Within*. Buffalo, NY: Prometheus Books, 1992.

Baker, Robert A. *They Call It Hypnosis*. Buffalo, NY: Prometheus Books, 1990.

Barden, R. Christopher, 'A Proposal to Finance Preparation of Model Legislation Titled "Mental Health Consumer Protection Act." ' August 1994. 4025 Quaker Lane North, Plymouth, MN 55441.

Barlow, David H. *Anxiety and Its Disorders: The Nature and Treatment of Anxiety and Panic*. NY: Guilford, 1988.

Barnicle, Mike, 'Absent But Not Without Guilt,' *Boston Globe*, Nov. 21, 1995.

Bartlett, Frederic C. *Remembering: A Study in Experimental and Social Psychology*. Cambridge, MA: Cambridge U. Pr., 1932, 1977.

Bartlett, Nigel, 'Facing the Unbelievable,' *Community Care*, Dec. 14, 1989.

Barton, Fiona, ' "Danger Therapy" Inquiry Ordered: Psychiatrists Act After Storm Over Memory Treatment,' *The Mail on Sunday*, Nov. 12, 1995, p. 23.

Barton, Fiona, with Margaret Jervis, 'Therapy of Danger,' *The Mail on Sunday*, Nov 5, 1995, p. 37–39.

Bass, Alison, 'Putting the Pieces Back Together Again,' *Boston Globe*, May 9, 1994.

Bass, Ellen and Laura Davis. *The Courage to Heal: A Guide for Women Survivors of Child Sexual Abuse*. 2nd ed. NY: HarperPerennial, 1988, 1992.

Bass, Ellen and Laura Davis. *The Courage to Heal: A Guide for Women Survivors of Child Sexual Abuse*. 3rd ed. NY: HarperPerennial, 1994.

Bass, Ellen, and Louise Thornton, eds. *I Never Told Anyone: Writings by Women Survivors of Child Sexual Abuse*. NY: Harper & Row, 1983.

Bauerlein, Monika, 'The Mirror Cracked,' *City Pages*, Aug. 23, 1995, p. 9–22.

Beard, George A. *American Nervousness: Its Causes and Consequences*. NY: G. P. Putnam Sons, 1881.

Beattie, Melody. *Codependent No More: How to Stop Controlling Others and Start Caring for Yourself*. NY: Harper/Hazelden, 1987.

Beaumont, Peter and Roland Howard, 'Fear and Loathing at the Hands of the Exorcist,' *The Observer*, Sept. 3, 1995, p. 10.

Beck, Aaron and Gary Emery, with Greenberg, Ruth L. *Anxiety Disorders and Phobias: A Cognitive Perspective.* NY: Basic Books, 1985.

Becker, Howard S. *Outsiders: Studies in the Sociology of Deviance.* NY: Free Press, 1963.

Bell, Ian. *Dreams of Exile: Robert Louis Stevenson: A Biography.* NY: Henry Holt, 1992.

Benedek, Elissa P. and Diane H. Schetky, 'Problems in Validating Allegations of Sexual Abuse,' *Journal of the Academy of Child & Adolescent Psychiatry* (1987), v. 26, p. 912–915.

Bennetts, Leslie, 'Nightmares on Main Street,' *Vanity Fair*, June 1993, p. 42–62.

Bikel, Ofra. 'Divided Memories,' *Frontline* TV Show, Parts I & II, April 4, 11, 1995, Shows No. 1312 & 1313.

Bikel, Ofra, 'Innocence Lost,' *Frontline* TV documentary, May 7, 1991. Show No. 918.

Bikel, Ofra, 'Innocence Lost: The Verdict,' Parts I & II, *Frontline* TV documentary, July 20, 21, 1993. Shows No. 1120 & 1121.

Bikel, Ofra. 'The Search for Satan,' *Frontline* TV Show, Oct. 24, 1995, Show 1402.

Biklen, Douglas. *Communication Unbound: How Facilitated Communication is Challenging Traditional Views of Autism and Ability-Disability.* NY: Teachers College Press, 1993.

Blake, William. *Complete Writings, with Variant Readings.* Ed. by Geoffrey Keynes. NY: Oxford U. Pr., 1972.

Blakeslee, Thomas R. *Beyond the Conscious Mind: Unlocking the Secrets of the Self.* NY: Plenum, 1996.

Bliss, Eugene L. *Multiple Personality, Allied Disorders, and Hypnosis.* NY: Oxford U. Pr., 1986.

Blood, Linda. *The New Satanists.* NY: Warner Books, 1994.

Blume, E. Sue, 'The Ownership of Truth,' *Journal of Psychohistory*, vol. 23, no. 2, Fall 1995, p. 131–140.

Blume, E. Sue. *Secret Survivors: Uncovering Incest and Its Aftereffects in Women.* NY: Ballantine, 1990.

Boakes, Janet, 'False Memory Syndrome,' *The Lancet*, Oct. 21, 1995, vol. 346, p. 1048–49.

'Boards of Registration: Disciplinary Actions,' *Boston Globe*, Nov. 27, 1995, p. 30.

Bodkin, J. Alexander, 'What Antidepressants Do,' May 9, 1994 speech to Friends of McLean Hospital, Belmont, MA.

Booker, Christopher, 'The Men Who Say My Truths Are All Lies,' *Sunday Telegraph*, Nov. 5, 1995, p. 36.

Borbely, Alexander. *Secrets of Sleep*, trans. Deborah Schneider. NY: Basic Books, 1986.

Bourguignon, Erika. *Possession*. San Francisco: Chandler & Sharp, 1976.

Bower, Bruce, 'Brain Scans Set Sights on Mind's Eye,' *Science News*, Dec. 2, 1995, vol 148(23), p. 372.

Boyd, Andrew. *Blasphemous Rumours: Is Satanic Ritual Abuse Fact or Fantasy?* London: HarperCollins, 1991.

Boyer, Peter J., 'Children of Waco,' *New Yorker*, May 15, 1995, p. 37–45.

Bradshaw, John. *Adult Children of Dysfunctional Families* [two cassette tapes, recorded live]. Houston, TX: John Bradshaw, [no date, 1990?]

Bradshaw, John. *Bradshaw on: The Family*. Deerfield Beach, FL: Health Communications, 1988.

Bradshaw, John. *Family Secrets: What You Don't Know Can Hurt You*. NY: Bantam, 1995.

Bradshaw, John, 'Incest: When You Wonder If It Happened To You,' *Lear's*, Aug. 1992, p. 43–44.

Bray, Madge. *Poppies on the Rubbish Heap: Sexual Abuse, the Child's Voice*. Edinburgh, Scotland: Canongate Press, 1991.

Breiner, Sander J. *Slaughter of the Innocents: Child Abuse Through the Ages and Today*. NY: Plenum, 1990.

Brenman, Margaret and Merton M. Gill. *Hypnotherapy: A Survey of the Literature*. NY: John Wiley & Sons, 1944.

Briere, John and Jon Conte, 'Self-Reported Amnesia for Abuse in Adults Molested As Children,' *Journal of Traumatic Stress*, v. 6(1), p. 21–31, 1993.

British Association for Counselling, 'Survey,' Rugby, BAC, April 1993.

'The British Inquisition,' *The Mail on Sunday*, March 10, 1991.

British Psychological Society. *Recovered Memories: The Report of the Working Party of the British Psychological Society*. Leicester, UK: BPS, Jan. 1995.

Britton, A. G., 'The Terrible Truth,' *Self*, Oct. 1992, p. 188–202.

Broadbent, Donald Eric. *Biology of Memory*. NY: Academic Pr., 1970.

Broadbent, Donald Eric. *In Defense of Empirical Psychology*. London: Methuen, 1973.

Brott, Armin, 'Who is Abusing the Children of Wenatchee?' *Sacramento Bee*, Oct. 8, 1995.

Brownmiller, Susan. *Against Our Will: Men, Women and Rape*. NY: Simon & Schuster, 1975.

Brunvand, Jan Harold. *The Vanishing Hitchhiker: American Urban Legends and Their Meanings*. NY: W.W. Norton, 1981.

Bryan, C. D. B., *Close Encounters of the Fourth Kind Alien Abduction, UFOs, and the Conference at M.I.T.* NY: Knopf, 1995.

Bufe, Charles. *Alcoholics Anonymous: Cult or Cure?* San Francisco, CA: See Sharp Pr., 1991.

Bulkley, Ed. *Only God Can Heal the Wounded Heart*. Eugene, OR: Harvest House, 1995.

Bunting, Madeleine, 'Evangelical Guide On Tackling Abuse,' *Guardian*, Nov. 15, 1995.

Burstow, Bonnie. *Radical Feminist Therapy: Working in the Context of Violence*. Thousand Oaks, CA Sage, 1992.

Butler, Katy, 'The Shadow Side of Therapy,' *Family Therapy Networker*, Nov./Dec. 1992, p. 14–23.

Butler, Katy, 'Surviving the Revolution,' *Family Therapy Networker*, March/April 1994, p. 28–29.

Butler, Katy, 'Too Good to Be True?' *Family Therapy Networker*, Nov./Dec. 1993, p. 3, 19–31.

Butler, Sandra. *The Conspiracy of Silence: The Trauma of Incest*. San Francisco, CA: New Glide Publications, 1978.

Butler-Sloss, Lord Justice Elizabeth. *Report of the Inquiry into Child Abuse in Cleveland 1987, Cmnd 412*. London: Her Majesty's Stationery Office, 1988.

Byrd, Kevin R., 'The Narrative Reconstructions of Incest Survivors,' *American Psychologist*, May 1994, v. 49(5), p. 439–440.

Campbell, Beatrix. *Unofficial Secrets*. London: Virago, 1988.

Campbell, Jeremy. *The Improbable Machine: What the Upheavals in Artificial Intelligence Research Reveal About How the Mind Really Works*. NY: Simon & Schuster, 1989.

Campbell, Terence W. *Beware the Talking Cure: Psychotherapy May Be Hazardous to Your Mental Health*. Boca Raton, FL: Upton Books, 1994.

Campbell, Terence W., 'Challenging Psychologists and Psychiatrists as Expert Witnesses,' *Michigan Bar Journal*, Jan. 1994, p. 68–72.

Carlson, Margaret, 'The Sex-Crime Capital,' *Time*, Nov. 13, 1995, p. 89–90.

Carroll, Lewis. *Alice's Adventures in Wonderland, Through the Looking-Glass and The Hunting of the Snark*. NY: Modern Library, nd.

Cartwright, Gary, 'The Innocent and the Damned,' *Texas Monthly*, April 1994, p. 101–156.

Castro, Stephen J., 'New Age Therapy: Higher Consciousness or Delusion?' *The Therapist*, Winter 1995, p. 14–16.

Ceci, Stephen J., 'Cognitive and Social Factors in Children's Testimony,' Master Lecture Presented at American Psychological Association, Toronto, Aug. 20, 1993.

Ceci, Stephen J. and Maggie Bruck. *Jeopardy in the Courtroom: A Scientific Analysis of Children's Testimony*. Washington, DC: American Psychological Association, 1995.

Ceci, Stephen J. and Maggie Bruck, 'Child Witnesses: Translating Research into Policy,' *Social Policy Report*, Society for Research in Child Development, Fall 1993, v. 7, 3, p. 1–30.

Ceci, Stephen J. and Maggie Bruck, 'Suggestibility of the Child Witness: A Historical Review and Synthesis,' *Psychological Bulletin*, 1993, v. 113, 3, p. 403–439.

Chafe, William H. *The Unfinished Journey: America Since World War II*. NY: Oxford U. Pr., 1986.

Charlton, Bruce, 'Can You Forget Sexual Abuse?' *London Times*, March 14, 1995.

Chesler, Phyllis. *Women and Madness*. Garden City, NY: Doubleday, 1972.

Chideya, Farai, 'The Language of Suspicion,' *Los Angeles Times Magazine*, Feb. 28, 1993, p. 34–36, 52–54.

'Child Sex Abuse Leaves Mark on Brain,' *Science News*, 1995, v. 147, p. 340.

Christianson, Sven-Ake and Elizabeth F. Loftus, 'Some Characteristics of People's Traumatic Memories,' *Bulletin of the Psychonomic Society*, 1990, v. 28(3), p. 195–198.

Cialdini, Robert B. *Influence: How and Why People Agree to Things*. NY: William Morrow, 1984.

CIBA Foundation. *Child Sexual Abuse Within the Family*. Edited by Ruth Porter. London: Tavistock, 1984.

CNN Special Assignment, reported by Kathy Slobogin, May 3, 1993.

Cockburn, Alexander, 'Beat the Devil,' *The Nation*, March 8, 1993, p. 296–297; April 5, 1993, p. 438–439.

Cohen, Stanley. *Folk Devils and Moral Panics: The Creation of the Mods and Rockers*. NY: St. Martin's, 1972, 1980.

Cohn, Norman. *Europe's Inner Demons: An Enquiry Inspired by the Great Witch-Hunt*. NY: Basic Books, 1975.

Coleman, Lee and Patrick E. Clancy, 'False Allegations of Child Sexual Abuse,' *Criminal Justice*, Fall 1990, p. 14–20, 43–47.

Coleman, Lee, 'Medical Examination for Sexual Abuse: Have We Been Misled?' *Issues in Child Abuse Accusations*, 1989, v. 1, 3, p. 1–9.

Coleman, Lee. *The Reign of Error: Psychiatry, Authority and Law.* Boston: Beacon, 1984.

Comprehensive Textbook of Psychiatry, ed. by Harold I. Kaplan, et al. 5th ed. Baltimore, MD: Williams & Wilkins, 1989.

Condon, Richard. *The Manchurian Candidate.* NY: New American Library, 1959.

'Conviction Overturned in Martensville Case,' *Financial Post*, May 3, 1995.

Coontz, Stephanie. *The Way We Never Were: American Families and the Nostalgia Trap.* NY: Basic Books, 1992.

Cornwell, John, 'True Lies,' *Sunday Times Magazine*, May 14, 1995.

Costin, Lela B., Howard Jacob Karger and David Stoesz. *The Politics of Child Abuse in America.* NY: Oxford U. Pr., 1996.

Council on Scientific Affairs, AMA, 'Clinical Ecology,' *JAMA*, Dec. 23/30, 1992, v. 268(24), p. 3465–3467.

Crews, Frederick. *The Memory Wars: Freud's Legacy in Dispute.* NY: New York Review, 1995.

Crews, Frederick. *Skeptical Engagements.* NY: Oxford U. Pr., 1986.

Crews, Frederick, 'The Unknown Freud,' *New York Review of Books*, Nov. 18, 1993, p. 55–66.

Croft, Adrian, 'Judge Throws Out Recovered Memory Conviction,' Reuters News Service, April 5, 1995.

Curtiss, Aaron, 'Some on Ritual Abuse Task Force Say Satanists Are Poisoning Them,' *Los Angeles Times*, Dec. 1, 1992.

The Cutting Edge: A Newsletter for Women Living With Self-Inflicted Violence. PO Box 20819, Cleveland, OH.

Daubert *vs.* Merrell Dow Pharmaceutical, 113 S. Ct. 2786 (1993), no. 92–102.

Davidson, Joy. *The Agony of It All: The Drive for Drama and Excitement in Women's Lives.* Los Angeles: Jeremy Tarcher, 1988.

Dawes, Robyn M. *House of Cards: Psychology and Psychotherapy Built on Myth.* NY: Free Press, 1994.

D'Emilio, John and Estelle B. Freedman. *Intimate Matters: A History of Sexuality in America.* NY: Harper & Row, 1988.

de Tocqueville, Alexis. *Democracy in America*, 2 vols. Trans by Henry Reeve, ed. by Phillips Bradley. NY: Vintage Books, [1835, 1840], 1958.

Demos, John. 'Entertaining Satan,' *American Heritage*, Aug./Sept. 1978, v. 29, p. 14–23.

Denfeld, Rene. *The New Victorians: A Young Woman's Challenge to the Old Feminist Order*. NY: Warner Books, 1995.

Department of Health. *Working Together*. London: HMSO, 1988, 1991.

Dershowitz, Alan M. *The Abuse Excuse: And Other Cop-outs, Sob Stories, and Evasions of Responsibility*. Boston: Little Brown, 1994.

Diagnostic and Statistical Manual of Mental Disorders, DSM-IV, Fourth edition. Washington, DC: American Psychiatric Association, 1994.

Dickinson, Emily. *Complete Poems*, ed. by Thomas H. Johnson. Boston: Little Brown, 1960.

Dijkstra, Bram. *Idols of Perversity: Fantasies of Evil in Fin-de-Siécle Culture*. NY: Oxford U. Pr., 1986.

Dissociative Identity Disorder: Theoretical and Treatment Controversies. Edited by Lewis Cohen et al. Northvale, NJ: Jason Aronson, 1995.

Dobson, Roger, 'Increase in "False Memory" Insurance,' *Independent*, Feb. 12, 1995.

Dolnick, Edward, 'What Dreams Are (Really) Made Of,' *Atlantic Monthly*, July 1990, p. 41–61.

'Doranda Blevins Counseling Center, Chesterfield, MO: A Cult?' KMOX-TV, Channel 4, St. Louis, MO, June 9, 1995.

DSM-IV Casebook, edited by Robert L. Spitzer et al. Washington, DC: American Psychiatric Press, 1994.

Dyer, Clare, 'Euro Appeal May Test Bar on Abuse Compensation,' *The Guardian*, March 8, 1993.

Dyer, Clare, 'It Has Affected Me in Every Area,' *The Guardian*, April 21, 1995.

Dyer, Clare, 'Victory for Victims of Child Abuse,' *The Guardian*, April 21, 1995.

Eberle, Paul and Shirley. *The Abuse of Innocence: The McMartin Preschool Trial*. Buffalo, NY: Prometheus, 1993.

Eliade, Mircea. *The Quest: History and Meaning in Religion*. Chicago: Univ. Chicago Pr., 1969.

Ellenberger, Henri F. *The Discovery of the Unconscious: The History and Evolution of Dynamic Psychiatry*. NY: Basic Books, 1970.

Ellis, Albert. *A New Guide to Rational Living*. Englewood Cliffs, NJ: Prentice Hall, 1975.

Ellis, Albert. *Reason and Emotion in Psychotherapy*. NY: Lyle Stuart, 1962.

Ellis, Bill, 'Satanic Ritual Abuse and Legend Ostension,' *Journal of Psychology and Theology*, 1992, v. 20(3), p. 274–277.

Engel, Beverly. *Divorcing a Parent: Free Yourself From the Past and Live the Life You've Always Wanted*. NY: Fawcett Columbine, 1990.

Enroth, Ronald M. *Churches that Abuse*, Grand Rapids, MI: Zondervan, 1992.

Epilepsy and Behavior, Ed. by Orrin Devinsky and William H. Theodore. NY: Wiley-Liss, 1991.

Epstein, Cynthia Fuchs. *Deceptive Distinctions: Sex, Gender, and the Social Order*. New Haven, CT: Yale U. Pr., 1988.

Epstein, Seymour, 'The Self-Concept Revisited, or a Theory of a Theory,' *American Psychologist*, May 1973, v. 28, p. 404–416.

Erickson, M. H., 'Negation or Reversal of Legal Testimony,' *Archives of Neurology and Psychiatry*, vol. 40, 1938, p. 548–553.

Estabrooks, G. H. *Hypnotism*. NY: E. P. Dutton, 1946.

Esterson, Allen. *Seductive Mirage: An Exploration of the Work of Sigmund Freud*. Chicago: Open Court, 1993.

The Evil Eye. ed. by Clarence Maloney. NY: Columbia U. Pr., 1976.

Exploring Female Sexuality, ed. by Carole S. Vance. Boston: Routledge & Kegan Paul, 1984.

Facilitated Communication: The Clinical and Social Phenomenon. Ed. by Howard C. Shane. San Diego: Singular Press, in press.

False Memory Syndrome: Therapeutic and Forensic Perspectives. Ed. by David A. Halperin. Washington, DC: American Psychiatric Press, in press.

False Memory Syndrome Foundation (FMSF) Newsletter, 3401 Market St., Suite 130, Philadelphia, PA 19104.

'A Family Betrayed,' videotape. Milwaukee, WI: VCY America, 1995.

Family Sexual Abuse: Frontline Research and Evaluation. Ed. by Michael Quinn Patton. Newbury Park, CA: Sage, 1991.

Family Violence. Ed. by J. Eckelaar and S. Katz. Toronto: Butterworths, 1978.

Farley, Christopher John, 'Growing Up With a Killer,' *Time*, June 20, 1994, p. 65.

Feldman, Marc D. and Charles V. Ford, with Toni Reinhold. *Patient or Pretender: Inside the Strange World of Factitious Disorders*. NY: John Wiley, 1994.

Feldman-Summers, Shirley and Kenneth S. Pope, 'The Experience of "Forgetting" Childhood Abuse: A National Survey of Psychologists,' *Journal of Consulting and Clinical Psychology*, 1994, v. 62, no. 1, p. 636–639.

Femina, Donna Della et al, 'Child Abuse: Adolescent Records vs. Adult Recall,' *Child Abuse & Neglect*, 1990, v. 14, p. 227–231.

Festinger, Leon. *A Theory of Cognitive Dissonance*. Stanford, CA: Stanford Univ. Pr., 1957.

Festinger, Leon et al. *When Prophecy Fails: A Social and Psychological Study of a Modern Group that Predicted the Destruction of the World.* NY: Harper Torchbooks, 1956.

Fife-Yeomans, Janet, 'Call to Ban Repressed Memory Evidence,' *Australian*, Sept. 27, 1995, p. 6.

Fine, Jason, 'Seeking Evil,' *California Lawyer*, July 1994, p. 50–55, 90–92.

Finkelhor, David, 'Current Information on the Scope and Nature of Child Sexual Abuse,' in *Sexual Abuse of Children, The Future of Children*, Summer/Fall 1994, vol. 4, no. 2, p. 31–53.

Finkelhor, David, 'Sexual Abuse in a National Survey of Adult Men and Women: Prevalence, Characteristics, and Risk Factors,' *Child Abuse & Neglect*, 1990, vol. 14, p. 19–28.

Finkelhor, David, et al. *A Sourcebook on Child Sexual Abuse.* Beverly Hills, CA: Sage, 1986.

Finkelhor, David and J. Dzubia-Leatherman, 'Victimization of Children,' *American Psychologist*, 1994, v. 49, p. 173–183.

Fitzgerald, F. Scott. *The Great Gatsby.* NY: Collier Books, 1925, 1992.

Fitzpatrick, Frank & Sara, *The Survivor Activist*, Spring 1993, Cranston, RI.

Fleming, Karl and Anne Taylor Fleming. *The First Time.* NY: Simon & Schuster, 1975.

'FMS: The Latest in Sexual Abuse Defense Ploys,' *Off Our Backs*, March 1993, p. 6.

Fogarty, Maggie, 'A Journey of Survival,' *Social Work Today*, June 23, 1988, p. 22.

Forward, Susan with Craig Buck. *Toxic Parents: Overcoming Their Hurtful Legacy and Reclaiming Your Life.* NY: Bantam, 1989.

Foster, Elaine. 'Legislative Update,' Aug. 31, 1994, Washington, DC.

Fox, Robin. *The Red Lamp of Incest.* NY: E. P. Dutton, 1980.

Fox, Sanford J. *Science and Justice: The Massachusetts Witchcraft Trials.* Baltimore, MD: Johns Hopkins Press, 1968.

Foxman, Paul. *Dancing with Fear: How to Recover from Anxiety and Stress without Drugs.* Unpublished manuscript. Family Therapy Associates, 15 Pinecrest Dr., Essex Junction, VT 05452.

Frank, Jerome D. *Persuasion and Healing: A Comparative Study of Psychotherapy.* Baltimore, MD: Johns Hopkins Univ. Pr., 1961, 1973.

Frankel, Fred H., 'Hypnotizability and Dissociation,' *American Journal of Psychiatry*, July 1990, v. 147(7), p. 823–829.

Frankl, Viktor E. *Man's Search for Meaning: An Introduction to Logotherapy.* NY: Washington Square Pr., 1959, 1963.

Franzini, Louis R. and John M. Grossberg. *Eccentric & Bizarre Behaviors*. NY: John Wiley, 1994.

Fraser, Sylvia, 'Freud's Final Seduction,' *Saturday Night*, March 1994, p. 18–21, 56–59.

Fraser, Sylvia. *My Father's House: A Memoir of Incest and Healing*. NY: Ticknor & Fields, 1988.

Fredrickson, Renee. *Repressed Memories: A Journey to Recovery from Sexual Abuse*. NY, London: Simon & Schuster, 1992.

Freud, Sigmund. *Cocaine Papers*, ed. by Robert Byck. NY: Stonehill, 1974.

Freud, Sigmund. *The Complete Letters of Sigmund Freud to Wilhelm Fliess, 1887–1904*, trans. and ed. by Jeffrey Moussaieff Masson. Cambridge, MA: Belknap Press, 1985.

Freud, Sigmund. *Standard Edition of the Complete Psychological Works of Sigmund Freud*, trans. by James Strachey. 24 volumes. London: Hogarth Pr., 1953–1974.

Friedan, Betty. *It Changed My Life*. NY: Random House, 1976.

Friedrich, William N. et al, 'Normative Sexual Behavior in Children,' *Pediatrics*, Sept. 1991, v. 88, 3, p. 456–464.

Friesen, James G. *Uncovering the Mystery of MPD*. San Bernadino, CA: Here's Life Publishers, 1991.

'From the Mouths of Babes,' *ABC News 20/20*, Oct. 22, 1993.

'From the Mouths of Children,' *Fifth Estate*, Canadian Broadcasting Corp., Feb. 15, 1994.

Frye v. U.S., 293 F. 1013, 1014 (D.C. Cir., 1923).

Ganaway, George K., 'Dissociative Disorders and Psychodynamic Theory: Trauma Versus Conflict and Deficit,' paper given at conference, 'Memory and Reality,' Valley Forge, PA, April 17, 1993.

Ganaway, George K., 'Historical versus Narrative Truth: Clarifying the Role of Exogenous Trauma in the Etiology of MPD and Its Variants,' *Dissociation*, Dec. 1989, v. 2(4), p. 205–220.

Ganaway, George K., 'Hypnosis, Childhood Trauma, and Dissociative Identity Disorder: Toward an Integrative Theory,' *International Journal of Clinical and Experimental Hypnosis* (in press).

Gangelhoff, Bonnie, 'Devilish Diagnosis,' *Houston Press*, July 6–12, v. 7, no. 27, p. 8–17.

Gardner, Howard. *The Mind's New Science: A History of the Cognitive Revolution*. NY: Basic Books, 1985.

Gardner, Richard A., 'Modern Witch Hunt – Child Abuse Charges,' *Wall Street Journal*, Feb. 22, 1993.

Gardner, Richard A. *Protocols for the Sex-Abuse Evaluation*. Cresskill, NJ: Creative Therapeutics, 1995.

Gardner, Richard A., *Sex Abuse Hysteria: Salem Witch Trials Revisited*. Cresskill, NJ: Creative Therapeutics, 1991.

Gardner, Richard A., *True and False Accusations of Child Sex Abuse*. Cresskill, NJ: Creative Therapeutics, 1992.

Gay, Peter. *Freud: A Life for Our Time*. NY: W. W. Norton, 1988.

Gelinas, Denise J., 'The Persisting Negative Effects of Incest,' *Psychiatry*, Nov. 1983, v. 46, p. 312–332.

Ghate, Deborah and Liz Spencer. *The Prevalence of Child Sexual Abuse in Britain: A Feasibility Study for a Large-Scale National Survey of the General Population*. London: HMSO, 1995.

Gibbs, Nancy, 'Angels Among Us,' *Time*, Dec. 27, 1993, p. 56–65.

Gilligan, Carol. *In a Different Voice: Psychological Theory and Women's Development*. Cambridge, MA: Harvard Univ. Pr., 1982.

Goffman, Erving. *Asylums: Essays on the Social Situation of Mental Patients and Other Inmates*. Garden City, NY: Anchor Books, 1961.

Goldstein, Eleanor, with Kevin Farmer. *Confabulations: Creating False Memories, Destroying Families*. Boca Raton, FL: SIRS, 1992.

Goldstein, Eleanor and Kevin Farmer. *True Stories of False Memories*. Boca Raton, FL: SIRS, 1993.

Goleman, Daniel, 'Miscoding Is Seen as the Root of False Memories,' *New York Times*, May 31, 1994.

Gomez, Lavinia, 'Satanist Abuse,' *Counselling*, May 1995, p. 116–120.

Goodman, Gail S., et al. *Characteristics and Sources of Allegations of Ritualistic Child Abuse*. Washington, DC: National Center on Child Abuse and Neglect, 1994.

Goodman, Felicitas D. *How About Demons? Possession and Exorcism in the Modern World*. Bloomington: Indiana University Pr., 1988.

Gordon, Betty N. et al, 'Children's Knowledge of Sexuality: A Comparison of Sexually Abused and Nonabused Children,' *American Journal of Orthopsychiatry*, April 1990, v. 60(2), p. 250–257.

Gould, Stephen Jay. *The Mismeasure of Man*. NY: Norton, 1991.

'Grandparents Being Sent to Jail for Sexually Abusing Grandkids,' *Donahue*, Transcript 3678, March 4, 1993.

Grant, Linda, 'Are Women Mad?' *Vogue* (U.K.), Feb. 1996, p. 46–48.

Gray, Frank. *Scoremanship*. NY: Bantam, 1969.

Gray, Paul, 'The Assault on Freud,' *Time*, Nov. 29, 1993, p. 47–51.

Gray, Peter. *Psychology*. NY: Worth, 1991.

Green, Gina, 'Facilitated Communication: Mental Miracle or Sleight of Hand?' *Skeptic,* 1994, v. 2(3), p. 68–76.

Grescoe, Paul, 'Things That Go Bump in the Night,' *Maclean's*, Oct. 27, 1980, p. 30–31.

Groff, William J. *Decree*. State of New Hampshire v. Joel Hungerford & John Morahan. Hillborough County Superior Court, Manchester, NH, 1995.

Groth, A. Nicholas, with H. Jean Birnbaum. *Men Who Rape: The Psychology of the Offender*. NY: Plenum, 1979.

Grünbaum, Adolf. *Foundations of Psychoanalysis*. Berkeley, CA: Univ. of California Pr., 1984.

Gudjonsson, Gisli H. *The Psychology of Interrogations, Confessions and Testimony*. NY: John Wiley, 1992.

Gustafson, Paul, 'Jury Awards Patient $2.6 Million,' *Star Tribune*, Aug. 1, 1995.

Haaken, Janice, 'The Debate over Recovered Memory of Sexual Abuse: A Psychoanalytic Feminist Perspective,' in press.

Haaken, Janice and Astrid Schlaps, 'Incest Resolution Therapy and the Objectification of Sexual Abuse,' *Psychotherapy*, Spring 1991, v. 28(1), p. 39–47.

Haberman, J. Victor, 'A Criticism of Psychoanalysis,' *Journal of Abnormal Psychology*, 1914, v. 9, p. 265–280.

Hacking, Ian, 'Two Souls in One Body,' *Critical Inquiry*, Summer 1991, v. 17(4), p. 838–867.

Hale, Nathan G., Jr. *Freud and the Americans: The Beginnings of Psychoanalysis in the United States, 1876–1917*. NY: Oxford U. Pr., 1971.

Hall, Calvin S. *The Meaning of Dreams*. NY: McGraw-Hill, 1953, 1966.

Hall, Liz and Siobhan Lloyd. *Surviving Child Sexual Abuse: A Handbook for Helping Women Challenge Their Past*. NY, Philadelphia, London: Falmer, 1989.

Hammond, D. Corydon, ed. *Handbook of Hypnotic Suggestions and Metaphors*. NY: W. W. Norton, 1990.

The Handbook of Emotion and Memory: Research and Theory. Ed. by Sven-Ake Christianson. Hillsdale, NJ: Lawrence Erlbaum, 1992.

Hansen, Chadwick. *Witchcraft at Salem*. NY: New American Library, 1969.

Hansen, Tracy. *Seven for a Secret: Healing the Wounds of Sexual Abuse in Childhood*. London: S.P.C.K., 1991.

Harper, Audrey, with Harry Pugh. *Dance With the Devil*. Eastbourne: Kingsway, 1990.

Harrington, Evan, 'Conspiracy Theories and Paranoia: Notes from a Mind Control Conference,' *Skeptical Inquirer*, in press, 1996.

Harris, Jonathan, 'Day Care Cases Summary,' 1994, MIT Room 66–450, 25 Ames St., Cambridge, MA 02139.

Harrison, Ted. *Stigmata*. NY: St. Martin's Press, 1994.

Hartung, John, 'Love Thy Neighbor,' *Skeptic*, vol. 3, no. 4, 1995, p. 86–99.

Haskew, Paul and Anne M. Donnellan. *Emotional Maturity and Well-being: Psychological Lessons of Facilitated Communications*. Madison, WI: DRI Press, 1993.

Hass, Nancy, 'Margaret Kelly Michaels Wants Her Innocence Back,' *New York Times Magazine*, Sept. 10, 1995, p. 37–41.

Hassan, Steven. *Combatting Cult Mind Control*. Rochester, VT: Park Street Pr., 1988, 1990.

Hayward, Ed and Tom Mashberg, 'Experts Split on Whether Memory Serves Us Right,' *Boston Herald*, Dec. 4, 1995.

Hayward, Ed and Tom Mashberg, 'Upheaval in '80s Put the Spotlight on Child Abuse,' *Boston Herald*, Dec. 3, 1995.

Heaton, Jeanne Albronda and Nona Leigh Wilson. *Tuning in Trouble: Talk TV's Destructive Impact on Mental Health*. San Francisco: Jossey-Bass, 1995.

Hebditch, David and Nick Anning, 'A Ritual Fabrication,' *Independent on Sunday*, Dec. 30, 1990.

Hedges, Lawrence E., 'Taking Recovered Memories Seriously,' *Issues in Child Abuse Accusations*, 1994, v. 6(1), p. 1–31. Excerpted from Hedges, *Remembering, Repeating, and Working Through Childhood Trauma*. NY: Jason Aronson, 1994.

Hellman, Lillian. *Pentimento*. Boston: Little Brown, 1973.

Hendricks, Bill, 'Insurance Invested Billions in Hospitals,' *San Antonio Express-News*, May 1992.

Herman, Judith, 'The Abuses of Memory,' *Mother Jones*, March/April 1993, p. 3–4.

Herman, Judith Lewis. *Trauma and Recovery*. NY: Basic Books, 1992.

Herman, Judith Lewis et al, 'Psychiatrist-Patient Sexual Contact: Results of a National Survey,' *American Journal of Psychiatry*, Feb. 1987, v. 144(2), p. 164–169.

Herman, Judith L. and Mary R. Harvey, 'The False Memory Debate: Social Science or Social Backlash?' *Harvard Mental Health Review*, April 1993, p. 4–6.

Herman, Judith Lewis, with Lisa Hirschman. *Father-Daughter Incest.* Cambridge, MA: Harvard U. Pr., 1981.

Herman, Judith Lewis and Emily Schatzow, 'Recovery and Verification of Memories of Childhood Sexual Trauma,' *Psychoanalytic Psychology*, 1987, v. 4, 1, p. 1–14.

Herman, Judith and Emily Schatzow, 'Time-Limited Group Therapy for Women with a History of Incest,' *International Journal of Group Psychotherapy*, Oct. 1984, v. 34(4), p. 605–616.

Herndon, Paul L., 'False and Repressed Memories Gain Media Spotlight,' *Practitioner Focus*, Feb. 1994, p. 3, 15.

Hertenstein, Mike and Jon Trott. *Selling Satan: The Tragic History of Mike Warnke.* Chicago, IL: Cornerstone Pr., 1993.

Hicks, Robert D. *In Pursuit of Satan: The Police and the Occult.* Buffalo, NY: Prometheus, 1991.

Hill, Frances. *A Delusion of Satan: The Full Story of the Salem Witch Trials.* NY: Doubleday, 1995.

Hill, Rob, 'The Many Hearts and Minds of William Adams,' *South Shore Sounds*, Olympia, WA, Nov. 1993, p. 3.

Hilts, Philip J. *Memory's Ghost: The Strange Tale of Mr. M. and the Nature of Memory.* NY: Simon & Schuster, 1995.

Hobbs, Chris and Jane Wynne, 'Buggery in Childhood: A Common Syndrome of Child Abuse,' *Lancet*, 1986, p. 792–796.

Hobson, J. Allan. *The Chemistry of Conscious States: How the Brain Changes Its Mind.* Boston: Little Brown, 1994.

Hobson, J. Allan. *The Dreaming Brain.* NY: Basic Books, 1988.

Hobson, J. Allan. *Sleep: Principles and Practices of Sleep Medicine.* NY: Scientific American Library, 1989.

Hochman, John, 'Recovered Memory Therapy and False Memory Syndrome,' *Skeptic*, 1994, v. 2(3), p. 58–61.

Hoffer, Eric. *The True Believer: Thoughts on the Nature of Mass Movements.* NY: Harper & Row, 1951.

Holmes, David S., 'Is There Evidence for Repression? Doubtful,' *Harvard Mental Health Letter*, June 1994, v. 10(12), p. 4–6.

Hopkins, Carol Lamb, 'Testimony,' May 24, 1995, U.S. Senate Subcommittee on Children and Families, Committee on Labor and Human Resources.

Horn, Miriam, 'Memories, Lost and Found,' *U.S. News & World Report*, Nov. 29, 1993, p. 52–63.

Horner, Thomas M. et al, 'The Biases of Child Sexual Abuse Experts: Believing is Seeing,' *Bulletin of the American Academy of Psychiatric Law*, 1993, v. 21, 3, p. 281–292.

Hornstein, Gail A., 'The Return of the Repressed: Psychology's Problematic Relations with Psychoanalysis, 1909–1960,' *American Psychologist*, Feb. 1992, v. 47(2), p. 254–263.

Howe, Mark L. and Mary L. Courage, 'On Resolving the Enigma of Infantile Amnesia,' *Psychological Bulletin*, 1993, v. 113(2), p. 305–326.

Howitt, Dennis. *Child Abuse Errors: When Good Intentions Go Wrong.* New Brunswick, NJ: Rutgers Univerity Pr., 1992.

Hsia, R. P-Chia. *The Myth of Ritual Murder: Jews and Magic in Reformation Europe.* New Haven, CT: Yale U. Pr., 1988.

Huber, Peter W. *Galileo's Revenge: Junk Science in the Courtroom.* NY: Basic Books, 1991.

Hudson, M., 'All Psyched Out,' *London Times*, Oct. 14, 1995.

Hufford, David J. *The Terror That Comes in the Night: An Experience-Centered Study of Supernatural Assault Traditions.* Philadelphia, PA: U. of Pennsylvania Pr., 1982.

Hughes, Robert. *Culture of Complaint: The Fraying of America.* NY: Oxford U. Pr., 1993.

Human Suggestibility: Advances in Theory, Research, and Application, ed. by John F. Schumaker. NY: Routledge, 1991.

Hunter, Mic. *Abused Boys: The Neglected Victims of Sexual Abuse.* Lexington, MA: Lexington Books, 1990.

Hyman, I. E, et al, 'False Memories of Childhood Experience,' *Applied Cognitive Psychology*, June 1995, v. 9, no. 3, p. 181–197.

Hypnosis and Memory, ed. by Helen M. Pettinati. NY: Guilford, 1988.

'I Am What We Are,' *All Things Considered*, NPR, July 23, 1994, Transcript 1552.

Innocence Lost – The Verdict, Part I and II, by Ofra Bikel. *Frontline*, WGBH-TV, Boston. Shows No. 1120 & 1121, July 20 & 21, 1993.

International Encyclopedia of Psychiatry, Psychology, Psychoanalysis, & Neurology, ed. by Benjamin B. Wolman. NY: Van Nostrand Reinhold, 1977.

Israels, Han and Morton Schatzman, 'The Seduction Theory,' *History of Psychiatry*, 1993, v. 4, p. 23–59.

Jacobs, David M. *Secret Life: Firsthand Documented Accounts of UFO Abductions.* NY: Simon & Schuster, 1992.

James, William. *The Principles of Psychology.* Chicago, IL: University of Chicago, 1952 [1891].

James, William. *The Varieties of Religious Experience: A Study in Human Nature.* NY: Collier Books, 1902, 1961.

Janov, Arthur. *The Primal Scream: Primal Therapy, The Cure for Neurosis.* NY: Dell, 1970.

Japenga, Ann, 'Rewriting the Dictionary of Madness,' *Los Angeles Times*, June 5, 1994.

Jaroff, Leon, 'Lies of the Mind,' *Time*, Nov. 29, 1993, p. 52–59.

Jaspers, Karl. *General Psychopathology*. Trans. by J. Hoenig and Marian W. Hamilton. Chicago, IL: Manchester U. Press, U. of Chicago Pr., 1963, [1923].

Jastrow, Joseph. *Wish and Wisdom: Episodes in the Vagaries of Belief*. NY: D. Appleton-Century, 1935.

Jenkins, Philip. *Intimate Enemies: Moral Panics in Contemporary Great Britain*. NY: Aldine de Gruyter, 1992.

Jenkins, Philip. *Pedophiles and Priests*. NY: Oxford U. Pr., 1996.

Jerome, Richard, 'Suspect Confessions,' *New York Times Magazine*, Aug. 13, 1995, p. 28–31.

Jervis, Margaret, 'Book Review: *The Filthy Lie*,' *BFMS Newsletter*, Dec. 1995, vol. 3, no. 2, p. 10–12.

Jervis, Margaret, 'Child Abuse Debate: Where's the Social Work Perspective?' *Social Work Today*, May 12, 1988, p. 8.

Jervis, Margaret, 'Dealing with Child Abuse by a Generic Approach,' *Social Work Today*, Aug. 11, 1988, p. 22–23.

Jervis, Margaret, 'Grey Area,' *Social Work Today*, April 11, 1991.

Jervis, Margaret, 'Judge and Fury,' *Social Work Today*, March 21, 1991, p. 27–28.

Jervis, Margaret, 'Objectivity Compromised, Says Cleveland Report,' *Social Work Today*, July 14, 1988.

Jervis, Margaret, 'Paediatrician's Confidence in Diagnostic Technique, *Social Work Today*, Nov. 23, 1987, p. 7.

Jervis, Margaret, 'Panic Over Satanic Abuse Strikes Again,' *New Statesman & Society*, Jan. 20, 1995, p. 11.

Jervis, Margaret, 'Paradox of Child Sexual Abuse,' *Social Work Today*, Nov. 23, 1987, p. 7.

Jervis, Margaret, 'Recall Totalled,' *Fortean Times*, Dec. 1995, vol. 84, p. 43–44.

Jervis, Margaret, 'Rise of the "Child Abuse Industry,"' *Sunday Telegraph*, June 26, 1994.

Jervis, Margaret, 'Spectral Evidence: Fear and Ignorance in the Courts,' *The Therapist*, Spring 1995, p. 13–15.

Jervis, Margaret, and Victoria Macdonald, 'Sex Trial Storm As Hypnosis Guide Ignored,' *Sunday Telegraph*, April 24, 1994.

Johnson, Donald, 'The "Phantom Anesthetist" of Mattoon: A Field Study in Mass Hysteria,' *Journal of Abnormal and Social Psychology*, April, 1945, p. 175–186.

Johnson, George. *In the Palaces of Memory: How We Build the Worlds Inside Our Heads*. NY: Knopf, 1991.

Jones, Landon Y. *Great Expectations: America and the Baby Boom Generation*. NY: Coward, McCann & Geoghegan, 1980.

Kafka, Franz. *The Trial*, trans. by Edwin and Willa Muir. NY: Knopf, 1925, 1937.

Kaminer, Wendy. *I'm Dysfunctional, You're Dysfunctional: The Recovery Movement and Other Self-Help Fashions*. NY: Vintage Books, 1992, 1993.

Kampman, Reima, 'Hypnotically Induced Multiple Personality: An Experimental Study,' *International Journal of Clinical and Experimental Hypnosis*, 1976, v. 24(3), p. 215–227.

Kandel, Eric and Minouche Kandel, 'Flights of Memory,' *Discover*, May 1994, p. 10, 32–38.

Karle, Hellmut. *The Filthy Lie: Discovering and Recovering from Childhood Abuse*. London: Hamish Hamilton, 1992.

Katz, Stan J. and Aimee Liu. *The Codependency Conspiracy: How to Break the Recovery Habit and Take Charge of Your Life*. NY: Warner, 1991.

Keillor, Garrison. *The Book of Guys*. NY: Viking, 1993.

Kelley, Charles R. and Eric C. *Now I Remember: Recovered Memories of Sexual Abuse*. Vancouver, WA: KR Publishing, 1994.

Kelley, Susan J., 'Parental Stress Response to Sexual Abuse and Ritualistic Abuse of Children in Day-Care Centers,' *Nursing Research*, vol. 39, no. 1, p. 25–29.

Kelley, Susan J., 'Ritualistic Abuse of Children: Dynamics and Impact,' *Cultic Studies Journal*, 1988, vol 5(2), p. 228–236.

Kelley, Susan J., 'Sexual Abuse in Day Care Centers,' *Child Abuse and Neglect*, 1993.

Kelley, Susan J., 'Stress Responses of Children to Sexual Abuse and Ritualistic Abuse in Day-Care Centers,' *Journal of Interpersonal Violence*, vol. 4, 1989, p. 502–513.

Kelly, Liz et al, 'An Exploratory Study of the Prevalence of Sexual Abuse in a Sample of 16–21 Year-Olds,' Child Abuse Studies Unit, Polytechnic of North London, 1991.

Kendall-Tackett, Kathleen, Linda Meyer Williams, and David Finkelhor, 'Impact of Sexual Abuse on Children: A Review and Synthesis of Recent Empirical Studies,' *Psychological Bulletin*, 1993, v. 113(1), p. 164–180.

Kenny, Michael G., 'Multiple Personality and Spirit Possession,' *Psychiatry*, v. 44, Nov. 1981, p. 337–357.

Kenny, Michael G., 'Paradox Lost: The Latah Problem Revisited,' *Journal of Nervous and Mental Disease*, 1983, v. 171(3), p. 159–167.

Kenny, Michael G. *The Passion of Ansel Bourne: Multiple Personality in American Culture*. Washington, DC: Smithsonian Pr., 1986.

Keyes, Daniel. *The Minds of Billy Milligan*. NY: Random, 1981.

Kihlstrom, John F., 'The Recovery of Memory in the Laboratory and Clinic,' April, 1993, unpublished paper.

Kilpatrick, Allie C. *Long-Range Effects of Child and Adolescent Sexual Experiences: Myths, Mores, and Menaces*. Hillsdale, NJ: Lawrence Erlbaum, 1992.

'King, Stephen Edwin,' *Contemporary Authors*, New Revision Series, v. 30, p. 216–225.

Kingsbury, Steven J., 'Where Does Research on the Effectiveness of Psychotherapy Stand Today?' *Harvard Mental Health Letter*, Sept. 1995.

Kinsey, Alfred C. et al. *Sexual Behavior in the Human Female*. Philadelphia: W. B. Saunders, 1953.

Kipnis, Aaron R. *Knights Without Armor*. NY: St. Martins, 1991.

Kirk, Stuart A. and Herb Kutchins. *The Selling of DSM: The Rhetoric of Science in Psychiatry*. NY: Aldine de Gruyter, 1992.

Kirsch, Irving and Steven Jay Lynn, 'The Altered State of Hypnosis,' *American Psychologist*, Oct. 1995, p. 846–858.

Kluft, Richard P., 'Clinical Presentations of Multiple Personality Disorder,' *Psychiatric Clinics of North America*, Sept. 1991, v. 14(3), p. 605–629.

Kluft, Richard, 'High-Functioning Multiple Personality Patients, Three Cases,' *Journal of Nervous and Mental Disease*, 1986, v. 174(12), p. 722–726.

Kluft, Richard P., 'Hospital Treatment of Multiple Personality Disorder: An Overview,' *Psychiatric Clinics of North America*, Sept. 1991, v. 14(3), p. 695–719.

Kluft, Richard, 'Treatment of Multiple Personality Disorder, A Study of 33 Cases,' *Psychiatric Clinics of N. Amer.*, March 1984, v. 7(1), p. 9–29.

Konker, Claudia, 'Rethinking Child Sexual Abuse: An Anthropological Perspective,' *American Journal of Orthopsychiatry*, Jan. 1992, vol 62(1), p. 147–153.

Kramer, Heinrich and James Sprenger. *Malleus Maleficarum*. trans. and introduction by Montague Summers. NY: Dover, [1486], 1971.

Kramer, Peter D. *Listening to Prozac*. NY: Viking, 1993.

La Fontaine, Jean. *Child Sexual Abuse*. London: Polity Press, 1990.

La Fontaine, J. S. *The Extent and Nature of Organised and Ritual Abuse*. London: HMSO, 1994.

Lakoff, Robin Tomach and James C. Coyne. *Father Knows Best: The Use and Abuse of POWER in Freud's Case of DORA*. NY: Teachers College Pr., 1993.

Laing, R. D. *The Politics of the Family and Other Essays*. NY: Vintage Books, 1969, 1972.

Langer, Lawrence. *Holocaust Testimonies: The Ruins of Memory*. New Haven, CT: Yale U. Pr., 1991.

Langner, Paul, 'Two Doctors Are Fined in U.S. Suit Over Drugs,' *Boston Globe*, March 15, 1995.

Lanning, Kenneth V. *Investigator's Guide to Allegations of 'Ritual' Child Abuse*, Jan. 1992, FBI Academy, Quantico, VA 22135.

Lasch, Christopher. *The Culture of Narcissism: American Life in an Age of Diminishing Expectations*. NY: W.W. Norton, 1978.

Lashley, Karl S., 'In Search of the Engram,' *Symposia of the Society for Experimental Biology*, 1950, v. 4, p. 454–482.

Laumann, Edward O., et al. *The Social Organization of Sexuality: Sexual Practices in the United States*. Chicago, IL: U. Chicago Pr., 1994.

Laurence, Jean-Roch and Campbell Perry. *Hypnosis, Will, and Memory: A Psycho-Legal History*. NY: Guilford, 1988.

Laurence, Jean-Roch and Campbell Perry, 'Hypnotically Created Memory Among Highly Hypnotizable Subjects,' *Science*, Nov. 4, 1983, v. 222, p. 523–524.

Laurence, Jeremy and Francis Gibb, 'Use of Recovered Memory in Evidence Raises Controversy,' *The Times*, March 29, 1995, p. 6.

Lawrence, Peter H. *The Hot Line*. Eastbourne: Kingsway, 1990.

Ledoux, Joseph E., 'Emotion, Memory and the Brain,' *Scientific American*, June 1994, p. 50–57.

Lee, Sharice A. *The Survivor's Guide*. Thousand Oaks, CA, London, UK: Sage, 1995.

Leman, Kevin and Randy Carlson. *Unlocking the Secrets of Your Childhood Memories*. Nashville, TN: T. Nelson, 1989.

Lerner, Harriet E., 'The Hysterical Personality: A "Woman's Disease,"' *Comprehensive Psychiatry*, March/April 1974, vol. 15, no. 2, p. 157–164.

Leutwyler, Kristin, 'Sick, Sick, Sick,' *Scientific American*, Sept. 1994, p. 17–18.

Lew, Mike. *Victims No Longer: Men Recovering from Incest*. NY: Perennial Library, 1988, 1990.

Lewis, I. M. *Ecstatic Religion: An Anthropological Study of Spirit Possession and Shamanism*. NY: Penguin, 1971.

Lewis, James, 'The Week in Britain,' *Guardian Weekly*, July 23, 1995, p. 9.

Lifton, Robert J. *Thought Reform and the Psychology of Totalism*. NY: Norton, 1961.

Lilienheim, Henry. *The Aftermath: A Survivor's Odyssey Through War-Torn Europe*. Montreal, Quebec: DC Books, 1994.

Lindner, Robert Mitchell. *Rebel Without a Cause: The Hypnoanalysis of a Criminal Psychopath*. NY: Grune & Stratton, 1944, 1968.

Lindsay, D. Stephen, 'Beyond Backlash: Comments on Enns, McNeilly, Corkery, and Gilbert,' *Counseling Psychologist*, April 1995, v. 23, no. 2, p. 280–289.

Lindsay, D. Stephen and J. Don Read, '"Memory Work" and Recovered Memories of Childhood Sexual Abuse: Scientific Evidence and Public, Professional, and Personal Issues,' *Psychology, Public Policy and the Law*, 1995, v. 1, p. 846–908.

Lindsay, D. Stephen and J. Don Read, 'Psychotherapy and Memories of Childhood Sexual Abuse: A Cognitive Perspective,' *Applied Cognitive Psychology*, 1994, p. 1–42, v. 8, p. 281–338.

Littauer, Fred and Florence. *Freeing Your Mind From Memories That Bind*. San Bernardino, CA: Here's Life Publishers, 1988.

Lockwood, Craig. *Other Altars*. Minneapolis: CompCare Publishers, 1993.

Loe, Victoria, 'Judge Dismisses 45 Child-Abuse Indictments,' *Dallas Morning News*, Nov. 7, 1995.

Loewenstein, Richard J., 'An Office Mental Status Examination for Complex Chronic Dissociative Symptoms and Multiple Personality Disorder,' *Psychiatric Clinics of North America*, Sept. 1991, v. 14, 3, p. 567–604.

Loftus, Elizabeth F., 'Desperately Seeking Memories of the First Few Years of Childhood: Comment on Usher & Neisser,' *Journal of Experimental Psychology: General*, in press.

Loftus, Elizabeth F. *Eyewitness Testimony*. Cambridge, MA: Harvard U. Pr., 1979.

Loftus, Elizabeth F., 'On the Permanence of Stored Information in the Human Brain,' *American Psychologist*, May 1980, v. 35(5), p. 108–121.

Loftus, Elizabeth F., 'The Reality of Repressed Memories,' *American Psychologist*, May 1993, v. 48, p. 518–537.

Loftus, Elizabeth, 'Remembering Dangerously,' *Skeptical Inquirer*, March/April 1995, p. 20–29.

Loftus, Elizabeth F., 'Repressed Memories of Childhood Trauma: Are They Genuine?' *Harvard Mental Health Review*, March 1993, p. 4–5.

Loftus, Elizabeth F., 'Therapeutic Recollection of Childhood Abuse:

When a Memory May Not Be a Memory,' *The Champion*, March 1994, p. 5-10.

Loftus, Elizabeth F., 'When a Lie Becomes Memory's Truth: Memory Distortion After Exposure to Misinformation,' *Current Directions in Psychological Science*, v. 1(4), Aug. 1992, p. 120-123.

Loftus, Elizabeth F. et al, 'Memories of Childhood Sexual Abuse,' *Psychology of Women Quarterly*, 1994, v. 18, p. 67-84.

Loftus, Elizabeth F. and Hunter G. Hoffman, 'Misinformation and Memory: The Creation of New Memories,' *Journal of Experimental Psychology: General*, 1989, v. 118(1), p. 100-104.

Loftus, Elizabeth and Katherine Ketcham. *The Myth of Repressed Memory: False Memories and Allegations of Sexual Abuse*. NY: St. Martin's, 1994.

Loftus, Elizabeth and Katherine Ketcham. *Witness for the Defense: The Accused, the Eyewitness, and the Expert Who Puts Memory on Trial*. NY: St. Martin's, 1991.

Loftus, Elizabeth F. and Geoffrey R. Loftus, 'The Repressed Memory Controversy,' *American Psychologist*, May 1994, v. 49(5), p. 443-445.

Loftus, Elizabeth F. and Jacqueline E. Pickrell, 'The Formation of False Memories,' *Psychiatric Annals*, Dec. 1995, vol. 25, no. 12, p. 720-725.

Loftus, Geoffrey R. and Elizabeth F. Loftus. *Human Memory: The Processing of Information*. Hillsdale, NJ: Lawrence Erlbaum, 1976.

Logan, Kevin. *Paganism and the Occult*. Eastbourne: Kingsway, 1990.

Loggins, Kirk, 'Divorced Fathers Told to Beware,' *The Tennessean*, July 24, 1994.

Lopez, F. et al, 'Prevalencia y Consecuencias del Abuso Sexual Al Menor en España,' *Child Abuse & Neglect*, 1995, vol 19, p. 1039-1050.

Lotto, David, 'On Witches and Witch Hunts: Ritual and Satanic Cult Abuse,' *Journal of Psychohistory*, Spring 1994, v. 21(4), p. 373-396.

Love, Patricia, with Jo Robinson, *The Emotional Incest Syndrome: What to Do When a Parent's Love Rules Your Life*. NY: Bantam, 1990.

Low, Abraham. *Mental Health Through Will-Training: A System of Self-Help in Psychotherapy as Practiced by Recovery, Incorporated*. Glencoe, IL: Willett Publishing, 1950, 1952, 1978.

Ludwig, Arnold M., 'Altered States of Consciousness,' *Archives of General Psychiatry*, September 1966, vol. 15, p. 225-234.

Ludwig, Arnold M. et al, 'The Objective Study of a Multiple Personality,' *Archives of General Psychiatry*, April 1972, vol. 26, p. 298-310.

Lutz, Tom. *American Nervousness, 1903*. Ithaca, NY: Cornell U. Pr., 1991.

Lyon, Kathryn. *The Wenatchee Report*. Kathryn Lyon, 4909 Shellridge Road, Olympia, WA 98502, 1995.

Lyons, Arthur. *Satan Wants You: The Cult of Devil Worship in America.* NY: Mysterious Press, 1988.

MacCurdy, John T., with a preface by W. H. R. Rivers. *War Neuroses.* Cambridge: At the University Press, 1918.

Mack, John E. *Abduction: Human Encounters with Aliens.* NY: Scribner's, 1994.

Mackay, Charles. *Extraordinary Popular Delusions and the Madness of Crowds.* London: Richard Bentley, 1841. [L. C. Page & Co., 1932, reprint].

MacLean, Harry N. *Once Upon a Time: A True Story of Memory, Murder and the Law.* NY: HarperCollins, 1993.

MacLean, Harry, 'Some Therapists Who Claim to "Recover" Memories May Actually Induce Them.,' *Denver Post,* Dec. 9, 1995.

Macmillan, Malcolm. *Freud Evaluated: The Completed Arc.* NY: North-Holland, 1991.

MacNamara, Mark, 'Fade Away: The Rise and Fall of the Repressed-Memory Theory in the Courtroom,' *California Lawyer,* March 1995, p. 36–41.

Madigan, Michael, '"Memory" Sex Cases Attacked,' *Courier-Mail* (Brisbane, Australia), Jan. 5, 1996, p. 6.

Magner, Ellis S., 'Recovered Memories: The Australian Position,' *Expert Evidence,* June 1995, vol. 3, no. 4, p. 151–154.

Maisch, Herbert. *Incest.* Trans. by Colin Bearne. London: André Deutsch, 1968, 1973.

Makarec, Katherine and Michael A. Persinger, 'Electroencephalographic Validation of a Temporal Lobe Signs Inventory in a Normal Population,' *Journal of Research in Personality,* 1990, v. 24, p. 323–337.

Malmquist, C. P., 'Children Who Witness Parental Murder: Post-traumatic Aspects,' *Journal of the American Academy of Child Psychiatry,* 1986, v. 25, p. 320–325.

Maltz, Wendy. *The Sexual Healing Journey: A Guide for Survivors of Sexual Abuse.* NY: HarperCollins, 1991.

Marano, Hara Estroff, 'Wave of the Future,' *Psychology Today,* July/August 1994, p. 22–25.

Markowitz, Laura M., 'Crossing the Line,' *Family Therapy Networker,* Nov./Dec. 1992, p. 25–31.

Marks, John. *The Search for the Manchurian Candidate.* NY: Times Books, 1979.

Martin, Judith A. and Elizabeth Elmer, 'Battered Children Grown Up: A Follow-up Study of Individuals Severely Maltreated as Children,' *Child Abuse and Neglect,* 1992, v. 16, p. 75–87.

Mashberg, Tom, 'Judge Nixes Amirault's Appeal for New Trial,' *Boston Herald*, Nov. 30, 1995.

Mashberg, Tom and Ed Hayward, 'Defense: Tapes Tell It All,' *Boston Herald*, Dec. 6, 1995.

Maslow, Abraham H. *Religions, Values, and Peak-Experiences*. NY: Viking, 1964, 1970.

Masson, Jeffrey Moussaieff. *Against Therapy: Emotional Tyranny and the Myth of Psychological Healing*. NY: Atheneum, 1988.

Masson, Jeffrey Moussaieff. *The Assault on Truth: Freud's Suppression of the Seduction Theory*. NY: HarperPerennial, 1984, 1992.

Masson, Jeffrey Moussaieff. *A Dark Science: Women, Sexuality and Psychiatry in the Nineteenth Century*. NY: Farrar, Straus & Giroux, 1986.

Matthews, Cathy Ann. *Breaking Through: No Longer a Victim of Child Abuse*. Sutherland, AU, Claremont, CA: Albatross Books 1990; Oxford, UK: Lion Publishing, 1990. (Part I originally published as *No Longer a Victim*. Canberra, AU: Acorn Pr., 1986.)

Mayer, Robert. *Through Divided Minds*. NY: Doubleday, 1988.

McCann, John et al, 'Genital Findings in Prepubertal Girls Selected for Nonabuse: A Descriptive Study,' *Pediatrics*, Sept. 1990, v. 86, 3, p. 428–439.

McCann, John et al, 'Perianal Findings in Prepubertal Children Selected for Nonabuse: A Descriptive Study,' *Child Abuse & Neglect*, 1989, v. 13, p. 179–193.

McDonald, Sally, 'An Ethical Dilemma: Risk Versus Responsibility,' *Journal of Psychosocial Nursing*, 1994, v. 32(1), p. 19–25.

McElroy, Susan L., and Paul E. Keck, 'Misattribution of Eating and Obsessive-Compulsive Disorder Symptoms to Repressed Memories of Childhood Sexual or Physical Abuse,' *Biological Psychiatry*, 1995, vol. 37, p. 48–51.

McElroy, Susan L. and Paul E. Keck, Jr., 'Recovered Memory Therapy: False Memory Syndrome and Other Complications,' *Psychiatric Annals*, Dec. 1995, vol. 25, no. 12, p. 731–735.

McGrath, Melanie. *Motel Nirvana: Dreaming of the New Age in the American Desert*. London: HarperCollins, 1995.

McGraw-Hill Encyclopedia of Science & Technology. 7th ed. 20 vols. NY: McGraw-Hill, 1990.

McHugh, Paul, 'History and the Pitfalls of Practice,' Draft Paper from author.

McHugh, Paul, 'Multiple Personality Disorder,' *Harvard Mental Health Letter*, v. 10(3), Sept. 1993.

McHugh, Paul R., 'Psychiatric Misadventures,' *American Scholar*, Autumn 1992, p. 497–510.

McHugh, Paul R., 'Psychotherapy Awry,' *American Scholar*, Winter 1994, p. 17–30.

McKain, Bruce, 'Ayr "Abuse" Case Closed,' *The Herald* (Glasgow), Oct. 18, 1995.

'The McMartin Pre-School,' produced by Lowell Bergman. *60 Minutes*, Nov. 2, 1986, v. 19(8).

McNamara, Eileen. *Breakdown: Sex, Suicide and the Harvard Psychiatrist.* NY: Pocket Books, 1994.

Meacham, Andrew, 'Call Me Mom,' *Changes*, Aug. 1992, p. 57–63.

Meacham, Jon, 'Trials and Troubles in Happy Valley,' *Newsweek*, May 8, 1995, p. 58–60.

Meehl, Paul E., 'Philosophy of Science: Help or Hindrance?' *Psychological Reports*, 1993, vol. 72, p. 707–733.

Melton, J. Gordon. *Encyclopedic Handbook of Cults in America.* NY: Garland, 1986.

Melton, J. Gordon and Robert L. Moore. *The Cult Experience: Responding to the New Religious Pluralism.* NY: Pilgrim Press, 1982.

Memory Distortion: How Minds, Brains, and Societies Reconstruct the Past. edited by Daniel L. Schacter. Cambridge, MA: Harvard U. Pr., 1995.

Memory in Context: Context in Memory, ed. by Graham M. Davies and Donald M. Thomson. NY: John Wiley, 1988.

Memory Observed: Remembering in Natural Contexts, selections and commentary by Ulric Neisser. San Francisco, CA: W. H. Freeman, 1982.

Memory Systems of the Brain, ed. by N. M. Weinberger et al. NY: Guilford Pr., 1985.

Merskey, Harold. *The Analysis of Hysteria.* London: Baillière Tindall, 1979.

Merskey, Harold, 'The Manufacture of Personalities: The Production of Multiple Personality Disorder,' *British Journal of Psychiatry*, 1992, vol. 160, p. 327–340.

Meyer, Donald. *The Positive Thinkers: Religion as Pop Psychology from Mary Baker Eddy to Oral Roberts.* NY: Pantheon, 1980.

Michelet, Jules. *Satanism and Witchcraft*, trans. by A. R. Allinson. NY: Citadel Press, 1992.

Miller, Alice. *Banished Knowledge: Facing Childhood Injuries*, trans. by Leila Vennewitz. NY: Doubleday, 1990.

Miller, Alice. *Breaking Down the Wall of Silence: The Liberating Experience of Facing Painful Truth*, trans. by Simon Worrall. NY: Dutton, 1991.

Miller, Sue. *Family Pictures*. NY: Harper & Row, 1990.

'Mind-Bending Treatments Need Testing,' *The Mail on Sunday*, Opinion, p. 28.

Minirth, Frank. *The Power of Memories: How to Use Them to Improve Your Health and Well-Being*. Nashville, TN: Thomas Nelson Publishers, 1995.

'Minirth-Meier New Life Clinic Betrays a Family?' *PsychoHeresy Awareness Letter*, Sept.-Oct. 1995.

Mitchell, B., 'Confessions and Police Interrogation of Suspects,' *Criminal Law Review*, Sept. 1983, p. 596–604.

Mitchell, Emily. 'Father of the Child Within,' *Time*, Nov. 25, 1991, p. 82–83.

Mithers, Carol Lynn. *Therapy Gone Mad: The True Story of Hundreds of Patients and a Generation Betrayed*. Reading, MA: Addison-Wesley, 1994.

Mollon, Phil, 'Clinical Psychologists, Recovered Memory and False Memory,' *Clinical Psychology Forum*, Dec. 1995, p. 17–20.

Montagu, Ashley. *Touching: The Human Significance of the Skin*. NY: Perennial Library, 1971, 1972.

Moore, R. I. *The Formation of a Persecuting Society: Power and Deviance in Western Europe, 950–1250*. Cambridge, MA: Basil Blackwell, 1987.

Morrow, Lance, 'Men, Are They Really That Bad?', *Time*, Feb. 14, 1994, p. 53–59.

Moya, Elena, 'Sparks Man Forms Group to Help People Falsely Accused,' *Reno Gazette-Journal*, Sept. 26, 1995.

'Multiple Personality Disorder Continues to Be Controversial Among Psychiatrists,' *APA Psychiatric News*, Nov. 20, 1992.

Multiple Personality Disorder From the Inside Out. Ed. by Barry M. Cohen et al. Baltimore, MD: Sidran Press, 1991.

Mulvihill, Maggie, 'No Reversal in Abuse Case,' *Boston Herald*, Aug. 18, 1995, p. 7.

Muram, D., 'Child Sexual Abuse: Genital Tract Findings in Prepubertal Girls,' *American Journal of Obstetrical Gynecology*, 1989, vol. 160, p. 328–333.

Narrative Psychology: The Storied Nature of Human Conduct, ed. by Theodore R. Sarbin. NY: Praeger, 1986.

Nash, Michael, 'What, if Anything, is Regressed About Hypnotic Age Regression? A Review of the Empirical Literature,' *Psychological Bulletin*, 1987, v. 102(1), p. 42–52.

Nathan, Debbie, 'Cry Incest,' *Playboy*, Oct. 1992, p. 84–88, 162–164.

Nathan, Debbie, 'McMartin Preschool Tunnel Claims: Evidence of a Hoax,' *FMSF Newsletter*, Sept. 1994, p. 5–6.

Nathan, Debbie, 'Reno Reconsidered,' *Miami New Times*, March 3–9, 1993, v. 7(46), p. 10–29.

Nathan, Debbie. *Women and Other Aliens*. El Paso, TX: Cinco Puntos Pr., 1991.

Nathan, Debbie and Michael Snedeker. *Satan's Silence: Ritual Abuse and the Making of a Modern American Witch Hunt*. NY: Basic Books, 1995.

Neimark, Jill, 'The Harvard Professor and the UFOs,' *Psychology Today*, March/April 1994, v. 27(2), p. 46–48, 74.

Neisser, Ulric. *Cognitive Psychology*. NY: Appleton-Century-Crofts, 1967.

Nelson, Sarah, 'Symbolic Rejection of Food Has a More Sinister Meaning,' *The Scotsman*, Nov. 15, 1995, p. 19.

Netzer, Carol. *Cutoffs: How Family Members Who Sever Relationships Can Reconnect*. Far Hills, NJ: New Horizon Press, 1996.

Nickell, Joe. *Looking for a Miracle: Weeping Icons, Relics, Stigmata, Visions & Healing Cures*. Buffalo, NY: Prometheus Books, 1993.

The Nineties. Ed. by Oliver Jensen. NY: American Heritage, 1967.

North, Carol S. et al. *Multiple Personalities, Multiple Disorders: Psychiatric Classification and Media Influence*. NY: Oxford U. Press, 1993.

Oakley, J. Ronald. *God's Country: America in the Fifties*. NY: Dembner Books, 1986.

Of Gods and Men: New Religious Movements in the West. Ed. by Eileen Barker. Macon, GA: Mercer Univ. Pr., 1983.

Ofshe, Richard, 'Coerced Confessions: The Logic of Seemingly Irrational Action,' *Cultic Studies Journal*, 1989, v. 6(1), p. 1–15.

Ofshe, Richard J., 'Inadvertent Hypnosis During Interrogation: False Confession Due to Dissociative State; Mis-Identified Multiple Personality and the Satanic Cult Hypothesis,' *International Journal of Clinical and Experimental Hypnosis*, 1992, v. 40(3), p. 125–156.

Ofshe, Richard and Margaret Singer, 'Attacks on Peripheral Versus Central Elements of Self and the Impact of Thought Reforming Techniques,' *Cultic Studies Journal*, 1986, v. 3(1), p. 2–24.

Ofshe, Richard and Ethan Watters, 'Making Monsters,' *Society*, March/April 1993, v. 30(3), p. 4–16.

Ofshe, Richard and Ethan Watters. *Making Monsters: False Memories, Psychotherapy, and Sexual Hysteria*. NY: Scribner's, 1994.

Okami, Paul, '"Child Perpetrators of Sexual Abuse": The Emergence of a Problematic Deviant Category,' *Journal of Sex Research*, Feb. 1992, v. 29(1), p. 109–130.

Olio, Karen, 'Truth in Memory,' *American Psychologist*, May 1994, v. 49(5), p. 442–443.

O'Neel, Kelley Ann and Constance J. Dalenberg, 'True and False Allegations of Physical Abuse: The Role of the Mother in Constructing a Believable Story,' 1994, California School of Professional Psychology, San Diego.

Orlans, Harold, 'Potpourri; Harvard Medical School's Investigation of Psychiatry Professor John Mack,' *Change*, Sept. 1995, p. 8.

Orne, Martin, 'The Use and Misuse of Hypnosis in Court,' *The International Journal of Clinical and Experimental Hypnosis*, 1979, v. 27(4), p. 311–341.

Orr, Marjorie. *Accuracy About Abuse Newsletter*. April 1994.

Orr, Marjorie, 'Accuracy About Abuse: The "False Memory Syndrome" Debate in the United Kingdom,' *Treating Abuse Today*, May/June 1995, p. 19–28.

Orr, Marjorie, '"False Memory" Syndrome,' *Self & Society*, July 1995, v. 23, no. 3, p. 24–27.

Orwell, George. *1984*. NY: New American Library, 1949, 1981.

Otani, Akira, 'Memory in Hypnosis,' *The Advocate*, August 1992, v. 16(1).

Palmer, Alasdair, 'Get the Baby, Go and Get the Baby!' *Spectator*, Aug. 6, 1994.

Parker, Gail Thain. *Mind Cure in New England: From the Civil War to World War I*. Hanover, NH: University Pr. of New England, 1973.

Parker, Russ. *Battling the Occult*. Downers Grove, IL: InterVarsity Press, 1990.

Parkin, Alan J. *Memory and Amnesia: An Introduction*. London: Basil Blackwell, 1987.

Parks, Penny. *Rescuing the 'Inner Child': Therapy for Adults Sexually Abused as Children*. London: Souvenir, 1990.

Parnell, June, 'Measured Personality Characteristics of Persons Who Claim UFO Experiences,' *Psychotherapy in Private Practice*, 1988, v. 6(3), p. 159–165.

Parton, Nigel. *The Politics of Child Abuse*. NY: Macmillan, 1985.

Passantino, Gretchen and Bob, and Jon Trott, 'Satan's Sideshow,' *Cornerstone*, Dec. 1989, v. 18(90), p. 23–28.

Patai, Daphne and Noretta Koertge. *Professing Feminism: Cautionary Tales from the Strange World of Women's Studies*. NY: BasicBooks, 1994.

Peck, M. Scott. *People of the Lie: The Hope for Healing Human Evil*. NY: Simon & Schuster, 1983.

Pedophilia: Biosocial Dimensions. Ed. by J. R. Feierman. NY: Springer-Verlag, 1990.

Peele, Stanton. *Diseasing of America: Addiction Treatment Out of Control.* Boston: Houghton Mifflin, 1989.

Pendergrast, Mark. *For God, Country and Coca-Cola: The Unauthorized History of the Great American Soft Drink and the Company That Makes It.* NY: Scribner's, 1993.

Penfield, Wilder. *The Mystery of the Mind.* Princeton: Princeton U. Pr., 1975.

Persinger, M. A., 'Elicitation of "Childhood Memories" in Hypnosis-like Settings is Associated with Complex Partial Epileptic-like Signs for Women But Not For Men: Implications for the False Memory Syndrome,' *Perceptual and Motor Skills,* 1994, v. 78, p. 643–651.

Persinger, Michael A. *Neuropsychological Bases of God Beliefs.* NY: Praeger, 1987.

Pert, Candace B., 'The Wisdom of the Receptors: Neuropeptides, the Emotions, and Bodymind,' *Advances,* Summer 1986, v. 3(3), p. 8–16.

Peters, Mason, 'Two Retrials Ordered in Rascals Case,' *Virginian-Pilot,* May 3, 1995.

Petersen, Betsy. *Dancing With Daddy: A Childhood Lost and Life Regained.* NY: Bantam, 1991.

Peterson, Judith A. 'When the Therapists Who Have Sat With Shattered Souls Are Themselves Shattered,' *Treating Abuse Today,* March/April 1994, v. 4 (2), p. 26–27.

Philipson, Ilene J. *On the Shoulders of Women: The Feminization of Psychotherapy.* NY: Guilford, 1993.

Piper, August, Jr. 'Multiple Personality Disorder: A Review,' *British Journal of Psychiatry,* 1994, v. 164, p. 600–612.

Piper, August, Jr., 'Treatment for Multiple Personality Disorder: At What Cost?' *American Journal of Psychotherapy,* 1994, v.48, p. 392–400.

Piper, August, Jr., '"Truth Serum" and "Recovered Memories" of Sexual Abuse: A Review of the Evidence,' *Journal of Psychiatry and Law,* in press.

Piper, August, Jr., 'Truth Serum and What Really Happened,' *FMSF Newsletter,* March 1994, p. 5–6.

Pipher, Mary. *Reviving Ophelia: Saving the Selves of Adolescent Girls.* NY: Ballantine, 1994.

Pipher, Mary. *The Shelter of Each Other: Rebuilding Our Families.* NY: Grosset/Putnam, 1996; London: Ebury Pr., 1996.

Pittman, Frank, 'Ask Dr. Frank,' *Psychology Today,* March/April 1994, p. 95–96.

Pleasure and Danger: Exploring Female Sexuality. Ed. by Carole S. Vance. Boston: Routledge & Kegan Paul, 1984.

Poole, Debra A. and D. Stephen Lindsay, 'Psychotherapy and the Recovery of Memories of Childhood Sexual Abuse: Doctoral-level Therapists' Beliefs, Practices, and Experiences.' (Version 1) Unpublished paper, 1994.

Poole, Debra A., D. Stephen Lindsay, Amina Memon, and Ray Bull, 'Psychotherapy and the Recovery of Memories of Childhood Sexual Abuse: U.S. and British Practitioner's Opinions, Practices, and Experiences,' *Journal of Consulting and Clinical Psychology*, 1995, v. 63, no. 3, p. 426–437.

Pope, Harrison G., Jr., '"Recovered Memories": Recent Events and Review of Evidence,' *Currents in Affective Illness*, July 1994, v. 13(7), p. 5–12.

Pope, Harrison G., Jr. et al, 'Childhood Sexual Abuse and Bulimia Nervosa: A Comparison of American, Austrian, and Brazilian Women,' *American Journal of Psychiatry* May 1994, v. 151(5), p. 732–737.

Pope, Harrison G., Jr. and James I. Hudson, 'Can Memories of Childhood Sexual Abuse Be Repressed?' *Psychological Medicine*, 1995, v. 25, p. 121–126.

Pope, Harrison G., Jr. and James I. Hudson, 'Is Childhood Sexual Abuse a Risk Factor for Bulimia Nervosa?' *American Journal of Psychiatry*, April 1992, v. 149(4), p. 455–463.

Pope, Kenneth S. 'Sexual Involvement Between Therapists and Patients,' *Harvard Mental Health Letter*, Aug. 1994, v. 11 (2), p. 5–6.

Pope, Kenneth S. and Barbara G. Tabachnick, 'Recovered Memories of Abuse Among Therapy Patients: A National Survey,' *Ethics & Behavior*, 1995, v. 5, no. 3, p. 237–248.

Poston, Carol and Karen Lison. *Reclaiming Our Lives: Hope for Adult Survivors of Incest*. NY: Bantam, 1989.

Powell, Russell A. and Douglas P. Boer, 'Did Freud Mislead Patients to Confabulate Memories of Abuse?' *Psychological Reports*, 1994, v. 74, p. 1283–1298.

Powers of Desire: The Politics of Sexuality, ed. by Ann Snitow et al. NY: Monthly Review Press, 1983.

Pransky, George S. *The Relationship Handbook: A Simple Guide to Satisfying Relationships*. Blue Ridge Summit, PA: Tab Books, 1992.

Price, Reynolds. *A Whole New Life: an Illness and a Healing*. NY: Atheneum, 1994.

Pride, Mary. *The Child Abuse Industry*. Westchester, IL: Crossway Books, 1986.

Prince, Morton. *The Dissociation of a Personality: A Biographic Study in Abnormal Psychology.* NY: Meridian Books, [1905, 1908], 1957.

Principles and Practices of Sleep Medicine, ed. by Meir H. Kryger et al. 2nd ed. Philadelphia: W. B. Saunders, 1994.

Prisoners of Silence, Frontline Show 1202, Oct. 19, 1993.

The Profits of Misery: How Inpatient Psychiatric Treatment Bilks the System and Betrays Our Trust. Hearing before the Select Committee on Children, Youth and Families, House of Representatives, April 28, 1992.

Pruett, Kyle D. *The Nurturing Father: Journey Toward the Complete Man.* NY: Warner, 1987.

Psychiatric Aspects of Epilepsy, ed. by Dietrich Blumer. Washington, DC: American Psychiatric Press, 1984.

Putnam, Frank W. *Diagnosis and Treatment of Multiple Personality Disorder.* London: Guilford, 1989.

Putnam, Frank W., 'Recent Research on Multiple Personality Disorder,' *Psychiatric Clinics of North America,* Sept. 1991, v. 14(3), p. 489–502.

Pynoos, R. S. and S. Eth, 'The Child as Witness to Homicide,' *Journal of Social Issues,* 1989, v. 2, p. 87–108.

Rabinowitz, Dorothy, 'A Darkness in Massachusetts,' *Wall Street Journal,* Jan. 30, 1995.

Rabinowitz, Dorothy, 'Darkness in Massachusetts II,' *Wall Street Journal,* March 14, 1995.

Rabinowitz, Dorothy, 'Wenatchee, A True Story, II,' *Wall Street Journal,* Oct. 13, 1995.

Rader, William C., 'Incest and Eating Disorders,' *Professional Counselor,* Feb. 1992, v. 6(4), p. 16.

Reconstructing Individualism, ed. by Thomas C. Heller et al. Stanford, CA: Stanford U. Pr., 1986.

Recovery From Cults. Ed. by Michael D. Langone. NY: Norton, 1993.

Redfield, James. *The Celestine Prophecy: An Adventure.* NY: Time Warner, 1993.

Reed, Graham. *The Psychology of Anomalous Experience.* Buffalo, NY: Prometheus Books, 1988.

Reid, D. H. S. *Suffer the Little Children: The Orkney Child Abuse Scandal.* St. Andrews, Scotland: Medical Institute for Research into Child Cruelty (Miric), 1992.

'Repressed Memories: True or False?' *Focus on the Family* Radio Program, Feb. 16 and 17, 1995.

Repression and Dissociation: Implications for Personality Theory, Psychopathology, and Health. Ed. by Jerome L. Singer. Chicago: U. of Chicago Pr., 1990.

The Retractor: Newsletter for Survivors of False Memories, ed. by Melody Gavigan. Reno, NV.

Rimmer, Janet, 'The Emperor's New Law Suit, Or, The Falsehoods in the False Memory Syndrome Debate,' *Human Potential*, Spring 1995, p. 28.

'Ritual Child Abuse: A Professional Overview,' videotape. CA: Cavalcade Productions, 1989.

Roberts, David, 'The Martensville Horror,' *Toronto Globe and Mail*, Feb. 19, 1994.

Roberts, Susan O., 'Multiple Realities,' *Common Boundary*, May/June 1992, p. 24–30.

Robbins, Russell Hope. *Encyclopedia of Witchcraft and Demonology*. NY: Crown, 1959.

Robbins, Thomas. *Cults, Converts & Charisma: The Sociology of New Religious Movements*. London: Sage, 1988.

Robinson, Kathryn, 'Memories of Abuse,' *Seattle Weekly*, Aug. 11, 1993, p. 18–28.

Rockwell, Robert B., 'One Psychiatrist's View of Satanic Ritual Abuse,' *The Journal of Psychohistory*, Spring 1994, v. 21(4), p. 443–460.

Roediger, Henry L. III, 'Implicit Memory: Retention Without Remembering,' *American Psychologist*, Sept. 1990, v. 45, no. 9, p. 1043–1056.

Roediger, Henry L. III, 'Memory Metaphors in Cognitive Psychology,' *Memory & Cognition*, 1980, v. 8, no. 3, p. 231–246.

Roesler, T., et al, 'Network Therapy Using Videotape Disclosures for Adult Sexual Abuse Survivors,' *Child Abuse & Neglect*, 1992, v. 16, no. 4, p. 575–583.

Rogers, Patrick, 'Farewell to the Couch?' *Newsweek*, June 6, 1994, p. 32.

Rogo, D. Scott, 'Is Religion in the Brain?' *Fate*, Nov. 1990, v. 43, p. 80–92.

Roiphe, Katie. 'Date Rape Hysteria,' *New York Times*, Nov. 20, 1991.

Roiphe, Katie. 'Making the Incest Scene,' *Harper's*, Nov. 1995, p. 65–72.

Roiphe, Katie. *The Morning After: Fear, Sex, and Feminism on Campus*. Boston: Little, Brown, 1993.

Rose, Elizabeth S., 'Surviving the Unbelievable,' *Ms.*, Jan./Feb. 1993, p. 40–45.

Rose, Steven. *The Making of Memory*. NY: Doubleday, 1992.

Rosen, R. D. *Psychobabble: Fast Talk and Quick Cure in the Era of Feeling*. NY: Atheneum, 1977.

Rosenberg, Charles E., 'The Place of George M. Beard in Nineteenth

Century Psychiatry,' *Bulletin of the History of Medicine* (1972), v. 36, p. 245–259.

Rosenfeld, Alvin et al, 'Determining Incestuous Contact Between Parent and Child: Frequency of Children Touching Parents' Genitals in a Nonclinical Population,' *Journal of the American Academy of Child Psychiatry*, 1986, v. 25, 4, p. 481–484.

Rosenfeld, Alvin et al, 'Familial Bathing Patterns: Implications for Cases of Alleged Molestation and For Pediatric Practice,' *Pediatrics*, Feb. 1987, v. 79, 2, p. 224–229.

Rosenfield, Israel. *The Invention of Memory: A New View of the Brain*. NY: Basic Books, 1988.

Rosenhan, D. L., 'On Being Sane in Insane Places,' *Science*, Jan. 19, 1973, v. 179, p. 250–258.

Ross, Colin A., 'CIA Mind Control' book proposal, circa 1993.

Ross, Colin A., 'Epidemiology of Multiple Personality Disorder and Dissociation,' *Psychiatric Clinics of North America*, Sept. 1991, v. 14(3), p. 503–517.

Ross, Colin A. *Multiple Personality Disorder: Diagnosis, Clinical Features, and Treatment*. NY: John Wiley, 1989.

Ross, Colin A. *The Osiris Complex: Case-Studies in Multiple Personality Disorder*. Toronto, ON, Buffalo, NY, London: U. Toronto Pr., 1994.

Ross, Colin A., 'President's Message,' *ISSMPD [International Society for the Study of Multiple Personality & Dissociation] News*, April 1994, v. 12(2), p. 1–2.

Ross, Colin. *Satanic Ritual Abuse: Principles of Treatment*. Toronto, ON: U. Toronto Pr., 1995.

Ross, Donald R., 'Discussion: An Agnostic Viewpoint on Multiple Personality Disorder,' *Psychoanalytic Inquiry*, 1992, v. 12(1), p. 124–138.

Rubel, Arthur J. et al. *Susto: A Folk Illness*. Berkeley, CA: Univ. of California, 1984.

Rubenstein, Robert and Richard Newman, 'The Living Out of "Future" Experiences Under Hypnosis,' *Science*, April 9, 1954, v. 119, p. 472–473.

Rubongoya, Joshua, 'Raising Our Children,' *Atlanta Journal/Constitution*, June 7, 1994.

Rush, Florence. *The Best Kept Secret: Sexual Abuse of Children*. Englewood Cliffs, NJ: Prentice-Hall, 1980.

Russell, Diana E. H. *The Secret Trauma: Incest in the Lives of Girls and Women*. NY: Basic, 1986.

Russett, Cynthia Eagle. *Sexual Science: The Victorian Construction of Womanhood*. Cambridge, MA: Harvard U. Pr., 1989.

Rymer, Russ. *Genie: An Abused Child's Flight from Silence*. NY: HarperCollins, 1993.

Sachs, Roberta G. and Peterson, Judith A. *Processing Memories Retrieved by Trauma Victims and Survivors: A Primer for Therapists*. Tyler, TX: Family Violence & Sexual Assault Institute, 1994.

Sagan, Carl. *The Demon-Haunted World: Science as a Candle in the Dark*. NY: Random House, 1996.

Salter, Stephanie and Carol Ness, 'Buried Memories, Broken Families' series, *San Francisco Examiner*, April 4–9, 1993.

Santrock, John et al. *The Authoritative Guide to Self-Help Books*. NY: Guilford, 1994.

Sargant, William. *Battle for the Mind: A Physiology of Conversion and Brain-Washing*. NY: Penguin, 1957.

The Satanism Scare, ed. by James T. Richardson et al. NY: Aldine de Gruyter, 1991.

Sayce, Liz, 'Looking Back in Anger and Confusion,' *The Guardian*, Jan. 7, 1994.

Schacter, Daniel L., 'Implicit Knowledge: New Perspectives on Unconscious Processes,' *Proceedings of the National Academic of Science USA*, Dec. 1992, v. 89, p. 11113–11117.

Schacter, Daniel. *Searching for Memory: The Brain, the Mind, and the Past*. NY: Basic Books, 1996.

Schacter, Daniel L. et al, 'Functional Retrograde Amnesia: A Quantitative Case Study,' *Neuropsychologia*, 1982, v. 20(5), p. 523–532.

Schacter, Daniel L. et al, 'Implicit Memory: A Selective Review,' *Annual Review of Neurosciences*, 1993, v. 16, p. 159–182.

Schacter, Daniel L. and Tim Curran, 'The Cognitive Neuroscience of False Memories,' *Psychiatric Annals*, Dec. 1995, vol. 25, no. 12, p. 726–730.

Schacter, Daniel L. and John F. Kihlstrom, 'Functional Amnesia,' in *Handbook of Neuropsychology*, v. 3. NY: Elsevier Science, 1989, p. 209–231.

Schatzman, Morton, 'Freud: Who Seduced Whom?' *New Scientist*, March 21, 1992, p. 34–37.

Schiff, Jacqui Lee, with Beth Day. *All My Children*. NY: M. Evans, 1970.

Schimek, Jean G., 'Fact and Fantasy in the Seduction Theory: A Historical Review,' *Journal of the American Psychoanalytic Association*, 1987, v. 35, p. 937–965.

Schissler, Henry, 'Avoiding the Truth Trap,' *Family Therapy Networker*, March/April 1994, p. 69–79.

Schoeneman, Thomas J. 'The Witch Hunt as a Culture Change Phenomenon,' *Ethos*, Winter 1975, v. 8 (4), p. 529–554.

Schreiber, Flora Rheta. *Sybil*. NY: Warner, 1973.

Schultz, Duane. *Intimate Friends, Dangerous Rivals: The Turbulent Relationship Between Freud & Jung*. Los Angeles: Jeremy P. Tarcher, 1990.

Schwarz, Ted. *The Hillside Strangler: A Murderer's Mind*. Garden City, NY: Doubleday, 1981.

Scotford, Roger, 'The Bjugn Case,' *Moderna Tider* (Sweden), Oct. 1994, v. 5, no. 48.

Scott, Roger and David Williams, 'A Father's Nightmare,' *Daily Mail*, March 29, 1995.

Seagrave, Ann and Faison Covington. *Free from Fears: New Help for Anxiety, Panic and Agoraphobia*. NY: Pocket Books, 1987.

Seligman, Martin E. P. *What You Can Change and What You Can't: The Complete Guide to Successful Self-Improvement*. NY: Knopf, 1994.

Sessums, Kevin, 'Really Roseanne,' *Vanity Fair*, Feb. 1994, p. 58–64, 113–116.

Shakespeare, William. *The Riverside Shakespeare*. Boston: Houghton Mifflin, 1974.

Shapiro, Laura, 'Rush to Judgment,' *Newsweek*, April 19, 1993, p. 54–60.

Sharkey, Joe. *Bedlam: Greed, Profiteering, and Fraud in a Mental Health System Gone Crazy*. NY: St. Martin's, 1994.

Shorter, Edward. *From Paralysis to Fatigue: A History of Psychosomatic Illness in the Modern Era*. NY: Free Press, 1992.

Sicherman, Barbara, 'The Uses of a Diagnosis: Doctors, Patients, and Neurasthenia,' *Journal of the History of Medicine*, 1977, v. 32, p. 33–54.

Siebers, Tobin. *The Mirror of Medusa*. Berkeley, CA: U. of California Pr., 1983.

Siegel, Shirley J. *What To Do When Psychotherapy Goes Wrong*. 5651 S. 144th St., Tukwila, WA 98168: Stop Abuse by Counselors, 1991.

Sileo, Chi Chi, 'Unearthed Memories Lose Ground in Court,' *Insight*, June 12, 1995, p. 14–15.

Simon, Richard, 'From the Editor,' *Family Therapy Networker*, Nov./Dec. 1993, p. 2.

Sinason, Valerie, ed. *Treating Survivors of Satanist Abuse*. London: Routledge, 1994.

Singer, Margaret Thaler, 'Coming Out of the Cults,' *Psychology Today*, Jan. 1979, p. 72–82.

Singer, Margaret Thaler, with Janja Lalich. *Cults in our Midst: The Hidden Menace in our Everyday Lives*. San Francisco: Jossey-Bass, 1995.

Sisterhood is Powerful: An Anthology of Writings from the Women's Liberation Movement, ed. by Robin Morgan. NY: Vintage, 1970.

Sizemore, Chris Costner. *A Mind of My Own*. NY: William Morrow, 1989.

Sizemore, Chris Costner, with E. S. Pittillo *I'm Eve!* Garden City, NY: Doubleday, 1977.

Skolnick, Arlene. *Embattled Paradise: The American Family in an Age of Uncertainty*. NY: Basic Books, 1991.

'Sleep Disorders, Part I,' *Harvard Mental Health Letter*, Aug. 1994, v. 11 (2), p. 1–4.

Smart, Ninian. *The Religious Experience of Mankind*. NY: Scribner's, 1969.

Smiley, Jane. *A Thousand Acres*. NY: Fawcett Columbine, 1991.

Smith, Marilyn Chapnik, 'Hypnotic Memory Enhancement of Witnesses: Does It Work?' *Psychological Bulletin*, 1983, v. 94(3), p. 387–407.

Smith, Mark, 'Haunted Dreams: Real or Implanted?' *Houston Chronicle*, Sept. 12, 1993.

Smith, Michelle and Lawrence Pazder. *Michelle Remembers*. NY: Pocket Books, 1980.

Smith, Susan. *Survivor Psychology: The Dark Side of a Mental Health Mission*. Boca Raton: Upton Books, 1994.

Smolowe, Jill, 'Dubious Memories,' *Time*, May 23, 1994, p. 51.

Smolowe, Jill, 'Making the Tough Calls,' *Time*, Dec. 11, 1995, p. 40–44.

Smolowe, Jill, 'Sex With a Scorecard,' *Time*, April 5, 1993, p. 41.

Sommers, Christina Hoff. *Who Stole Feminism? How Women Have Betrayed Women*. NY: Simon & Schuster, 1994.

Spanos, Nicholas P. and Jack Gottlieb, 'Demonic Possession, Mesmerism, and Hysteria: A Social Psychological Perspective on Their Historical Interrelations,' *Journal of Abnormal Psychology*, 1979, vol. 88 (5), p. 527–546.

Spanos, Nicholas P. and Joanne McLean, 'Hypnotically Created Pseudomemories: Memory Distortions or Reporting Biases?' *British Journal of Experimental and Clinical Hypnosis*, 1985–86, v. 3(3), p. 155–159.

Spanos, Nicholas P. et al, 'Hypnotic Amnesia as a Strategic Enactment: Breaching Amnesia in Highly Susceptible Subjects,' *Journal of Personality and Social Psychology*, 1985, v. 47(5), p. 1155–1169.

Spanos, Nicholas P. et al, 'Hypnotic Interview and Age Regression Procedures in the Elicitation of Multiple Personality Symptoms: A Simulation Study,' *Psychiatry*, Nov. 1986, v. 29, p. 298–311.

Spanos, Nicholas P., et al, 'Multiple Personality: A Social Psychological Perspective,' *Journal of Abnormal Psychology*, 1985, v. 94 (3), p. 362–376.

Spanos, Nicholas P. et al, 'Secondary Identity Enactments During Hypnotic Past-Life Regression: A Sociocognitive Perspective,' *Journal of Personality and Social Psychology*, 1991, v. 61(2), p. 308–320.

Spear, Caroline C., 'The Healing Circle,' *The Healing Woman*, August 1994, p. 1, 7–8.

Spence, Jonathan D. *The Memory Palace of Matteo Ricci*. NY: Viking, 1984.

Spencer, Judith. *Suffer the Child*. NY: Pocket Books, 1989.

Spiegel, Herbert 'The Grade 5 Syndrome: The Highly Hypnotizable Person,' *International Journal of Clinical and Experimental Hypnosis*, 1974, v. 22, p. 303–319.

Spiegel, Herbert, and David Spiegel. *Trance and Treatment: Clinical Uses of Hypnosis*. NY: Basic, 1978.

Squire, Larry R. *Memory and Brain*. NY: Oxford, 1987.

'A Star Cries Incest,' *People*, Oct. 7, 1991, p. 84–88.

State Comparison of Laws Regulating Social Work. Washington, DC: National Association of Social Work, 1993.

Steinem, Gloria. *Revolution From Within: A Book of Self-Esteem*. Boston: Little Brown, 1992, 1993.

Stevens, Suzanne, 'Post Therapy,' *The Therapist*, Winter 1995, vol. 2, no. 4, p. 46.

'Stigmatics.' Interview with Ted Harrison, 'Outlook' radio program, British Broadcasting Corporation, March 31, 1994.

Stone, W. Clement and Norma Lee Browning. *The Other Side of the Mind*. Englewood Cliffs, NJ: Prentice-Hall, 1964.

Stratford, Lauren. *Satan's Underground*. Eugene, OR: Harvest House, 1988.

Strauss, William and Neil Howe. *Generations: The History of America's Future, 1584 to 2069*. NY: William Morrow, 1991.

Streiker, Lowell D. *Mind Bending: Brainwashing, Cults, and Deprogramming in the '80s*. Garden City, NY: Doubleday, 1984.

The Suggestibility of Children's Recollections, ed. by John Doris. Washington, DC: American Psychological Association, 1991.

Sulloway, Frank J. *Freud, Biologist of the Mind: Beyond the Psychoanalytic Legend*. NY: Basic Books, 1979.

Summit, Roland C., 'The Child Sexual Abuse Accommodation Syndrome,' *Child Abuse and Neglect*, 1983, v. 7, 2.

Summit, Roland C., 'The Dark Tunnels of McMartin,' *The Journal of Psychohistory*, Spring 1994, v. 21(4), p. 397–416.

Survivors of Incest Anonymous (SIA) literature, PO Box 21817, Baltimore, MD 21222.

Sykes, Charles J. *A Nation of Victims: The Decay of the American Character.* NY: St. Martin's, 1992.

Szasz, Thomas, 'Diagnoses Are Not Diseases,' *Skeptic*, 1994, v. 2(3), p. 86–89.

Tate, Tim. *Children for the Devil: Ritual Abuse, and Satanic Crime.* London: Methuen, 1991.

Tavris, Carol. *Anger: The Misunderstood Emotion.* NY: Simon & Schuster, 1982.

Tavris, Carol, 'Beware the Incest-Survivor Machine,' *New York Times Book Review*, Jan. 3, 1993.

Tavris, Carol, 'The Illusion of Science in Psychiatry,' *Skeptic*, 1994, v. 2(3), p. 77–85.

Tavris, Carol. *The Mismeasure of Woman.* NY: Touchstone, 1992.

Taylor, Gordon Rattray. *The Natural History of the Mind.* NY: E. P. Dutton, 1979.

Taylor, John, 'The Lost Daughter,' *Esquire*, March 1994, p. 76–87.

Taylor, John, 'Salem Revisited,' *New York*, April 12, 1993, p. 10–12.

Taylor, Peggy, 'Family Man,' *New Age Journal*, July/August 1995, p. 65–68.

Temple, Robert. *Open to Suggestion: The Uses and Abuses of Hypnosis.* Wellingborough, Northamptonshire: Aquarian Press, 1989.

Terr, Lenore. *Too Scared To Cry: Psychic Trauma in Childhood.* NY: Basic Books, 1990.

Terr, Lenore. *Unchained Memories: True Stories of Traumatic Memories, Lost and Found.* NY: Basic Books, 1994.

Terr, Lenore, 'What Happens to Early Memories of Trauma? A Study of Twenty Children Under Age Five at the Time of Documented Traumatic Events,' *Journal of the American Academy of Child & Adolescent Psychiatry*, 1988, v. 27, p. 96–104.

Theories of Hypnosis, edited by Steven Jay Lynn and Judith W. Rhue. NY: Guilford Press, 1991.

Thigpen, Corbett H. and Hervey M. Cleckley, 'A Case of Multiple Personality,' *Journal of Abnormal and Social Psychology*, 1954, v. 49, p. 135–151.

715

Thigpen, Corbett H. and Hervey M. Cleckley, 'On the Incidence of Multiple Personality Disorder: A Brief Communication,' *International Journal of Clinical and Experimental Hypnosis,* 1984, v. 32(2), p. 63–66.

Thigpen, Corbett H. and Hervey M. Cleckley. *Three Faces of Eve.* NY: McGraw-Hill, 1957.

Thomas, David. *Not Guilty: The Case in Defense of Men.* NY: Morrow, 1993.

Thomas, Gordon. *Journey Into Madness: The True Story of Secret CIA Mind Control and Medical Abuse.* NY: Bantam, 1989.

Thornton, E. M. *The Freudian Fallacy: An Alternative View of Freudian Theory.* Garden City, NY: Dial Press, 1984.

Tillman, Jane et al, 'Does Trauma Cause Dissociative Pathology?' in *Dissociation: Clinical, Theoretical and Research Perspectives,* ed. by S. J. Lynn. Washington, DC: American Psychological Association, in press.

Timms, Robert and Patrick Connors. *Embodying Healing: Integrating Bodywork and Psychotherapy in Recovery from Childhood Sexual Abuse.* Orwell, VT: Safer Society Pr., 1992.

Tong, Dean. *Don't Blame ME, Daddy: False Accusations of Child Sexual Abuse.* Norfolk, VA: Hampton Roads Pub., 1992.

Torrey, E. Fuller. *Freudian Fraud: The Malignant Effect of Freud's Theory on American Thought and Culture.* NY: HarperCollins, 1992.

Tower, Cynthia Crosson. *Secret Scars: A Guide For Survivors of Child Sexual Abuse.* NY: Penguin, 1989.

Trace, Robert, 'Research Findings Fail to Support Early Claims by Advocates of FC,' *Advance for Speech-Language Pathologists & Audiologists,* March 21, 1994, p. 6–7, 20–21.

Trauma and Its Wake: The Study and Treatment of Post-traumatic Stress Disorder. Ed. by Charles R. Figley. NY: Brunner/Mazel, 1985.

Trauma and Its Wake: Vol. II: Traumatic Stress Theory, Research and Intervention. Ed. by Charles R. Figley. NY: Brunner/Mazel, 1986.

Treating Survivors of Satanist Abuse. Ed. by Valerie Sinason. London, NY: Routledge, 1994.

Trevor-Roper, H. R. *The European Witch-Craze of The Sixteenth and Seventeenth Centuries and Other Essays.* NY: Harper & Row, 1969.

The Troops for Trudi Chase. *When Rabbit Howls.* NY: E. P. Dutton, 1987.

Trott, Jon. 'The Grade Five Syndrome,' *Cornerstone,* v. 20(96), p. 16–26.

Trott, Nancy Roberts, 'Campuses Too Politically Correct?' *Burlington Free Press,* Dec. 3, 1995, p. 6A.

Twitchell, James B. *Forbidden Partners: The Incest Taboo in Modern Culture*. NY: Columbia University Pr., 1987.

Tulving, Endel. *Elements of Episodic Memory*. NY: Clarendon Pr., 1983.

Tulving, Endel. *Organization of Memory*. NY: Academic Pr., 1972.

Udolf, Roy. *Handbook of Hypnosis for Professionals*. NY: Van Nostrand Reinhold, 1981.

Underwager, Ralph and Hollida Wakefield, 'Interview,' *Paidika* (Amsterdam), 1993, v. 3(1), p. 2–12.

Underwager, Ralph and Hollida Wakefield, 'Misinterpretation of a Primary Prevention Attempt,' *Issues in Child Abuse Accusations*, 1994, v. 6(2), p. 96–107.

Underwager, Ralph and Hollida Wakefield. *The Return of the Furies: Analysis of Recovered Memory Therapy*. Chicago, IL: Open Court, 1994.

Underwager, Ralph and Hollida Wakefield, 'Statement of Ralph Underwager and Hollida Wakefield in Response to Criticism of *Paidika* Interview,' Northfield, MN: Institute for Psychological Therapies, 1993.

'U.S. Attorney Settles Drug Lawsuit with Cambridge Psychiatrist,' *PR Newswire*, July 5, 1995.

Usher, JoNell Adair and Ulric Neisser, 'Childhood Amnesia and the Beginnings of Memory for Four Early Life Events,' *Journal of Experimental Psychology: General*, 1993, v. 122(2), p. 155–165.

Vaillant, George E. *The Wisdom of the Ego*. Cambridge, MA: Harvard U. Pr., 1993.

Van Biema, David, 'Abandoned to Her Fate,' *Time*, Dec. 11, 1995, p. 32–36.

Vance, Ralph, 'After the Fall,' *Chicago Tribune Magazine*, Feb. 27, 1994, p. 14–20.

Vanderbilt, Heidi, 'Incest: A Chilling Report,' *Lear's*, Feb. 1992, unpaged reprint.

Van der Kolk, Bessel A., 'The Body Keeps the Score: Memory and the Evolving Psychobiology of Post-traumatic Stress,' *Harvard Review of Psychiatry*, Jan/Feb. 1994, p. 253–265.

Van der Kolk, Bessel A. and Rita Fisler, 'Dissociation and the Fragmentary Nature of Traumatic Memories: Overview and Exploratory Study,' *Journal of Traumatic Stress*, 1995, vol. 8, no. 4, p. 505–525.

Van der Kolk, Bessel A. et al. *Psychological Trauma*. Washington, DC: American Psychiatric Pr., 1987.

Veith, Ilza. *Hysteria: The History of a Disease*. Chicago, IL: U. of Chicago Pr., 1965.

Verny, Thomas, with John Kelly. *The Secret Life of the Unborn Child*. NY: Summit Books, 1981.

Victor, Jeffrey S. *Satanic Panic: The Creation of a Contemporary Legend*. Chicago, IL: Open Court, 1993.

Walker, Andrew. *Restoring the Kingdom: The Radical Christianity of the House Church Movement*. London: Hodder & Stoughton, 1985, 1989.

Walker, Moira. *Surviving Secrets*. Buckinghamshire: Open University Press, 1992.

Waller, Douglas, 'The Vision Thing,' *Time*, Dec. 11, 1995, p. 48.

Wallerstein, Judith S. and Sandra Blakeslee. *Second Chances: Men, Women, and Children a Decade After Divorce*. NY: Ticknor & Fields, 1989.

Walling, William H. *Sexology*. Philadelphia: Puritan Publishing Co., 1904.

Ward, Elizabeth. *Father-Daughter Rape*. NY: Grove Press, 1985. [London: Women's Press, 1984.]

Warrington, Elizabeth K. and Larry Weiskrantz, 'Amnesia: A Disconnection Syndrome?' *Neuropsychologia*, 1982, vol. 20(3), p. 233–248.

Wasserman, Saul and Alvin Rosenfeld, 'An Overview of the History of Child Sexual Abuse and Sigmund Freud's Contributions,' in *The Sexual Abuse of Children: Theory and Research*, v. 1, ed. by William O'Donohue and James H. Geer. Hillsdale, NJ: Lawrence Erlbaum, 1992.

Wassil-Grimm, Claudette, *Diagnosis for Disaster: The Devastating Truth about False Memory Syndrome and Its Impact on Accusers and Families*. Woodstock, NY: Overlook, 1995.

Waterhouse, Rosie, 'Families Haunted by Accusations of Childhood Abuse,' *The Independent*, May 24, 1993.

Waterhouse, Rosie, 'NSPCC Questions Led to Satan Cases,' *Independent on Sunday*, Sept. 30, 1990.

Waterhouse, Rosie, 'Satanic Cults: How the Hysteria Swept Britain,' *Independent on Sunday*, Oct. 12, 1990.

Waterhouse, Rosie, 'Satanic Inquisitors from the Town Hall,' *Independent on Sunday*, Oct. 28, 1990.

Waterhouse, Rosie, 'Therapist's Role in Notts Case,' *Independent on Sunday*, April 7, 1991.

Waterhouse, Rosie, 'Witch Hunt,' *New Statesman and Society*, Sept. 6, 1991.

Waterloo, Carol, 'Remembering Past Trauma is Possible,' *McKeesport Daily News*, March 11, 1994.

Watkins, John G. *Hypnotherapy of War Neuroses*. NY: Ronald Press, 1949.

Watson, Bruce. 'Salem's Dark Hour: Did the Devil Make Them Do It?'
Smithsonian, April 1992, v. 23, p. 116–131.

Webster, Richard. *Why Freud Was Wrong: Sin, Science and Psychoanalysis.*
London: HarperCollins; NY: Basic Books, 1995.

Weiskrantz, Larry and Elizabeth Warrington, 'Conditioning in Amnesic
Patients,' *Neuropsychologia*, 1979, vol. 17, p. 187–194.

Weiskrantz, Larry, 'Problems of Learning and Memory: One or Multiple
Memory Systems?' *Phil. Trans. R. Soc. Lond. B*, 1990, vol. 329, p. 88–108.

Weiss, Mitch, 'Citizens Group Casts Doubt on Victims Aid,' *Plain Dealer*,
Sept. 17, 1995.

Weldon, Fay. *Trouble.* NY: Penguin, 1993. [Published in the U.K. as
Affliction, HarperCollins, 1994.]

Wexler, Richard. *Wounded Innocents: The Real Victims of the War Against
Child Abuse.* Second Edition. Buffalo, NY: Prometheus, 1995.

Wheatley, Dennis. *The Devil Rides Out.* London: Arrow, [1934], 1966.

Whitfield, Charles. *Healing the Child Within: Discovery and Recovery for
Adult Children of Dysfunctional Families.* Deerfield Beach, FL: Health
Communications, 1987.

Whitfield, Charles L. *Healing the Child Within . . . Continued: Trauma,
Memory and PTSD*, Tapes 1–8, Sept. 28 & 29, 1995, Philadelphia,
PA: J & K Seminars.

Whitfield, Charles L. *Memory and Abuse: Remembering and Healing the
Effects of Trauma.* Deerfield Beach, FL: Health Communications,
1995.

Whitley, Glenna, 'Abuse of Trust,' *D Magazine*, Jan. 1992, p. 36–39.

Whitley, Glenna, 'The Seduction of Gloria Grady,' *D Magazine*, Oct.
1991, p. 44–49.

Wilkinson, Paul, 'Father Freed Over "False Memory" Abuse Claims,' *The
Times*, March 29, 1995, p. 1.

Williams, Linda Meyer, 'Recall of Childhood Trauma: A Prospective
Study of Women's Memories of Child Sexual Abuse,' *Journal of
Consulting and Clinical Psychology*, 1994, vol. 62, no. 6, p. 1167–1176.

Williams, Linda M., 'Recovered Memories of Abuse in Women with
Documented Child Sexual Victimization Histories,' *Journal of Traumatic
Stress*, 1995, vol. 8, no. 4, p. 649–673.

Wills, Garry. *Reagan's America: Innocents at Home.* Garden City, NY:
Doubleday, 1987.

Wilson, Ian. *All in the Mind.* Garden City, NY: Doubleday, 1982.

Wisniewski, Laura, 'Technique for Teaching Autistic Children Still
Divides Educators, Parents,' *Atlanta Journal/Constitution*, May 25, 1994.

Woffinden, Bob and Margaret Jervis, 'Out of the Mouths of Babes,' *Independent*, Oct. 8, 1995.

Woititz, Janet Geringer. *Adult Children of Alcoholics*. Deerfield Beach, FL: Health Communications, 1983.

Wolfe, Tom, 'The "Me" Decade and the Third Great Awakening,' *New York*, Aug. 23, 1976, p. 26–40.

Wood, Garth. *The Myth of Neurosis: Overcoming The Illness Excuse*. NY: Harper & Row, 1986.

Woodhull, Tim, 'McMartin Held On to Her Faith After Accusations Took Everything Else,' Torrance *Daily Breeze*, Dec. 19, 1995, p. A5-A6.

Woodward, Kenneth L., 'Angels,' *Newsweek*, Dec. 27, 1993, p. 52–57.

Woodward, Kenneth L., 'Was It Real or Memories?' *Newsweek*, March 14, 1994, p. 54–55.

Woolger, Roger J. *Other Lives, Other Selves: A Jungian Psychotherapist Discovers Past Lives*. Garden City, NY: Doubleday, 1987.

Wright, Lawrence. *Remembering Satan: A Case of Recovered Memory and the Shattering of an American Family*. NY: Knopf, 1994.

Wylie, Mary Sykes, 'Endangered Species,' *Family Therapy Networker*, March/April 1994, p. 20–27, 30–33.

Yapko, Michael, 'The Seductions of Memory,' *Family Therapy Networker*, Sept./Oct. 1993, p. 31–37.

Yapko, Michael D., 'Suggestibility and Repressed Memories of Abuse: A Survey of Psychotherapists' Beliefs,' *American Journal of Clinical Hypnosis*, Jan. 1994, v. 36(3), p. 163–171.

Yapko, Michael D. *Suggestions of Abuse: True and False Memories of Childhood Sexual Traumas*. NY: Simon & Schuster, 1994.

Yates, Frances A. *The Art of Memory*. Chicago: U. of Chicago Pr., 1966.

Yoachum, Susan, 'Democrat Schroeder Says She Won't Run Again,' *San Francisco Chronicle*, Nov. 30, 1995.

Zilbergeld, Bernie. *The Shrinking of America: Myths of Psychological Change*. Boston: Little Brown, 1983.

Index

(A small n after a number refers to a footnote in the main text.)